ANDY WARHOL

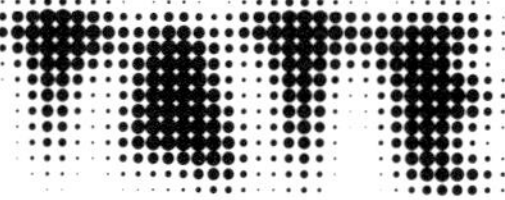

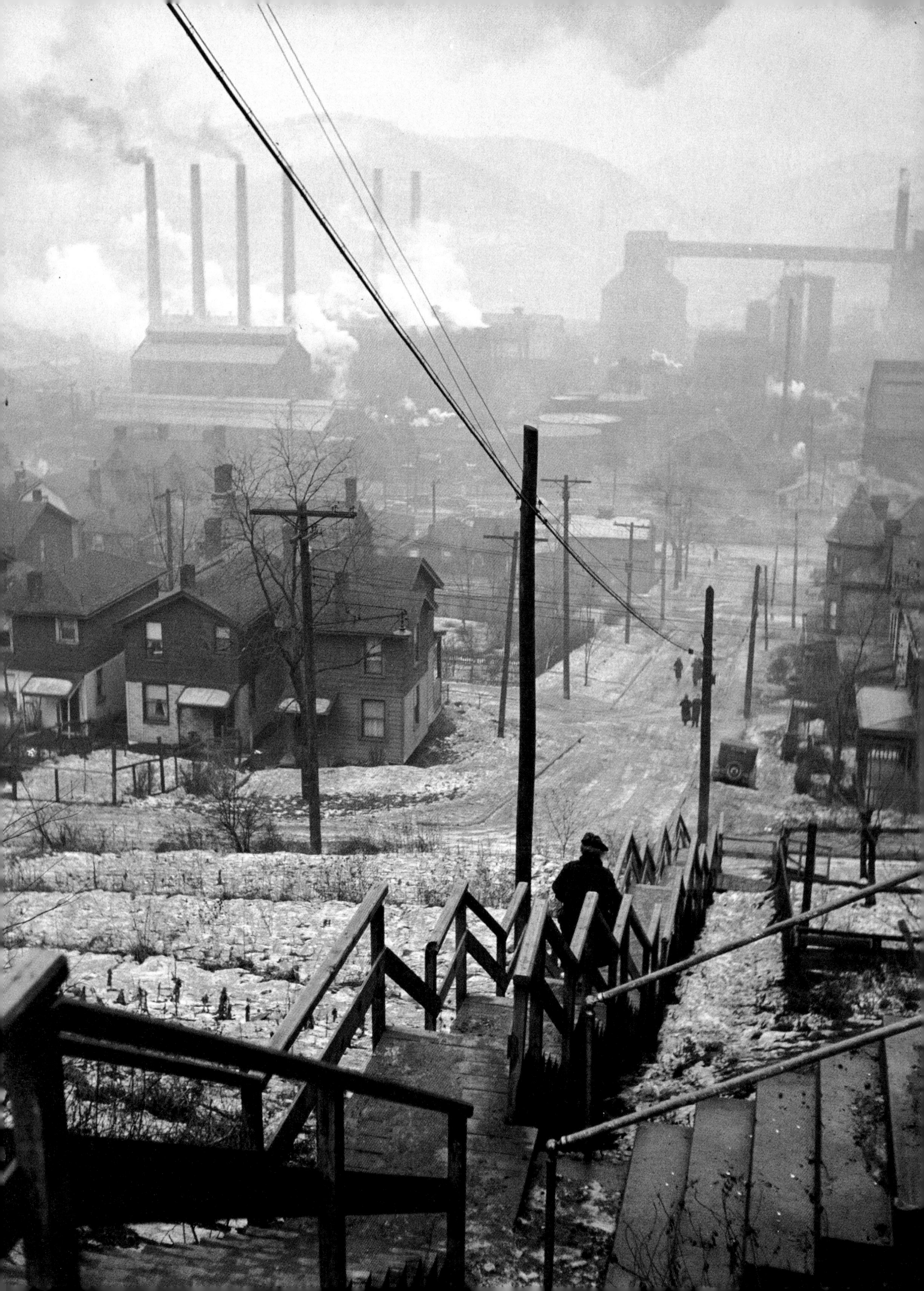

ANDY WARHOL

Edited by Gregor Muir and Yilmaz Dziewior

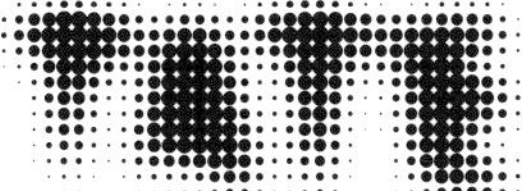

Tate Modern, London
12 March – 6 September 2020

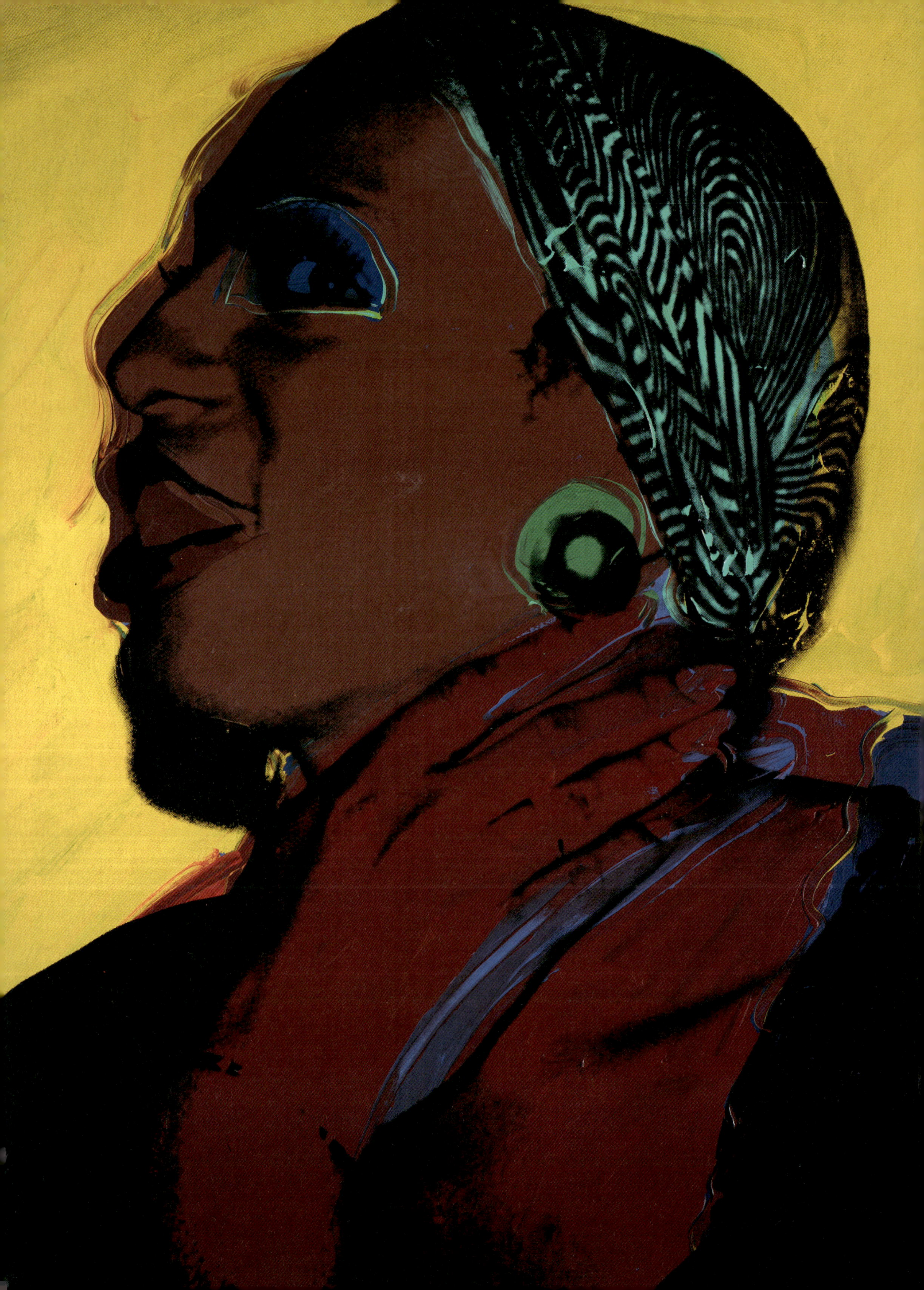

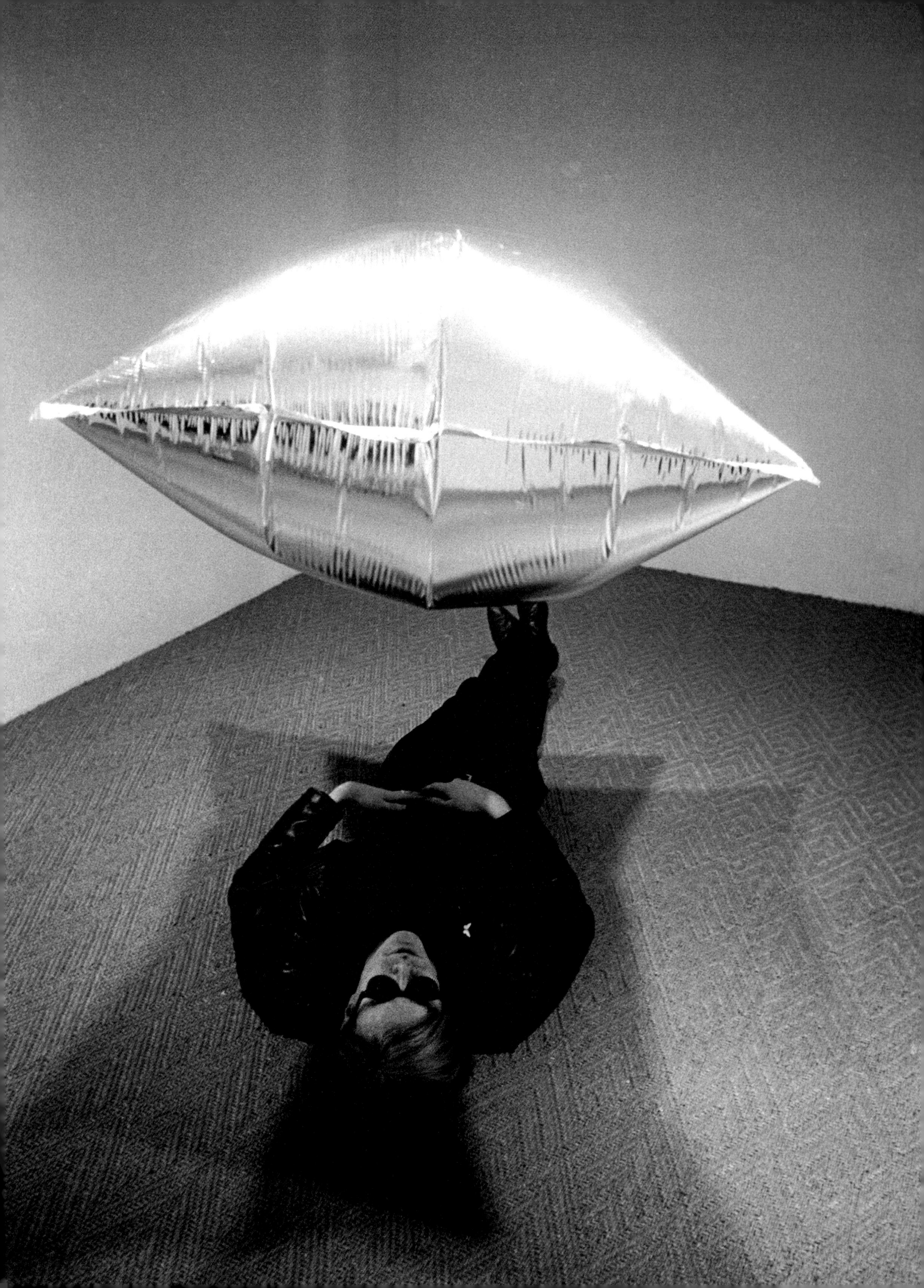

SPONSOR'S FOREWORD

At Bank of America we believe in the power of the arts to help economies thrive, educate and enrich societies, and create greater cultural understanding. That is why we are a leader in helping the arts flourish across the globe, supporting more than 2,000 not-for-profit cultural institutions each year. The Bank of America Art Program is part of the company's commitment to grow responsibly while bringing value to economies, society and the communities we serve.

We are pleased to support Tate Modern with the exhibition *Andy Warhol*. This is our seventh partnership with the gallery, including providing a grant from the Bank of America Art Conservation Project to conserve Warhol's *Marilyn Diptych*, which is featured in the exhibition.

Tate plays an integral role in the UK economy and the global cultural landscape. We are honoured to work with the institution once again.

Brian Moynihan
Chairman of the Board and Chief Executive Officer
Bank of America

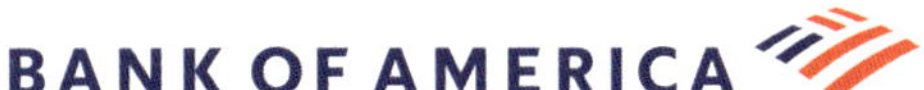

DIRECTORS' FOREWORD

Everyone has their own Warhol. Or gets the Warhol they deserve, as suggested by the late Douglas Crimp. Depending on where we look, we find Warhol the commercial artist, pop artist, or filmmaker; Warhol the business executive, celebrity, or sell-out. In many respects the artist courted or made little attempt to counter these personae, therefore it is easy to forget that Andy Warhol was someone who chose to create art at a particular moment in time in ways that continue to hold relevance.

The exhibition *Andy Warhol* (titled *Andy Warhol. Now* in Cologne) attempts to move beyond the surface to present a humanistic meditation on Warhol's life and work. In putting the show together, the curators frequently returned to the question of how this shy gay man from an immigrant family forged his own distinct path to perfectly reflect America. Rather than focusing solely on his position as the preeminent pop artist, *Andy Warhol* asks the visitor to contemplate the influences that his family history, his deeply-held beliefs, and his gay identity may have had on his view of the world. This intimate exchange is signalled in the opening rooms of the exhibition where the five-hour film *Sleep* 1963, documenting Warhol's lover, the poet John Giorno, is presented alongside line drawings of men from the 1950s. From this position, and from between the usual headlines, other stories emerge: pop works are placed against a time of immense political and social change; Warhol's performative approach to the myth of artistic genius is revealed, and we see how, after his near-fatal shooting, he continued to flamboyantly and tirelessly find new ways of imaging the world that he inhabited. As we continue to develop and expand the way we think about the histories of art, *Andy Warhol* provides the perfect opportunity to contemplate how an artist who is so familiar and yet so alien can speak to the concerns of today.

The exhibition is the result of a close collaboration between Tate Modern and Museum Ludwig, Cologne whose respective collections have enabled us to bring together an exceptional presentation. We have also been supported by the other venues on the exhibition tour: Art Gallery of Ontario in Canada and Dallas Museum of Art in the United States. Such an ambitious project was made possible with the enthusiastic support of the Andy Warhol Foundation for the Visual Arts in New York, and we would like to extend our immense gratitude to Joel Wachs, President of the Foundation; Michael Hermann, Director of Licensing; and Neil Printz, Editor of the *Andy Warhol Catalogue Raisonné* who assisted with a number of loan requests. We are also most grateful to the Andy Warhol Museum in Pittsburgh and to its Director Patrick Moore for supporting the project. Special thanks are due to Jessica Beck, José Carlos Diaz, Kenneth Marshall, Amber Morgan, Erin Byrne, Geralyn Huxley, Gregory Pierce, Matt Gray and Patrick Seymour for both welcoming the curators to Pittsburgh and assisting in their research. We are thankful to Martin Cubjak and Michal Bycko of the Andy Warhol Museum of Modern Art in Medzilaborce, Slovakia who welcomed Gregor Muir on a trip that greatly influenced his research. We remain extremely grateful for the important conversations that we had with the following people about the project: Mandy Argenio, Bruno Bischofberger, Marina Clerici and Sofia Rasini, Bob Colacello, Tommaso Corvi-Mora, Donna DeSalvo, Roberto Di Giacomo, Nicola Erni, Vincent Fremont, Anita Froehlich, Alison Gingeras, Pauline Karpidas, Olivia Laing, Charlie Porter, Howard Reid, Jennifer Sichel, and Jean Wainwright.

A project of this scale relies heavily on the support of many. We are extremely grateful for the generosity with which works have been loaned from public and private collections and send our sincere thanks to Andy Warhol Museum, Pittsburgh; Art Gallery of Ontario, Toronto; ARTIST ROOMS; Fondation Louis Vuitton, Paris; Herbert F. Johnson Museum of Art, Ithaca; Hirshhorn Museum and Sculpture Garden, Washington D.C.; KOLUMBA, Cologne; Kunstmuseum Basel; Kunstsammlung Nordrhein-Westfalen, Düsseldorf; Museum für Angewandte Kunst, Frankfurt; Museum Brandhorst, Munich; Museum für Moderne Kunst, Frankfurt; Museum Ludwig; Museum of Applied Arts Cologne/ Collection Ulrich Reininghaus; Museum of Contemporary Art, Chicago; The Doris and Donald Fisher Collection at the San Francisco Museum of Modern Art; Exhibition records of the Contemporary Wing of the Finch College Museum of Art, Archives of American Art; Staatliche Museen zu Berlin, Berlin; Städtische Galerie im Lenbachhaus und Kunstbau Munich; Städtisches Museum Abteiberg Mönchengladbach berg; Tate; Tate Library, London; Whitney Museum of American Art, New York; Galerie des Modernes, Paris; the Udo and Anette Brandhorst Collection, Munich; John Cheim; Cheim & Reid, New York; Nicola Erni Collection; Froehlich Collection, Stuttgart; Larry Gagosian; the Peter and Irene Ludwig Foundation; Gregor Muir; the Private Collection of Phyllis and Jerome Lyle Rappaport; Collection Thaddaeus Ropac, London, Paris, Salzburg; the Paul Warhola Family Collection; Yageo Foundation, Taipei; and those lenders that wish to remain anonymous.

We would like to express our gratitude to the following individuals who helped to make specific loans possible: Susan Cary, Josh T. Franco and Craig Schiffert at Archives of American Art, Smithsonian Institution; Nicola Erni and Valentina Frug at the Nicola Erni Collection; Francis Outred and Jutta Nixdorf at Christie's;

Julia Peyton-Jones; Thaddaeus Ropac; Pierre Chen and Carol Huang at Yageo Foundation, Taipei.

We would like to thank the exhibition curators Gregor Muir, Director of Collection (International Art) and Fiontán Moran, Assistant Curator at Tate Modern; Stephan Diederich, Curator, Collection of Twentieth-Century Art at Museum Ludwig; and also Kenneth Brummel from Art Gallery of Ontario and Katherine Brodbeck at Dallas Museum of Art.

At Tate Modern, many thanks are due to Achim Borchardt-Hume, Director of Exhibitions and Programmes; Helen Sainsbury, Head of Exhibitions and Programme Management; and Rachel Kent, Senior Programme Manager, International Collaborations, each of whom offered support and advice on a range of matters. Samantha Crawford, Personal Assistant to Gregor Muir, provided essential assistance. Many thanks to Carol Burnier Magno, Exhibitions Registrar, for negotiating the loan agreements and coordinating the transportation of the artworks, and to Caroline McCarthy and Emma Denness for organising the display of works from the Tate and ARTIST ROOMS collections. Thanks to Neil Casey, Business and Operations Manager for his assistance with the budget, and to Genevieve Barton, Exhibitions Assistant, for her support on a range of curatorial tasks. Special thanks to the installation team: Phil Monk, Design and Production Manager, Richard Install, Art Installation Manager, Justina Budd, Art Installation Assistant, Glen Williams, Senior Art Handling Technician, and the art handlers. Thanks to our colleagues in Conservation, especially to Rachel Chrome, Charity Fox, Annette King, Louise Lawson, Jack McConchie and Alexandra Nichols, and colleagues in the Tate Library and Archive, especially Hayley Webb, Mina Gibaud and Anna Golodnitsky. Thanks to the LGBTQ+ Network for their support. We would like to thank our colleagues in Press and Marketing including Stephanie Biddle, Jessye Bloomfield, Elli Cartwright, Lee Cheshire, Duncan Holden, La Kingsbeer, Kitty Malton, Lindsay O'Leary, Liat Rosenthal, Johanna Sandler, Alex Stiles, and Rachael Young. Many thanks to David Hingley and Sandra McLean from Visitor Experience and all of the attendants that supervise the galleries;

Richard Martin and Jennifer Shearman for crafting the public programme; Kirsteen McSwein and Sophie Nibbs for their work on interpretation; Mark Crowley for the exhibition design, and North for the advertising campaign. Additional thanks are due to the Development team, including Charlotte Reeves, Margot Sprague-Davies, Sophie Busby, Nia Aronoffsky, Jonathan Howe and Laura Edwards.

For the catalogue, immense gratitude is due to Project Editor Emma Poulter, Picture Researcher Emma O'Neill and Production Manager Bill Jones, and of course to Kenneth Brummel, Bob Colacello, Stephan Diederich, Diedrich Diederichsen, Olivia Laing, Fiontán Moran, Gregor Muir, Charlie Porter and Martine Syms for their insightful contributions. Special thanks to The Bon Ton for their wonderful design.

At Museum Ludwig many thanks are due to the entire team; to Leonie Radine, Curatorial Assistant to the Director; Helena Kuhlmann and Simone Schmahl who assisted Stephan Diederich during the preparation of the exhibition; Antonella Müller who took care of the fundraising together with Maren Wohlenberg; the Registrars Anna Höfinghoff, Rachel Schumann, Petra Oepen and Christin Wähner; the Conservation Department with Katrin Keßler, Petra Mandt, Kristof Efferenn, Sophia Elze, Yvonne Garborini, Isabel Gebhardt and Astrid Schubert; the team of carpenters including Leif Lenzner, Michael Bangert, Milan Scharf, Max Rommeswinkel, Katrin Schwarz and Philipp Hawlitschek; Marc Dreckmann, Dirk Otter, Krzysztof Wojewoda and Leo Donauer for the building management; Iris Maczollek and Helen Meßler for the exhibition management; Guido Fassbender, Christian Gotte, Thomas Loerzer, Uwe Mode, Peter Pier, Isa Uzun, Ingo Weber, Andreas Wischum and Michael Zorn for the technical management; Artefact for setting up the exhibition; the Art Handlers Paul Eßer and Jürgen Koll; Katrin Sauerländer for taking care of the German edition of this catalogue; the Press and Public Relations Department with Kirsten te Brake, Sonja Hempel, Anne Niermann, Donata Rahnenführer, Judith Specht, Paulina Thillmann and Meliha Schadwinkel; Angelika von Tomaszewski and Diana A. Schuster for the education programme; the Archivists Anina Baum, Beate Bischoff and Meike Deilmann; Axel Kuhn for the storage management; Ulla Bönnen, Brit

Meyer and Morgaine Schäfer of the Collection of Prints and Drawings; and the Administration with Angela Coenen, Marion Funken, Alexander Bach, Melanie Evers, Nicole Faust, Ilona Orban-Boysen and Ella Krüger.

Museum Ludwig thanks the city of Cologne for the additional support of the exhibition *Andy Warhol. Now*. We would like to thank the cultural policy spokespersons for their substantial support. In particular, we are grateful to the Head of the Department of Culture Susanne Laugwitz-Aulbach for her commitment.

The Peter and Irene Ludwig Foundation has been a substantial supporter of the museum for many years, to which we would like to express our thanks, especially to Isabel Pfeiffer-Poensgen and Brigitte Franzen. Thanks also to the Gesellschaft für Moderne Kunst am Museum Ludwig e.V., the team, its members, the Managing Directors Carla Cugini and Adelheid Komenda, and Executive Board, especially Mayen Beckmann.

Museum Ludwig would also like to thank for their generous support the CEO of the REWE Group, Lionel Souque, along with the Head of Corporate Communication, Martin Brüning. And our thanks also go to the Strabag Real Estate and its Managing Director Rainer M. Schäfer, as well as Marcus Kaller.

The *Andy Warhol* exhibition at Tate Modern is presented in The Eyal Ofer Galleries. This exhibition is in partnership with Bank of America, with additional support from the Andy Warhol Exhibition Supporters Circle, including long-standing Tate supporters Lydia and Manfred Gorvy; Tate Americas Foundation, Tate International Council, Tate Patrons and Tate Members, to whom we would like to thank for generously supporting the exhibition.

The exhibition in London has been made possible by the provision of insurance through the Government Indemnity Scheme. Tate Modern would like to thank HM Government, and the Department for Digital, Culture, Media and Sport and Arts Council England for arranging the indemnity.

Frances Morris, Director, Tate Modern

Yilmaz Dziewior, Director, Museum Ludwig

ANDY WARHOL
OUTSIDER ON THE INSIDE?

Gregor Muir & Yilmaz Dziewior

'When I think of my high school days, all I can remember, really, are the long walks to school, through the Czech ghetto with the babushkas and the overalls on the clothesline, in McKeesport, Pennsylvania. I wasn't amazingly popular, but I had some nice friends. I wasn't very close to anyone, although I guess I wanted to be, because when I would see the kids telling one another their problems, I felt left out. — Andy Warhol[1]'

This could start out, as many introductions do, by positioning Warhol as a cultural icon: one of the most influential figures of the twentieth century. This may well be true; however, there is a predictability with which Warhol is upheld as some form of psychedelic messiah: his life seen as one unbroken success story set against a backdrop of the Silver Factory. Some go further, citing elements of the world around us as a reflection of his enduring presence. Take, for instance, the closed-circuit world of 'reality TV', or the concept of 'famous for being famous'. Then there is the arrival of social media such as Facebook and Instagram, consensual networks where active participants self-promote at the touch of a button. Whereas Warhol pre-dates our digitally enabled culture, we nevertheless sense how the artist was ahead of his time and that he, unlike many of his contemporaries, remains well placed to help us make sense of our present day – Warhol having patented the future a long time ago. Ultimately, what we should take from all this enthusiasm is that Warhol's influence won out, more so than that of any other artist who would daunt him during his lifetime.

Warhol is eternal. In a highly prized in-game commercial during the 2019 Super Bowl, the most expensive intermission in the world, one hundred million people were treated to a forty-five-second advertisement showing the artist, clear as day, eating a Burger King 'Whopper': a slowly unfolding scene ending with the hashtag #EatLikeAndy (fig.1). While the fixed-camera shot of someone doing not that much chimes with the underlying principles of a Warhol *Screen Test*, the scene was actually a collaboration with Danish poet and filmmaker Jørgen Leth, and formed part of Leth's 1982 film work *66 Independent Scenes*. At the time of the Super Bowl airing, Warhol would have been ninety years old. Enshrined in the very media that once employed him, the artist – seen momentarily struggling to pour ketchup from a bottle – seems unchanged, timeless. It's as though he never left us.

Furthermore, the voice-over of a Coca-Cola commercial, aired during the same Super Bowl, resurrected Warhol once again: 'A Coke is a Coke, is a Coke. You can get one anywhere. It's the same for everyone ...' In an attempt to emphasise

Fig.1 Still from the Burger King advert, aired during the 2019 Super Bowl. The scene ('Andy Warhol Eating a Hamburger') is one of the scenes from Jørgen Leth's *66 Independent Scenes* 1982

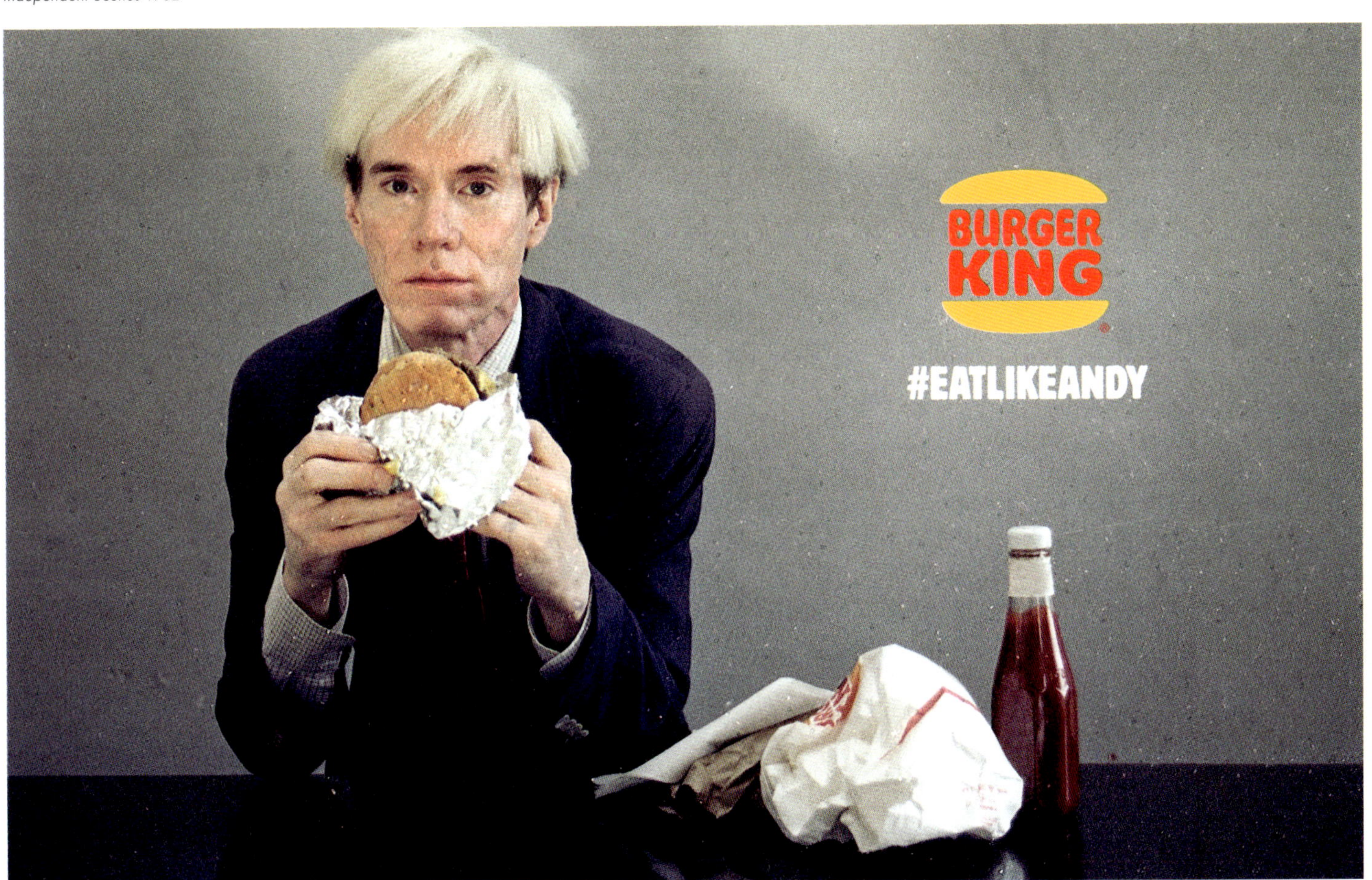

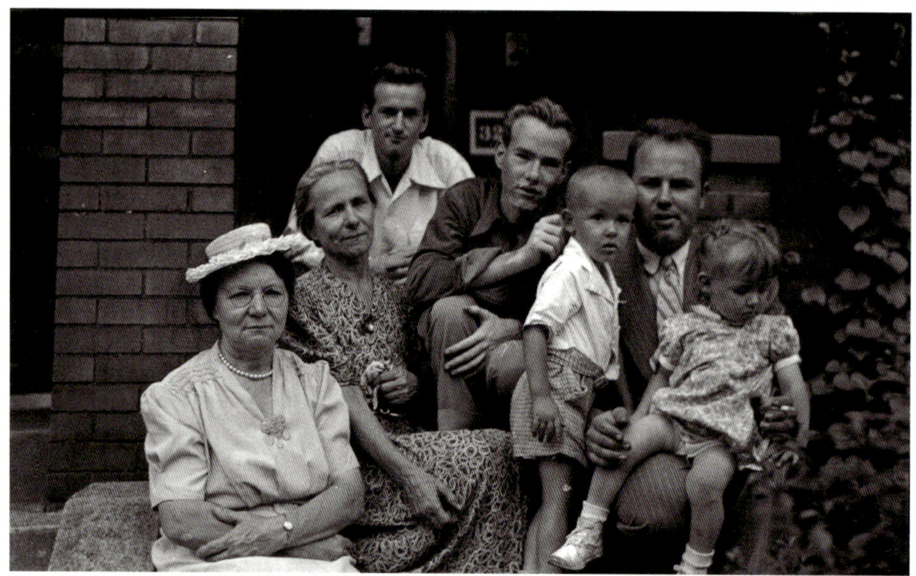

Fig.2 *Warhola Family*
1946–7
Photograph; black and
white negative 7 x 11.7
The Andy Warhol
Museum, Pittsburgh

its diverse customer base, Coca-Cola's
catchline inevitably returns us to a quote
from *The Philosophy of Andy Warhol:
From A to B and Back Again*: 'A Coke is
a Coke and no amount of money can get
you a better Coke than the one the bum
on the corner is drinking. All the Cokes
are the same and all the Cokes are good.
Liz Taylor knows it, the President knows
it, the bum knows it, and you know it ...'[2]
Democratisation, equality, the joining of
the circle between socialism and capitalism
... it is somewhere in here that Warhol
once hoped to position his work as a form
of 'Commonism', merging 'common' with
'Communist'.[3] 'Commonism' was a term he
preferred to the imported British definition
'pop art', which he thought sounded awful.
In more recent years, Slavoj Žižek
– the Slovenian philosopher whose
relationship with Coca-Cola is at best arch
– has referred to the product's invisible,
transcendent essence. 'It was already
[Karl] Marx who long ago emphasised that
a commodity is never just a simple object
that we buy and consume. A commodity
is an object full of theological, even
metaphysical, niceties.'[4] Given its mystery
and allure, as Žižek would have it, Coca-
Cola remains one of America's best-
known entities, much like Warhol himself.

To hold a mirror up to America,
Warhol's focus had to be on the most
American of products, including dollar
bills (p.99), tabloid imagery, Hollywood
stars and ultimately Andy himself. His total
immersion in the American Century would
imbue him with a gum-chewing all-American

persona, one that would help define
a nation to which he expressed a sense
of belonging. If we read the more prolific
and defining statements about Warhol,
we find reference to his being the most
famous American artist in the world,
indeed one of the world's most famous
Americans. In his book *America*, Warhol
reflects on his condition: 'We all came
here from somewhere else, and everybody
who wants to live in America and obey
the law should be able to come too, and
there's no such thing as being more or less
American, just American.'[5] Those last two
words, 'just American', seem to hang in the
air. In his lifetime, Warhol saw out many US
presidents, including Roosevelt, Eisenhower,
JFK, Nixon, Carter and Reagan. How,
then, might 'just American' play out in the
emotional wake of the Trump era?

In posing such a question in the
age of 'Make America Great Again',
the organisers of this exhibition felt a
fundamental need to be reminded of who
Andy Warhol actually was. Furthermore,
how can it be that one of America's
greatest artists, possibly *the* greatest, would
find it difficult to gain acceptance under the
present administration, as an effeminate
gay man born into an immigrant family?
From this vantage point, might we look on to
a life shaped by his family's roots, as well
as his mother's religious conviction, which
in Warhol's case just goes to show how the

Fig.3 *Living Room* 1948
Watercolour on paper
38.1 x 50.8
Paul Warhola Family
Collection

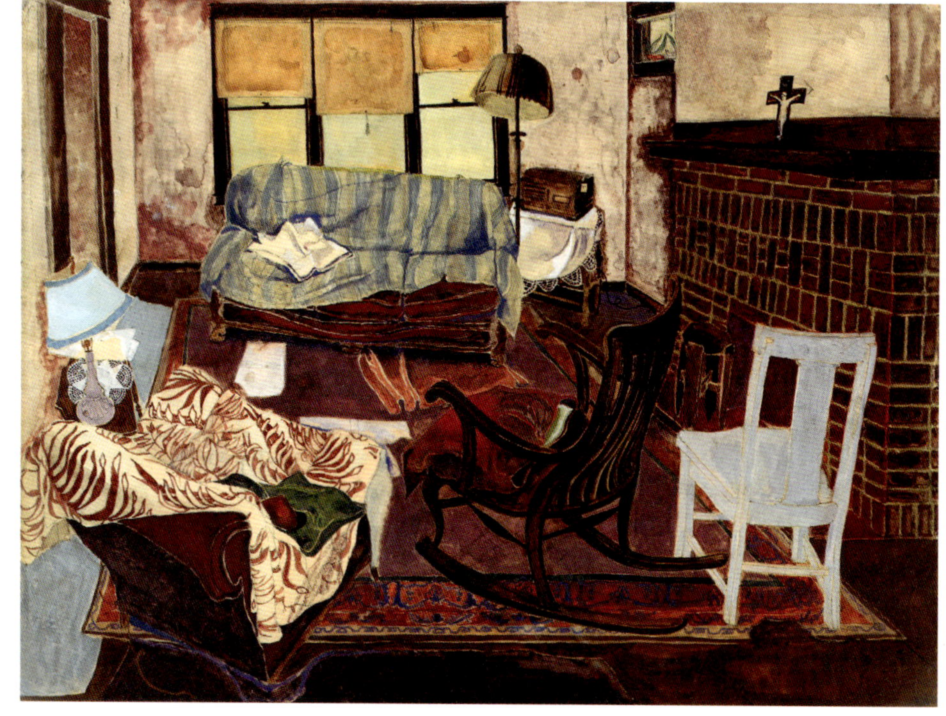

apple doesn't fall far from the tree. Then there is the artist's lifelong obsession with death, both in close-up and from afar, spanning the *Death and Disaster* paintings to the moment of his own shooting, while taking into account his spiritual reckonings as a man of faith. Consequently, the three main headings began to form: 'Immigrant', 'Queer', 'Death/Religion'. It is through these lenses that we wanted to return to Andy Warhol.

Rather sweetly, and anticipating his later work, Warhol made audio recordings of his mother, Julia Warhola, singing traditional folk songs from the old country, which he also had printed as vinyl records. Her forlorn vibrato rising above the crackles, Julia sings old Rusyn songs, such as 'Červena Ruža Trojaka' (A Rose with Three Shades of Paint), which recounts the fortunes of a woman who flees her drunken husband on a ship, waving goodbye with a flick of a scarf. In another recording Julia recites a religious chant, marking a distinct shift in mood as she assumes a more monotonous drone; as a young woman, Julia knew the liturgy and other services by heart. Reminiscent of her distant past, Julia's voice takes us back to her birthplace, the remote village of Miková, situated in the Eastern Carpathians or Lower Beskid Hills, just below Slovakia's northern border with Poland.

The sixth of fifteen children, Júlia Justína Zavacká was a force of nature who suffered serious hardship from early adulthood right through to her son's shooting in 1968. In 1911, unable to raise a doctor, Julia lost her first child and only daughter, Maria (also cited as Justina), after just six weeks. In 1918 her mother, Justína Zavacká, died, leaving Julia orphaned at the age of twenty-six to raise her younger siblings (Julia's father had died in 1909). Such traumas were endured in the absence of her husband, Andrej Varchola, also from Miková, whom she married in 1909. (Different sources cite Andrej as Andrij or Ondreij.) When they first met, Julia was seventeen. Andrej – having just returned from America – was twenty. Finding him a handsome man, it nevertheless took the efforts of a local priest, and a box of chocolates from her courting husband-to-be, to persuade Julia of the merits of marrying Andrej, or 'Andy' as she always knew him. Fearing conscription to the army, Andrej would later return to America, having run across

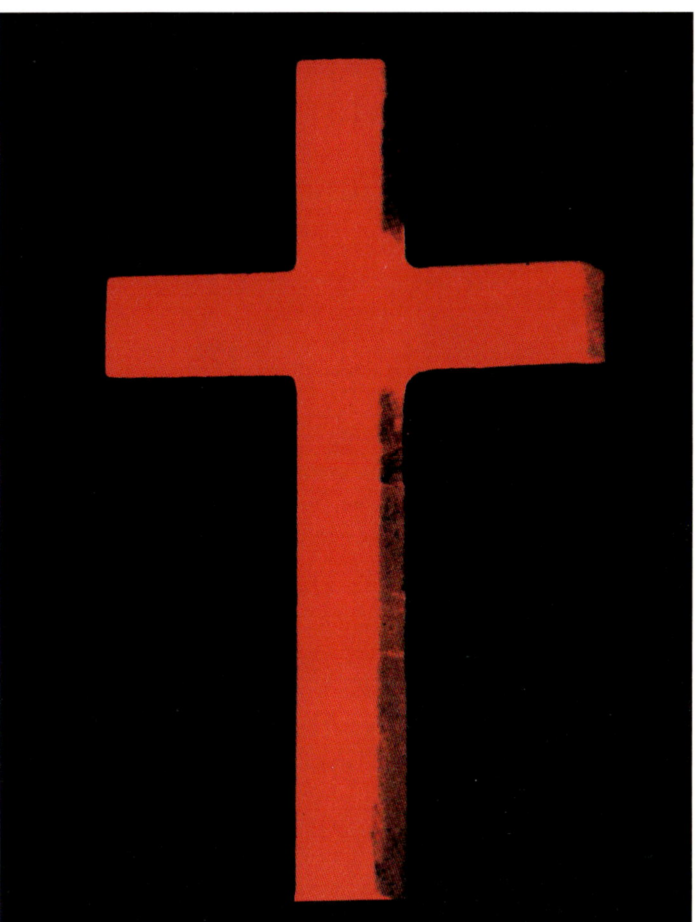

Fig.4 **Cross** 1981–2
Acrylic paint and screenprint
on canvas 229 x 178
Kolumba Museum, Cologne

the border under cover of night to nearby Poland, leaving Julia behind to eke out a frugal existence that would see out the First World War. Following a long period of separation from her husband, Julia finally negotiated a loan from the Church so she could cross the Atlantic to be with Andrej in 1921.

The Warholas (fig.2) had undertaken an epic journey from Miková to Prague, Prague to Hamburg, and then by steamship to Ellis Island, where their entry to the United States is recorded on the American Immigrant Wall of Honor. In Pittsburgh they were by no means alone, joining other 'new immigrants',[6] predominantly from Czechoslovakia, who came to settle in the surrounding areas, alongside those from other Eastern Europe countries such as Hungary, Poland, Romania and Slovenia. Lured by the promise of a new life, others came from Belgium, France and Holland. For Julia, events would again take a turn for the worse when her husband died in 1942. Andrej, a hardworking man by all accounts, became ill on a construction job in West Virginia after drinking toxic water. According to Paul, the eldest of the three Warhola brothers: 'We were told that Dad died of liver problems. He had never been ill before, never taken any medicines and then he was suffering for six weeks and slowly dying, until he passed away.'[7] In accordance with the family's wishes, Andrej's body was laid to rest at home for three days. Much has been said about Warhol's fear of death with particular reference to this tragic event: the young Andy hid in his bedroom, unable to venture downstairs for fear of confronting his father's corpse. In 1944 having nursed Andy through various ailments from scarlet fever to St Vitus's dance, Julia developed colon cancer, requiring extensive surgery and hospitalisation. Once again, the mortality of a family member was at stake, only this time their prayers were answered. Julia survived her operation.

The Warhola story is truly an immigrant story: something that reveals itself not only in the need to leave Miková for Pittsburgh, thousands of miles away, but in incremental changes to the family name, which in the first instance changed from Varchola to Varhola – a misspelling from the time of the establishment of the Czechoslovak Republic in 1918. (The Czechoslovak Republic would become the Independent Slovak Republic in 1939, before being renamed Czechoslovakia in 1945, followed by a period of Communist rule from 1948 until the ironically named Velvet Divorce in 1989, paving the way for modern-day Slovakia). Now in America, the family name changed from Varhola to Warchola, as recorded by a Pittsburgh registry official in 1922, following the birth of Andy's brother Paul. From Warchola, the name changed yet again to Warhola, after the birth of Andy's second brother John in 1925. And finally a young Andrew Warhola chose to omit the last 'a' from his surname, as immigrants were known to do to seem more American. As John Warhola recounts: '[Andy] told me that when he first started it was hard for him to get a job. With a name like Warhola everyone knew he was either a Slovak or an Italian. When he dropped the "a" at the end, they didn't know if he was a German, or where he was from. So he just took the "a" off.'[8] And so Varchola became Warhol.

It is unsurprising, then, that this tight-knit family – bonded through adversity yet fearlessly aspirational (epitomised by Andy's graduation from Carnegie Institute

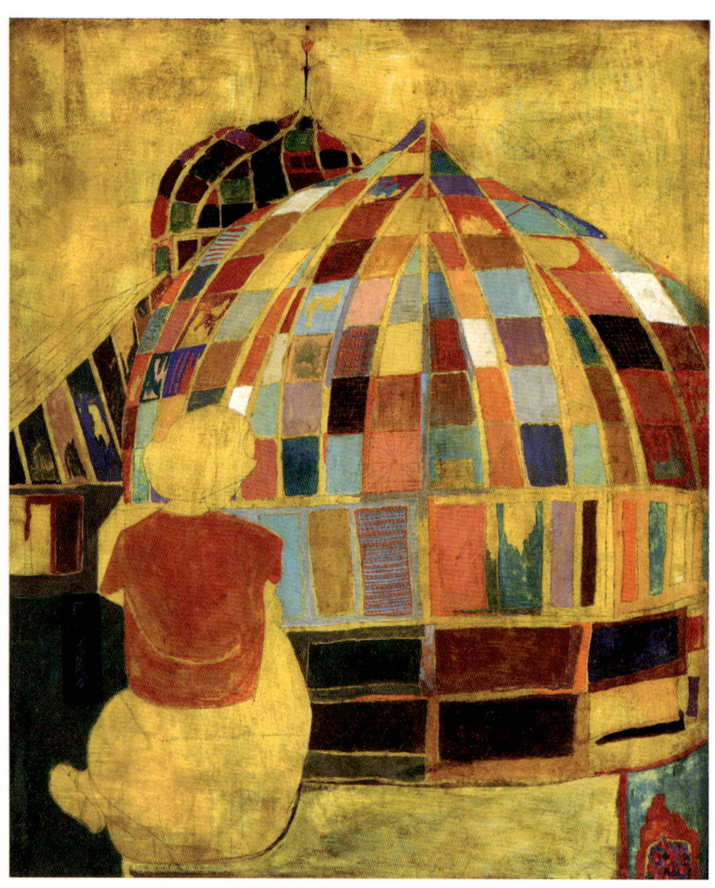

Fig.5 *Girl in Park* 1948
Tempera on Masonite
61 x 50.8
Paul Warhola Family
Collection

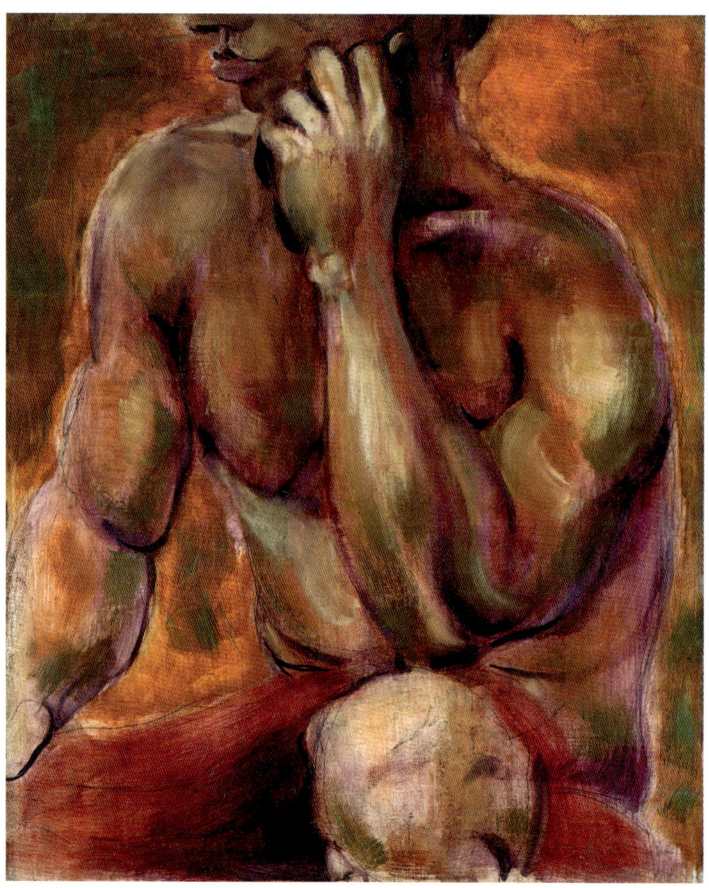

Fig.6 *Male Figure* 1948
Tempera on Masonite
61 x 50.8
Paul Warhola Family
Collection

of Technology in 1949) – would now find its nucleus in the relationship between Andy and his mother. Through her he became familiar from an early age with the fanciful folk decoration, like the embroidery on pillows or the crocheted tablecloths that he depicted in his painting *Living Room* 1948 (fig.3). In the same painting a crucifix stands prominently on the mantelpiece, and hints at the omnipresent religious spirit of their home in Pittsburgh. It was also his mother who spoke to him in the first language he would learn, Rusyn, which the family spoke at home.

Eventually purchasing a narrow townhouse in 1959 with funds from his flourishing advertising career, Julia came to live with Andy at 1342 Lexington Avenue for the best part of twenty years. It is hard to imagine how Warhol could have escaped Julia's Carpatho-Rusyn past and her ongoing devotion to the Ruthenian Greek-Catholic Church of the Byzantine Rite – or, as upheld by Miková, the old Russian faith. Sensitive of his upbringing and being labelled a 'Hunkie',[9] Warhol's first artistic collaboration would nevertheless be with his mother, whose beautiful ornate handwriting adorned his early commissions and books (p.84). Having co-opted Julia into the heart of his burgeoning artistic practice, Julia's calligraphic flourishes remain resolutely bound to the old world, which raises the question of whether Warhol ever let go. (As one of the great hoarders, did he ever let go of anything?) It seems inconceivable that certain aspects of Warhol's upbringing could be cosmetically erased overnight, religion being one. His artistic involvement with religious themes is not only reflected in the composition and formal structure of some of his works, in which he used, for example, golden backgrounds, or when he created *Round Marilyn* in 1962 (p.101). There is also evidence of religious influences in the iconography in his works, such as *Cross* 1981–2 (fig.4) and *Sixty Last Suppers* 1986 (pp.204–5), or as early as 1948 in *Girl in Park* (fig.5), in which he depicted a girl in front of a cupola resembling a Greek Orthodox church.

Another aspect of Warhol's personality, which comes up time and time again and yet seems strangely unresolved, is his perceived asexuality. Shortly after arriving in New York, Warhol entered a world of like-minded men, which is where we find a newly emboldened young buck,

photographed wearing a preppy blazer and tie outside his favourite café, Serendipity 3 on the Upper East Side (fig.7). As his sexuality began to assert itself, his line drawings became more risqué, more explicit. Might these early drawings of men with flowers, men in tight jeans, male profiles, male nudes (fig.6, pp.74–9) and so forth come under the heading *asexual*? Warhol also portrayed women, but it is in his depictions of men that the artist's direction of travel is confirmed. Was the term *asexual* allowed to flourish around Warhol as a means of covering up his queer identity? Was it a dealer term, to help with the more prudish clients, interchangeable with terms like ambiguous? It is hard not to be amused by Wayne Koestenbaum's contrasting, head-on approach: 'How gay was Warhol? As gay as you can get.'[10]

A recently unearthed recording of an interview between Warhol and the young art critic Gene Swenson – held in the presence of studio assistant Gerard Malanga and two friends called John and Rory – helps shed further light. Heavily redacted versions of the interview appeared in two articles published

Fig.7 Andy Warhol
and Stephen Bruce at
Serendipity 3, c.1962
Photo by John Ardoin
Private collection

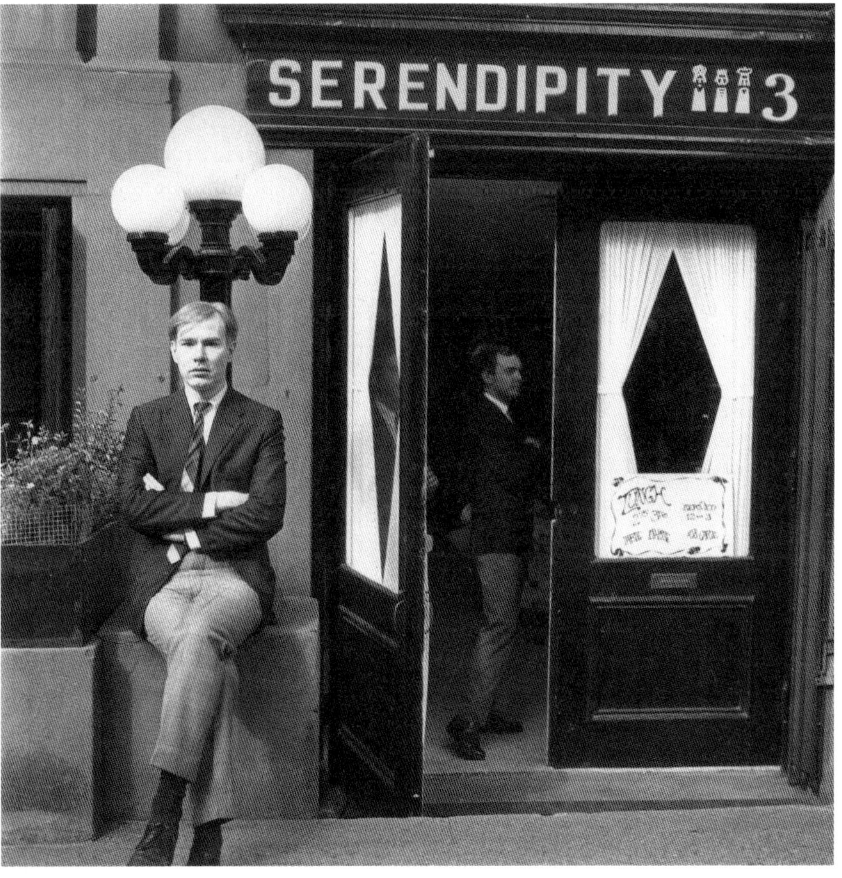

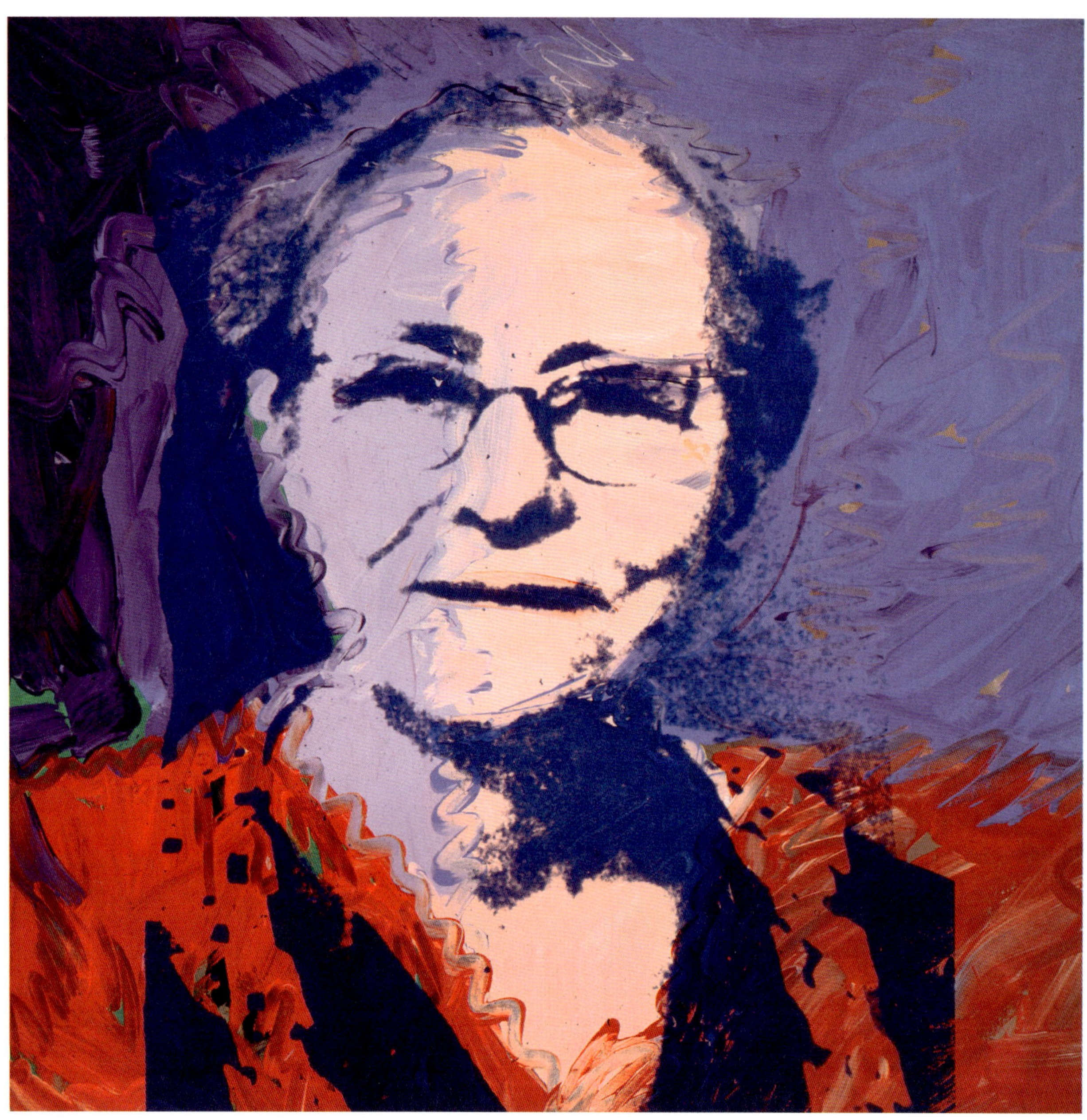

Fig.8 *Julia Warhola* 1974
Acrylic paint and screenprint
on canvas 101.6 x 101.6
The Andy Warhol Museum,
Pittsburgh, PA

in *ARTnews* in November 1963 and February 1964. The recording jumps in on the gathering of young men giving male abstract expressionist artists female names: whereby Norman Bluhm becomes Norma Bluhm, Michael Goldberg becomes Michele Goldberg and the dealer Ivan Karp becomes Eva Karp (more likely to be Ivanka, presently). Soon after, Warhol declared how the entire interview should be about homosexuality, proposing that other artists should be drawn on the subject, artists such as Jim Dine or Claes Oldenburg. The recording continues with Warhol rounding on the idea of how 'everybody should like everybody', that pop art is about 'liking things' and 'liking things is being like a machine'. Warhol then makes mention of how we 'do the same thing every time', all the time, and that, in a non-discriminatory way, everything we do uses things up, 'like you use people up'. Swenson challenges this: 'And you approve of it?' Warhol responds, 'Yes. Because it's all a fantasy.'[11] Swenson then hits upon the idea of confronting artists with the question 'Do you think Pop Art is queer?' Throughout the interview, what predominates is a certain knowingness that in the early 1960s the word 'queer' stands in for a view of the world (and art) in much the same way as it does today. As Jennifer Sichel summarised:

The new revelation that Warhol constructed his 'fantasy' about everybody being a machine and liking everybody explicitly as a 'kind of different' strategy to speak on the record about homosexuality in a fantastical way that could be generative, open, and ambiguous – or, in a word, queer – indeed confirms what scholars have long surmised: that even as Warhol's work addresses consumerism, serial production, and modernist myths of authenticity and creativity, it is also and fundamentally about queer ways of feeling and being in the world.[12]

Warhol held back from entering the fray of the gay liberation movement, although his own brand of radicalism would always stand for a great deal. In the 1960s Warhol represented an alternative to the heteronormative world of the abstract expressionists: the Factory becoming a refuge for those who broadened the spectrum of New York's underground scene. However, by the late 1960s Warhol had alienated, as well as been alienated by, counterculture's hardening wing, which sought to express itself through militant forms of activism. Warhol's infatuation with the rich and famous was unlikely to square with the ideals of those taking to the streets to protest against the Vietnam War, sexual repression or gender inequality.

The optics on Warhol would soon change forever as the naivety and playfulness of the early years were abruptly shattered. Warhol was shot at the Union Square Factory on 3 June 1968.

[Solanas] waited while [Warhol] took a call from Viva and when he hung up, she pumped three bullets into his chest and abdomen from a few feet away. She then shot Mario Amaya, a visiting curator, and aimed her .32-caliber automatic pistol at Fred Hughes, but it jammed. Andy was rushed to Columbus-Mother Carbrini Hospital on East 19th Street, where he was pronounced clinically dead at 4.51 P.M. His chest was cut open and his heart massaged, and then five doctors operated for five hours on his lungs, liver, gallbladder, spleen, esophagus, intestines and pulmonary artery. – Bob Colacello[13]

Because of his lifestyle, Warhol had exposed himself to personal risk, especially during the Silver Factory years. However, the open-door policy was now at an end. Warhol would never be the same again. For a time, shy Andy became reclusive Andy. Social projects were dropped.

Death would always be at Warhol's core, reinforced by his religious belief, the traumatising effects of his father's passing and events surrounding his mother's past. Still recovering from being shot and learning to live life in a medical corset, Warhol would have been crushed by news of his mother's death in 1972, not ambivalent as some have speculated. His insistence on a frugal service would have been in keeping with his mother's wishes; Andy had already paid for Julia's Pittsburgh nursing home, followed by a funeral he would never attend. Fearing death to such a degree that he would ask drivers to detour around hospitals, Warhol would have been incapable of facing his mother's funeral. Moreover, the intense secrecy he maintained around his mother's passing suggests a pathological need to conceal Julia's memory from everyone's view, even his own: a spell that to some extent was broken with a series of paintings of his mother in the style of the celebrity portraits, which appeared in 1974 (fig.8).

By the early 1970s Warhol had thrown himself back into his work, returning as the painter he had once set out to be prior to the *Silver Clouds* exhibition at the Leo Castelli Gallery in 1966, which was supposed to signal his retirement from painting. The paintings of *Mao* (p.158), *Hammer and Sickle* (p.159), *Ladies and Gentlemen* (pp.162–71), *Torso* (fig.9 and p.179), *Oxidation Painting* (pp.180–1) and *Shadow* (pp.182–3) would all follow in rapid succession (a prolific period of production, especially given his physical condition). From 1972 onwards, *Andy Warhol's Interview* – with its beautifully airbrushed covers by Richard Bernstein – contributed to the decade's signature style (pp.174–7). By the late 1970s he was a regular attendee at Studio 54 and a permanent fixture on New York's disco scene. By the early 1980s Warhol fused his artistic interests with television and music videos, becoming increasingly linked with artists such as Jean-Michel Basquiat or Blondie's Debbie Harry.

Warhol's activities had the potential to open minds as well as connecting people across the world by making subculture appeal to the masses. Issues and topics that seemed far away from everyday life found their way into American households through his publishing output. With *Interview*, Warhol provided cultural icons from the worlds of fashion, music, film, photography, religion and so on with a platform on which to communicate in an unredacted and unapologetic manner.

The contrast between the intimacy and privacy of subculture and its outspoken representation can also be traced in his work for the screen. Films like *Sleep* 1963 (pp.25, 122) and the *Screen Tests* 1964–6 (pp.124–6) communicate subcultural elements in a quieter, more visually focused and subtle way compared to the excessive and provocative films, or the TV series conceived for cable networks and the broader public. The TV productions in particular brought a usually very tight-knit community of celebrities with their glamourous, dark charm into people's living rooms. Almost making subculture mainstream by not hiding but exposing its protagonists, these works contributed to increased tolerance for certain personalities or topics by arousing curiosity about those on TV and what they stood for. This transformation of subculture into pop culture coincided with the emergence of the LGBTQ+ movement.

By exploring the subject of the male body and its characteristic features in his early drawings (pp.74–9) in a more private, quiet manner than in his later works, Warhol seemed to capture fleeting but intimate moments between the often-anonymous subject and the artist. The private and homey nature of those drawings stands in contrast to the glamorous and colourful paintings of the *Ladies and Gentlemen* series of the 1970s (pp.162–71). Warhol's approach of taking Polaroids and using them as templates was also a sign of personal interaction and closeness between the artist and those portrayed. However, here the subject matter – the drag queens and transwomen – step out of the personal relationship with Warhol into the colourful limelight of interaction with the beholder. This series is a pioneering depiction of drag and trans culture as well as of queerness. Bringing these ladies or, in another example, male body features such as those in the *Torso* paintings (fig.9 and p.179), to the large canvas, opened up subculture to mainstream pop culture.

By showing explicit imagery of the male body and drug consumption in various forms of artistic expression, Warhol, like nobody else, provoked, commented on and, most importantly, represented what was a controversial reality at the time. He also depicted personalities such as Grace Jones, Roy Halston Frowick and Diana Ross. These subjects raised the public's awareness of the discussions and topics circulating around these figures and marked a milestone in the fight for equality and more inclusive understanding. Meanwhile, throughout the 1980s the spectre of HIV/AIDS would start to impact on the lives of many in Warhol's circle.

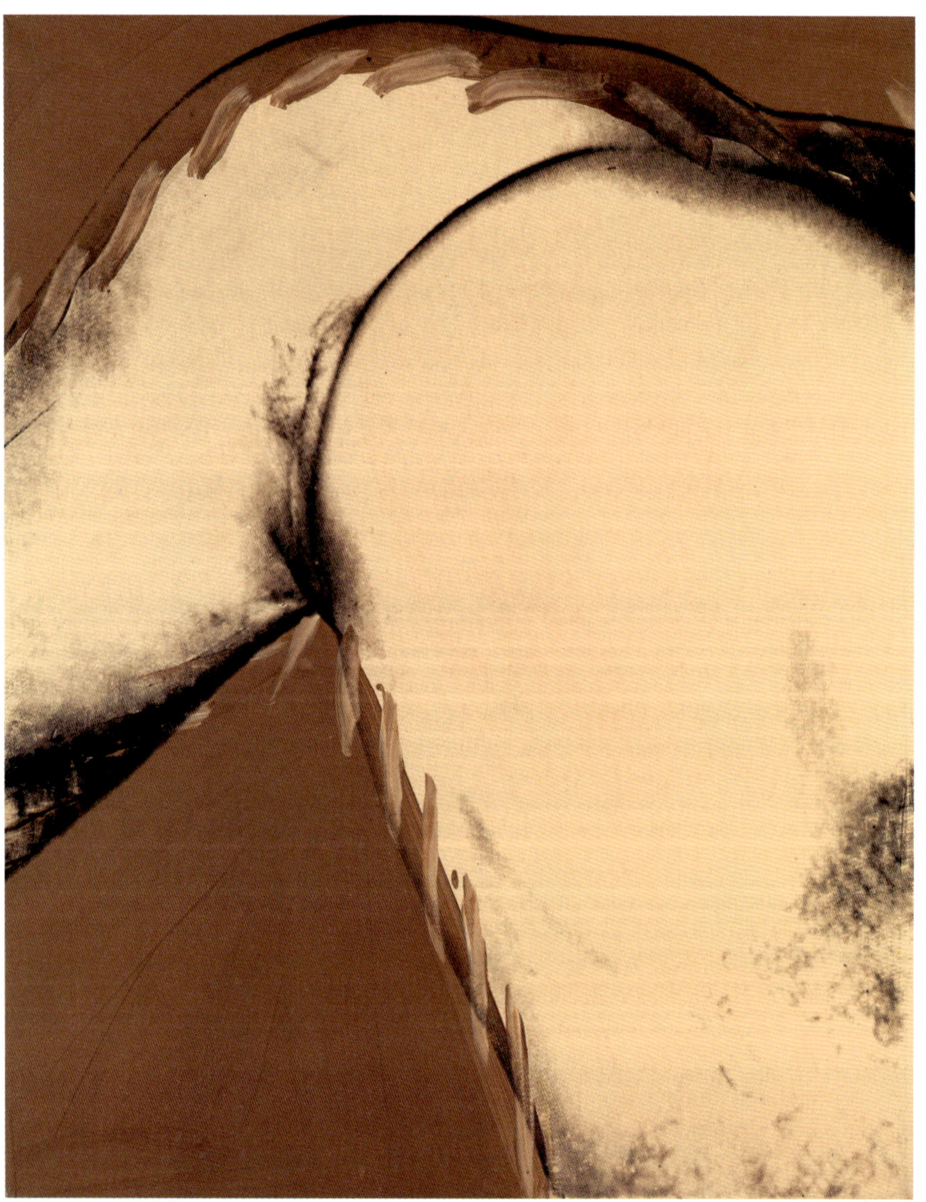

Fig.9 *Torso* 1977
Acrylic paint and screenprint
on canvas 127 x 101.5
Private collection

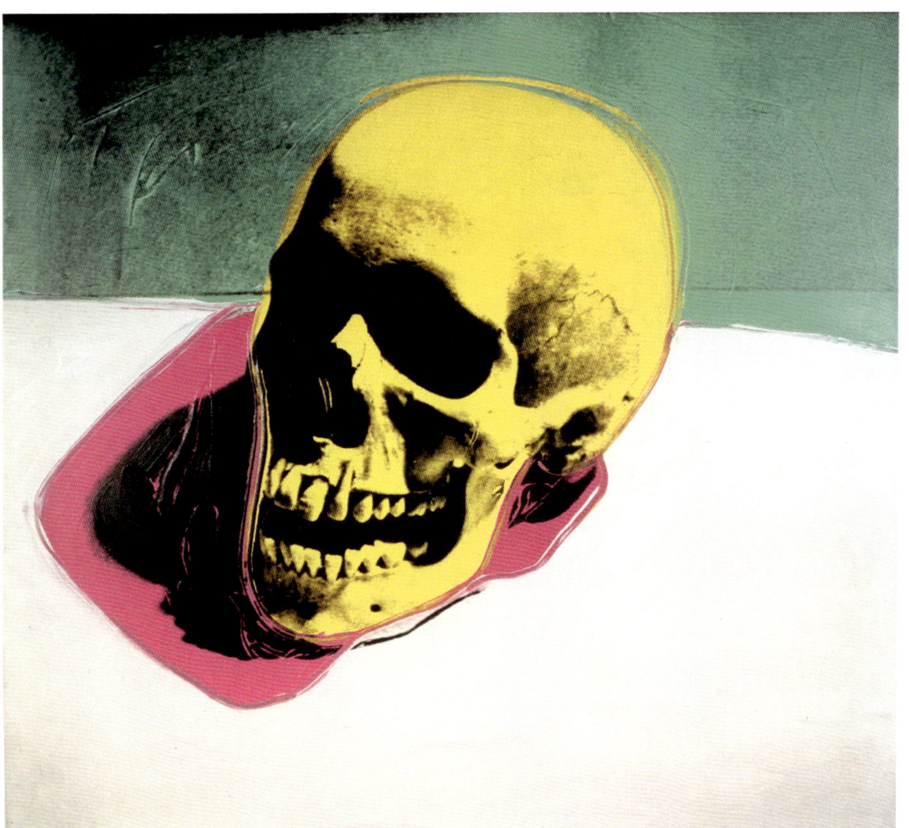

Fig. 10 *Skull* 1976
Acrylic paint and screenprint
on canvas 183.5 x 203.8
Froehlich Collection, Stuttgart

Given the dazzling urgency of the 1970s and early 1980s, and Warhol's perceived fame, it may come as a surprise to hear talk of the artist being washed up, of being yesterday's man. However, ever since the *Mao* paintings in 1972, it appears few people had a good word to say about Andy. While his public profile was high, his art kudos was low, or at least faltering, after too many concessions to fame and money.

Having thrown himself back into life after the shooting, Warhol now started to concern himself with the dreaded return to hospital for a much-needed gallbladder operation, which he desperately tried to postpone for as long as possible. (As his condition worsened, Warhol was advised to admit himself to hospital immediately, but instead chose to stash jewellery and other valuables in his bedroom safe at 57 East 66th Street.) This was to be a major operation, not routine surgery as previously claimed. Warhol saw fit to hire a private nurse, Min Chou, while checking himself in as 'Bob Robert'. The operation must have come with an air of inevitability, Warhol's father having had his gallbladder removed in 1928. However, unlike his father, Warhol was a sick man whose body had never recovered from the shooting. His operation was so long overdue that his gallbladder was said to have disintegrated upon removal. Warhol survived the operation, but suffered a heart attack during recovery. At 6.21 am on 22 February 1987 Warhol died at the New York Hospital aged fifty-eight.

Having inscribed himself in the world around us, to the point where his eating a burger was deemed worthy of a Super Bowl commercial, Warhol remains a constant force. We didn't have to meet Andy to know Andy. Just like him, we too are consumed by surfaces, and are happy to meet him there, just where he said he would be, on the surface of his work and personae. As Jack Bankowsky brilliantly confessed: 'As a forever Warhol devotee, I feel proprietary, cranky, when it comes to other people's Andys.'[14] He is not alone. We all carry a version of Andy with us. For some he is a cartoon character, epitomised by a pop-era can of soup. For others, he is the silver-wigged hipster who discovered the Velvet Underground, or Andy the experimental filmmaker, or Andy promoting a Commodore Amiga computer. Even Warhol must have held a version of Andy in mind: a mental projection of himself to which he would aspire in everyday life – a world of lotions and potions as time went by. And throughout all of this, there was a sense of dread, as befitting a man who had been shot, and had already died. In this way, the skull paintings and 'fright-wig' self-portraits become his death mask, and the *Last Supper* paintings his final incarceration in art. Warhol always knew something was coming, and it wasn't just the future.

A LA LA LA
AN ANDY WARHOL
ALPHABET

Olivia Laing

A
IS FOR ANDY

'I'm nobody',[1] Andy Warhol once said, and made himself one of the most recognisable people alive by exaggerating all his defects, transforming untouchable into iconic. As a young man in New York City, he was poor, ugly, unpopular, the child of immigrants, queer, cripplingly shy, an outsider in every way.

B
IS FOR BEAUTY

In despair at his own appearance, Warhol venerated beauty. But his definition of beauty was generous, encompassing, radically open. 'I've never met a person I couldn't call a beauty',[2] he said, and abandoned a film project called *The Beauties* because he didn't want to exclude anyone from it. He made art out of the most democratic materials he could find, dismantling the barrier between the art object and the ordinary, intricate world outside. Soup cans, dollar bills, car crashes and celebrities: nothing should be excluded, everything deserved a closer look. He wanted to call pop art 'Common Art', that is, not exclusive, for us, never mind the prices it commands today. Get this: 'America is really The Beautiful. But it would be more beautiful if everybody had enough money to live.'[3]

C
IS FOR CATHOLIC

You could call this a religious motivation, along the lines of Christ in the Gospel of St Matthew enjoining his followers to care for the 'the least of these', although you shouldn't discount the layers of Factory-wrought irony. Andy was raised in the Ruthenian Greek Catholic Church. Even in the 1980s, when he was a staple on the party circuit, he went to Mass most days at St Vincent Ferrer, a block from his house at 57 East 66th Street. He sat at the back, embarrassed, he said, because he crossed himself the wrong way. Christmas, Easter and Thanksgiving were spent serving up lunch and pouring coffee for the homeless, anonymously, at the Church of Heavenly Rest.

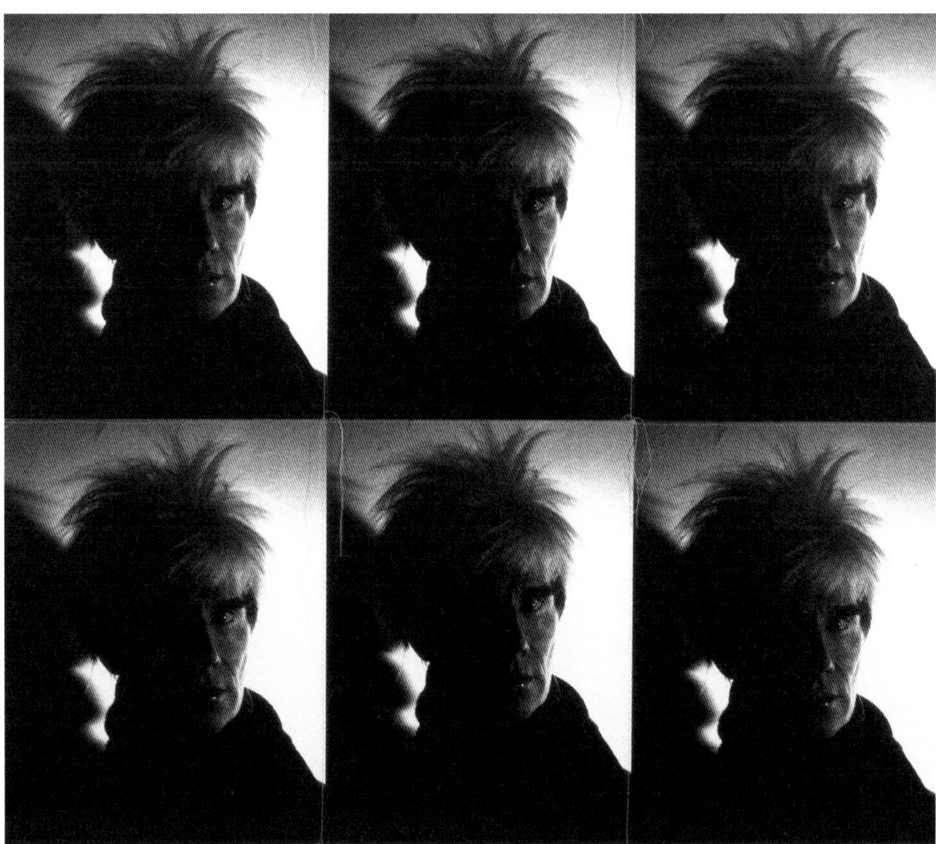

Fig.1 *Self-Portrait*
1976–86 (detail)
6 photographs; gelatin silver prints on paper and thread
96.2 x 106.4 (overall)
ARTIST ROOMS Tate and National Galleries of Scotland

D
IS FOR DEATH

The first time Andy died was on 3 June 1968, when he was shot with a .32 Beretta by Valerie Solanas. The bullet passed through most of his major organs, wounding him so gravely that during surgery his heart stopped beating and he was clinically dead for a minute and a half. He'd always been terrified of death. When he was a kid he hid under the bed during his father's wake. He was also phobic about hospitals. He called them 'the place',[4] and took detours to avoid them, which is why he kept delaying surgery for his gangrenous gallbladder. He died for the second time during recovery from the long-postponed operation, in New York Hospital at 6.21 am on 22 February 1987. This time his heart stopped for good.

E
IS FOR EXTINCTION

But death was also part of his repertoire, especially the industrialised, mechanised, politicised and perpetually reproduced deaths of twentieth-century America. In the *Death and Disaster* series, begun in 1962, he screenprinted images culled from newspapers of race riots, car crashes and electric chairs. It could all stop at any time. Maybe you'd eat a tin of poisonous tuna, or fall out of the sky or, like the man in *Green Car Crash (Green Burning Car I)* 1963, find yourself in the evening papers, suspended dumbly from a tree.

F
IS FOR FACTORY

It's not that he was cheapening death, more that he understood a new kind of approach was needed. Abstract expressionism was over. Jackson Pollock had killed it, posing in *Life* magazine in paint-smattered overalls. Authenticity and high seriousness were in grave danger of toppling into pretentiousness and kitsch. You could not make art like that anymore, so how about side-stepping painting altogether? By using screenprints, Warhol automated the process of art-making.

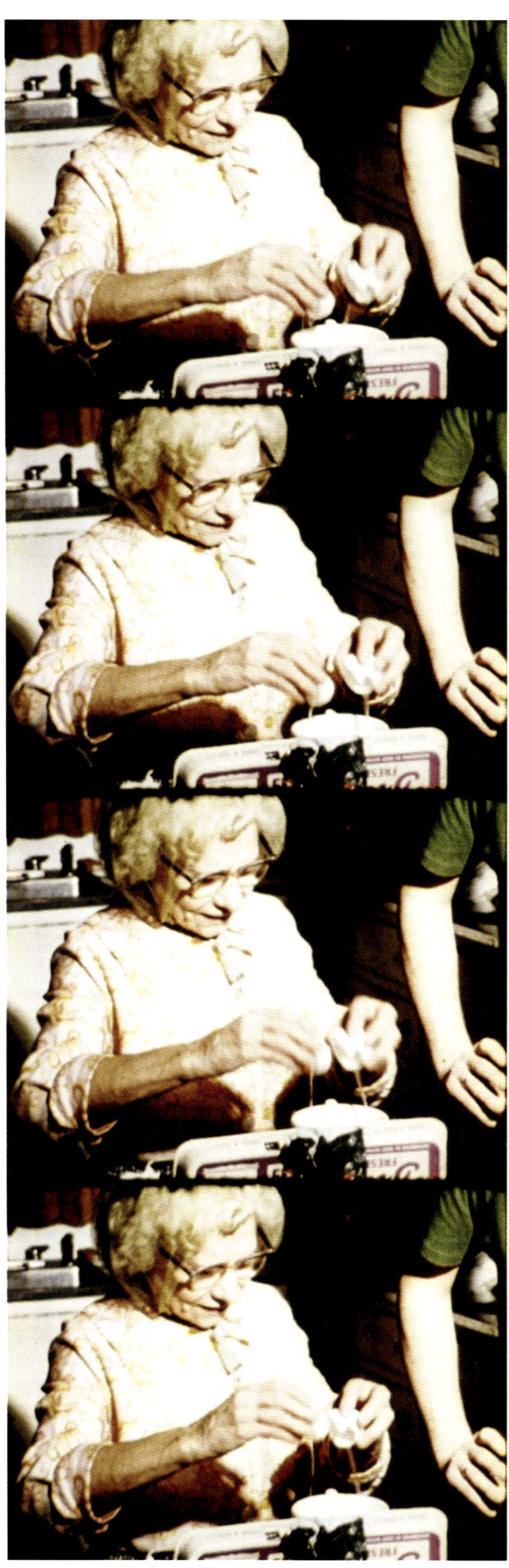

Fig.2 *Mrs. Warhol* 1965
16mm film, colour, sound
67 minutes
The Andy Warhol Museum,
Pittsburgh, PA

There wasn't one unique work but many, infinitely variable and drawn from life, sifted from the replication machine of newspapers and reproduced in fabulous new palettes. Play it again: the mesmeric effect of a repeating wall of Marilyns, her face degenerating into ink, or multiple Elvises cocking their triggers, receding sets of silver conjoined twins.

G
IS FOR GENDER SWAP

Imagine if Andy had been a girl. Would he have been Edie Sedgwick, rich, beautiful, hopeless, incapable of being alone, or would he have been Valerie Solanas, poor, queer, out of kilter, desperate to make a mark? In the *Ladies and Gentlemen* series he documented drag queens and transsexuals; in June 1981 he spent two days posing for the photographer Chris Makos dressed as a woman. In *The Philosophy of Andy Warhol* he described himself as a mama's boy, a sissy, a butterboy (not a word you hear today), but what you see in these photographs is a human whose beauty, delicacy and awkwardness do not quite fit into either gender box.

H
IS FOR HANDS

Andy didn't like his hands – too big – and he also didn't like evidence of the hand. Brilliant at drawing, he was avid to mechanise the process, to speed it up, to facilitate replication and also to introduce the possibility of error, upheaval, surprise. As a student, he invented the blotted line technique that became the signature of his 1950s commercial artwork: a homemade, lo-fi version of the printing press 'When you do something exactly wrong, you always turn up something'[5]: an Andy aphorism.

I
IS FOR INTERVIEW

Tongue-tied in interviews ('can I just answer a-la-la-la?',[6] he once asked), in real life Warhol was inordinately fond of talk, especially gossip and especially over the phone, a preferred medium for facilitating closeness while ensuring privacy and seclusion. Many of his non-visual art projects were actually speech works. In 1968 he produced the anti-novel *a*, composed entirely of real conversations with his speed-freak friends, recorded over five exhausting days, typed up by a quartet of high-school girls and students, and published with all errors intact. Gertrude Stein, eat your heart out. Even his epic *Diaries*, which span ten years and 807 pages, were actually transcribed from daily phone calls with his secretary Pat Hackett. In 1969 he founded *Interview* magazine, in which stars turn the microphone on each other. It might have looked like a gossip rag, but it was actually Andy in the guise of avant-garde anthropologist, out to capture the enlivening oddities of human speech.

J
IS FOR JOKE

The Warhol of the *Diaries*: vacuous, canny, relentlessly attentive, witty, cruel, generous, hilarious, self-mocking. On threatening to fire an employee: 'I'll give her a pink slip. I'll give her dogs pink slips. Fame and Fortune will be fired.'[7]

K
IS FOR KIN

As an adult, Andy lived with his mother for twenty years. She occupied the basement of his house, cooking him soup and tending to her dynasty of Siamese cats. Julia Warhola was his first assistant, her exquisitely erratic lettering adorning his commercial products of the 1950s. When she died in 1972, he didn't tell his friends, but he did keep some of her things in a cardboard box: Woolworths paper bags; a newspaper clipping about a mass baptism; a marzipan cow, now brown; a record by The Dixie Gentlemen; an apron with a thank-you note in the pocket dating from 1953; and, saddest of all, a used and crumpled paper towel with a border of blue flowers.

L
IS FOR LIMELIGHT

Fame is a centripetal force. Warhol drew celebrities to him by promising to record and magnify their fame, to make an enduring record. The Factory was a machine for disseminating Superstars. A star's wattage is amplified by attention, and Andy had enough attention for everyone.

M
IS FOR MAKE-UP

He also had bad skin. As a little boy in Pittsburgh he was nicknamed Spot for his vitiligo and teased for his scarlet nose. Bodies are embarrassing. The screenprint style he developed was a process of beautification, oddities edited out, features reduced to eyes and bee-stung lips. With the help of pancake make-up and an uplight, he took time off everyone, gave them back their face as product, impermeable as plastic. The celebrity portraits are the twin of the camouflage paintings, both fed by the desire to be disguised, Warholised, to fit in. In real life beauty stands out. In Warhol's world it was the default state. Anyone could be anointed.

N
IS FOR NEW YORK

Andy arrived in New York in 1949 and it remained his home until his death. No Bahamas paradise for him. He once listed the island's smells, seventy-five items that included shoeshine stands, hot-dog carts, pretzels, truck exhaust and the banana smell of dry cleaners. 'Ghetto space is wrong for America', he added. 'It's wrong for people who are the same type to go and live together. In America it's got to be mix 'n' mingle. If I were President I'd make people mix 'n' mingle more.'[8]

O
IS FOR OXIDATION

One of the first portraits Warhol drew at art school was of a boy picking his nose. He liked putting the grosser elements of bodily experience to his own ends. I'm thinking particularly of the 1977–8 *Oxidation* paintings, which utilised piss on copper paint to achieve their sublimely damaged surfaces. Piss-shy himself, Andy persuaded many comely Factory visitors to open their flies in the service of art. The resulting series is a joke on abstract expressionism, paintbrush literally transfigured into penis, yet somehow manages to possess the lovely uneasiness of a Pollock in its own right.

P
IS FOR PROXIES

It was hardly the only time he deployed a proxy. Andy loved having people to hide behind, who could speak for him or serve as his public face. In the 1960s Edie Sedgwick played doomed twin, more charismatic but by no means as hardy. In the 1980s it was Jean-Michel Basquiat. Twinship was different from sex or marriage. It meant play and pleasure – dressing alike in kindergarten stripes, even painting on a shared canvas – but it was also rife with fears of invasion and abandonment. In the end, though, it was Warhol who left a grieving Basquiat behind.

Q
IS FOR QUEER

One of the reasons Warhol's career as artist rather than commercial illustrator was slow to start was that he was considered too gay, too out, too swishy by the galleries he longed to show in. He never hid his orientation. It was always there in plain sight. Look, for example, at the famous *Flowers* 1964, with its jungly palette of green and pink, blue, coral, ochre, yellow. Andy took a Patricia Caulfield photograph of hibiscus blossom as his source image, but during the copying process airbrushed most of the detail out. Now look at the centre of the bottom two flowers: two assholes, surrounded by petals and hung on the wall at Leo Castelli.

R
IS FOR RECORDING MACHINES

But Andy was married! In 1964 he was given a Phillips tape recorder that for the next decade he took everywhere with him, referring to it as 'my wife'.[9] All recording devices held a special charm, from the 16mm Bolex on which he recorded his *Screen Tests* to the Polaroid for documenting friends and strangers. Recording meant having a copy, the raw material for future work, but the device itself had a function too. It was a way of luring strangers to him, documenting his participation while keeping himself occupied and separate, therefore safe. It's not that Warhol invented the iPhone; more that he was the forerunner, even prototype, of the personality who would need one.

S
IS FOR STITCH

After Valerie Solanas's bullet blew him apart, Warhol had to be stitched back together with needle and thread, the sort of handwork his own art despised. In Richard Avedon's portrait, taken fourteen months after the event, he's still clearly under construction. His chest has been carved from nipple to nipple, each stitch and incision visible as a dot-dot-dash of keloid. There are two more train-track slashes on his flank, above a hole like a second navel. Under his leather jacket you can just make out a dressing still gummed to his back. Typical Andy, he got in on the act, introducing needlework into his own repertoire. He started stitching together multiples of black-and-white photographs. Many are of breakable objects, like skeletons, or white ceramic jugs, or a bed of tulips behind a sign that warns, as any fragile body might wish to, 'PROTECTED KEEP OFF'.

T
IS FOR TIME

The reason Warhol's early films feel so dreamy is that he recorded them at normal speed, twenty-four frames a second, but played them back at silent-movie speed, which is sixteen frames a second. Time hangs heavy, thick as honey, a fluid in which essences – Mario Montez, Taylor Mead, Susan Sontag, Nico – are preserved like flies.

U
IS FOR UNION SQUARE

For a brief while in 2011 there was a silver statue of Warhol in Union Square, New York, made by Rob Pruitt. It stood opposite the Decker Building, where the Silver Factory once was: preppy Andy, in a jacket and tie, probably Brooks Brothers, his wig askew, Levi's 501s crumpled at the knee. He had a Polaroid camera around his neck and a Bloomingdale's medium brown bag full of *Interview* magazines in his right hand, ready to give away: a miner's son, an icon of self-creation, alien, instantly recognisable, still undeniably the colour of the future.

V
IS FOR VAMPIRE

Whip-cracking Warhol Superstar Mary Woronov once described Andy as a vampire, a white worm feeding on other people's souls. His nickname in the 1960s was Drella, a portmanteau of Dracula and Cinderella: part bloodsucker, part lost little girl. But the other role he liked to play was Daddy, bringing home the bacon, getting on with business ('working is art', another aphorism[10]) while the kids raised hell around him.

W
IS FOR WASTE

He was voracious, it's true, despite the affectless aura. He often said he didn't want to leave anything behind, but he even transformed his trash into art, devising an ingenious way of getting rid of things while preserving, maybe even monetising, them at the same time. In 1974 he started putting all sorts of detritus – letters, invitations, artworks, photographs, movie theatre stubs, gifts, perfume bottles, catalogues, exhibition announcements, diaries, pencils, gloves – into brown cardboard boxes measuring 14 by 10 by 18 inches. He kept one at home and one in his studio and when they were full he would seal them, send them to storage and start again. At his death, there were 610 *Time Capsules*, each one a tiny archive, a snapshot of a very particular twentieth-century life: green ticket stub from the Metropolitan Opera; *Time* magazine, 30 October 1972; shoe last; a broken bit of window sash.

X
IS FOR X-RATED

Sex hums through Warhol's work, sometimes sublimated and sometimes explicit: Mario Montez, raising a phallic banana to a painted mouth; the multiple meeting lips of *Kiss* 1963; the five longing hours and twenty minutes of an unconscious John Giorno shifting and smiling in *Sleep* 1963. In the 1950s Andy made playful blotted-line drawings of dicks swathed in ribbon or served up on plates. In the 1970s whimsy gave way to the harder-edged *Torso* and *Sex Part* series, a cock-and-balls story of abstracted and unashamed flesh.

Y
IS FOR YES

'No' is restrained, elegant, demure; 'yes' risks being vulgar, indecent, tacky. Andy went for it anyway. He was an experimental artist who overflowed every medium, including the commercial: advertising, books, fashion, films, magazines, photography, sculpture. He longed to be on television; in 1979, tired of waiting, he created his own show. At the end of his life, he returned to the hand, two decades after he'd put the knife into painting, making over one hundred versions of Leonardo's *Last Supper*. He didn't copy Leonardo's original, but rather the prints made after it, producing some of his versions-of-versions of this icon of religious art as screenprinted multiples and some as freehand paintings. Was he serious? The answer to that is yes, too.

Z
IS FOR ZERO

In the original of Leonardo's *Last Supper* the wall behind Christ has three windows, out of which you can see a landscape and sky. In the Warhol version I'm looking at now this detail has been effaced. With it the focus shifts backwards to what are now three blaring regions of emptiness, a counter point to the drama within. That is Warhol in a nutshell, replicating the whole world, but never omitting the space, the blank, into which everything else keeps vanishing.

Fig.3 *Sleep* 1963
16mm film, black and white, silent
5 hours 21 minutes at 16 frames per second
The Andy Warhol Museum, Pittsburgh, PA

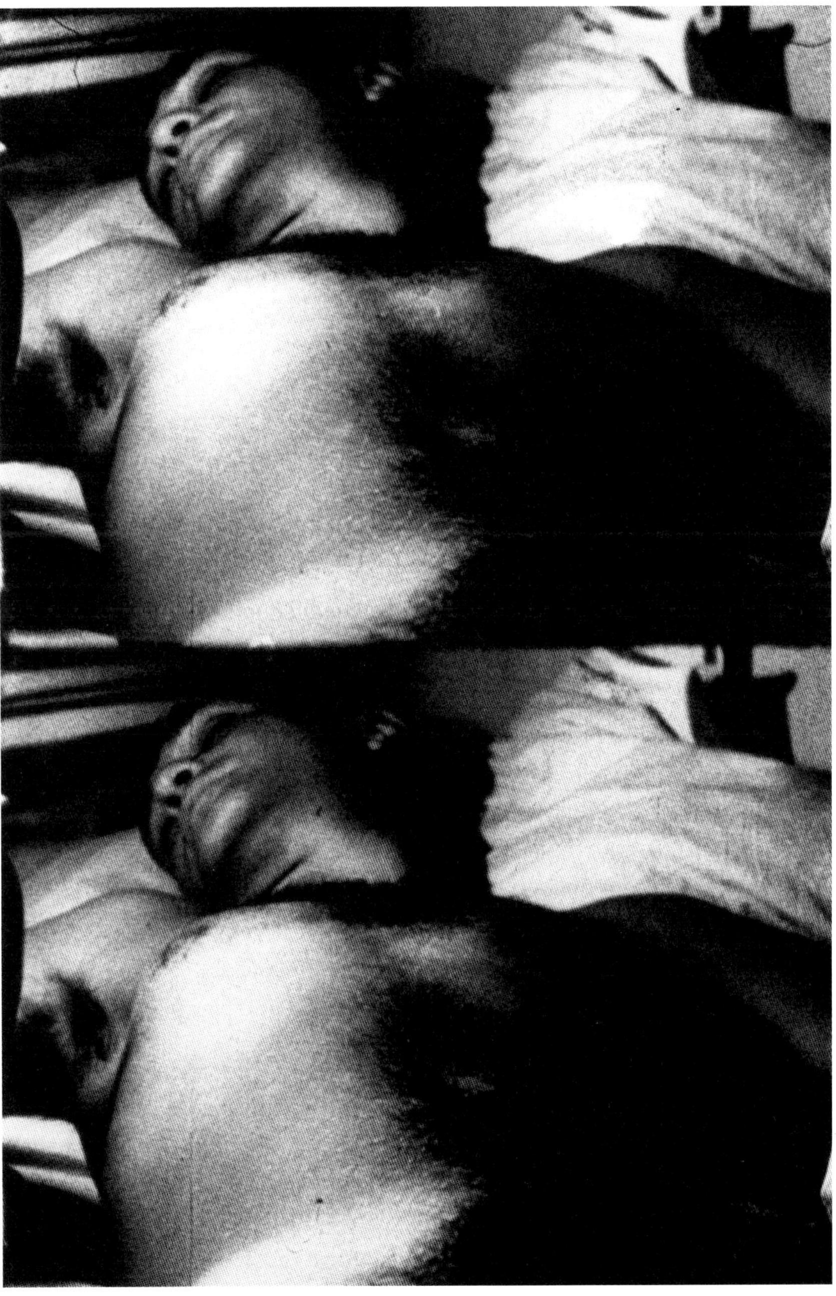

SILVER CLOUDS

MAKING DONALD JUDD FLOAT

Kenneth Brummel

Made out of Scotchpak, a silver laminate sourced by the Bell Laboratories engineer Billy Klüver that Warhol and his assistants cut, folded and sealed before inflating it with helium, Andy Warhol's *Silver Clouds* (1965–6) had its first unveiling at Leo Castelli Gallery, New York, on 2 April 1966 (fig.1).[1] The 'pillows', as they are often called, captivated the gallery-goers. Glinting under the lights, their steely, metallic surfaces occasionally disappeared into the space around them. Lightly anchored to the floor with lead fishing weights,[2] the floating masses also drifted and turned as they responded to shifts in the air currents and to the actions of passersby. According to one reviewer, *Silver Clouds* was a huge hit: everyone crowded around this work on opening night (fig.2), leaving the back room where Warhol hung his *Cow Wallpaper* 1966 conspicuously empty.[3]

Part of the attraction of *Silver Clouds* at the Castelli debut was its performative aspect. That evening Warhol opened one of the gallery's windows and liberated one of his Scotchpak constructions.[4] As the silver rectangle sailed up and above New York City's rooftops, Warhol, in his typically deadpan manner, dryly declared, 'That would be the end of painting.'[5] He later elaborated, 'I thought that there must be a way that I have to finish [painting] off, and I thought the only way is to make a painting that floats.'[6]

When Warhol pronounced painting dead at Castelli, he was directly mocking the American artist Donald Judd, who famously told the art critic Bruce Glaser in a February 1964 radio interview that European painting was 'over with'.[7] One aspect of European painting Judd regarded as outmoded was the deeply rooted practice of part-by-part composition. Also known as 'relational painting',[8] this more traditional mode of composing concentrates on the relationships between different parts of a picture: a mark in one corner of the canvas must be counterbalanced by a comparable mark in another corner. Rather than strike compositional balances between different areas of a given canvas, Judd wanted to create art that communicates its meaning through streamlined objects that presented themselves as unified wholes.[9] As Judd explained, 'When you start relating parts, in the first place, you're assuming you have a vague whole – the rectangle of the canvas – and definite parts, which

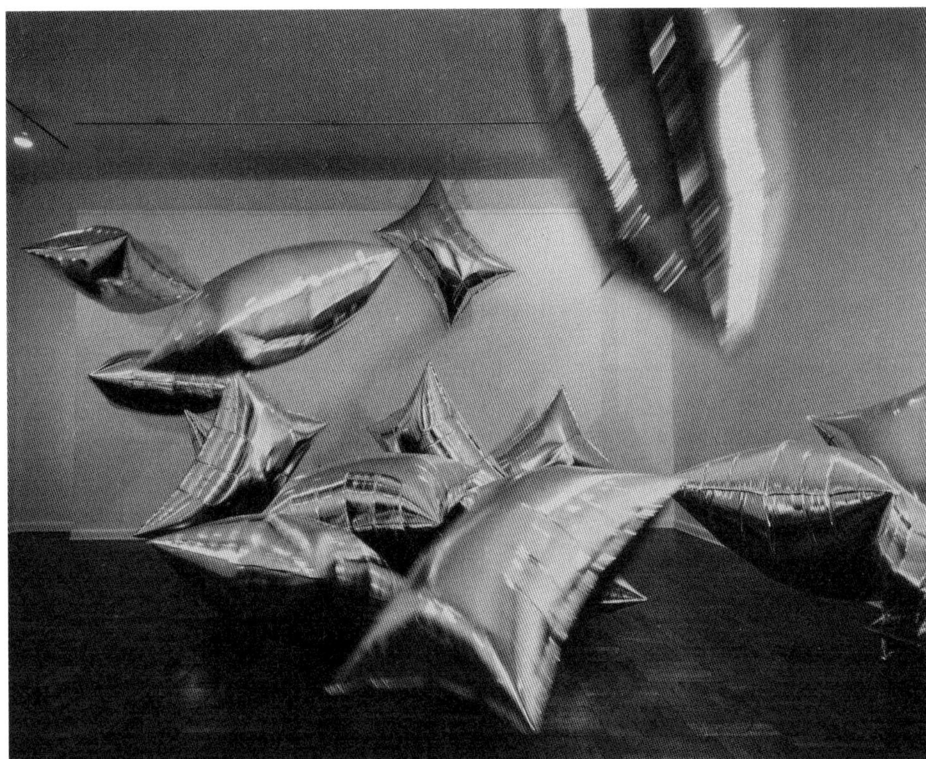

Fig.1 Installation shot of Andy Warhol's *Silver Clouds* at Leo Castelli Gallery, New York 1966. Scotchpak and helium. Dimensions variable. Photo by Rudy Burckhardt. Archives of American Art, Smithsonian Institute, Washington, DC

is all screwed up, because you should have a definite *whole* and maybe no parts, or very few.[10] Another characteristic of European painting Judd considered obsolete was illusionism.[11] Rejecting painting's long history of depicting fictional objects and spaces on two-dimensional planes, Judd opted instead to fabricate real objects that occupied three dimensions. To quote Judd: 'I'm using actual space because when I was doing paintings I couldn't see any way out of having a certain amount of illusionism.'[12]

Formalising these views in his 1965 article 'Specific Objects', Judd illustrated them with American artist Frank Stella's *Charlotte Tokayer* 1963 (fig.3).[13] Everything about this work supported Judd's bold assertion that a new three-dimensional art had supplanted traditional European painting: its concentric bands of aluminium paint articulate a relatively flat and unified surface that acknowledges and repeats the shape of the whole canvas; its thick stretcher pushes the two-dimensional plane of the canvas off the wall and into the physical space of the beholder, making it feel three-dimensional; and its pentagonal format underlines the fact that *Charlotte Tokayer* is not an illusionistic image but a shaped, material object.

Warhol had reason to parody these and other ideas espoused by Judd.

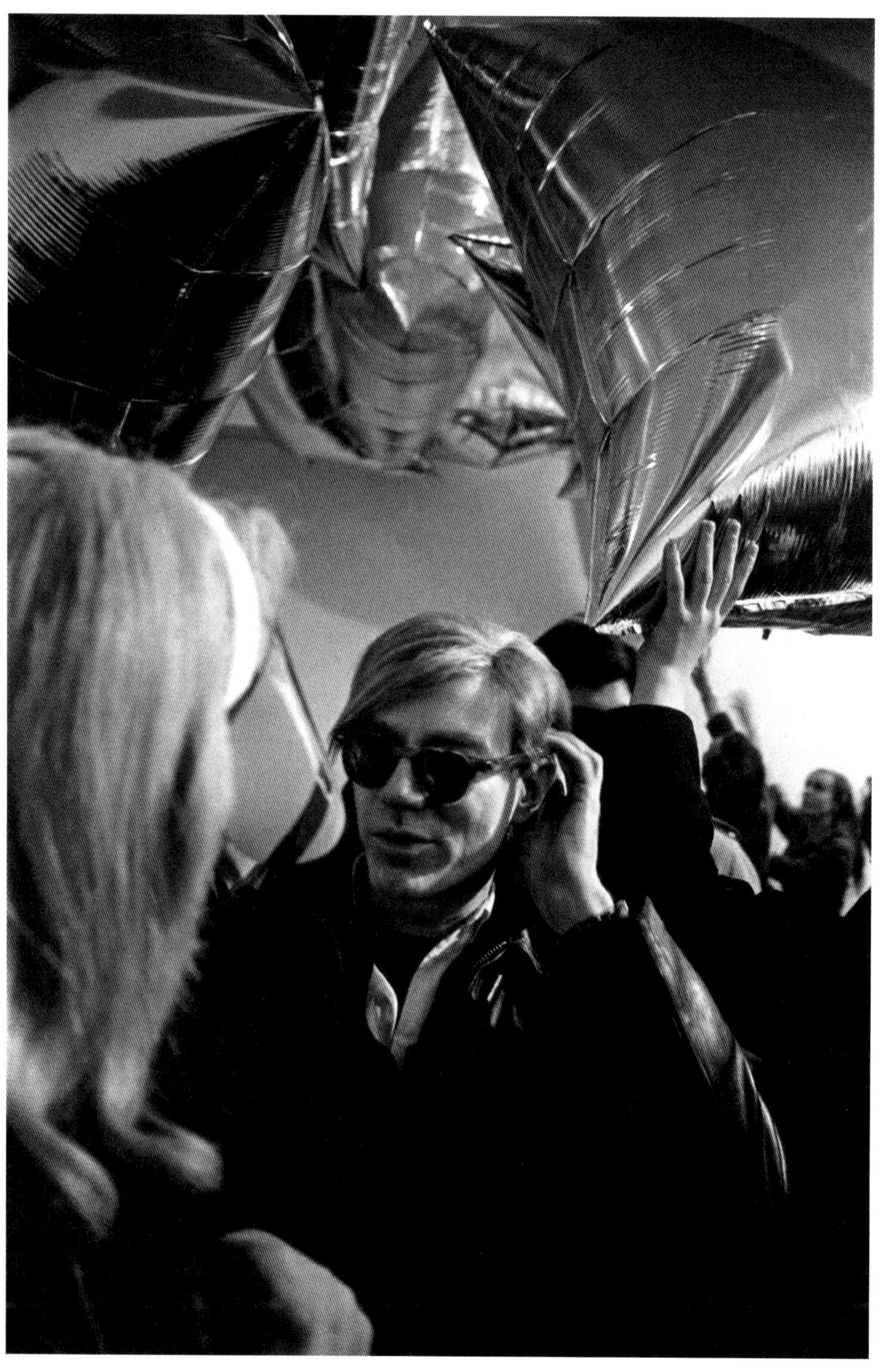

Fig.2 Andy Warhol with
Silver Clouds at Leo Castelli
Gallery, 1966.
Photo by Nat Finkelstein

Throughout the mid-1960s, Judd was openly hostile to Warhol and his work.[14] In the May–June 1963 issue of *Arts Magazine*, for example, Judd flippantly dismissed Warhol in one of his exhibition reviews as an artist who could 'only paint'.[15] Coming from an art critic who the same year wrote that painting had 'to go entirely',[16] Judd's remark was meant to be brutal. Two years later, in 'Specific Objects', Judd cast similar aspersions when he belittled Warhol for creating only 'a small amount' of three-dimensional work.[17] Downplaying the importance and relevance of the box sculptures Warhol exhibited on two occasions in 1964,[18] this last comment was inaccurate and unfair. Even if Warhol was not one to worry about vicious put-downs or negative reviews – to him they were just free publicity[19] – he must have felt compelled to respond.

His April 1966 exhibition at Castelli provided the perfect opportunity, as it followed on the heels of Judd's solo show at the same gallery from 5 February to 2 March 1966. At Castelli, Judd installed for the first time in North America one of his now-famous vertical 'stacks' (fig.4).[20] Having had ample opportunity to study Judd's column of seven galvanised iron boxes while working with Castelli's staff in February 1966,[21] Warhol explicitly lampooned these objects' three-dimensionality and unified, metallic surfaces when he presented his boxlike *Silver Clouds* just two months later in the same exhibition space. Aggressively engaging Judd in a game of 'anything-you-can-do-I-can-do-too',[22] Warhol hoped to demonstrate with *Silver Clouds* that he was indeed capable of producing more than just 'a small amount' of three-dimensional art. Warhol also seems to have attempted to establish that Stella, contrary to Judd's interpretation, was an illusionistic painter.[23] When Warhol encountered Judd's stack of evenly spaced and identically sized boxes at Castelli in February 1966, he understood how they referenced the concentric bands of silver aluminium paint Stella applied at equal widths to the surfaces of works such as *Charlotte Tokayer*. Judd, after all, was the one who referred to Stella's repeated stripes as 'one thing after another' in the final paragraph of 'Specific Objects'.[24] Warhol evidently accepted this reading, for he employed a similar method of serial repetition when he and his assistants cut

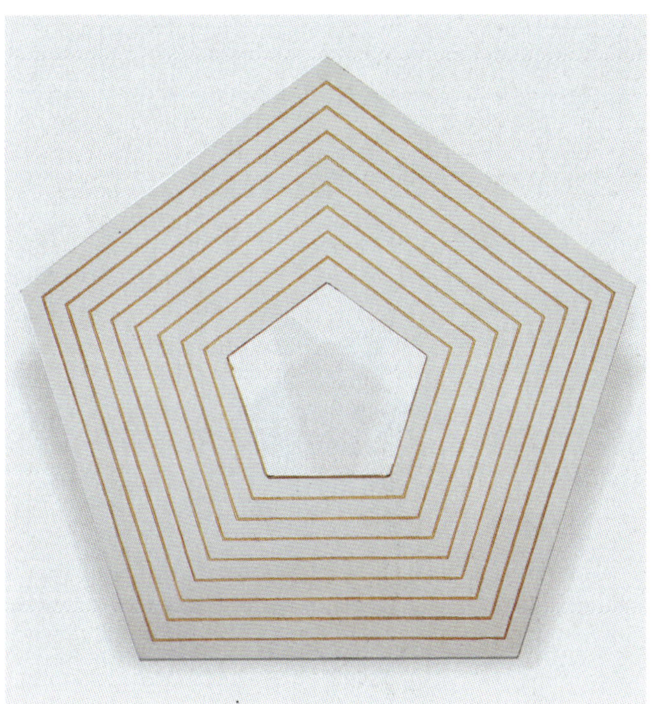

Fig.3 Frank Stella
Charlotte Tokayer 1963
Metallic paint on canvas
221.6 x 232.4
San Francisco Museum of
Modern Art

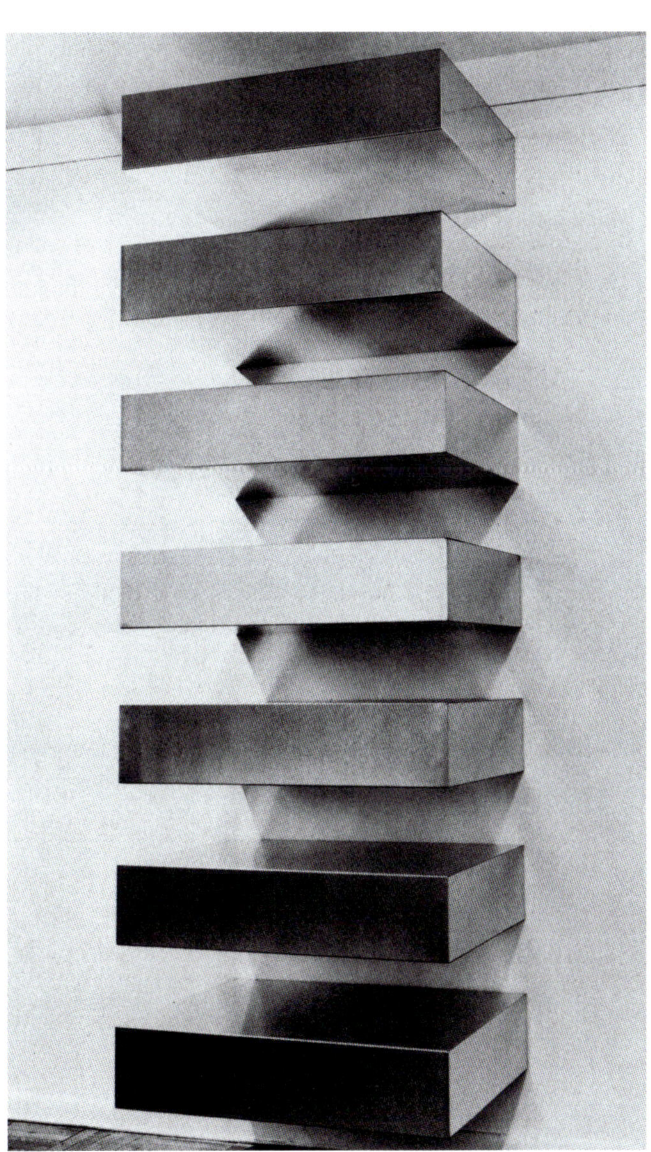

Fig.4 Installation shot of
Donald Judd's 'stack' at Leo
Castelli Gallery, New York,
1966. Galvanised iron
7 units; 23 x 101.6 x 78.7
(each) with 23-cm intervals

and shaped Klüver's Scotchpak material into identical rectangular units during the manufacturing process of *Silver Clouds*. What Warhol could not brook about Judd's stack, however, was its transformation of Stella's silver aluminium paint into metal. Judd had been likening Stella's paint to metal since at least his February 1964 radio interview with Glaser and Stella. After Glaser mentioned how Stella's thick stretchers gave his shaped canvases a 'distinctly sculptural presence', Judd confessed that he had always thought of Stella's aluminium paintings 'as slabs, in a way'.[25] Judd reiterated this view one year later in 'Specific Objects'. Affirming that everything about Stella's work, including its colour, was 'specific, aggressive and powerful', Judd, in so many words, argued that Stella's silver aluminium paint did not generate illusionistic images but instead solely functioned to underline the weight and physical presence of Stella's large and bulky canvases.[26]

For Warhol, nothing could be further from the truth. When looking at a work such as *Charlotte Tokayer*, Warhol did not see Judd's slabs of metal; what he most probably observed was the illusion of receding and projecting trapezoidal planes pivoting around the shaped canvas's empty pentagonal centre. This optical experience of Stella's work informed the highly enigmatic and utterly indeterminate appearance of Warhol's *Silver Liz as Cleopatra* 1963 (fig.5). One of the many silver paintings of 1962 and 1963 that were prompted by Stella's use of aluminium pigment,[27] this canvas with its hand-painted, sensuous silver background creates an ambiguous, almost impalpable atmosphere in front of which the four horizontal strips of Elizabeth Taylor's repeated silkscreen image appear to curl and hover. Filling his silver Scotchpak rectangles with helium and suspending them in mid-air, Warhol recuperated his and Stella's disembodied illusionism and literalised it in *Silver Clouds*. 'I've always said that silver was my favorite color because it reminded me of space', wrote Warhol in 1975.[28] He also once said, 'Silver was the future, it was spacy – the astronauts wore silver suits.'[29] Referring to the gravity-defying aluminised Mylar costumes of American astronauts John Glenn and Gus Grissom, Warhol surely was also alluding to the spatial illusionism of his and Stella's silver canvases.

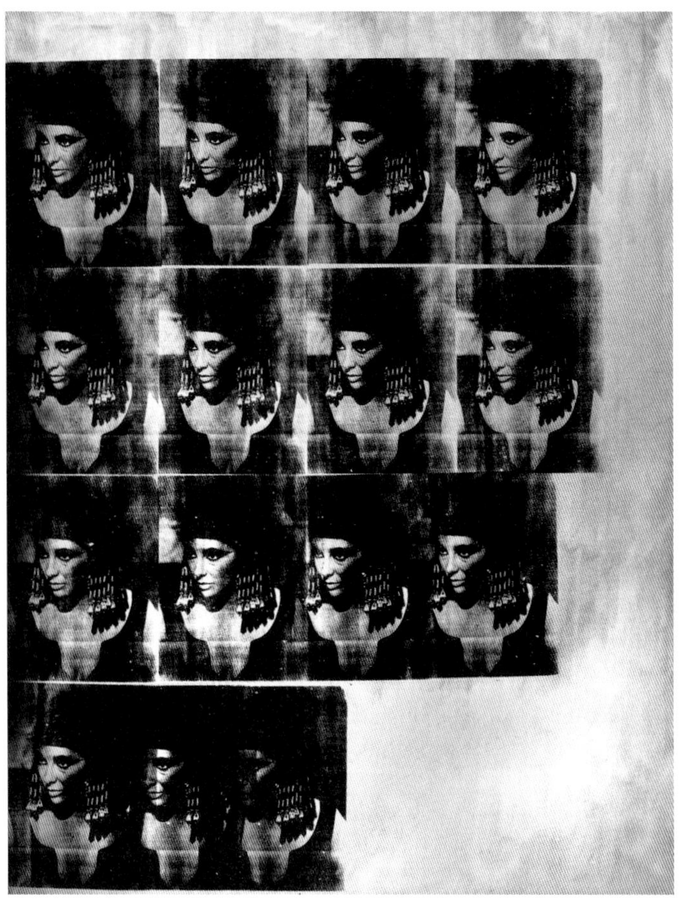

the part-by-part compositions of European paintings had been replaced by objects that were single, unified wholes. If Judd were to have acknowledged that *Cloud* was just one of many parts of a larger installation, he would have had to contradict one of the central tenets of his belief that a new three-dimensional art had rendered European painting obsolete. As one would expect, he was unable and unwilling to do this, which is probably why the conclusion of his review of Morris's exhibition is one grand equivocation: 'The work looks well together, but it isn't an environment; there are seven separate pieces. If Morris made an environment it would certainly be one thing.'[31]

Here Judd was clearly grasping at straws, and Warhol, who in the wake of Judd's many jabs must have been an engaged reader of his art criticism, took notice. Not only did the title of Warhol's work openly refer to *Cloud*,[32] the one sculpture that seemed to have put Judd and his art criticism in a conceptual tailspin in the mid-1960s, but also Warhol's preference to have *Silver Clouds* 'float scattered'[33] across the room flew directly in the face of Judd's belief that 'you should have a definite *whole* and maybe no parts, or very few.' Warhol's assault on Judd's desire for unified wholes did not end there, however. Releasing one of his Scotchpak concoctions out of Castelli's window on the night of *Silver Clouds*'s debut, Warhol

In addition to challenging Judd's metalisation of Stella's aluminium paint, *Silver Clouds* likewise questioned the validity of Judd's analysis of the American artist Robert Morris's *Cloud* 1964 (fig.6). Morris's *Cloud* was one of seven painted plywood sculptures the artist exhibited at Green Gallery, New York, from 16 December 1964 to 9 January 1965 (fig.7). Essentially a box painted Merkin Pilgrim Gray, the sculpture, which was suspended from the ceiling, rested in mid-air, serving as a counterbalance to the right-angled table sculpture situated to the left side of the giant plywood bar bisecting the gallery's floor. Although *Cloud* was clearly part of a carefully composed environment in which spectators were asked to wander, Judd insisted in his review of Morris's show that the sculpture was a separate, unified entity. Portraying it as one 'enormous column', that occupies the space above and below it, he argued that *Cloud* was an independent object that had 'specific' qualities.[30] All this was, of course, in keeping with the formal logic of Judd's stacks as well as the artist's contention in the 1964 radio interview with Glaser and Stella that

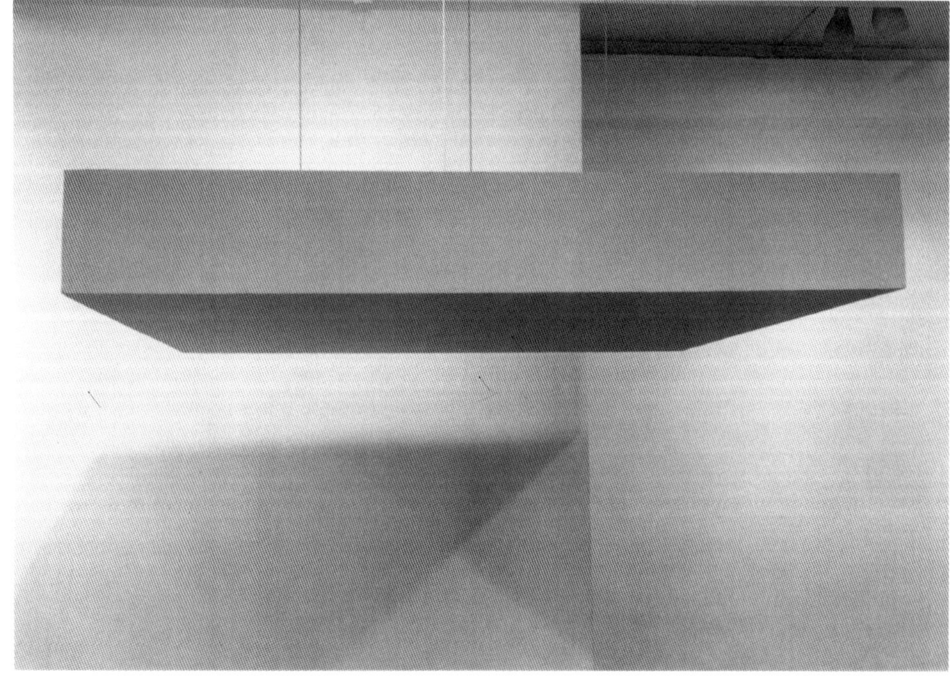

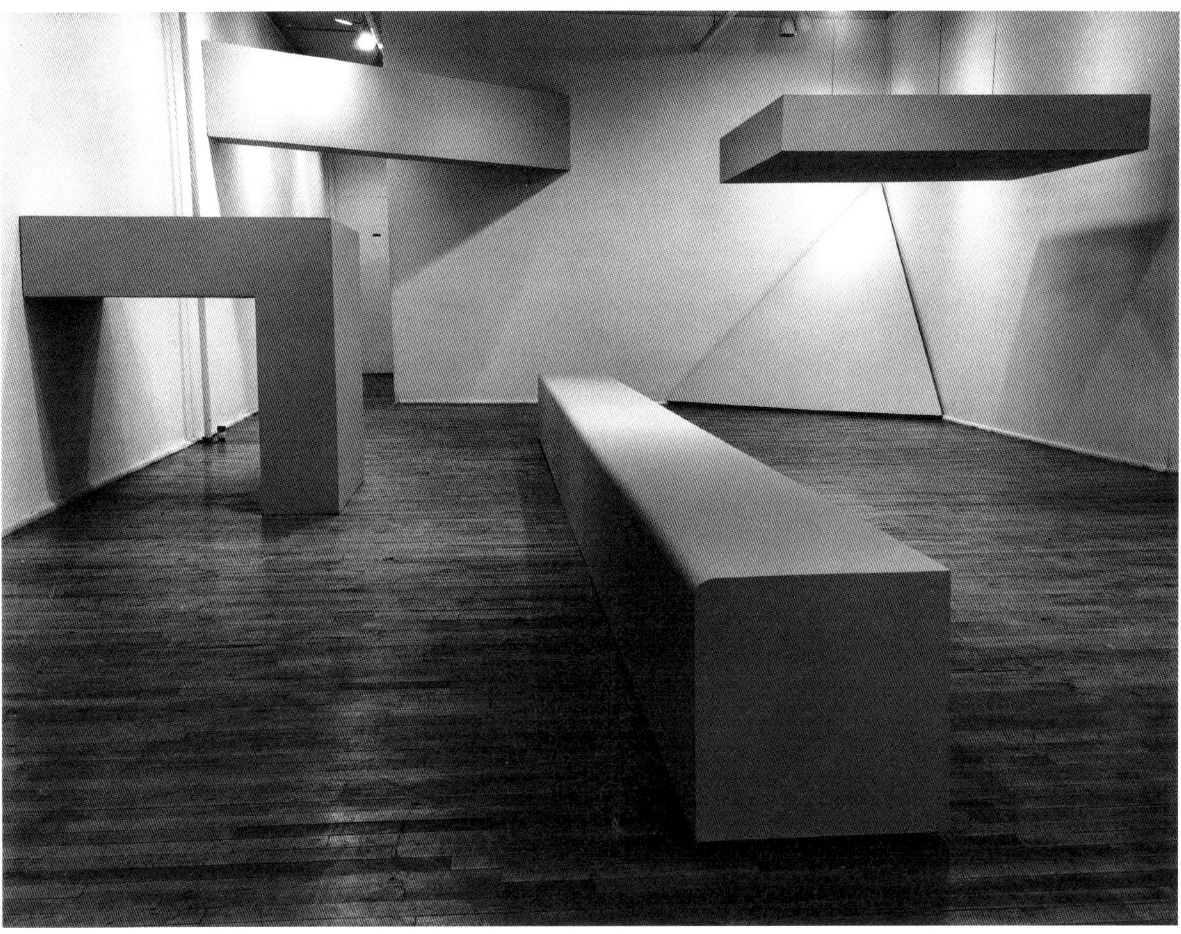

Fig. 7 Installation of Robert Morris's solo exhibition at Green Gallery, New York, 16 December 1964–9 January 1965
Photographer unknown
Sonnabend Gallery, New York

made it abundantly clear to everyone present that his work was not a sacrosanct unity but a loose and constantly shifting assemblage of removable and replaceable parts. Instead of uttering 'that would be the end of painting' when he freed one of the boxlike *Silver Clouds* on 2 April 1966, Warhol might have been more literal and less ironic, simply stating, 'That would be the end of Donald Judd.'

Warhol also could have declared, 'That would be the end of interpretation.' One year later, in 1967, when he was asked about the meaning of his art, Warhol's response was both cryptic and categorical: 'When you talk about what I make, do not say Marilyn, Liz, Flowers, only say 'the things he loves' or 'the clouds.' There are no Marilyn or Flowers or Electric Chairs; there are only my clouds.'[34] How different Warhol's understanding of art and signification was than that of Judd, who in 'Specific Objects' wrote that the 'chief interests' of a three-dimensional work are 'obvious' and that any and all references of a work of art should be 'single and explicit'.[35]

Refusing Judd's mandate for univocal, unambiguous meanings with his cheeky citation of his 'clouds', Warhol was right in line with some of the most innovative thinkers of his time. On 21 October 1966 the French philosopher Jacques Derrida announced at the International Colloquium on Critical Languages and the Sciences of Man at Johns Hopkins University, Baltimore, Maryland, that a new form of interpretation that 'affirms free-play' and lacks any 'reassuring foundation' was poised to revolutionise the arts and humanities.[36] Describing at one point in his lecture a 'floating signifier'[37] that has a surplus of meanings that are impossible to pin down, Derrida might well have used Warhol's less academic term 'clouds'. For similar to the floating signifier, Warhol's 'clouds' were always already oriented toward infinity.[38] A 'painting that floats', *Silver Clouds*'s lack of a stable centre and ground buoyed it and all the advanced art that followed towards a future none of us can adequately name or pretend to actually know.

REPRODUCTION AND REALITY

Diedrich Diederichsen

Andy Warhol erased a concept that had been relevant to Western art for a very long time (and still applies to the market today): that of uniqueness (including that of aura, originality and all that relates to it).[1] At the same time he introduced another concept that, albeit in a very dubious, namely exploitative sense, has become increasingly successful in art and the cultural industry: the aura of the recorded, unique body, with involuntary physicality as a source of attraction. Both concepts were first brought together, though not very systematically, by Walter Benjamin.

The connection between Benjamin and Warhol was first made by the German art historian Rainer Crone, who in the 1960s pointed out in his doctoral thesis the various links between them. Benjamin is partly responsible for the fact that, for a long time, the focus of media studies has not been the ability of technical media to record living things and somehow to preserve mortal life, but rather their capacity to reproduce (art objects, 'reality', and so on). Warhol addressed issues of reproduction and the status of reproduced images by treating works produced by technologies of reproduction as auratic original works of art in the traditional sense.

The other approach to uniqueness also appears in an essay by Benjamin called 'Little History of Photography',[2] where he asks 'isn't every square inch of our cities a crime scene? Every passer-by a culprit?'[3] and derives from this forensic theory of photography and other recording media the idea that they contain (indexical) traces of objective reality that account for their capacity to preserve uniqueness: the uniqueness of the living human being. This ability possessed by the photographic arts then returns in the essay 'The Work of Art in the Age of Its Technological Reproducibility' as the 'right' of every human being to be filmed: a general and universal right to one's own peculiarity. It is no longer a matter of the offender's fingerprints being recorded in order to obtain a conviction, or of a petty-bourgeois individualism, but of a materialistically understood basis of human individuality, which belongs to all people and can be documented. In this way the asymmetry between producers and consumers is abolished: 'In terms of film, the newsreel proves in no uncertain terms that every single individual can be filmed. But this possibility is not enough. Every human being today is entitled to be filmed. [...] Thus, the distinction between author and audience is about to lose its fundamental character.'[4]

However, Crone rightly points out that, in Warhol, this uniqueness has nothing to do with and even flagrantly contradicts the ideology of the uniqueness of the bourgeois subject as communicated and celebrated in the fetish of biography. Rather, he suggests, Warhol is concerned with a dialectical approach to uniqueness, the basis of which is likeness. According to Crone, Warhol himself identified this as an idea derived from Brecht[5]; he felt that all people are indeed alike, they think alike and should not pin their uniqueness on the criteria defined by the cult of genius and the laws of copyright but on their physical appearance as recorded by the technical image – an appearance that they themselves transcended: 'The lighting is bad, the photography is bad, the projection is bad, but the people are fabulous.'[6]

The property of everyone to be 'fabulous', solely because of the somehow proven uniqueness of their physical presence in an objective recording medium, was Warhol's other major theme. He used it in his *Screen Tests*, his middle-period films[7] and later in his various television projects. As long as we encounter only empirical people in everyday life, we have no criterion for

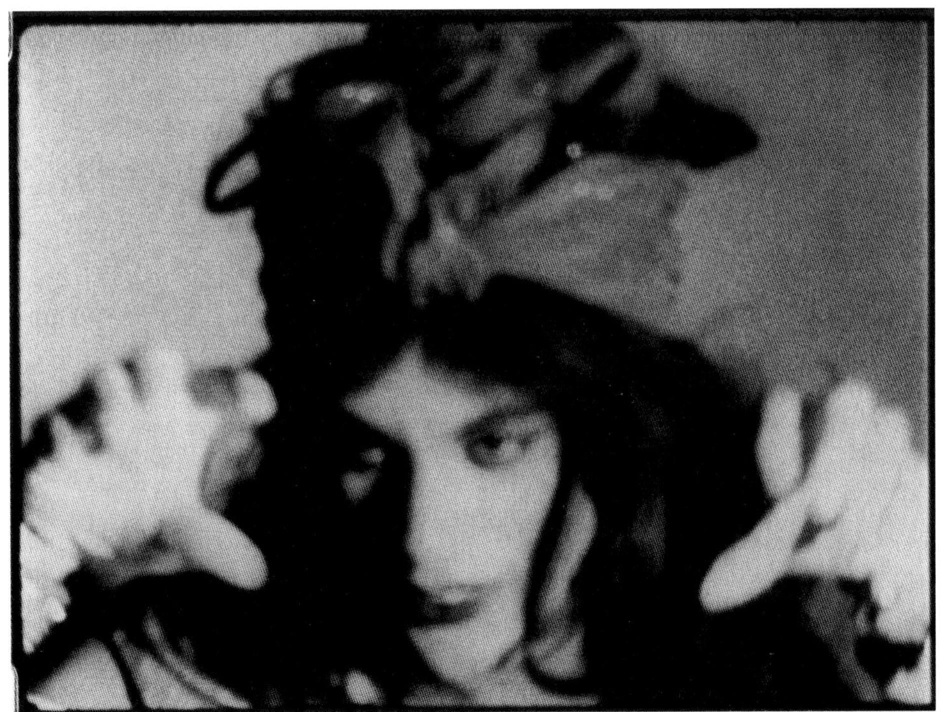

Fig. 1 *Screen Test #2* 1965
16mm film, black and white,
sound, 66 minutes
The Andy Warhol Museum,
Pittsburgh, PA

their uniqueness. On the contrary, since in an individualistic culture they appear as irreplaceable and individual beings, but often resort to identical or similar rhetorical and bodily gestures, we empirically tend, almost out of a spirit of contradiction, to perceive only what is common and similar between them: since their differences are part of the always already installed unmarked individualist ideology. Only the photographic (and thus also the cinematic) image, with its twofold testimony, provides a criterion for uniqueness: the moment itself, and the body in the moment beyond that, are unique precisely because they are objectively passé: always already lost. This is the price to be paid for that objective document, just as life itself is always on the verge of being lost forever. This mortal human being is the one who is 'fabulous' in Warhol's sense.

But what can an artist or director who works with this fabulousness actually do? Warhol's discovery that sheer aliveness – if recorded – exceeds any attraction of ability, virtuosity and other learnable skills could well lead to the artist becoming unemployed. His job could be limited to switching a machine on and off, and Warhol often described himself that way. The fact that he wanted to be like a machine was related to the consummate artistry of Warhol's technical activities as a cameraman. In many of his films he did not move his camera, and if he did, he tended to use drastic zooms rather than sensitive panning shots. The length of his films, which were always based on the industry standard of commercially available film rolls, points in the same direction. For most of the more than 400 *Screen Tests*, there were succinct instructions. However, the celebrities and the denizens of the Factory he portrayed behaved in remarkably different ways – and that too was fabulous.

Dealing with the objective trace of pure aliveness was not limited to the realms of the mechanical and the passive. Warhol also intuited that the goal of observing pure aliveness could involve something more than just a fabulous pose, even though this too was soon to develop into an art of its own (more about that later). At first, there were a few films (*Screen Test #2, Suicide, Beauty #2* 1965) in which, in addition to Warhol's rigid or zooming camera, there was another person behind the camera getting ready to intervene. This was sometimes true, for example,

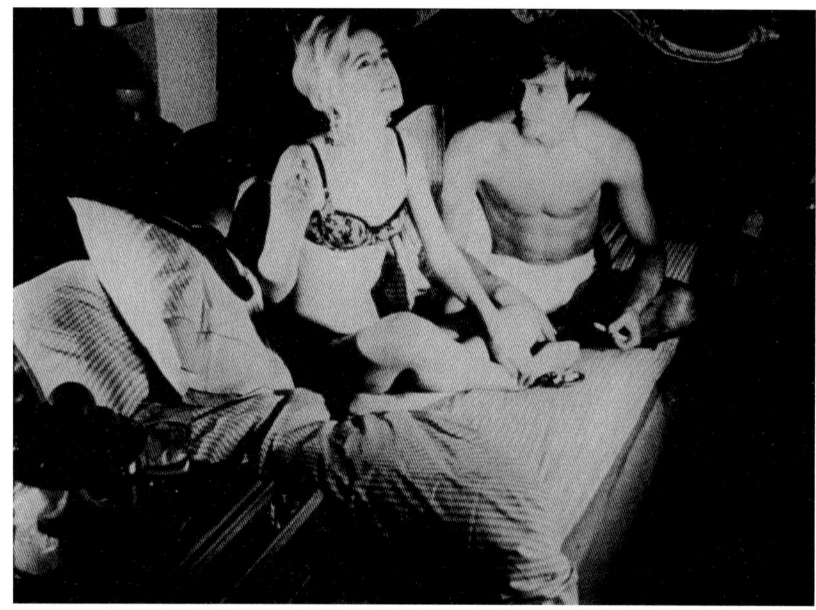

Fig.2 *Beauty #2* 1965
16mm film, black and white, sound, 66 minutes
The Andy Warhol Museum, Pittsburgh, PA

of Ronald Tavel, the author of the scripts that all of those middle-period Warhol films came with: scripts that he also used for the stage such as *The Life of Juanita Castro*. On other occasions, it was Chuck Wein who played this extra part behind the camera. The function of this role was simply to torture and unsettle the fabulous person in front of the camera. Mind games and deliberately sadistic insults based on the weaknesses and secrets of the people targeted were the tried and tested means deployed. In the unusually long *Screen Test #2* (fig.1), Tavel unsettled Warhol's actor Mario Montez, who among other things played drag roles for Jack Smith and often went 'into costume', as he called it (he wanted to avoid the term 'drag queen'). With deliberate malice, Tavel also questioned Montez's gender identity, finally asking him to unzip his trousers. In *Beauty #2* (fig.2), Wein obviously saw it as his job to make Edie Sedgwick cry. Traces of pure aliveness are intensified into traces of wetness: tears and sexual body fluids (this became the cultural-industrial truth of the porn industry). Here, the concepts of objective trace and fleeting aliveness were even further intensified into a dehumanising, de-subjectivating, instantaneously squandered corporeality, at once celebrating and denouncing desire and shame. Douglas Crimp highlights this relationship with his witticism 'misfitting together',[8] in reference to a maliciously shared sense of difference among the Factory crowd, a bond in which physical attraction, with its excessive load of information and its surplus traces of reality, constantly came up against the impossibility of symbolising such states. All the displacement activities and the aggression, including Warhol's own sadism – to which several Superstars eventually fell prey – were countered by the cool objectivism of mechanical filming (and documentation in other media, such as tape recordings).

But apart from the mechanical nature of the camera and the sadism of the voice-over, there was a third way of dealing with the new condition. It was perhaps the most consequential.

To make this clear, I need to approach things from a tangent. Warhol did not have to do this: it was obvious to him. The discovery of the lost but irreducible aliveness found in recording media, and the availability of people who would allow themselves to be depicted in this way, making their aliveness available as corporeality, was hardly discussed in theoretical terms before Roland Barthes's famous photo-theoretical treatise *Camera Lucida* (1980). In this work Barthes, drawing on the emotions he feels on looking at old photos of his recently deceased mother, distinguishes between the referential content of a photo (for example three men and a woman in summer clothes, kneeling down in front of a dog), which he calls the *stadium*, and what fascinates and pierces the viewer of an image – the place where a subject participates in some way in the ontology of the image: the fact that we can here see living people who will one day die or have been dead for a long time. This 'piercing' place (as Barthes calls it) can be different for everyone: he calls it the *punctum*.

Today, this account is familiar to anyone concerned with the theory of photography; in Warhol's time there was no such theory, yet Warhol tried to work with the punctum even though one of Barthes's central statements is precisely that it is quite impossible to exploit it in any deliberate, artistic way. The punctum experience happens to the viewer like a natural event. The quality that constitutes our mortal uniqueness, our irreplaceability, does not follow our ability to acquire and accumulate characteristics and abilities. This means that our many friends, and those who live on after our obituaries have been written, can document the successful

growth of our social capital. Rather, our uniqueness resides in the documentation of the fleeting and involuntary features of our living corporeality. How are these features to be staged?

The answer to this lies in a certain ability to be passive, to wait, to hang about, to be open and ready without becoming active. In Craig Owens's theory of the pose,[9] he compares it to the third voice that, in ancient Greek, stands between the active and passive voices familiar to us from other European languages: in Greek it is known as the 'middle' voice. It can be translated by a reflexive: 'to show oneself' rather than 'to show' or 'to be shown' – to use an example quite close to the techniques used at Warhol's Factory.

Of course, rock bands of his particular kind are particularly suited to this technique in which the intention is not to actually bring something about, but just to let something happen. The bands of the second half of the 1960s that emerged from the classic Beat generation did not as yet idolise the phallocratic soloists on guitar but worked on the basis of the guitar rhythm, as was the general rule shortly before the explosion of the psychedelic trend; they provided a model for the performance of a certain absorption. They were busy rhythmically beating out the chords, but without making any particularly eloquent gestures and without any self-expression. In this posture

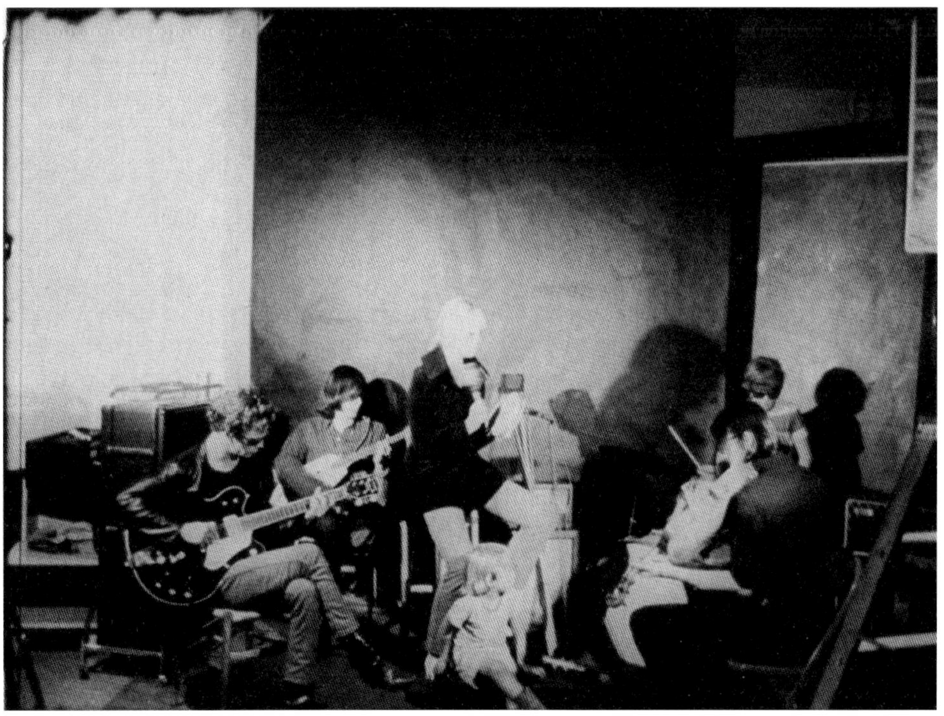

Fig.3 *The Velvet Underground and Nico* 1966
16mm film, black and white, sound, 66 minutes
The Andy Warhol Museum, Pittsburgh, PA

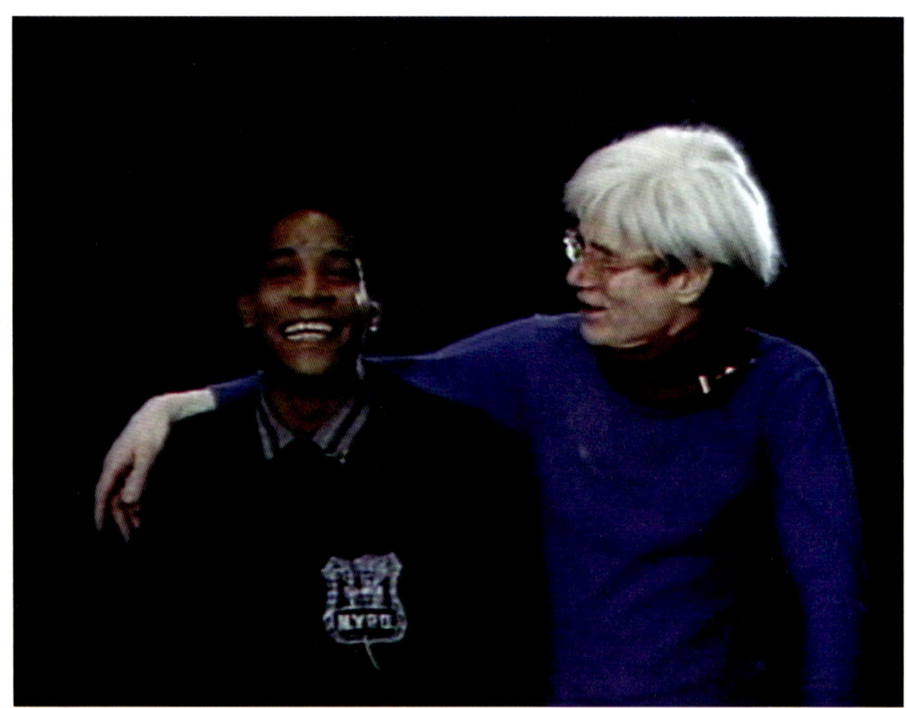

Fig.4 *Andy Warhol's TV*
[episode 9] 1983
1-inch videotape, colour,
sound, 30 minutes
The Andy Warhol Museum,
Pittsburgh, PA

they offered the audience a surface that resembled a living image, a human object derived from a photographic pose in which there was now plenty of time to discover touching details even when these did not seem intended.

It was no coincidence that Warhol's house band The Velvet Underground, along with other styles and specialities, performed exactly the same rhythmic guitar-strumming with relatively few solos, adding to the viola drones derived from minimal music that John Cale had already developed with La Monte Young and Tony Conrad. The resulting flat, static sound was ideal for doing nothing while letting a lot happen. In Warhol's film *The Velvet Underground & Nico* 1966 (fig.3), the group inaugurates its repertoire of non-expressive depiction techniques: rhythmic strumming, 'psychedelic' oriental-sounding garlands and dark sunglasses.

All three techniques of punctum effects – a stoical deployment of the camera, a certain sadism, and posing – have over time enjoyed a career in the industrial production of uniqueness. But between the success story of so-called reality TV as the cheapest method of producing certain definite effects on the one hand, and the Factory on the other, lie the many television experiments that Warhol initiated himself. First came a media experiment that combined the techniques just described: the installation film *Outer and Inner Space* 1965 (pp.136–7),

which shows Edie Sedgwick reacting to a television running a video of her that Warhol had recorded earlier. Here, again, Sedgwick was being used as a guinea pig in an experiment about how an actor could be forced into involuntary reactions: in this case by looking at herself via the then brand-new medium of video.

The way film and television actors have long been able to observe and alter their performance thanks to monitors is not the only thing that this installation prefigures. The close-ups of Sedgwick's head, and her intonation, use different resolutions, sound qualities and image types to establish two media worlds: indeed, two separate ontologies, each of which has the same level of reality on which the body leaves its mark, while each world still looks different and is different. The surprised (or sometimes ostentatiously bored) Sedgwick, Warhol's good friend and also possibly his favourite victim, would leave the Factory in December of the same year because he yet again suggested that she foot the restaurant bill for his whole entourage (she was rich, wasn't she?). Sedgwick was already well established as a witness to the particular kind of reality that Warhol's films produced, and now testified to a deeper or second reality.

Warhol's first production for television then followed, in 1979, a quite different era. It comprised the ten episodes of a series titled *Fashion*, which was provisionally intended to deal with the world of fashion. In fact, a number of people constantly active in Warhol's circle around 1980 made repeat appearances, as in his magazine *Interview*: Debbie Harry, Henry Geldzahler, Diana Vreeland and Fran Lebowitz – another group of people who were fabulous in themselves. The now conventional argument that they were famous is not quite true: Geldzahler and Vreeland were known only to insiders in their respective fields (art and fashion), Lebowitz was known only through Warhol's magazine, and Debbie Harry was indeed a pop star, but was here being spotlighted far from the world of her successes. Yet again, the Factory model prevailed. You just have to let people be, let them show themselves between action and passion: then, just by themselves, they are great. You just select those who happen already to be in your circle. Nevertheless, it was not the simplest format that was chosen (such as a talk show); rather, an artistically fashioned environment (such as Vreeland's lavishly

decorated floral living room) was part of
the deal, a part representing the whole:
the person was no longer just a body, but
provided a suitable content for the setting.

In the next series – *Andy Warhol's TV*
1980–3 – only people known to a wider
audience were now brought before the
camera: John Waters, Steven Spielberg,
Louise Bourgeois, Keith Haring, Frank
Zappa and Yoko Ono, together, of course,
with Warhol's closest friends, such as Jean-
Michel Basquiat (fig.4) and Debbie Harry.
The productions were even more specific,
partly repeating scenes from Warhol's
middle-period films. Steven Spielberg
and Bianca Jagger on a bed in a hotel
room are reminiscent of *Beauty #2* (fig.2).
Also, the old idea was again trotted out
that it was through tackling taboo subjects
and asking potentially shameful questions
that fabulousness could be derived from
embarrassment, although this was done in
a distinctly more low-key and less personal
way than in the 1960s.

His last television project, *Andy Warhol's
Fifteen Minutes* 1985–7 (figs.5–6), referred
in its title to one of Warhol's most famous
sayings, which conveys about the same
amount of information as Walter Benjamin's
demand that every person on earth should
have a right to be filmed. It is almost banal
to add that this condition has actually now
been achieved; more interesting in this
context is the fact that Warhol sold this
series, each episode of which actually ran
for fifteen minutes, to MTV, while the first
two television projects had been shown on
local cable channels in Manhattan. Slowly
the mainstream became prepared to accept
the performance of physical uniqueness
(reduced to physical symptoms) as a
business model and source of entertainment;
soon it would be producing such shows
itself. Thus Warhol almost managed in
his own lifetime to inaugurate the era of
modern reality TV – which, according to
some historical accounts began with the
series *An American Family* 1973, in which
the son, Lance Loud even has a Warhol
poster on the wall – although in actual fact
only modern talent shows, with their fake
outbursts of emotion and involuntary
performances, continue to promote Warhol's
theory of fabulousness in the present state of
cultural-industrial atrophy.

The slightly sadistic irony that physical
uniqueness can indeed be recorded and
thus celebrated, but that it fully unfolds its
attractiveness only when it turns against the

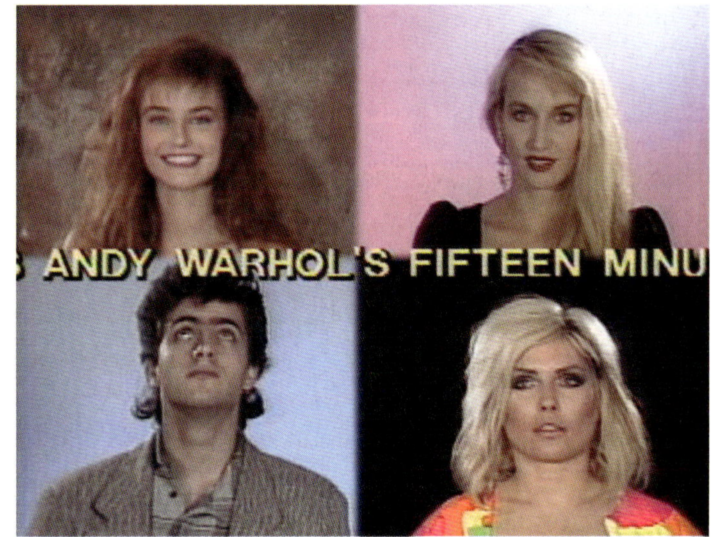

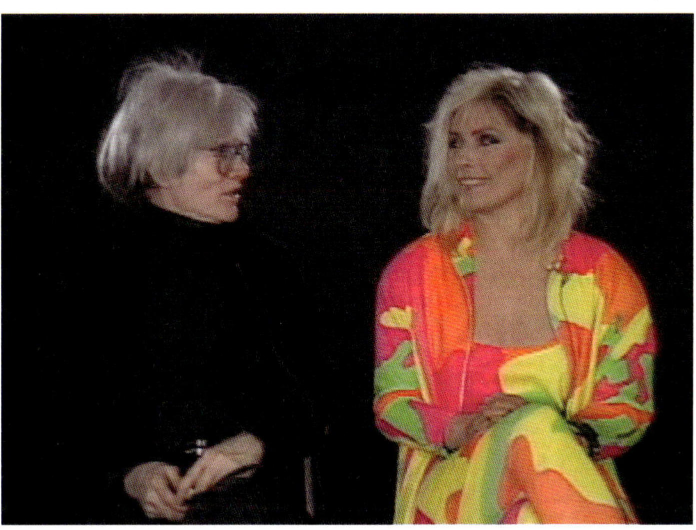

Figs.5–6 *Andy Warhol's
Fifteen Minutes* [episode 1]
1986
1-inch videotape, colour,
sound, 30 minutes
The Andy Warhol Museum,
Pittsburgh, PA

classic individualistically conceived identity
of the person thus shown, was for Warhol
the sign of a new, great form of tragedy –
and it achieved cathartic effects of the kind
described by Douglas Crimp.[10] Today, the
successors of this movement live on only in
the genuineness of their humiliation and the
ideological establishment of a normative
cult of authenticity, in which being identical
with oneself has long meant not that one
is released from one's role, but that one is
condemned to spiritual incarceration.

THE FACES OF WARHOL

Stephan Diederich

'Nowadays, whether I'm depicting a shoe or a Coca Cola bottle, or presenting a fresh face in an interview, a film or on cable TV, I'm invariably producing portraits. That may be down to that fact that I find other people so much more interesting than myself. – Andy Warhol[1]'

'I've always believed that despite his funny remarks and nonchalant attitude, Andy was as serious about his commissioned portraits as he was about all of his work. [...] "They all have to be the same size," he said, "so they'll fit together and make one big painting called 'Portrait of Society'. That's a good idea, isn't it? Maybe the Metropolitan Museum would want it someday."' – Bob Colacello[2]

Many people consider Andy Warhol's standardised commissioned portraits to be strategic stunts in the field of commercial art production. Their abiding popularity has elevated his Marilyns and Jackies almost to the level of icons, with art prints adorning the walls of countless doctors' waiting rooms, while the originals are the highlights of renowned collections. Even Goethe's likeness is familiar to us not from Tischbein's original portrait, but rather from Warhol's camper version. Nevertheless, Warhol's ubiquitous portrait images still manage to elude definition as much as they ever did.

He immortalised over a thousand people on classical canvas alone, from Sylvester Stallone to Yves Saint Laurent, Mohammad Reza Shah Pahlavi to Jean-Michel Basquiat, Liza Minnelli to Golda Meir. In the commissioned piece *The American Man (Portrait of Watson Powell)* 1964 he placed the prototype of the American go-getter in an even grid made up of thirty-two panels: one for each year that his subject had worked at the American Republic Insurance Company (fig.1). Yet he also depicted nineteen New York drag queens and transwomen of colour in the brilliant yet sensitive series *Ladies and Gentlemen* (pp.162–71).

Time and time again, Warhol used himself, or rather the roles into which he slipped, as the subject, which makes his supposed lack of interest in himself, as expressed in the opening quotation, seem a somewhat coquettish pose, just as his most memorable sayings should be approached with a certain scepticism. In turn, Warhol's anthropomorphisation of objects was symptomatic of his deep-seated fascination with people. As early as the mid-1950s, some of his 'shoe drawings' already served as portraits of those celebrities who fascinated him so much. For example, he used gold-leaf and appliqué-embellished footwear and shoe-covered legs with names like Elvis Presley, Mae West, Truman Capote and transgender pioneer Christine Jorgensen (pp.82–3). Much later, when he had an entire career as an artist behind him, he was still playing the game, albeit in another guise, by trying to land a commission at a party at the Waldorf Astoria to mark the

Fig.1 *The American Man (Portrait of Watson Powell)*
1964
Acrylic paint and screenprint on canvas
Thirty-two panels;
163.8 x 272.3 overall
Bill Bell collection

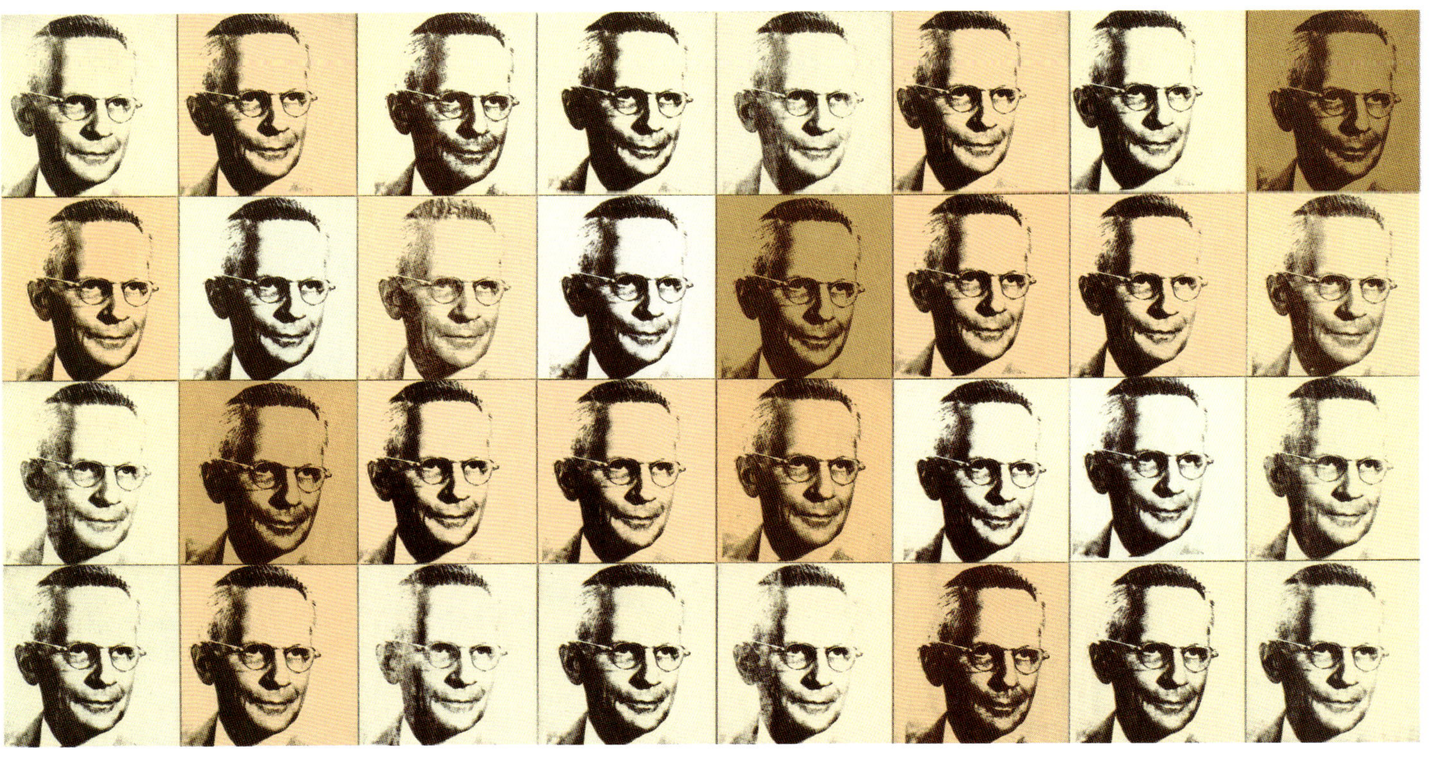

seventy-fifth birthday of the Oreo cookie:
'I was dressed in black and white so
I looked like an Oreo, and when the
cameras were on I ate the cookies and
said, "Miss Oreo needs her portrait done".
So I hope the bigwigs get the hint.'[3]

With provocative understatement,
Robert Rosenblum entitled his catalogue
essay for the exhibition of Warhol's
commissioned portraits from the 1970s at
the Whitney Museum in New York 'Andy
Warhol: Court Painter to the 70s'. While he
saw the photo- and media-based images
as a fitting contribution to the long line of
great portrait painters throughout history,
most of the critics' reviews were crushing,
whether due to a fundamental denial of
the portrait as a contemporary form of art
or simply due to the sheer commercial taste
of the pieces in question.[4] In a review in
the *New York Times*, the conservative art
critic Hilton Kramer described the pieces
as banal, barely modified photographic
prints with decorative colours,[5] while in
Time magazine Robert Hughes called
the standardised dimensions, serial
presentation and typical use of bold
colours 'autistic cake icing'.[6] As Richard
Meyer remarks, such critics misjudged
a fundamental facet of the exhibition:
'Warhol had captured something
irresistible about the zeitgeist of American
culture in the 1970s.'[7] Even a cursory
glance at contemporaneous portraits of
people whose way of life or position within
society interested Warhol is enough to
contradict the general accusation of
a lack of depth. In 1976, for instance, he
immortalised the charismatic spokesman
of the American Indian Movement Russell
Means in a heartfelt pictorial homage
(fig.2). By contrast, with scathing irony,
Warhol came out for the Democrats in the
1972 electoral campaign by producing
an image of a diabolically green-faced
Richard Nixon with the slogan 'Vote
McGovern': the artistic approach applied
to the likeness made a striking point in the
political struggle (fig.3).

When the most comprehensive
exhibition of his portraits, *Le grand monde
d'Andy Warhol*, opened in 2009 at the
Grand Palais in Paris, the untranslatable,
ambiguous exhibition title echoed both
the high-society factor and the enduring,
manifold value of Warhol's portraits.
Although categorisation under headings
such as 'Glamour', 'Royals and Politics'
and 'Geniuses' inhibited a sweeping

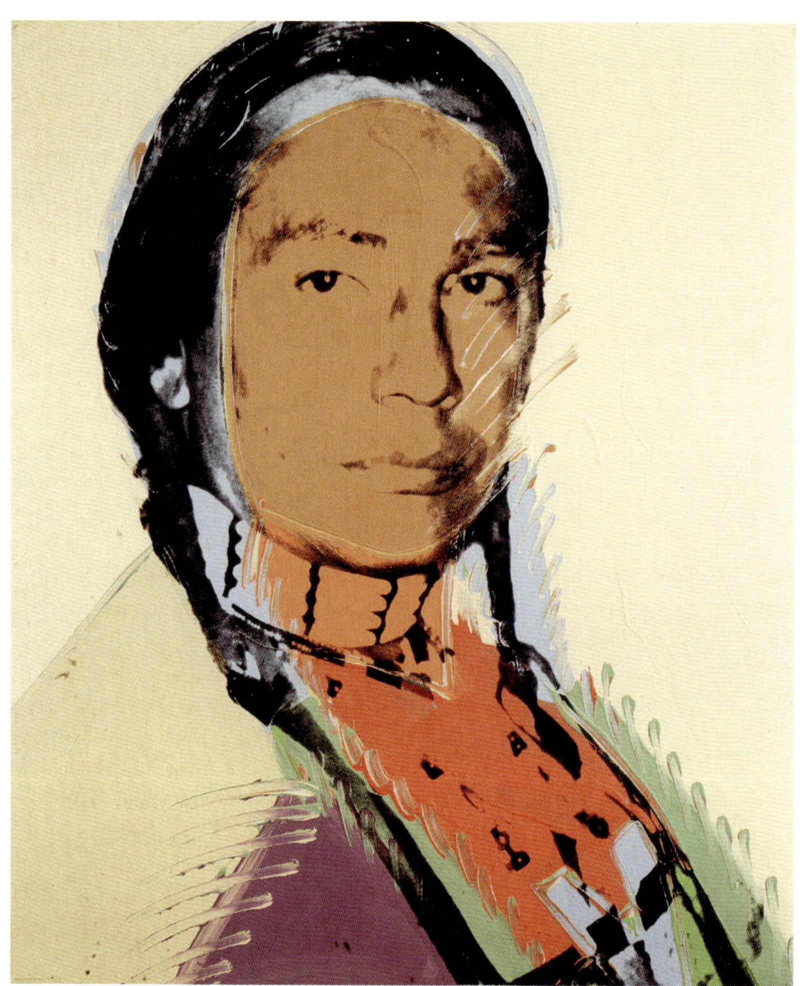

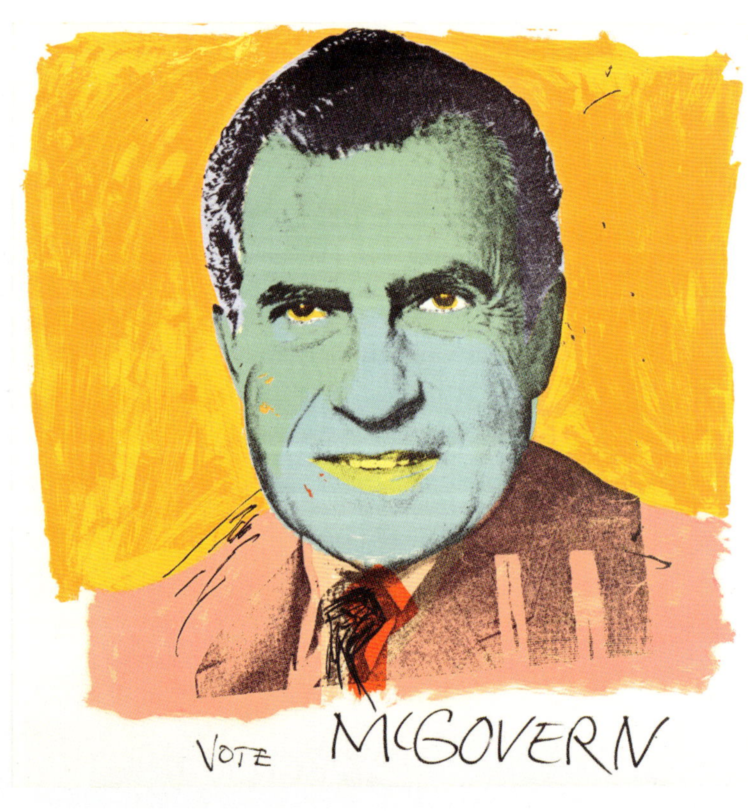

oversight of the artist's works and ran counter to Warhol's possible desire for an overall view, the curator Alain Cueff managed to draw attention away from the superficial pop art label, instead highlighting allegorical and religious aspects.[8] The working-class boy, the son of Eastern European immigrants to Pittsburgh, had been struck by the Orthodox Catholic icons in church at Sunday Mass, and through his vast output sought to create a contemporary equivalent to those very iconostases of his childhood. The light that Cueff's co-curator Émilia Philippot shed on the complex process of creating the works, using the portrait of *Debbie Harry* 1980 (pp.186–7) as an example, did even more to exonerate the comissioned portraits from the charge of being trite products for mass consumption.

Warhol received his first portrait commission in 1963 from the New York taxi mogul and art collector Robert Scull, the archetypal self-made man and a representative of New Money. 'Bob and Spike are the folk heroes of every social climber who ever hit New York',[9] wrote Tom Wolfe of Robert and Ethel Scull, using their nicknames. Scull envisaged something similar to Warhol's charged homage to the deceased Marilyn Monroe, created the previous year. Warhol intuitively knew the difference: Ethel Scull's face did not have cult status, nor was it strikingly memorable; it was her charisma that he needed to convey. The rest is history. Warhol took the astonished Mrs Scull to a series of public photo booths, inserted coins and encouraged his model to adopt more relaxed poses by cracking jokes: good, normal American fun. Of around 300 photos, he selected seventeen snapshots and arranged them in a chequerboard pattern of thirty-six different-coloured panels, further enhancing their dynamism and range of expression by adding bright hues. As Keith Hartley notes, *Ethel Scull 36 Times* 1963 (pp.134–5) 'gives the impression of a budding actress practising her repertoire of roles'.[10] The subject herself was delighted: 'What I liked about it mostly, was that it was a portrait of being alive.'[11] Warhol used psychological skills and techniques learned from his work in advertising to bring a powerful sense of life to an unfamiliar face and give it significance, thus deliberately creating a counterpart to his iconic Marilyn.[12]

That single photograph of Monroe, refined over and over again in thirty-seven paintings in different colourways and formats, in sequences, grids or in isolation, over August and September 1962, has helped to shape the afterimage of a star like virtually no other portrait. Based on a face-only section from the publicity still for the film *Niagara* (1953), Warhol created what is surely the most striking visual metaphor for the fame and tragedy that made Monroe the quintessential Hollywood star and gave her such media appeal. The piece's reception among the general public and academics alike was founded on a fascination with 'the sublimity of a tragic life combined with the lustre of her glittering, artificial world',[13] as Thomas Miessgang puts it, thus embedding 'MM as an all-purpose icon in a wide array of social spheres'. In spite of this, or perhaps precisely because of it, Warhol deserves credit among the flood of artistic treatments of Marilyn Monroe, with his keen sense for the metaphorical nature of a face giving rise to a picture of exceptional appeal and timelessness. Cueff describes Warhol's work as loaded with pathos yet striking at the very heart of its subject due to the artist's instinct for the distinctive nature and

essence of a being who is destined to become an image, presenting themselves in a completely patent way, while also retaining their absolute mystery. A consummate symbol of happiness made flesh becomes an abstraction from one day to the next. This woman's demise at the age of 36 allowed her to leave the world of present appearances, placing her instead in a mythological dimension where appearances are eternal and the gaze reigns sovereign.[14]

It is no coincidence that Jane Daggett Dillenberger draws a parallel between Warhol's commissioned portrait *Katie Jones* 1973 (fig.4) and Egyptian mummy portraits[15]: the faces of those who have passed from this world, painted as they were in life, gazing fixedly both at the viewer and at a point outside time. In Warhol's paradigmatic Marilyn motif, the three variations of the painting set against a gold background suggest that the artist was approaching the image in an almost religious way, reflecting the kind of sacralisation practised in that ancient tradition. Cueff was not the only one to find Warhol's conspicuously icon-like depiction of Marilyn reminiscent of the images of saints that the young Andrew Warhola would have seen on attending Mass at the Church of Saint John Chrysostom in Pittsburgh (fig.5).[16] His attachment to two cultures, the US pop and consumer era and a Byzantine Catholic upbringing with his mother, found particular expression in the fusion of both types of images. In drawings dating back to the 1950s, many of the shoe portraits and some of the large-format erotic portrait drawings of idealised young men on gilt paper, he created a prime, gilded version of the objects of his desire. Alongside Warhol's liking for Victorian opulence and decadence, the allure of that style of sacred image certainly played a part, whether as a blasphemous resistance to the rigid conventions of the Church or out of wistful yearning for a state of paradisaical freedom.[17]

One of the counterparts to Marilyn was Warhol's versions of press photographs of Jackie Kennedy, created following the assassination of President John F. Kennedy in November 1963, and which fall chronologically and thematically in among his *Death and Disaster* paintings, where death is ubiquitous, in the suicide of a film star (p.106) or a nameless person, or in a plane crash or traffic accident (p.98), not to mention food poisoning, atom bomb explosions or the electric chair (pp.107, 154–5).[18] Warhol made reference to the merciless images of calamities taken from mass media by selecting and repeating eight press photos that show Jackie over the period just four days before and after the attack on Kennedy in *Jackie (The Week that Was)* 1963 and *Jackie Frieze* 1964 (pp.116–17). The political tragedy and Jackie's public widowhood were made the subject of permanent live broadcasting to an unprecedented degree. A single face, expressing carefree joy or mute grief and desolation, becomes a mirror of historic events and the collective mood; an individual woman and her portrayal in the media merge into one another. Warhol also depicted Jackie using a religious pictorial formula on several occasions, including the altar-like panels of the *Jackie Triptych* 1964 (pp.118–19) with its mirrored, staggered three-part grieving woman, which made use of a press photo of the introverted First Lady taken at the burial at Arlington Cemetery. Warhol zoomed in on her face beaming into the crowd just moments before the attack that would change everything, placing her against a golden background in his *Round Jackie*, with a glimpse of her smiling husband behind. The snapshot is duplicated by a second disc in monochrome gold. Warhol had already used the empty, contemplative afterimage in some of his *Death and Disaster* scenes (pp.112–13) as well as in a double tondo, showing Marilyn next to a plain golden disc. The question remains: does this depict presence and absence, life and death, the visualisation of someone who has ceased to exist or reached everlasting perfection? Or is it simply a formal counterpart, introduced to balance the composition?

In this sense the human image was already explored in terms of its existential contradictions and its media relevance by Warhol prior to the mid-1960s. In his following so-called 'Business Portraits', this view of the person undergoes, at least apparently, some kind of distortion. 'Business art is the step that comes after Art. I started as a commercial artist, and

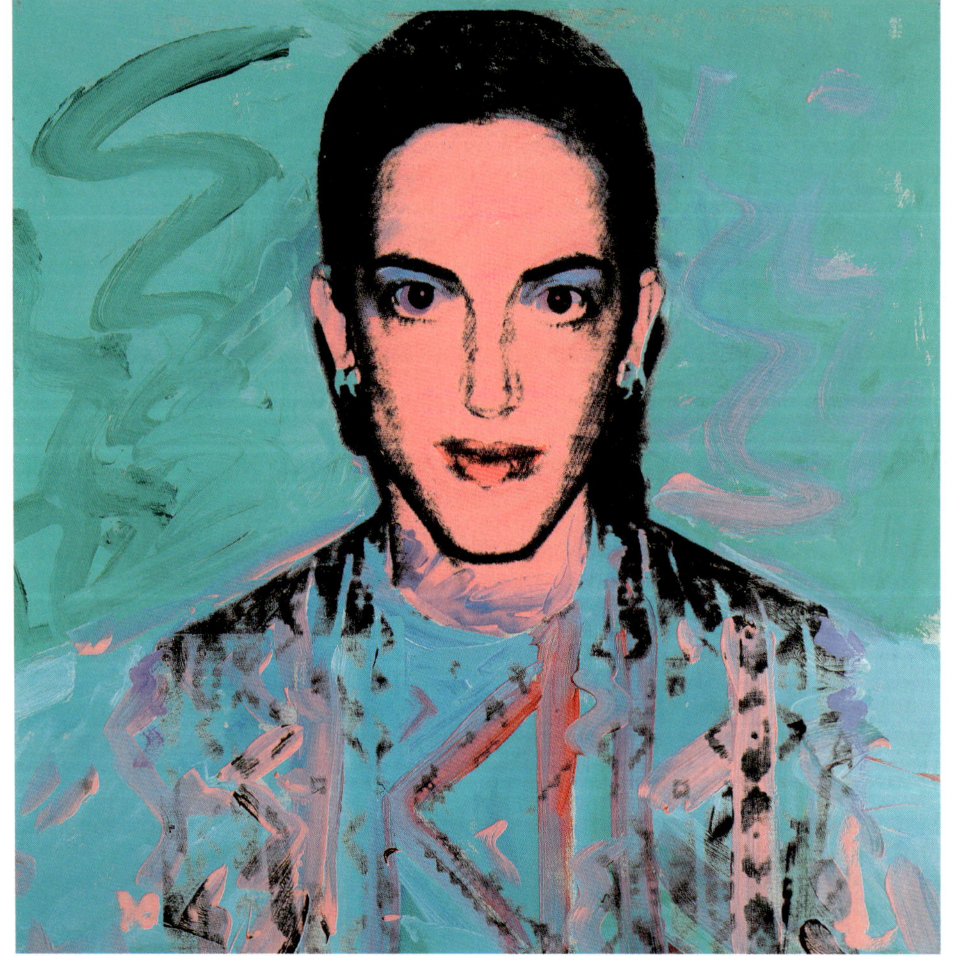

Fig.4 *Katie Jones* 1973
Acrylic paint and screenprint
on canvas 101.6 x 101.6
Private collection

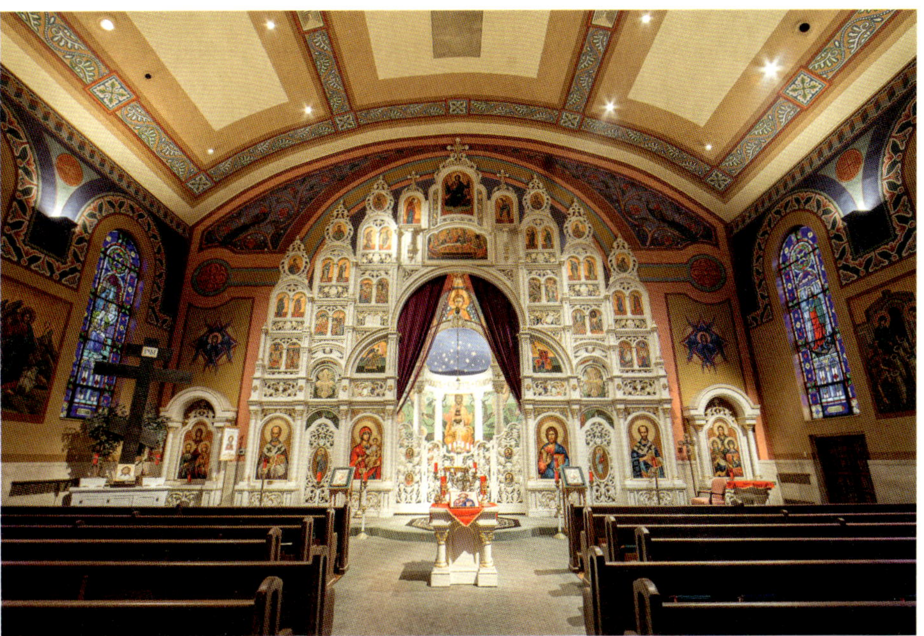

Fig.5 Iconostasis of Saint John Chrysostom in Pittsburgh, Pennsylvania, USA. This is an image of the updated church, renovated in the 1970s.

I want to finish as a business artist. [...] Being good in business is the most fascinating kind of art.'[19] As Richard Meyer states, this typically atypical statement by Warhol 'shaped both the production and (often negative) critical reception of his work throughout the 1970s and 1980s'.[20] In particular, this may account for the view of the commissioned portrait genre as a lucrative and fundamental area of business for Warhol. From the early 1970s until his death in 1987, he created hundreds of these images according to economic principles.

As early as 1969, Warhol produced the first portraits with 40 by 40 in. (101.6 by 101.6 cm) dimensions, which quickly became his standard format. This size ensured a larger-than-life, striking output that was instantly recognisable and suitable for most uses and forms of presentation: big enough to stand out, yet compact enough to ensure easy production and widespread use. Like the format, the price also became standard. At the outset, each of the initial portrait panels cost $25,000, with subsequent ones priced at $15,000. As Bob Colacello explained:

> One was never enough. Clients were encouraged to commission additional panels, at US$15,000 each, of the same portrait in different colors, and those who didn't were considered 'cheap'. We were all trained to tell

clients, 'Repetition is a very important element of Andy's aesthetic.' Of course, it really was, and the more serious collectors usually did order four more panels.[21]

Over the years, the price has increased many times over, and even this commercial factor can, in hindsight, be considered to have given rise to interpretations of the pieces themselves. Alain Cueff speculates that, together with inflation, 'something quite different was going on. Paying for your own ever-vanishing image is something remarkable. Warhol was fully aware of that and brought a remarkable symbolic dimension to that phenomenon by demanding not only a simple payment, but indeed a ransom.'[22] The resulting revenue, which was considerable, went largely towards Warhol's far more blatant experimental projects, films, his *Interview* magazine and his various TV series. 'I have Social Disease. I have to go out every night',[23] he writes at the beginning of his photobook *Andy Warhol's Exposures*, which he produced in 1979 with Colacello, providing a fulsome insight into the carnivalesque existence of his celebrity friends. However, he was driven not only by a fear of missing out, but also by a desire for entertainment. Warhol and his team were constantly on the lookout for clients, and his legendary omnipresence as a partygoer and permanent fixture at the trendy club Studio 54[24] was also instrumental in making and maintaining contacts, as well as acquiring new portrait commissions. A professional and socially astute management team also did much to build 'networks of clients, patrons, and fans in various tribal settings, from the new gay monthlies (*Christopher Street* and *Blueboy*) to the *Social Register*'.[25] Warhol thus played with different clienteles, deploying his superb understanding of the psychological and social mechanisms behind societal longings and affiliations, profiting from the reflected glow of celebrities and providing the newly wealthy with an echo of the cultural scene by depicting figures from both worlds. 'Of course, the quality of the portrait was all the greater if Andy was impressed by his model', reports Henry Geldzahler.[26] After an inspiring tour of the collection of the Centre Pompidou in Paris with Pontus Hulten in May 1977, Warhol himself cast a quizzical sidelong glance at the long-standing, comfortable monotony of his commissioned portraits, noting, 'This took two hours [...] but I had energy and wanted to just rush home and paint and stop doing society portraits.'[27]

In view of all this, as Émilia Philippot insightfully reveals, using *Debbie Harry 1980* (pp.186–7) as an example,[28] the complex process of creating a typical Warhol portrait should not be underestimated. The setting for the basic photoshoot was, admittedly, bare and nonspecific – a simple chair against a white wall – which made sittings outside the studio easier when external clients were involved. Warhol used a Polaroid Big-Shot camera, whose fixed depth of field required the photographer to experiment with distances from the model until he found the right shot, usually at less than a metre away. That made the whole thing more relaxed, especially when Warhol chatted away casually as he gave instructions, sometimes over the course of several hours. The subsequent joint viewing of the photographic material was a clever way of making the model feel involved in the choice of image, although the decision would ultimately be down to the artist alone. Of more than a hundred Polaroids, he would keep just four or five, which one of his employees would further process for him. Firstly, small-format preliminary versions were produced as black-and-white positives on acetate film. Warhol often used these as the raw material for a radical transformation of the subject that might be compared to a cosmetic procedure performed by a plastic surgeon. The composition and contrast were altered, as were the mouth and nose, the proportions balanced and blemishes retouched. These treated films were enlarged to the painting size, usually 101.6 by 101.6 cm. Warhol marked up any final corrections to these scaled-up pre-print copies in red felt-tip pen. Creating the actual image on canvas required a further series of complex steps to be performed by Warhol and his assistants: the coloured canvas primer coat (which might be either a single block colour, divided into coloured sections or generously applied in gestural brushstrokes), the copying of the film outlines, the subsequent masking and addition of the coloured areas with a brush, and the application of the prepared screenprint using acetate film and the silkscreen ink, usually in black, with a scraper. Sometimes Warhol would lay

a second screenprint on top, as he did with the *Lips* book c.1975, a collection of lip images that he used to alter and enhance the facial appearance of his models (fig.7).

When used together, photography, painting and screenprinting offered Warhol manifold possibilities for correcting, smoothing and refining his models, not to mention distorting and appropriating them. The radicalism of Warhol's portraits lies in this nonstop manipulation within the production process, particularly for his commissioned pieces, as Simon Watney notes:

> Warhol's portraits exemplify his disinterest in any appeals to psychological or biographical notions of 'depth' or 'insight'. Warhol's portraits scrupulously refuse banal notions of 'character', supposedly revealed in physiognomy. On the contrary, his portraits carefully rob their subjects of individuality, as they become 'Warhols', objects in a market economy, defined by simple and clearly recognizable stylistic resemblances. What they register is the sitter's prior position in the much larger system of public representations, of *personas*.[29]

The notion of the 'persona' is essential to Warhol's conception of people, his way of working and his own self-portrayal, put on display to the public, as a schematised role within the social value structure, is deliberately overlaid with that of the personality.

Fig.6 Andy Warhol shooting Peter Ludwig for his portrait, Cologne, 1980
Peter and Irene Ludwig Foundation

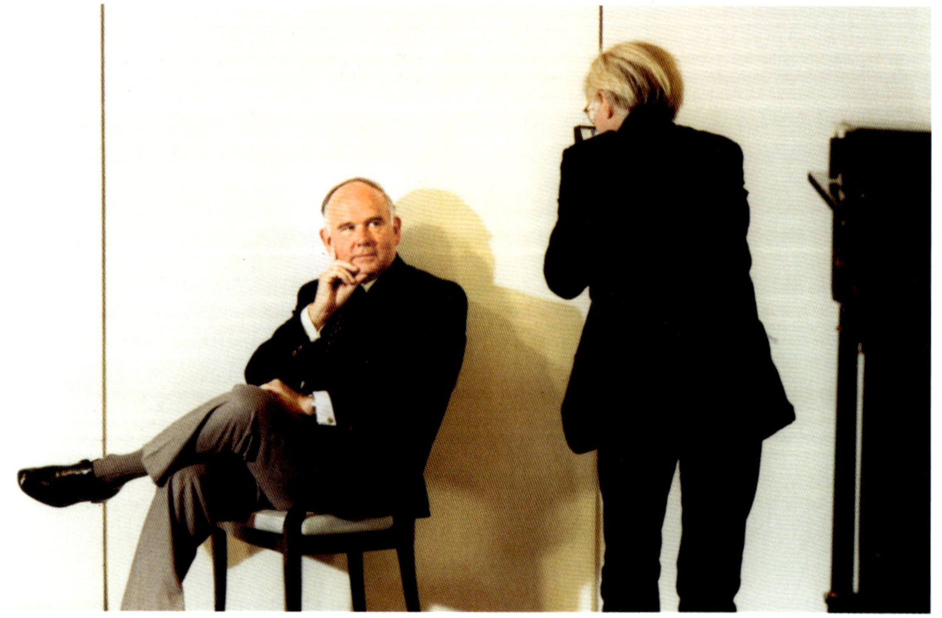

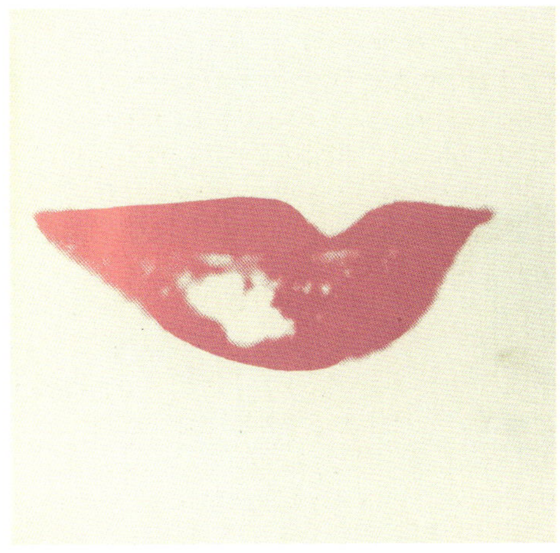
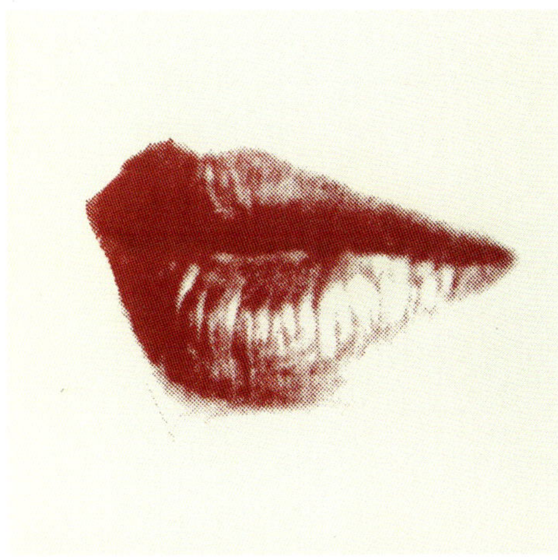
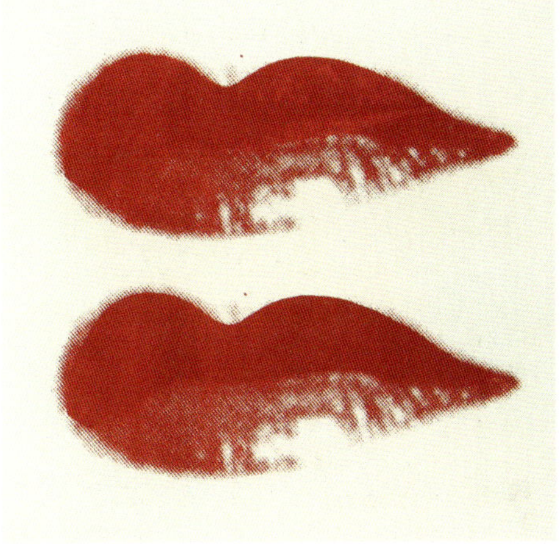
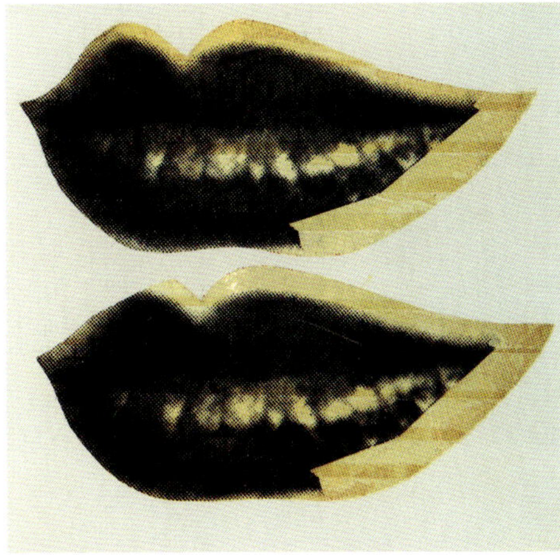

Fig.7 *Lips* c.1975
Screenprint and tape on
Ragston S-N paper
20.3 × 45.7 (open book)
The Andy Warhol Museum,
Pittsburgh, PA

Such allocations of roles should, however, never be mistaken for naïve stereotyping. The original commission for the *Ladies and Gentlemen* series in 1975 indicates that the client envisaged something informed by stereotypical images and a certain voyeurism, yet Warhol produced a brilliantly playful yet obviously respectful gallery of portraits on the theme of New York's drag culture. The Italian art dealer Luciano Anselmino had requested a series of 'impersonal, anonymous' pictures of 'transvestites', with the title of the series intended as a cheap joke.[30] At $900,000 for 105 canvases, this was Warhol's most lucrative commission, and the portraits were presented without names, as requested in Italy in 1975. What Warhol actually did was to create an empathetic series based on over 500 Polaroids, a masterpiece of affinity with the depicted people precisely by virtue of accentuating the personae that they put on show (fig.8). These African-American and Latinx transwomen look feminine, self-confident and strong. They include the activist Marsha P. Johnson (p.169), who

played a major role in the Stonewall Riots in 1969 and was later involved in the LGBT movement. Clear indications of deprivation – a missing tooth, cheap jewellery – which are visible in the photos were removed in Warhol's paintings; instead he offset these 'imperfections' with a vital and beautiful sense of personality, expressing complex individuality that runs across the series.

Watney sees Warhol's campness, which is also evident in such images, as a fundamental survival strategy that became deeply rooted within him early in his life.[31]

Not for nothing did Warhol joke as a child that he came from another planet. It was a joke and not a joke. Such fantasies speak almost too accurately (and painfully) of the experience of queer childhood, before the acquisition of an affirming identity grounded in homosexual desire. [...] Thus when other fifties homosexuals such as Frank O'Hara and Truman Capote gave him the cold shoulder because, in their times, he was too 'swishy', too much of a window dresser, something very profound was at stake. They had accepted a deal that was not available to Warhol. They had, if you will, dehomosexualized themselves, especially in their social role as artists or critics.[32]

In *Ladies and Gentlemen* Warhol forged a link between his earlier sensitive drawings based on photographs of his friend Otto Fenn in drag with the Polaroids of his self-portraits in drag in the early 1980s. According to Geldzahler, creating the series using the medium of the classic canvas image gave Warhol an opportunity to 'blur the self-imposed boundaries between the private and the socially acceptable for the first time', and perhaps even grow out of a role that he was still constantly enforcing with tape recorders and video cameras during the 1960s and 'which he had concocted for the public: the "naughty boy" syndrome, as it might be described'.[33]

The fact that Warhol was able to confront gender-related issues with a light-footed irony of his own is demonstrated by his images of Chairman Mao. On the recommendation of his Zurich gallerist Bruno Bischofberger that he commence his much-vaunted 1972 return to painting with a universally familiar figure, Warhol chose Mao Zedong, who had been named in

Life magazine as the most famous person in the world. Warhol transformed Mao's officially prescribed portrait, published millions of times for the frontispiece of his *Little Red Book*,[34] and the very antithesis of a flamboyant image, into a whole series of subtly differentiated versions, some of them in a giant format with red-painted lips, blue eyelids and rouge on his cheeks, blurring the gender identity of the subject of this propaganda image (p.158).[35] Using the example of this ostensibly immovable political colossus, Warhol was almost imperceptibly exercising the basic freedom of the principle of transgenderism in a playful way, from beneath the protective cloak of art.

'As far as Andy was concerned, the portrait was an idealised interpretation of someone's personality',[36] writes Vincent Fremont, with acute perception. From that vantage point, modifications, corrections and embellishments could be made, but did not have to necessarily correspond with the subject's own self-assessment or the image that they usually presented to the public. The way Warhol wanted the image of the subject to be, and how this fitted into his image, played a key role, and this was true of both his sitter and himself. 'When I did my self-portrait, I left all the pimples out because you always should. Pimples are a temporary condition and they don't have anything to do with what you really look like.'[37] This deliberately flippant statement reveals not only Warhol's sense of pragmatism and self-mockery, but also his understanding of the individual's character and abiding essence, which must be immortalised in the portrait. This distinguishes Warhol's drawn, painted and printed images from all of his other methods of portrayal.

In countless interviews Warhol was the one asking or answering the questions, mastering the art of the evasive response and camouflage like no other.[38] He conducted and documented his psychological studies through pared-back recordings that sometimes aimed at and lingered on his fellow men with a trace of sadism, whether the medium was a tape recorder or a 16-mm camera. In hundreds of *Screen Tests* he provoked his subjects into confrontation with the camera in much more powerful attempts at self-representation, and sometimes clumsier efforts at self-reflection or uncontrolled emotional outbursts than the classic portrait

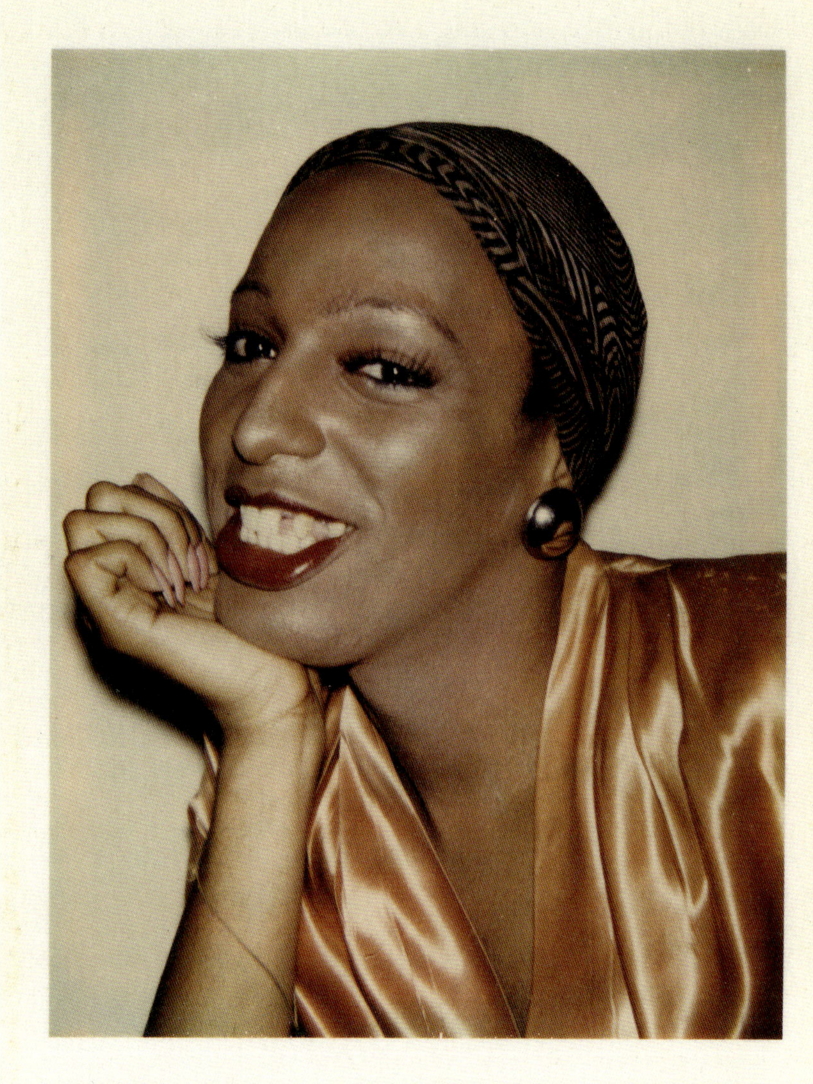

Fig.8 *Wilhelmina Ross* 1974
Polaroid™ 10.8 × 8.6
The Andy Warhol Museum,
Pittsburgh, PA

conventionally demanded. In the photo-booth images that served as the basis for Ethel Scull's portrait, the fact that Warhol was there too, making silly faces, had negated the lonely feeling of helplessness at being in the hands of the machine and brought some levity to the situation, but now Warhol left his test subject alone for a full three minutes, exposed to the merciless running of the camera. Meanwhile, Andy would usually be elsewhere, throwing himself into the hustle and bustle of the Factory or, as Cueff writes: 'Instead of the helpful presence of the other's gaze, which reveals to the subject what he is and allows him to become aware of himself as ego and potentially experience catharsis, Warhol turns the dead eye of a machine on him, transforming Freud's couch into an electric chair.'[39] Warhol's role in the painted pictures was quite different; here the person portrayed had a certain assurance of corrections and the artist's benevolent intervention. This was where Warhol usually blotted out any blemishes, although he did so not only with the intention of flattering his clients and drumming up business. Rather, he allowed everyone the potential to be beautiful, to be able to feel good under their protective mask. Whether his criticism was applied to himself, as in the case of the much-cited 'corrected' passport photo of Warhol from 1956 (indeed, it made the cover of the catalogue for the 2018 retrospective exhibition at the Whitney), with pencil marks around the nose and hairline, or the *Before and After* paintings from 1961–2 (pp.88–9), based on nose-job advertisements, or again the plastic surgery-like procedures that he customarily performed in the production of his commissioned portraits, such modifications made in the interest of making the subject more attractive fell somewhere between irony and genuine empathy, and sought to boost the sitter's self-esteem. His *Lips* book c.1975 (fig.7), which contain pages of screenprinted lips in all possible shapes and colours, and from which he would choose as the need arose,[40] speak volumes here. Perhaps the most striking example of his attempt to create the perfect face of a star were his drawings from 1962, made up of the mouths, noses, eyes and foreheads of idols such as Greta Garbo and Sophia Loren, collaged to create different options.[41] Sometimes he even had better-looking employees act as his double, thus jokingly referring to the film industry's penchant for presenting historical figures as more attractive than they were in real life. 'Who wants the truth? That's what show business is for – to prove that it's not what you are that counts, it's what they *think* you are.'[42]

Having grown up with albums full of collector's cards of film stars and dreaming about looking like them or playing their roles, and having later become a successful commercial illustrator who soon set about applying the clean, simple lines of his training to idealised drawings of young men, Warhol was undoubtedly geared towards a media-influenced, romantic and highly conventional, cultivated beauty from an early stage. In his last interview he was asked what had the power to stop him in his tracks. He answered laconically, 'A good display in a window … I don't

know … a good looking face.'[43] This did not mean, however, that he sought to dispel reality from his life: away from the glare of the media spotlight he looked after homeless people at the church-run soup kitchen in his New York district, for instance.[44] Rather, the fact that Warhol wanted to make his models as alluring as possible should perhaps be seen as an act of compassionate charity; his employee and confidante Pat Hackett said of his cosmetic alterations, 'In short, he would do unto others as he would wish others to do unto him.'[45] Examining the vast field of Warhol's self-portraits would go beyond the scope of this essay. As Dietmar Elger notes, they are all 'enactments, role plays that to an astonishing degree fulfil both his need for exhibitionist display and public presence, and for anonymity and privacy'.[46] This is perhaps most evident in one of his earliest portraits, *Nosepicker I: Why Pick on Me* 1948 (p.72), or as the despairing yet self-assured original title has it, *The Lord Gave Me My Face, But I Can Pick My Own Nose*. At this point, the twenty-year-old had not yet developed or refined his later strategy of camouflage: he defiantly jams his finger into his bulbous nose, which he saw as an imperfection.[47] Far more sophisticated is the interplay between public display and physical disappearance in *Invisible Sculpture* 1985, which Warhol set up in the Area nightclub in New York, the quintessential place of self-projection. His body, familiar to viewers through the media, was exhibited in a glass cabinet, clearly visible yet at the same time separated from the viewers by the pane of glass. Once he left the showcase, only the empty plinth labelled *Andy Warhol, USA; Invisible Sculpture; mixed media, 1985* remained. The 'paradoxical entanglement of self-expression and self-disguise'[48] that Barbara Straumann attributes to the bashfully camp Warhol proved to be the best strategy for survival, given his combined desire to belong and fear of losing himself. Being omnipresent while at the same time leaving everyone in the dark about himself as a person became his hard-won image. From early on, it was a matter not so much of hiding his queerness, but rather of the privilege of not being tied down. What Eve Kosofsky Sedgwick describes in *Epistemology of the Closet* as a fatally necessary protective pattern adopted either overtly or latently in the context of gay

self-revelation was transformed by Warhol into a masterfully controlled second skin.[49] This is vividly apparent in his late self-portraits with camouflage, and to various degrees also underlies all of his assumed roles, references to vanitas paintings with skulls or shadows, and dandy-like poses and wigs, in which Warhol makes the element of hiding obvious, calls out its regrettable necessity and at the same time asserts it as a fundamental right.

Having applied this complex practice to himself, Warhol's modifications, beautifications and enhancements also gave almost all of his countless subjects their desired outward appearance, as well as their own protective mask. Just as the golden background of the iconostases that he admired brings everything together, at once elevating and containing the subject, the 101.6 x 101.6-cm dimensions of Warhol's canvases ennoble and level everyone in the same way, forming the vast Warhol community. Not only did Warhol clairvoyantly anticipate today's increasing demands for constant self-publicising, with people capturing their every obsession, fleeting moment, revelation and deception, their image shaped by social media, but through his foresight, irony and empathy he also pointed the way to an approach that might work in response.

LIKE 2 LOOK / MAKE THEM SEE YOU

Martine Syms

Andy Warhol was an artist, he liked to look,
and he didn't get much sleep. We have
those things in common.

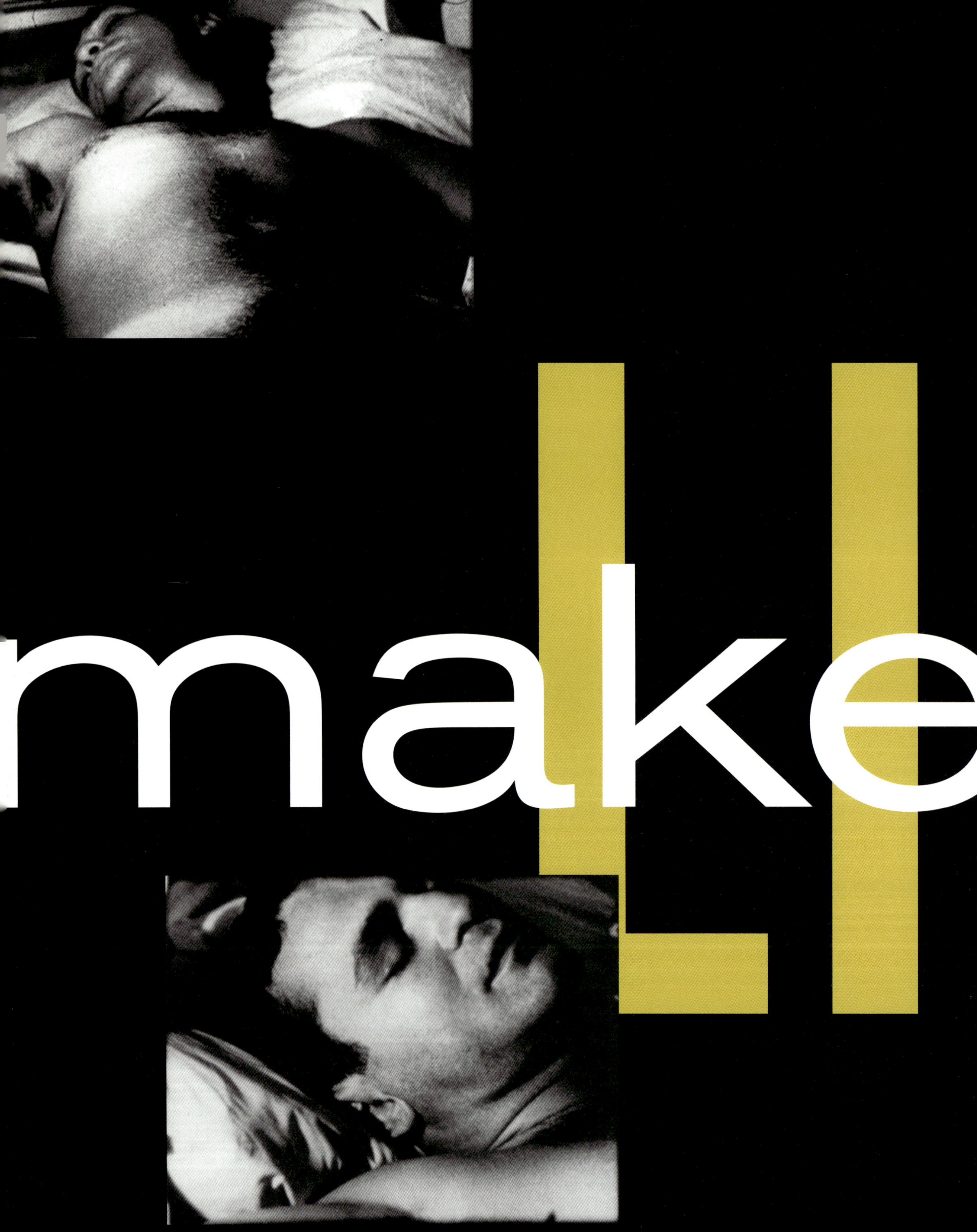

them

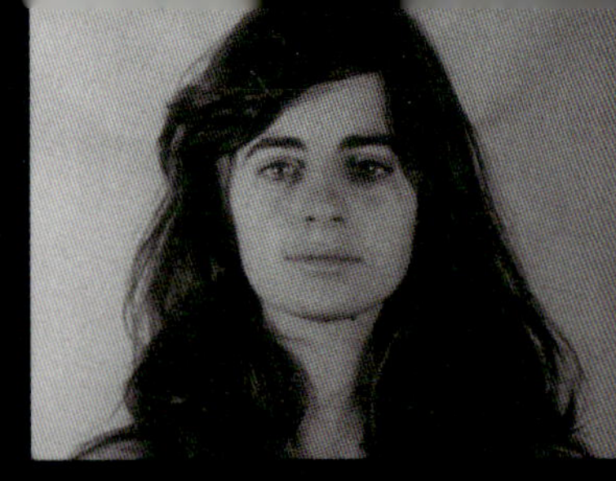
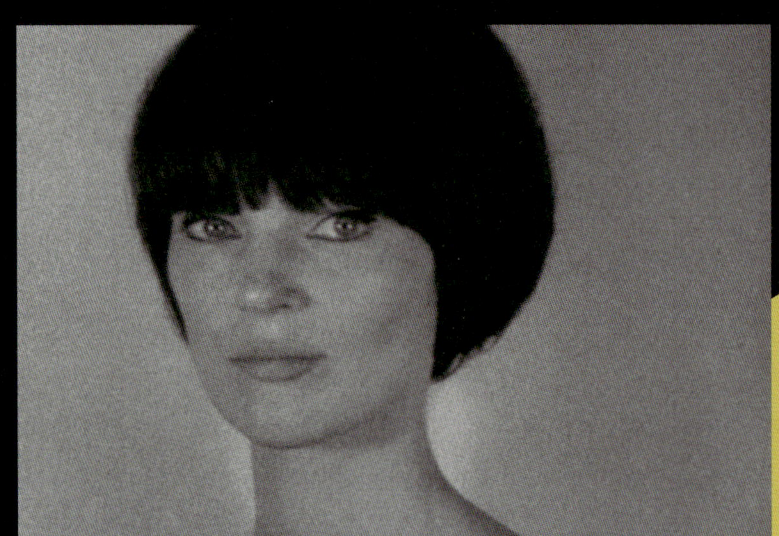
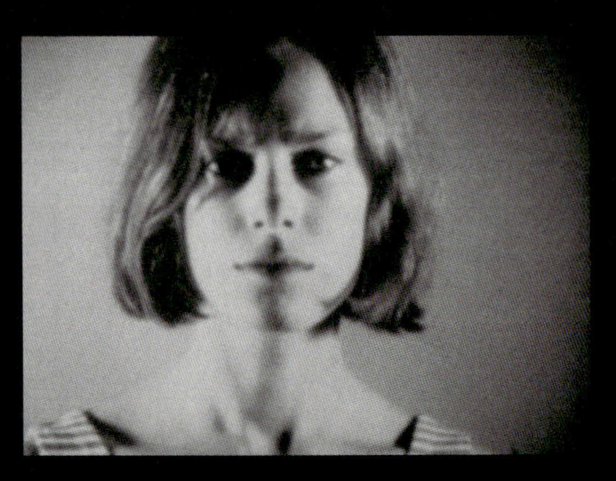
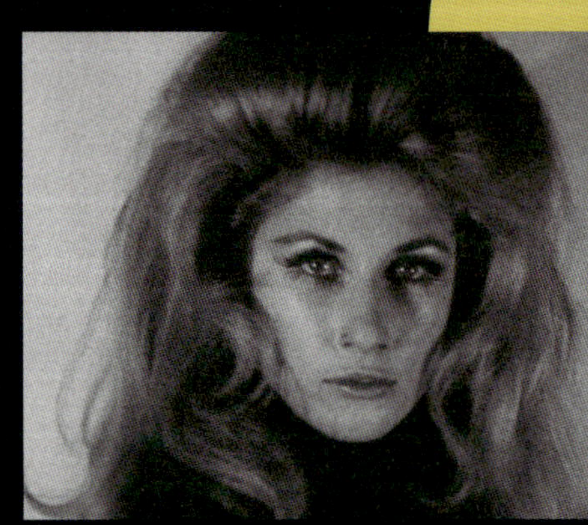

e ther

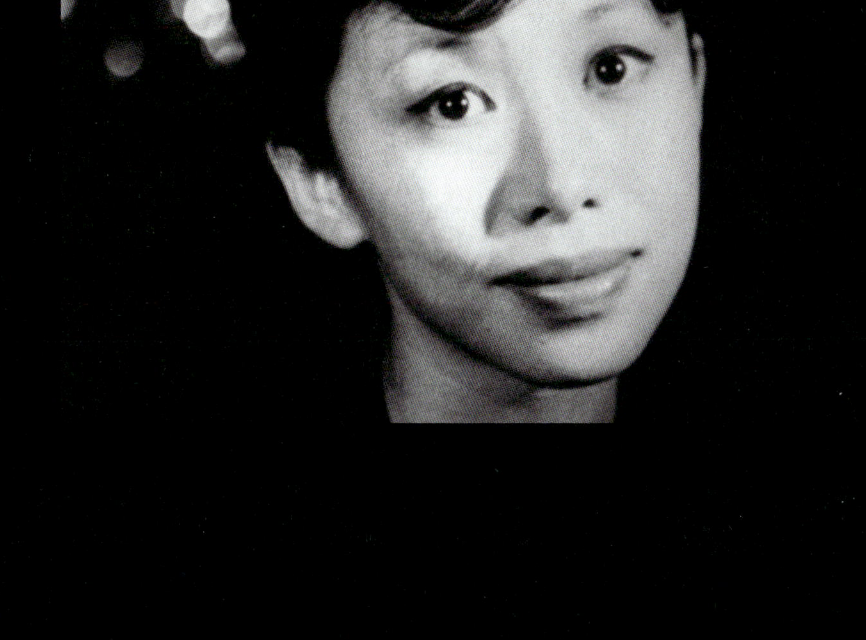

n see

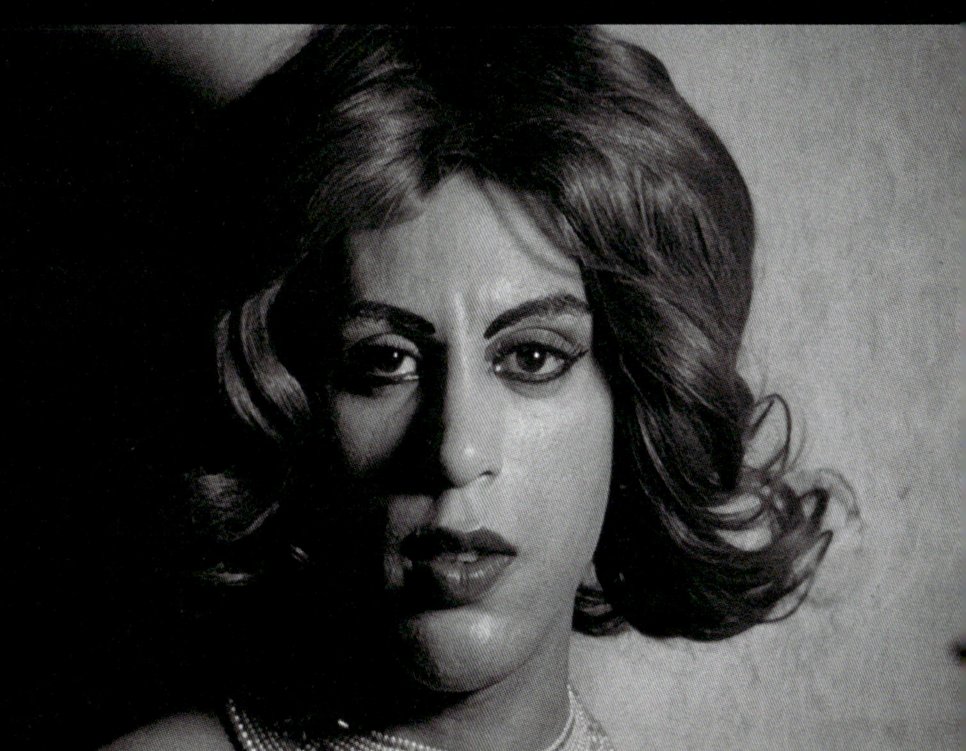

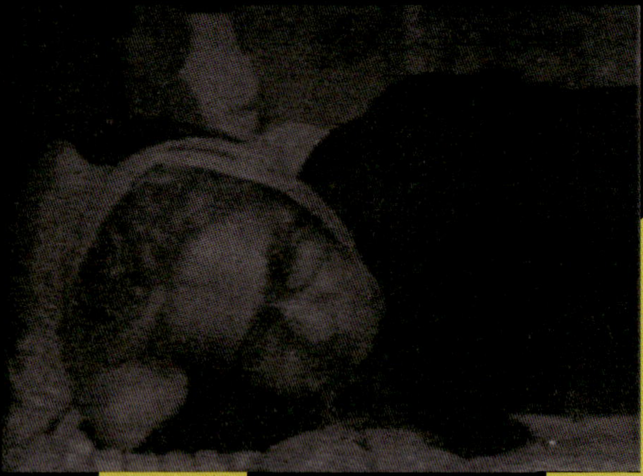

em L0 se

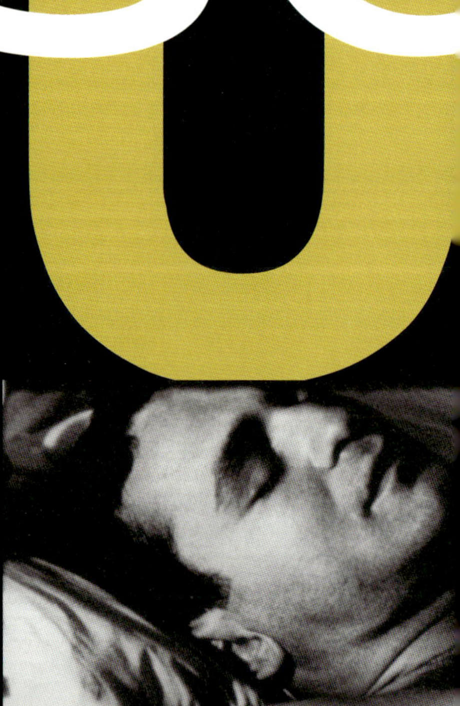

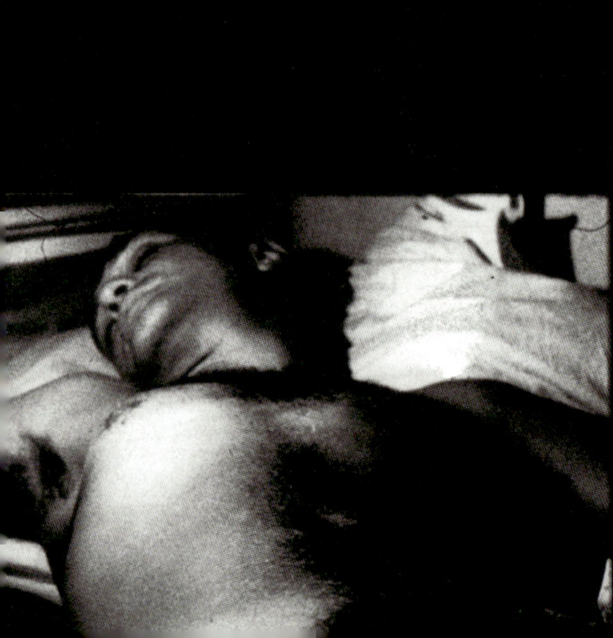

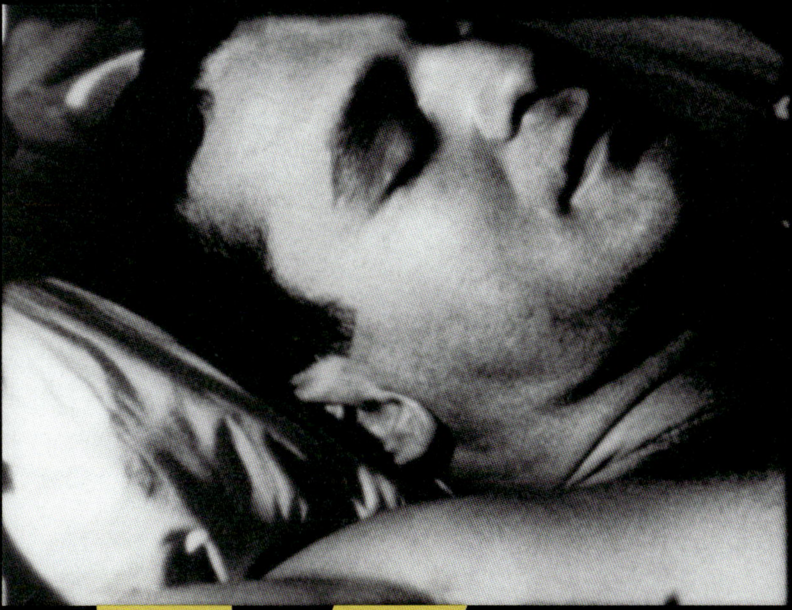

OK
e you

EXHIBITIONISM

Fiontán Moran

'Everybody posed. If you didn't pose – nobody saw you.' – Mary Woronov[2]

In 1969 Andy Warhol found himself underground yet again, only this time he was in the storage vaults of Rhode Island School of Design's Museum of Art. Like many other institutions looking to make their collection accessible to a younger audience, the museum had, on the suggestion of art collectors Dominique and John de Menil, asked the famous artist to curate the first in what was meant to be a series of exhibitions entitled *Raid the Icebox*.[3] Warhol's selection showed little concern for conventional art historical or monetary value by presenting paintings by famous and unknown artists alongside indigenous craft and applied arts, in a display that replicated the museum's overcrowded storage arrangements. Bartolomeo Passarotti's *Portrait of a Cavalier with his Hunting Dogs* c.1570–80 was propped sideways against the wall along with Matthias Stom's *Christ at the Column* c.1635 and kept in place with sandbags (fig.1), rows of spare American Windsor chairs were laid out as though in an antique store, while a cabinet full of shoes that the curators had considered 'a collective problem to maintain' was shown with its doors left wide open.[4] As requested by the artist, each item was carefully recorded in a catalogue accompanying the exhibition.

Warhol's presentation initially surprised the museum's director, Daniel Robbins, who recalled:

There were exasperating moments when we felt that Andy Warhol was exhibiting 'storage' rather than works of art, that a series of labels could mean as much to him as the paintings to which they refer. And perhaps they do, for in his vision, all things become part of the whole and we know that what is being exhibited is Andy Warhol.[5]

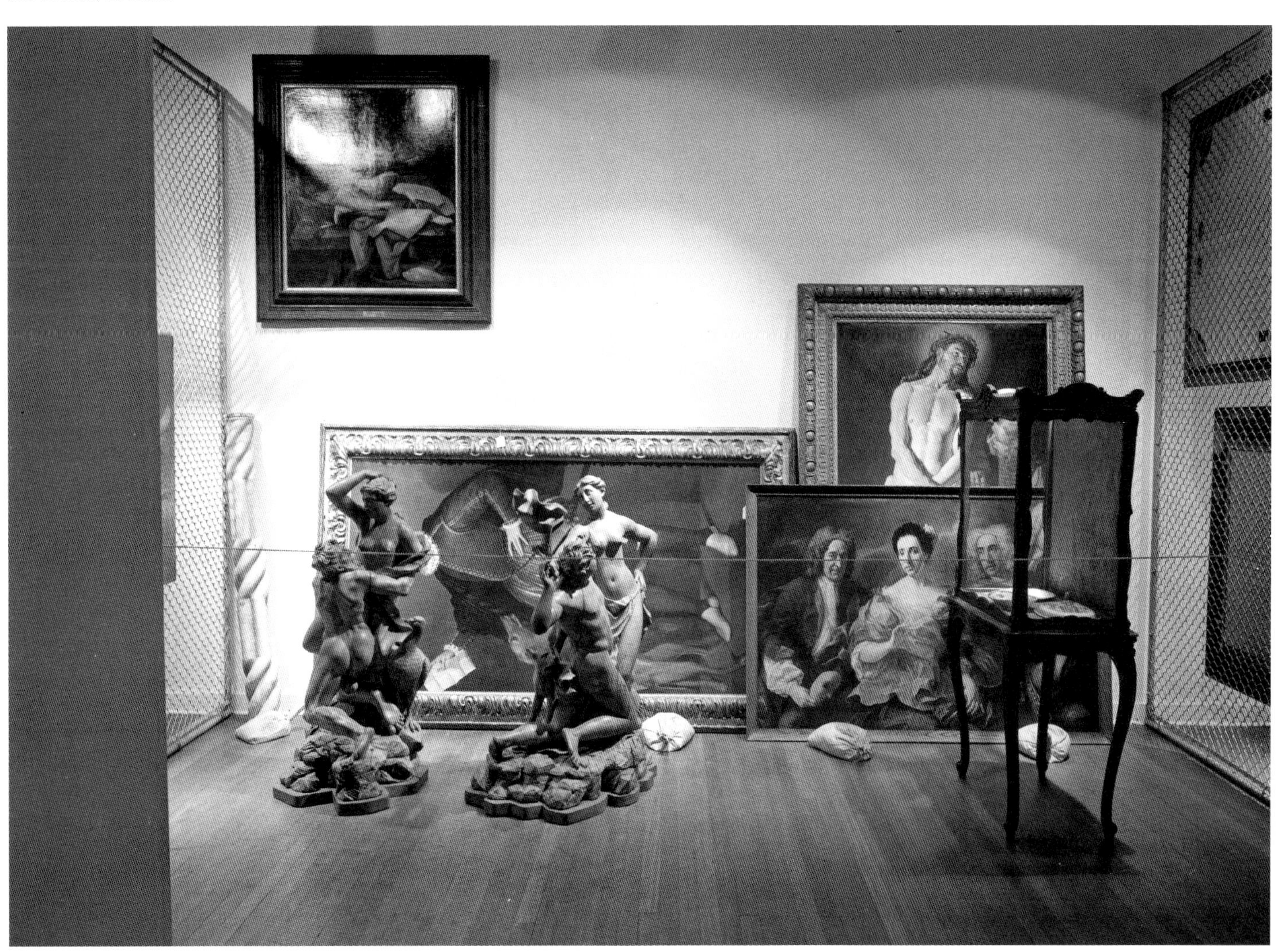

Fig.1 Installation shot of *Raid the Icebox*, Museum of Art, Rhode Island School of Design, 1970
RISD Museum, Providence

The decision to exhibit 'storage' did
indeed recall Warhol's displays of serial
Campbell's Soup Can paintings on a shelf
at the Ferus Gallery in 1962 (p.94), the
stacks of *Brillo Box* sculptures that filled
the Stable Gallery two years later (p.96),
and the conception of Warhol's studio
as 'The Factory'. Yet *Raid the Icebox* also
pointed to how he challenged systems
of identification and display to create
alternate meanings for objects, people and
his artistic identity. Thinking like a curator,
Warhol reimagined painting, photography,
film and stardom – through his so-called
'Superstars' who performed for his camera
– as parts of a wider social situation, one
that involved a type of exhibitionism, in a
manner that was performative and rooted
in a camp relation to the world.[6]

As Esther Newton described in *Mother
Camp: Female Impersonators in America*
(1972), camp involves a 'relationship
between things, people, and activities
or qualities, and homosexuality' that
shifts attention from 'what a thing *is* to
how it *looks*, from *what* is done to *how* it
is done'.[7] Warhol explicitly referenced the
subject in his 1965 film *Camp* (fig.2) that
was created in response to the publication
of Susan Sontag's influential text 'Notes
on "Camp"' the previous year. However,
while Sontag's analysis largely buried the
homosexual subtext by focusing on camp
as an adjective that merely prioritises
style over content, it is important to
remember that initially camp was a private
code rooted in gay communities. This is
suggested by the finale of Warhol's film
where, after performances by the dancer
Paul Swan, socialite Jane Holzer and the
model Donyale Luna among others, the
artist Jack Smith points towards a cabinet
and asks, 'Should I open the closet
now, Andy?'[8]

With the publication of *Pop Out: Queer
Warhol* in 1996, Warhol came to be
repositioned as an artist who was not 'out'
in a political sense but who – for the editors
José Esteban Muñoz, Jennifer Doyle and
Jonathan Flatley – created gestures that
'had the effect of transfiguring, exploding,
or reworking the kinds of categories by
which he might be policed or judged'.[9]
Subsequently Warhol's work and world
has been reinterpreted as enacting a queer
sensibility at a time when homosexuality
was illegal. As Samuel R. Delany explains,
the New York of the 1950s and 1960s
was a time when 'camp' and 'camping'

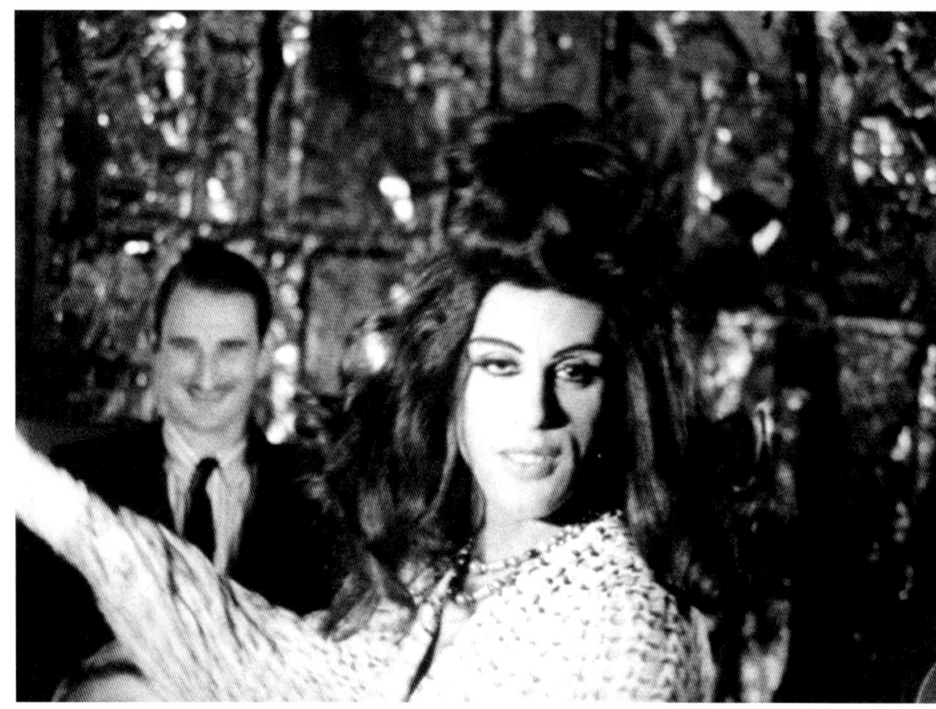

Fig.2 Mario Montez and Jack
Smith in *Camp* 1965
16mm film, black and white,
sound, 66 minutes
The Andy Warhol Museum,
Pittsburgh, PA

Fig.3 Leila Davies Singelis
Making the Rounds 1950
Gelatin silver print
20.8 × 20.3
The Andy Warhol Museum,
Pittsburgh, PA

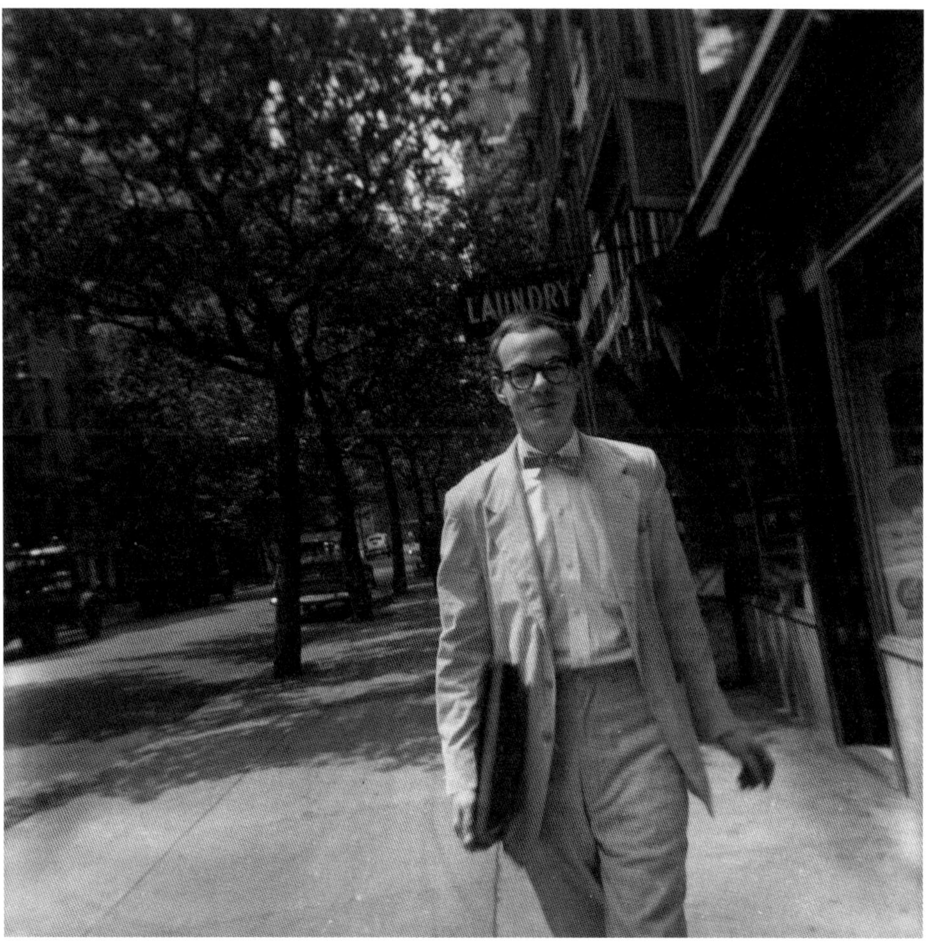

were acts of 'flaunting the customs' of the queer world, a time when 'coming out' was a matter of 'bodily practice' that brought one into communion with similar individuals.[10] Rather than the later politicised meaning associated with 'coming out of the closet', usually in order to be visible to a heterosexual public, pre-Stonewall coming out was about 'counterpublic space, appropriation, and relation': strategies that are quintessentially Warholian.[11]

In *POPism: The Warhol Sixties* (1980), Warhol recalls how his 'swish' identity, then a common term for an effeminate homosexual, his art collecting and career as a commercial illustrator initially acted as a barrier to the art world of the 1950s, but that it was something he chose to embrace:

> And as for the 'swish' thing, I'd always had a lot of fun with that – just watching the expressions on people's faces. You'd have to have seen the way all the Abstract Expressionist painters carried themselves and the kinds of images they cultivated, to understand how shocked people were to see a painter coming on swish. I certainly wasn't a butch kind of guy by nature, but I must admit, I went out of my way to play up the other extreme.[12]

What is revealing here is that Warhol recognised his camping, or 'swishing', as just one type of performance that existed alongside the cultivated images of heteronormative identity that were associated with the New York School of abstract expressionist painting. It was through performance, as related to theatricality but also to the concept of performativity, whereby identity is understood to be *socially* constructed through what Judith Butler describes as the 'stylised repetition of acts', that Warhol's artistic project can be best understood.[13]

Of course, Warhol was by no means the only gay in Greenwich Village, and it is important to consider the influence of Jack Smith's flamboyant films and performances, but also the use of everyday movement in the dances of Lucinda Childs and Fred Herko at Judson Theater, who would both appear in his early silent movies.[14] In her study on the history of performance in contemporary art, Catherine Wood explains that artists of the 1960s and 1970s began to reconceive subjectivity as 'constructed and projected towards the world, shaped in relation to

social norms and expectations' and that from this position came to consider that the superficial surface 'might be more truthful than what lies beneath'.[15] Viewed from this perspective, Warhol's famous statement that, 'If you want to know all about Andy Warhol, just look at the surface: of my paintings and films and me, and there I am. There's nothing behind it', takes on renewed significance, especially as the statement was the result of interviewer Gretchen Berg combining her comments with Warhol's laconic responses.[16] Looking to the surface of his works, to their material components, Warhol's techniques of mechanical reproduction, appropriation and 'stylised repetition' often drew attention to the way they were constructed, to replace visibility with ambiguity, authenticity with theatricality. This can be seen in his blot printing technique of the 1950s drawings, his over-and-under-inking of silkscreens in works such as *Marilyn Diptych* 1962 (pp. 102–3) where the face appears to be both mask-like and ethereal, in the loose scripting and staging of his films, and the performance of his own instantly recognisable yet elusive persona.

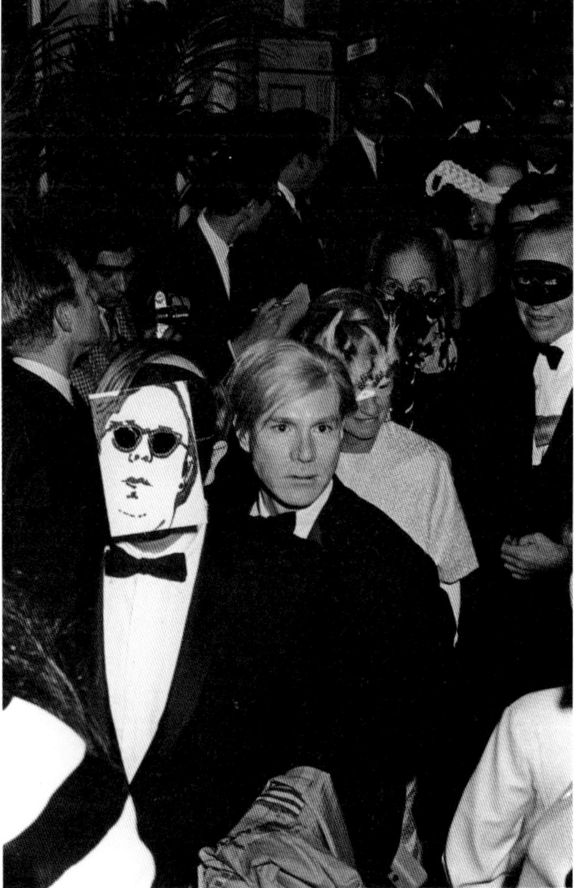

Fig. 4 Warhol standing alongside curator Henry Geldzahler and Frank Sinatra at Truman Capote's Black and White Ball, Plaza Hotel, New York, 28 November 1966
Photo by Bernard Gotfryd

This persona was astutely and campily performed when, in 1966, Warhol was invited to Truman Capote's now legendary masquerade 'Black and White Ball' where, moving through the crowds at the Plaza Hotel in New York, next to eminent figures such as Lee Radziwill, Mia Farrow, Frank Sinatra and Lauren Bacall wearing custom-made masks, he chose to wear only his face (fig.4). As if to suggest that his wig and nonchalant attitude was enough of a façade, this also unveils Warhol's understanding of identity as a construction that is performed in public and associated with style. Forever self-conscious about his skin problems, bulbous nose and premature balding, Warhol used clothing to transform himself in ways that often reflected his artistic endeavours. While working as a commercial illustrator he was known as 'raggedy Andy' due to his penchant for ill-fitted suits that complemented the craft-like aesthetic of his designs and suggested to art directors that he really did need the job (fig.3). With the adoption of a light brown, then grey wig that later became whiter, Warhol's career as an artist saw him move from formal suits to the iconic combination of leather jacket, boots and sunglasses

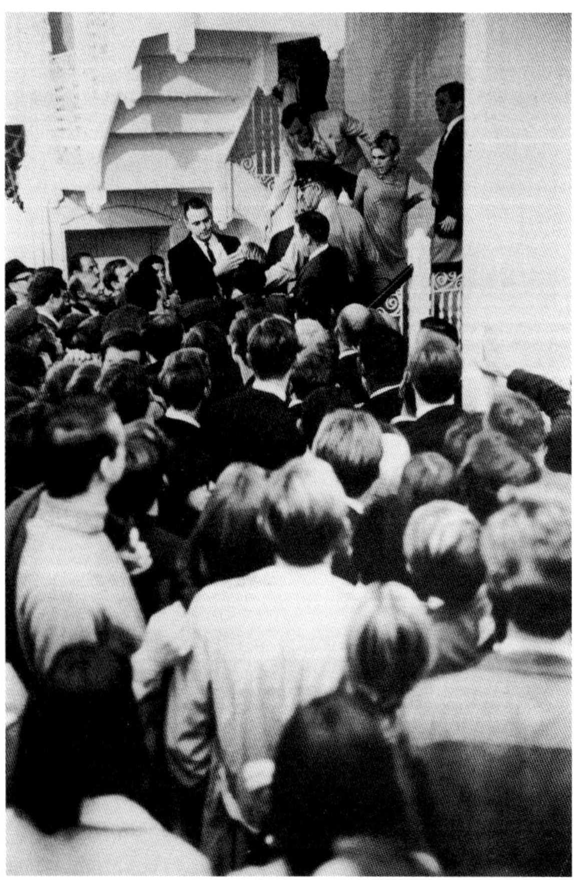

Fig.5 Curator Sam Green helps Edie Sedgwick, Gerard Malanga and Andy Warhol escape the crowds at the Institute of Contemporary Art Philadelphia, 1965

that were associated with biker and gay subcultures. In the 1970s, as he entered into the realm of so-called 'business art', Warhol created his own version of 'executive realness' that consisted of a shirt, tie and blazer with the then-unusual combination of blue jeans. By contrast, as he started to collaborate with younger artists in the 1980s and attend nightclubs such as Danceteria and Area, Warhol adopted a predominantly black wardrobe so that his head and large white wig appeared to float as immortalised in the 'fright-wig' self-portraits of 1986 (p.207).

With each iteration Warhol was able to turn his visage and attitude into an abstract entity, an act, that could be easily copied and then applied like a brand to both products and people.[17] For instance, in 1967 he had the actor Allen Midgette dress up as him for a tour of college campuses stating that he 'made a much better Andy Warhol than I did', and in 1971 had an actor portray him in the play *Pork*.[18] This also extended to his loose concept of authorship as evidenced in his appropriation of found imagery for his pop paintings, and his film and television projects that relied upon the division of labour to create products for 'Andy Warhol Enterprises'. Even when he began to author books Warhol required the assistance of other people. His often-quoted publications *The Philosophy of Andy Warhol* (1975), *Andy Warhol's Exposures* (1979), *POPism* (1980) and *America* (1985) channel the tradition of the ghostwritten celebrity biography by being the product of Factory staff members Pat Hackett, Bob Colacello, Vincent Fremont and Brigid Berlin, who elaborated on Warhol's brief statements and learned to enact his 'voice'.[19]

Warhol's slippery presentation of identity and artistry, of making the personal social, and the social personal, was at the heart of the pop experiment, as he explained: 'Pop Art took the inside and put it outside, took the outside and put it inside.'[20] One of the most explicit ways in which Warhol was able to achieve this was through the 'Superstars' – poets, socialites, drag queens, dancers and others – who populated his films, hung around the Factory, accompanied him to events and collectively became a living artwork. For example, Warhol was delighted when his paintings had to be removed from the walls of his exhibition at the Institute of Contemporary Art in Philadelphia in 1965 due to the large crowd that had gathered to

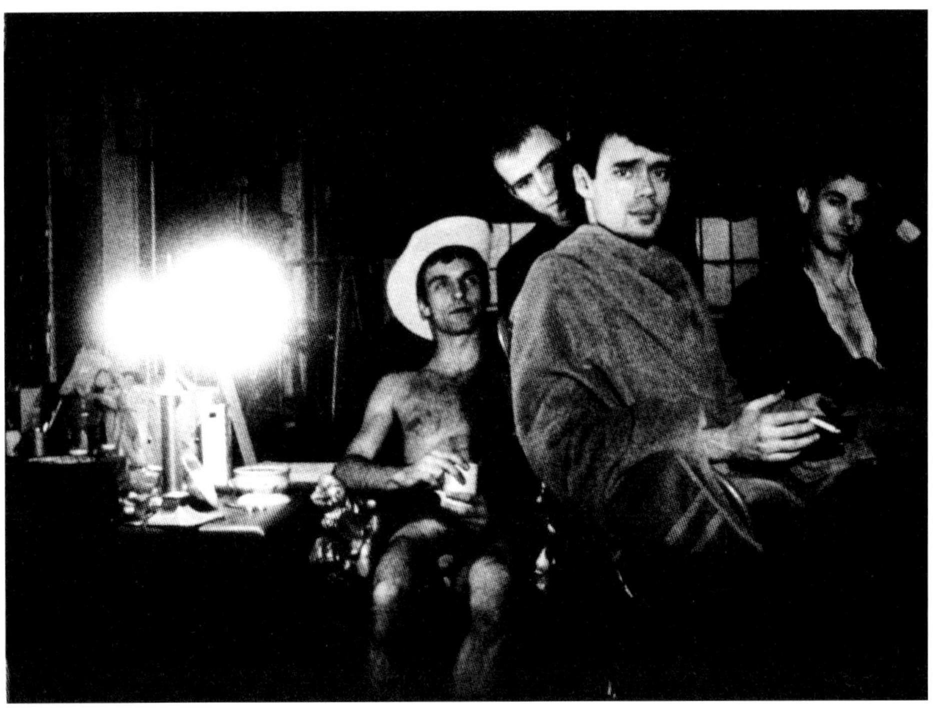

Fig.6 Fred Herko, Billy Name,
John Daley and James
Waring in *Haircut (No.1)*
1963
16mm film, black and white,
silent, 27 minutes
The Andy Warhol Museum,
Pittsburgh, PA

see Andy, Edie, Gerard and co. (fig.5).
'It was fabulous: an art opening with no
art!' Warhol recalled, 'We weren't just at
the art exhibit. We *were* the art exhibit.'[21]
The importance of the social world around
the artist was affirmed when the catalogue
for his exhibition at Moderna Museet in
1968 afforded more space to photographs
of the Factory taken by Stephen Shore and
Billy Name (Linich) than to the paintings,
sculptures and films.

It was through film, influenced
by Smith's co-opting of Hollywood
conventions and star mythology, that
Warhol created a space for his Superstars
to perform, but also to imagine queer
forms of relationality. His first movies were
shot with a static camera, silent, often
unedited, and focused on intimate scenes
of everyday activities such as sleeping
(*Sleep* 1963, p.122), fellatio (*Blow Job*
1964), haircuts (*Haircut (No.1)* 1963,
fig.6), kissing (*Kiss* 1963) or, in the case
of *Empire* 1963, the passing of time. With
the purchase of an Auricon camera in
the summer of 1964, Warhol began to
introduce sound and (loose) narrative. His
minimal technique incrementally developed
with haphazard zooms and pans across the
mise en scène, followed by jump cuts made
by turning the camera off and on. This
acted to demarcate the limits of the picture
frame and revealed the films to be closer
to stage shows performed for an invisible

audience rather than the 'magic of cinema'.
One notebook from 1969 in the archives
of The Andy Warhol Museum in Pittsburgh
lists ideas for scenarios that combine
simple directions such as 'the same story
done by two different actresses', 'making
love to a motorcycle', and 'undressing
and dancing at same time' that suggest
sensual live compositions.[22] Within this
framework Superstars were free to fall in
and out of character or to simply improvise
and exhibit themselves. For Richard Dyer,
Hollywood stars represented 'typical
ways of behaving, feeling and thinking in
contemporary society, ways that have been
socially, culturally, historically constructed',
so by blurring the line between fact and
fiction, Warhol found a way to reimagine
and obfuscate not only identity but also
those 'social, cultural and historical'
constructions.[23] Meanwhile, the Superstar
'talkers' introduced a greater theatricality
to proceedings, most notably Ondine
(Robert Olivo). His infamous role as 'The
Pope' in *Chelsea Girls* 1966 (pp.140–1)
featured him storming off camera after
verbally and physically attacking Ronna
Page, which further tore at the imaginary
space of theatrical performance.

'But drag, like violence, is as American
as apple pie.' – Esther Newton[24]

Gender experimentation also frequently
featured throughout Warhol's career: from
his 1950s drawings of photographer Otto
Fenn in drag, his film stars Mario Montez,
Holly Woodlawn, Candy Darling and
Jackie Curtis, through to 1981 when he
donned various wigs for a photoshoot with
Christopher Makos.[25] However, gender
identity is given its most considerable
attention in painting with the series
Ladies and Gentlemen of 1975, which
depicts African-American and Latinx drag
queens and transwomen in New York.
Commissioned by Warhol's Italian dealer,
Luciano Anselmino, who came up with
the theatrical title and asked him to depict
'funny looking' drag queens, it was a time
when gender fluidity was gaining cultural
capital, as shown by the emergence of
glam rock, stars such as Divine, the musical
The Rocky Horror Show (1973) and the
influential exhibition *Transformer: Aspekte
der Travestie* (1974) at the Kuntsmuseum
Lucerne, which featured the stars of the
Warhol and Paul Morrisey film *Women
in Revolt* (1971): Darling, Woodlawn

and Curtis.[26] While the originator of
the commission appears to have been
indifferent to the real lives of the subjects
depicted, all of whom were sourced by
Warhol's assistants, paid the standard
modelling fee, and whose identities were
until recently mostly unknown, the large
number of paintings created for the *Ladies
and Gentlemen* series reveals Warhol's
acute understanding of how gender is both
performed and visualised.[27]

One of the ways this is evidenced is
through Warhol's play with the layers of
the painted ground and the silkscreened
prints made from his Polaroid photographs.
Whereas the works of the 1960s used
block colour to vaguely correspond to
the features of the photographic image,
in *Ladies and Gentlemen* the forms are
loosely delineated with gestural brush
marks, finger painting and dynamic colour
combinations that border on abstraction,
which emphasise and confuse how
the composition is constructed. Through
this process the works dramatise the
Renaissance debate about the use of vivid
colour (*colore*) in painting, which was
associated with naturalism and spontaneity,
and drawing (*disegno*), in which composition
and form were associated with reason,
to productive effect. For instance, in the
set of smaller paintings depicting Alphanso
Panell (pp.163–4), the contrasting colours
of the ground at times obscure and then
reveal the photographic silkscreen image,
while the portrayal of trans and gay
liberation activist Marsha P. Johnson
uses green for the silkscreen print, which
makes it more difficult to determine which
layer was applied first (p.169). When
used in the depiction of non-white trans
individuals whose lives would have been
subject to systematic oppression and
surveillance, Warhol's handling of colour
resists so-called classical approaches to
representation based upon the accurate
depiction and identification of a subject.
Instead, the paintings propose a fluid
conception of gender identity and also
the impossibility for a single portrait to
truly represent the complications of life. It is
through collective display that the works of
Ladies and Gentlemen perform at their best.
When placed together the ricochet of colour
and visibly worked surfaces activate the
static poses of the photographs to convey
a sense of pageantry in a similar manner
to the drag balls that created a safe space
for gender expression.[28]

Public spaces are essential to the
construction of identity, whereby social
performances are learned and performed
by individuals based upon unspoken rules
and conventions.[29] As Warhol moved
into the 1970s and 1980s, from the Silver
Factory to his 'Office', from the Iranian
Embassy to Studio 54, his own publicised
socialising, or social climbing, was widely
dismissed as 'selling out'. While Warhol
certainly understood that the performance
of being an artist and of being seen had
economic value, as shown by his obsession
with securing more portrait commissions and
advertisements for his magazine *Interview*,
it can be regarded as having a social value
too for the way it formed new connections
between various creative communities
and society. As chronicled by Pat Hackett
in his *Diaries* (1976–87), Warhol's so-
called 'social disease' of going out every
night was approached with a democratic
zeal as suggested in the opening pages
of *Exposures* (1979) in which Warhol (or
Colacello) declares that he would happily
attend the 'opening of anything, including a
toilet seat'.[30] This is reflected in the thousands
of photographs that were taken with his
small Minox 35EL that allowed him to easily
point-and-shoot any scene. Aesthetically
no different from the paparazzi shots of Ron
Galella (who Warhol happened to admire),
they provide a vital portrait of the times
but also function as a framing device that
throws into focus the theatricality of social
performances that have become all too
familiar in an age of social media (fig.7).

It is a social scene that forms the basis
of *Sixty Last Suppers* 1986 (pp.204–5),
which repeats a copy of Leonardo da Vinci's
depiction of Christ and his apostles, sixty
times in black and white, across a 10-metre-
wide canvas. Much like the close-framing of
his Polaroid portraits and films, the dramatic
perspectival composition of the *Last Supper*
places the scene within a tight stage-set
where the pose of each figure has been
carefully defined. Just as Warhol's films
reveal the poetry in the everyday, the *Last
Supper* depicts an everyday scenario that
has great significance in Christian history
and is re-enacted as a public and collective
action during the Mass, like those that
Warhol attended with his mother. Jessica
Beck has noted that through the depiction
of the Christ figure, surrounded by men,
at a moment of suspicion around who will
betray him, Warhol's *Last Supper* series can
be interpreted as his attempt to deal with the

escalating AIDS crisis, which was unfolding at this time and had already claimed the lives of a number of Warhol's friends including his former boyfriend, Jon Gould.[31] By repeating an image depicting collective activity between men, loaded with symbolic value, *Sixty Last Suppers* becomes a moving portrayal of endless loss, and the merging of private and public realms at a time when the gay community suffered insensitive scrutiny by the media and took to the street in protest against the inaction of the government.

While Warhol was not a queer activist who joined marches or made political declarations to the press, his works are a reminder of the importance of queer forms of belonging and relationality. By creating spaces – in galleries, in film and in his social life – for different ways of being, exhibiting and performing in the world, Warhol reimagined what art, an artist or superstar could be. Just as *Raid the Icebox* played with the institution's classification and display of objects, through the stages Warhol created for the 'stylised repetition of acts', for forms of exhibitionism, he dramatised the fractures in everyday reality to productive effect. Rather than suggest that identity and meaning are stable, the use of repetition, theatricality and ambiguity in Warhol's work enacts a processional character that refuses easy definition and continues to be interpreted anew. His work performs a 'coming out' as described by Samuel R. Delany that is a 'gradual, continual, and constantly modulating process of becoming who we are', one that is set within a broader event field to make room for those collections of objects left in storage, those communities kept underground and those yet to be discovered.[32]

Fig.7 *Contact Sheet August*
1976: Andy Warhol, Bianca Jagger, Halston, Diane de Beauvau, Bethann Hardison at Elton John concert; In the back of a limousine; At Halston's apartment, Andy Warhol photographing Bianca Jagger shaving in the living room.

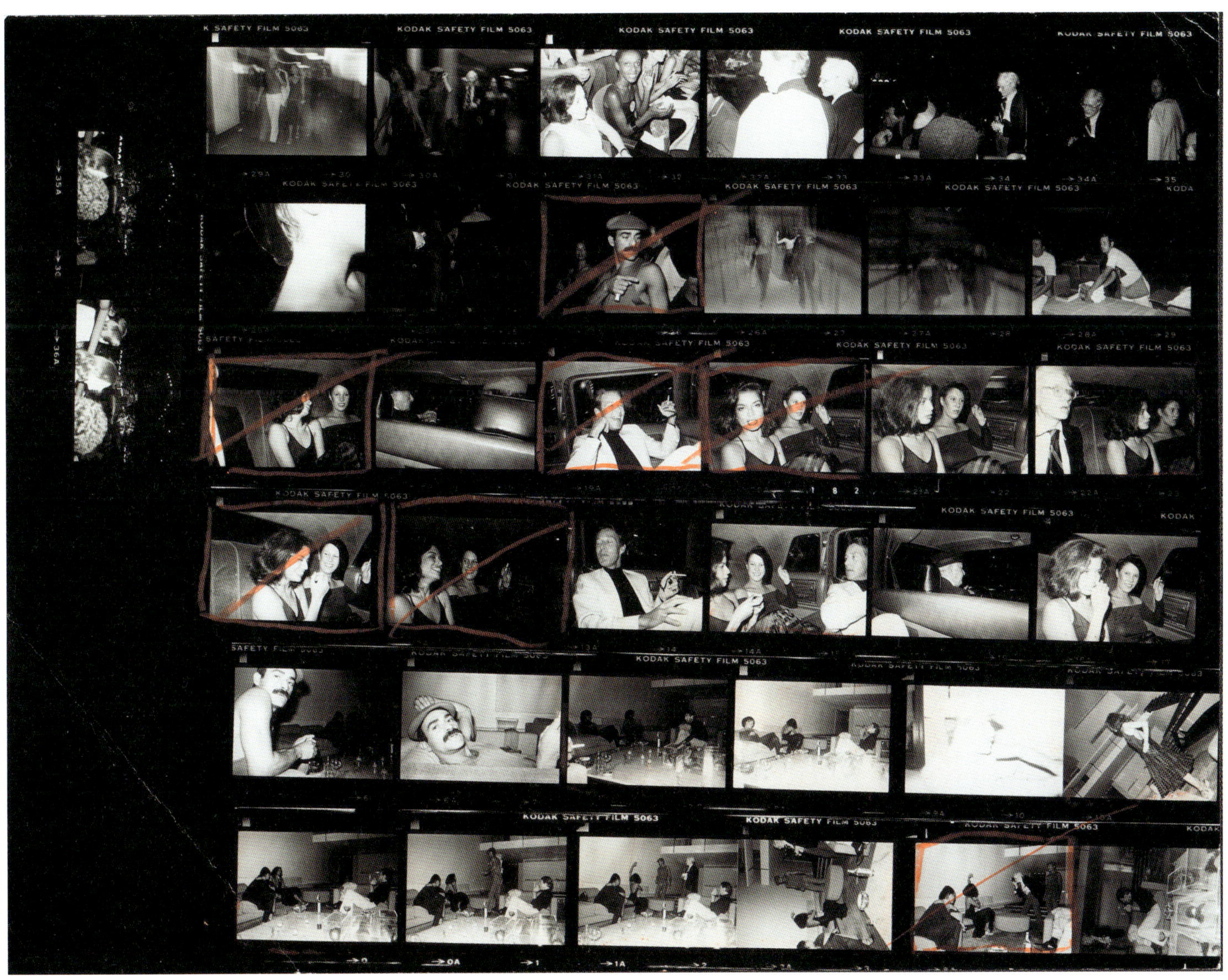

ANDY WARHOL THROUGH THE EYES OF BOB COLACELLO

Charlie Porter

'Bob, don't you realise I'm living my life through your life? – Andy Warhol[1]

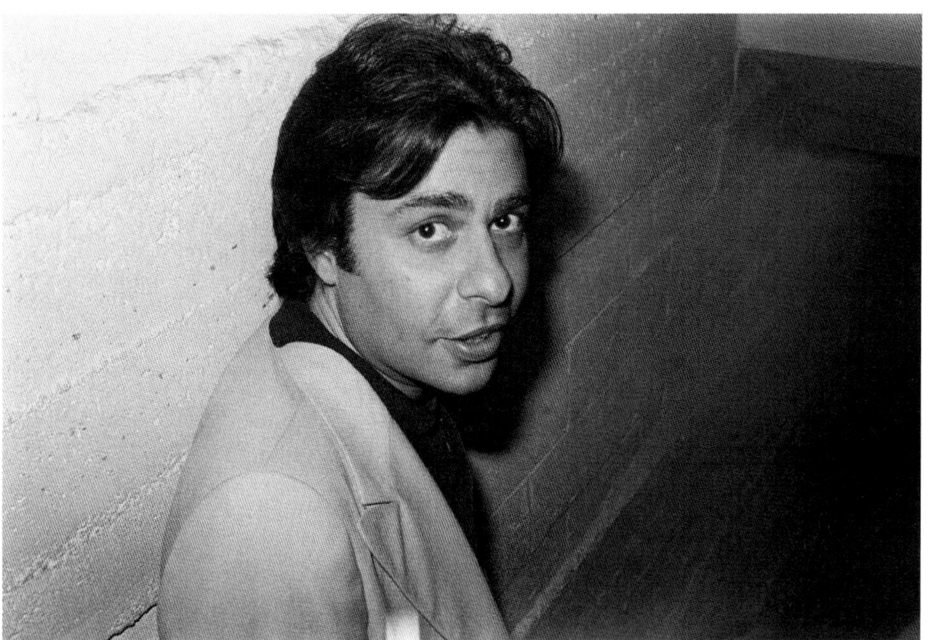

Fig.1 Bob Colacello
Self Portrait c.1976
Gelatin silver print
43.2 x 53.4 (framed)
Private collection

Bob Colacello was an editor of *interVIEW*, renamed *Andy Warhol's Interview*, renamed *Interview*, from 1970 to 1983. He took the top title of Executive Editor in 1974, running the magazine until his exit. When he started, Colacello was twenty-three years old; Warhol was forty-two. The magazine's office was at the Factory, first at 33 Union Square West, then 860 Broadway, placing Colacello at the heart of Warhol's life for twelve years.

Colacello was in charge of the magazine's editorial and helped gather advertising. He wrote its famed social column OUT. But there was so much more to his work. He got paid commission by Warhol to arrange society portraits. He was witness to what Warhol did and said. He socialised with Warhol, partied with Warhol, travelled the world with Warhol. He told Warhol all his secrets – Warhol was constantly asking for his secrets – and the secrets he had heard about other people, too.

Throughout, Colacello kept meticulous diaries, which he used to write *Holy Terror*[2], his insightful and heartfelt account of life with Warhol. In my opinion, it is the best book on Warhol yet published.

Much of Colacello's life has revolved around the recorded word. *Interview* was a gleeful magazine of style and fashion and culture and glamour, based on conversations with the magazine's friends, who also happened to be celebrities, like cover stars Diana Ross, Marisa Berenson, Fran Lebowitz or Diane von Furstenberg. These conversations were part of Warhol's wider obsession with the recorded word. Warhol recorded any conversation he could with his tape recorder, a constant companion he referred to as 'my wife'.

I met with Colacello at his apartment on the Upper East Side to record a conversation about Warhol. In 97 minutes, Bob spoke 9,628 words. He probably said as many again when we had lunch afterwards, off the record, at the Italian across the road. The usual modus operandi for journalists is to condense interviews, compress them, chop and stitch together and pretend that conversations are neat and compact. I want to move away from that. Here, I am just going to quote directly from Colacello, use as many quotes as I can fit in the space, maybe tidying the odd sentence up for clarity. He says so much, his words should stand for themselves.

Bob on Bob: *[just after I press the Voice Memos button on my iPhone]* I have the face of a priest. People tell me things, people I hardly know.

On not asking questions
One thing I learned from Andy, and also that was just in my nature, was I never really liked asking questions very much. I found that, when you didn't ask questions – especially about the elephant in the room – if you don't bring it up, they bring it up, because they know you want to talk about it.

Young people, open door
Another thing I learned from Andy is to have younger friends, and to work with younger people. It's just fun, it's interesting to engage with all generations. That was so core to what Andy did, to just have an open-door policy, not being afraid to put people together you'd think would never get along, and they did.

Shyness, Garbo
Andy was a combination of real shyness, and also liking to play Garbo, also understanding that mystery was part of what made you famous. If you were mysterious and didn't give all the answers and even lied sometimes, journalists then had to come back to correct lies or get more out of you.

Andy like a child: annoying and entertaining

He was a child who didn't grow up. He could be very annoying like a child could be. He was like a child, the way a child keeps repeating the same stupid thing. On the other hand, sometimes his childishness, I miss that side of his childishness. You'd go to these fancy parties and fancy apartments and Andy would be like the child who noticed that the dog just peed on the rug. He would be like, I think the husband's gay. *[adopt's Andy's voice]* 'Oh Bob, you know he has a problem.' He would never say gay. 'He has a problem.'

Andy as observer, Andy as voyeur

Andy took it all in, he really didn't miss a trick. He was a very acute observer. The more you're an observer, the harder it makes it to really engage. I think there's always a price to be paid. There was a point where observing becomes voyeurism, and he certainly crossed that line.

When people say voyeurism, they immediately think of watching people have sex, which Andy, with Victor Hugo, managed to do a little bit of, in the Polaroid sessions for the *Torso* and *Sex Part* series. But voyeurism for Andy was more like holding the tape recorder in your face in the taxi going uptown after work and saying, 'Oh so what happened at 54, did you get that boy, who did you go home with, who did so-and-so go home with?' I was saying, 'Andy, I'm not telling you, just stop asking me all these questions.' He was like, 'Bob, don't you realise I'm living my life through your life?'

Andy as control freak, influence of his background

He wanted to control the lives of all of us kids, in a way like a peasant parent from the Carpathian mountains, where his parents were from, from the borderlands of Poland, Slovakia, the Ukraine, this nowhere part of Europe. His brother said, 'We didn't even know what language we were speaking. We knew it wasn't Slovak, it wasn't Ukranian.' It was something called Rusyn, which was closer to Russian. Andy was a control freak and he was extremely manipulative, but in a way you couldn't really hold against him. On the one hand it was funny, and on the other hand you sort of felt sorry for Andy. You felt you had to protect him physically and also

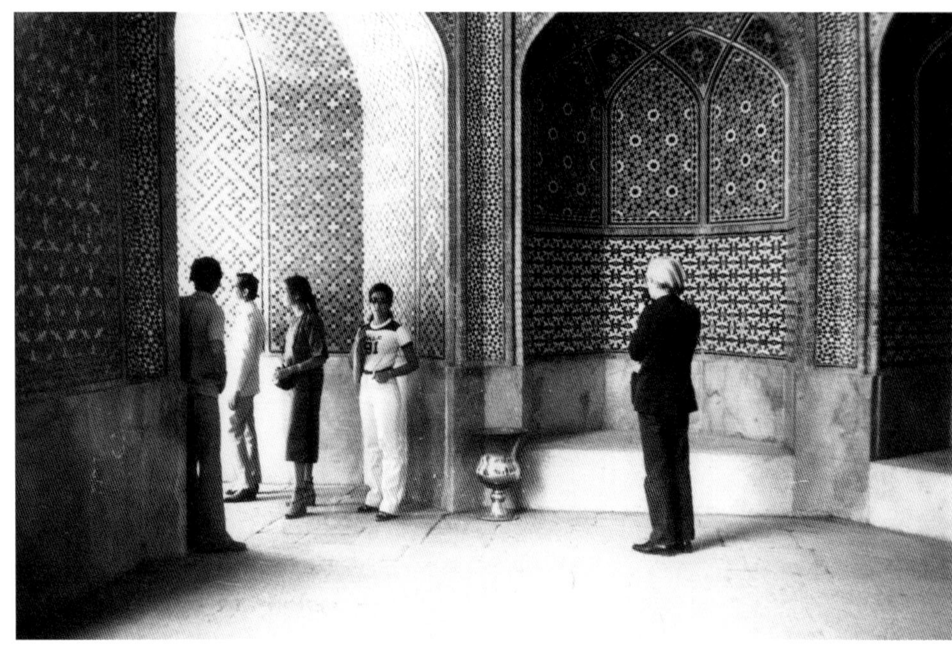

Fig.2 Bob Colacello
Andy, Isfahan, Iran 1976
Vintage gelatin silver print
20.3 x 25.4
Private collection

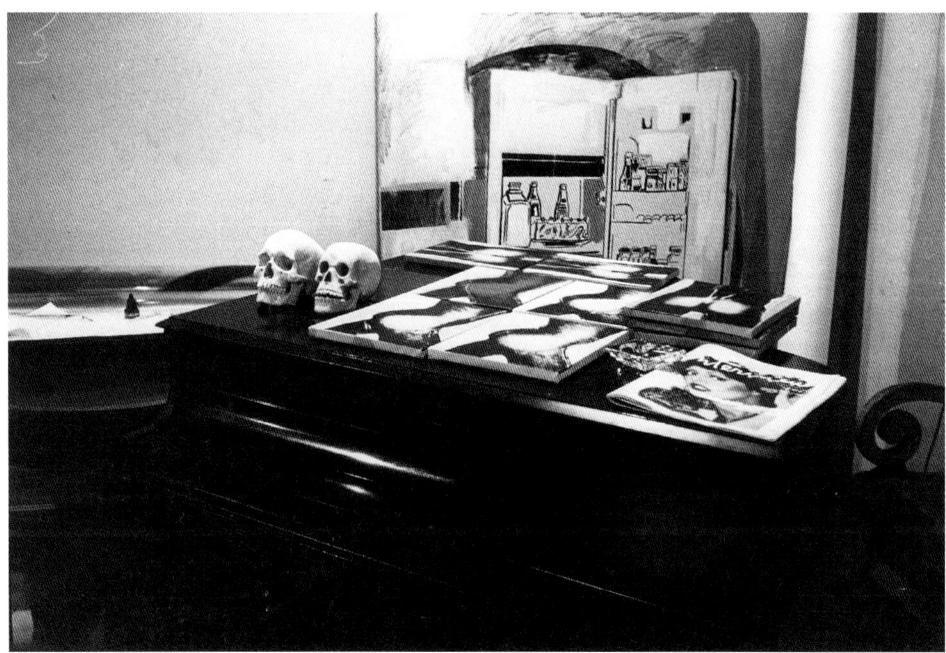

Fig.3 Bob Colacello
*Andy's Studio at the Factory,
860 Broadway, New York*
1977
Vintage gelatin silver print
20.3 x 25.4
Private collection

psychologically, socially, like you had to be the bridge between him and other people.

Protecting Andy
He just seemed so vulnerable, and he had been shot and he had almost died. That was an omnipresent thought. Valerie Solanas would call every so often and would say, 'is Warhol there?' in this gruff voice, then we would go on high alert, Joe Dallesandro would whisk Andy into a taxi with Jed Johnson and they'd go home to the house on 66th Street, or before that 89th and Lex.

The importance of Andy's family history
His parents were immigrants who didn't even speak English. His connection to the 'old world' as it was called was fresh. Andy moved his mother to New York like a year after he got here and he made a little money. Andy's mother, who didn't speak English. When he started doing fashion illustration in the 1950s, the handwritten captions were done by Andy's mother, whose language was written in Cyrillic, not Roman. She had this funny way of writing Roman because she only knew how to write in Cyrillic, and Andy liked this kind of curly, fancy writing.

Andy always said he was Czech, because the village in far eastern Slovakia where his parents were from was technically Czechoslovakia. I remember once we were in the airport in Rome or Paris or somewhere, Zurich, and a flight landed from Prague, and all these Czechs came off carrying shopping bags, and we didn't make the connection that in Communist countries they couldn't afford real luggage, and Andy was always carrying shopping bags, and we said, 'We can't believe it, look there's your people, Andy, they're all carrying shopping bags.'

Teasing Andy – and here Bob spoke for a moment in the present tense, as if Andy was still alive
You can tease Andy, you can have fun with Andy, he was not the least bit pretentious or pompous. The only time he would show a little anger or resentment was when someone said something not very nice, like, 'You're not an artist, Andy, you're a photographer', or, 'I collect impressionism, that's real art.' Then he'd be, 'Who do they think they are, I hate him, I hate him, I'm never having dinner with him again Bob. He'll have to beg me to do his wife's portrait.'

Andy's sexuality
His brothers told me, you know he was kind of an effeminate and sickly child. They said the way he got the neighbourhood toughs to like him was by drawing their portraits. He'd have them come into the house and, if you've ever had your portrait drawn or painted, it's very different from having your photograph taken. It seems like magic almost, in order for the artist to do it, they have to look at you really intensely. And then they produce this thing that resembles you. And he really won over the kids that way.

His mother was very protective of him, but I think a lot of gays dealt with their outward identity in the 1940s and 1950s by becoming eccentrics, so people wouldn't say 'Oh he's so gay', they didn't use the word until the 1970s. 'Oh he's such a fag', or 'He's such a sissy', they would say, 'Oh he's weird', 'he's really colourful'. I think that Andy was like Truman Capote. People didn't think of Capote so much as gay, they thought of him as more of this great eccentric, you made yourself into a character, oh what a character. Or you played it very straight, but Andy couldn't pull off the Wall Street look or the country club look.

Andy and social climbing
Andy never stopped being from a working-class immigrant family. He didn't put on airs. Whereas Kenny Lane [Kenneth Lane, a costume jewellery designer] would say, 'I'm from De-troite', it would be a joke, not Detroit. I mean Halston was one big air, even Truman, they were much more affected.

People started putting Andy down for social climbing. His more bohemian friends like David Bourdon [an art critic], he'd be like, 'Andy's become such a social climber with Fred Hughes and Bob Colacello now as the assistant social climber.' But the so-called American Dream, that's what it was. Andy's parents were more limited, but when Andy was eleven he was enrolled in this programme to go to the Carnegie Museum every Saturday. This bus would take him from the poorest neighbourhood through the upper middle class into the rich neighbourhood where the museum was. He started interacting with higher classes at a very early age, and you can't help be attracted to people as a child in bigger houses with better food and nicer clothes. And in a city like Pittsburgh, it was almost

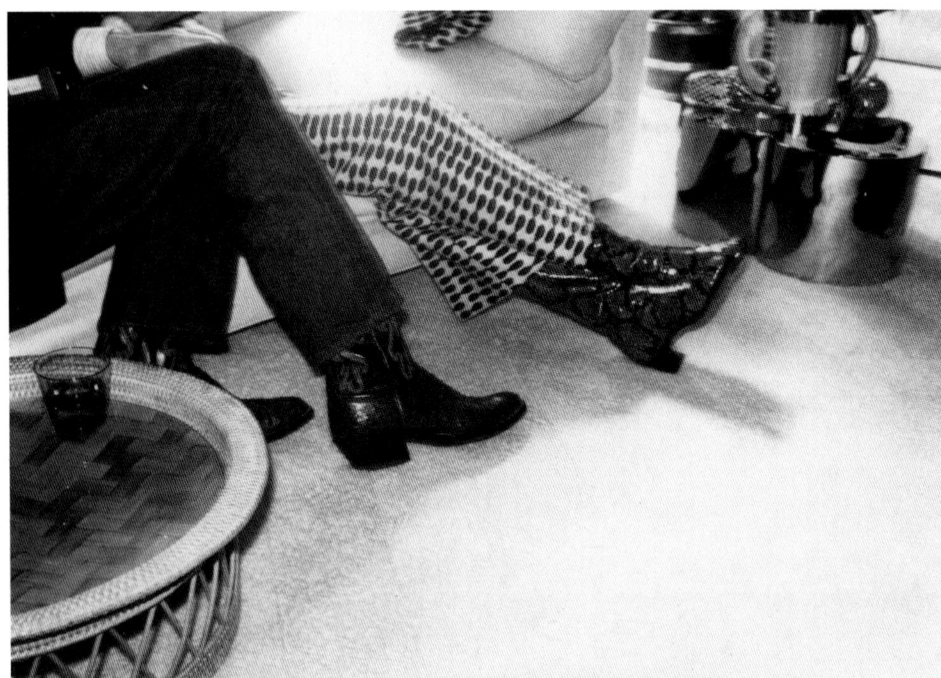

feudal. There were the Mellons and the Carnegies, and everything was named after them, so suddenly Andy's meeting their grandchildren. He channelled that brilliantly into the commissioned portraits.

Andy and money

To his credit, he didn't put that money in the bank. He poured it into *Interview*, he poured it into Vincent Fremont's videos, he hired more young people, we raised the fees we paid for interviews and photographs in *Interview*, we had a pension plan starting in the mid-1970s at the Factory, we got annual raises, we had little bonuses, he gave us art. Yes, he kept salaries low, but that then gave us an incentive, like in my case to start the *Philosophy* project [*The Philosophy of Andy Warhol: From A to B and Back Again*, ghostwritten by Colacello]. I own half of that book. He was a great manager, a great entrepreneur. He practised what he preached in terms of liberalism. When he made more money, he shared some of it with his workers.

Fast. Cheap. Easy. Modern.

Andy had this phrase. He thought everything we did and he did should be fast, cheap, easy and modern. He felt if it didn't come easy or if it cost too much, it was like you weren't meant to be doing it, and he meant modern like new. The more we stuck to that at *Interview*, the more

we had success. We were never going to be *Time* magazine, but having 100,000 of the coolest hippest people everywhere from Amsterdam to Seattle, and lots of little towns in between where we had one or two subscribers, the advertisers loved this.

We started doing readership surveys and it was through the roof, the income level, the education level and the young age, so they could try out new advertising campaigns in *Interview* for very little money, they could reach the people who were going to be the first to buy products. You didn't actually directly ask people if they were gay in the survey, but we had a high percentage of single people. The marketing people at the advertising agencies, they figured this thing was starting that when gay people went to clubs, everyone went to clubs, when gay people bought a certain product, a year later everyone bought it. When gay people went into a certain neighbourhood, it started gentrifying. The whole of the 1970s was really the decade when homosexuality became accepted on a large scale.

Camp

Susan Sontag wrote this book on camp [*Notes on Camp*]. It was a camp. The Factory was like the camp camp. I didn't go to Andy to learn about Oscar Wilde or Cocteau, I already knew all that stuff. I'd read every word Sartre ever wrote, and Camus and Kafka. At Georgetown

[*the university where Colacello studied*] we were brainwashed on Kierkegaard. Andy was so impressed when I said something like, 'Kierkegaard said the erotic and the spiritual and the aesthetic are all closely interrelated', and Andy would say, 'Oh gee, you know all that stuff.' He, I don't know, was just sort of meant to be.

It never stopped. If, for a moment, I was mad at Andy, thinking I should do something else, and he knew he'd crossed a line or got me really mad, then it would be, 'Oh, err ...'; he wouldn't say he was sorry, he'd be more like, 'You want to go for tea with Dalí?', or, 'Do you want to go to Jackie's Christmas party?' He knew you couldn't be mad at him. In that sense, I was as curious as a normal person. I guess the part of me that is a journalist, I mean I was like, this is going to be a great scene for my diary.

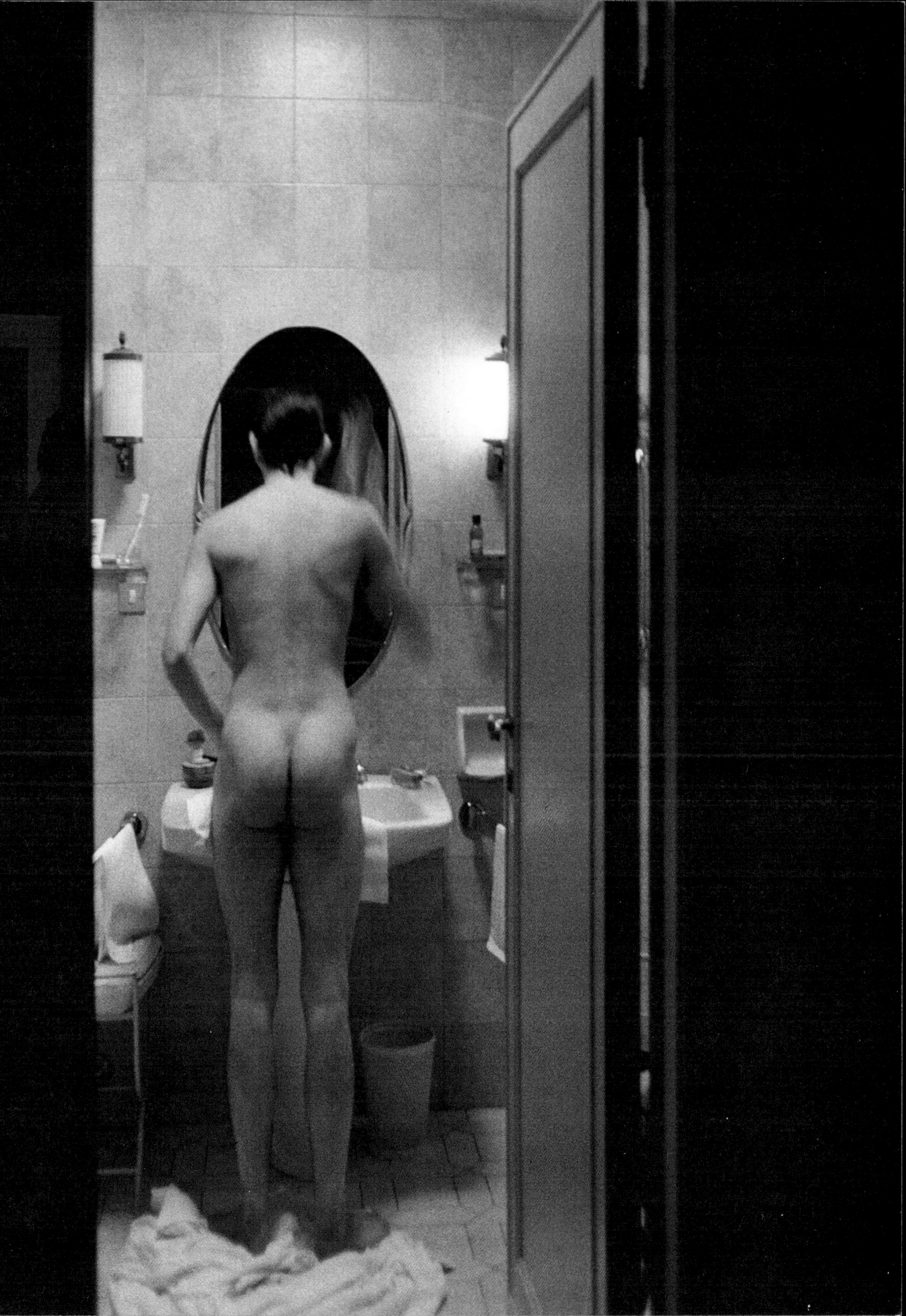

T H E

WORKS

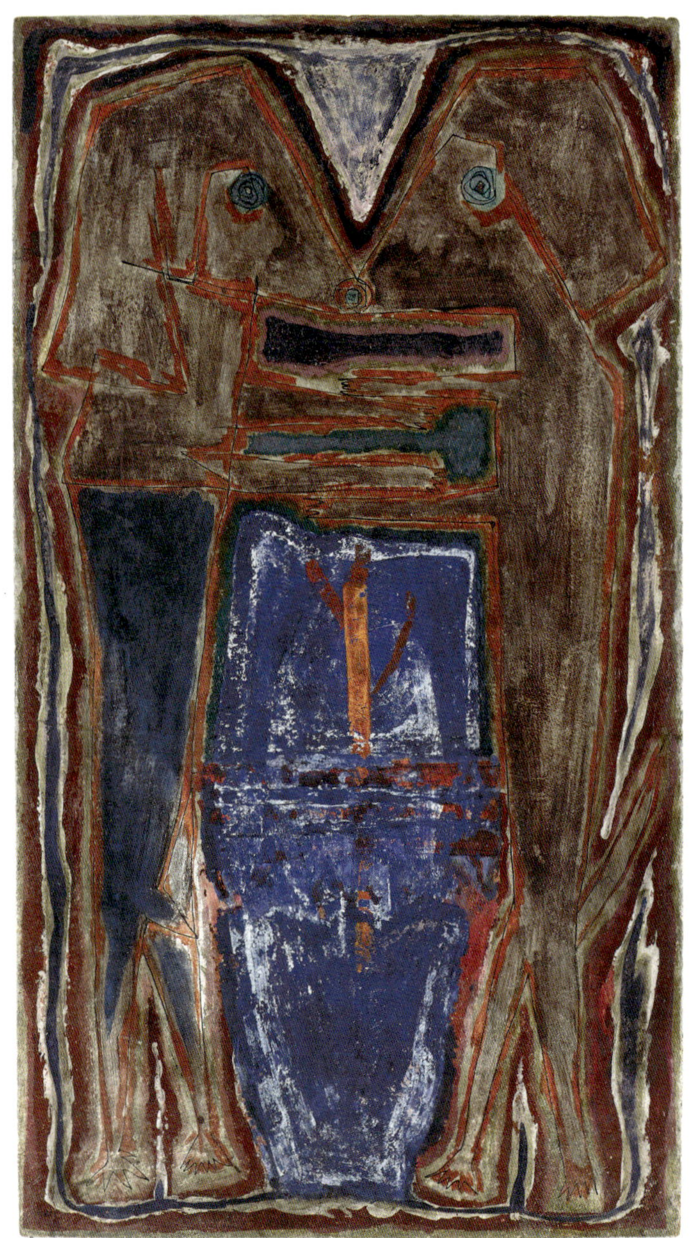

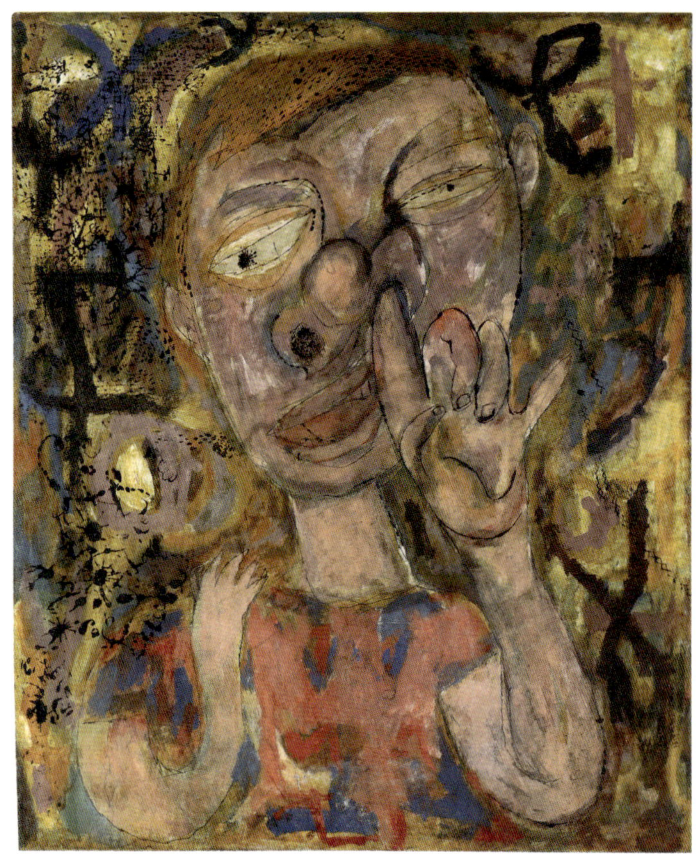

Two Dogs Kissing 1949
Tempera on Upson Board
94 x 61

*Nosepicker I: Why Pick on
Me* 1948
Tempera and ink on Masonite
76 x 63.5

I Like Dance 1947
Oil paint on board
61.7 x 61.7

Three Children 1949
Tempera and ink on Masonite
86.4 x 122

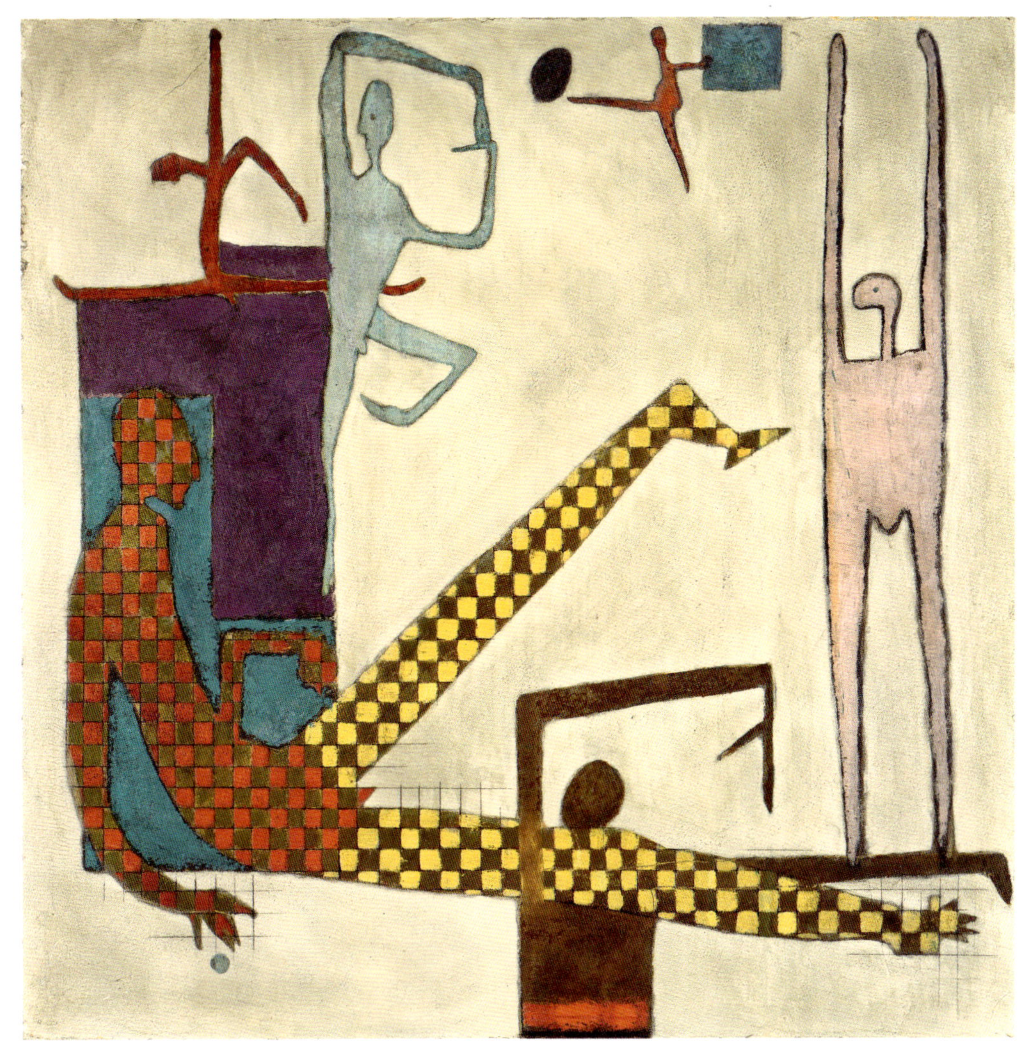

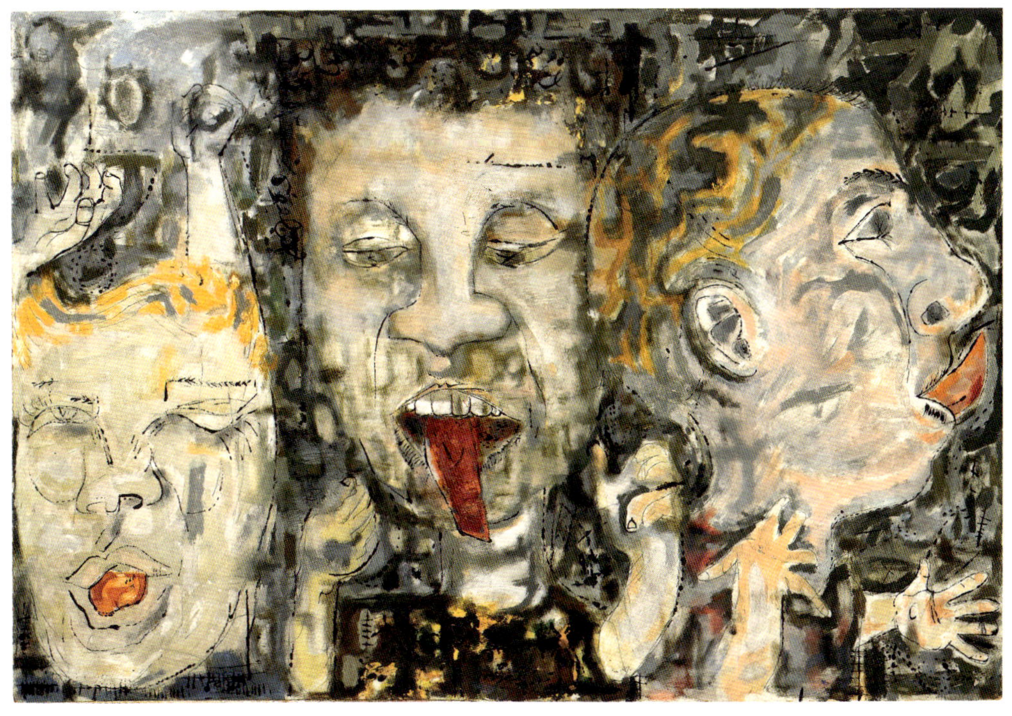

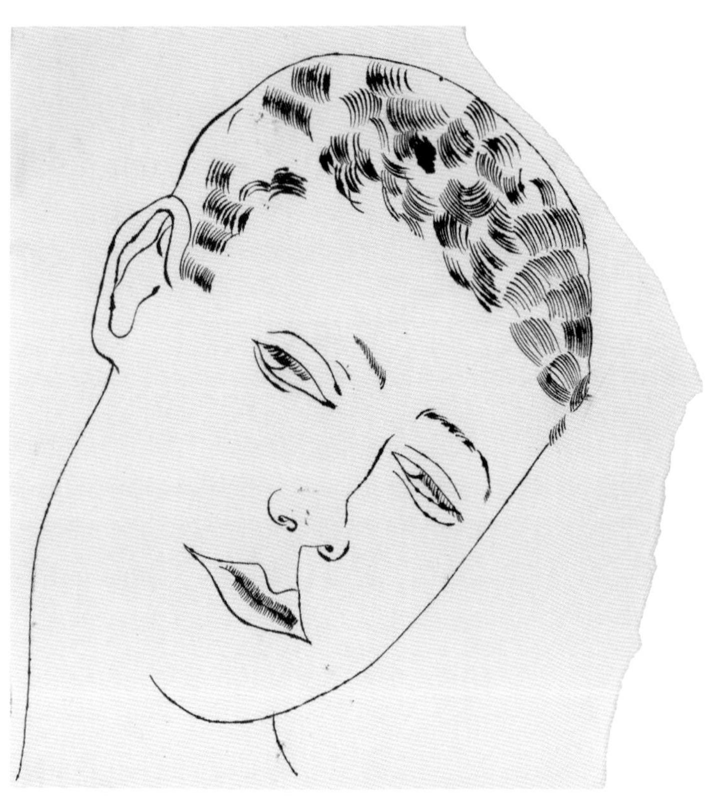

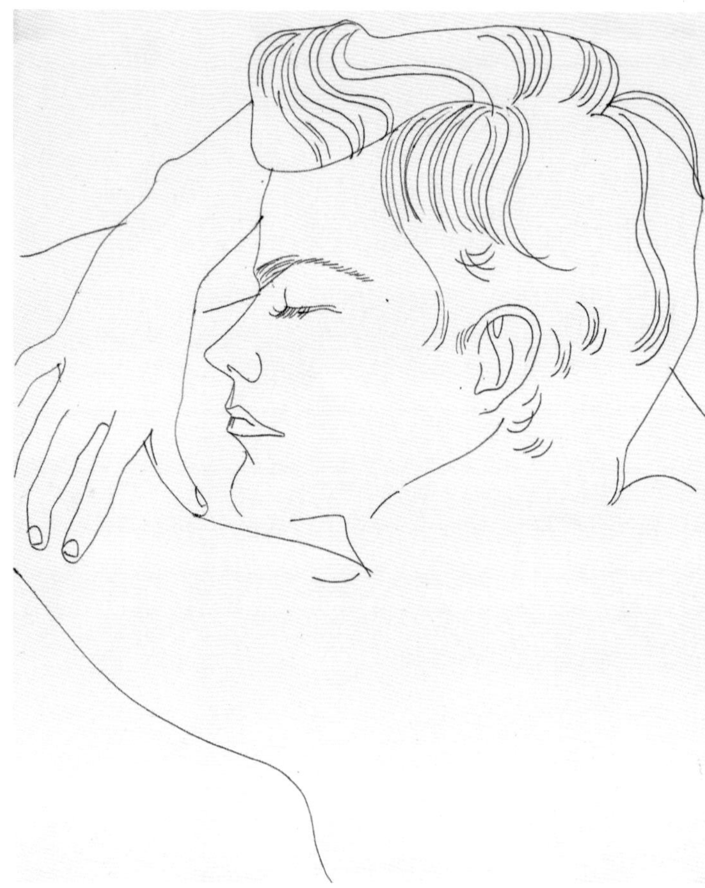

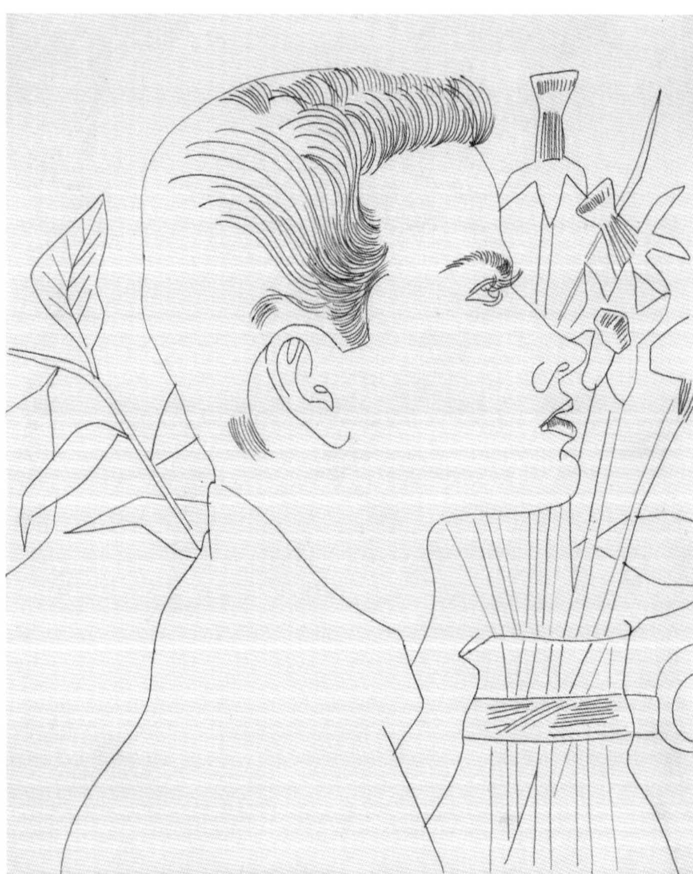

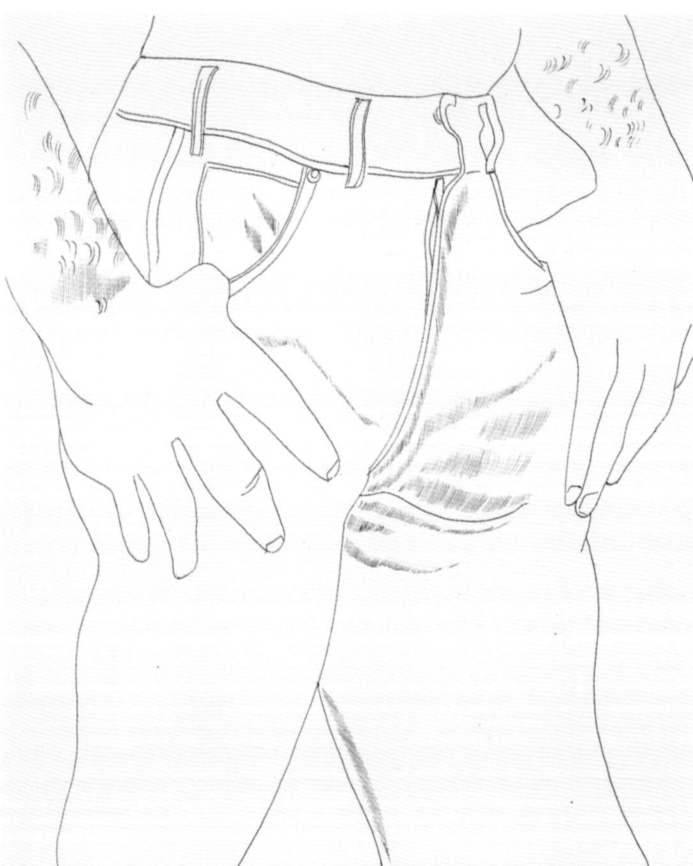

From left to right
Untitled [Head of a Man] 1956
Ink, graphite and gold leaf on paper
45.4 x 42.2

Resting Boy 1955–7
Ink on paper
41.8 x 34.5

Boy with Flowers 1955–7
Ink on paper
42.5 x 35

Male Torso 1956
Ink on paper
42.5 x 34.5

Oppostie page
Male Heads c. 1953
Ink on paper
73.6 x 58.4

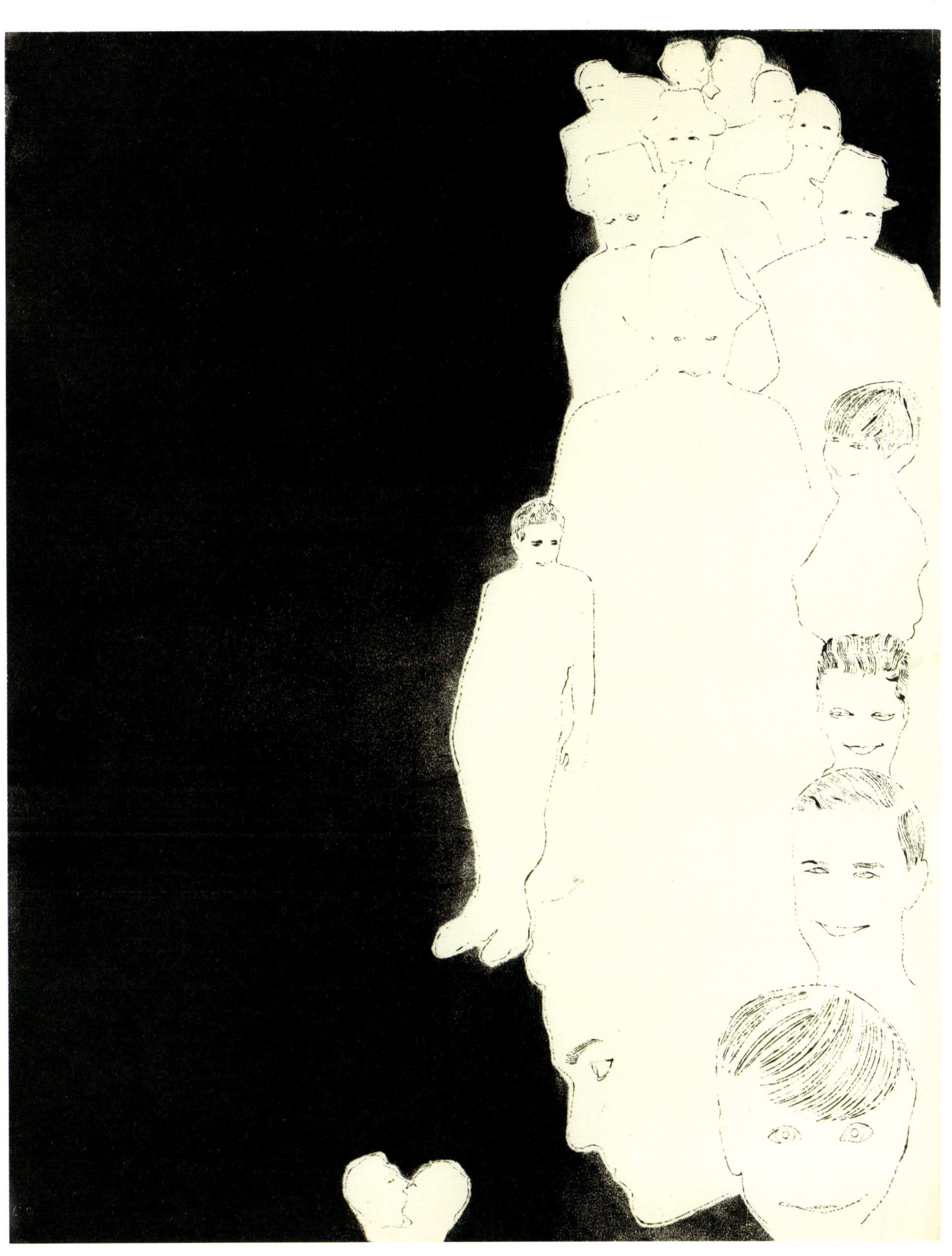

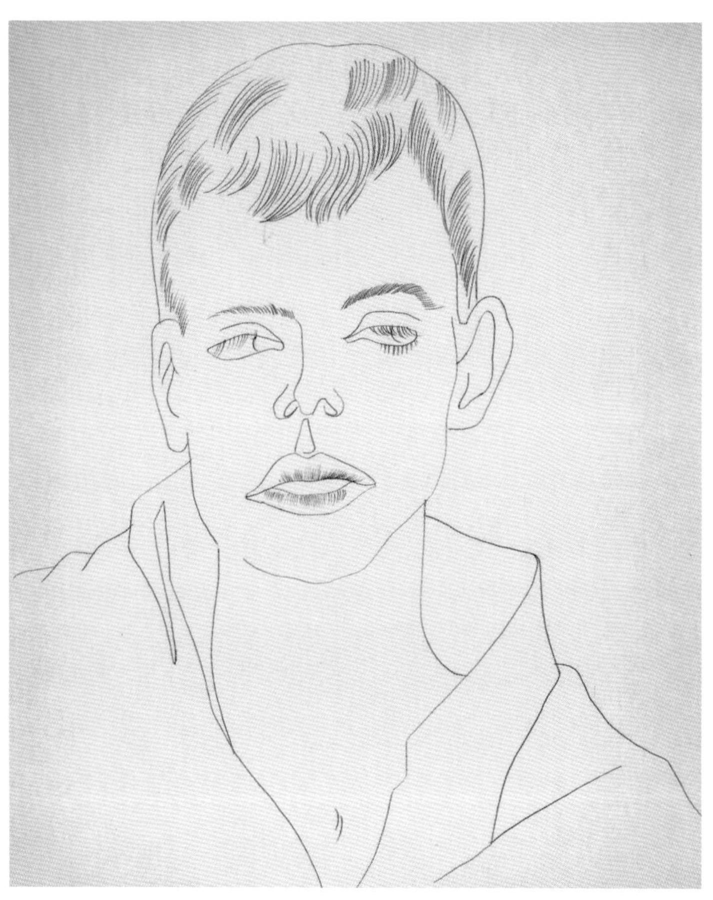

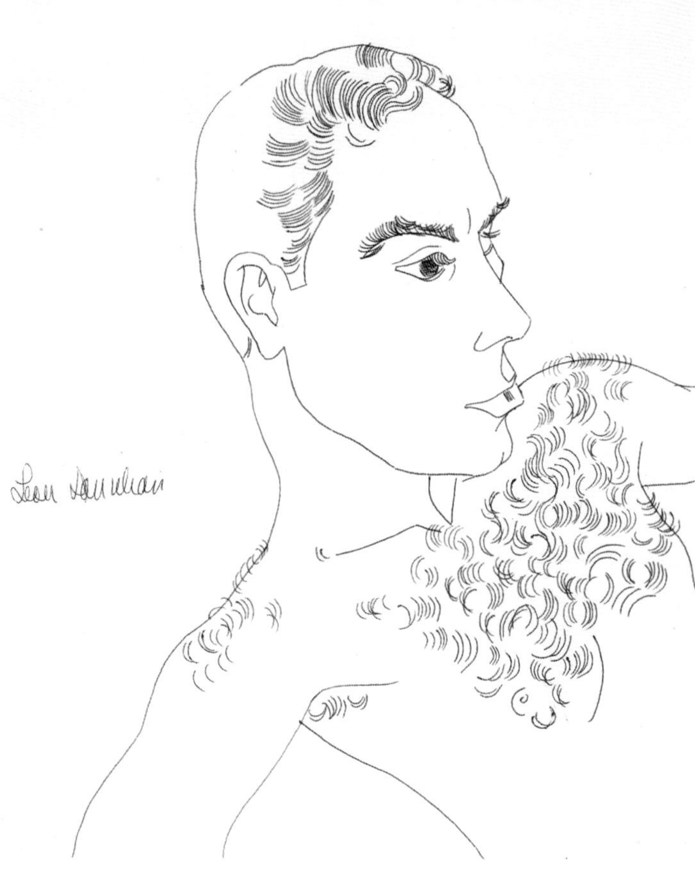

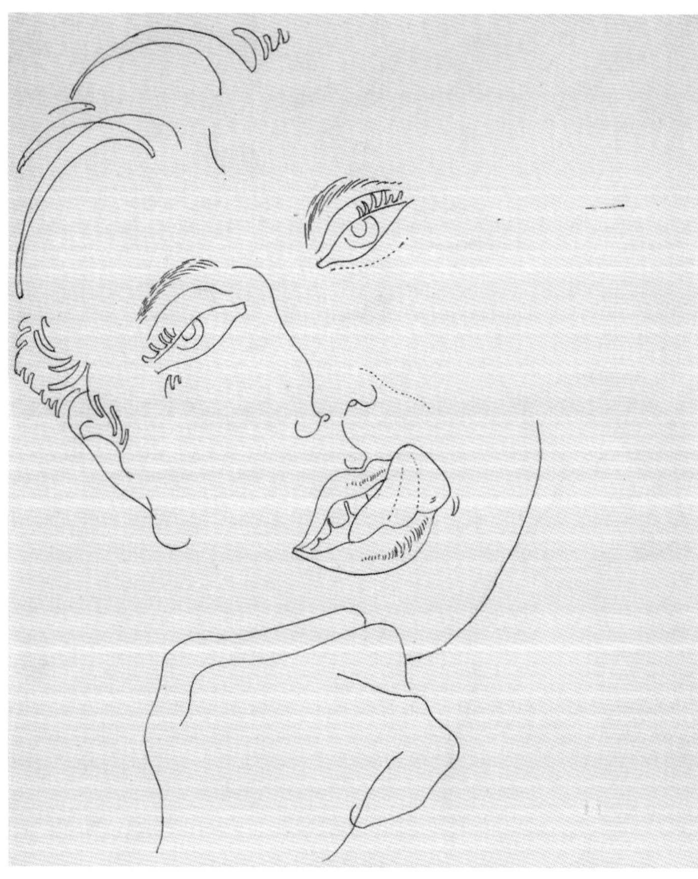

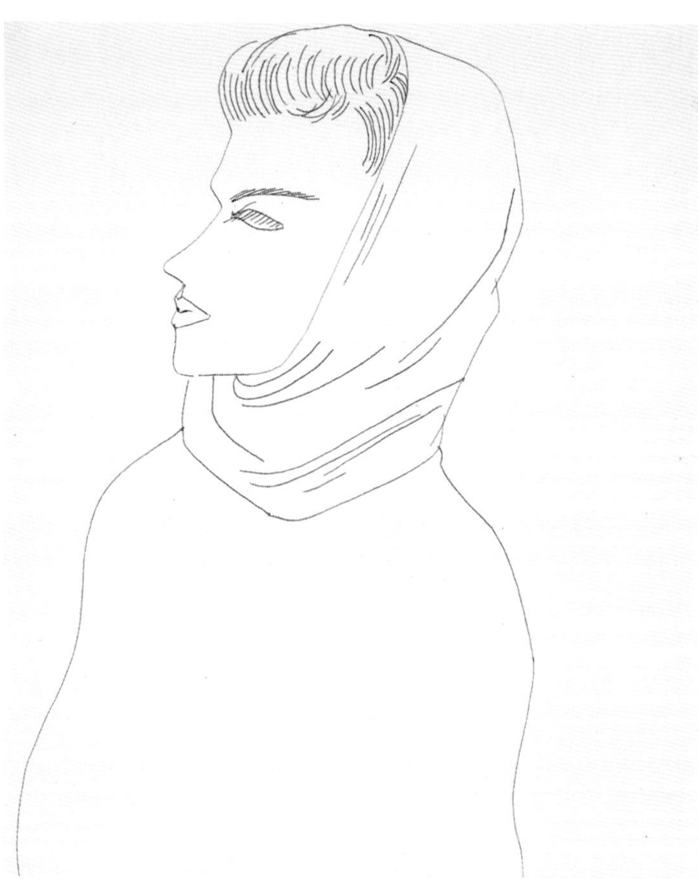

From left to right
Unidentified Male c.1956
Ink on paper
43.2 x 35.5

Leon Danielian c.1956
Ink on paper
42.5 x 35.5

Boy Licking his Lips 1956
Ink on paper
42 x 35.5

Unidentified Female c.1956
Ink on paper
42.5 x 35.5

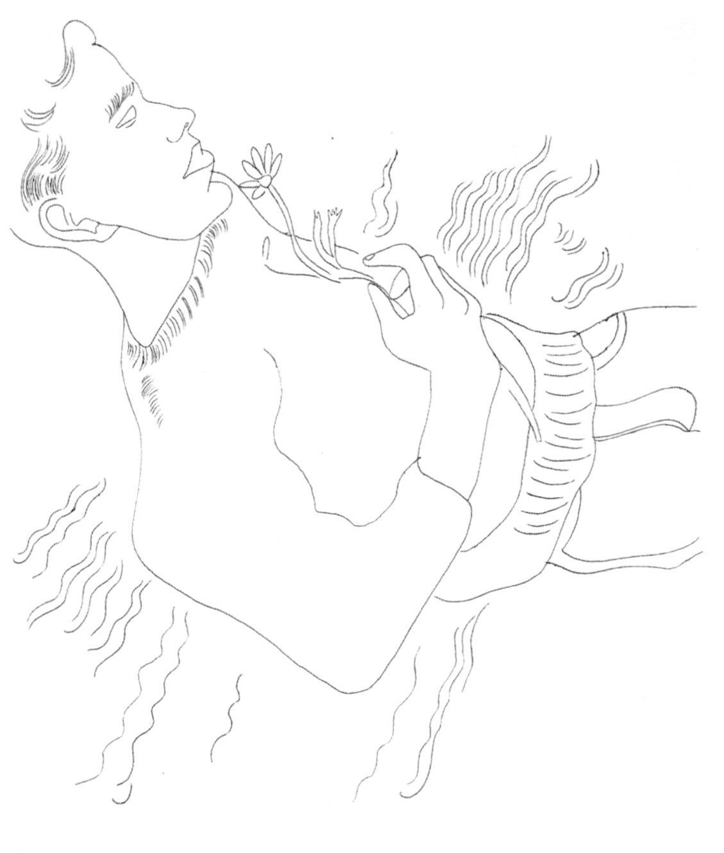

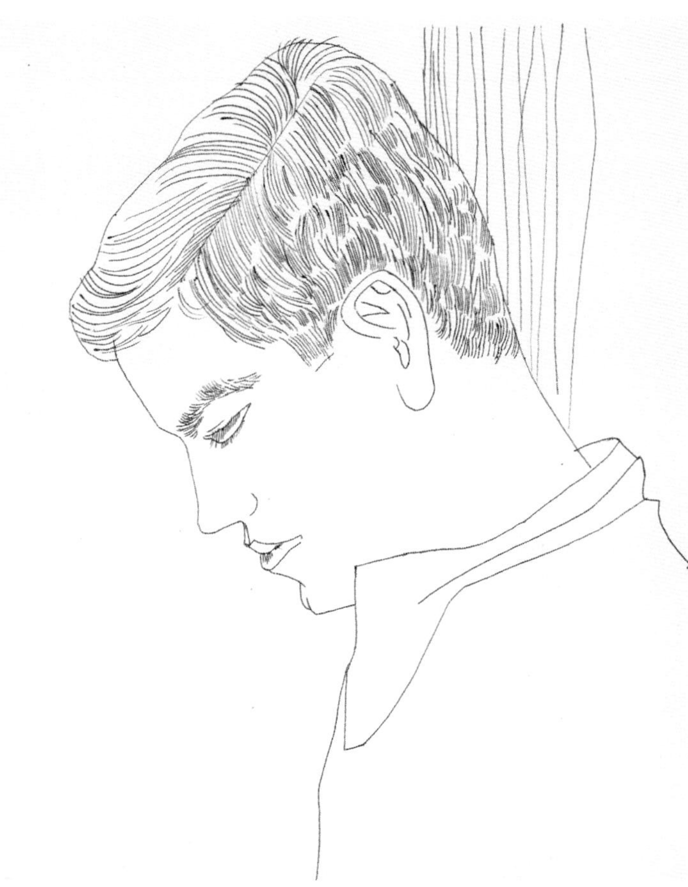

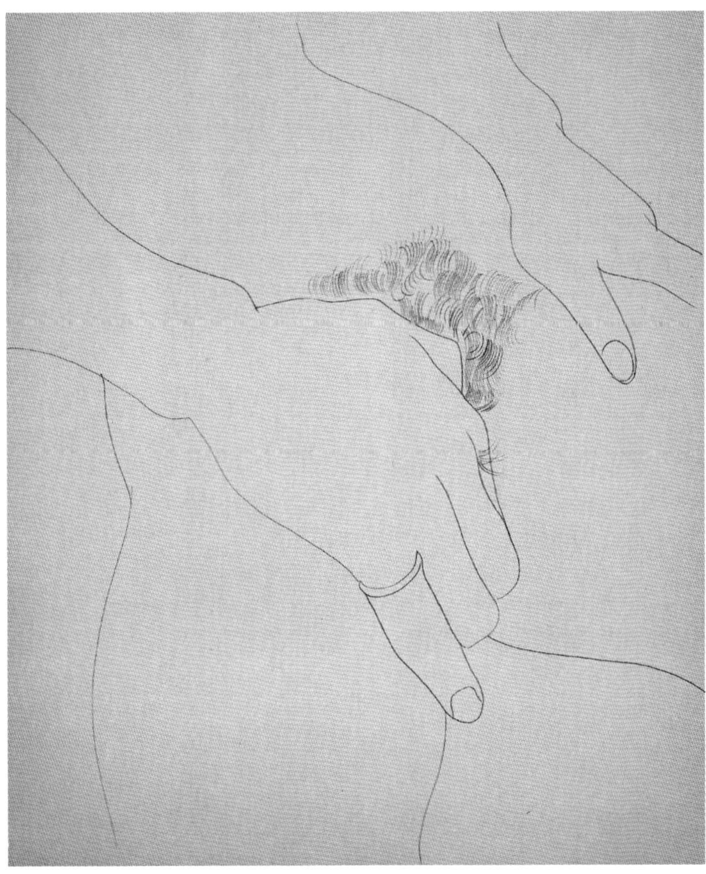

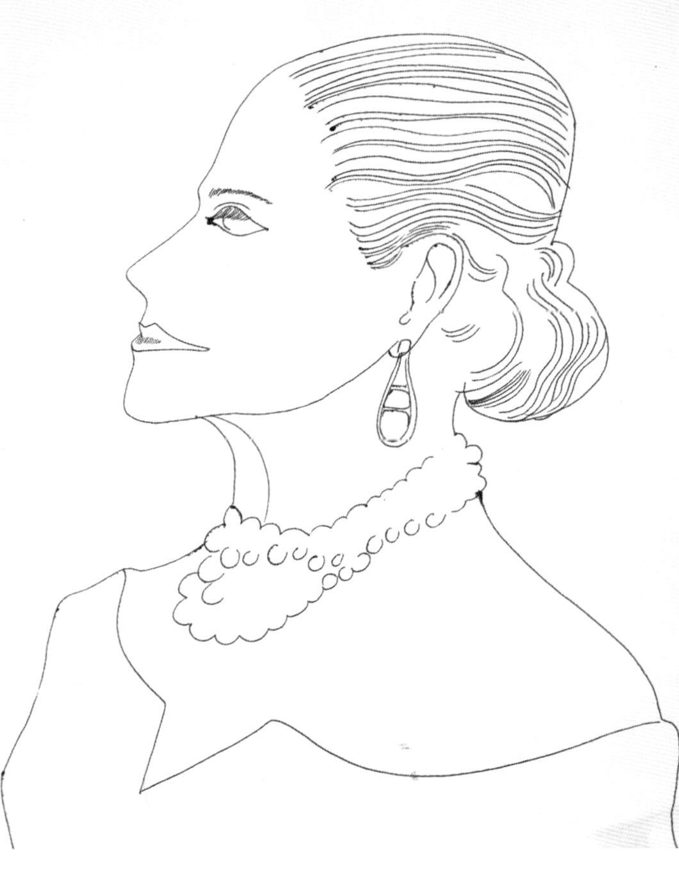

From left to right
Reclining Male c.1956
Ink on paper
42.5 x 35.5

Charles Lisanby c.1956
Ink on paper
42.5 x 35.5

Male Nude 1956–7
Ink on paper
42.5 x 35.5

Madame Helena Rubinstein 1956–7
Ink on paper
43.2 x 35.5

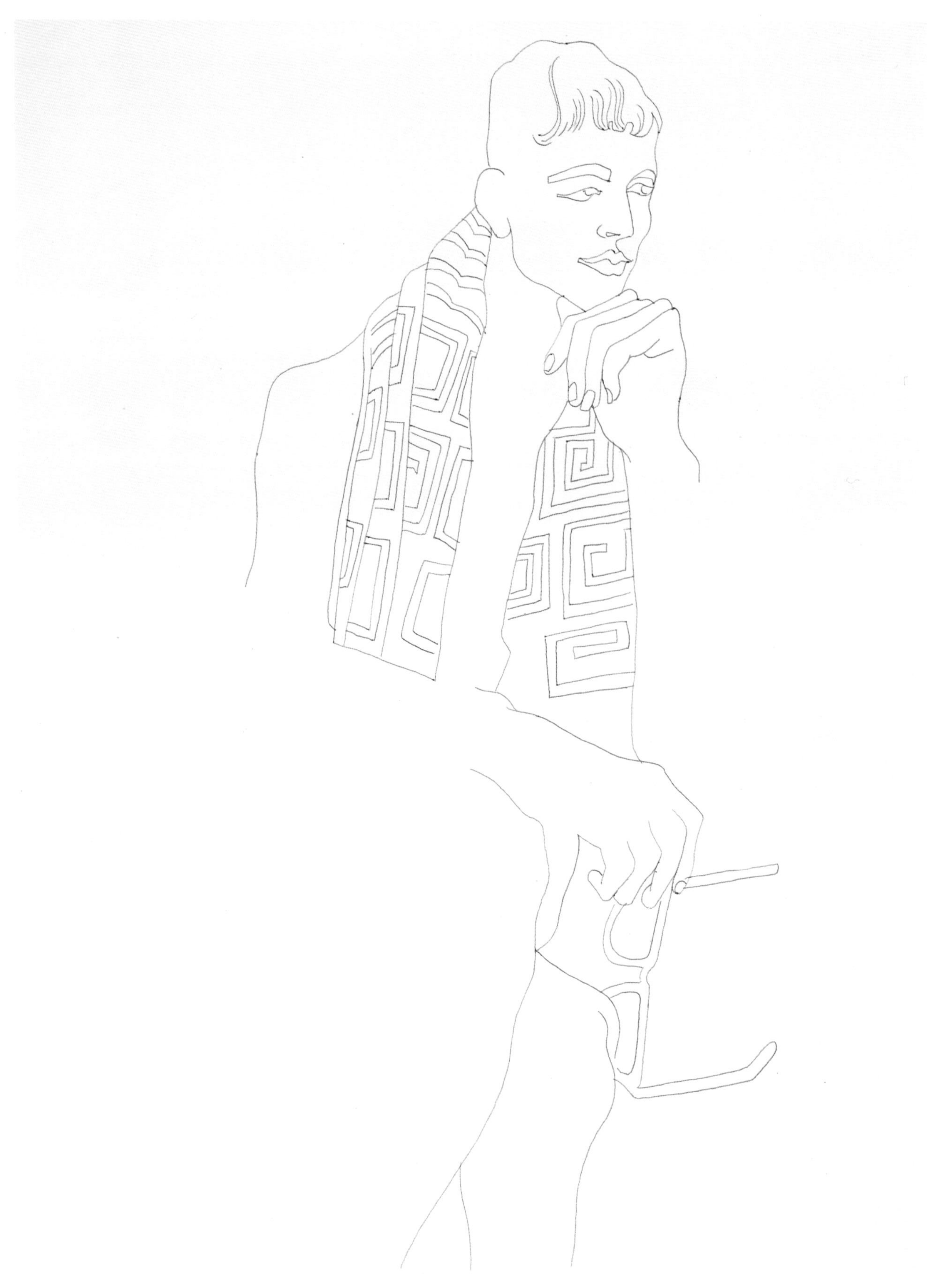

Standing Male c.1957
Ink on paper
61 x 46

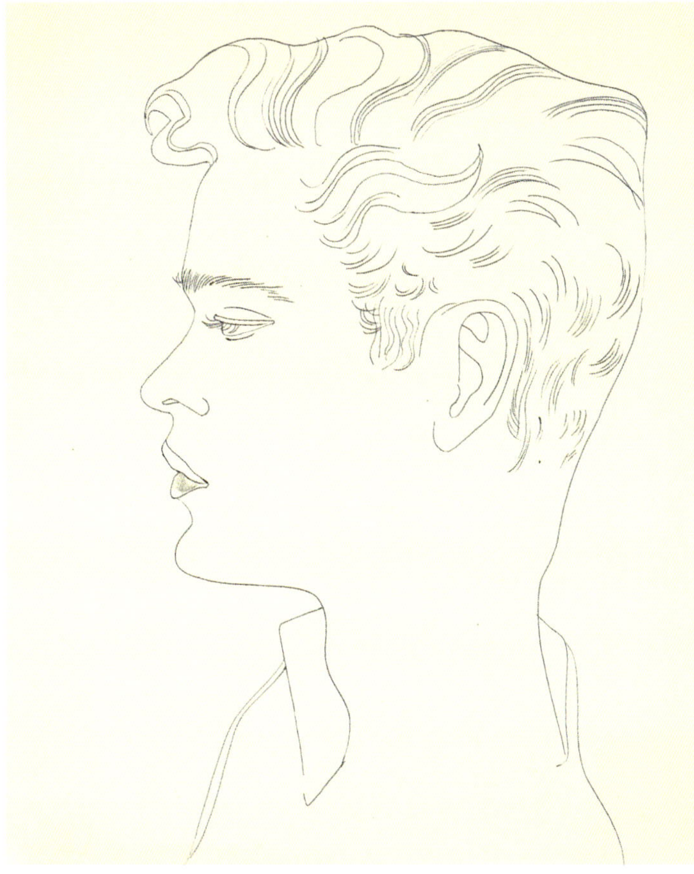

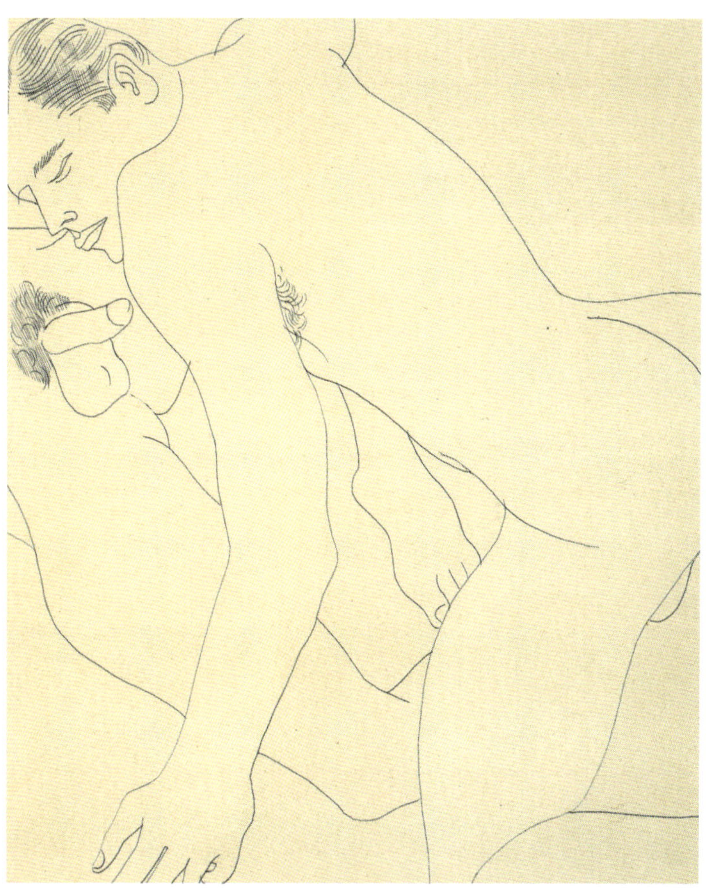

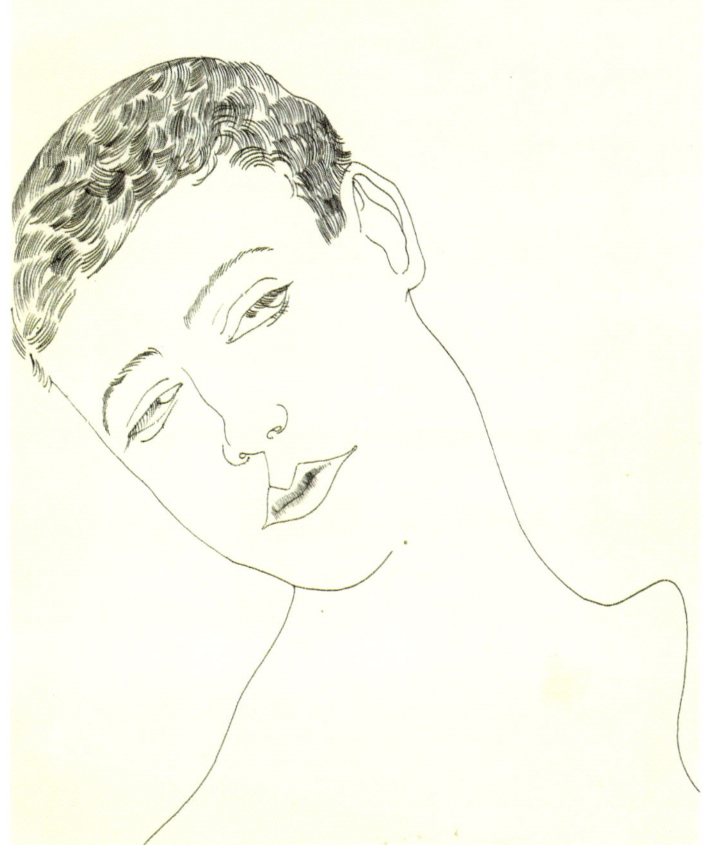

From left to right
Unidentified Male c.1957
Ink on paper
42.5 x 35.5

*Kneeling Male Over Male
Lower Torso* 1955–7
Ink on paper
42.7 x 35.3

Unidentified Male c.1956
Ink on paper
42.5 x 35.2

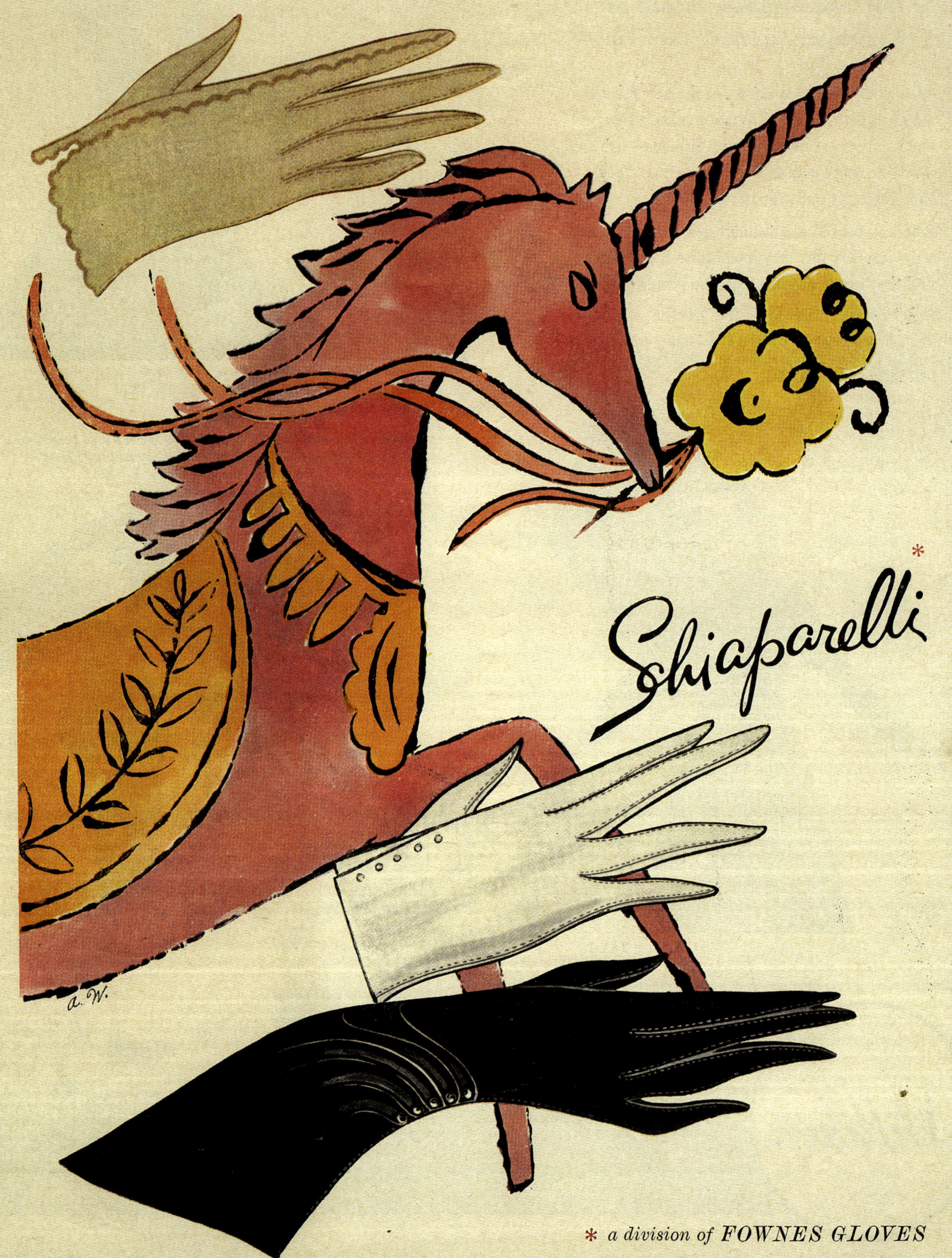

Perfection is fact…not fantasy…in DOETTE® fabric gloves by FOWNES. Top, GADABOUT $3.50. Center, BON BON $4.00. Bottom, FANTASIA $5.00. At fine stores everywhere or write: FOWNES GLOVES, 411 Fifth Avenue, New York 27.
Schiaparelli
* a division of FOWNES GLOVES

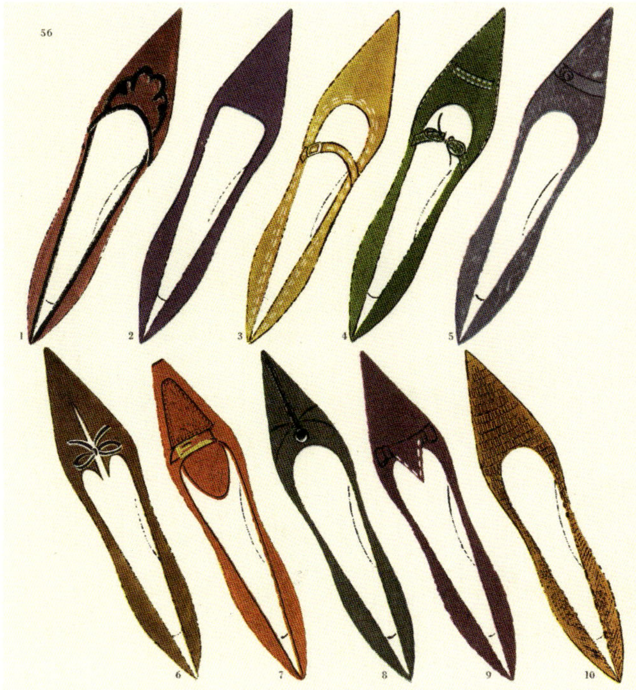

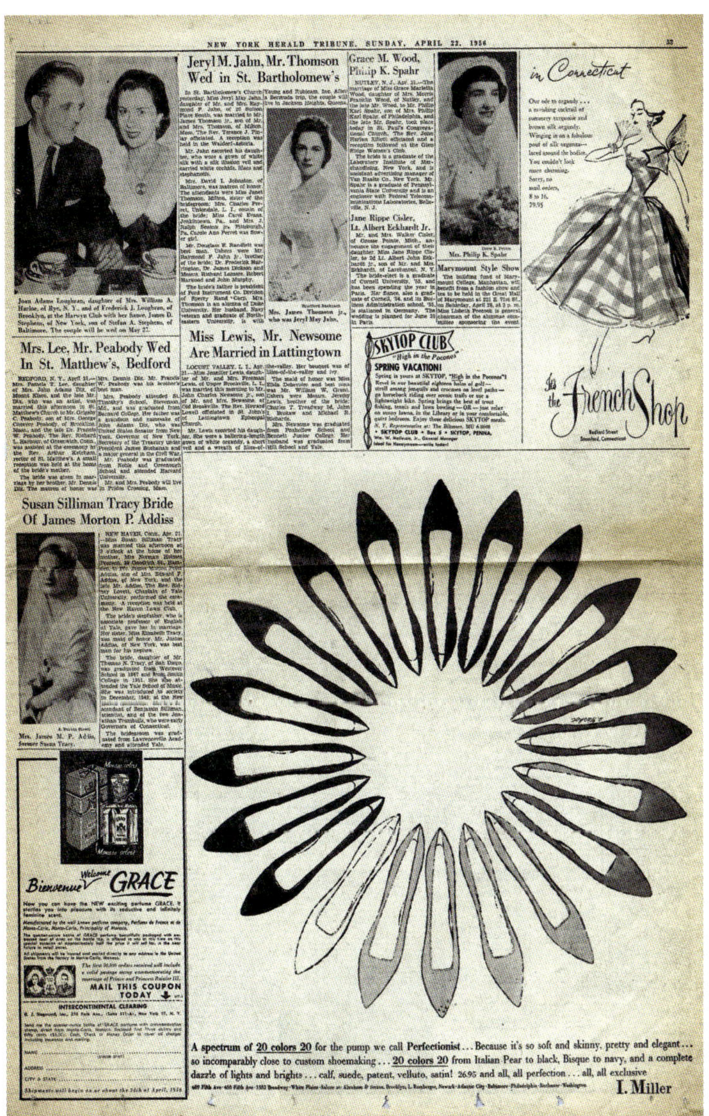

Opposite page
Schiaparelli gloves (Vogue)
1957
Printed ink on paper
32.4 x 23.5

Newspaper advertisement
'20 Colors 20' for I. Miller, The New York Times, April 22, 1956 1956
Printed ink on newsprint
28.6 × 38.1

Magazine advertisement
'Leather News: Color, Color, Color', Harper's Bazaar, July 1958 1958
Printed ink on coated paper
32.4 x 24.1

Next pages
'Crazy Golden Slippers'
1957
Printed ink on coated paper
on board
39.4 x 58.4

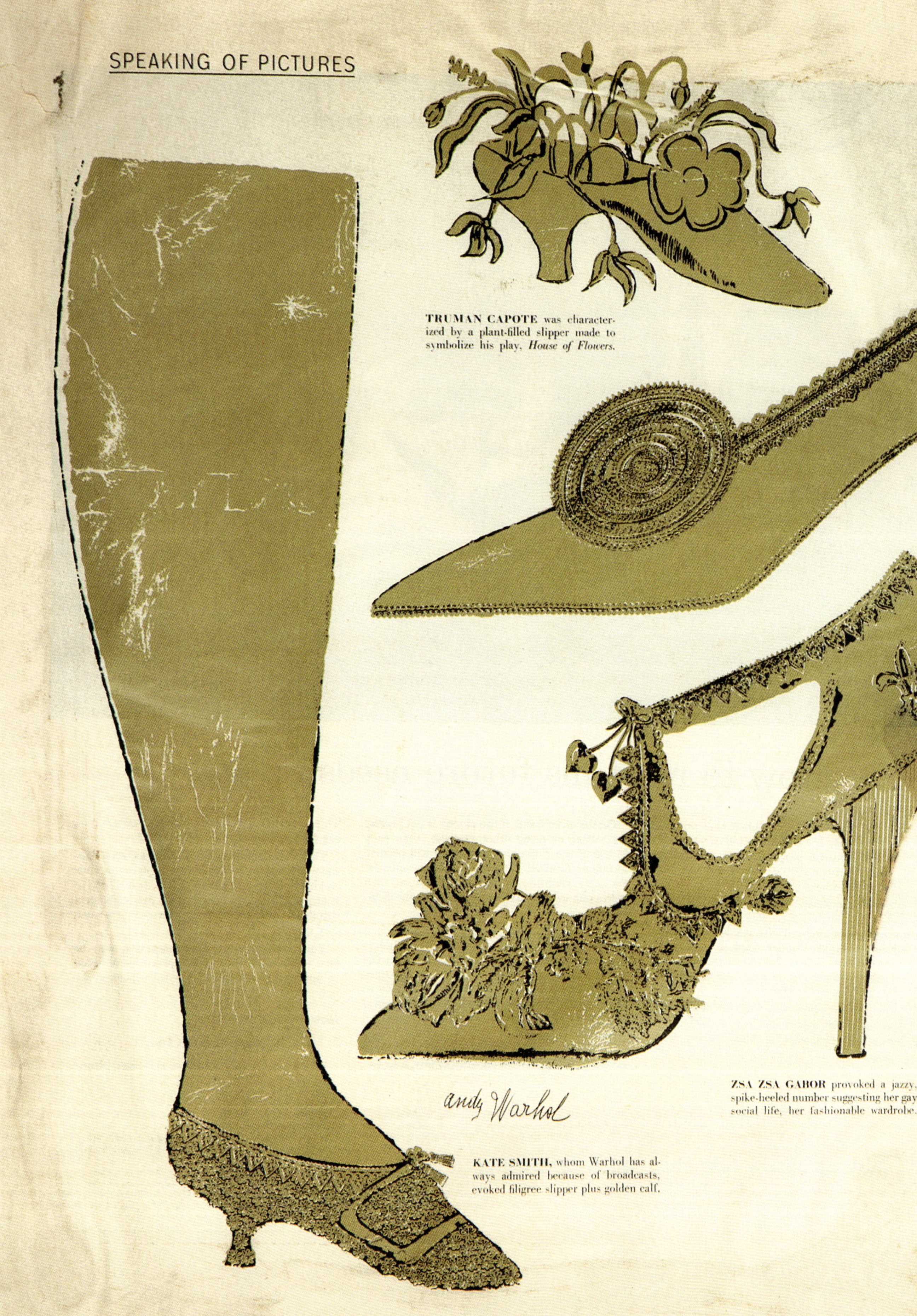

TRUMAN CAPOTE was character-
ized by a plant-filled slipper made to
symbolize his play, *House of Flowers.*

andy Warhol

ZSA ZSA GABOR provoked a jazzy,
spike-heeled number suggesting her gay
social life, her fashionable wardrobe.

KATE SMITH, whom Warhol has always admired because of broadcasts,
evoked filigree slipper plus golden calf.

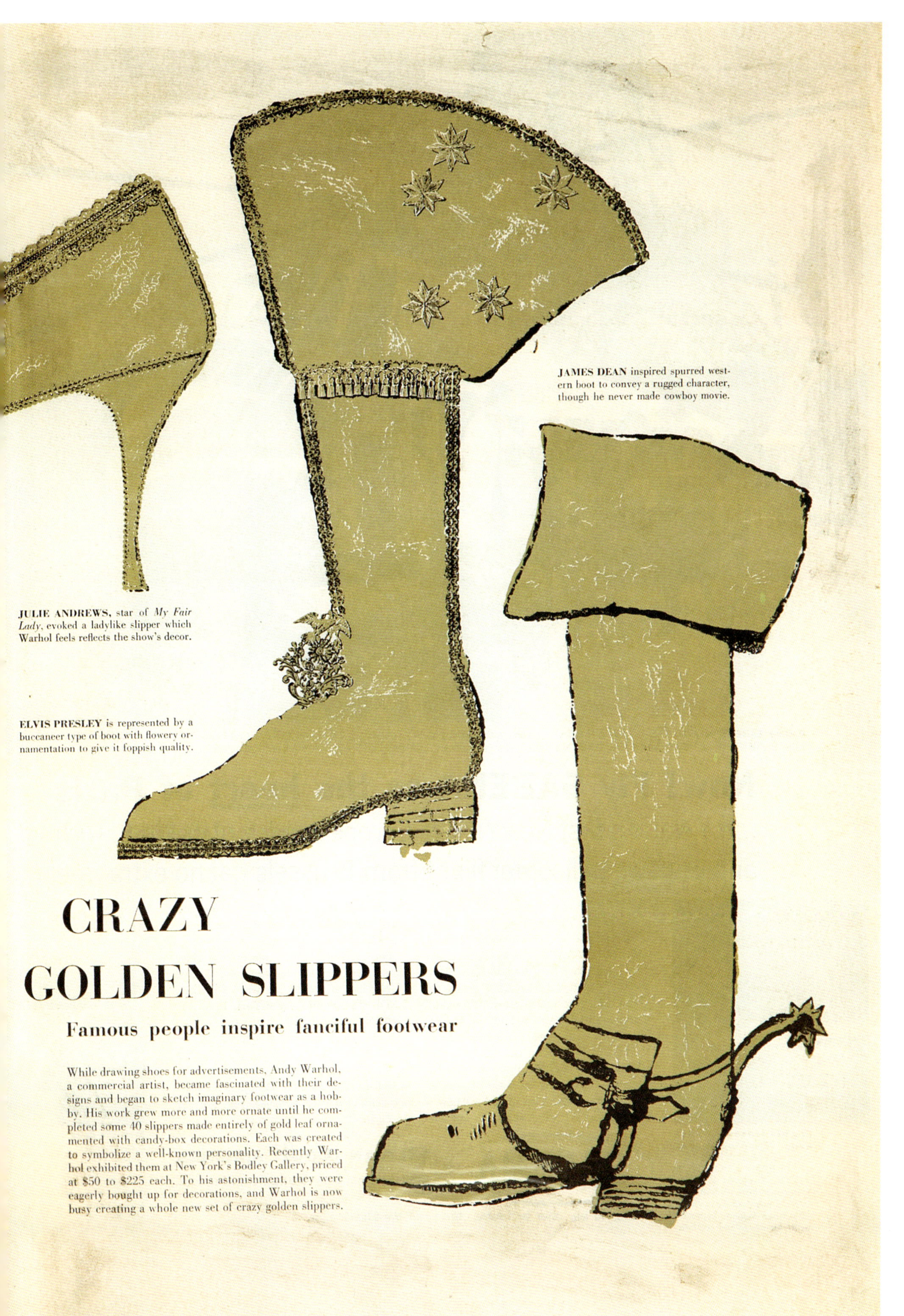

CRAZY GOLDEN SLIPPERS

Famous people inspire fanciful footwear

While drawing shoes for advertisements, Andy Warhol, a commercial artist, became fascinated with their designs and began to sketch imaginary footwear as a hobby. His work grew more and more ornate until he completed some 40 slippers made entirely of gold leaf ornamented with candy-box decorations. Each was created to symbolize a well-known personality. Recently Warhol exhibited them at New York's Bodley Gallery, priced at $50 to $225 each. To his astonishment, they were eagerly bought up for decorations, and Warhol is now busy creating a whole new set of crazy golden slippers.

A Gold Book,
by,
Andy Warhol,

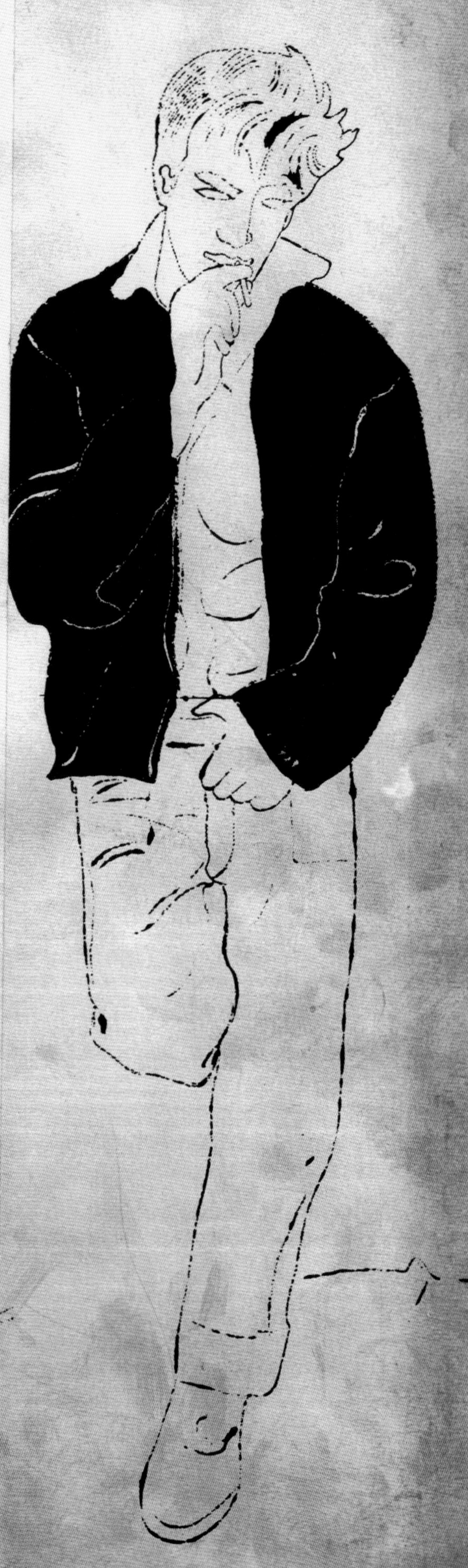

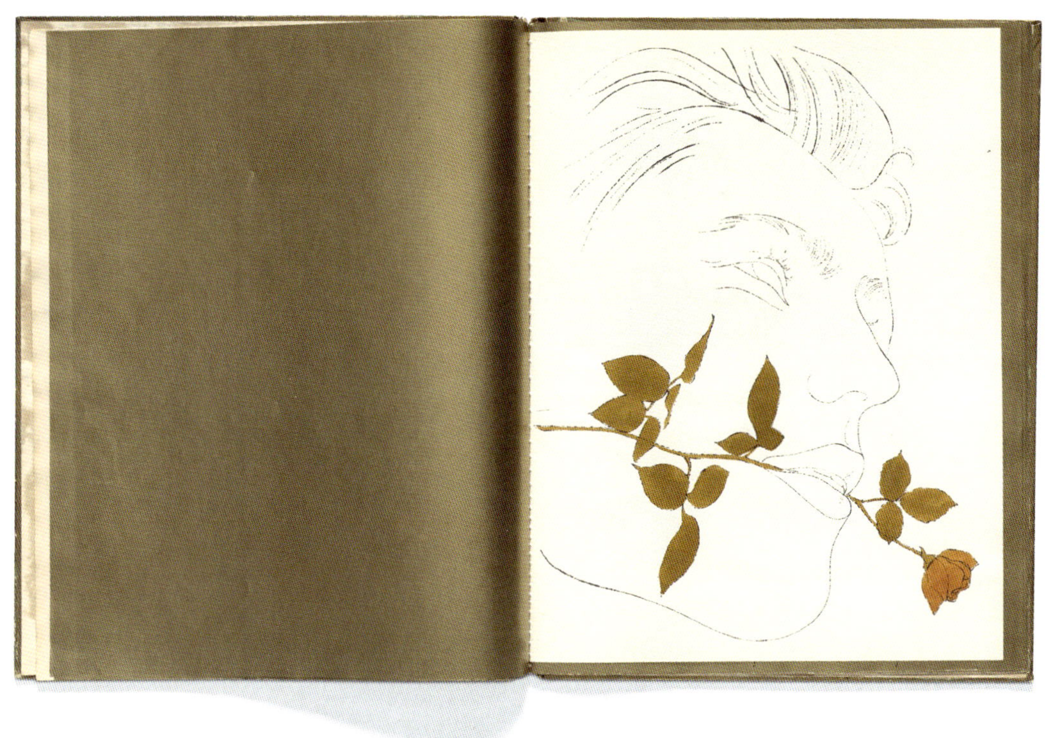

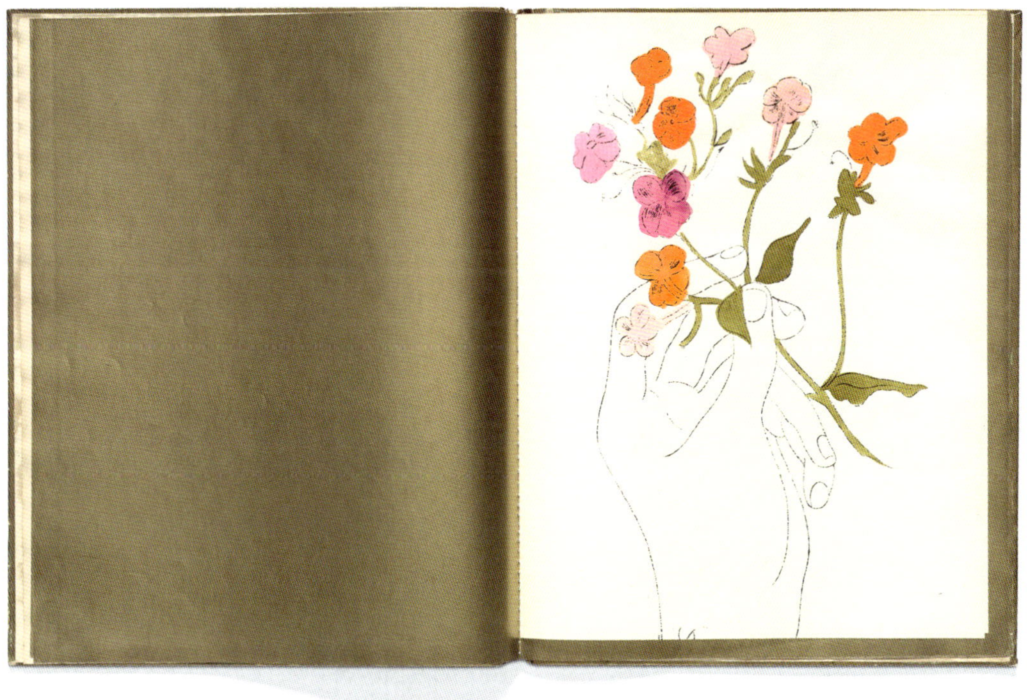

A Gold Book 1957
Artist's book (with lettering
by Julia Warhola); 22 pages
with 19 illustrations, offset
lithograph and Dr Martin's
Aniline dye on paper and
coated metallic paper,
with buckram board cover
38.1 x 29.3 x 1.3

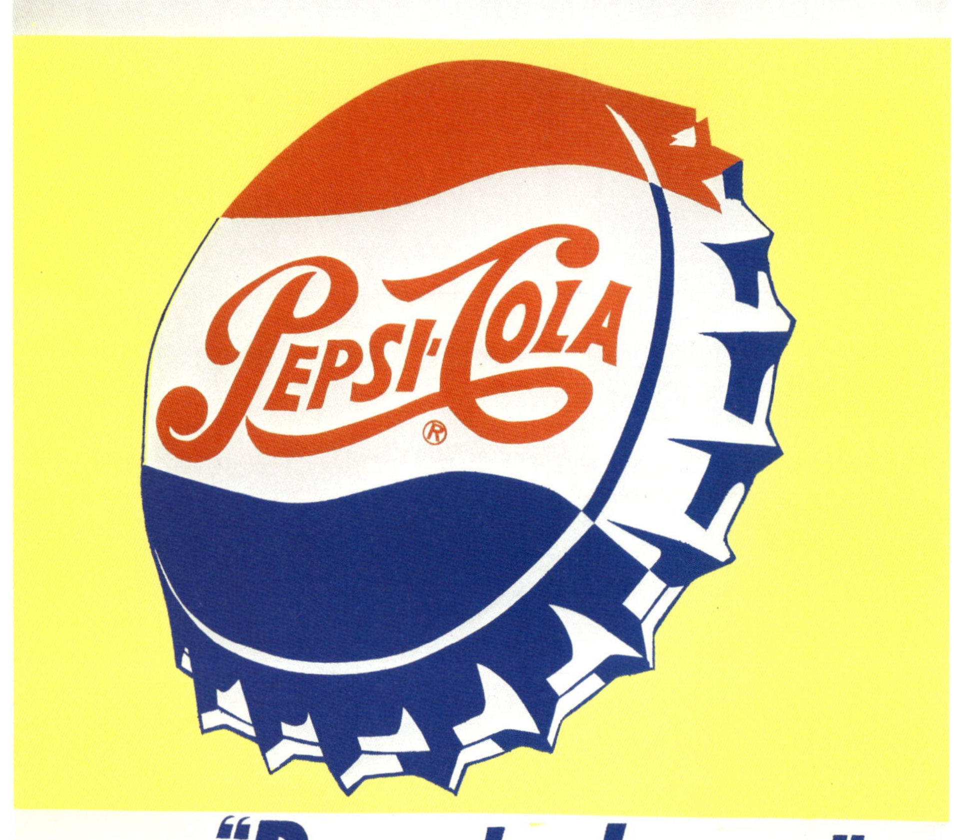

*Close Cover Before Striking
(Pepsi Cola)* 1962
Acrylic paint and sandpaper
on canvas
183 x 137

Opposite page
Advertisement 1960 (detail)
Acrylic paint and wax crayon
on canvas
183 x 137

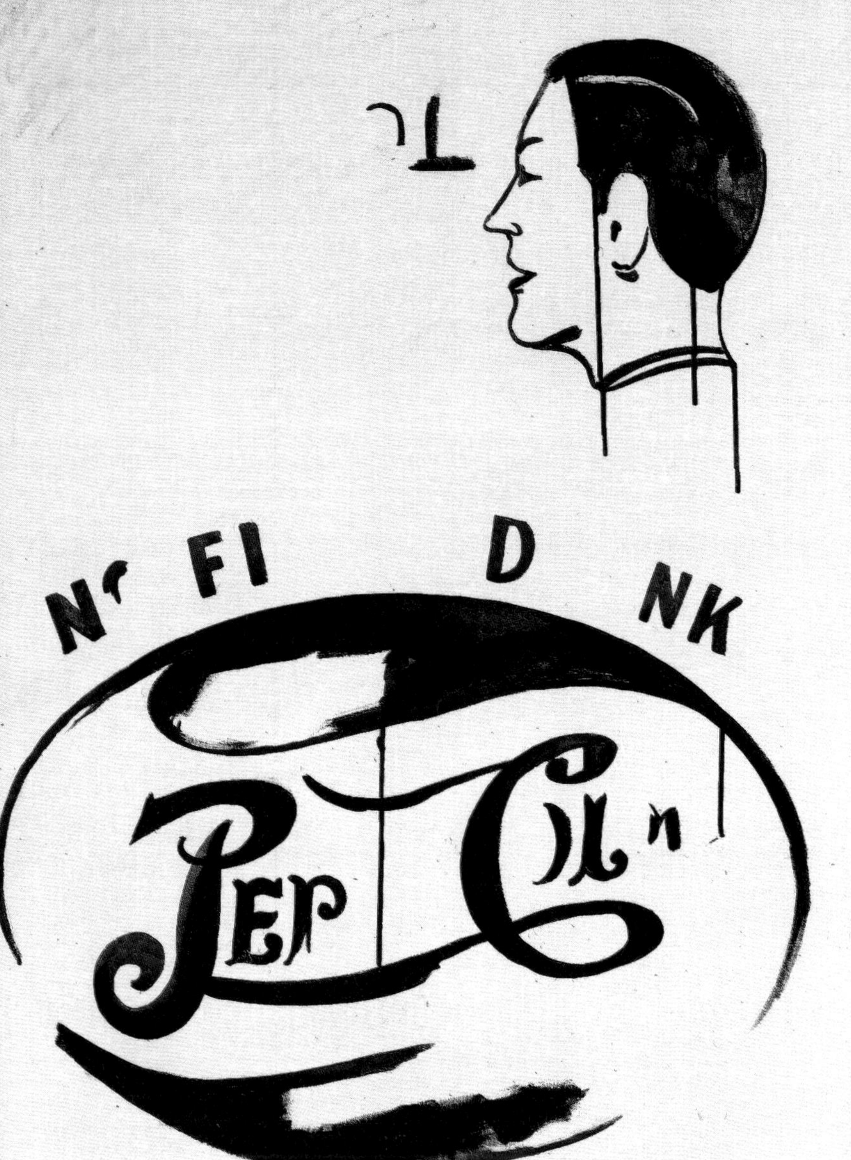

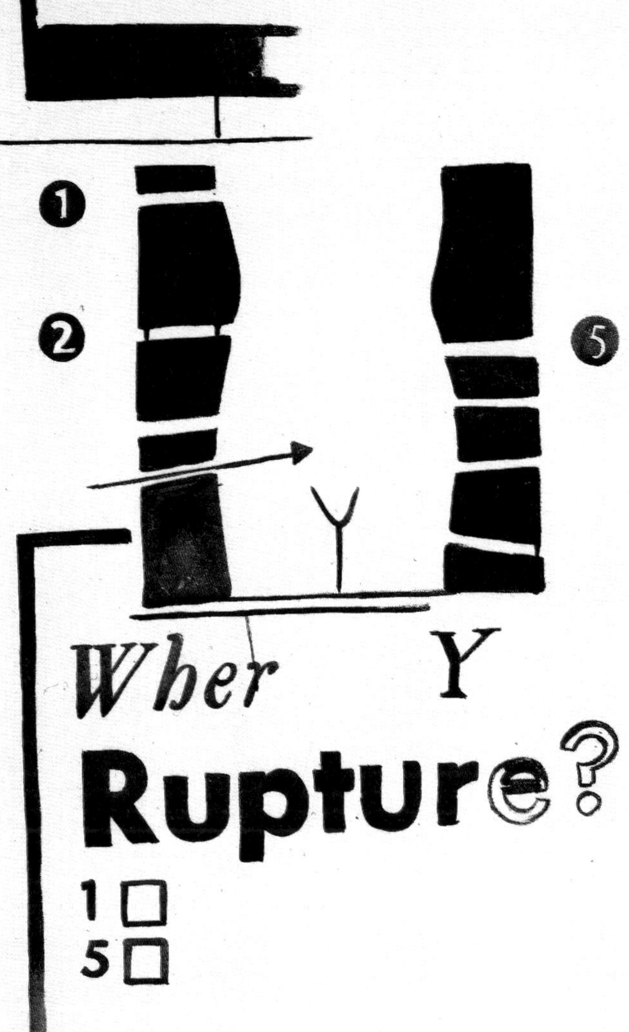

ST   G ARMS

NOSES RESHAPI

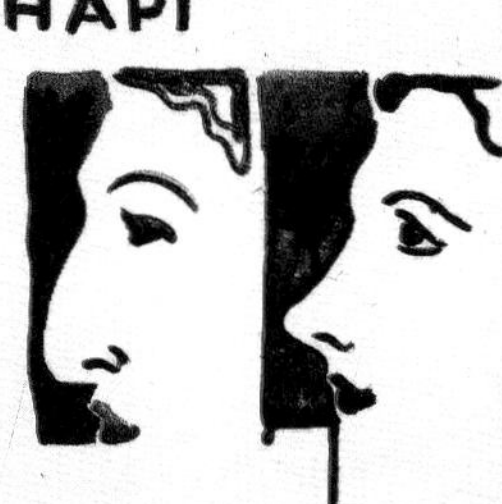

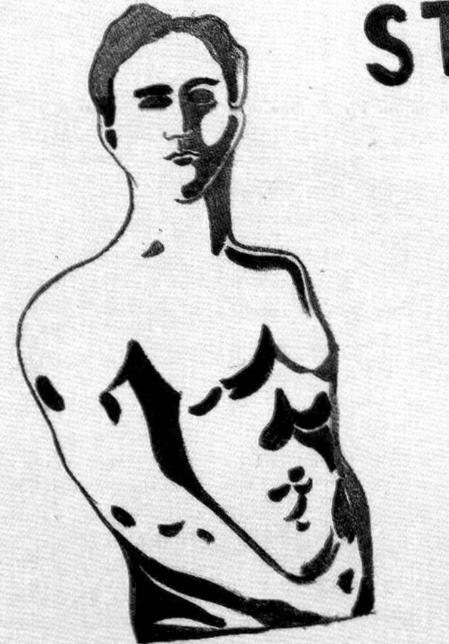

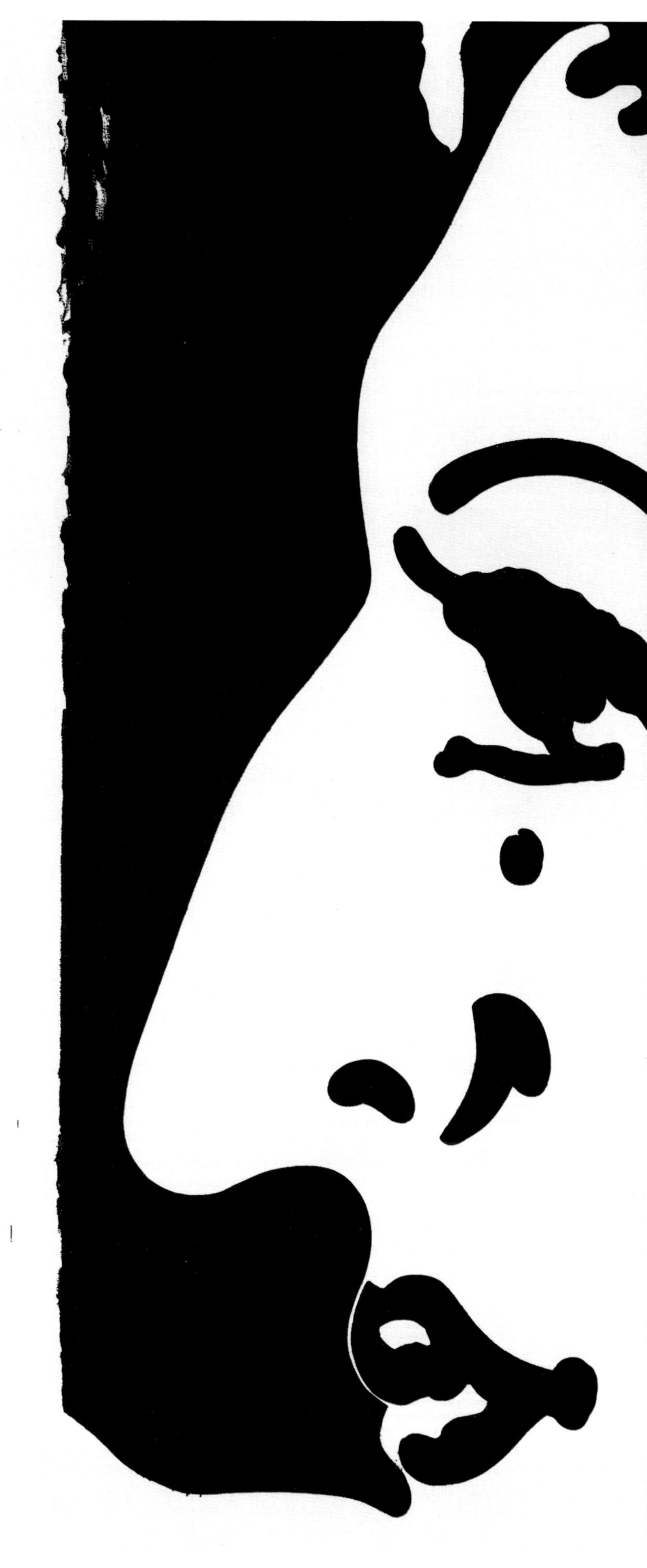

Before and After [3] 1961
Casein paint on canvas
137.5 x 178.4

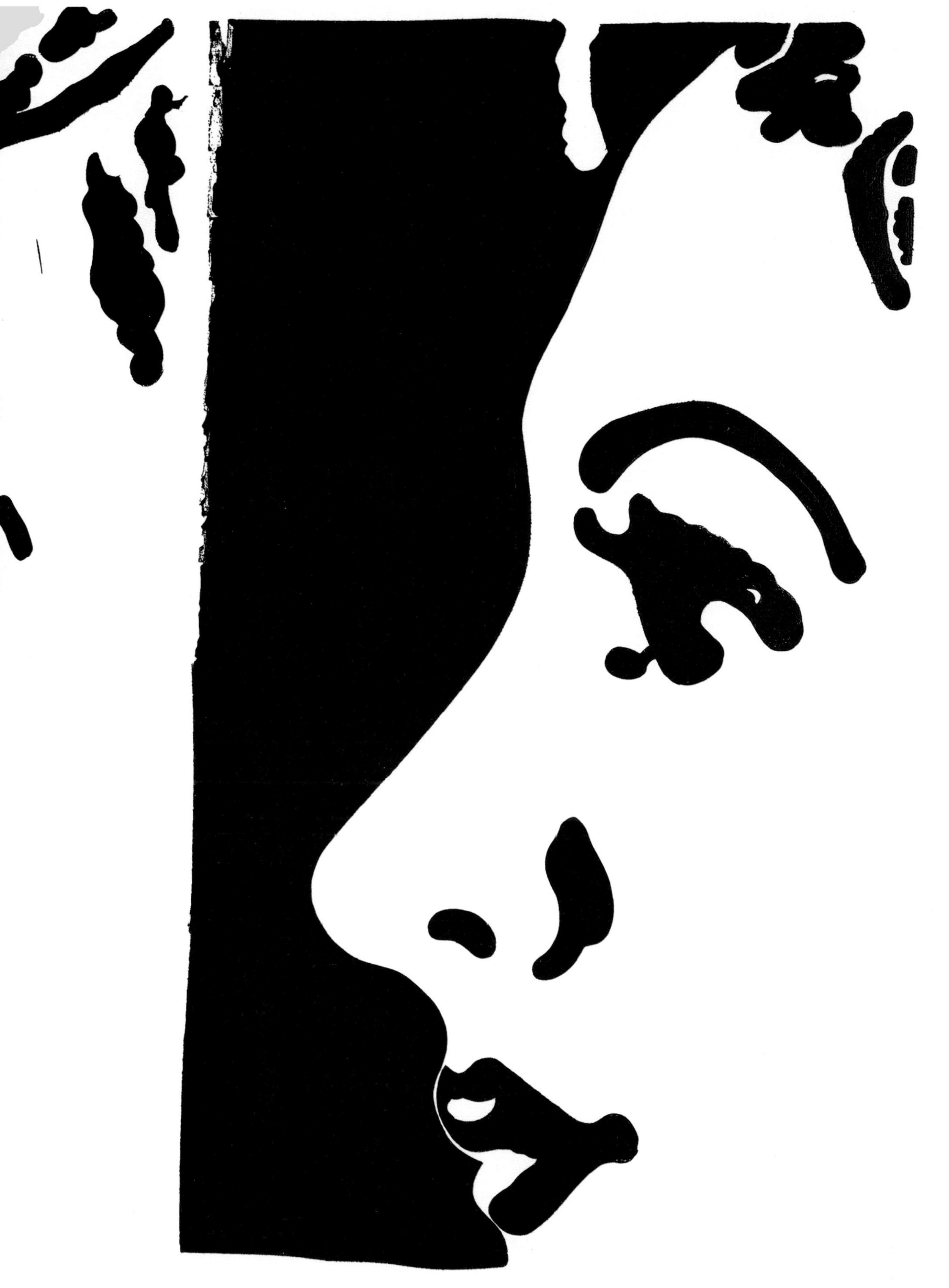

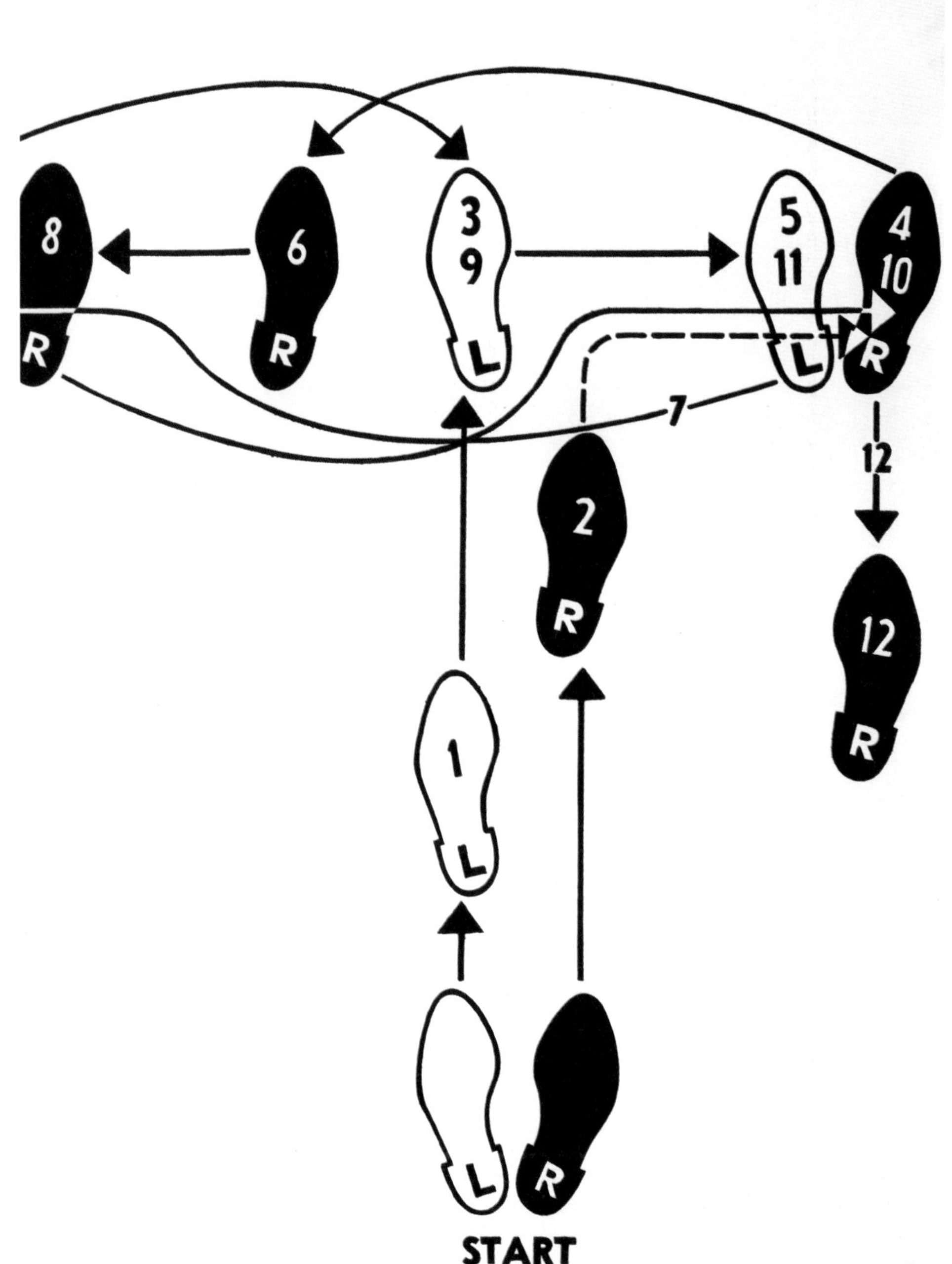

Dance Diagram [1]
[Fox Trot: 'The Double
Twinkle-Man'] 1962
Casein and graphite
on canvas
183.5 x 137.8

Opposite page
Do It Yourself 1962 (detail)
Acrylic paint, graphite and
Letraset on canvas
177.2 x 137.5

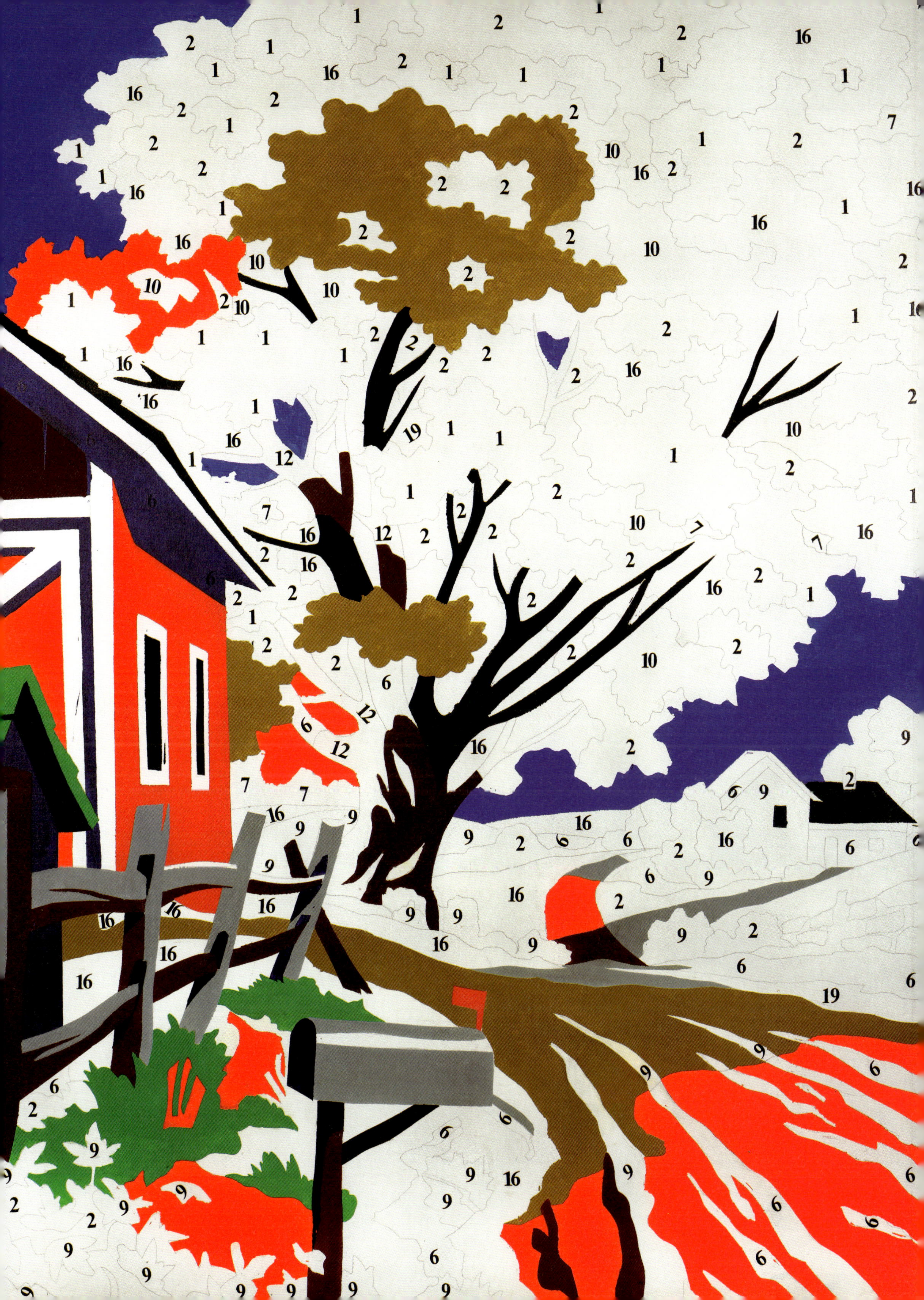

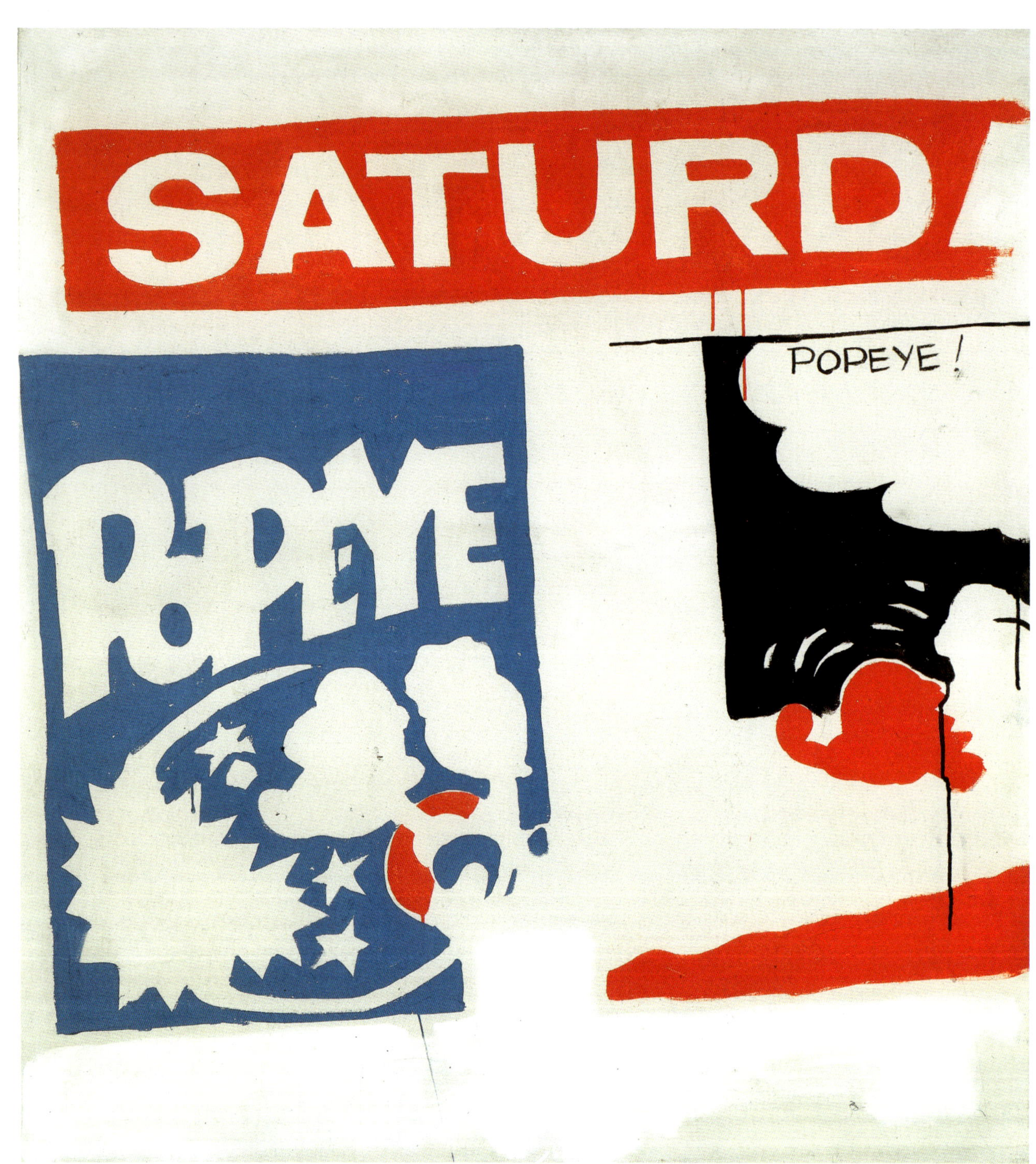

Saturday's Popeye 1961
Casein on canvas
108.5 x 98.7

Opposite page
$199 Television 1961 (detail)
Acrylic paint and oil stick
on canvas
172.7 x 132.7

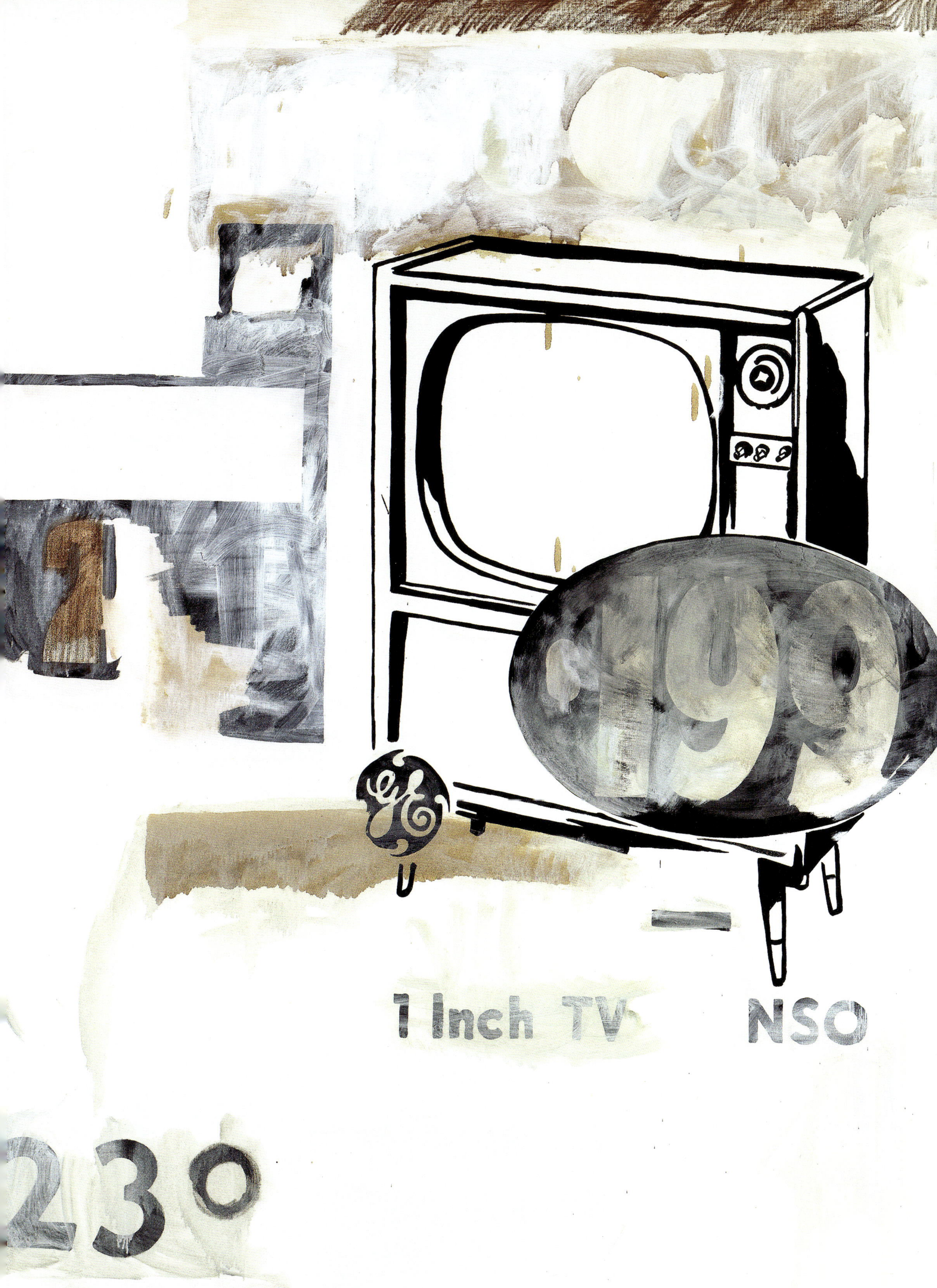
1 Inch TV   NSO
23°

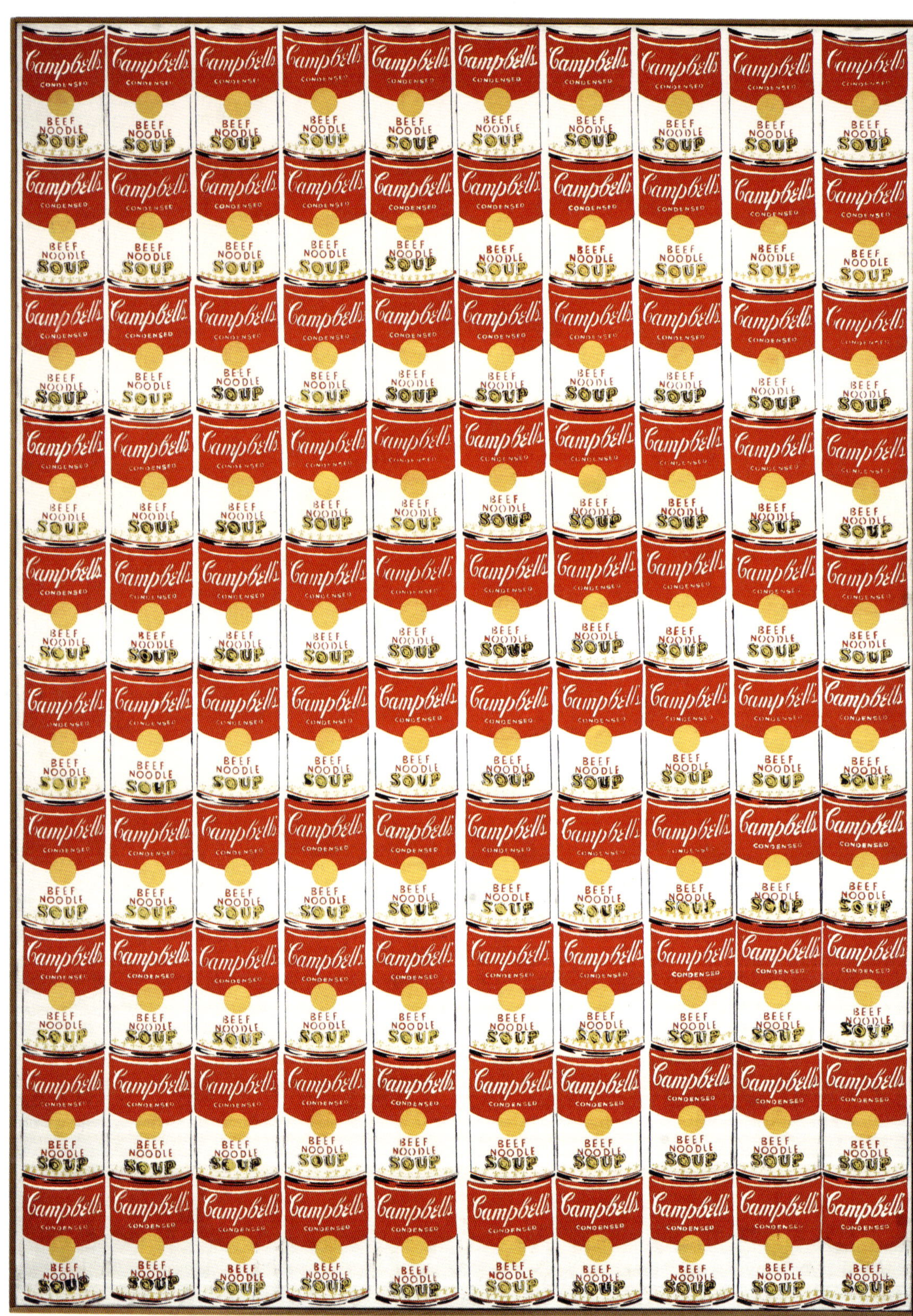

100 Campbell's Soup Cans
1962
Casein, acrylic paint and
graphite on canvas
182.9 x 132.7

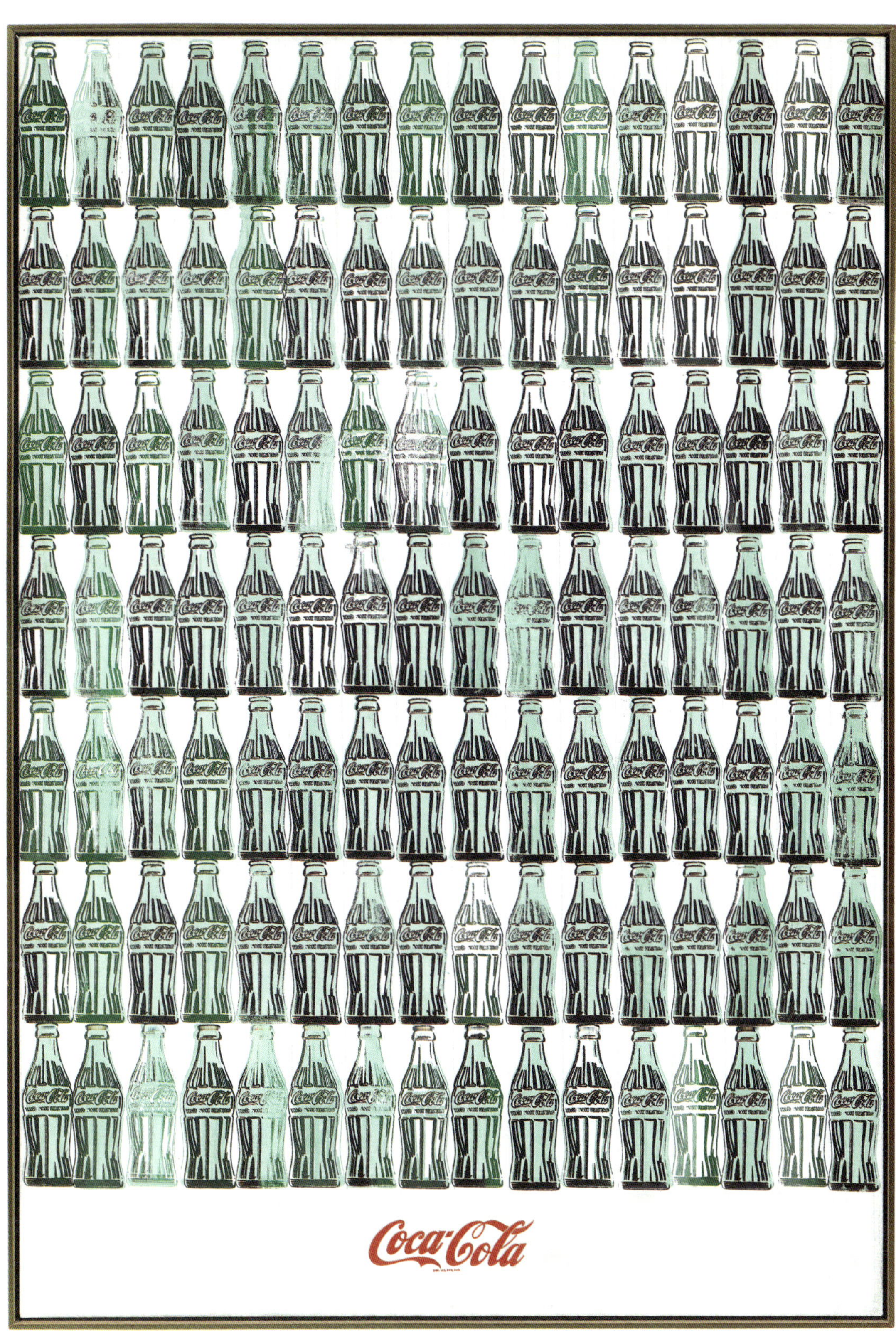

Green Coca-Cola Bottles
1962
Acrylic paint, screenprint
and graphite on canvas
210.2 x 145.1

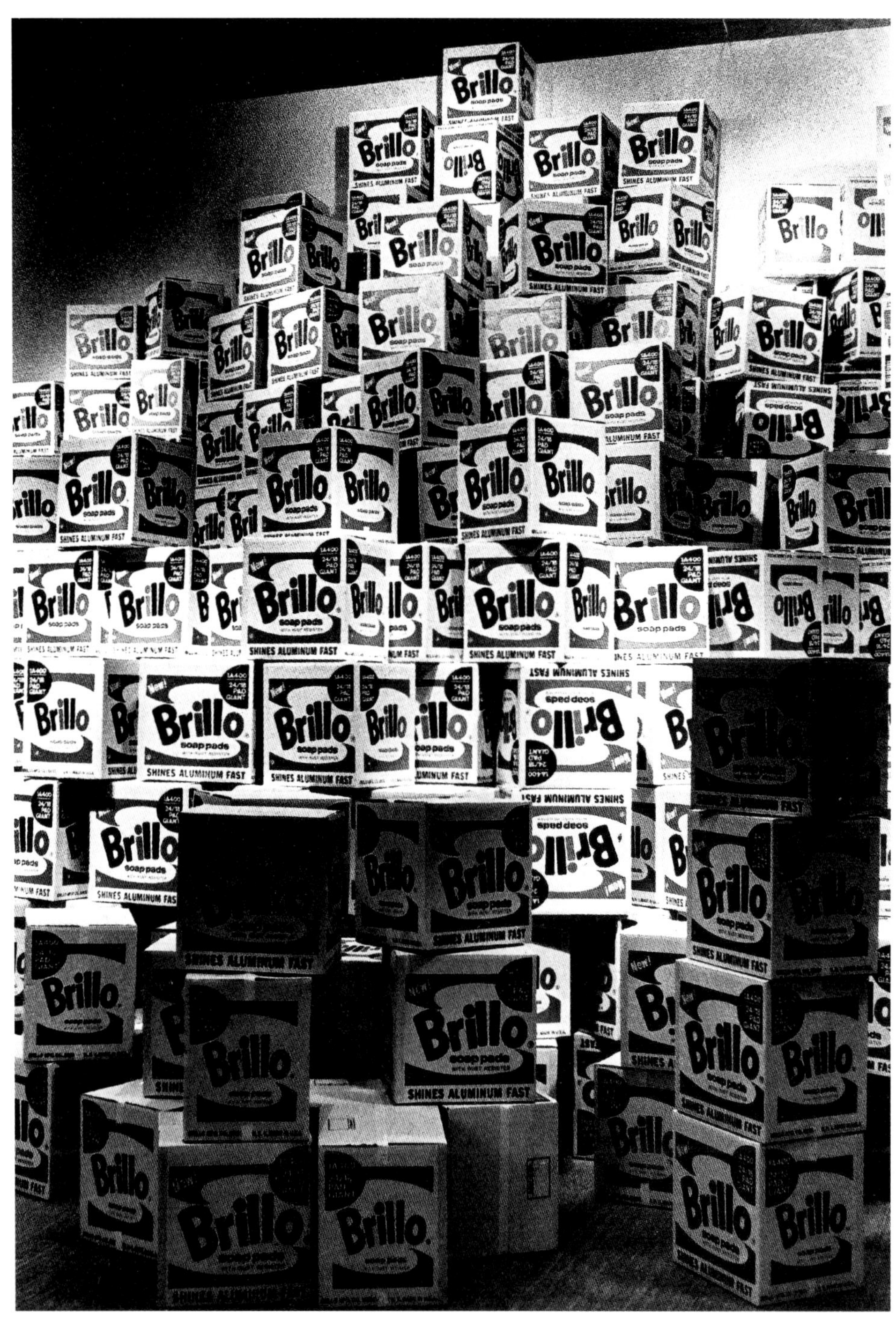

White Brillo Boxes 1964
Screenprint on wood
44 x 43 x 35.5 (each)
Installation shot from the Andy
Warhol exhibition at Moderna
Museet in Stockholm, 1968.
Photo by Nils-Göran Hökby

Opposite page
Campbell's Boxes 1964
Screenprint on wood
25.5 x 48 x 24 (each)
Installation shot from the
Stable Gallery, New York,
1964. Photo by Ken Heyman

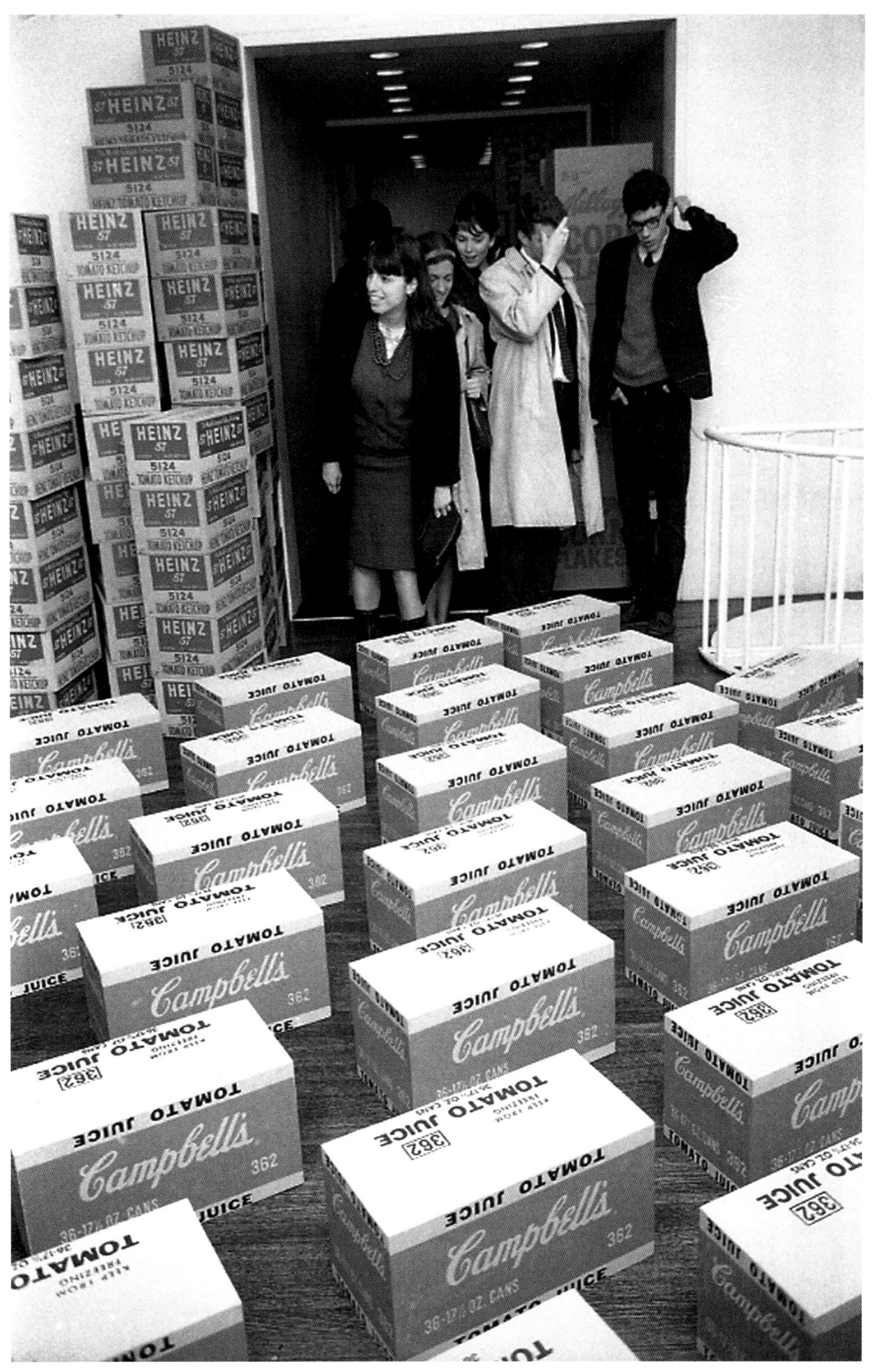

HEINZ
57
5124
TOMATO KETCHUP
TOMATO JUICE
362
Campbell's
36-17 1/2 OZ CANS
KEEP FROM
FREEZING

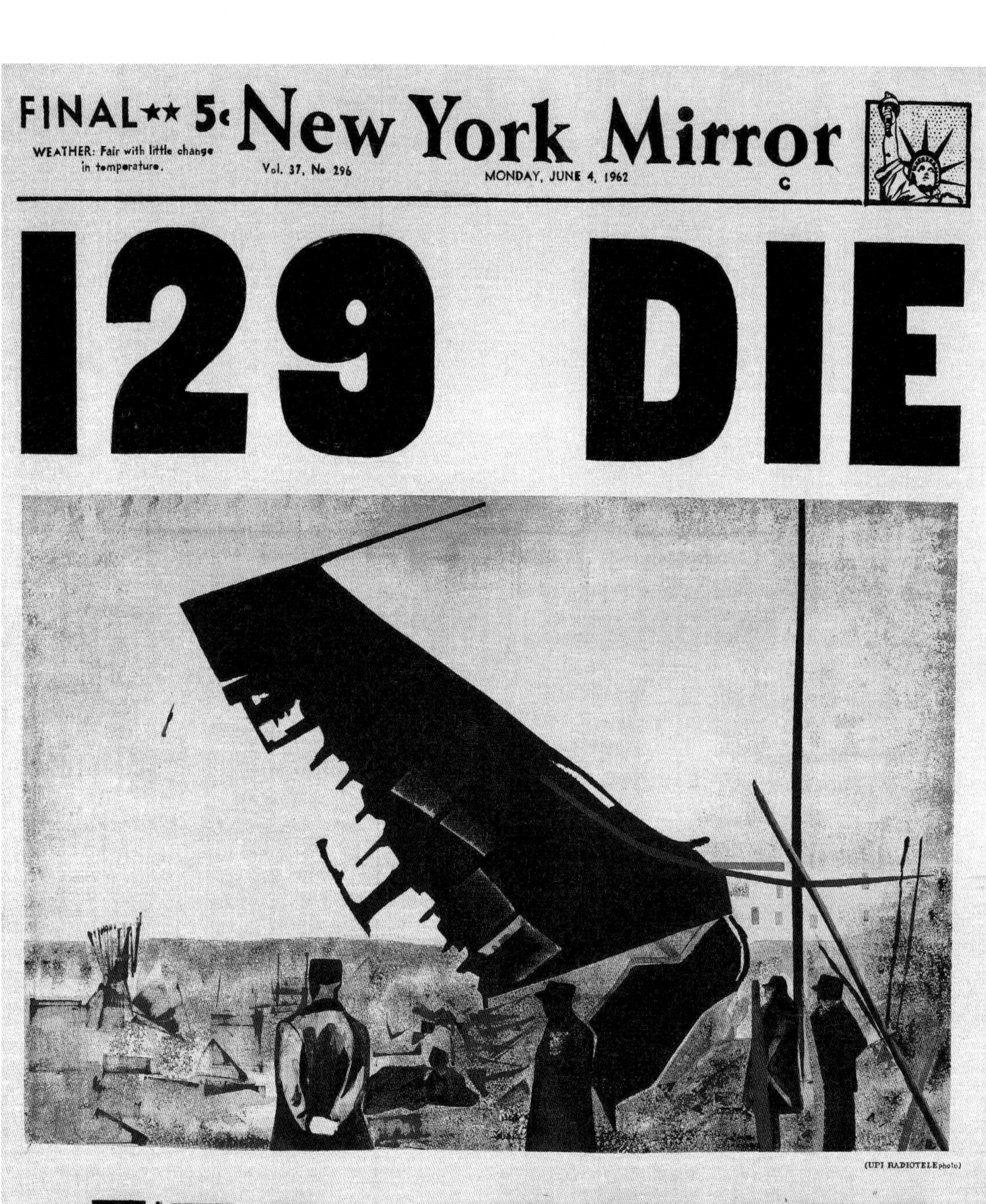

129 Die in Jet! (Plane Crash)
1962
Acrylic paint and graphite
on canvas
254.5 x 182.5

Opposite page
Two Dollar Bills (Front and Rear) 1962 (detail)
Screenprint on canvas
210 x 96

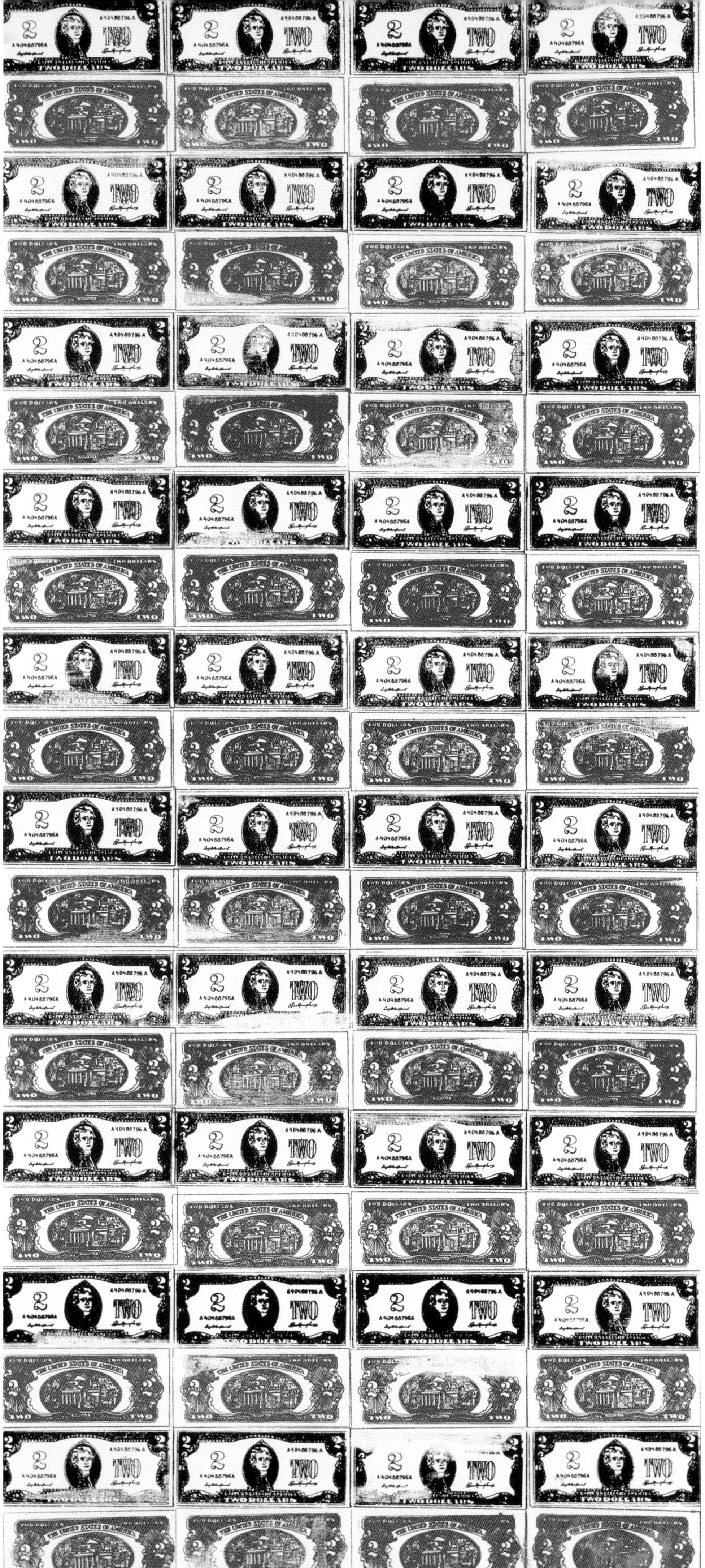

Round Marilyn 1962
Acrylic paint, screenprint and
metallic paint on canvas
Diam. 45.2

Next pages
Marilyn Diptych 1962
Acrylic paint on two canvases
205.4 x 144.8 (each)

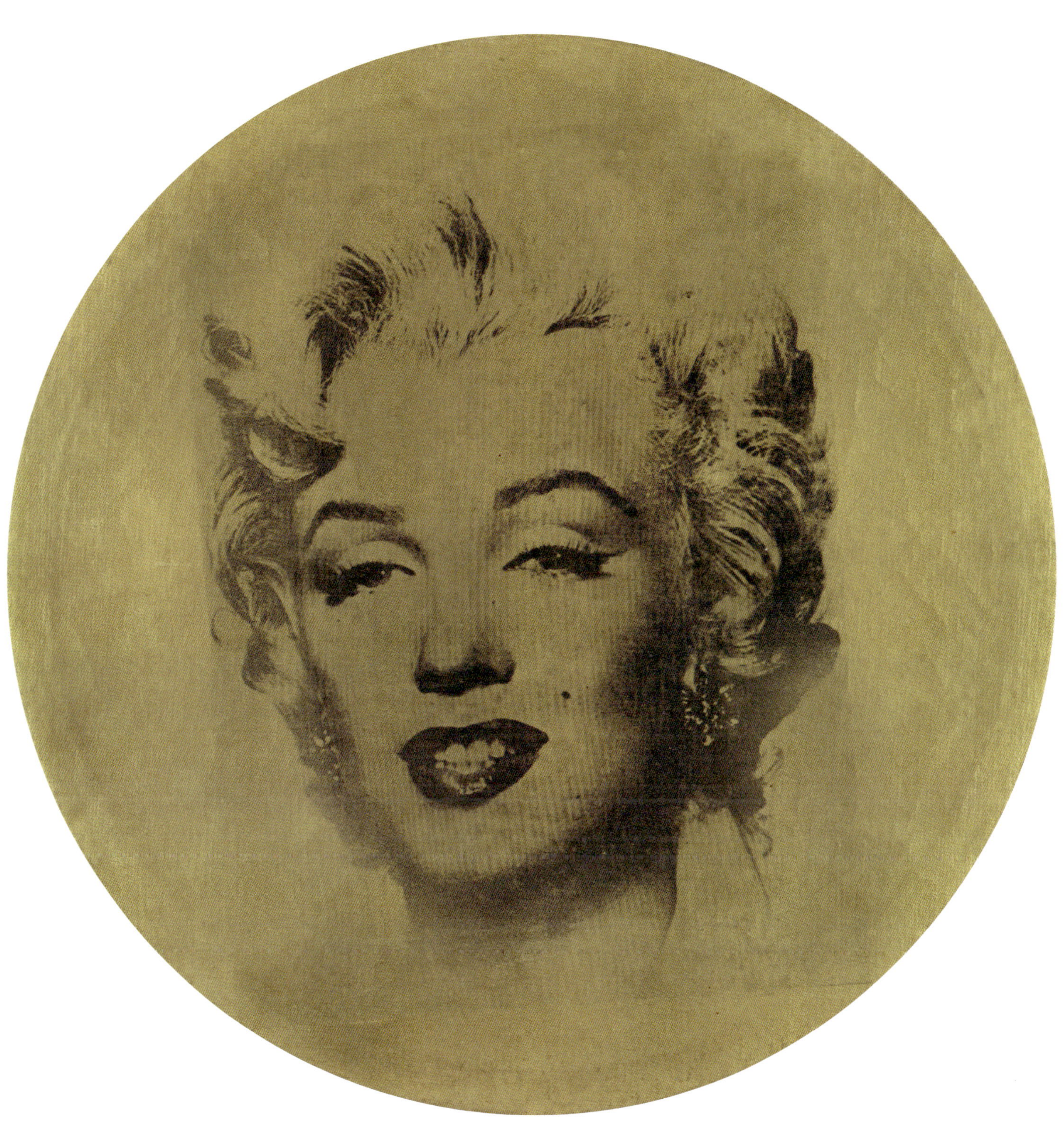

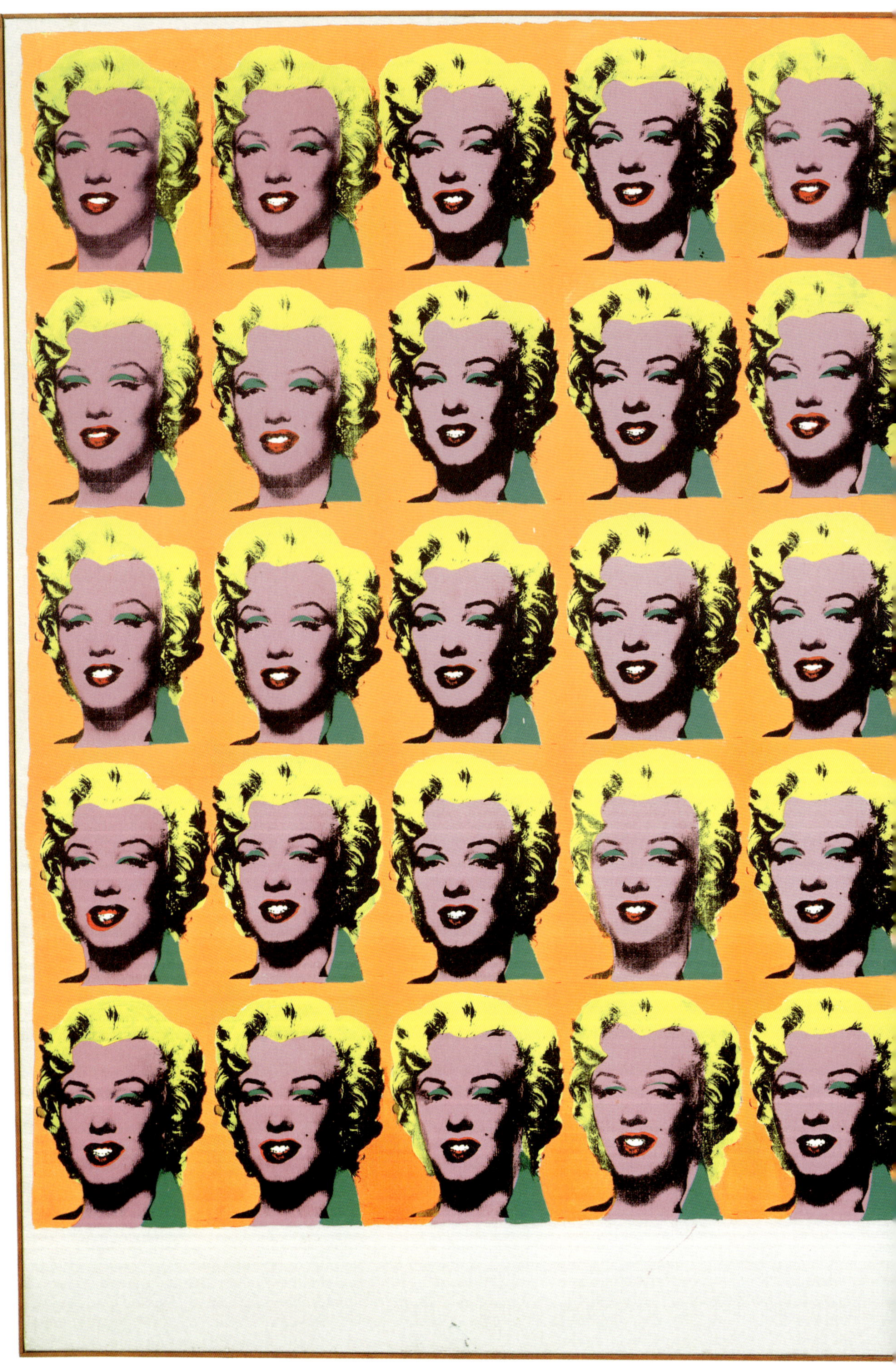

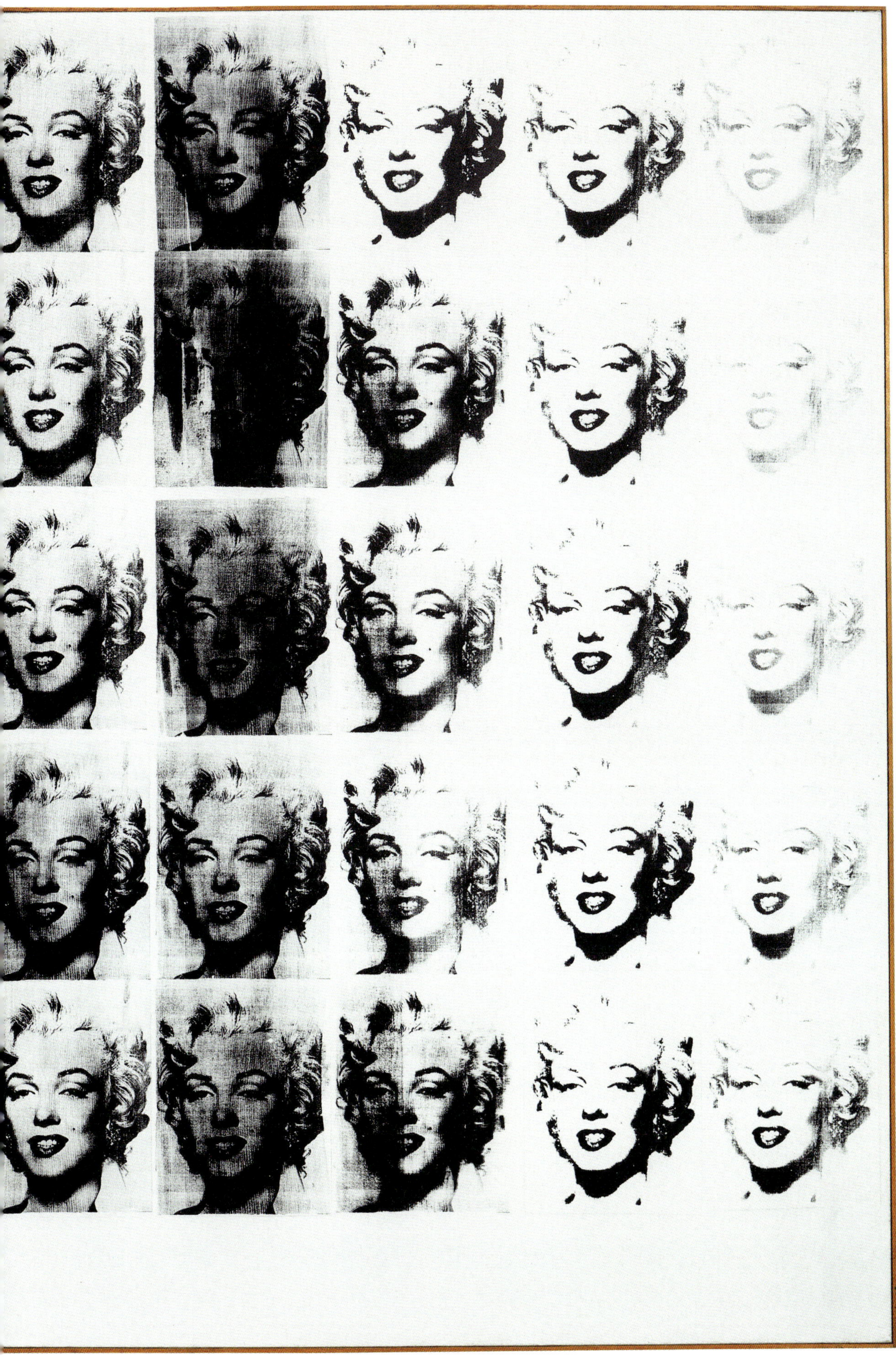

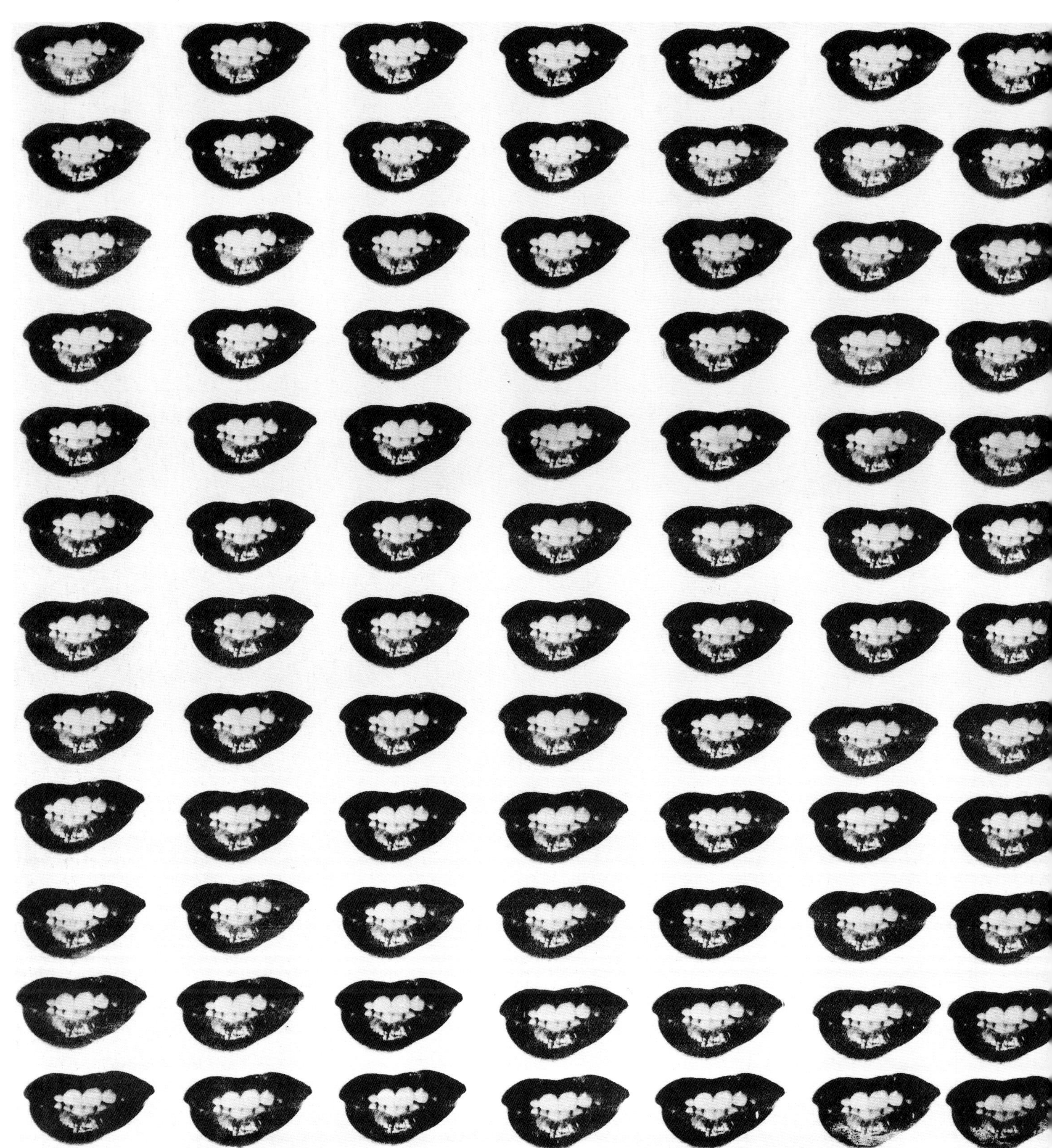

Marilyn Monroe's Lips 1962
Acrylic paint, screenprint and
graphite on two canvases
210.2 x 205.1;
210.2 x 209.2

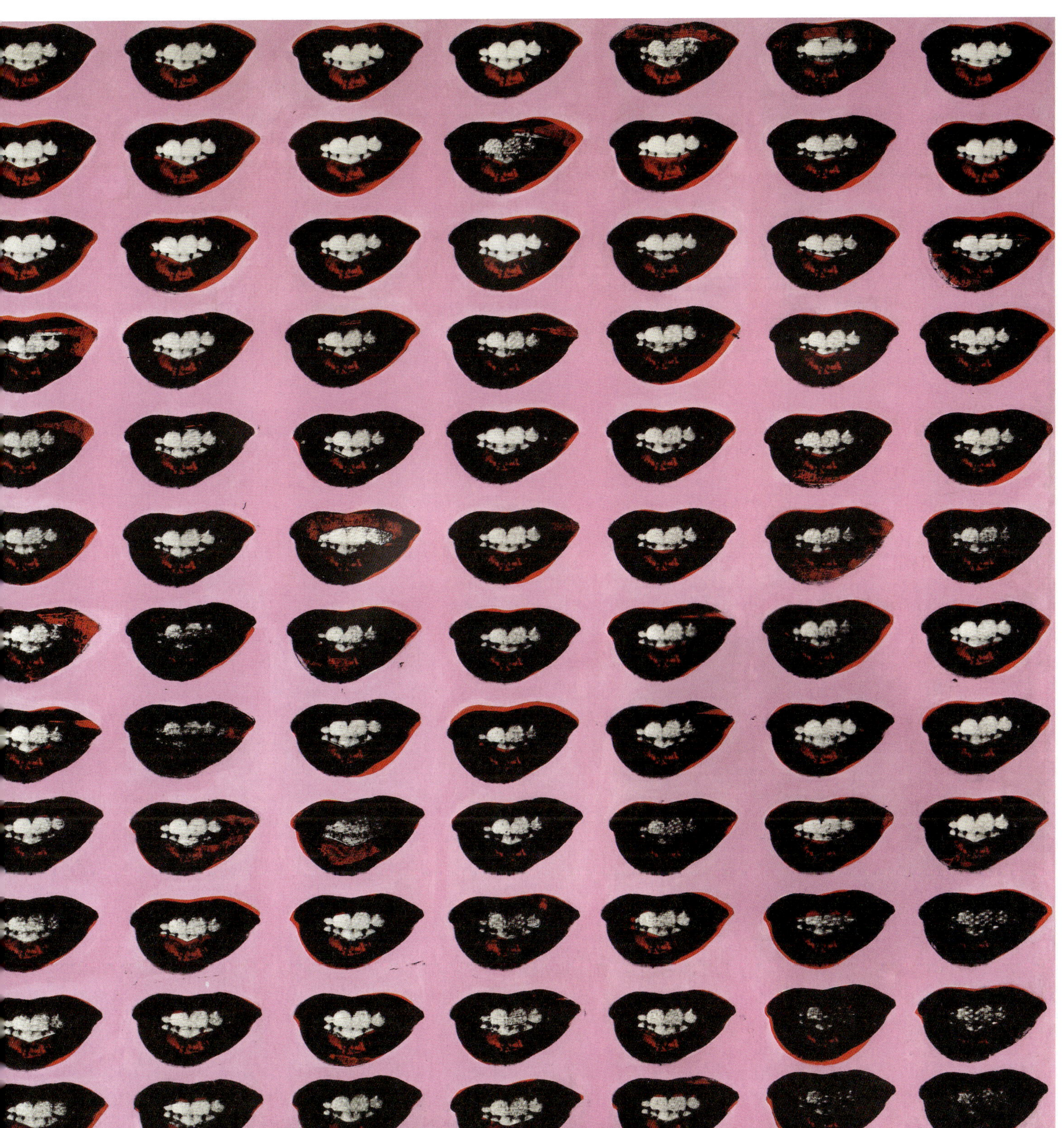

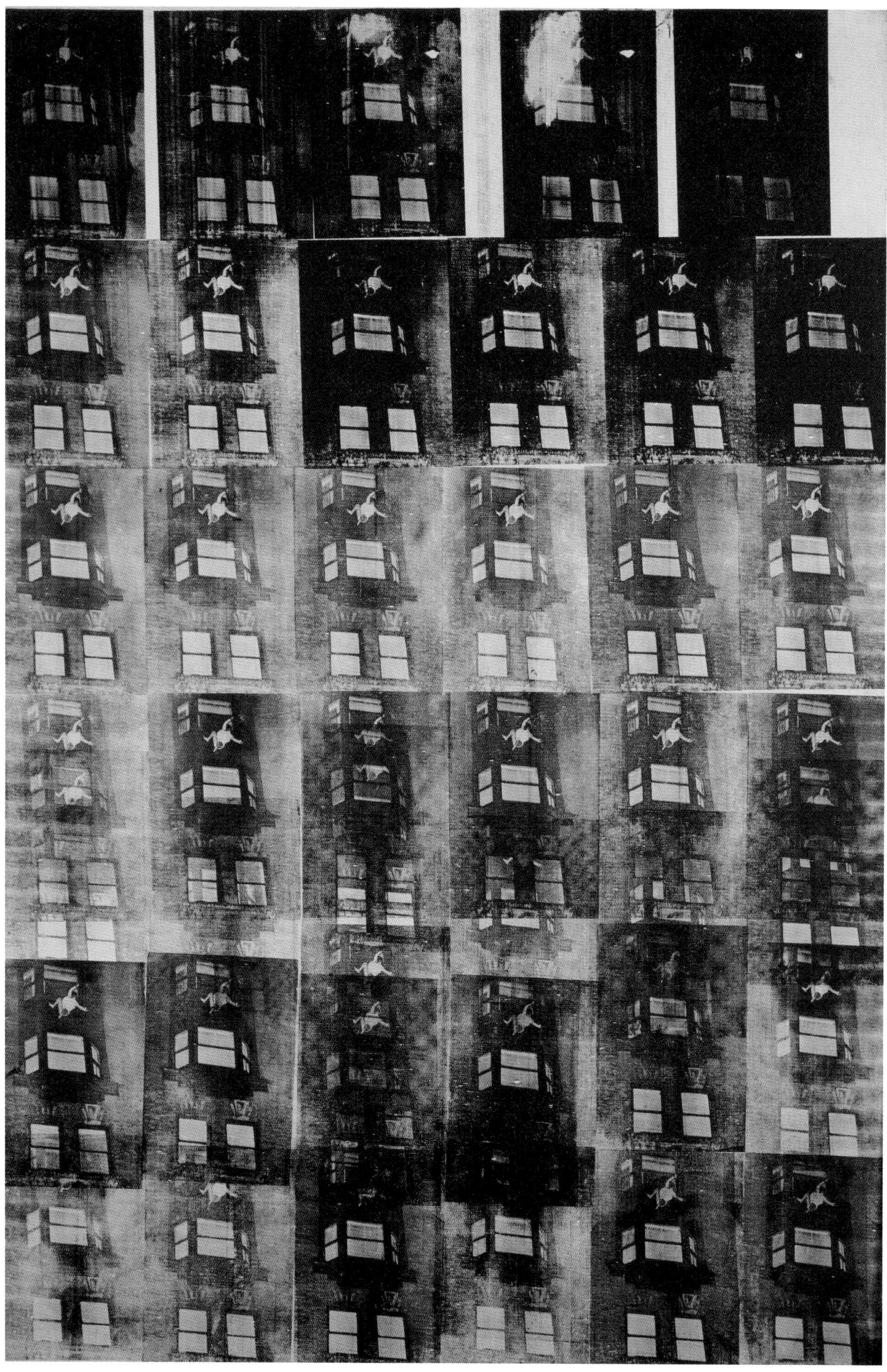

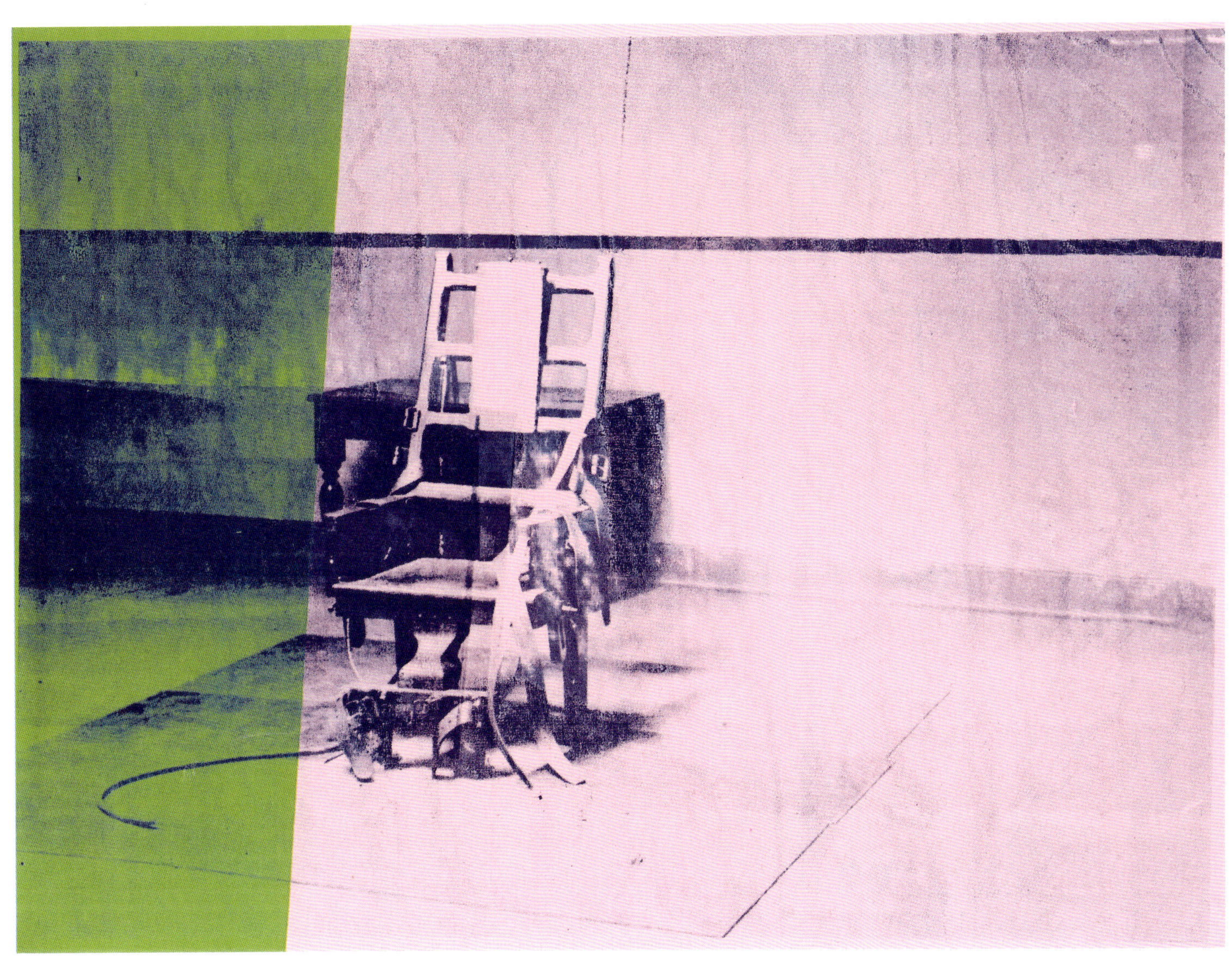

Big Electric Chair 1967
Acrylic paint and screenprint
on canvas
137.2 x 185.5

Opposite page
A Woman's Suicide 1962
Screenprint and graphite
on canvas
313 x 211

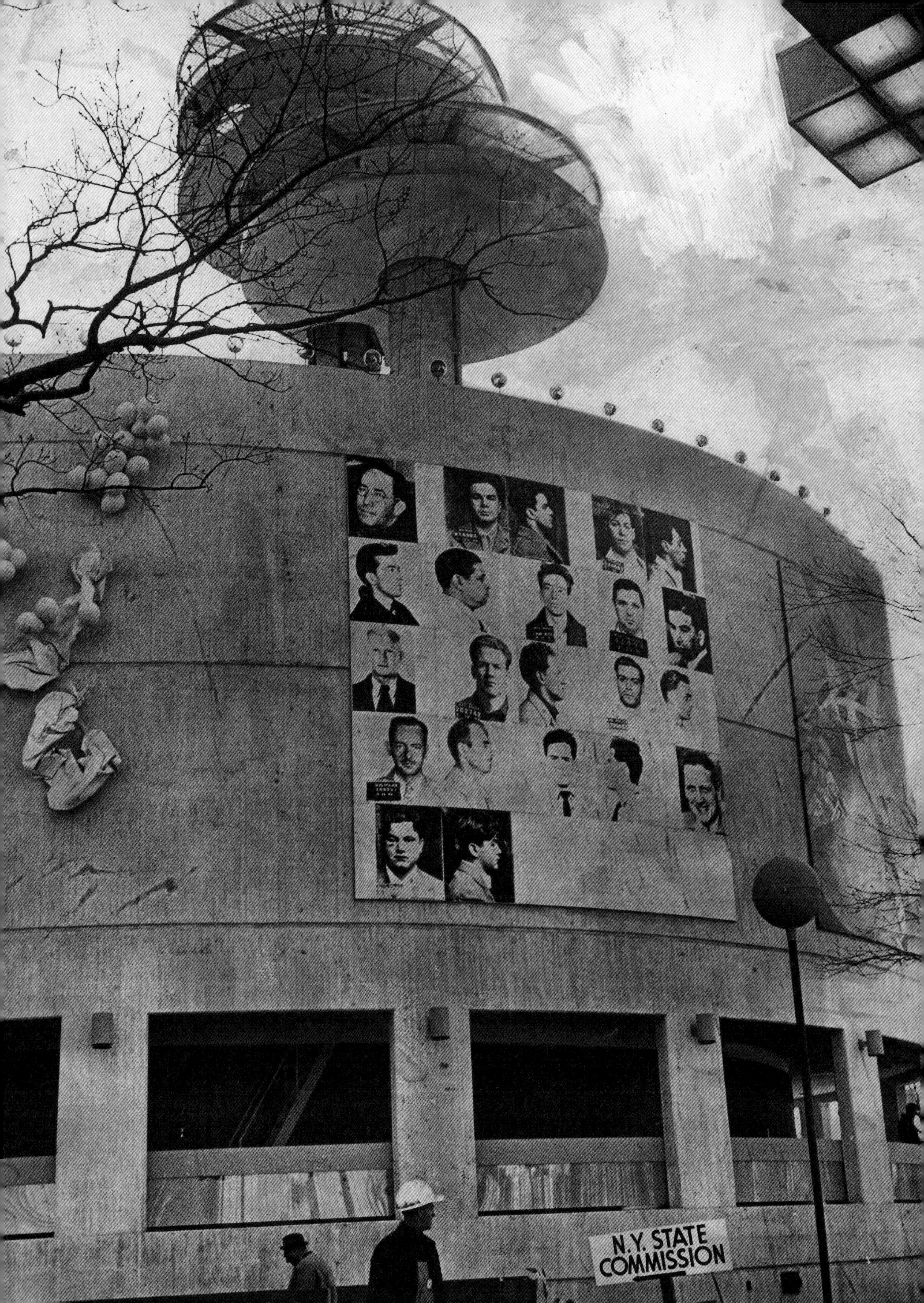

N.Y. STATE
COMMISSION

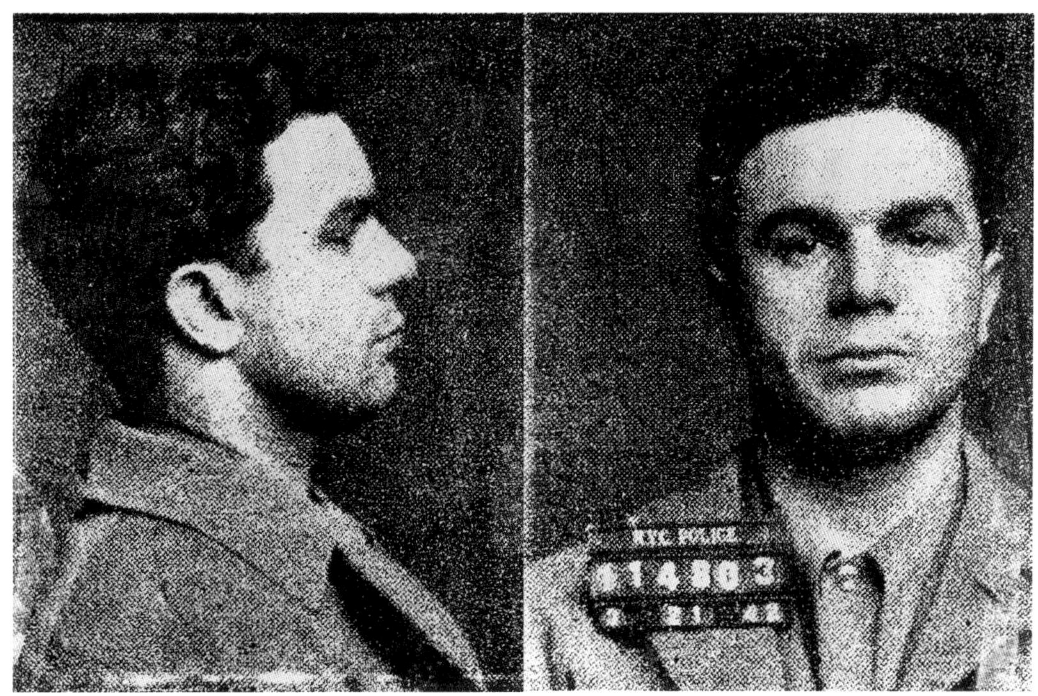

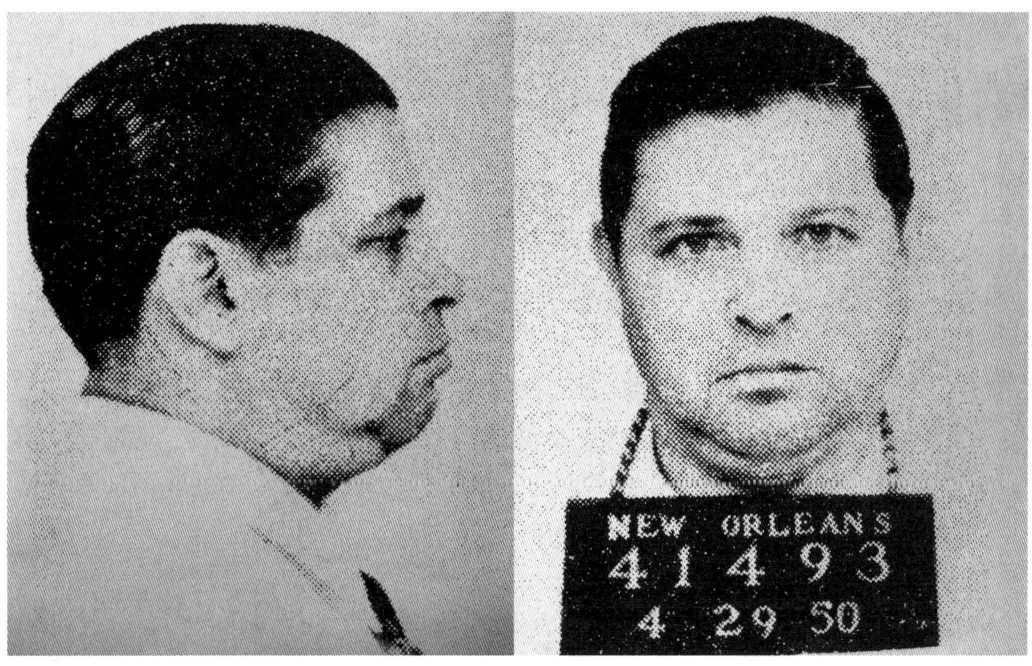

Opposite page
Thirteen Most Wanted Men
Mural for the New York State
Pavilion at the 1964 World
Fair, Flushing Meadows,
New York. Photo by Patrick
A.Burns/New York Times

*Most Wanted Men No.1,
John M.* 1964
Screenprint on two canvases
124.5 x 95.9 (each)

*Most Wanted Men No.7,
Salvatore V* 1964
Screenprint on two canvases
199 x 99 (each)

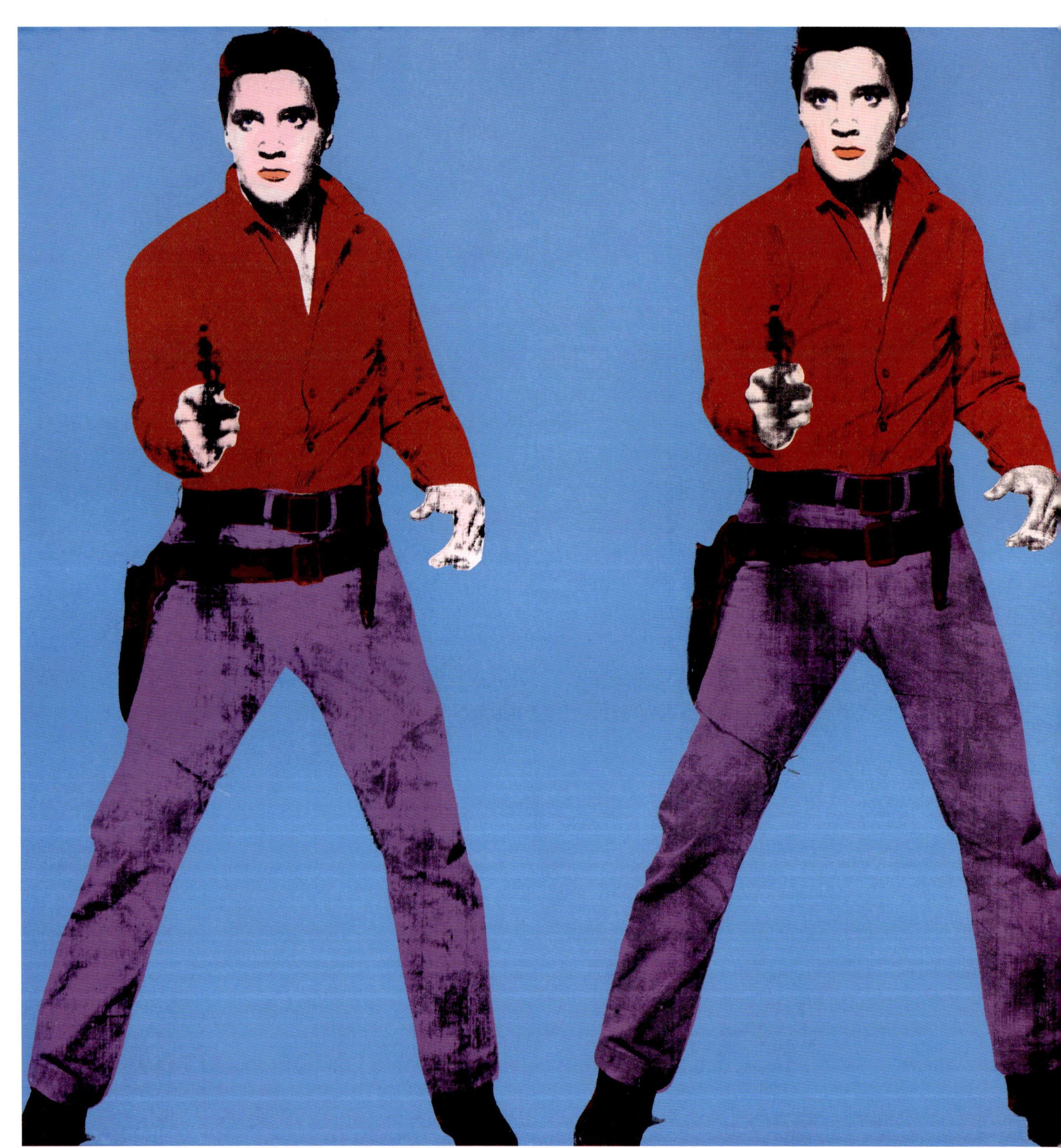

Elvis I and II 1963–4
Screenprint and acrylic
paint (blue panel); screenprint
and spray paint (silver panel)
on canvas
208.3 x 208.3 (each)

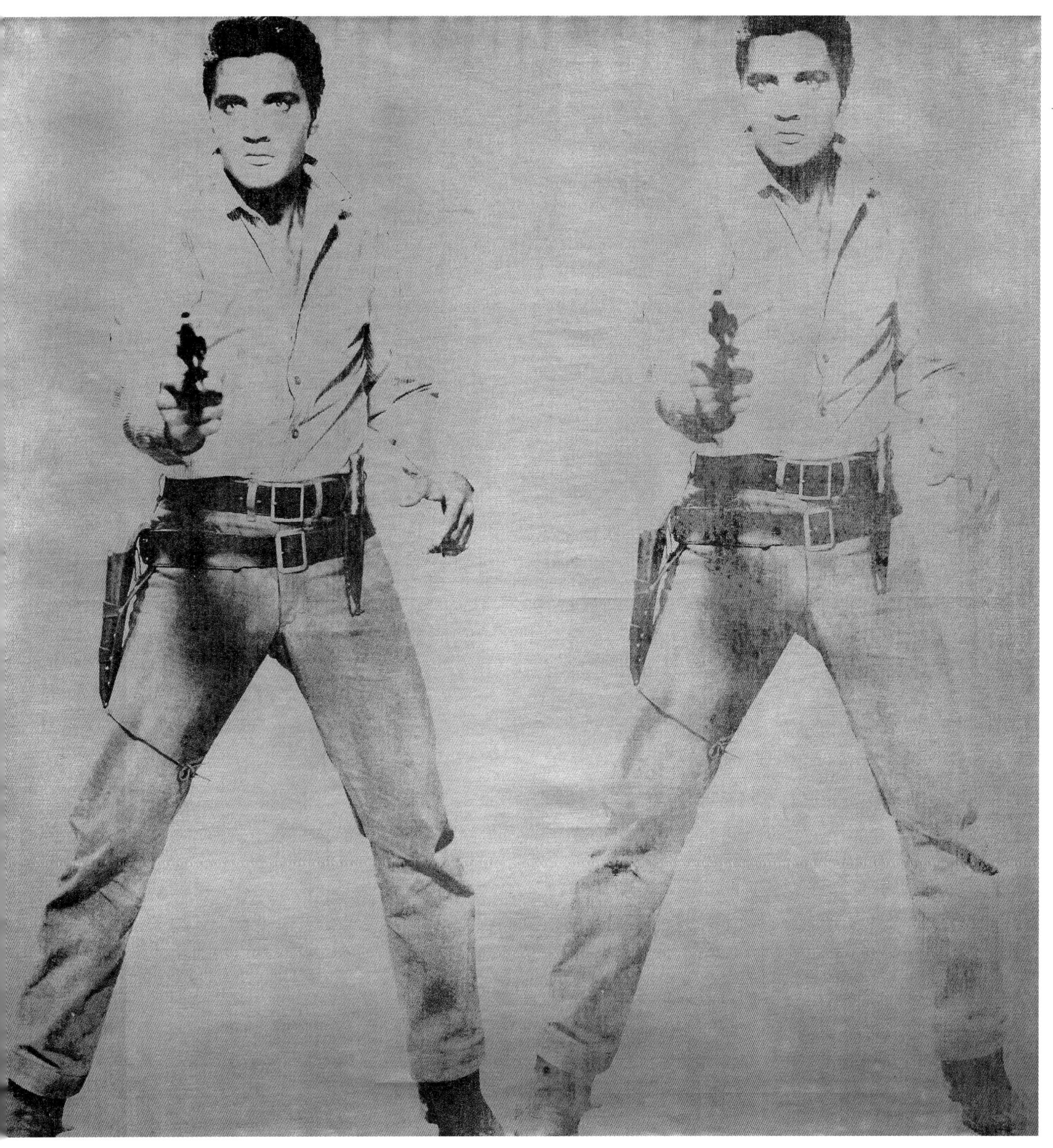

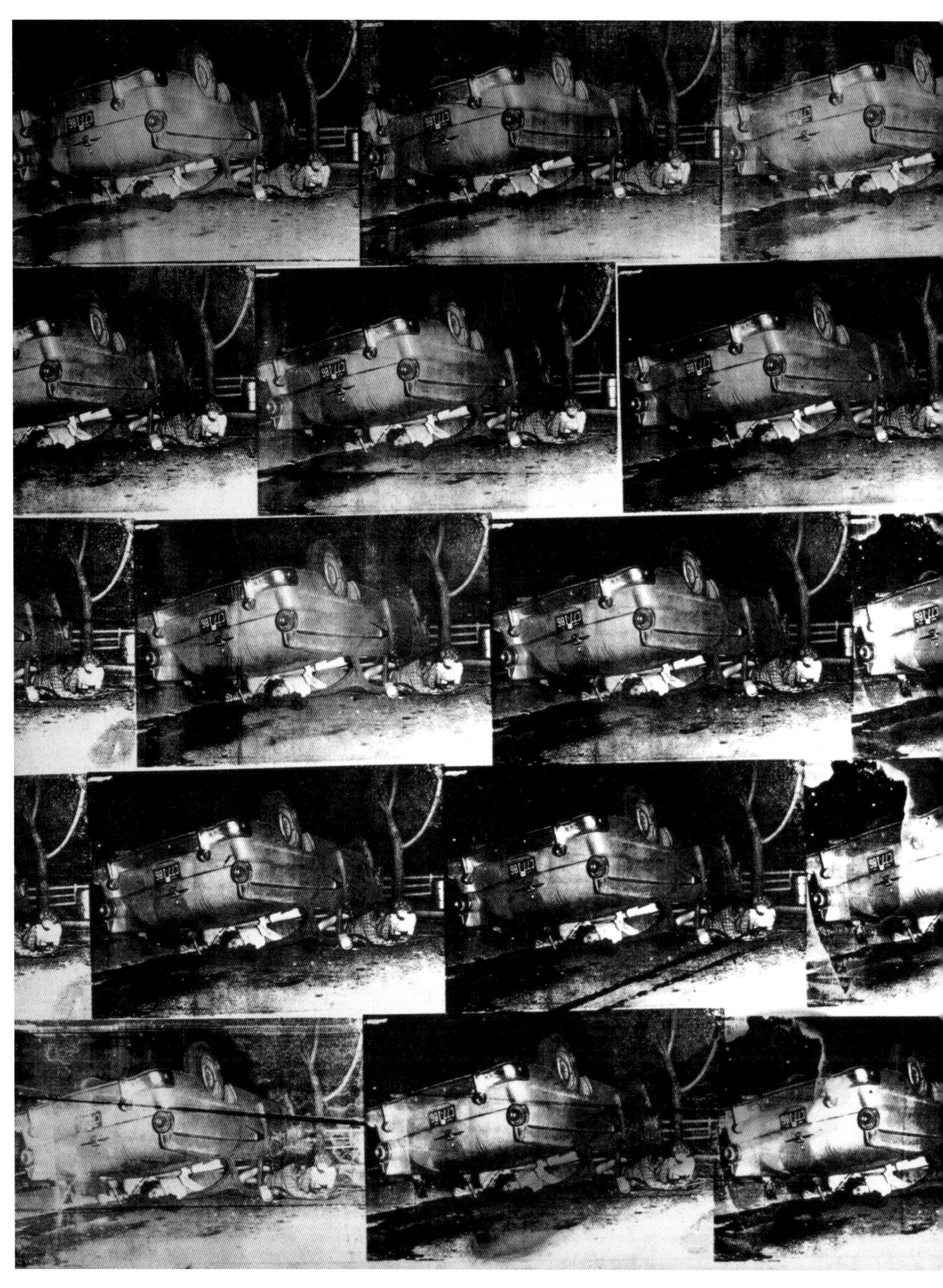

*Black and White Disaster #4
(5 Deaths 17 Times in Black
and White)* 1963
Acrylic paint, screenprint and
graphite on two canvases
261.9 x 209 (each)

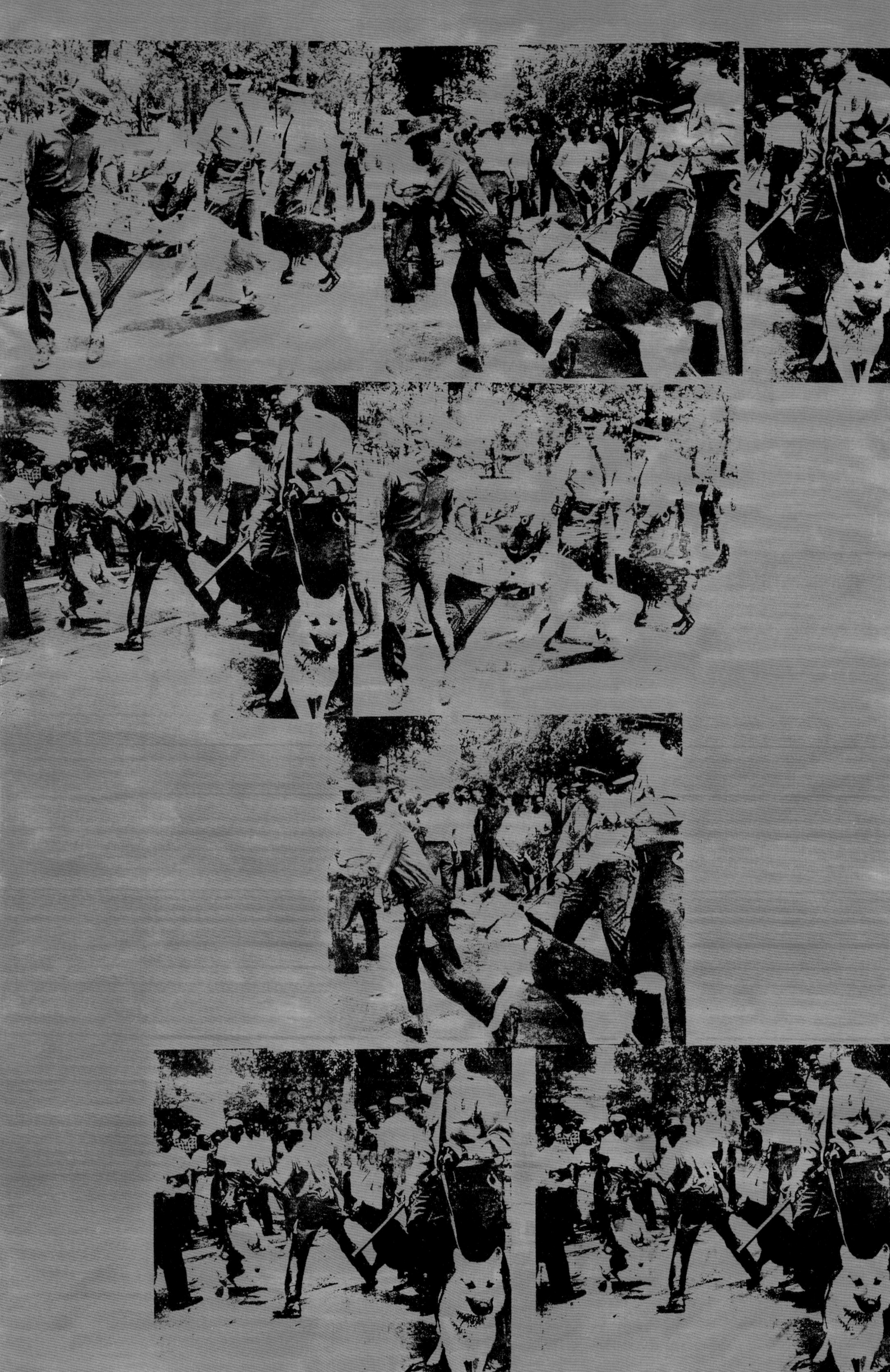

Opposite page
Red (Pink) Race Riot 1963
Screenprint and acrylic paint
on canvas
325.8 x 210.8

Life Magazine, 17 May 1963
Photo by Charles Moore/
Life Magazine

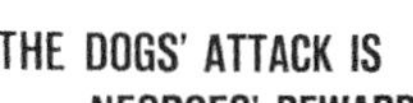

THE DOGS' ATTACK IS
NEGROES' REWARD

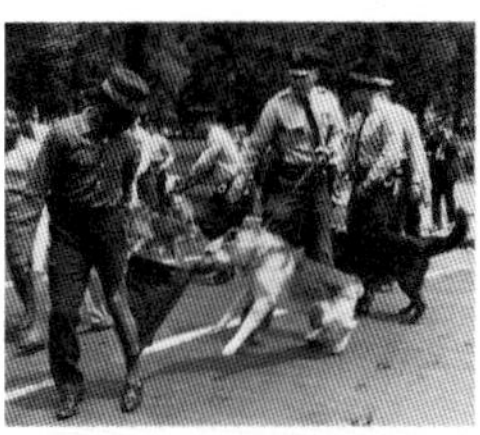

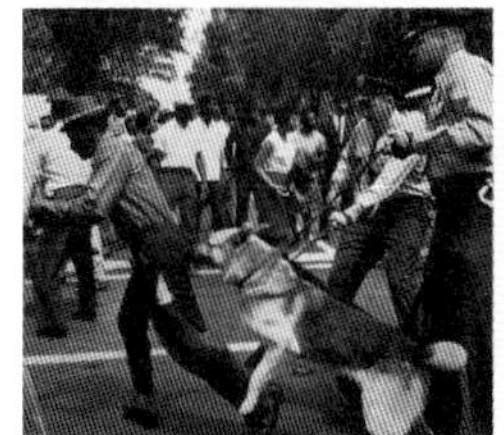

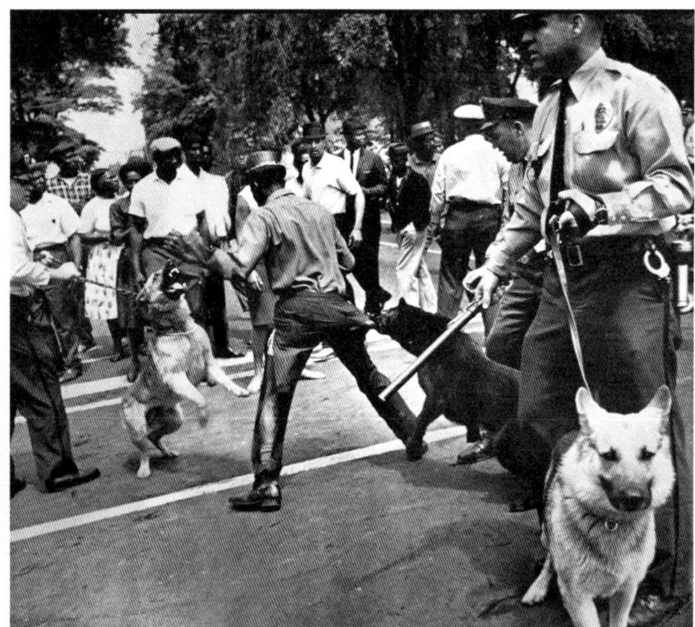

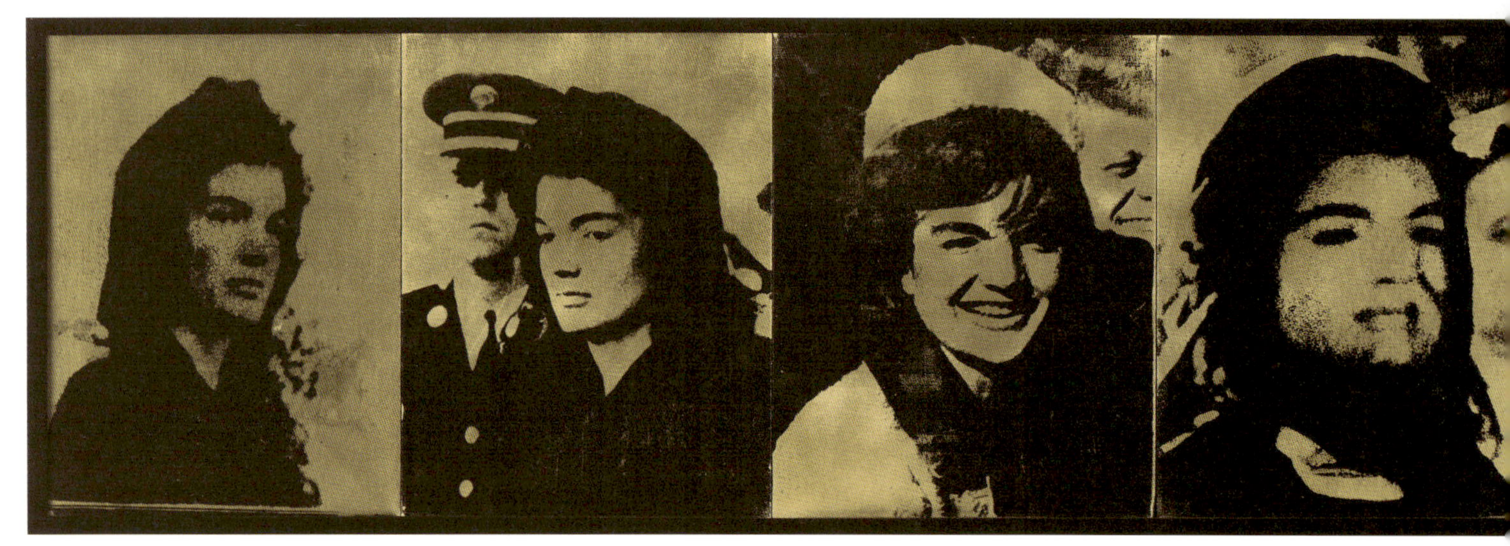

Jackie Frieze 1964
Screenprint, acrylic paint and
metallic paint on canvas
50.8 x 325

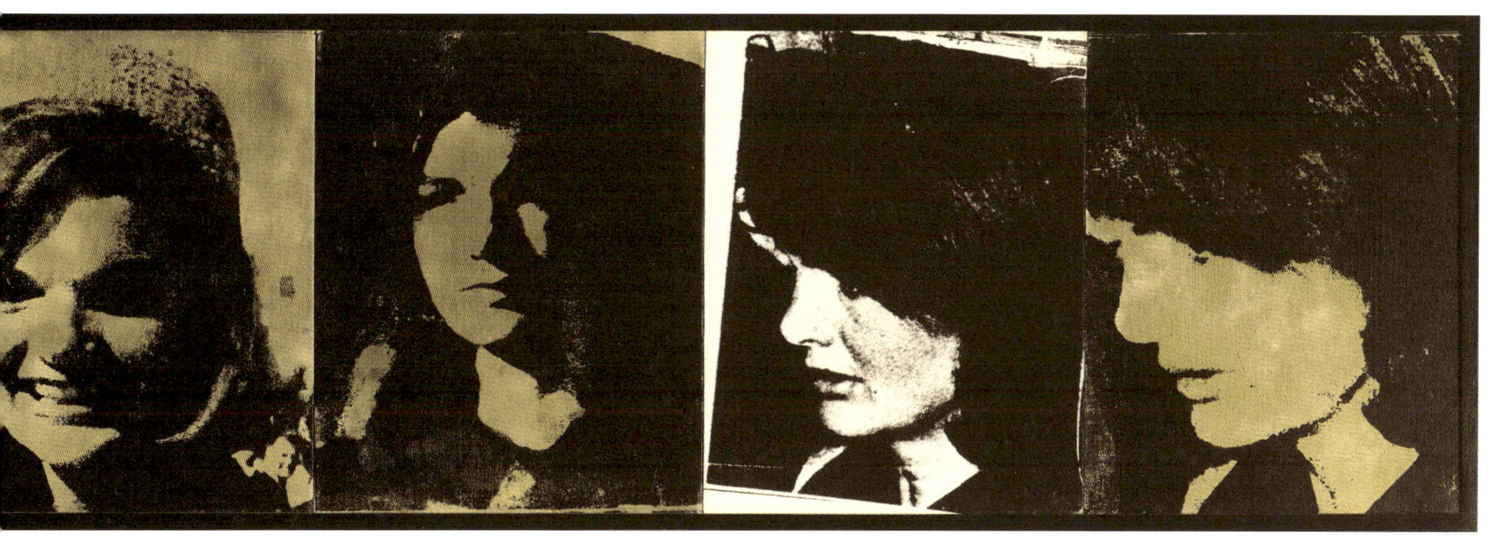

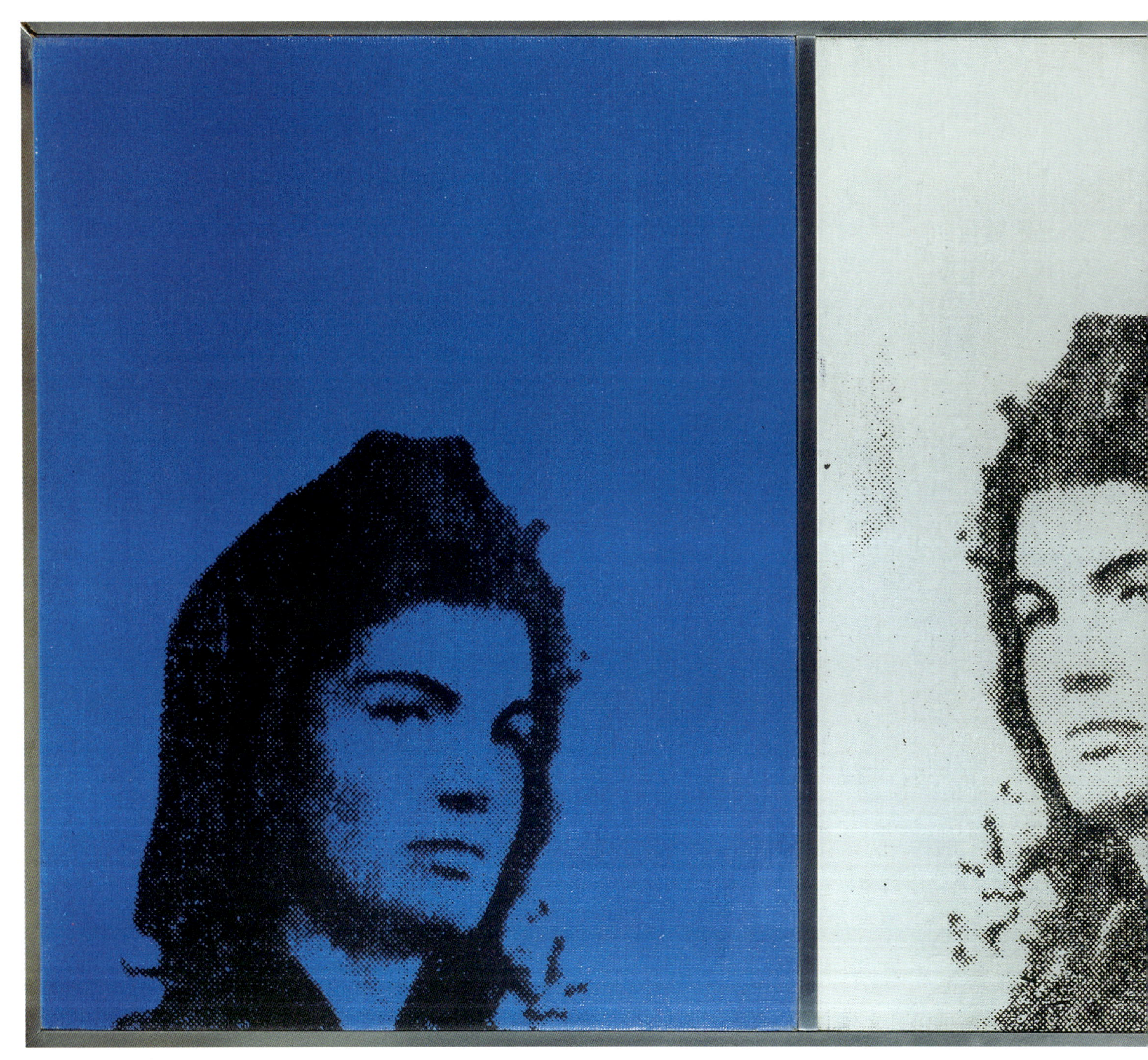

Jackie Triptych 1964
Screenprint and acrylic paint
on three canvases
53 x 124 (overall)

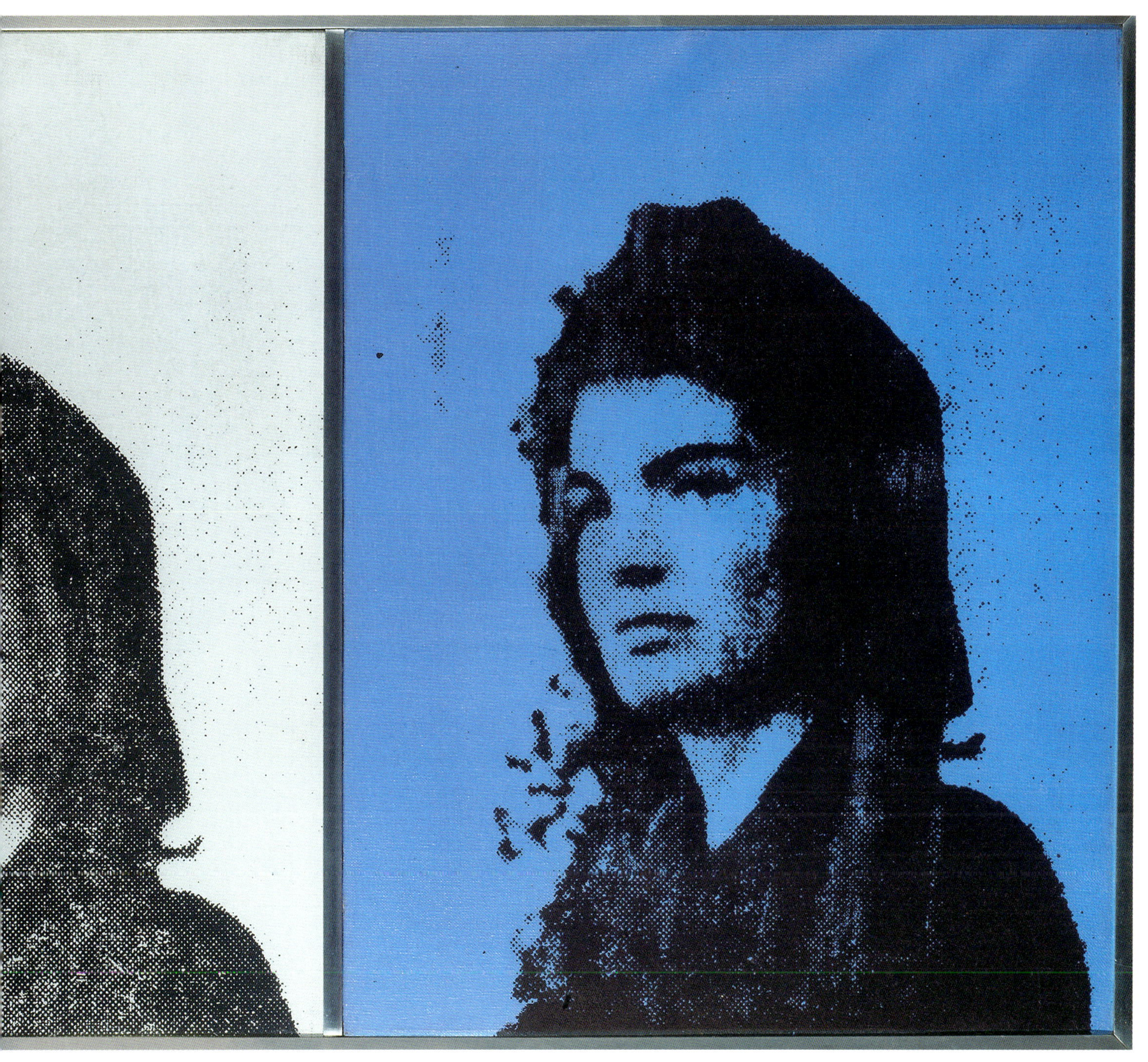

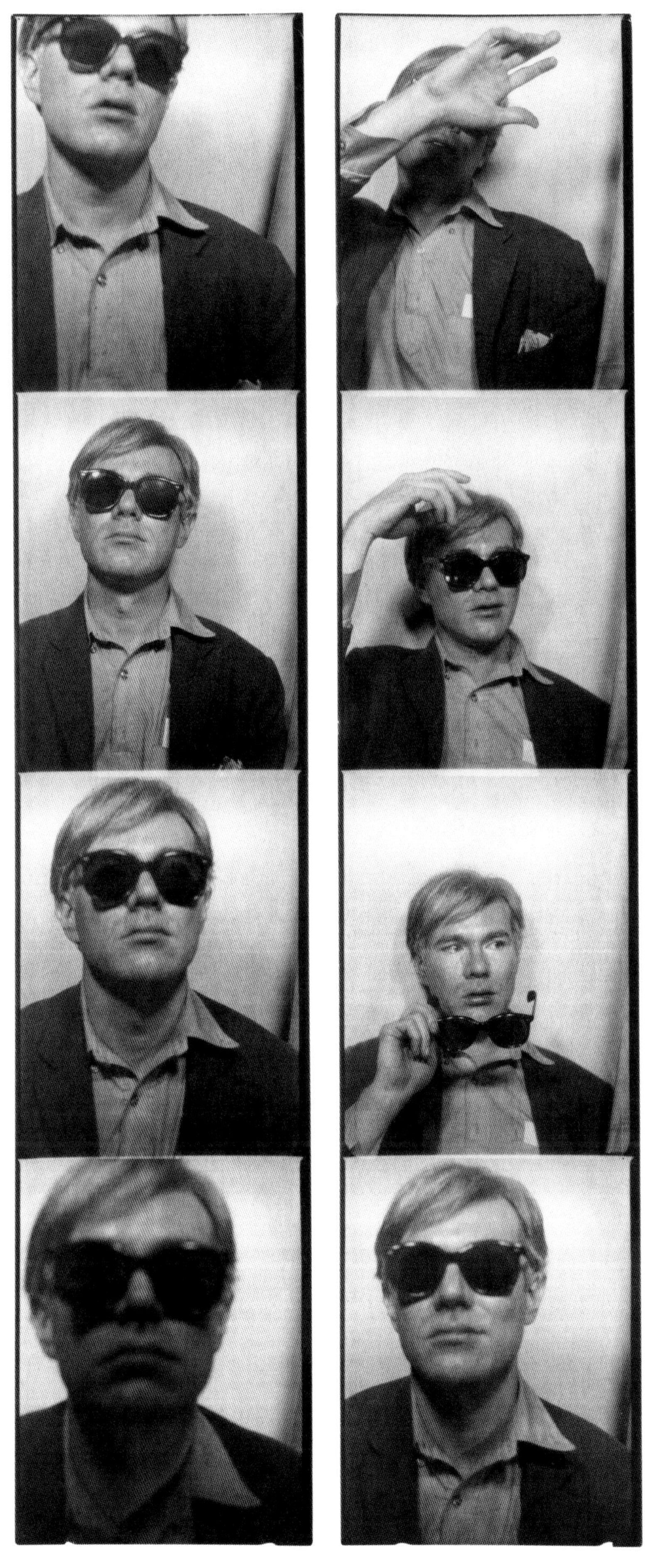

Photobooth Self-Portrait
c.1963
Gelatin silver print
19.6 x 3.6

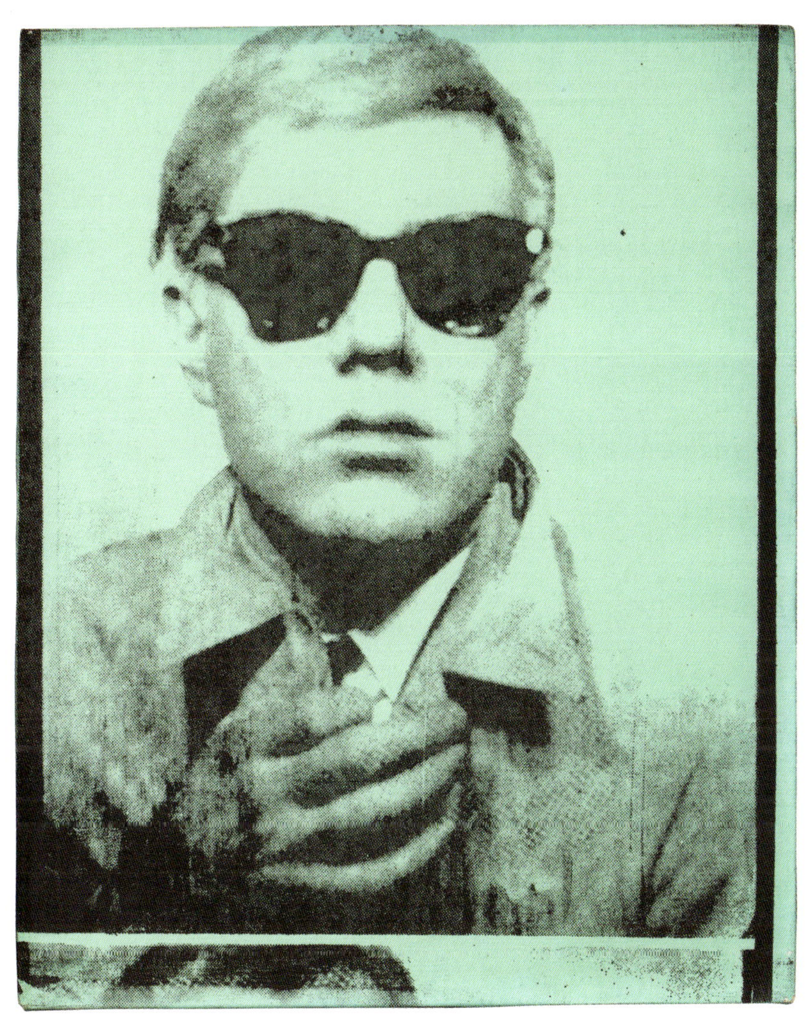

Self-Portrait 1964
Acrylic paint and screenprint
on canvas
50.8 x 41.2

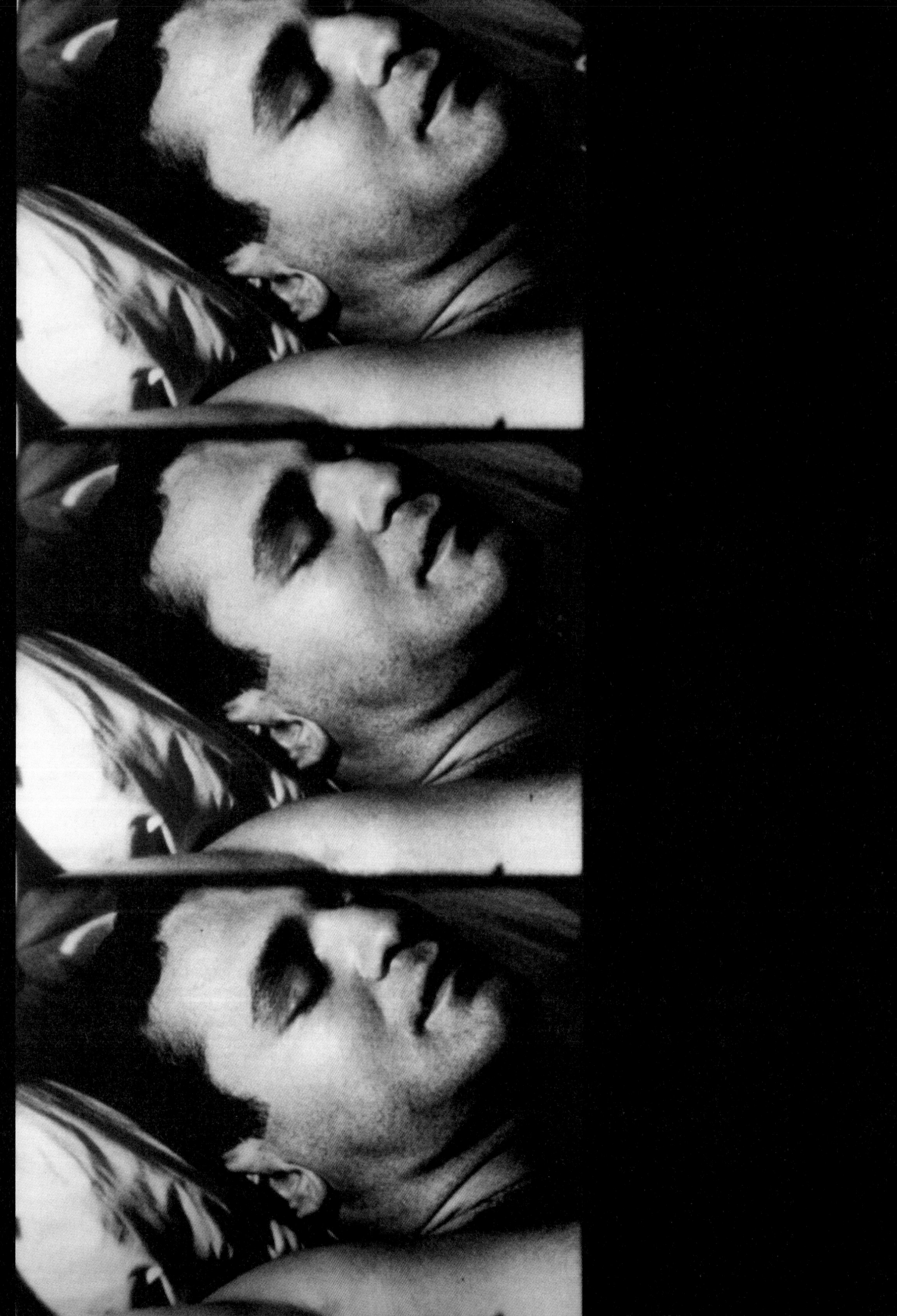

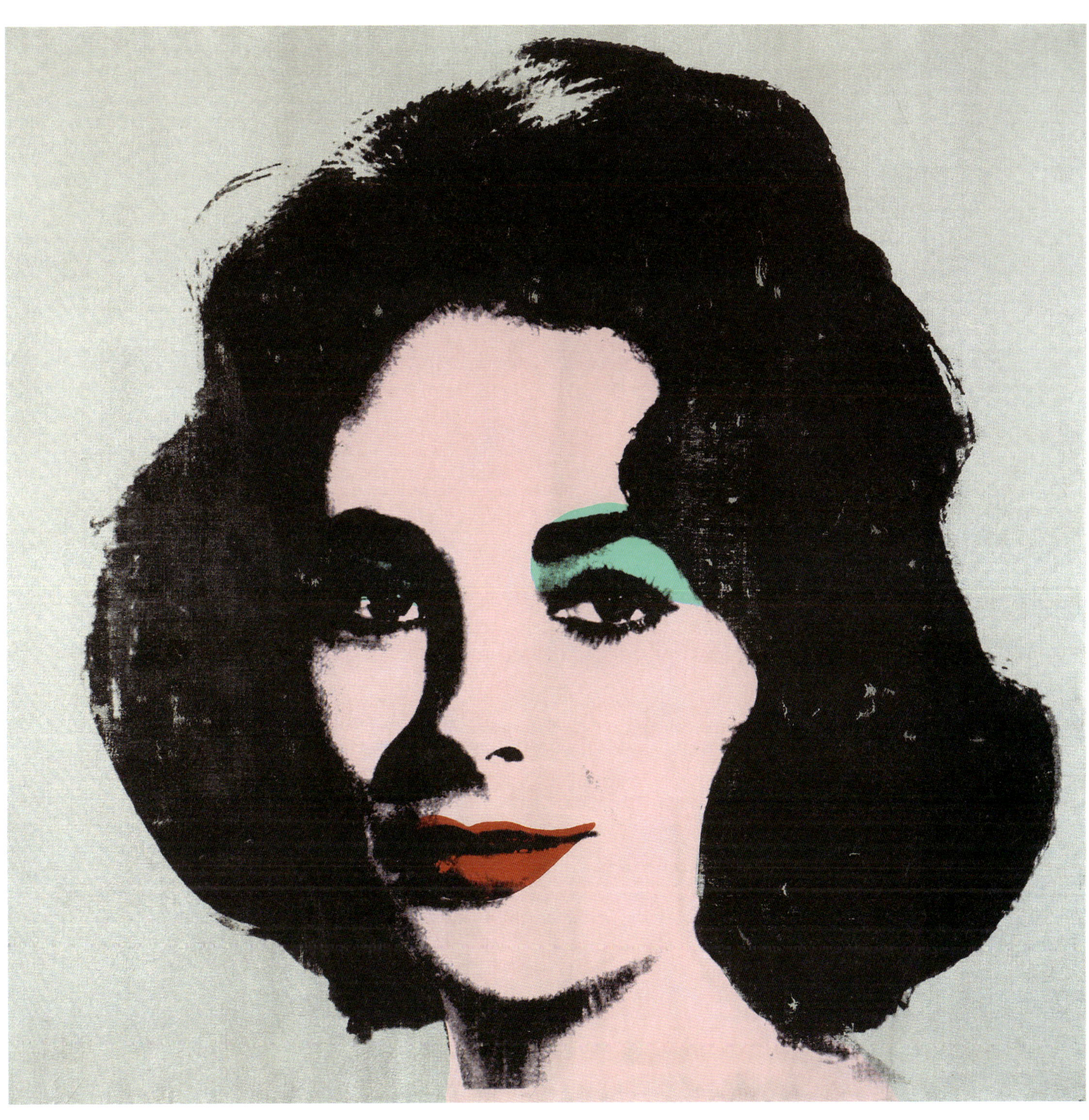

Silver Liz (aka Liz Taylor)
1963
Aluminium paint and
screenprint on canvas
104.1 x 107.9

Opposite page
Sleep 1963
16mm film, black and white,
silent
5 hours, 21 minutes at
16 frames per second

Next pages
Screen Tests 1964–6
16mm film, black and white,
silent
Approximately 4 minutes
30 seconds each

From left to right:
Jack Smith
Ann Buchanan
Lucinda Childs
Kyoko Kishida

Rufus Collins
Ivy Nicholson
Dennis Hopper
Peter Hujar
Mario Montez
Jane Holzer
Susan Sontag
Marcel Duchamp
Bob Dylan
Allen Ginsberg
(See *Exhibitied Works*
list for full details)

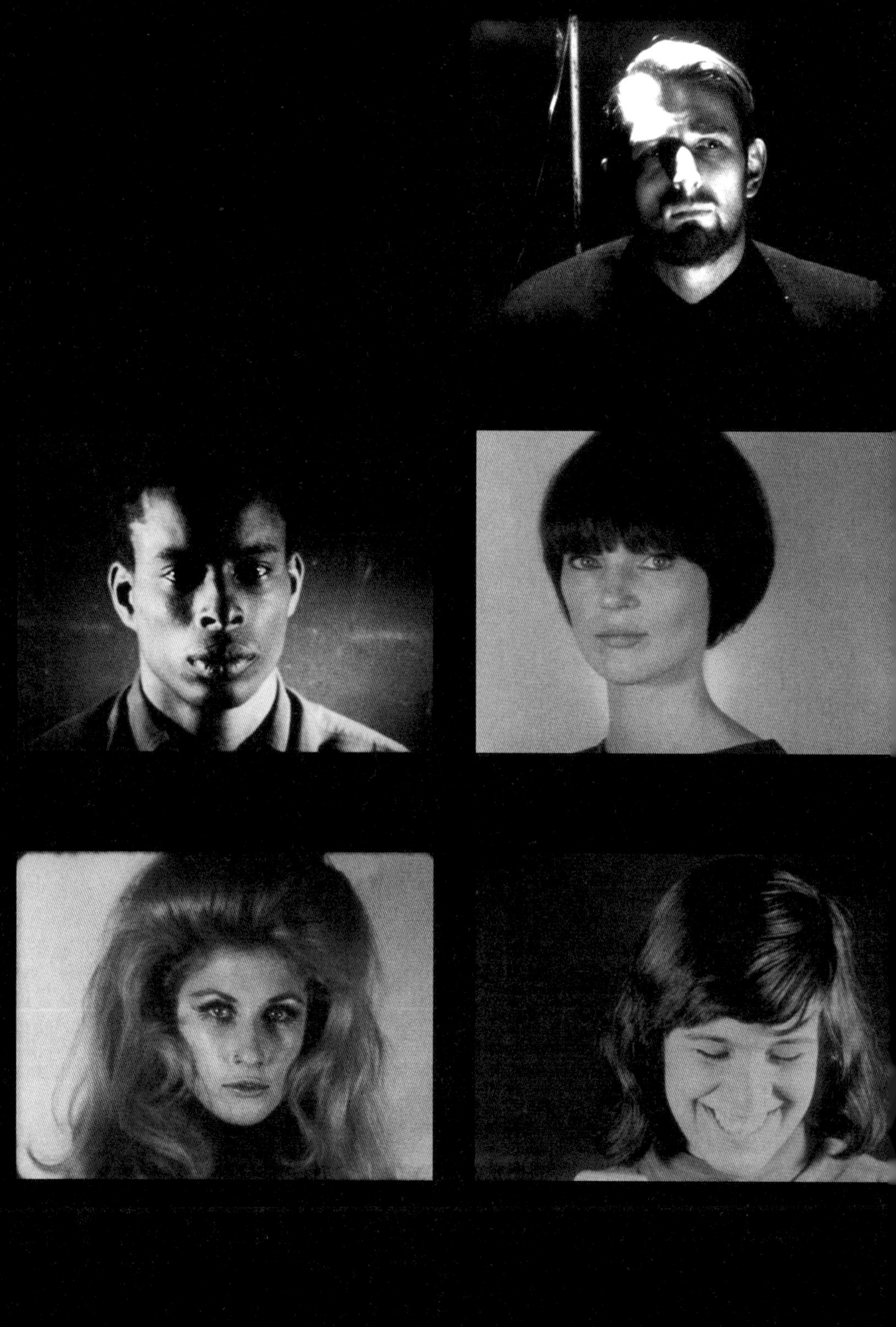

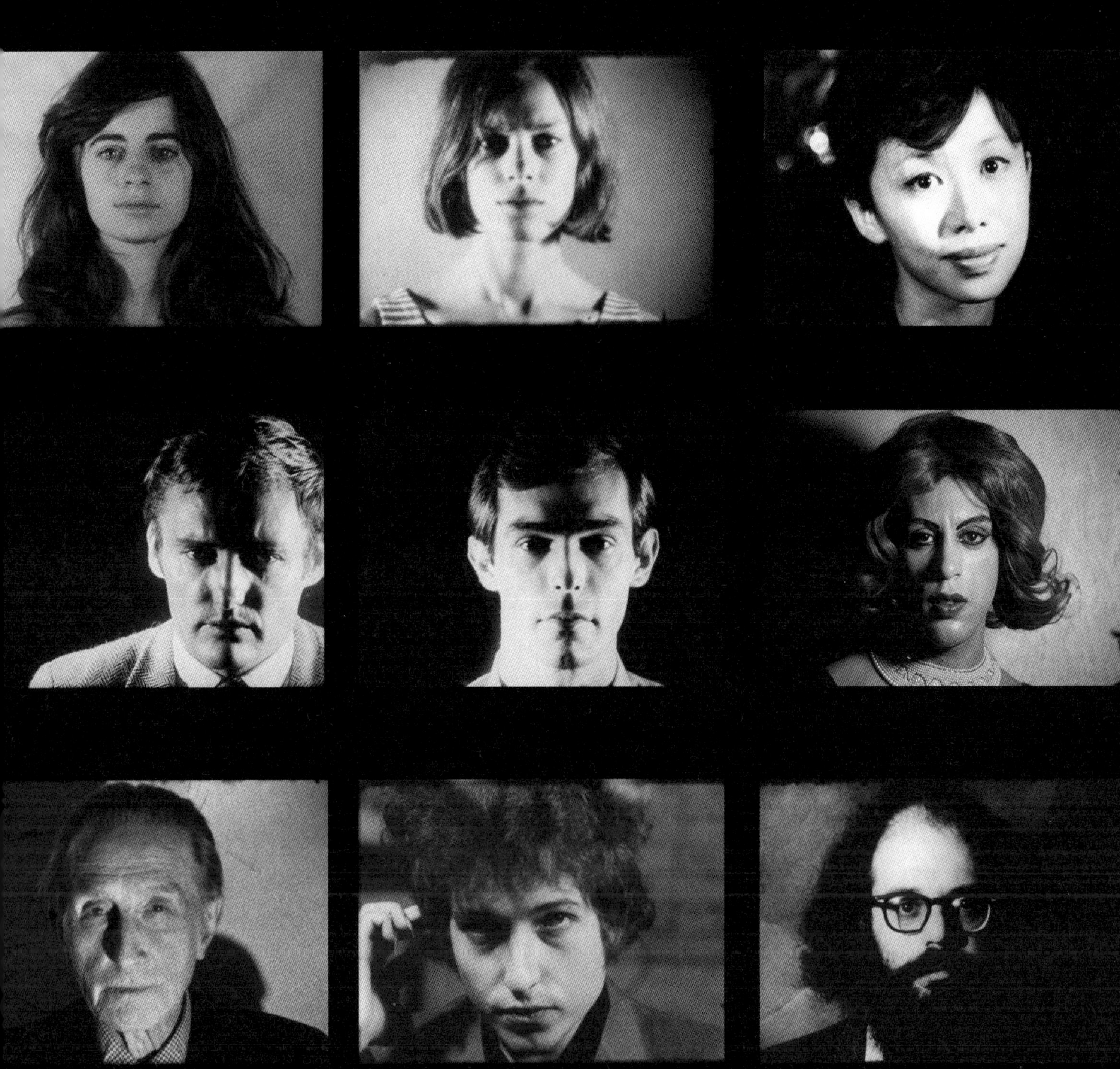

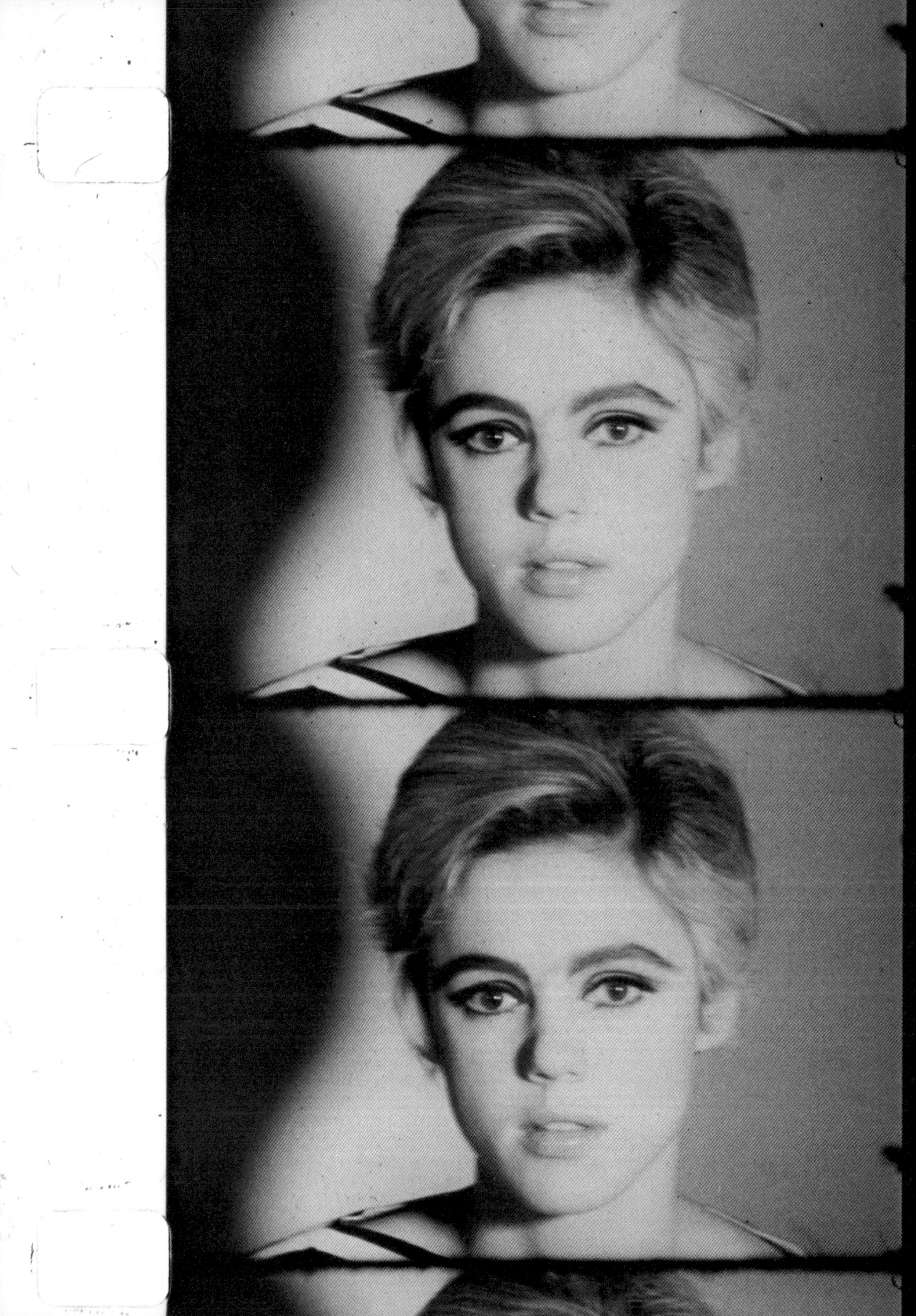

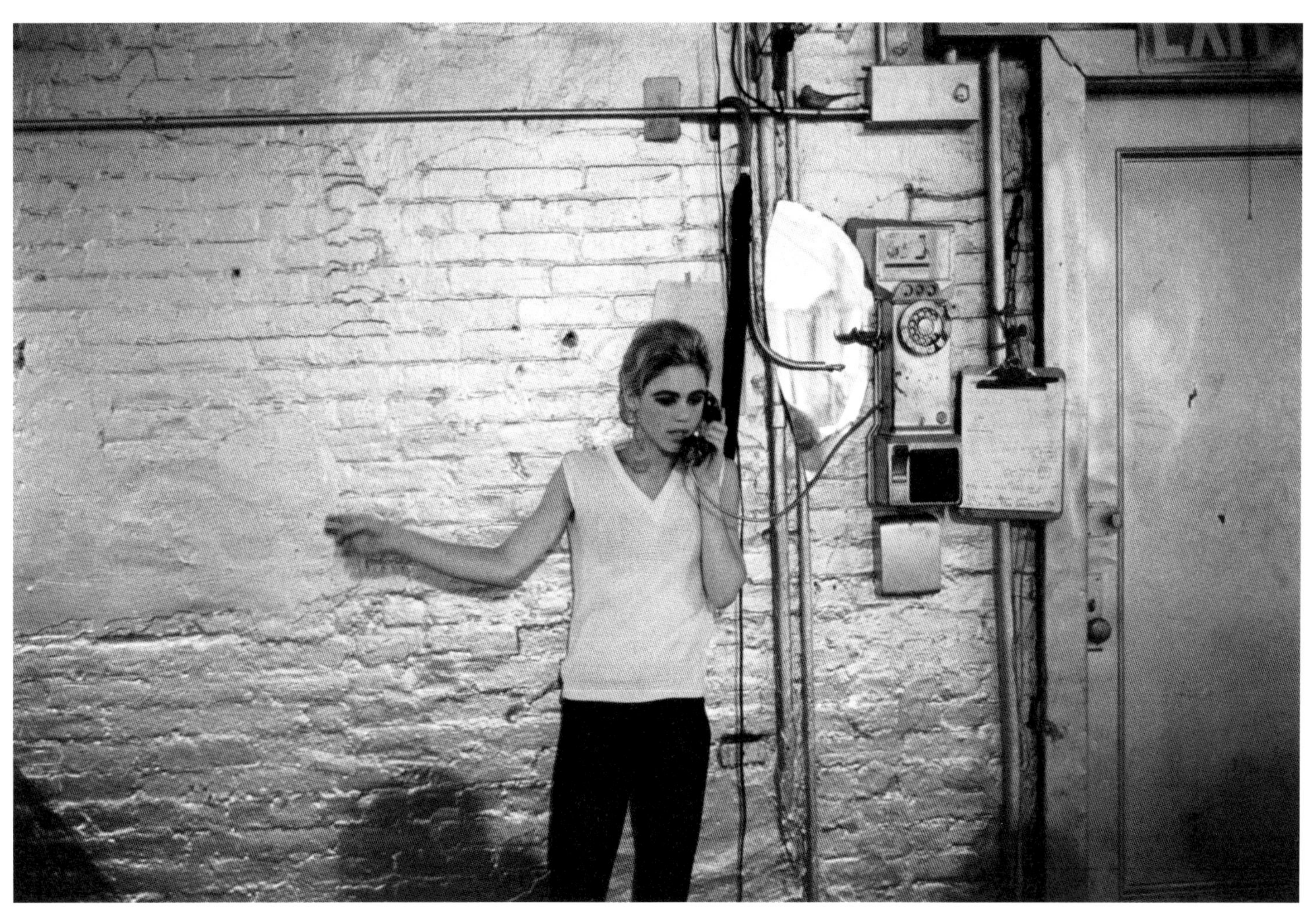

Edie Sedgwick 1965–7
Photograph by Stephen Shore
Fibre-based gelatin silver print
on paper
32.4 x 48.3

Opposite page
Screen Test: Edie Sedgwick
1965
Film; 16mm, black and white,
silent
4 minutes, 36 seconds

Next pages
Andy Warhol & Lou Reed
1965–7

Paul Jasmine & Gino Piserchio
1965–7

*Edie Sedgwick & Ingrid
Superstar* 1965–7

*Edie Sedgwick, Andy
Warhol, unidentified guests*
1965–7

Photographs by
Stephen Shore
Fibre-based gelatin silver
prints on paper
32.4 x 48.3

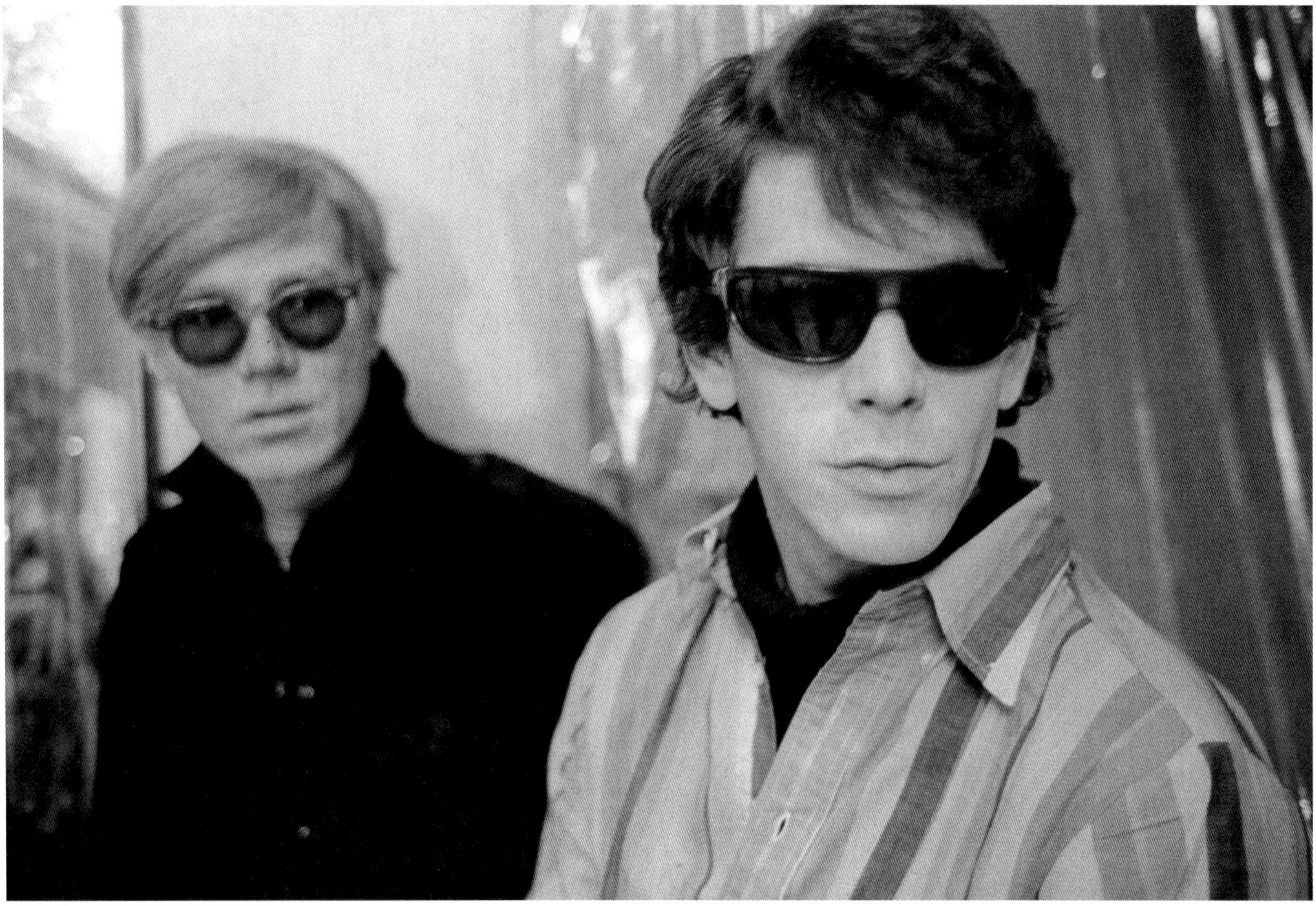

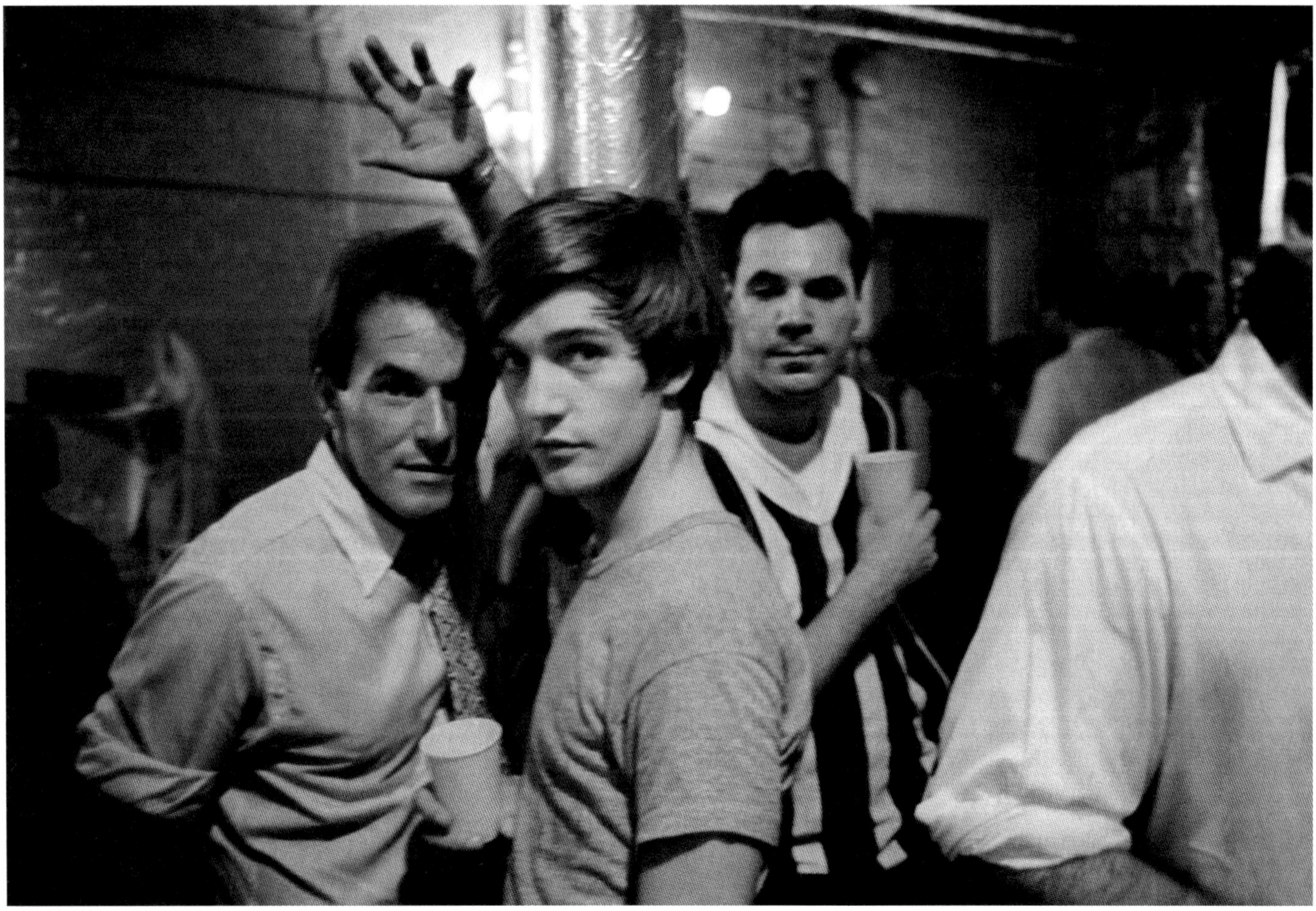

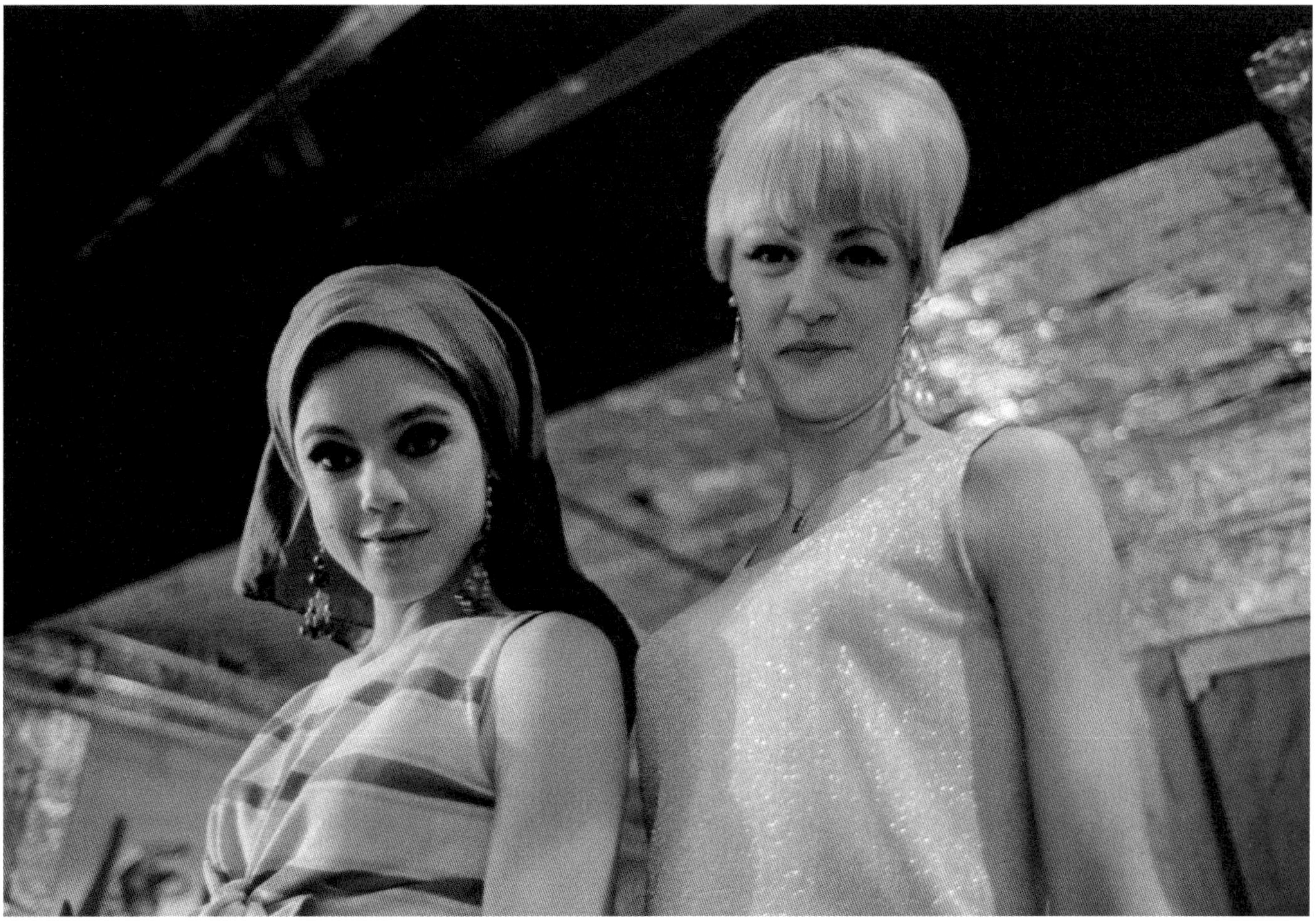

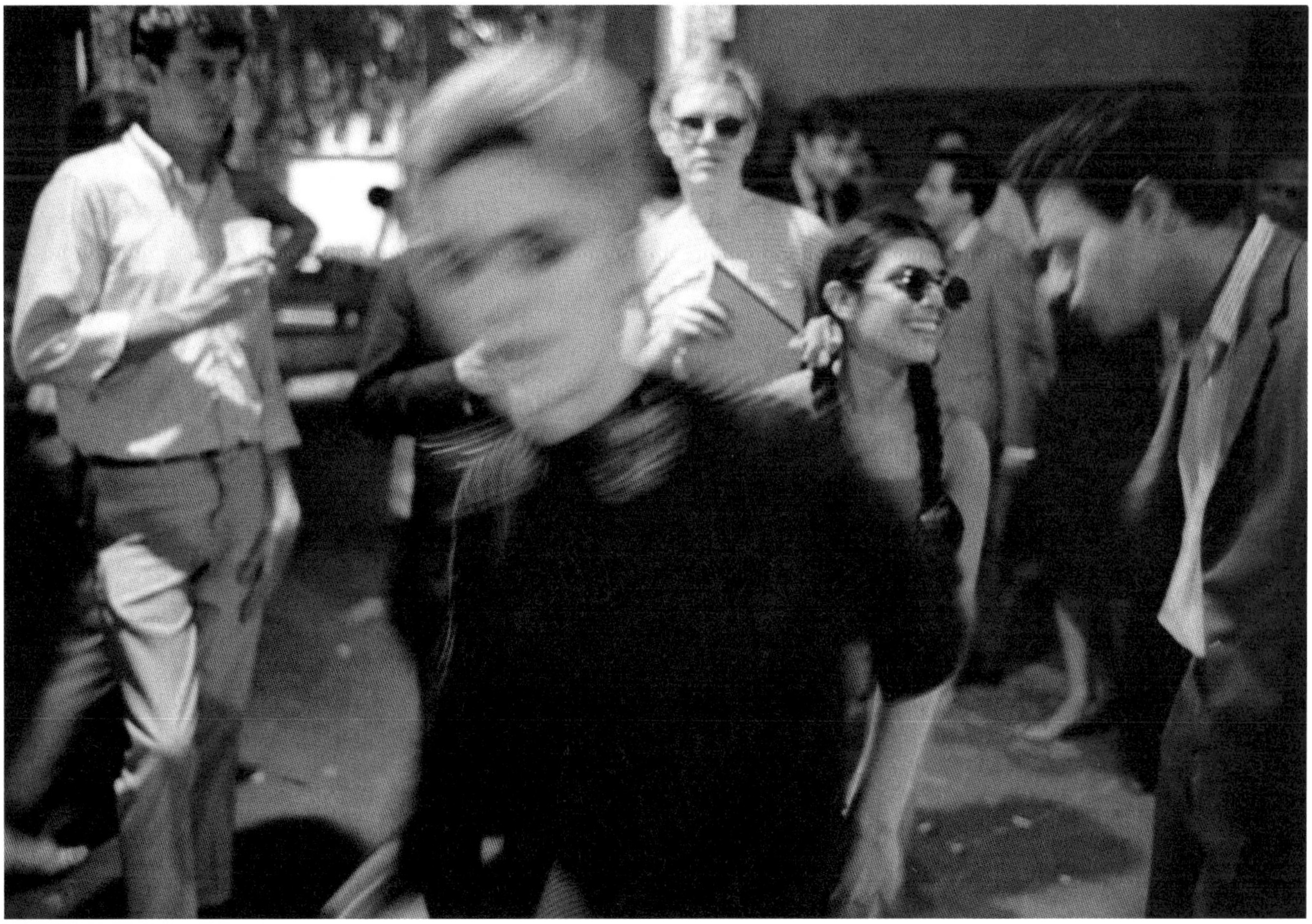

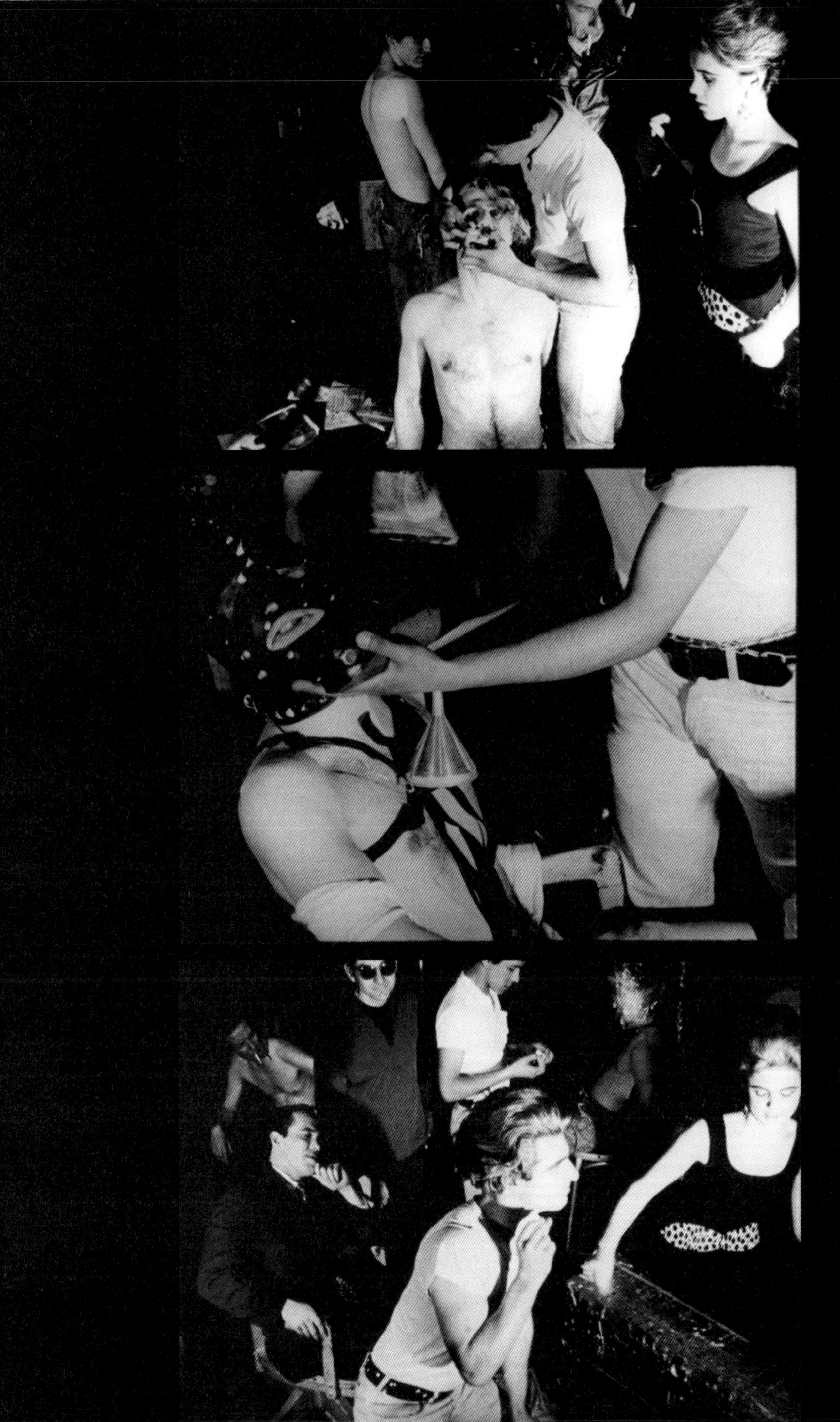

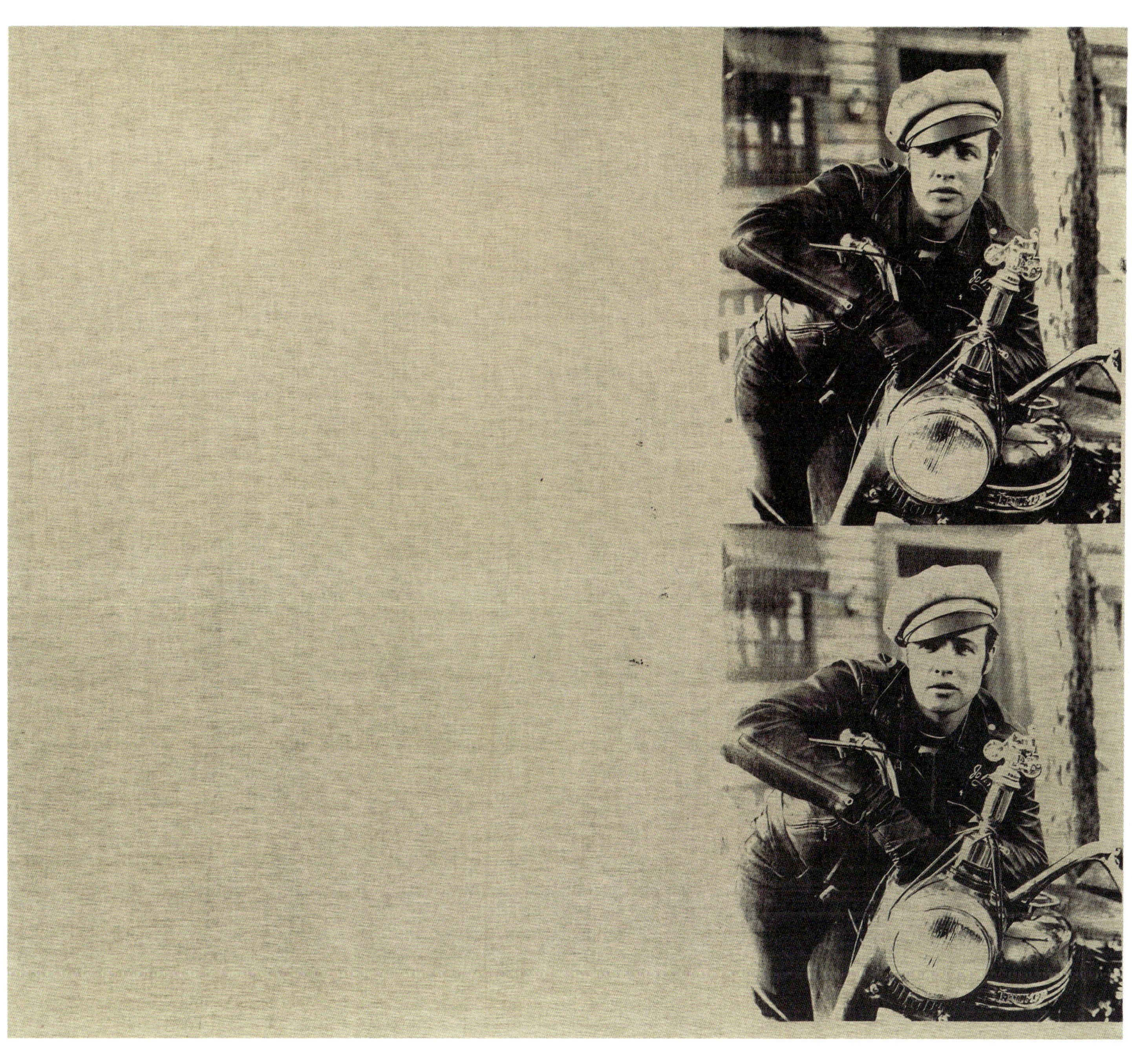

Vinyl 1965
16mm film, black and white, sound
67 minutes

Double Marlon 1966
Screenprint on unprimed canvas
213.4 x 243

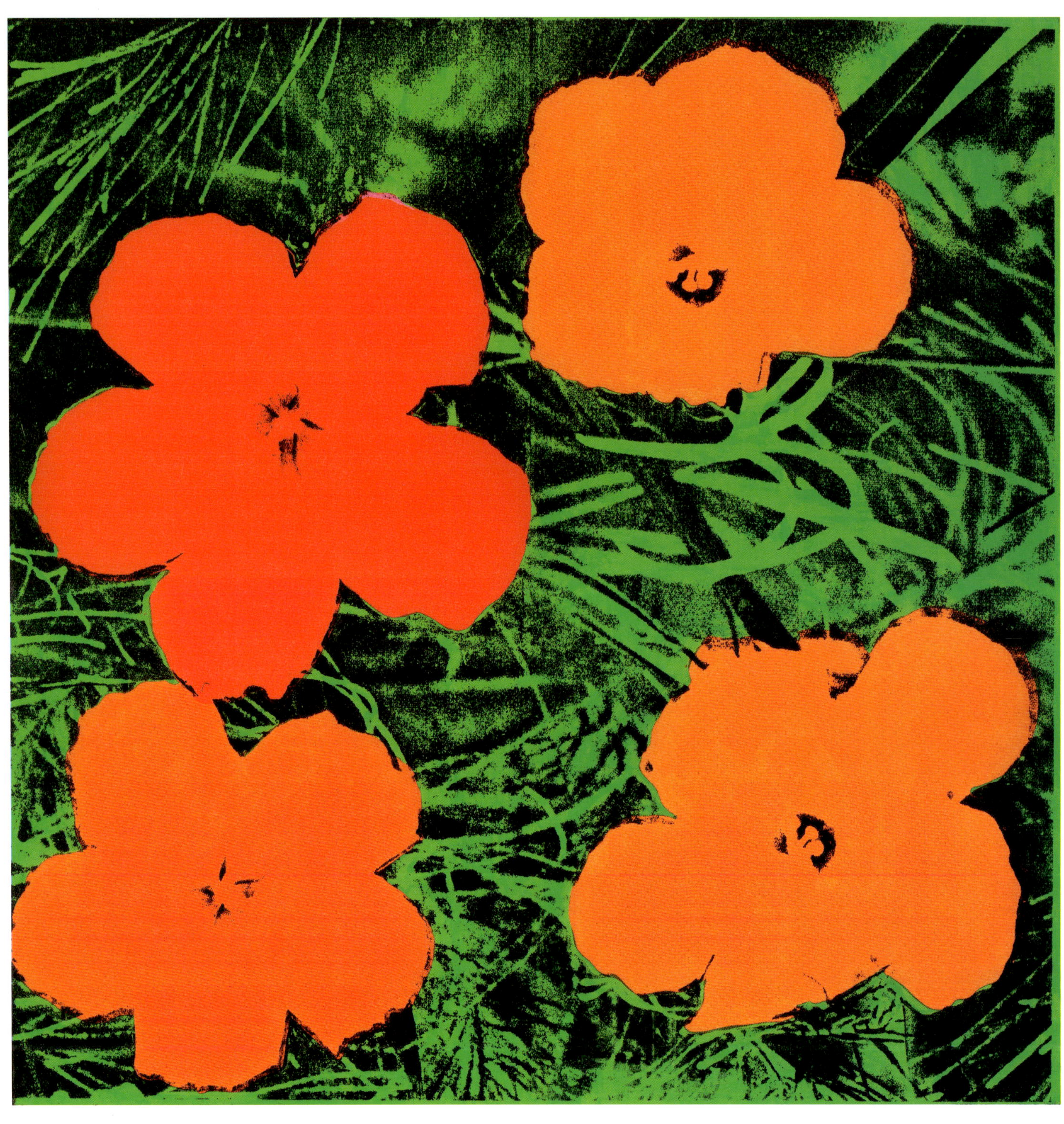

Flowers 1964
Fluorescent paint and
screenprint on canvas
208.3 x 208.3

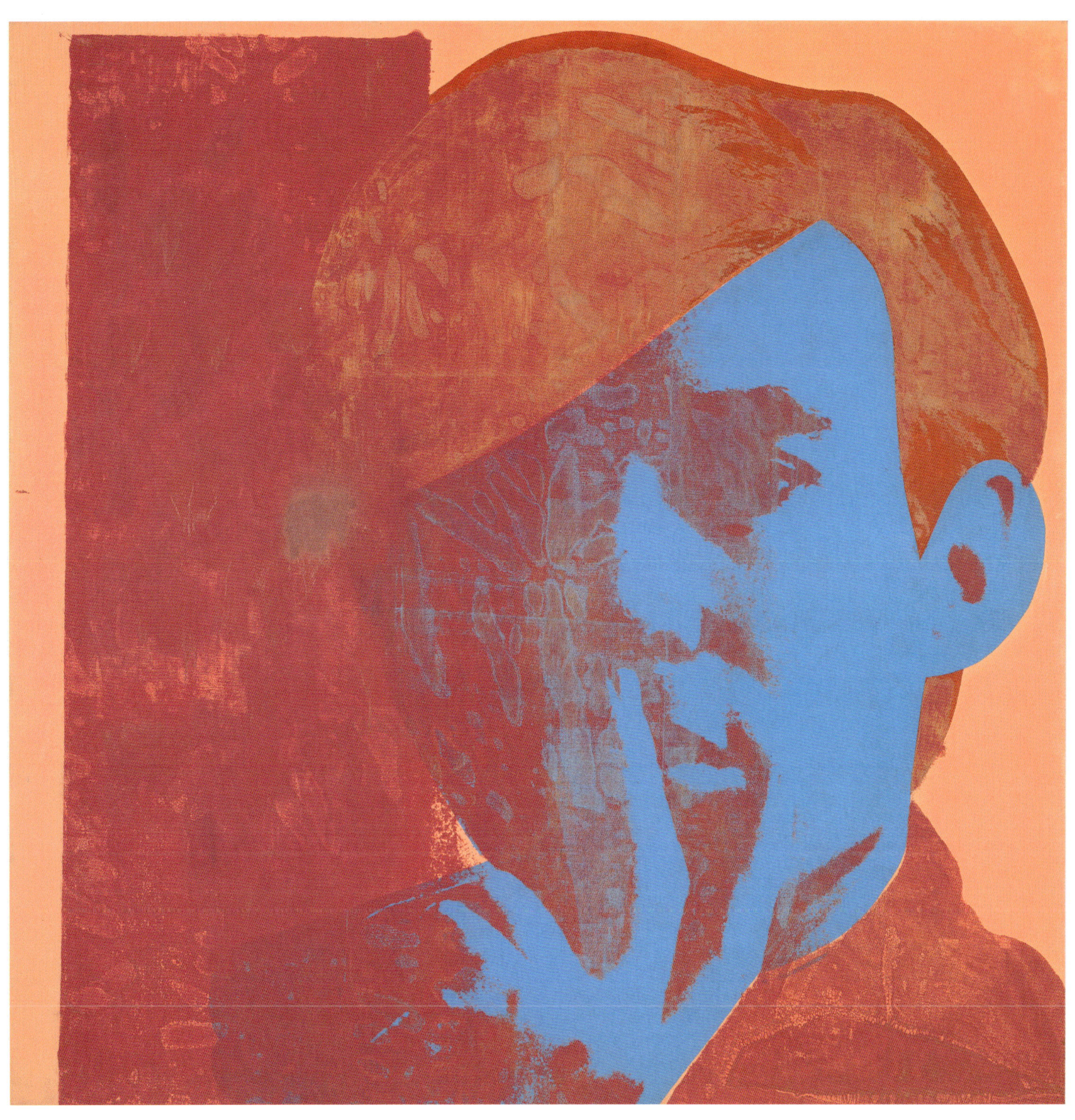

Self-Portrait 1967
Acrylic paint and screenprint
on canvas
183.2 x 183.2

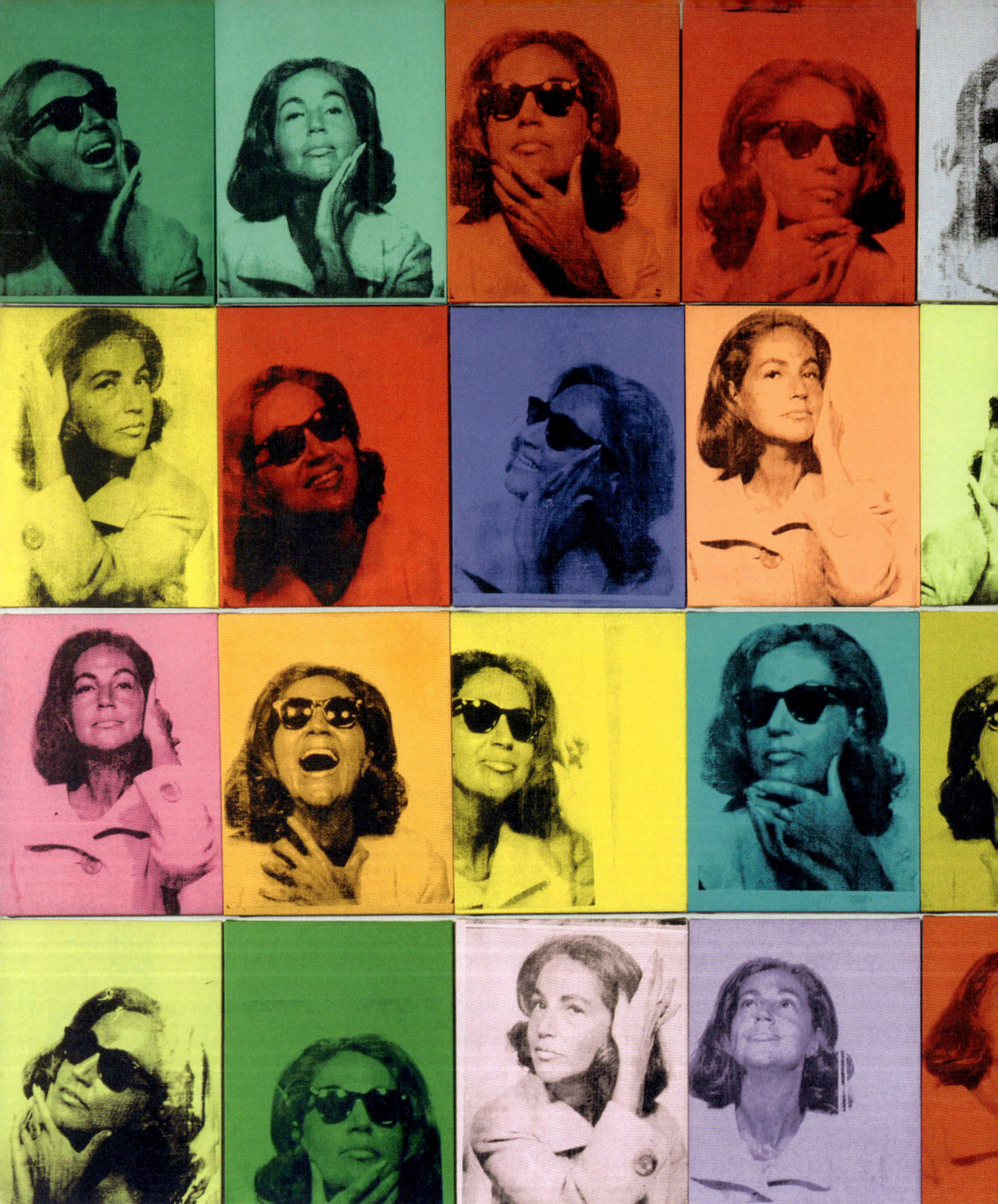

Ethel Scull 36 Times 1963
Acrylic paint and screenprint
on canvas
203.2 x 365.8

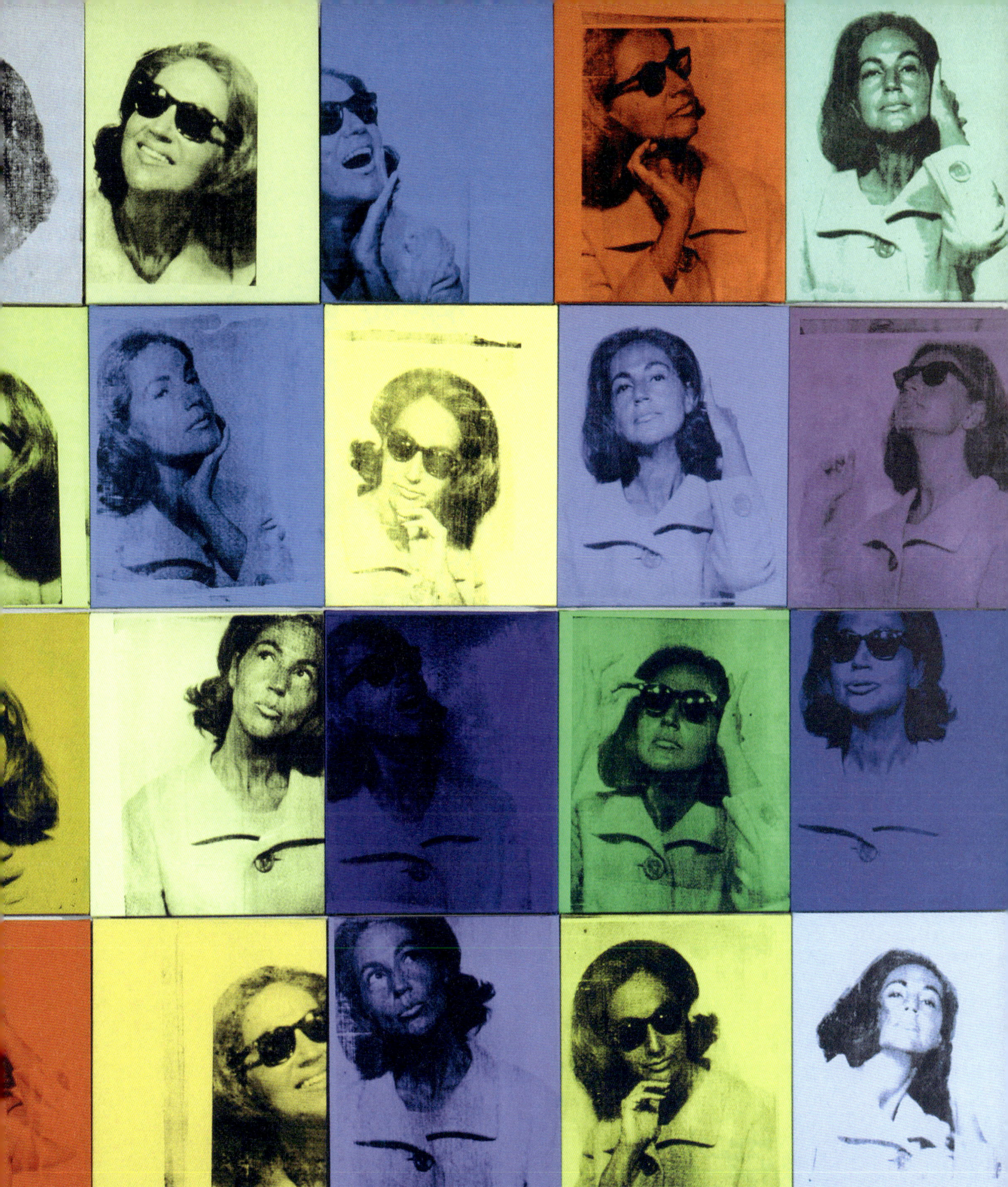

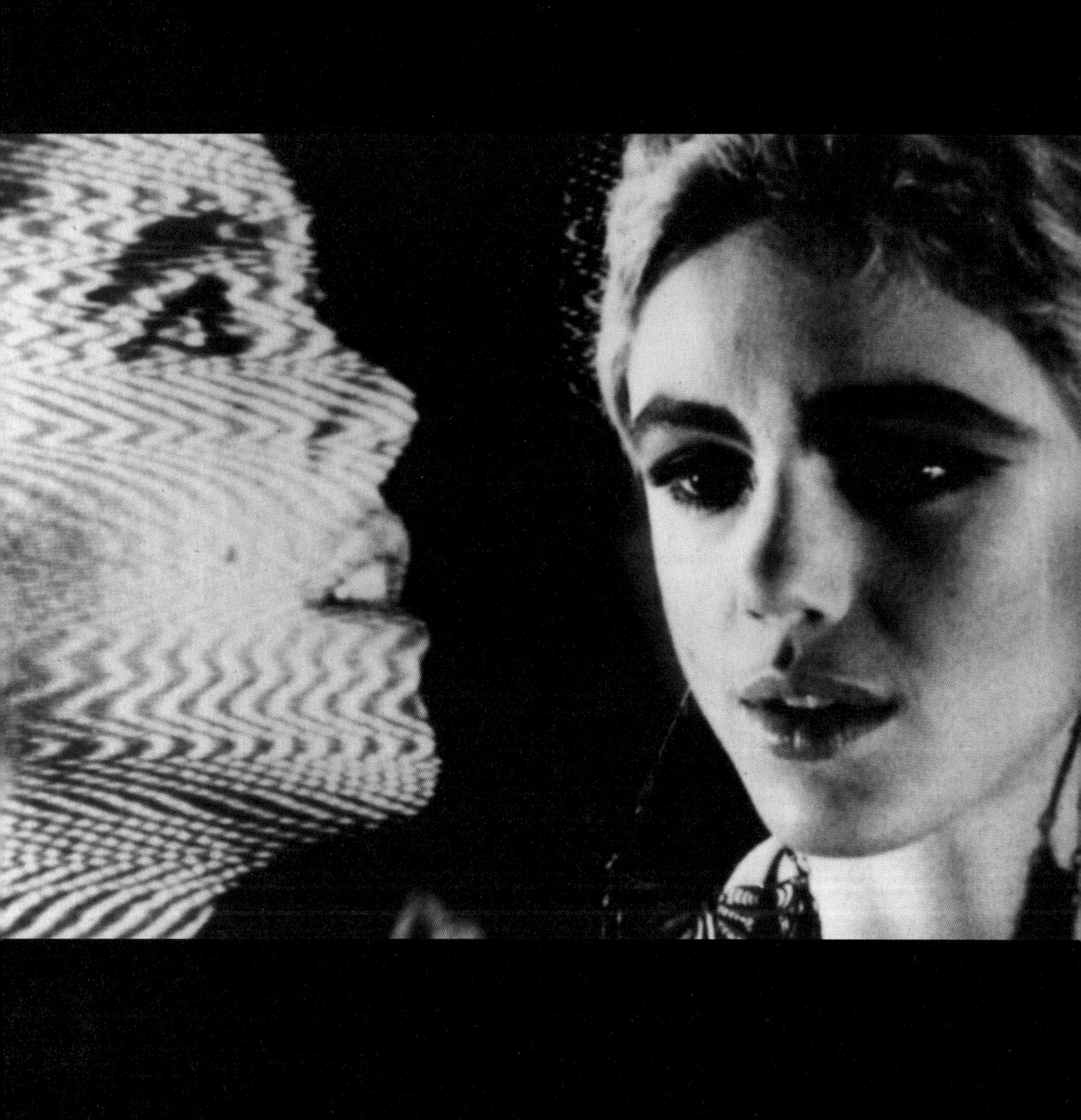

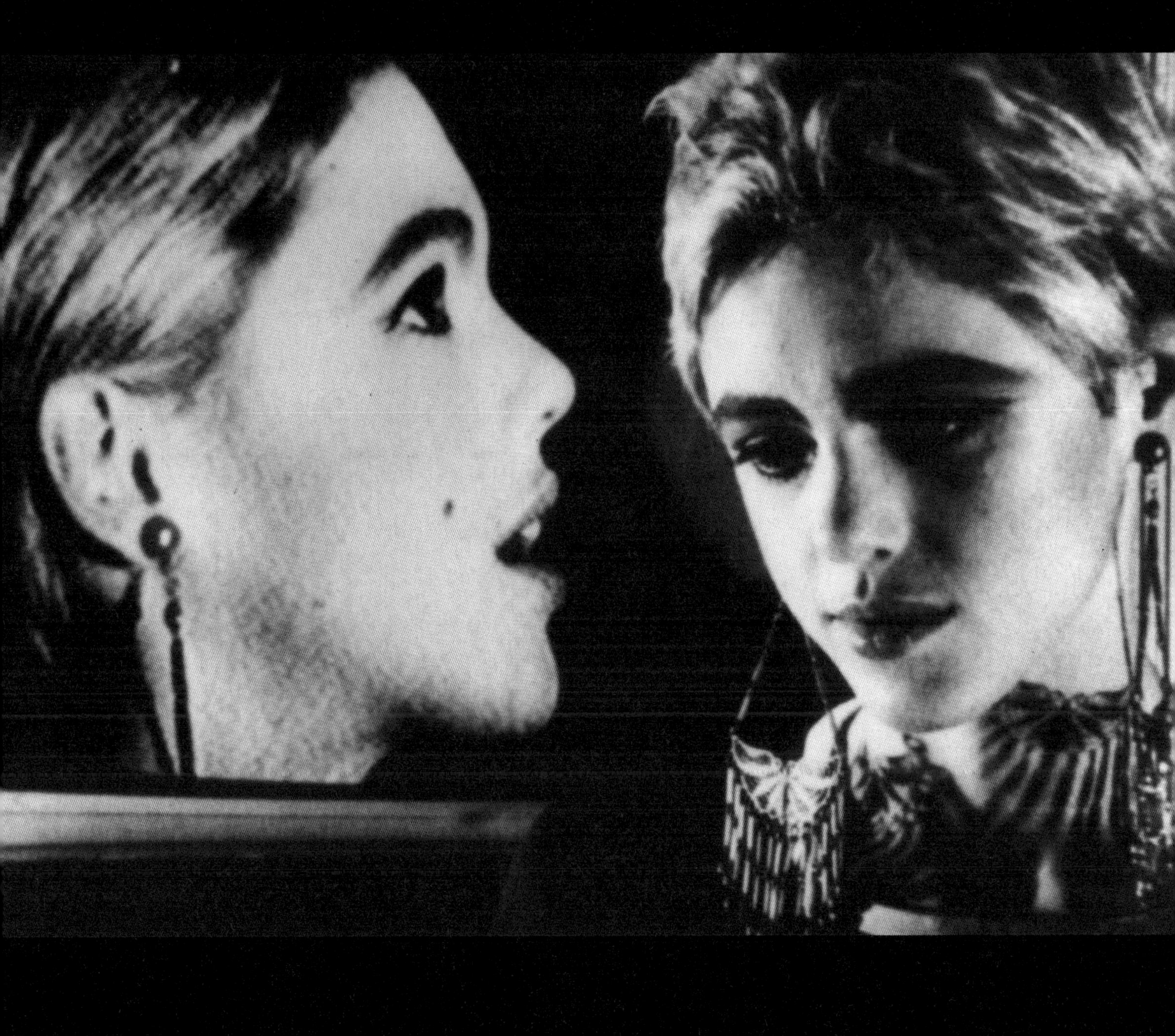

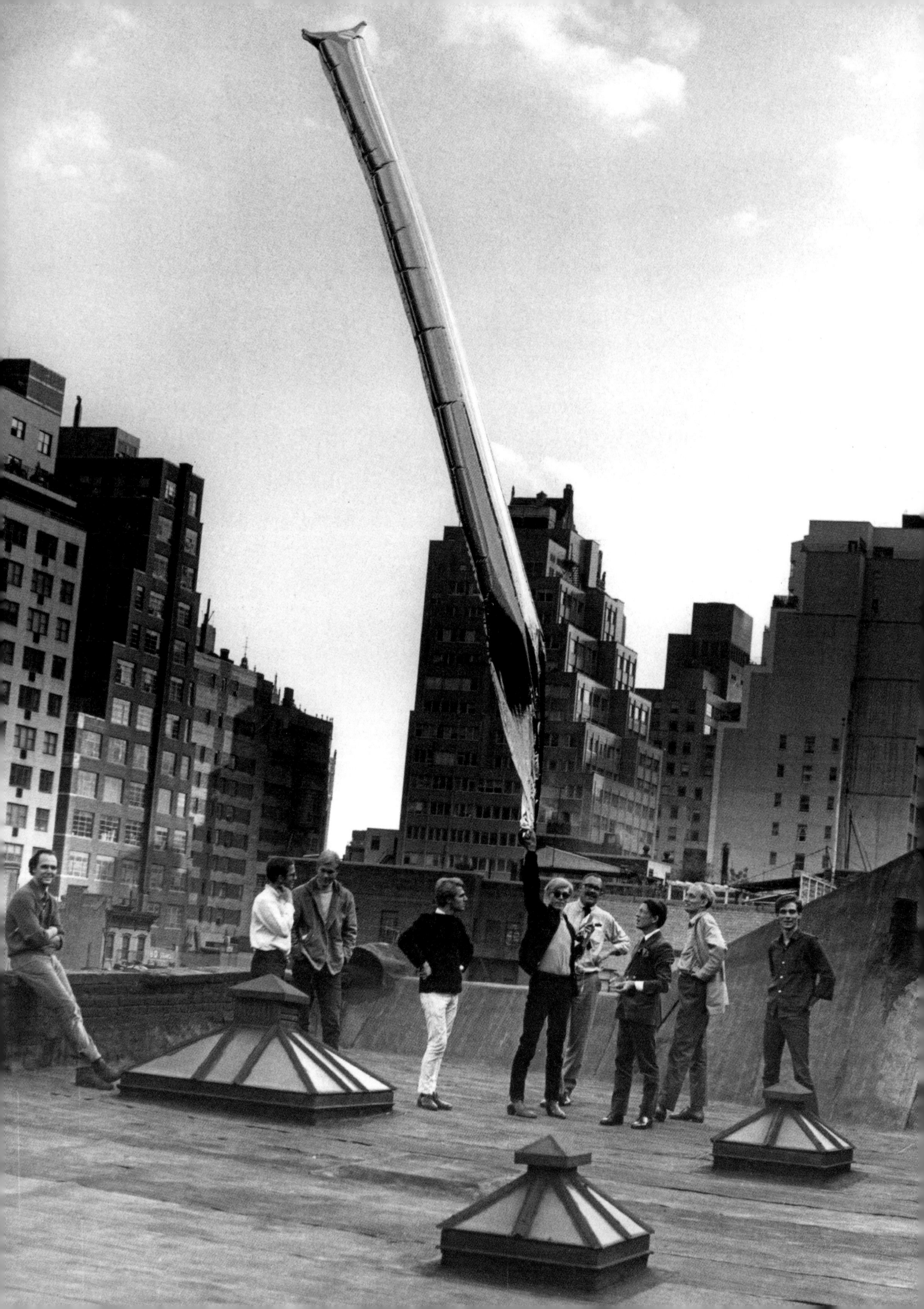

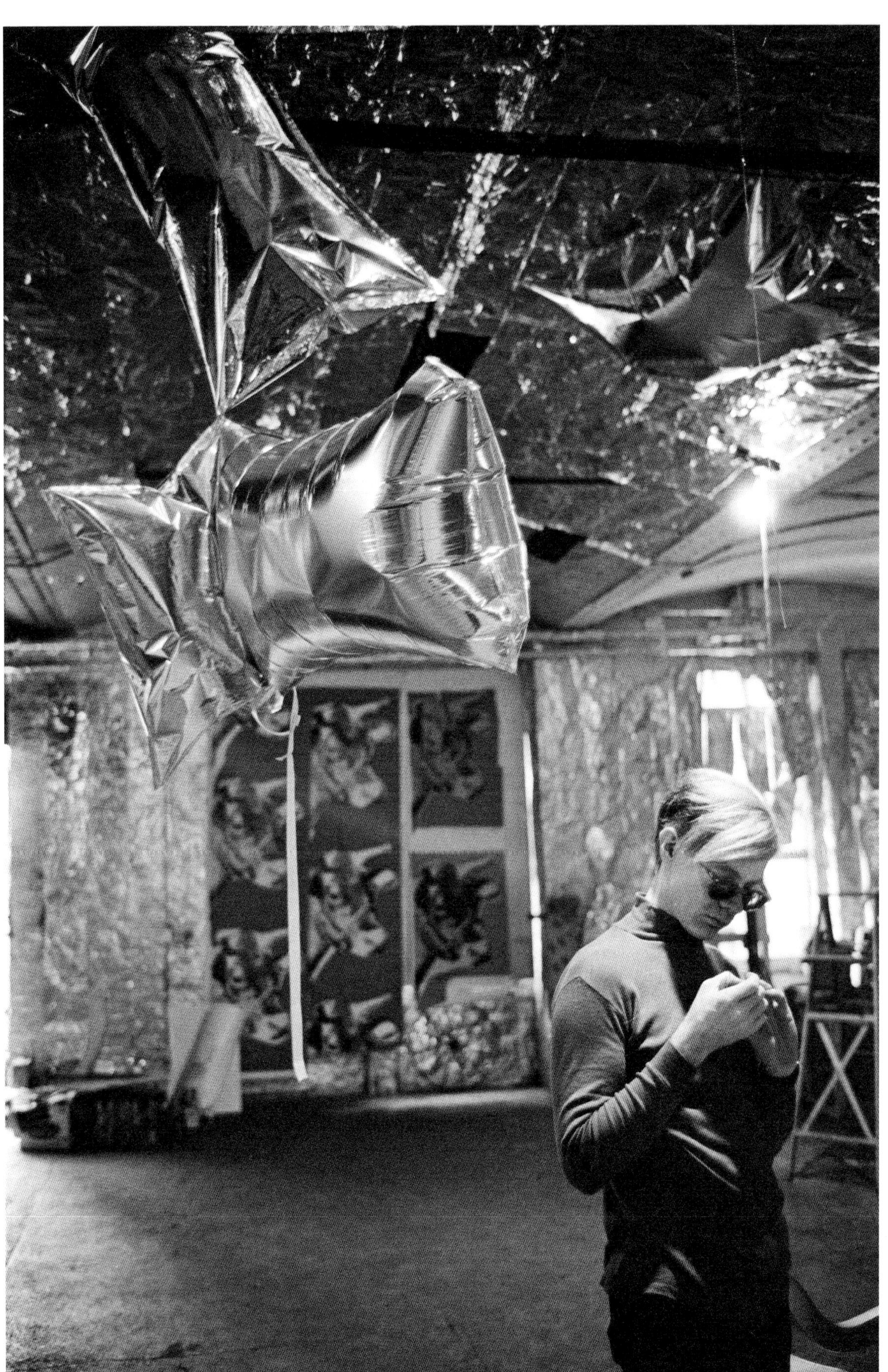

Previous pages
Outer and Inner Space 1965
16mm film, black and white,
sound
66 minutes (33 minutes in
double screen)

This page
*Andy Warhol with Silver
Clouds, the Factory,
New York, New York*
1965–7
Photo by Stephen Shore
Black and white photograph
48.3 x 31.8

Opposite page
*Andy Warhol with 'Infinite
Sculpture' on the roof of the
Factory on E47th St, New
York* 1965
Photo by Billy Name

Following pages
Chelsea Girls 1966
16mm film, black and white
and colour, sound
204 minutes in double screen

Pages 142–3
The Velvet Underground
performing on stage during
Andy Warhol's Exploding
Plastic Inevitable 1966
Photo by Steven Schapiro

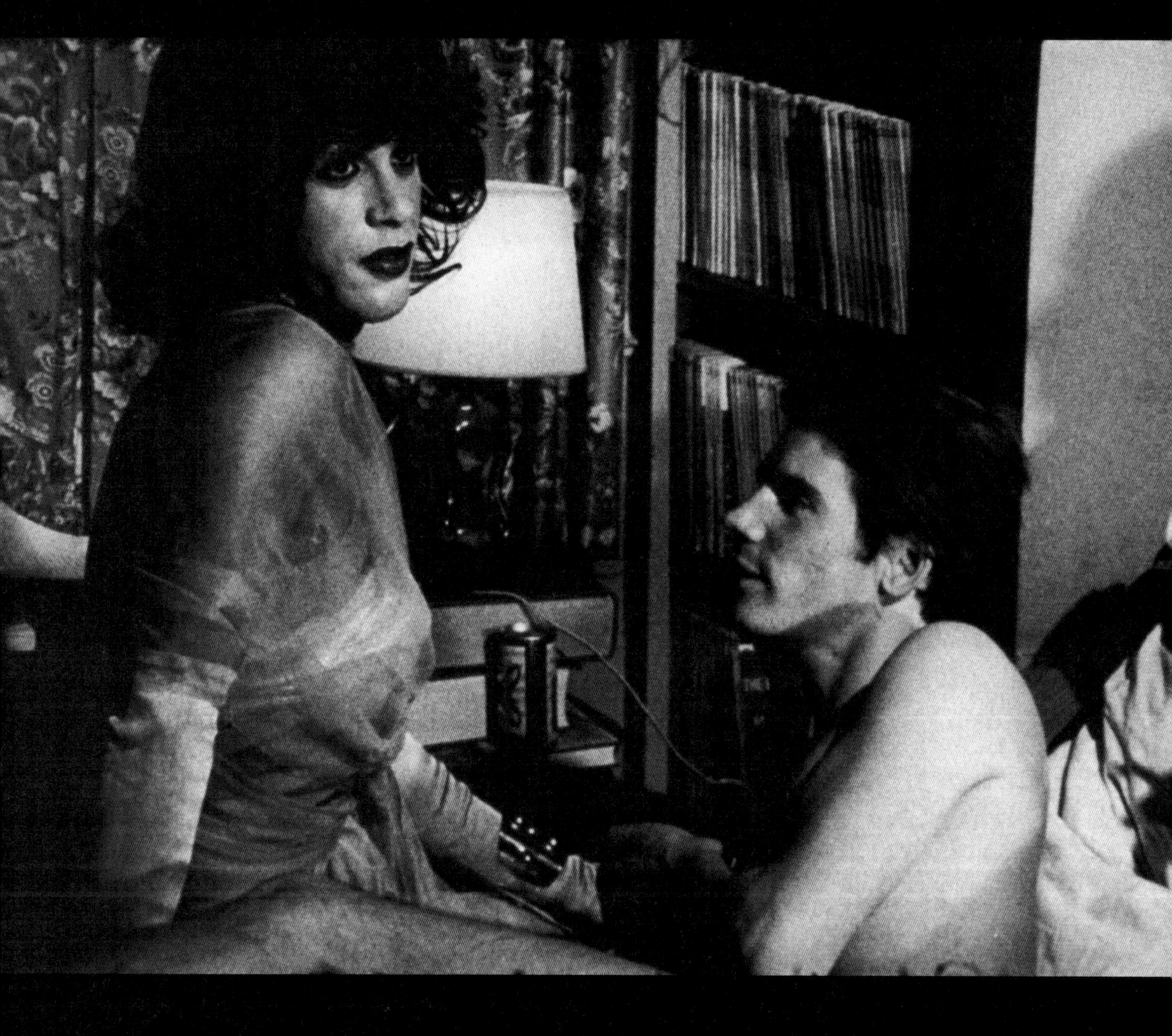

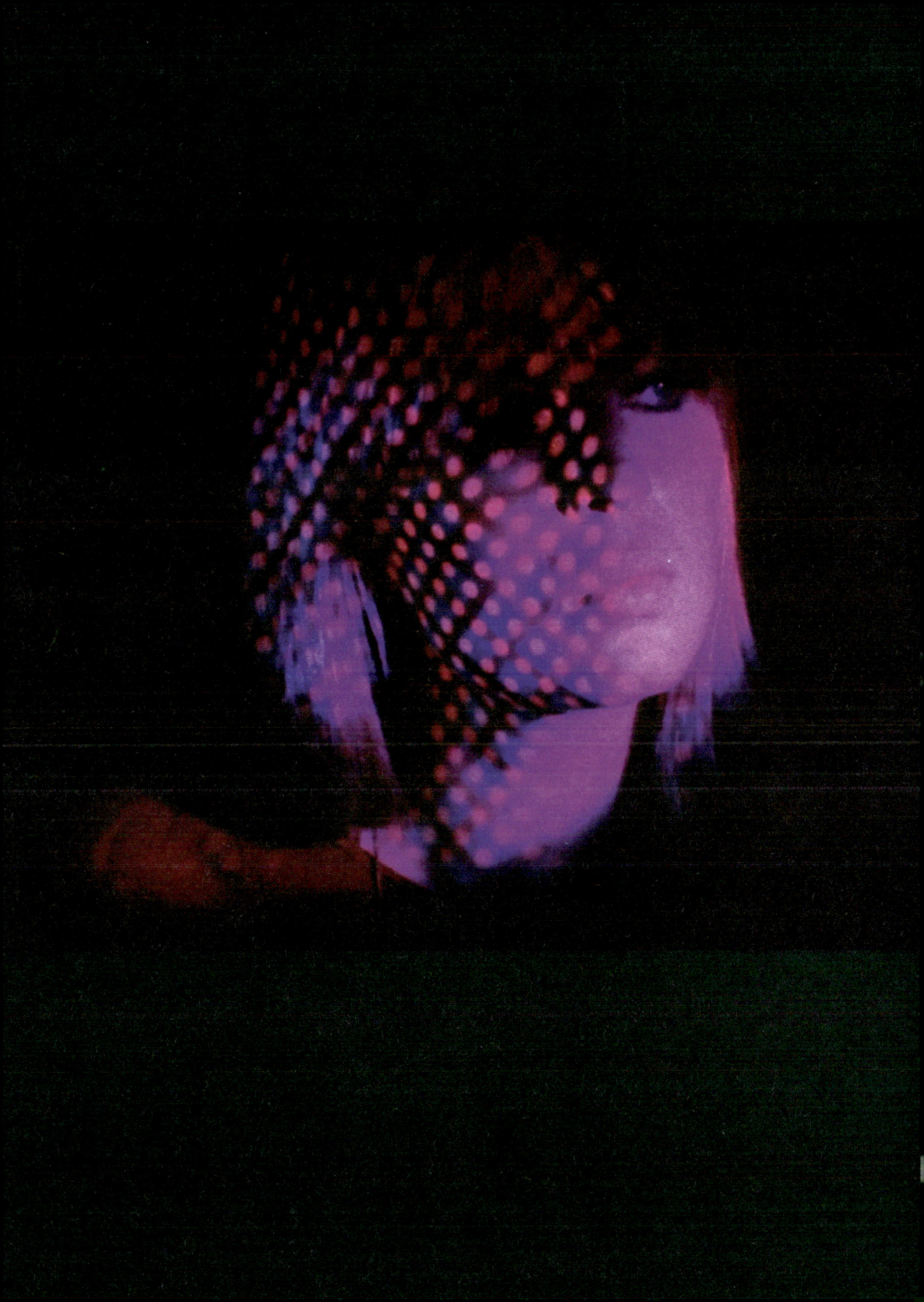

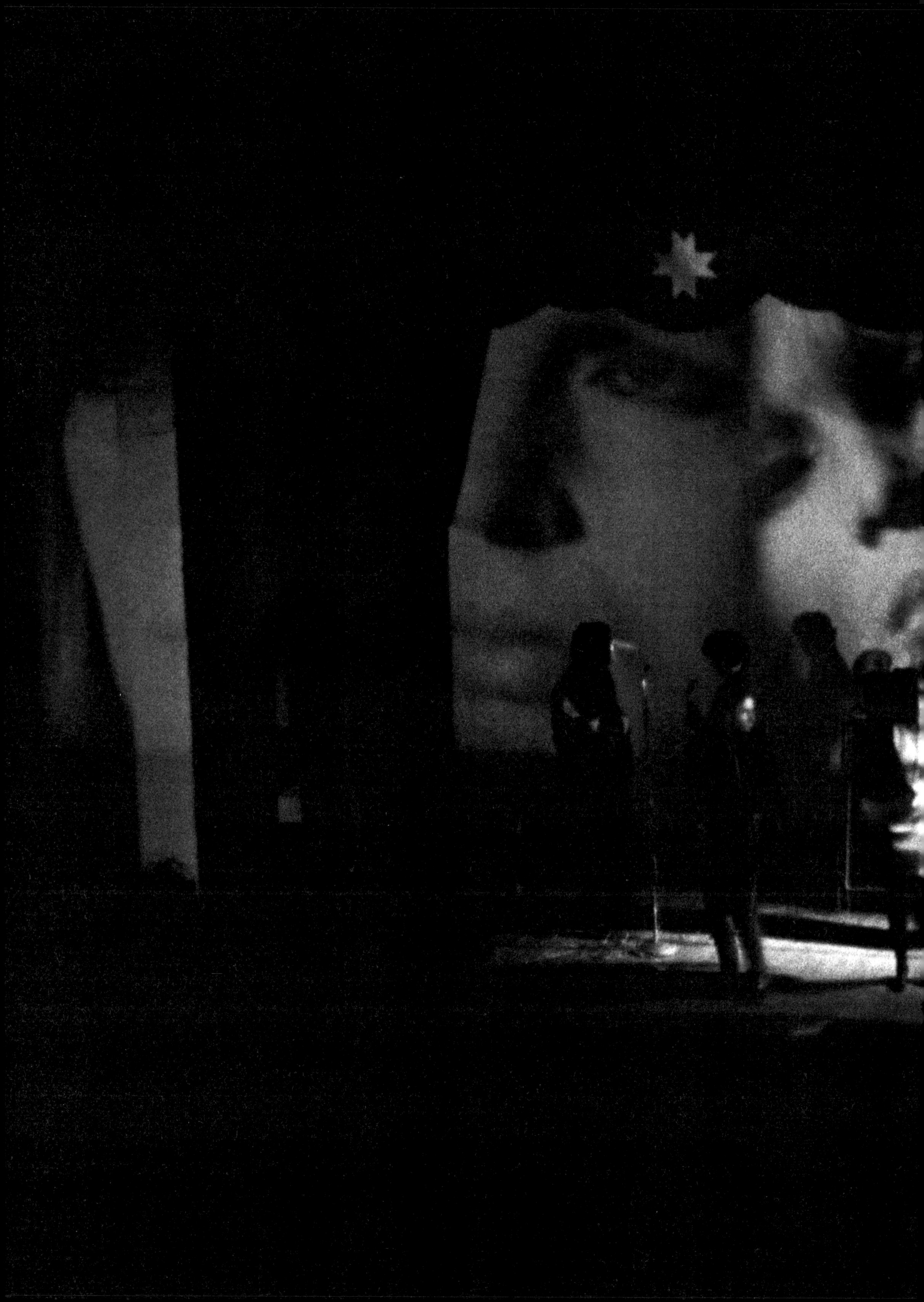

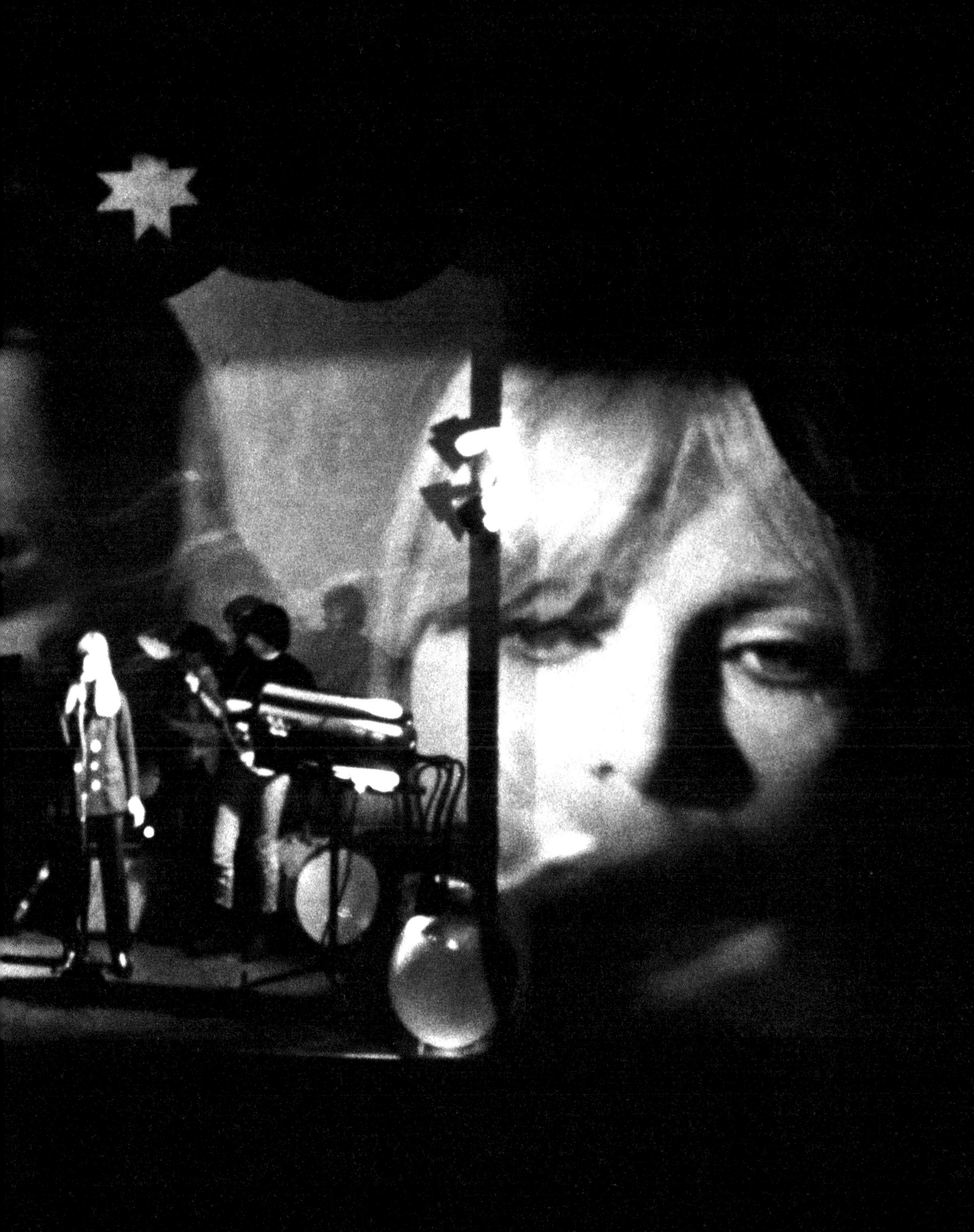

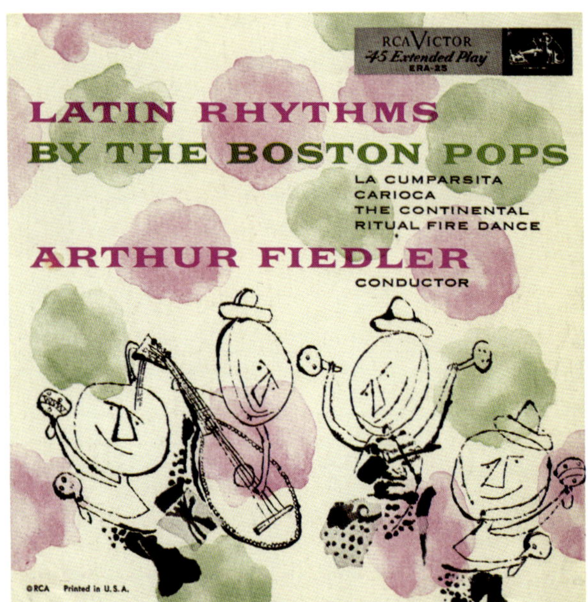

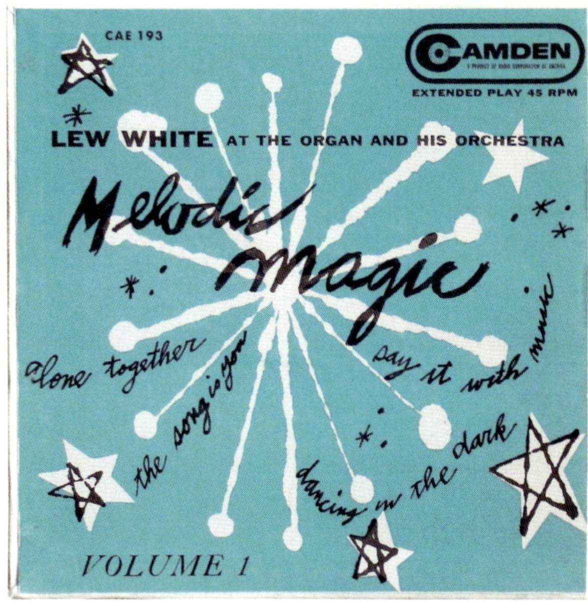

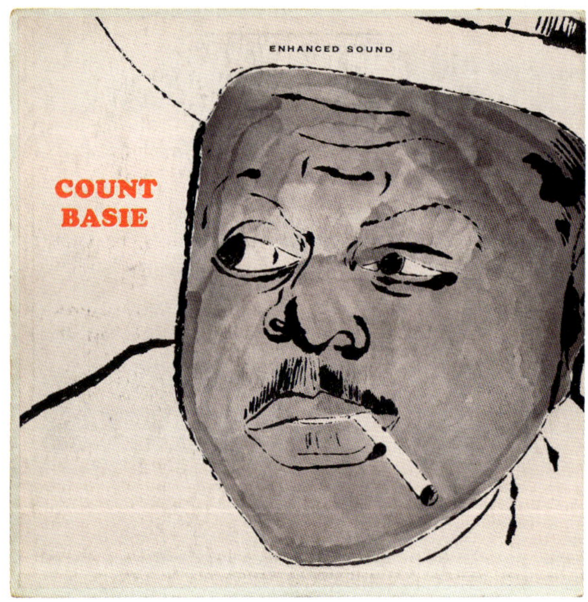

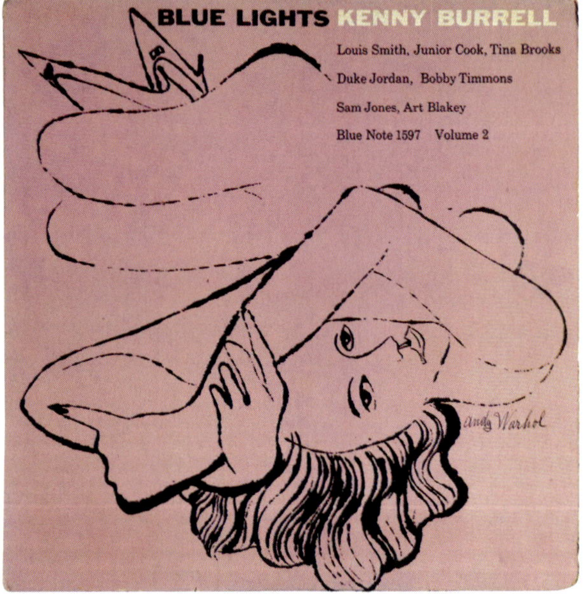

Record covers by
Andy Warhol

The Boston Pops
Latin Rhythms c.1952

Lew White and His Orchestra
Melodic Magic Vol.1 1953

Count Basie
Count Basie 1955

Kenny Burrell
Blue Lights Vol.2 1958

The Velvet Underground
& Nico
*The Velvet Underground
& Nico* 1967

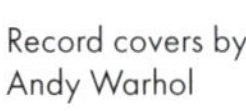

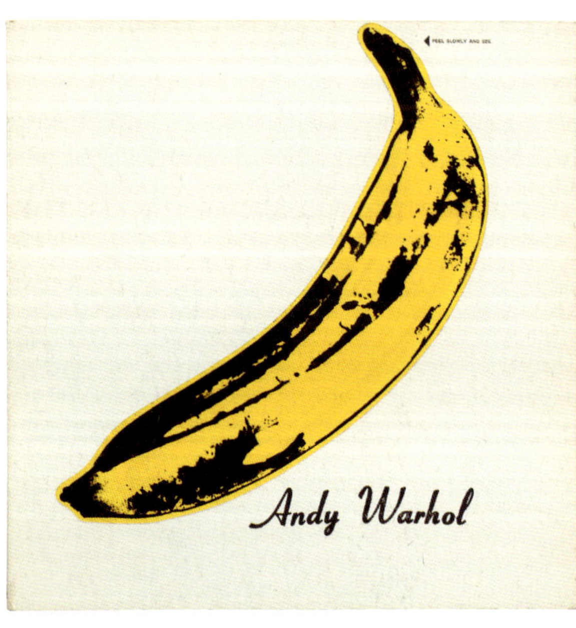

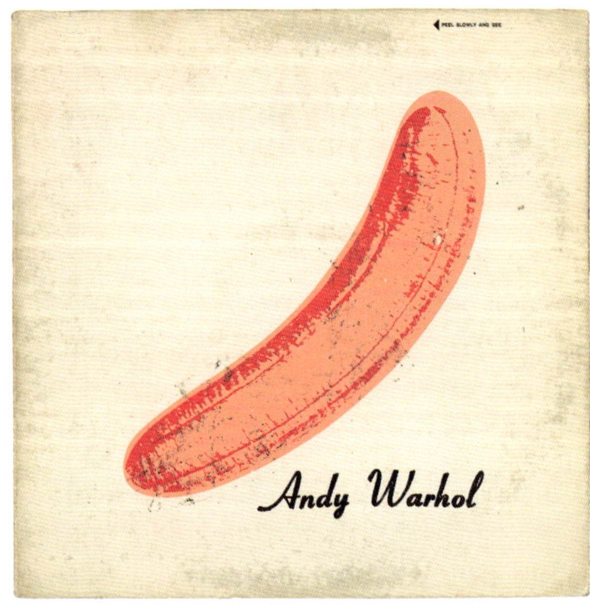

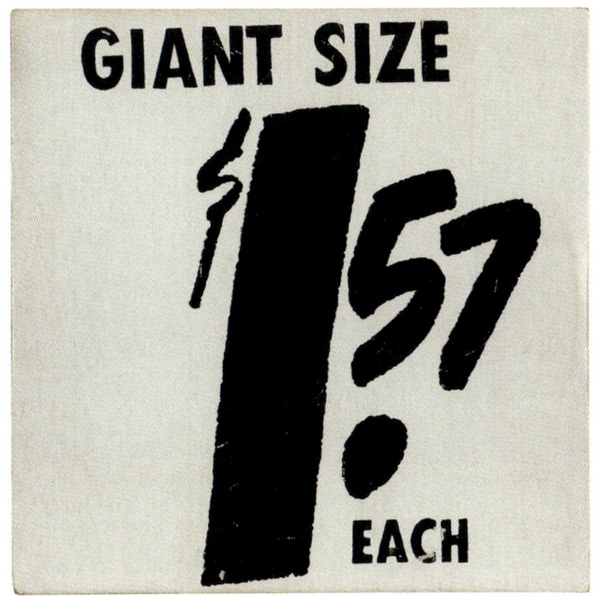

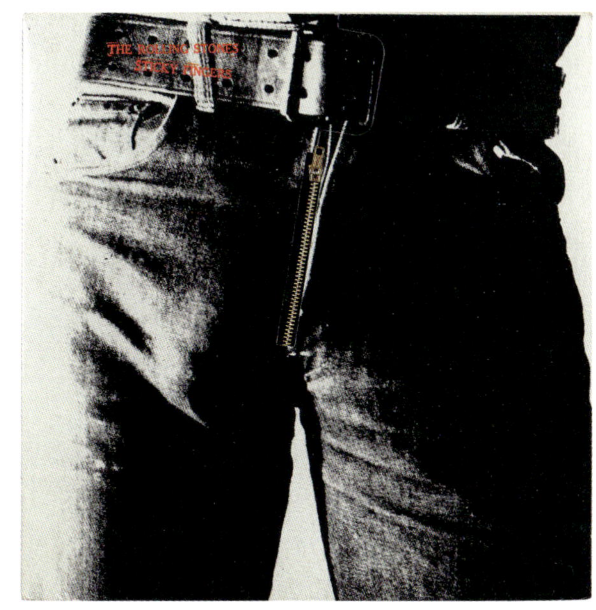

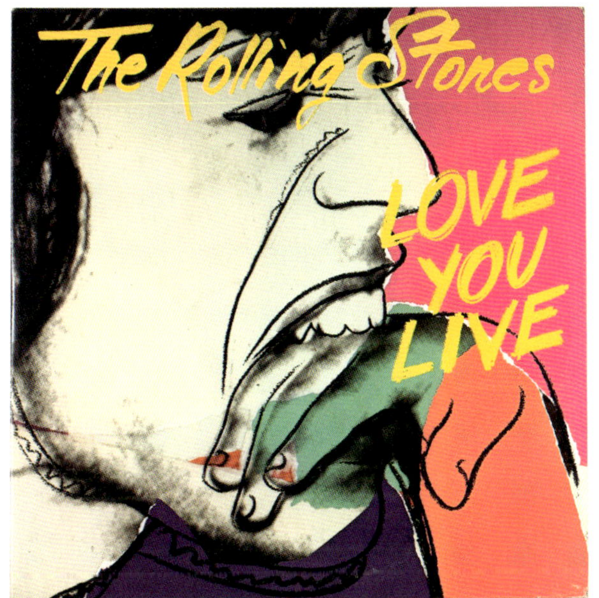

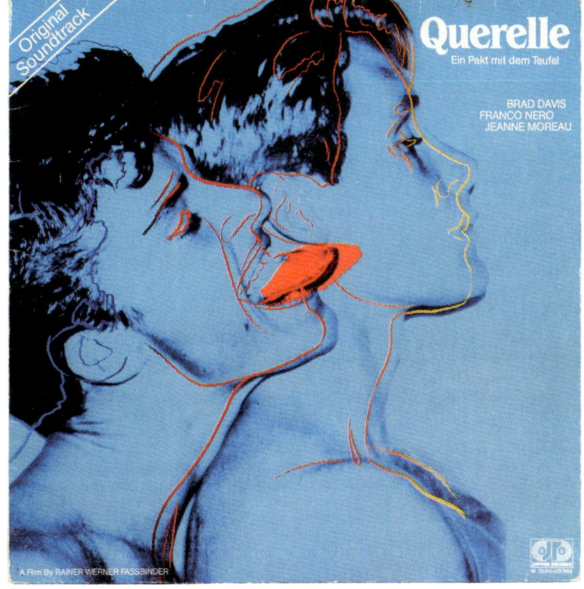

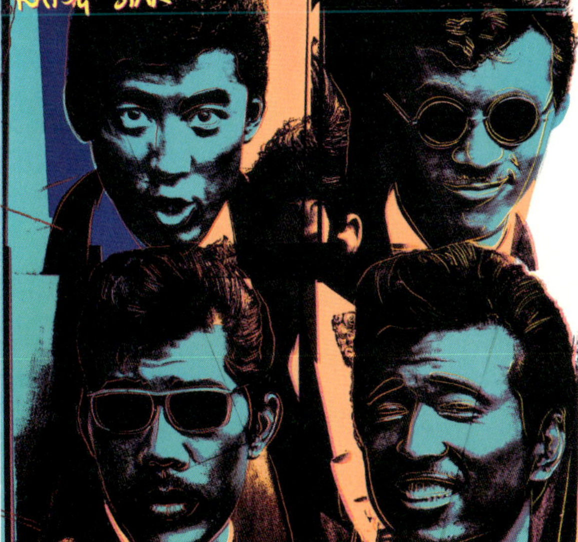

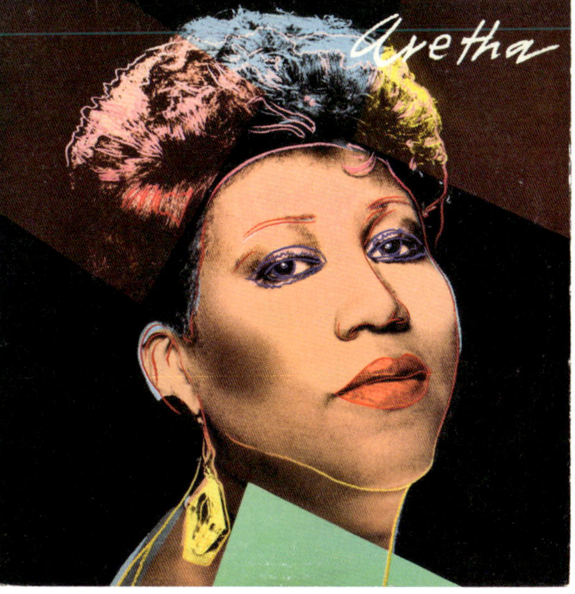

George Brecht
Giant Size $1.57 Each 1963

The Rolling Stones
Sticky Fingers 1971

The Rolling Stones
Love you Live 1977

Querelle: A Deal with the
Devil
Querelle 1982

Rats & Star
Soul Vacation 1983

Aretha Franklin
Aretha 1986

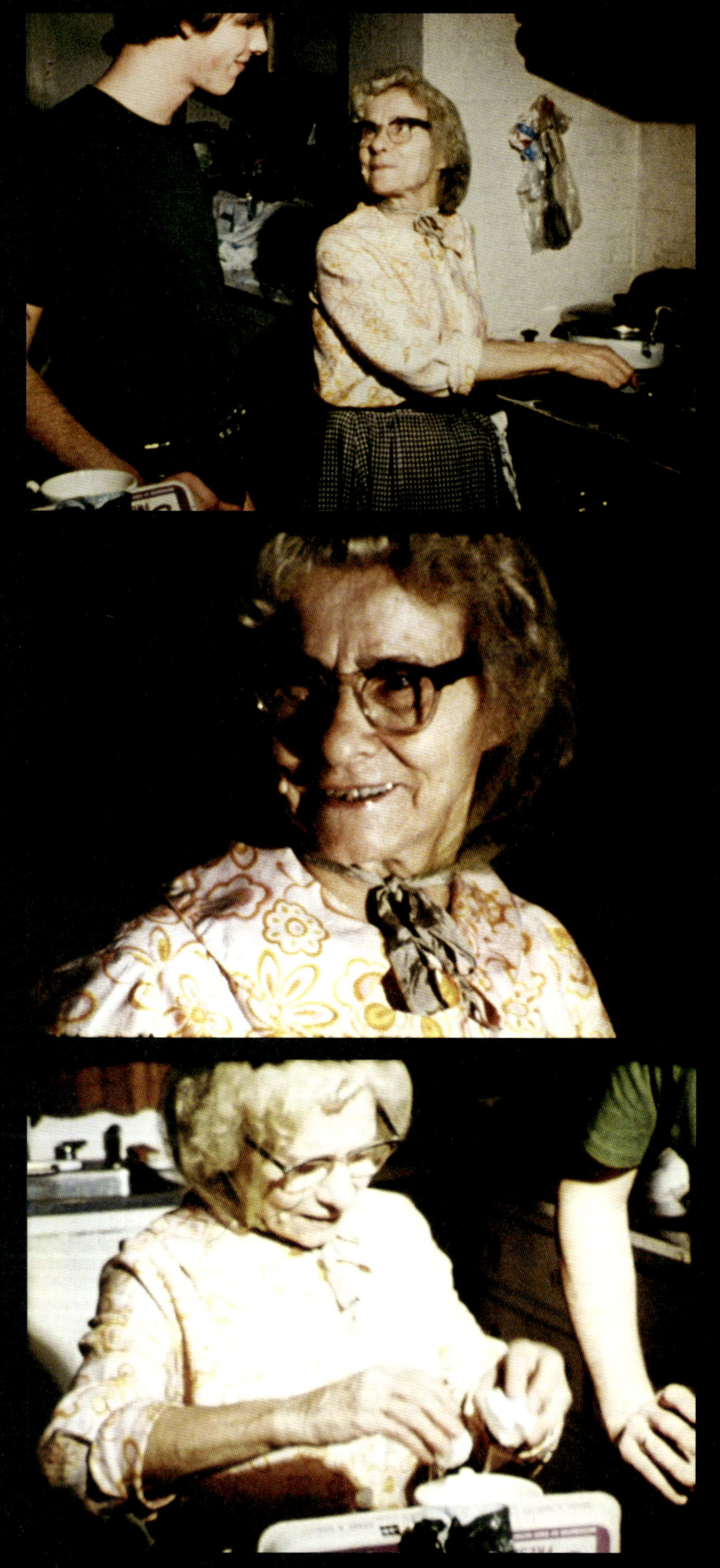

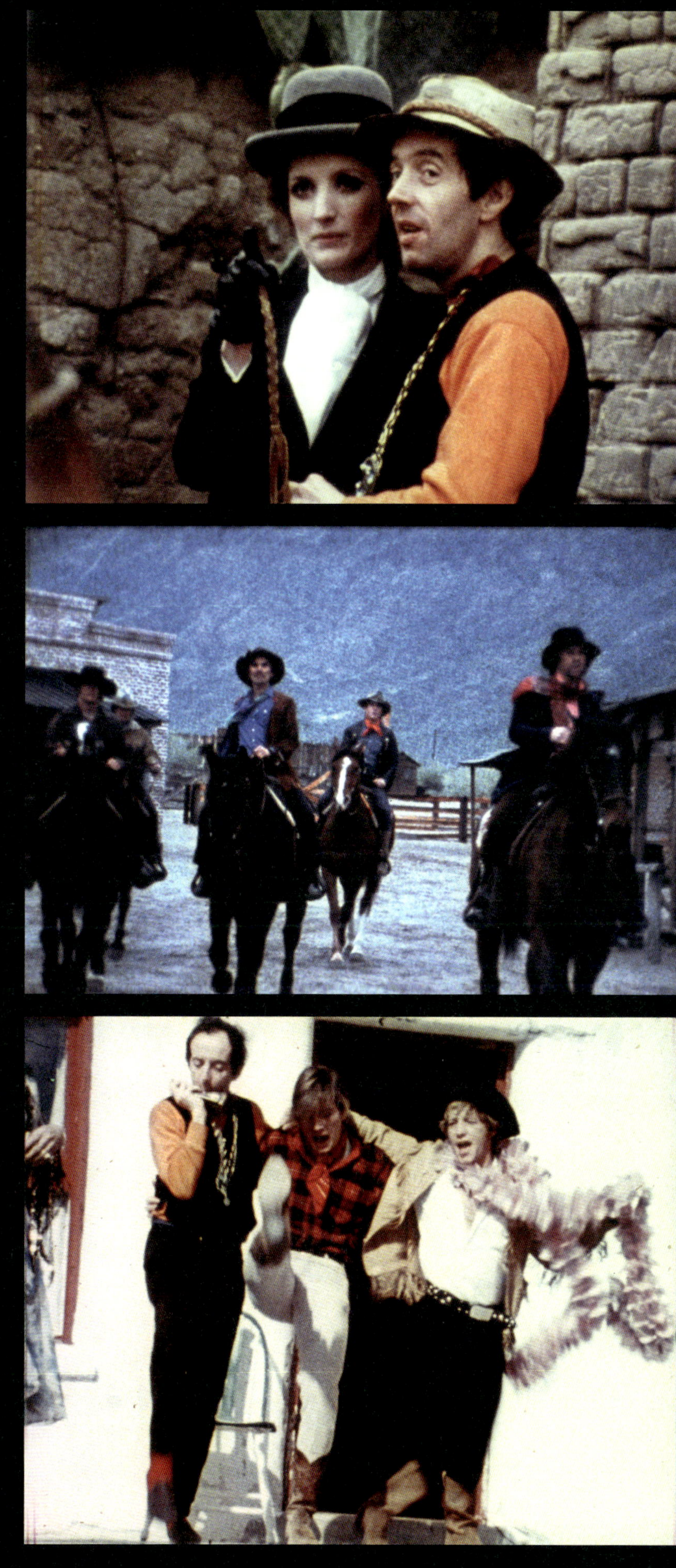

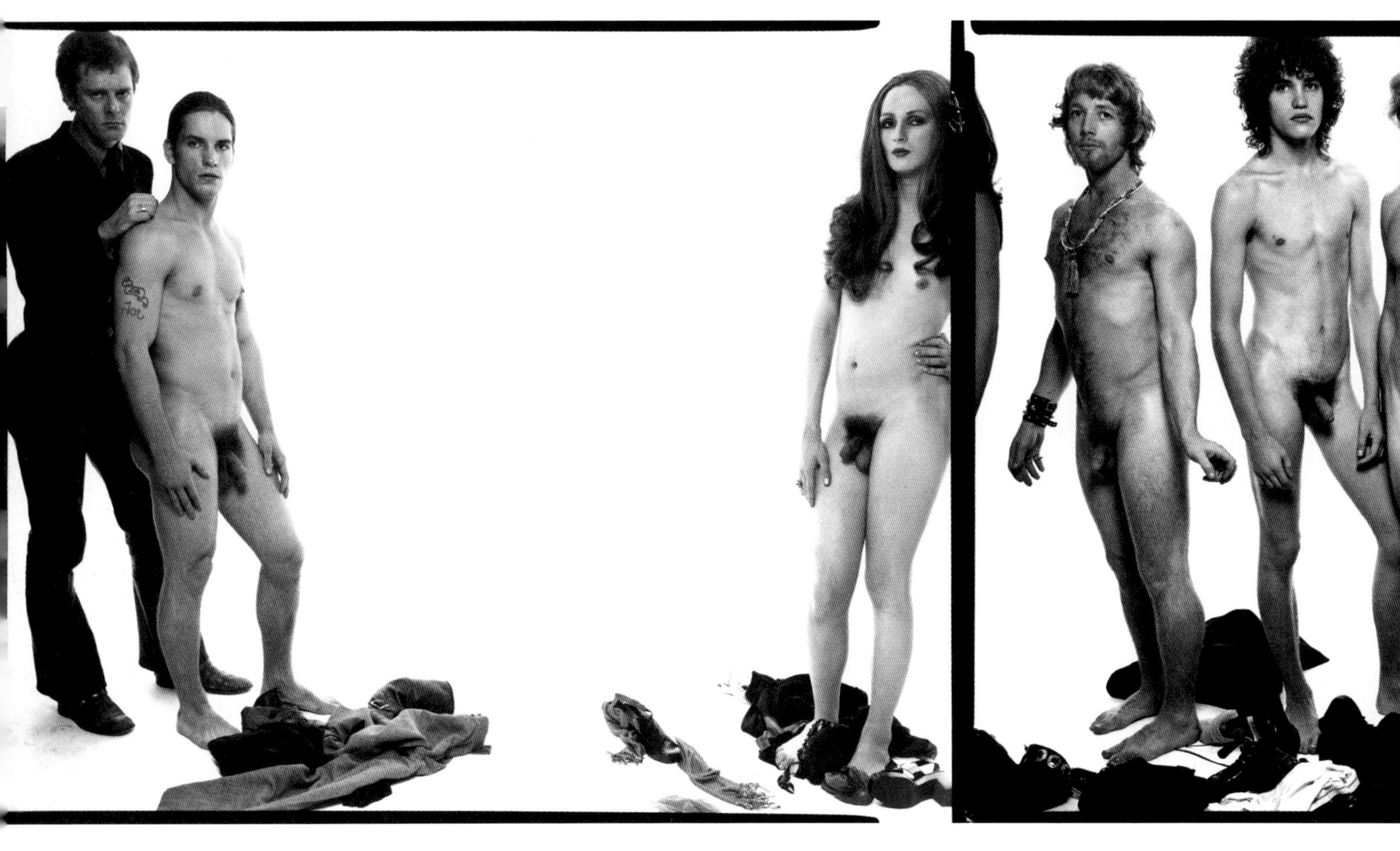

Previous pages
Mrs Warhol 1966
16mm film, colour, sound
67 minutes

Lonesome Cowboys 1967–8
16mm film, colour, sound
109 minutes

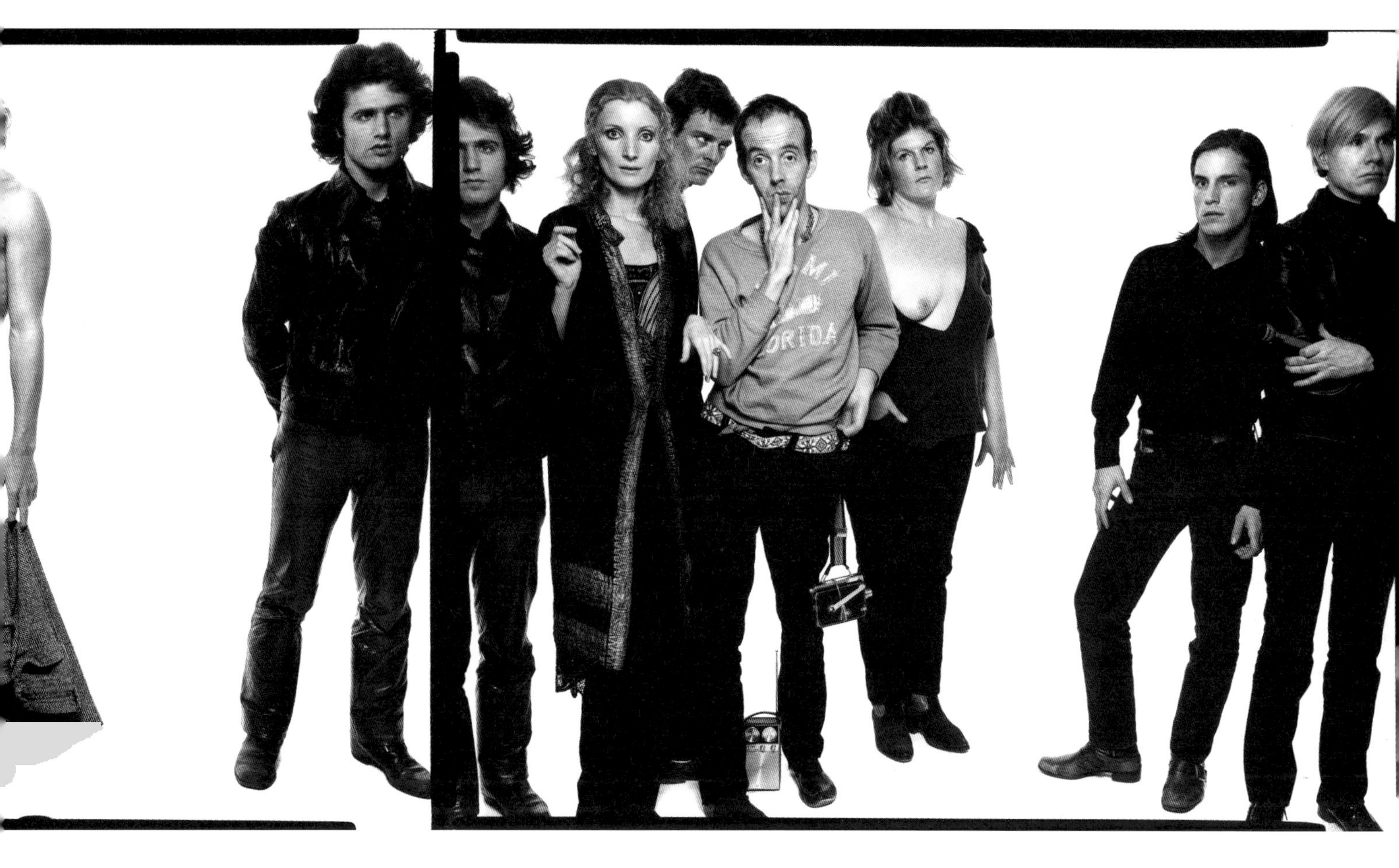

Andy Warhol and members of the Factory:
Paul Morrissey, director; Joe Dallesandro, actor; Candy Darling,
actor; Eric Emerson, actor; Jay Johnson, actor; Tom Hompertz,
actor; Gerard Malanga, poet; Viva, actress; Paul Morrissey;
Taylor Mead, actor; Brigid Polk, actress; Joe Dallesandro;
Andy Warhol, artist, New York,
30 October 1969
Photograph by Richard Avedon
Three photographs; gelatin silver prints on paper
20 x 25 (each)

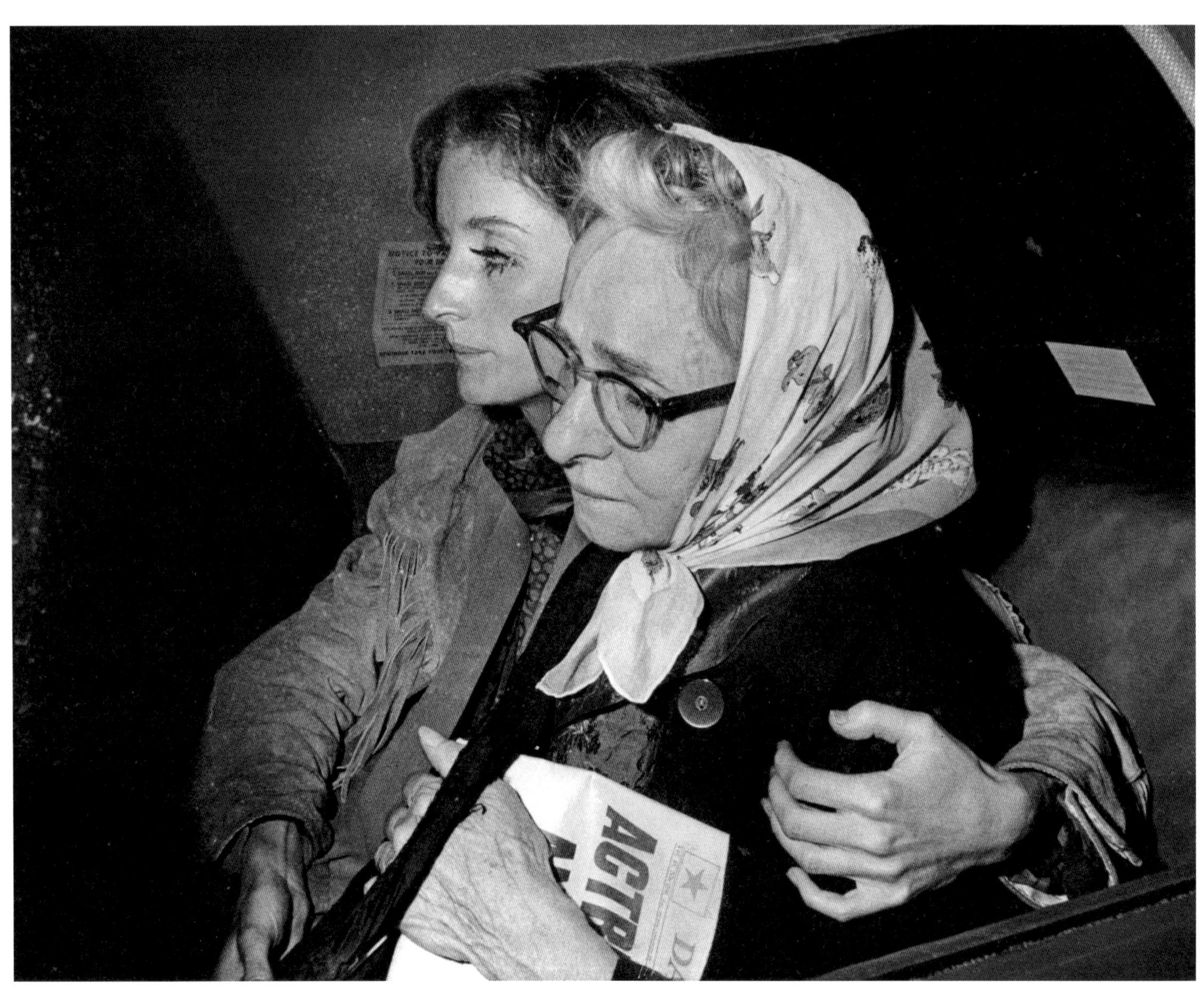

Andy Warhol's mother, Julia Warhola is comforted inside a
taxicab by actress Viva, as the pair leave Columbus Hospital
in Manhattan on 3 June 1968. Warhol had been shot earlier
in the day at his studio by Valerie Solanas.
Photo by Stan Wolfson

Opposite page
The *Daily News* reporting the
event, 4 June 1968
Facsimile from an original
newsprint clipping
39.4 x 27.9

DAILY 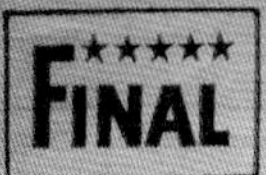 NEWS

NEW YORK'S PICTURE NEWSPAPER ®

8¢

10¢ OUTSIDE L.I. AND SUBURBS

Vol. 49. No. 296   Copr. 1968 News Syndicate Co. Inc.   New York, N.Y. 10017, Tuesday, June 4, 1968★   WEATHER: Sunny and warm.

ACTRESS SHOOTS ANDY WARHOL

Cries 'He Controlled My Life'

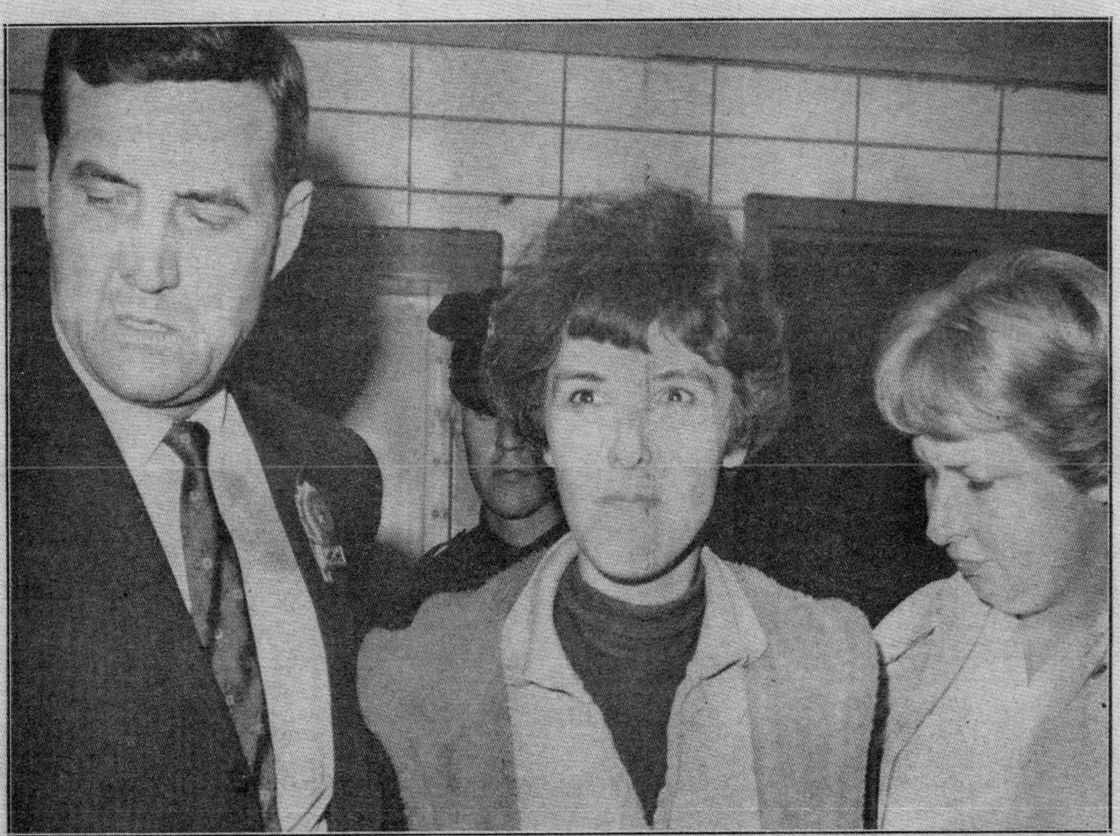

'Flower Child' Surrenders. Detective and policewoman (r.) escort actress Valerie Solanas, 28, into E. 21st St. station to be booked in shooting of pop art movie man Andy Warhol at his 33 Union Square West office yesterday. Last night, Valerie surrendered to a cop in Times Square, allegedly admitting shooting, and saying: "I am a flower child." Warhol is in critical condition. His associate, Mario Amaya of London, also was shot. —*Stories p. 3; other pics. centerfold*

NEWS photo by Frank Russo

Andy Warhol, artist, New York,
20 August 1969 1969
Photograph by Richard Avedon
Gelatin silver print on paper
147.5 x 118

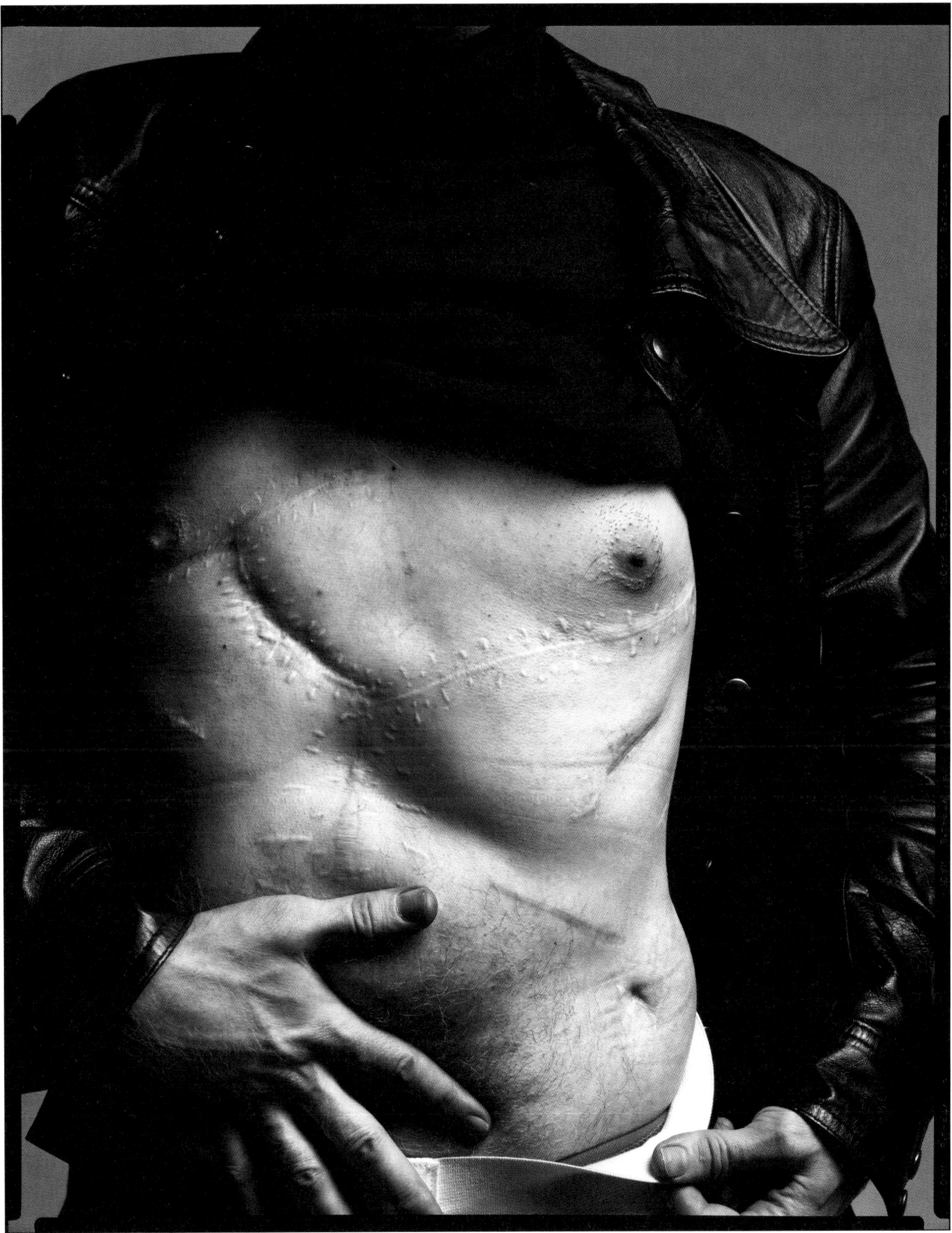

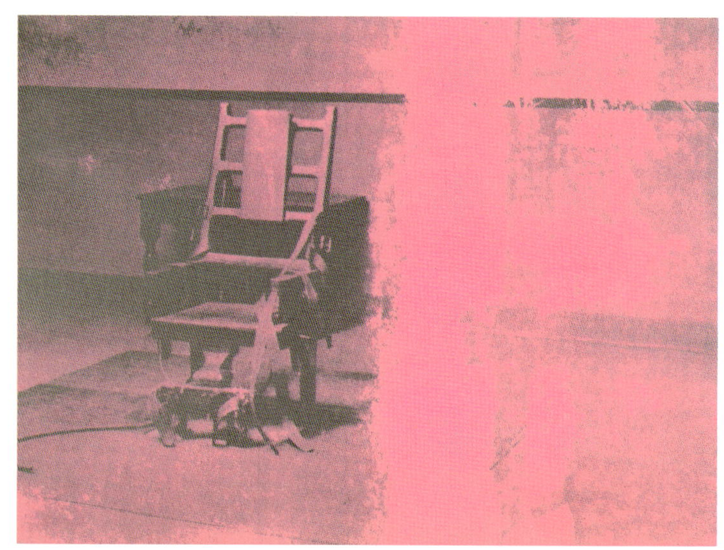

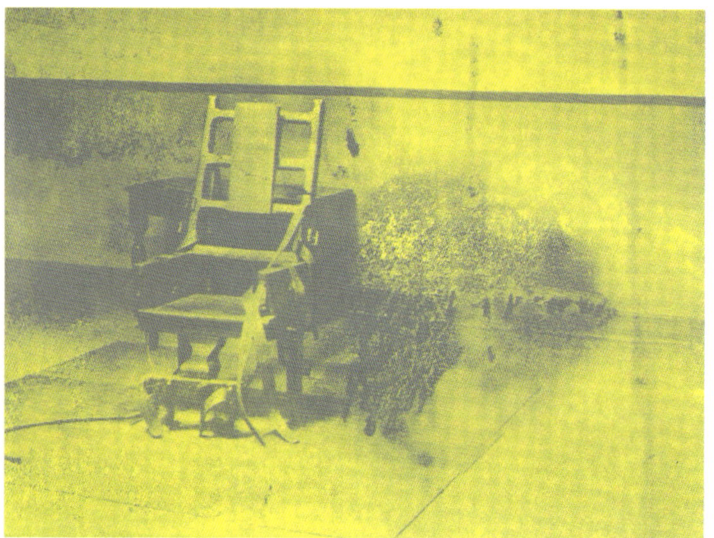

[No title] 1971
From the series *Electric Chair*
Screenprint on paper
90 x 121.6 (each)

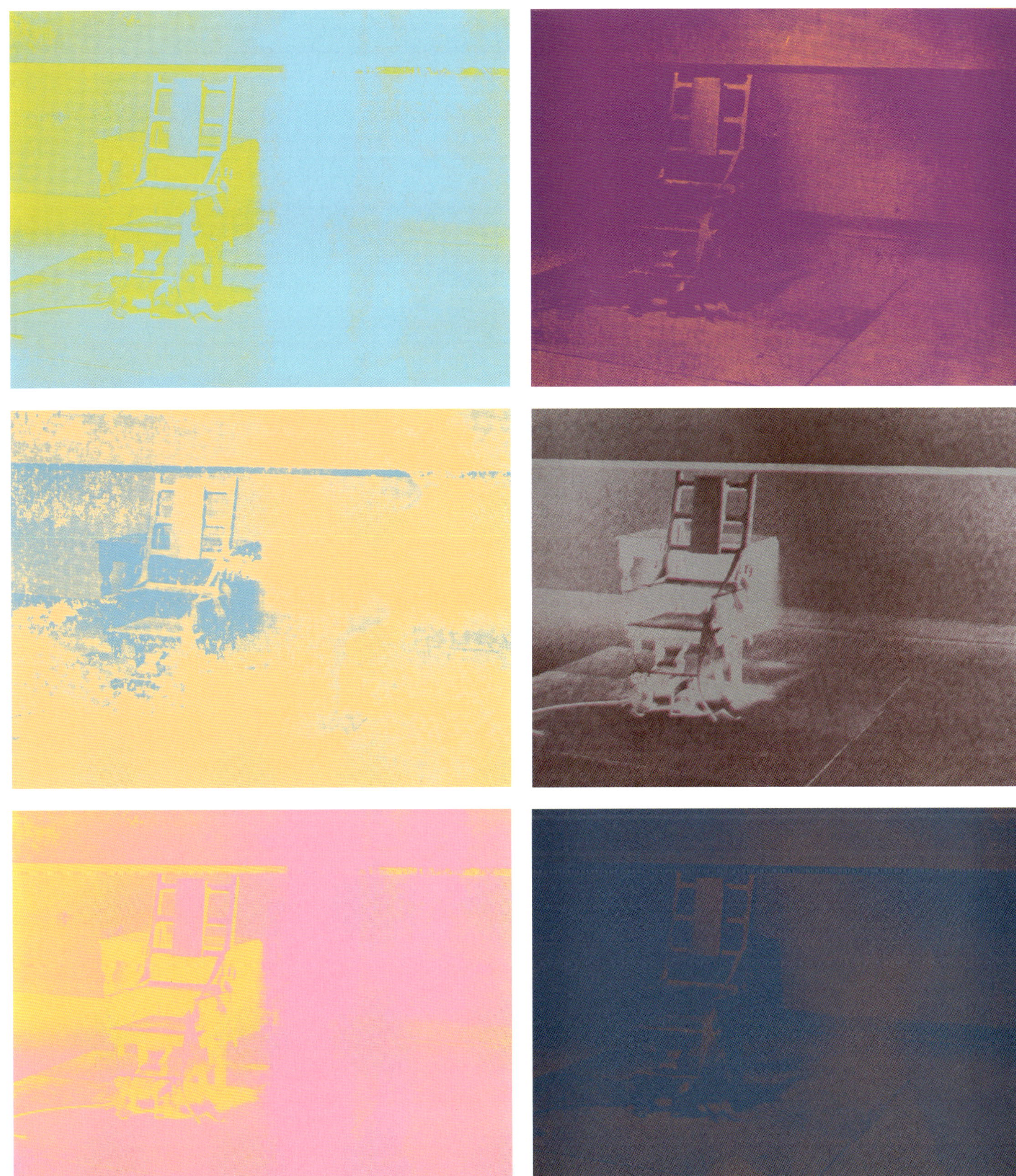

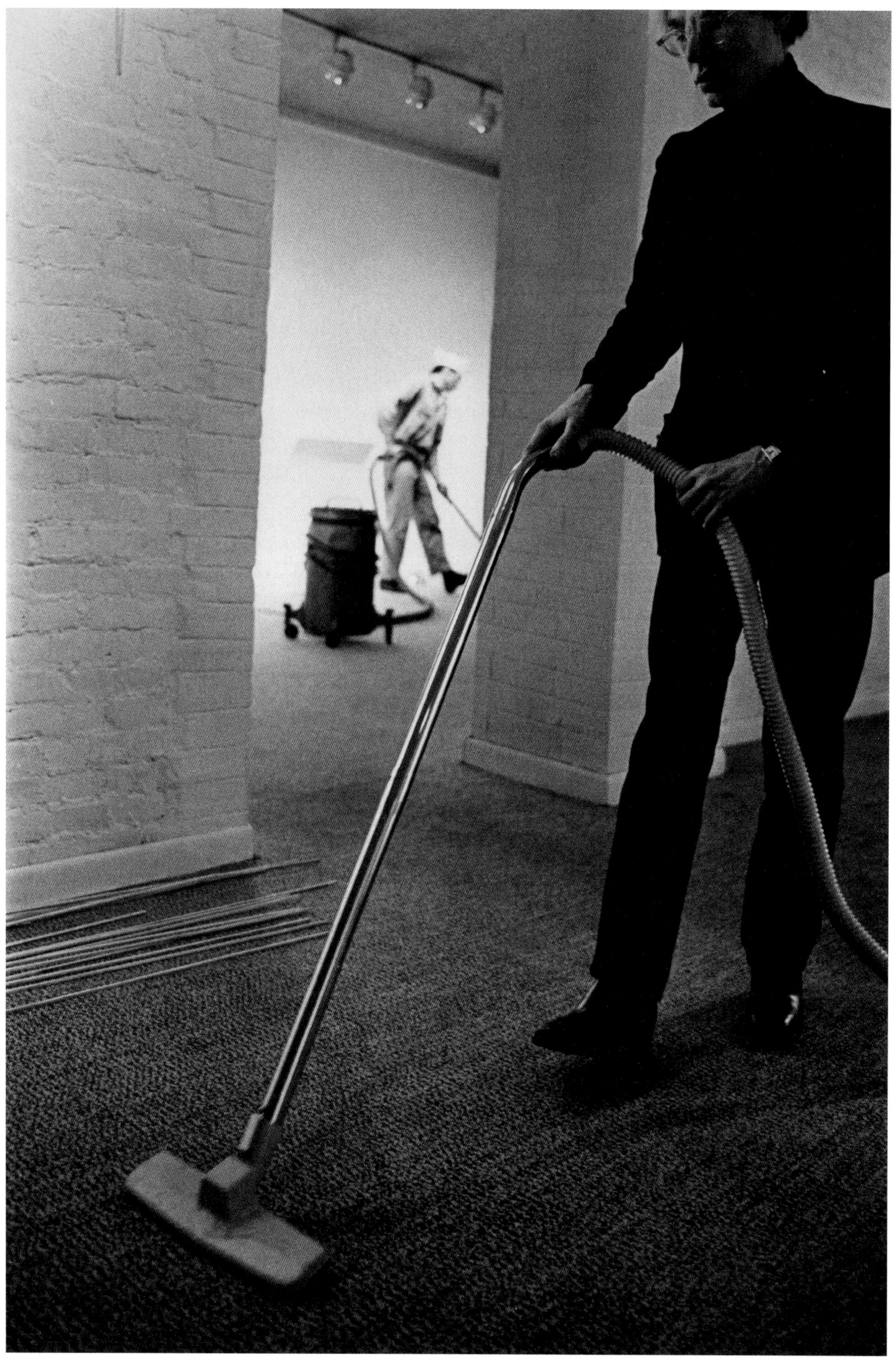

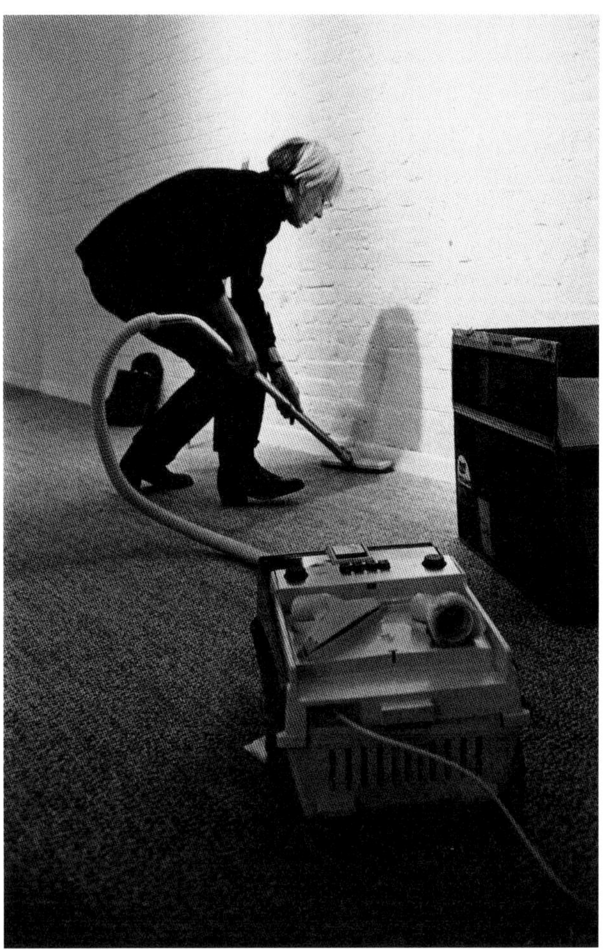

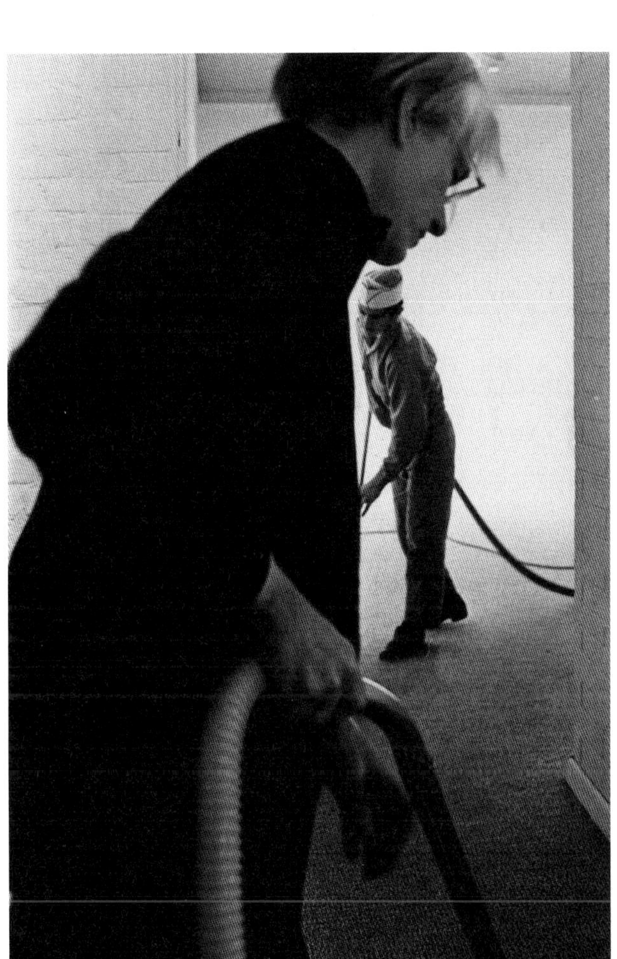

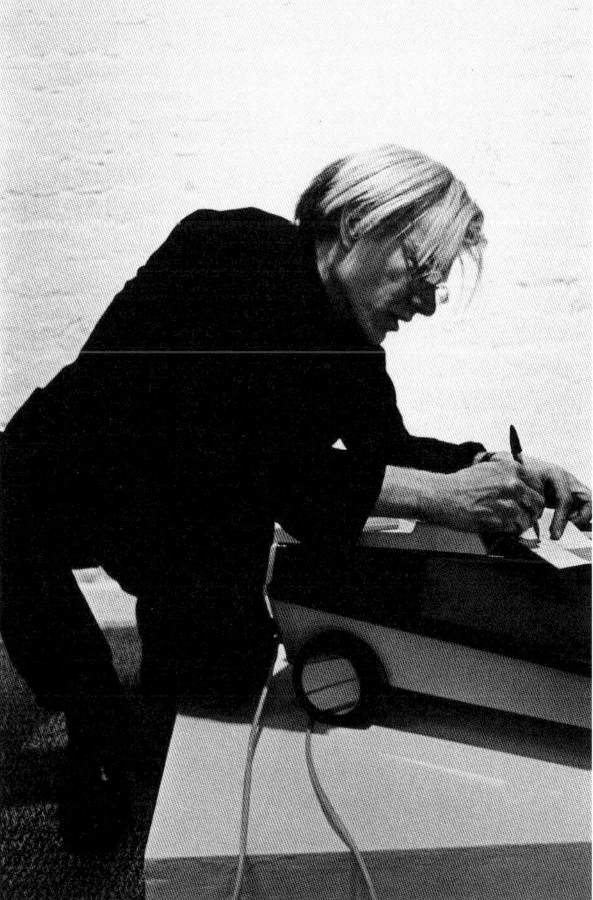

Photographs of Andy Warhol's
contribution to the *Art in Process
V exhibition* at Finch College
Museum of Art 1972
Photographs by Michael Kostiuk
Prints on paper
26 x 21 (each)

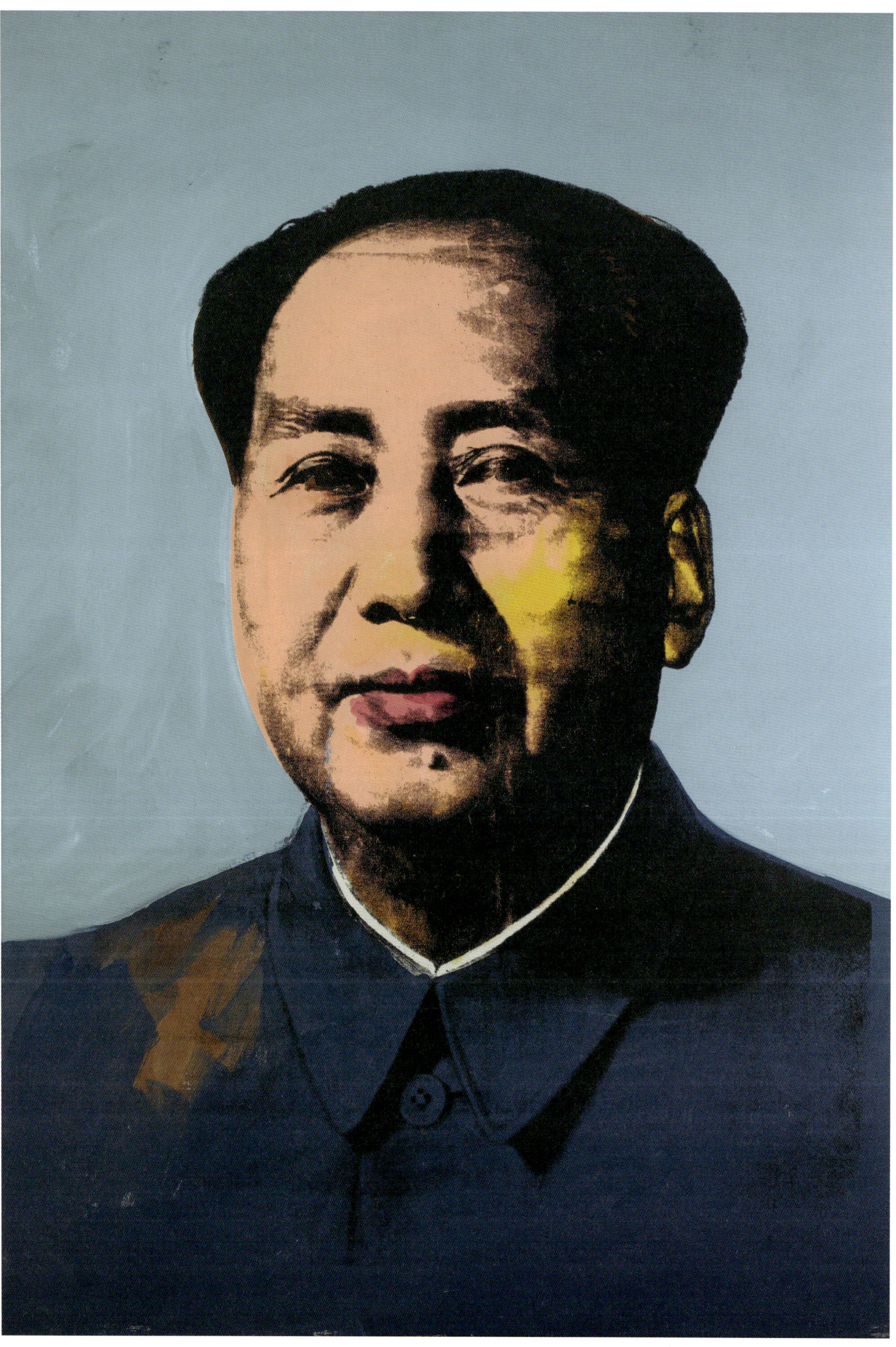

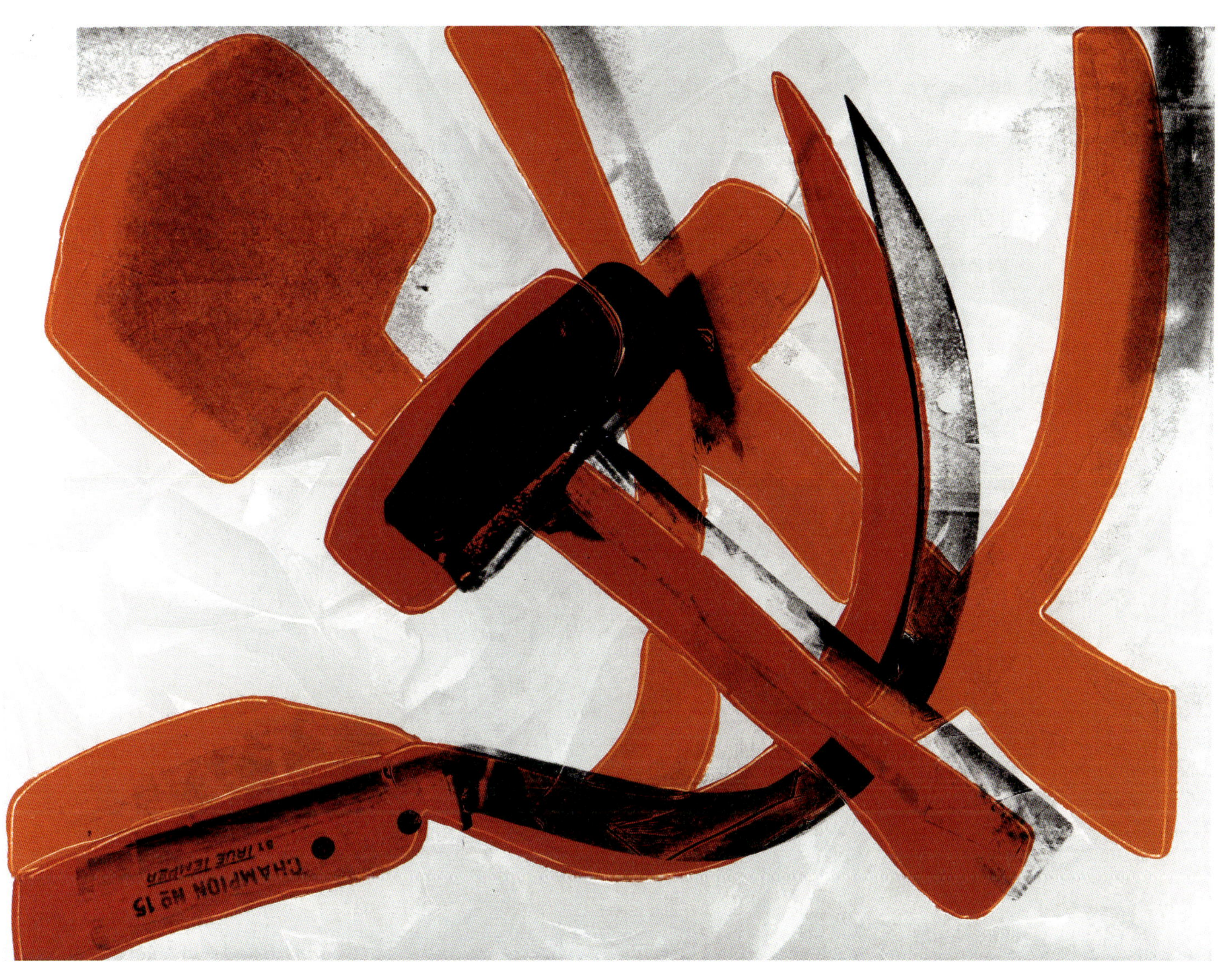

Hammer and Sickle 1976
Acrylic paint and screenprint
on canvas
305 x 407.5

Opposite page
Mao 1972
Acrylic paint and screenprint
on canvas
208.3 x 144.8

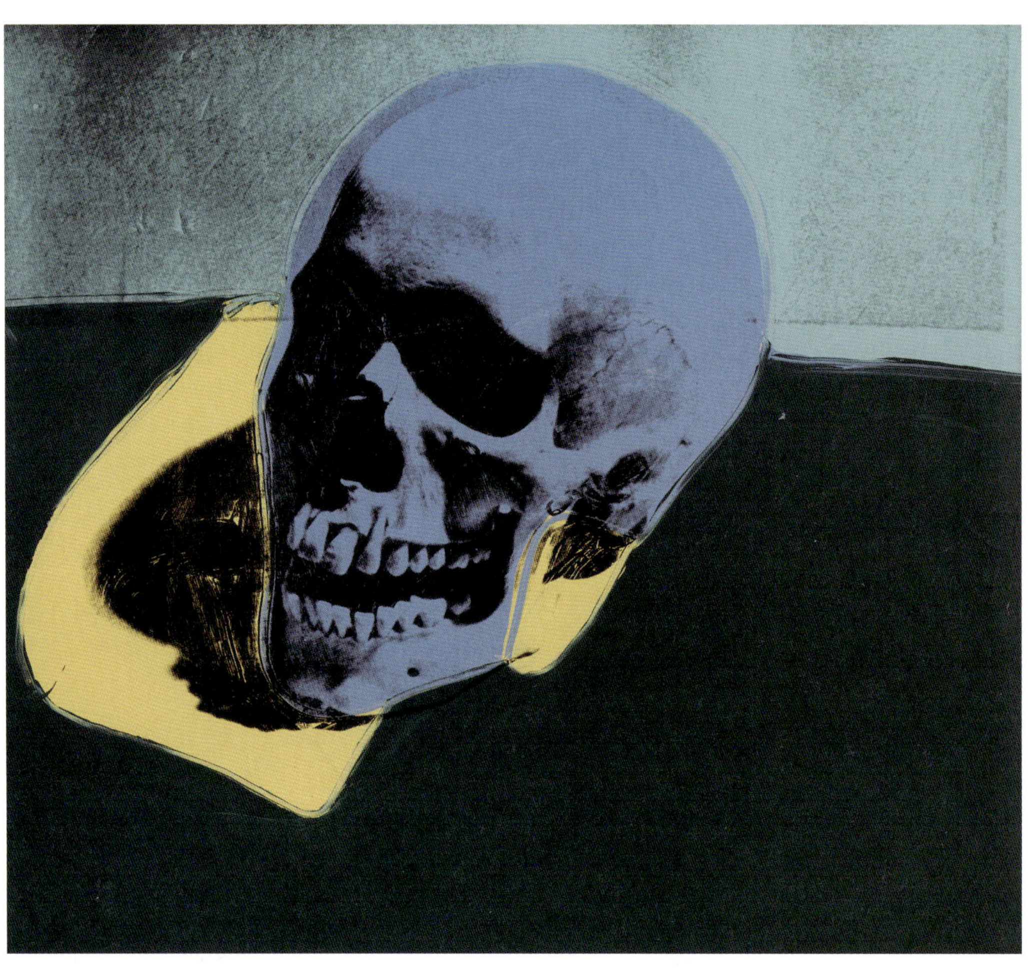

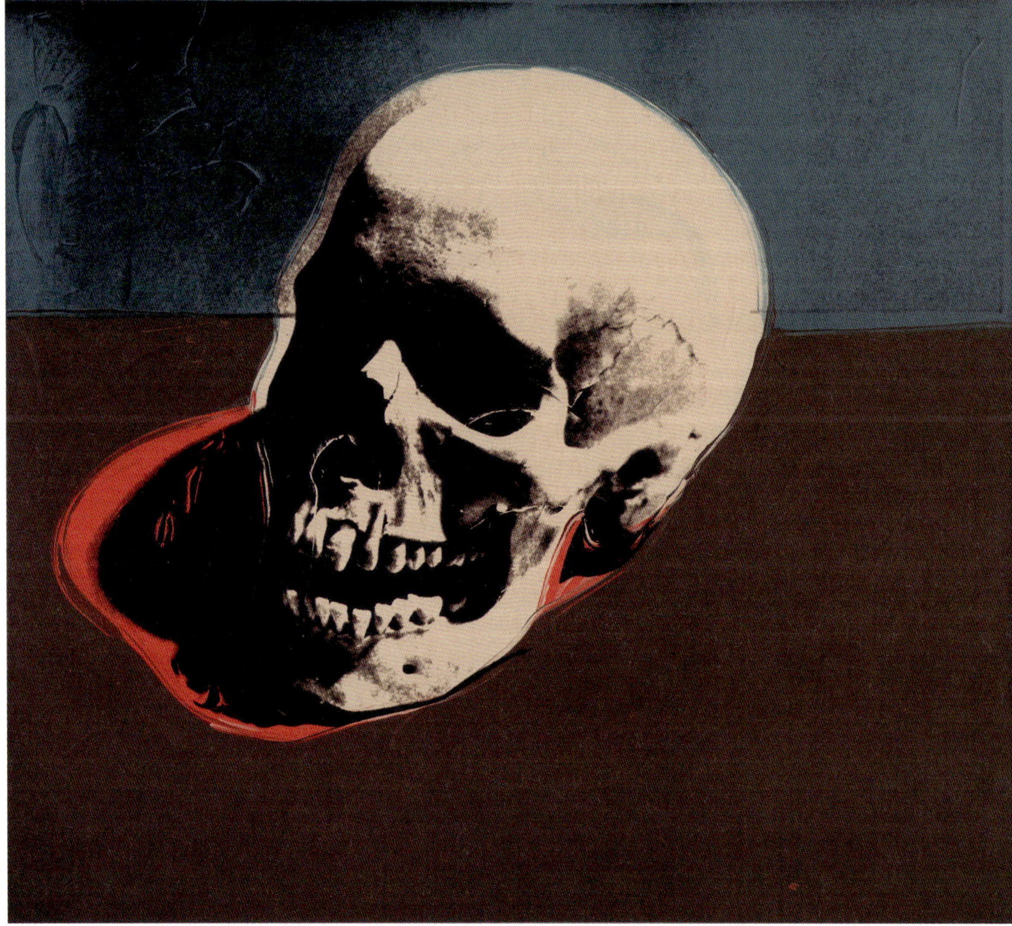

Skull 1976
Acrylic paint and screenprint
on canvases
Approx. 182 x 203 (each)

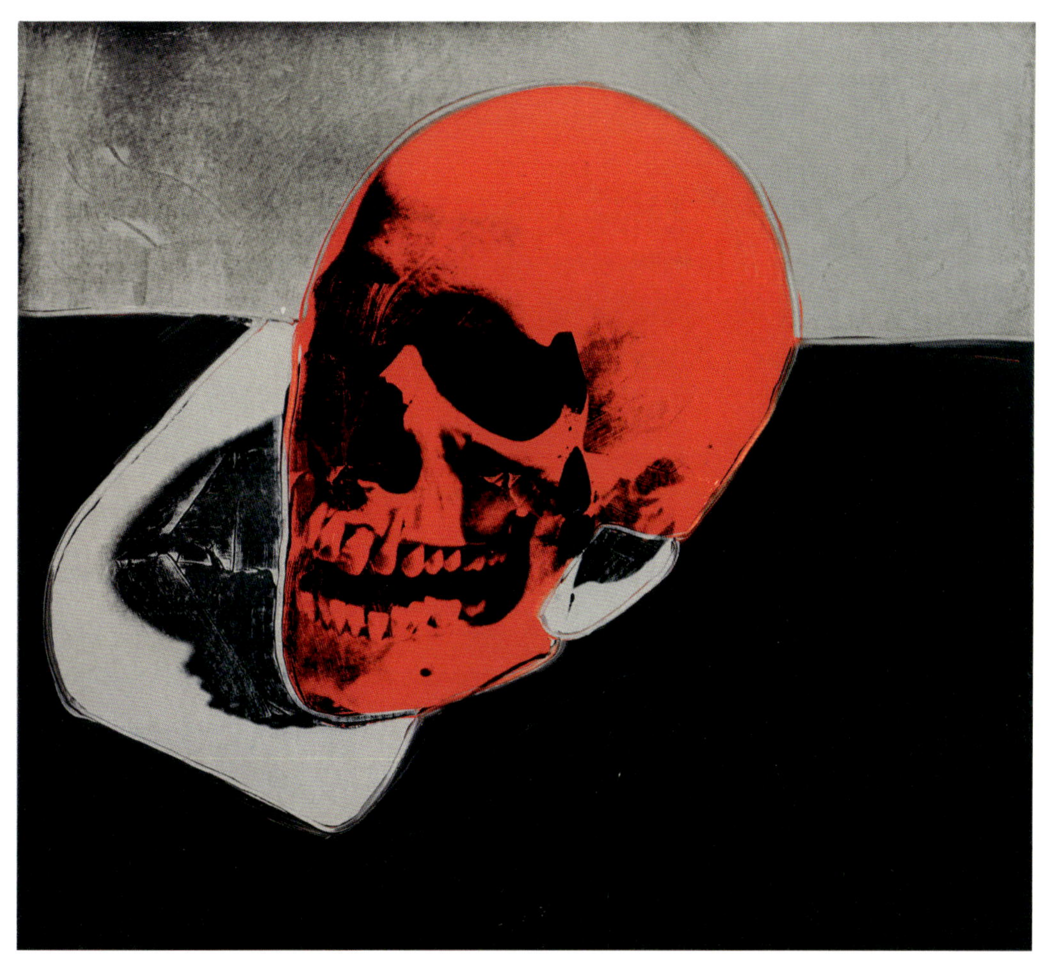

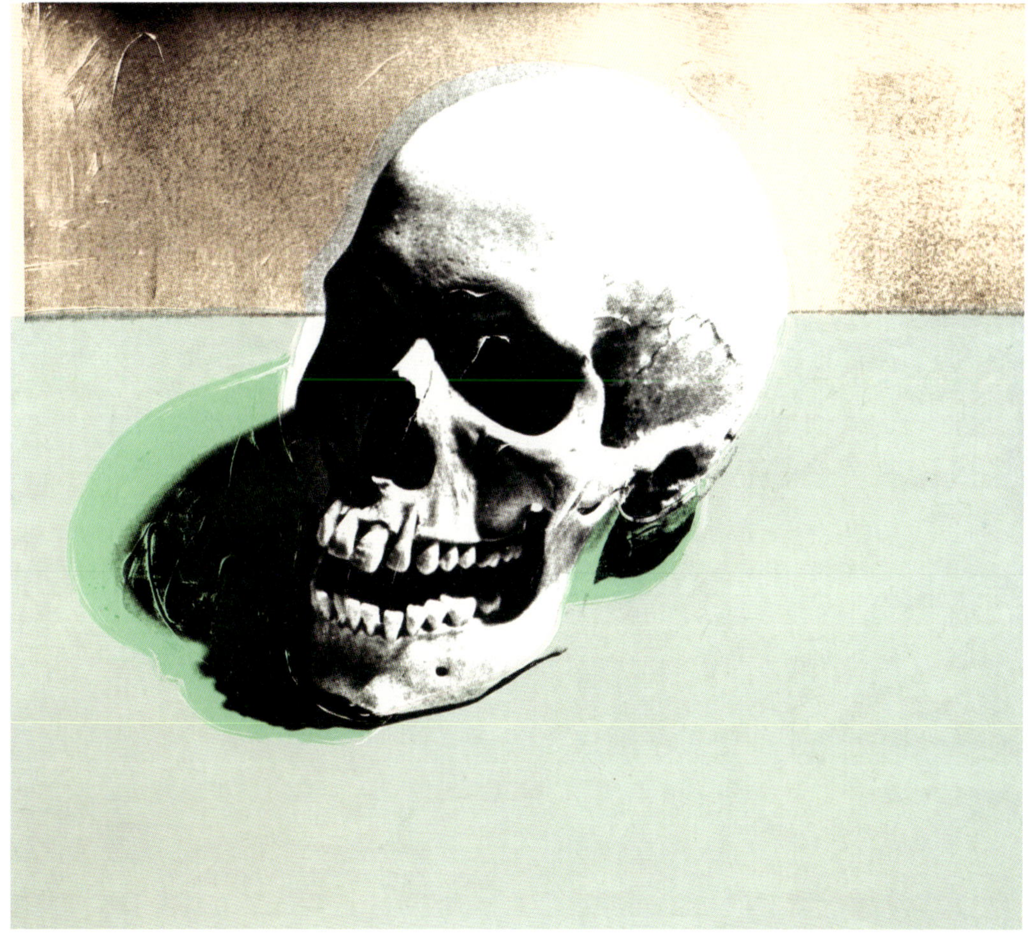

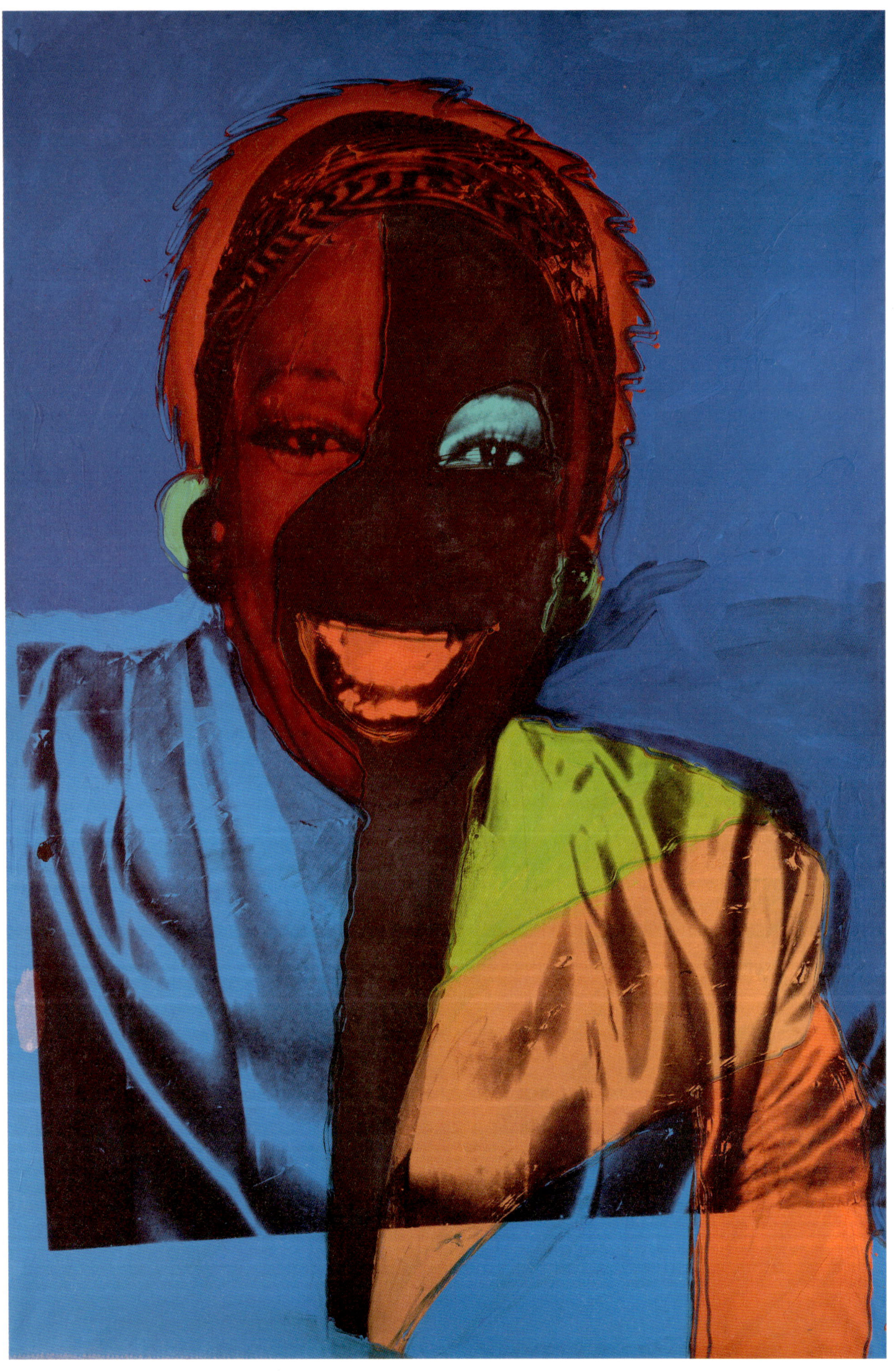

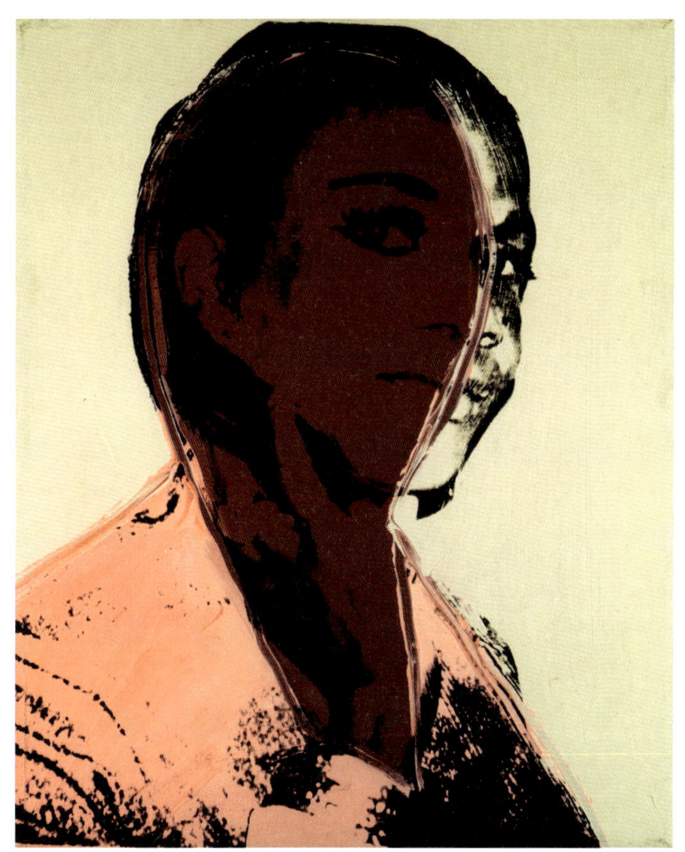

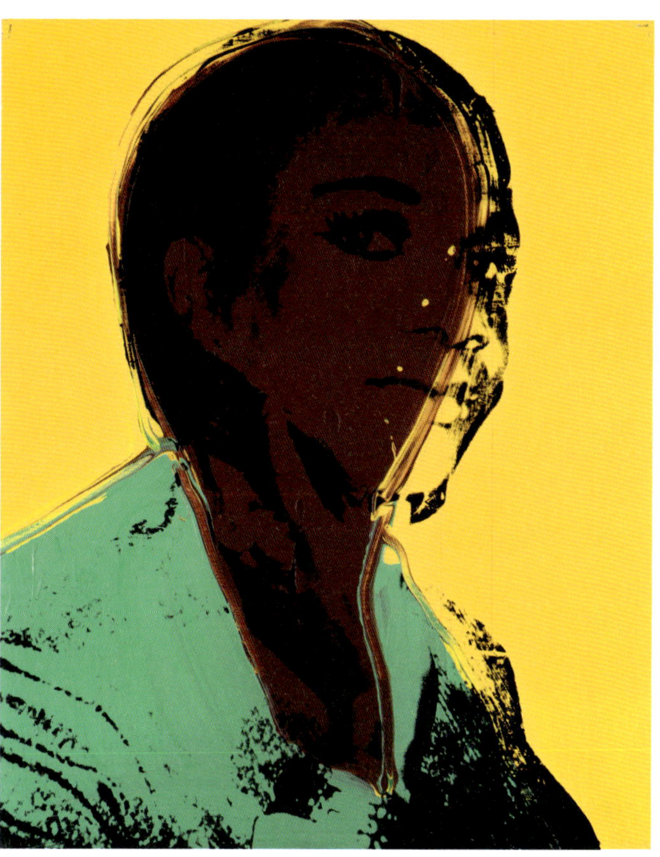

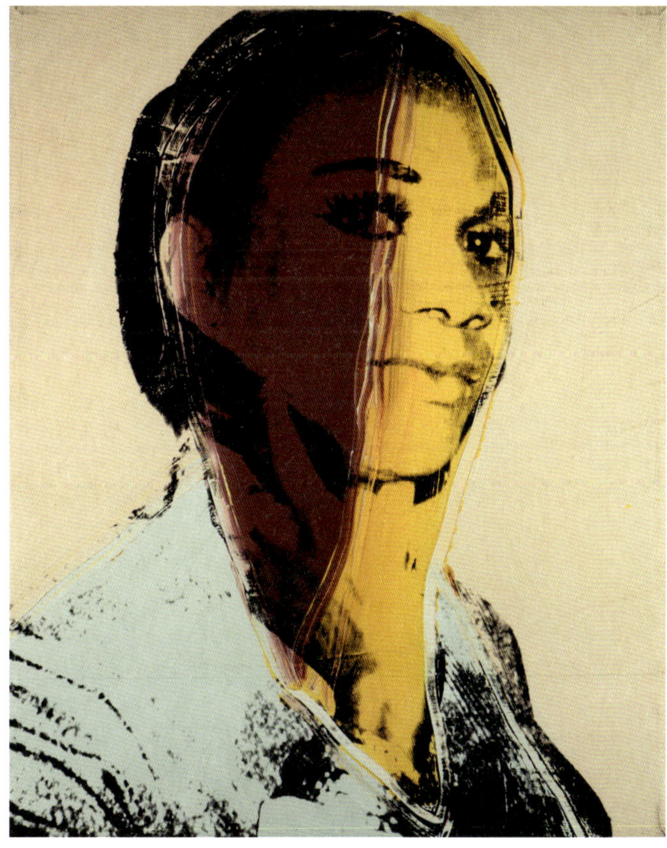

*Ladies and Gentlemen
(Wilhelmina Ross)* 1975
Acrylic paint and screenprint
on canvas
300 x 200

*Ladies and Gentlemen
(Alphanso Panell)* 1975
Acrylic paint and screenprint
on canvas
81.3 x 66

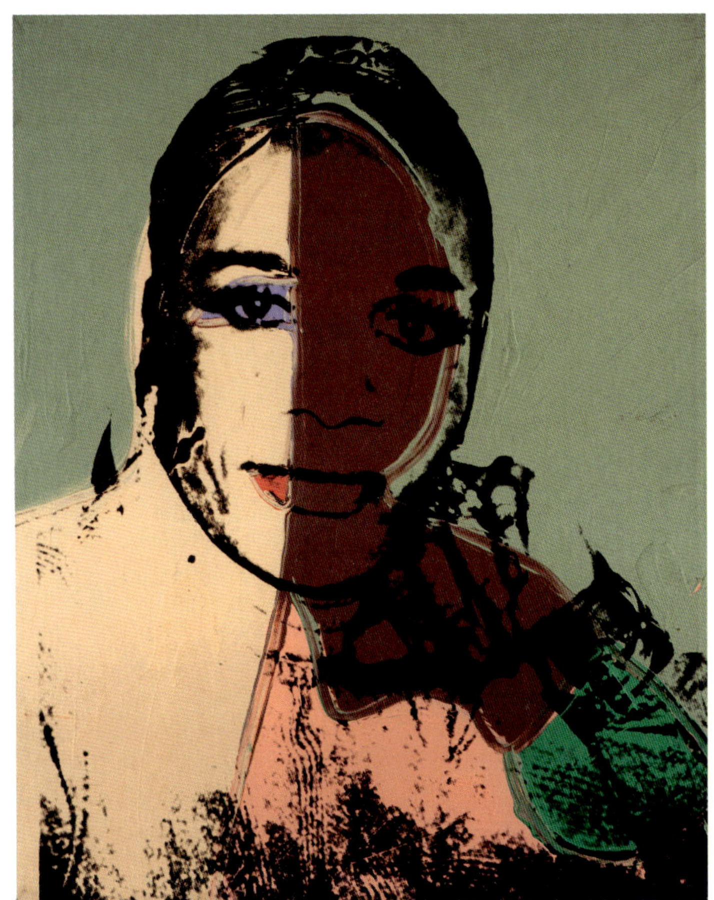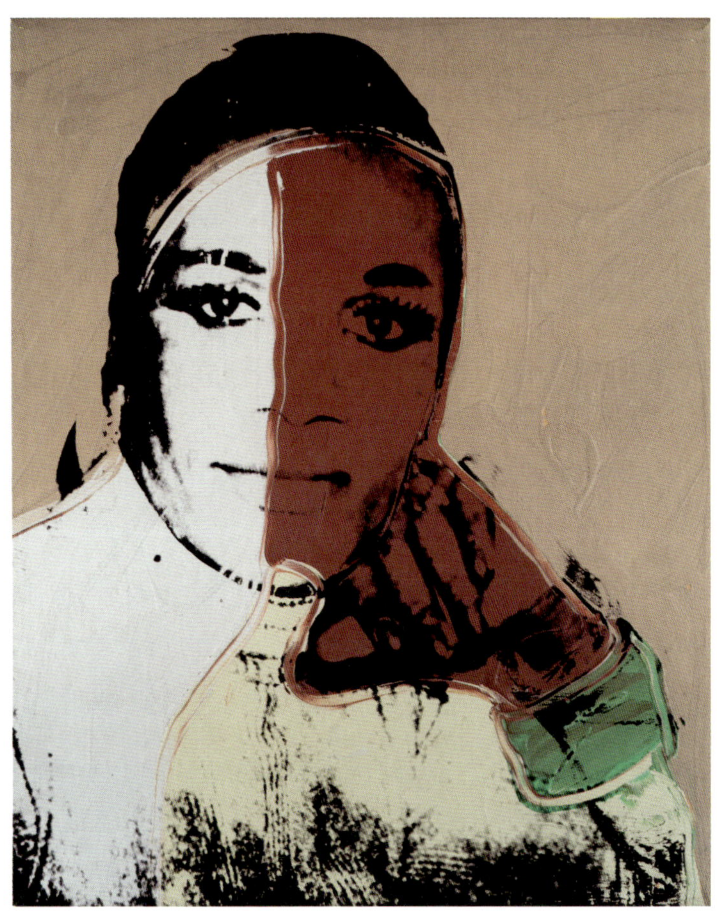

Ladies and Gentlemen
(Alphanso Panell) 1975
Acrylic paint and screenprint
on canvas
81.3 x 66 (each)

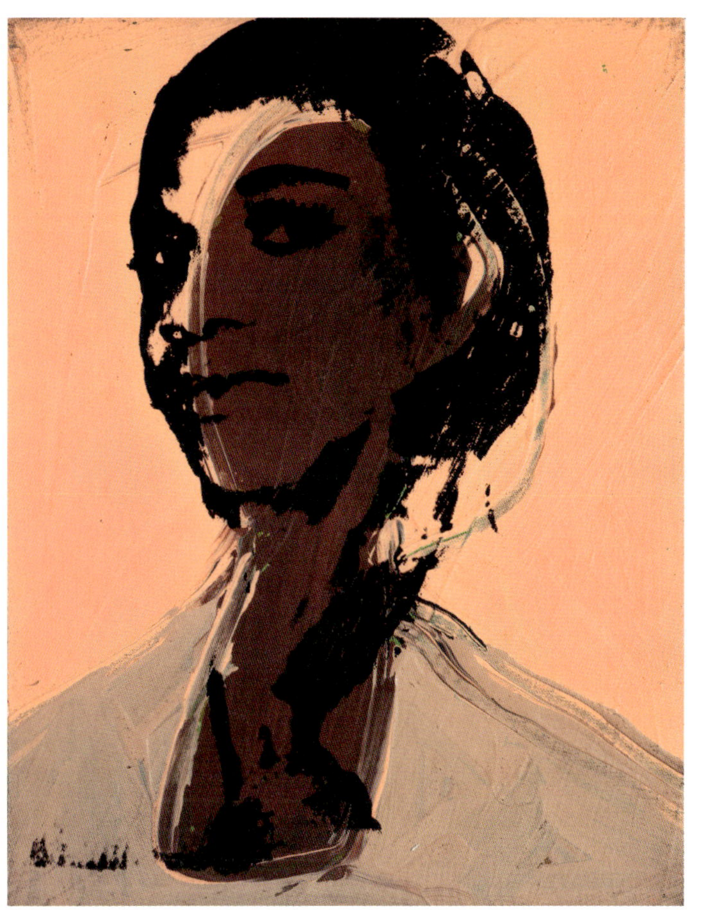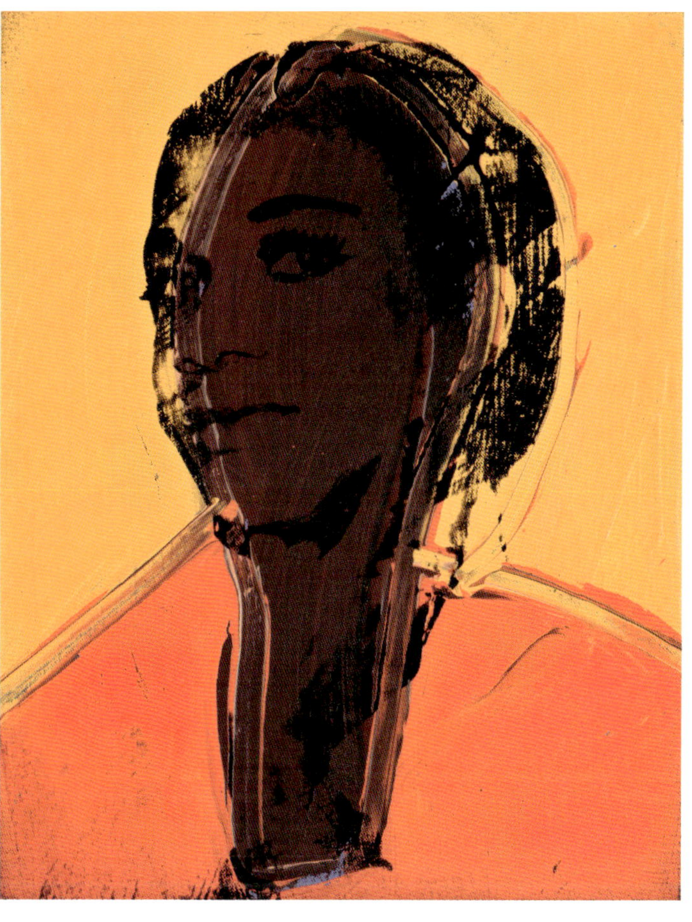

This page
*Ladies and Gentlemen
(Alphanso Panell)* 1975
Acrylic paint and screenprint
on canvas
35.6 x 27.9 (each)

p.166
*Ladies and Gentlemen
(Broadway)* 1975
Acrylic paint and screenprint
on canvas
35.6 x 27.9 (each)

p.167
*Ladies and Gentlemen
(Helen/Harry Morales)*
1975
Acrylic paint and screenprint
on canvas
35.6 x 27.9

p.168
*Ladies and Gentlemen
(Lurdes)* 1975
Acrylic paint and screenprint
on paper
127 x 101.6

p.169
*Ladies and Gentlemen
(Marsha P. Johnson)* 1975
Acrylic paint and screenprint
on canvas
27 x 101.6

pp.170–1
Ladies and Gentlemen (Iris)
1975
Acrylic paint and screenprint
on canvas
35.6 x 27.9 (each)

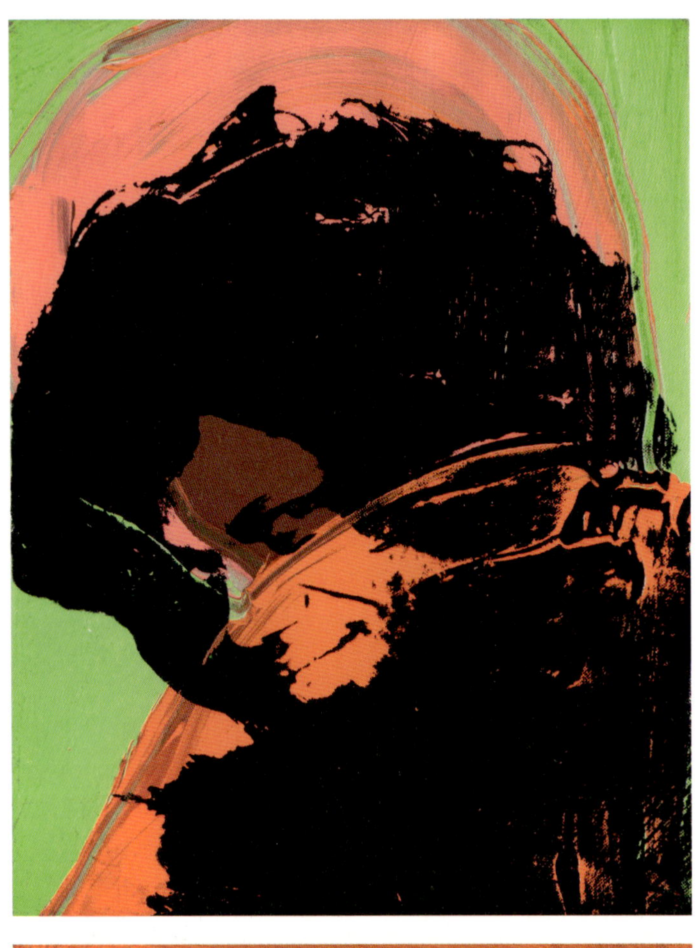
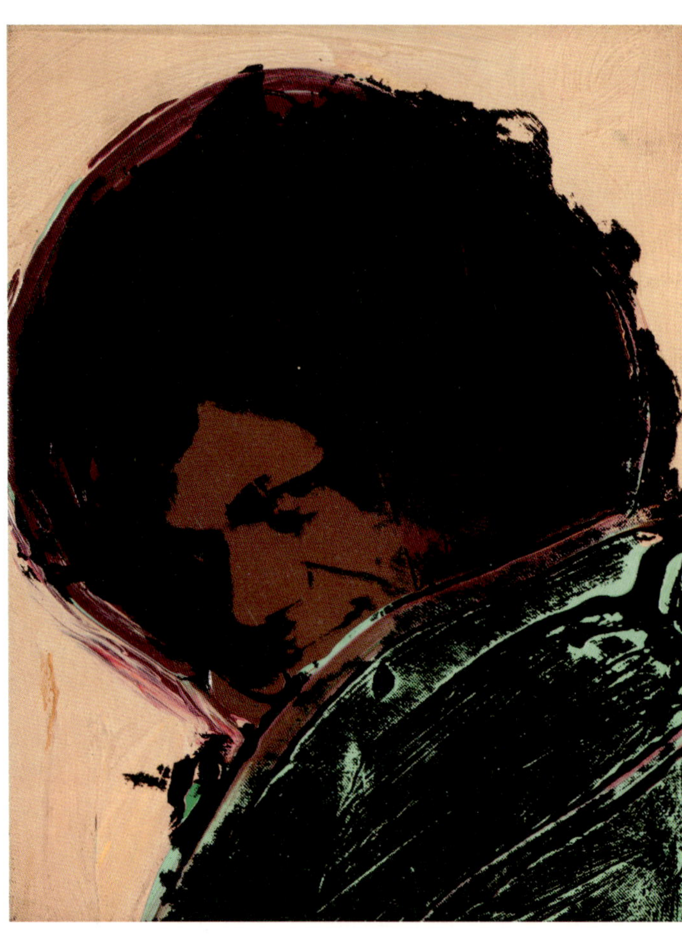
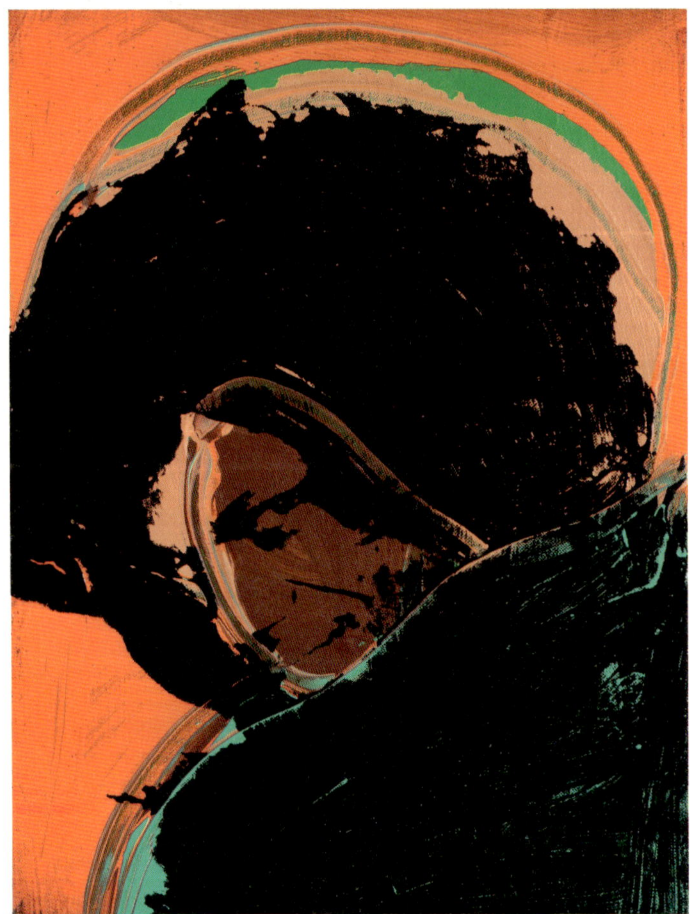
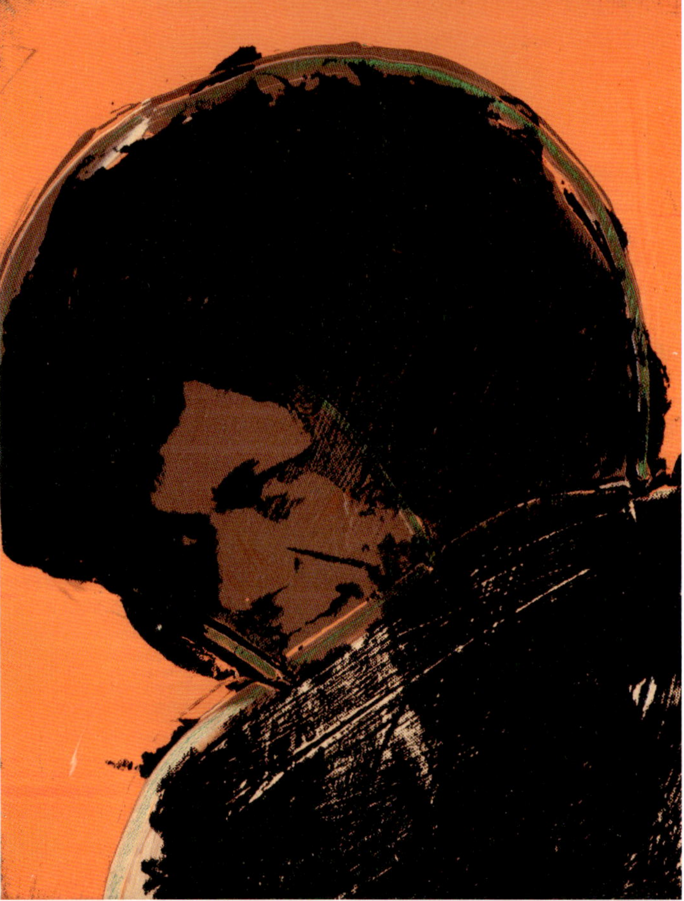

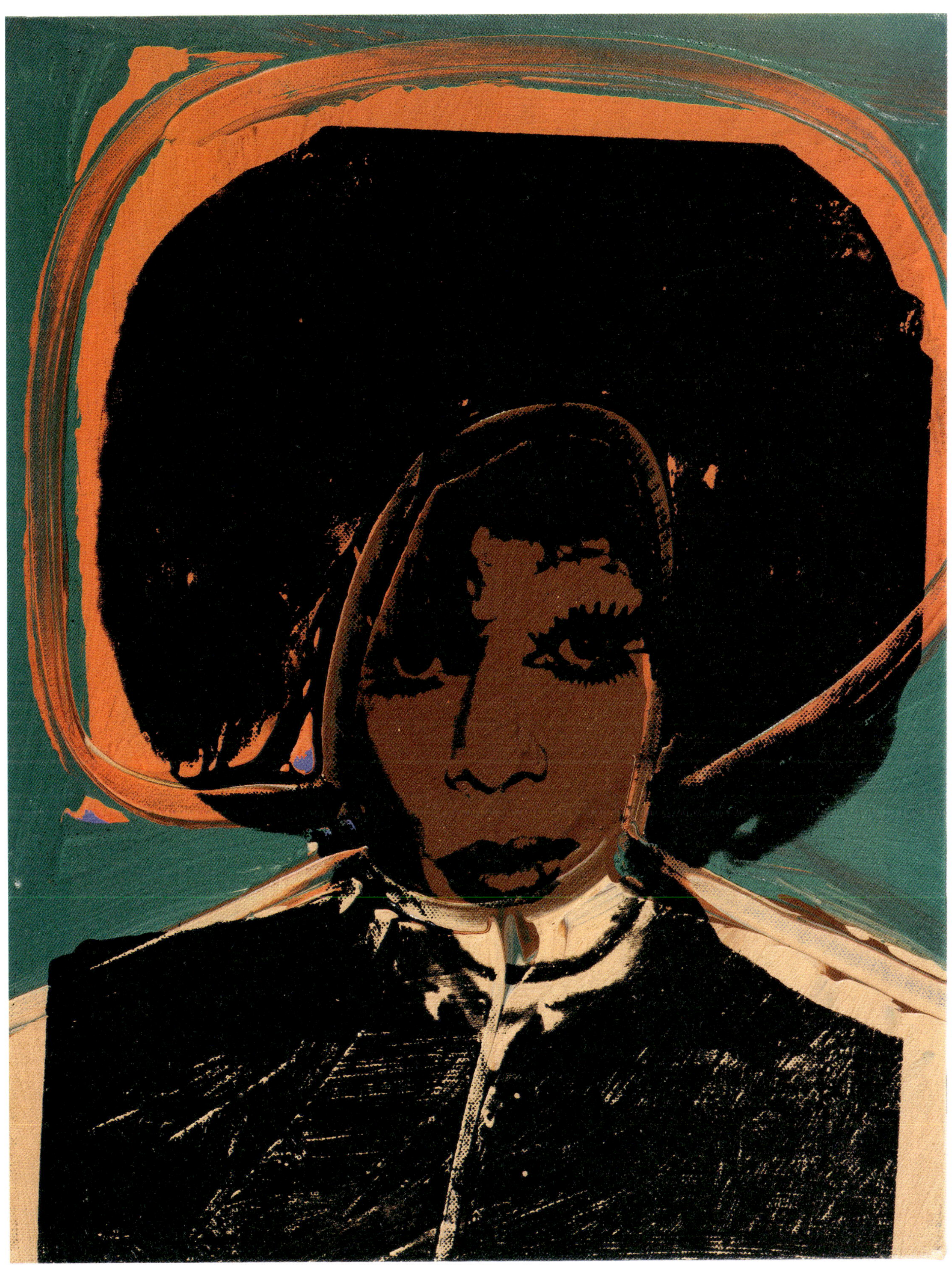

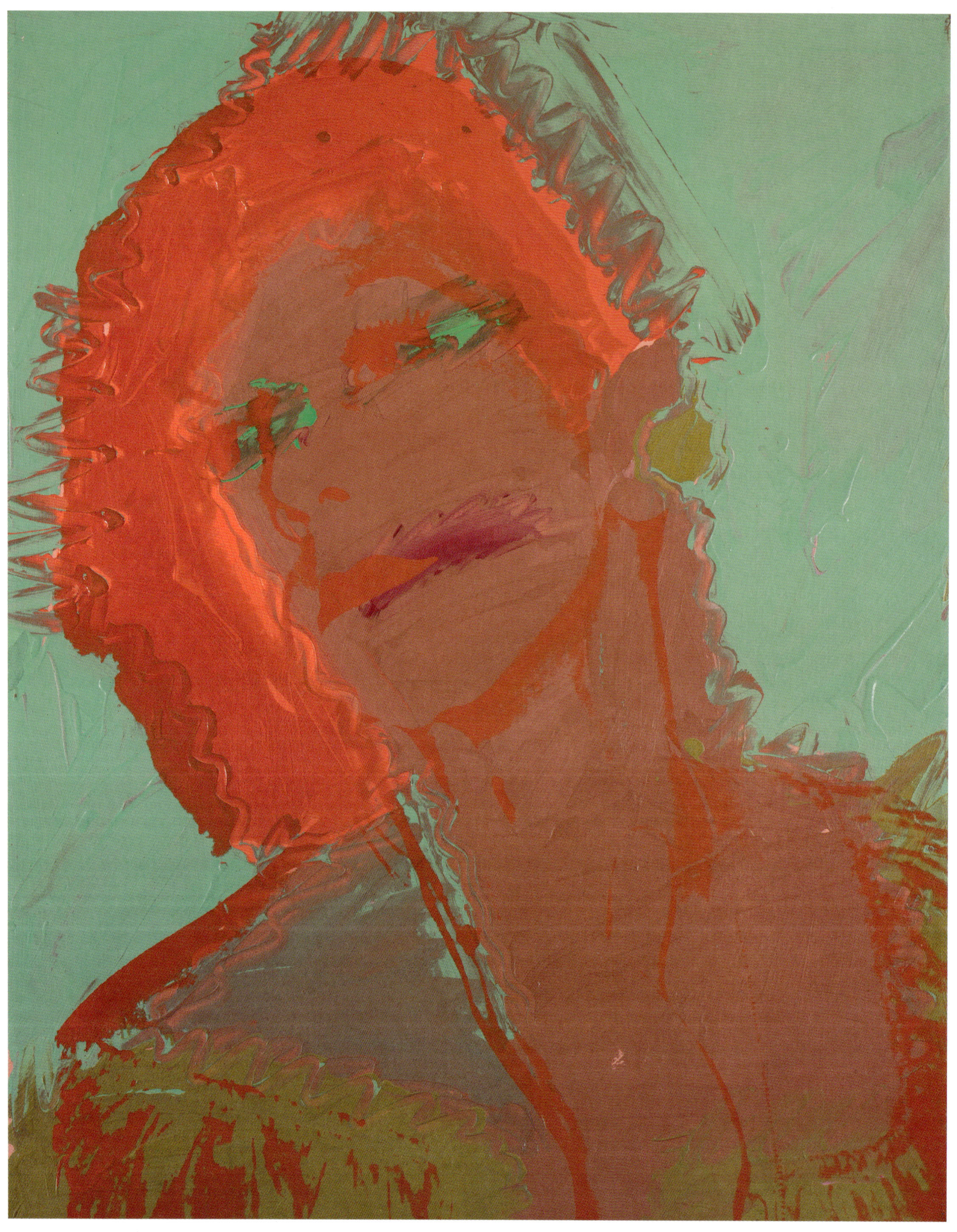

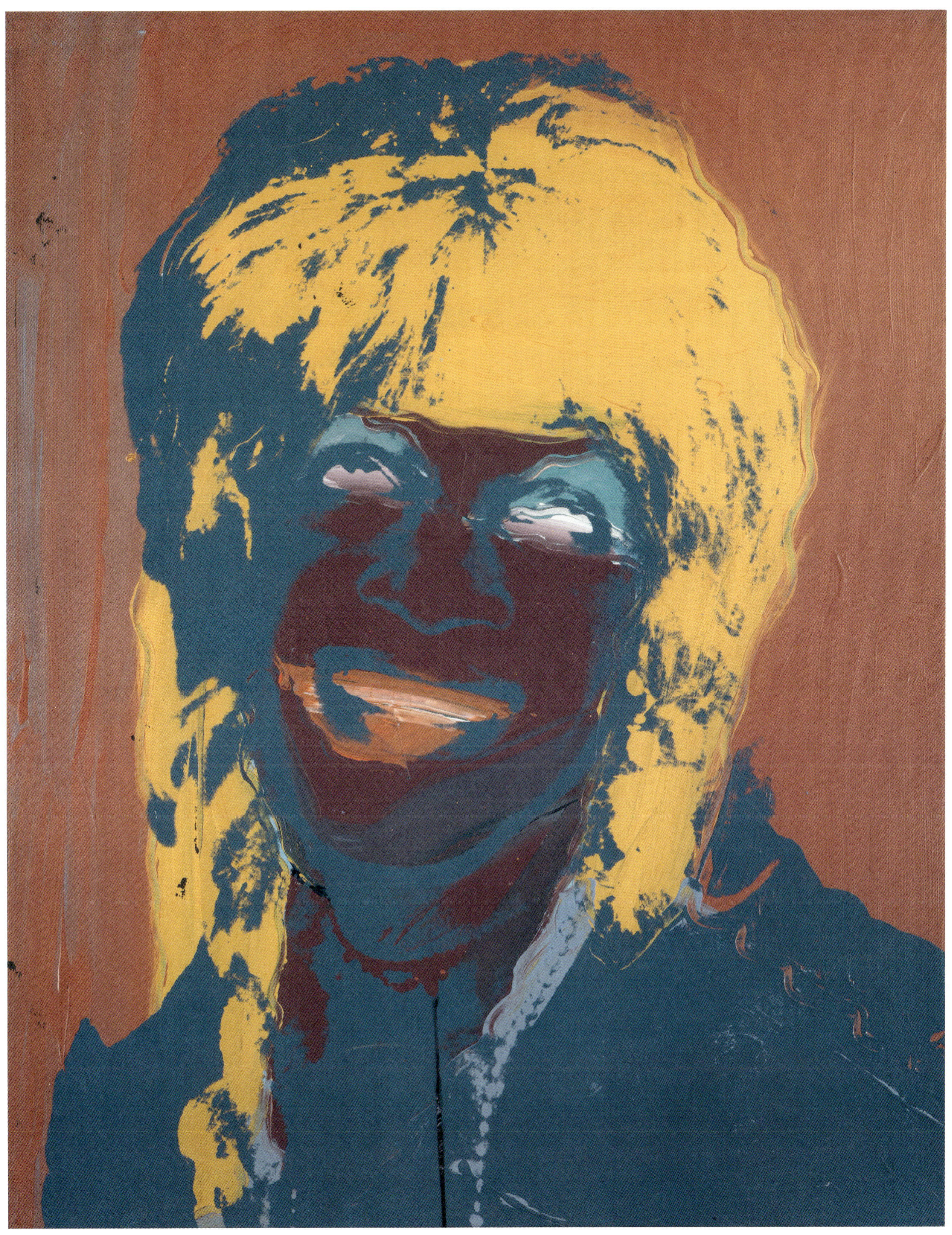

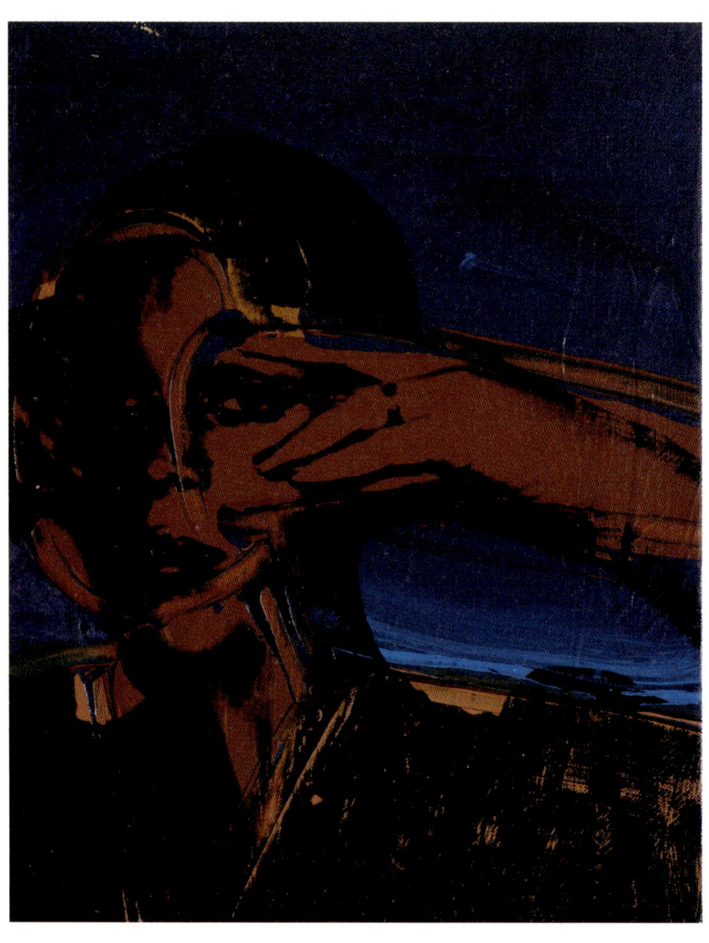
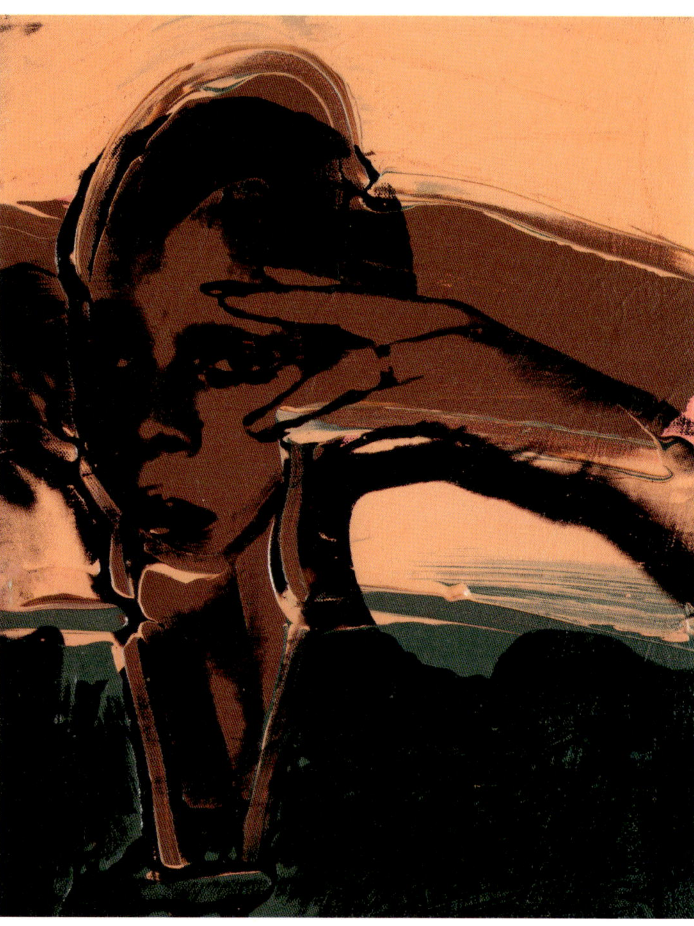
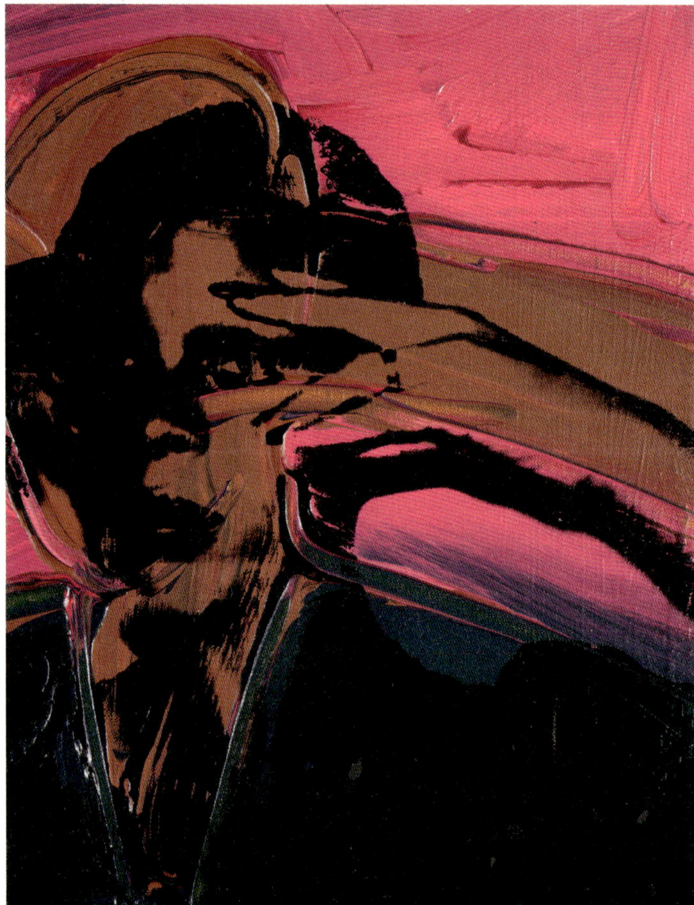
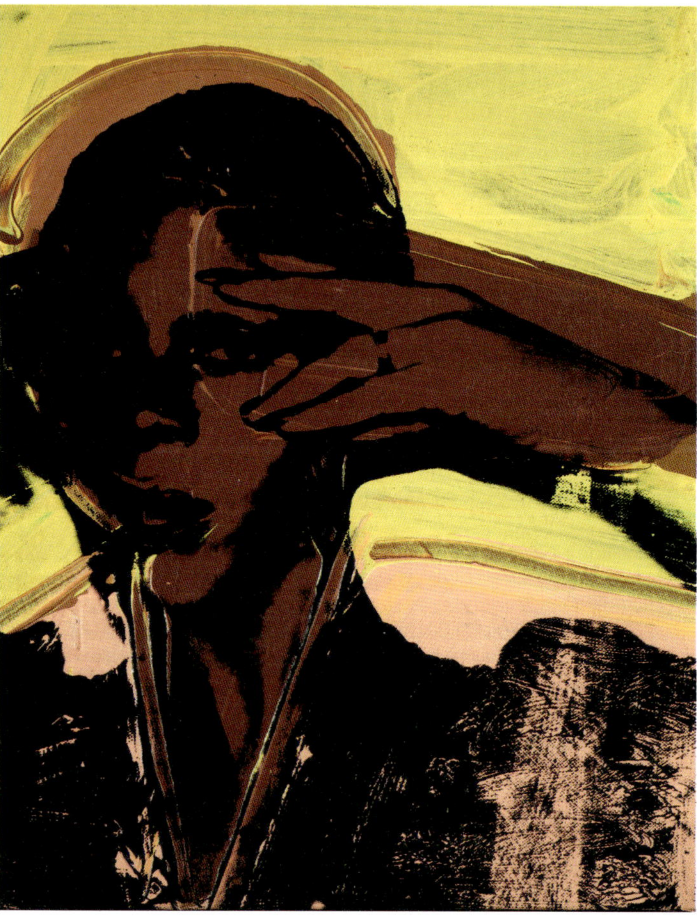

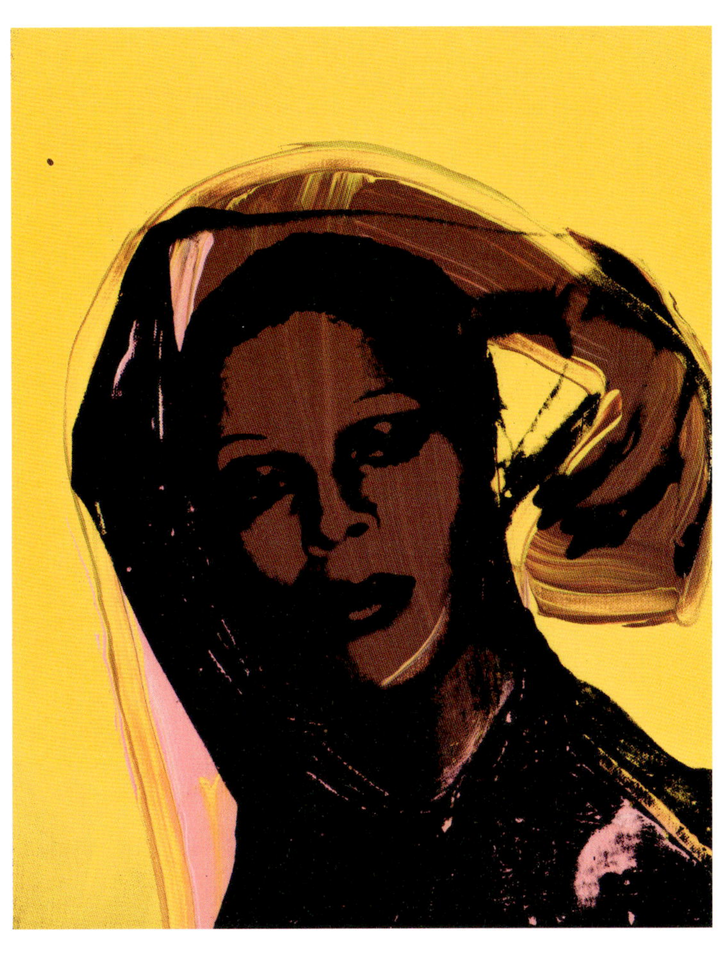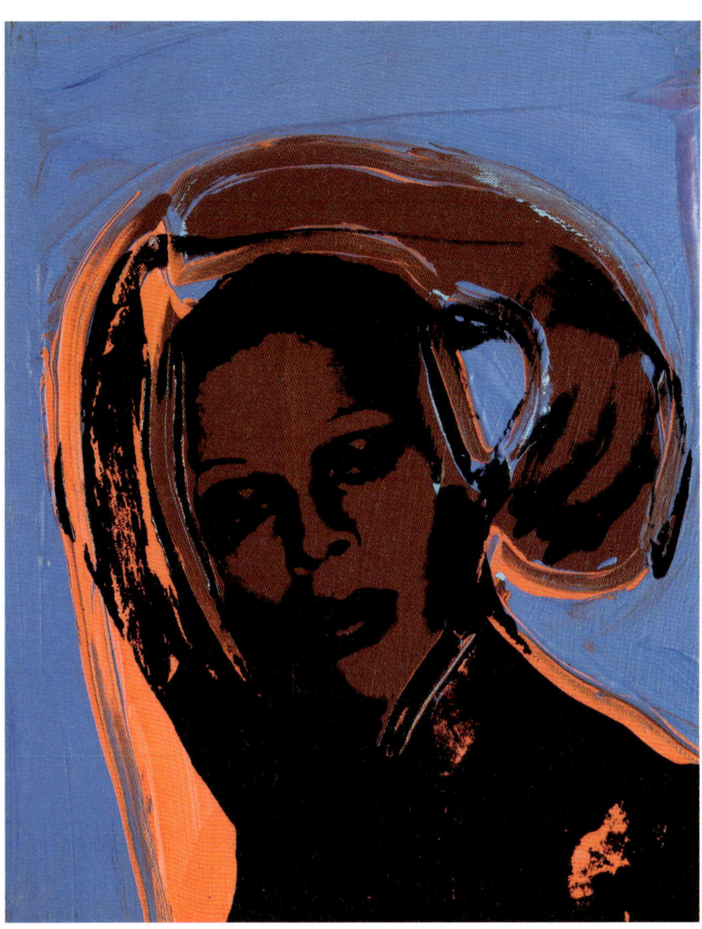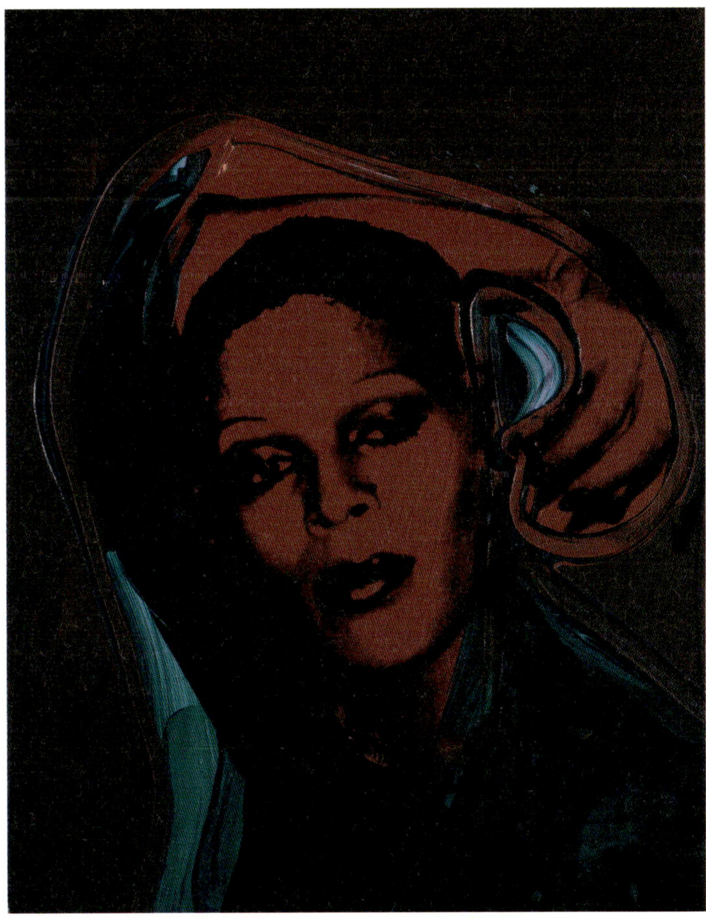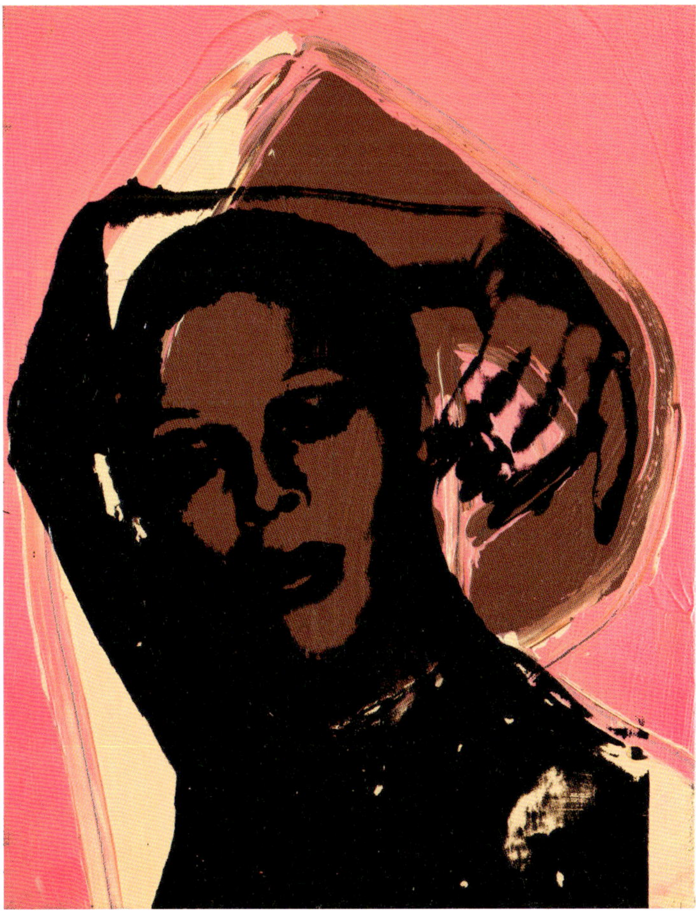

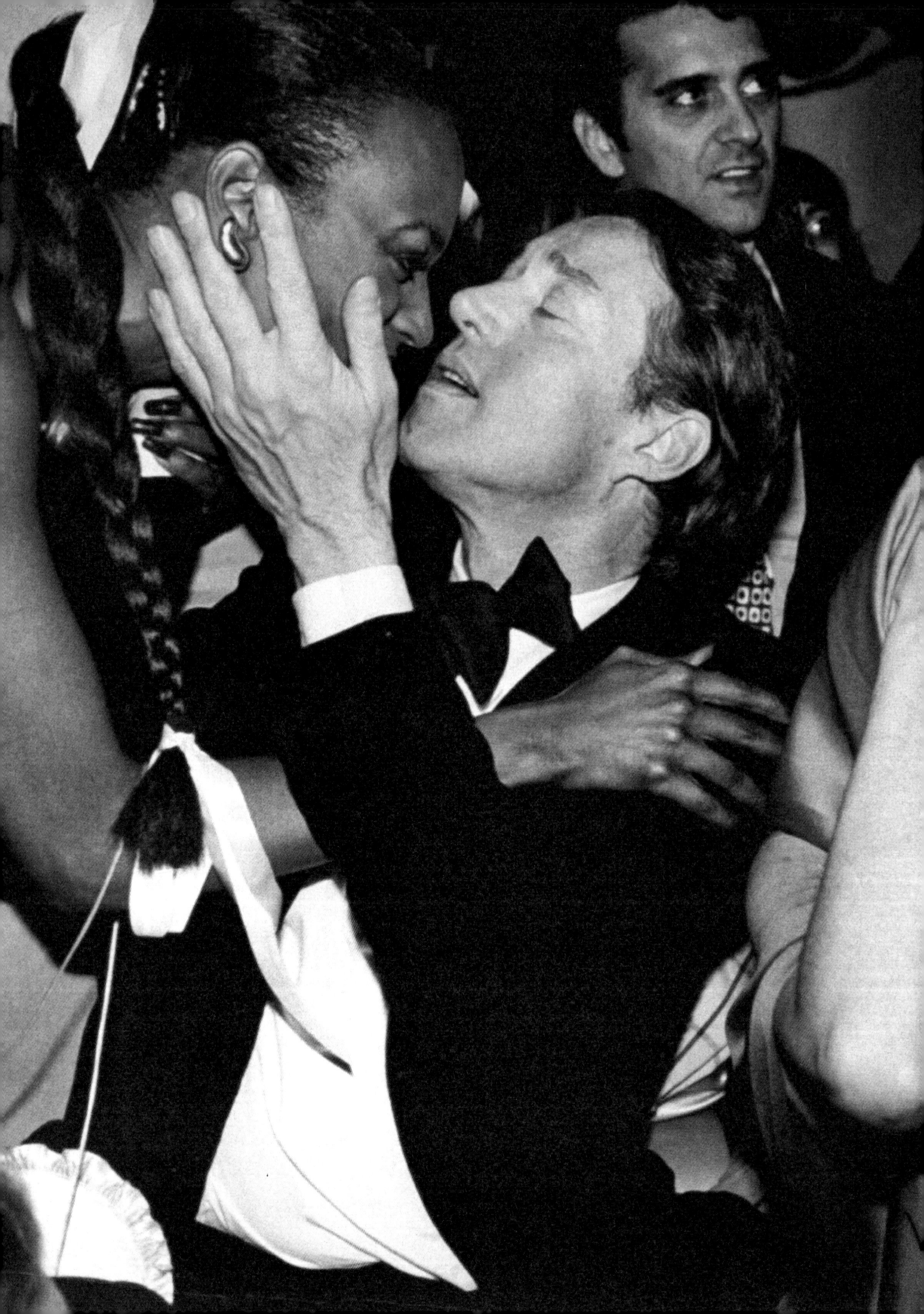

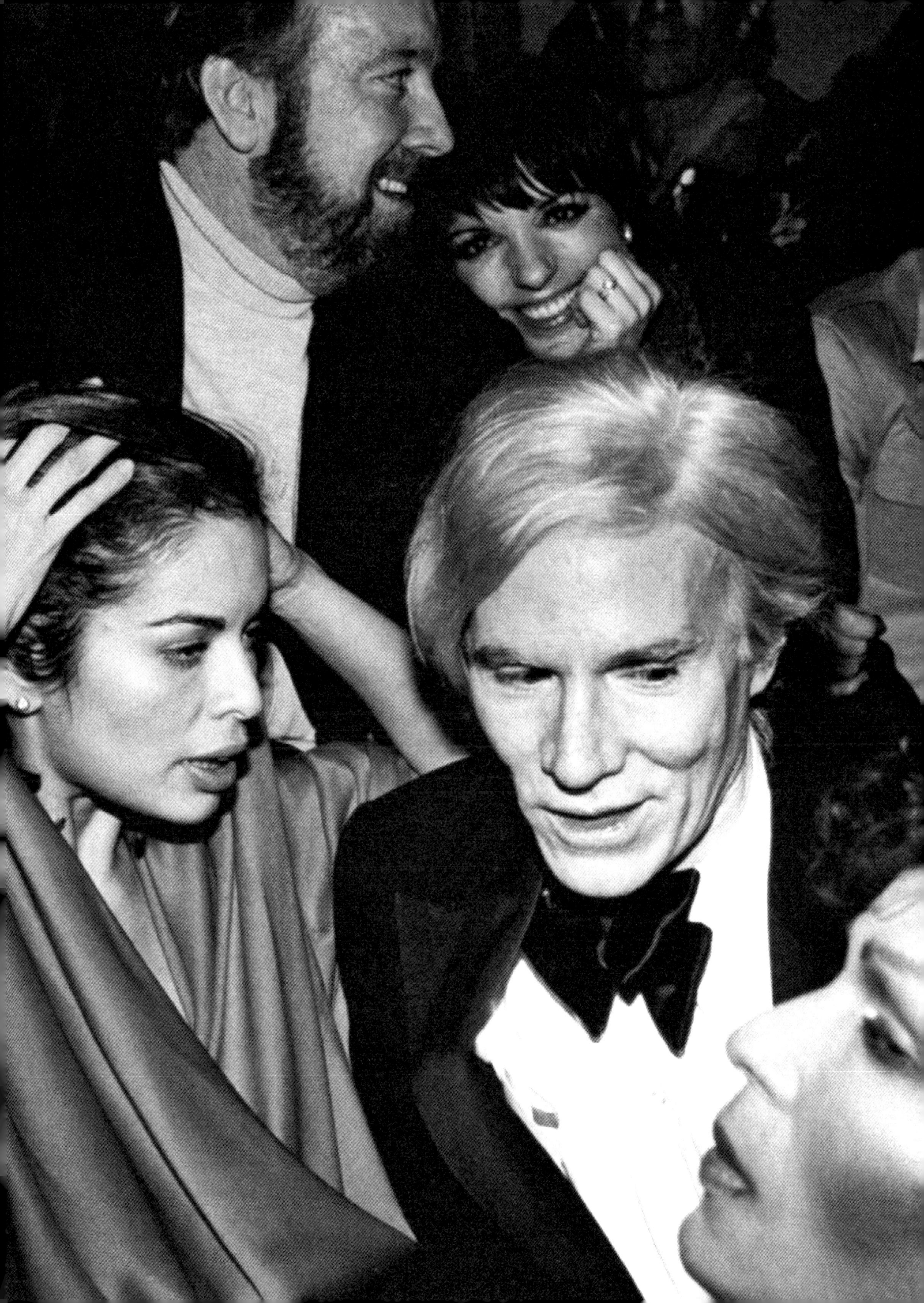

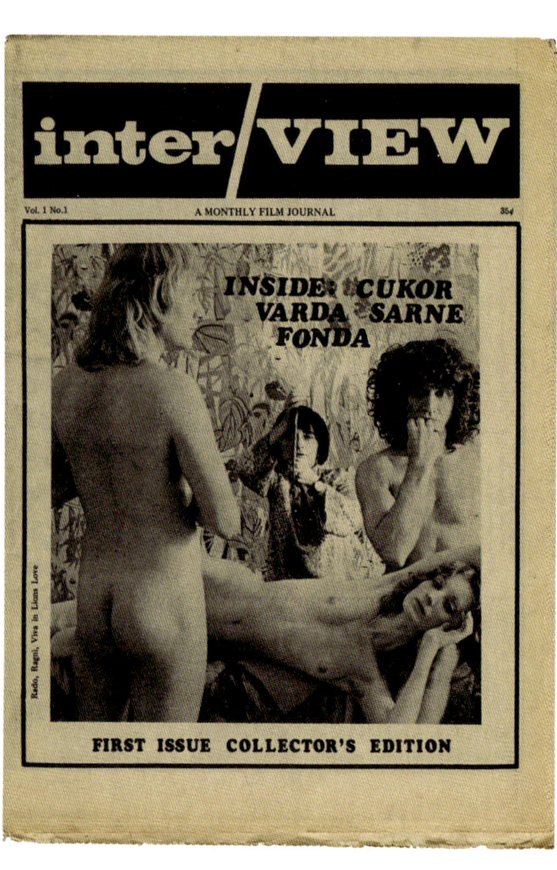

Previous pages
Celebrities during a New
Year's Eve party at Studio 54
(from left to right): Halston,
Bianca Jagger, Jack Haley
Jr. and wife Liza Minnelli,
Andy Warhol. Photo by Robin
Platzer/Twin Images/Time
Life Pictures/G

From top to bottom
Interview vol. 1, no. 1 1969
Printed ink on newsprint
41.9 x 29.5

*Andy Warhol's Interview,
December 1972* (Warhol
and Naomi Sims) 1972
Cover design by
Richard Bernstein
Printed ink on newsprint
29 x 37.8

Opposite page
*Andy Warhol's Interview,
June 1979* (Debbie Harry)
1979
Cover design by
Richard Bernstein
Printed ink on newsprint
43 x 28.2

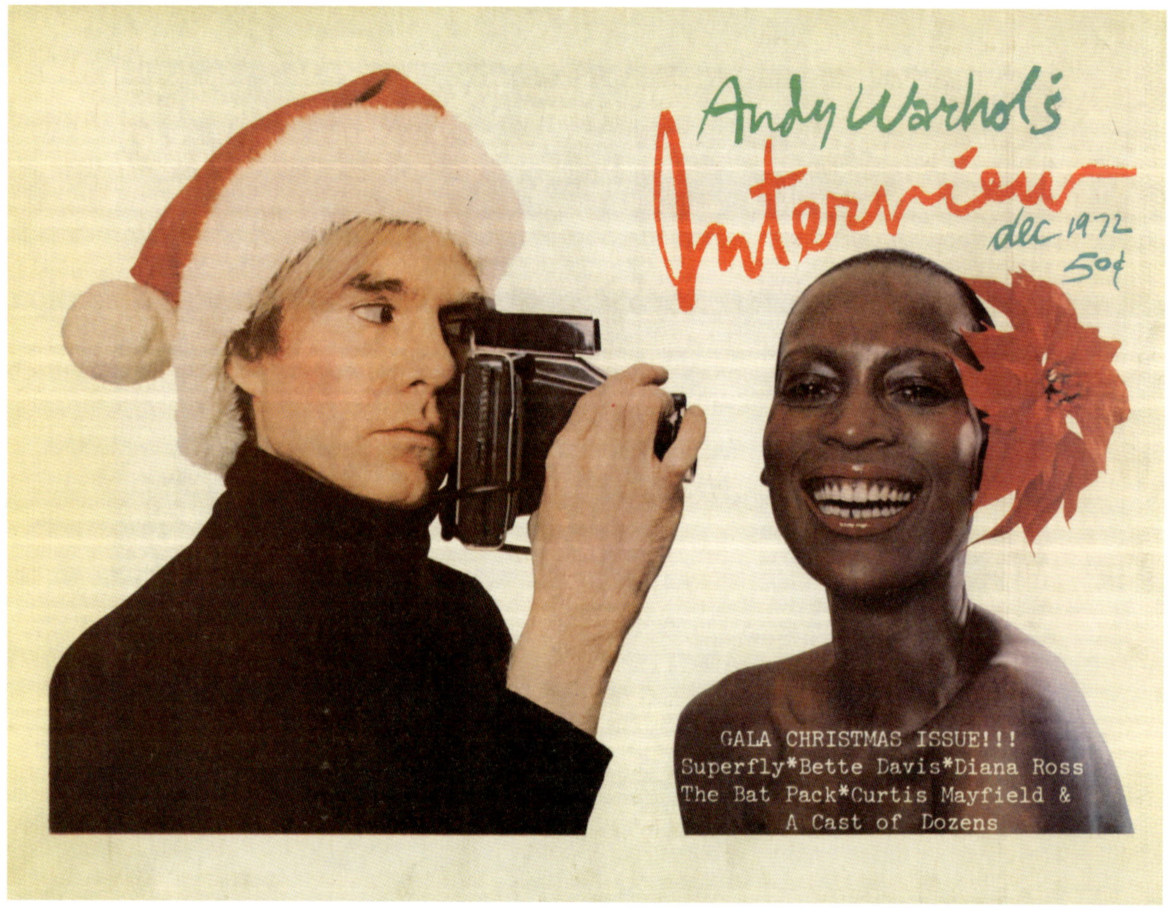

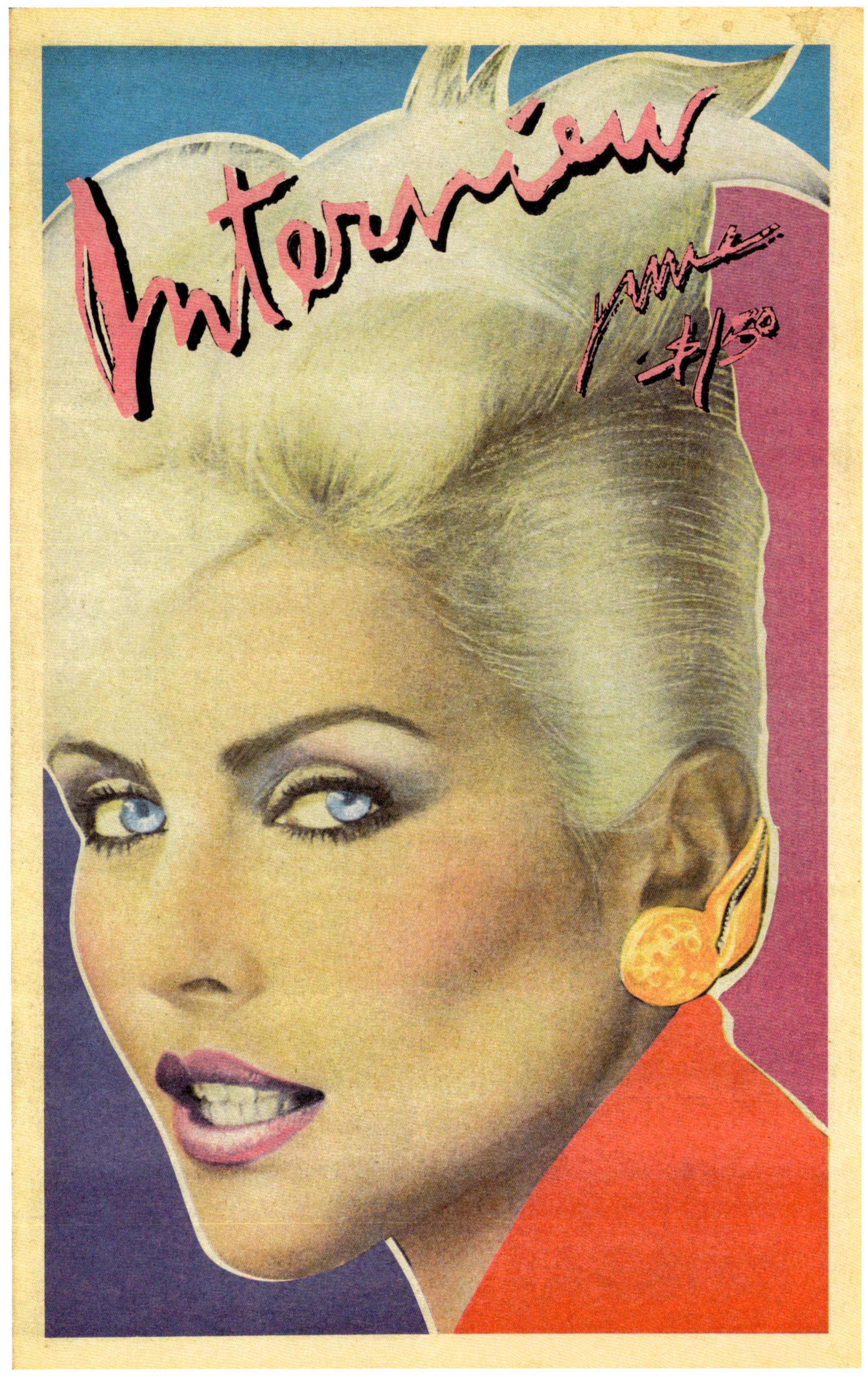
Interview
June. $1.50

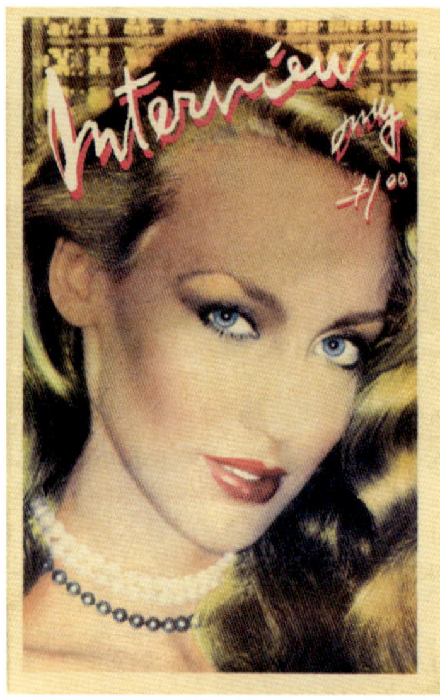
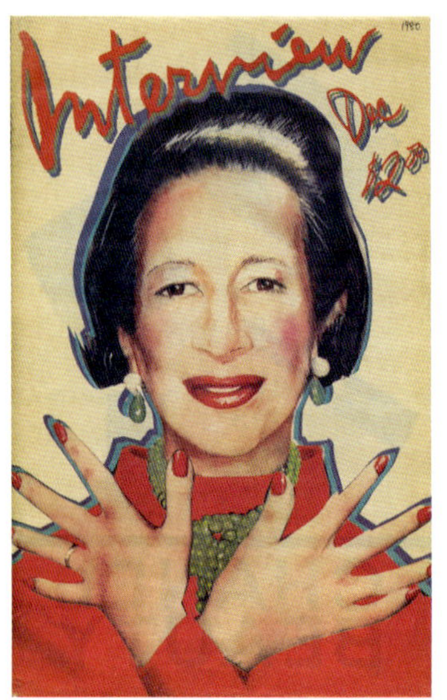
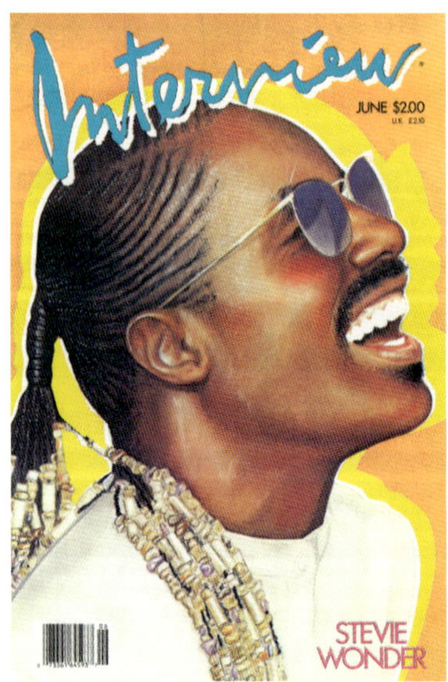
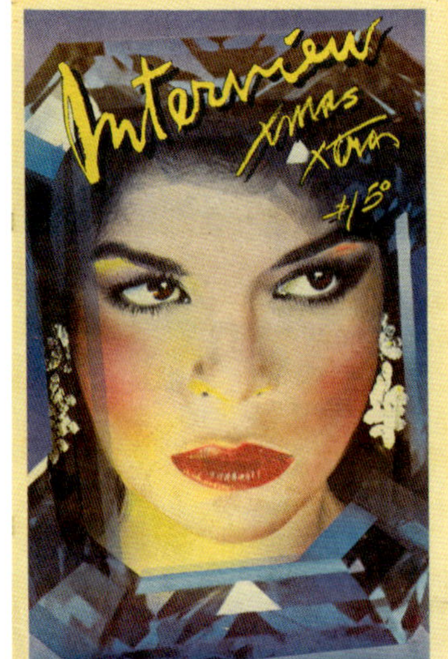
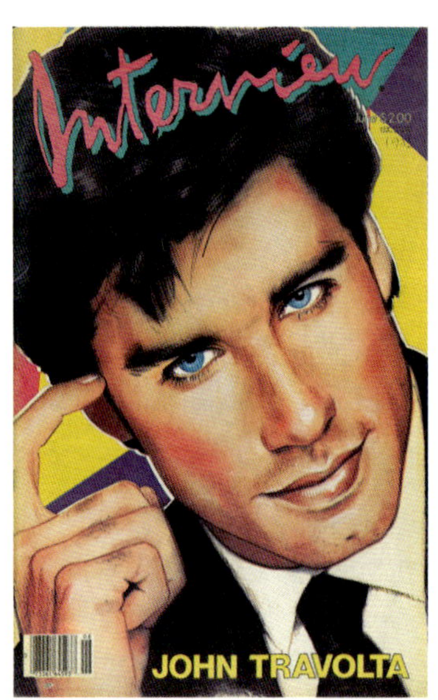

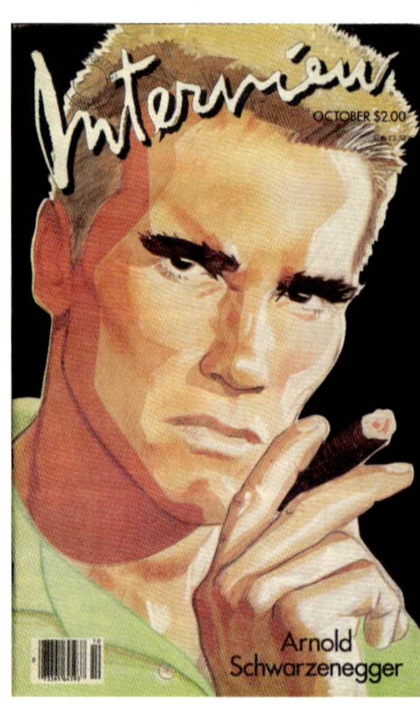
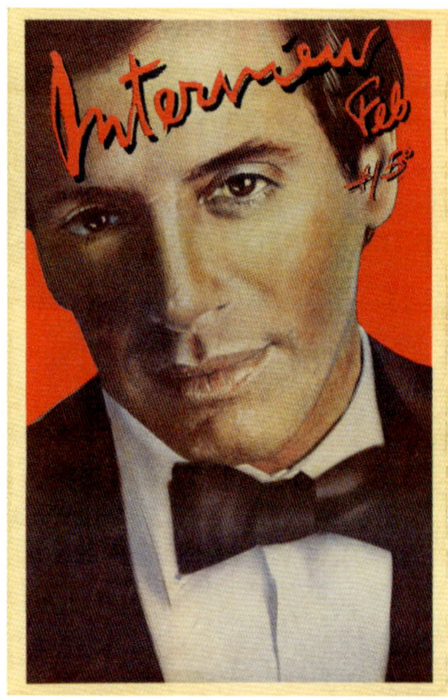
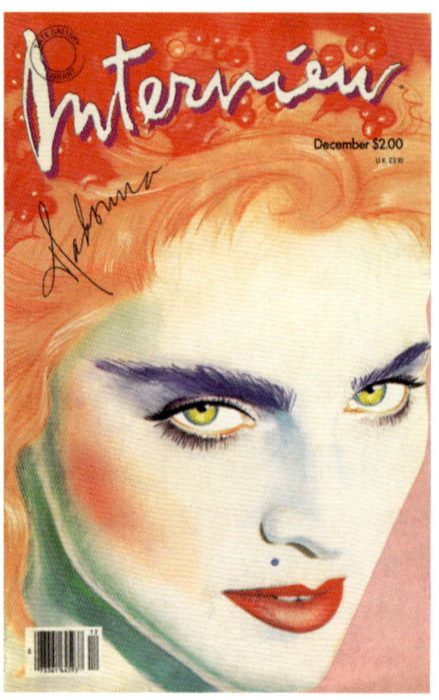

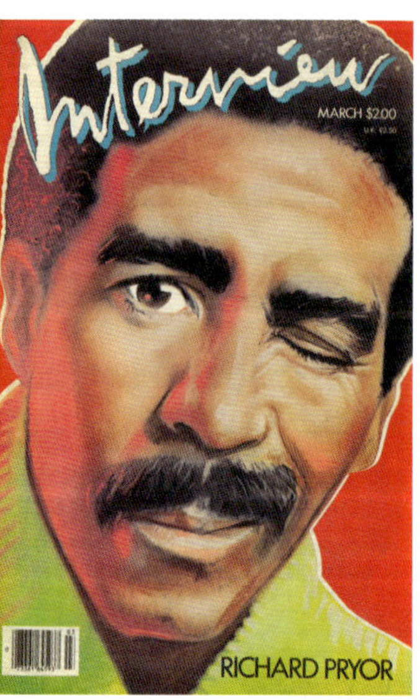

Interview 1978–86
Covers designed by Richard Bernstein
Printed ink on newsprint
43 x 28.2

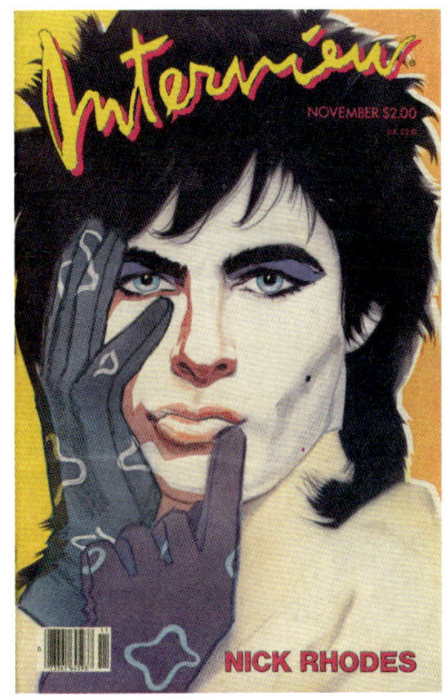

Interview
NOVEMBER $2.00
NICK RHODES

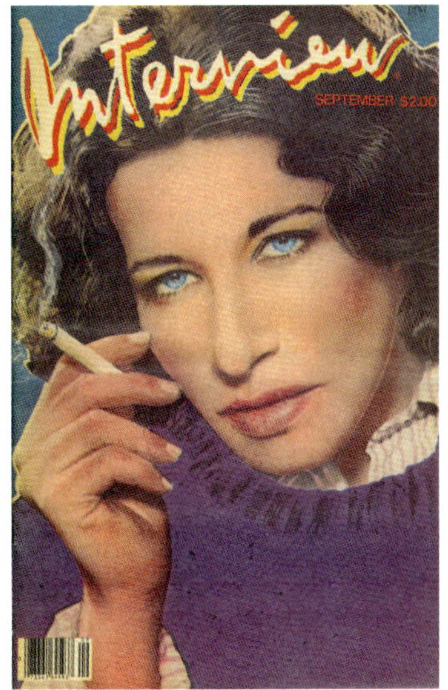

Interview
SEPTEMBER $2.00

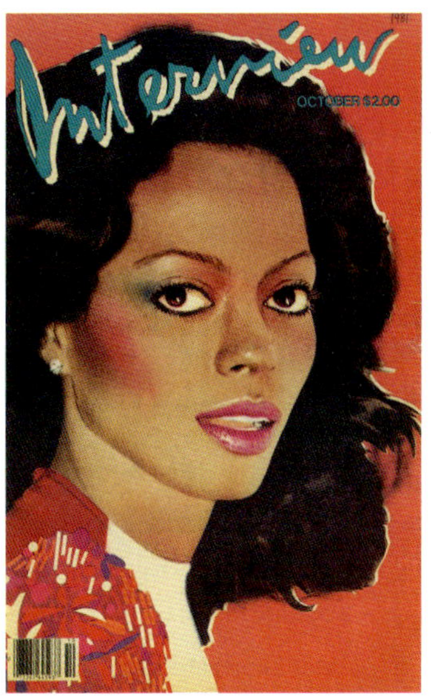

Interview
OCTOBER $2.00

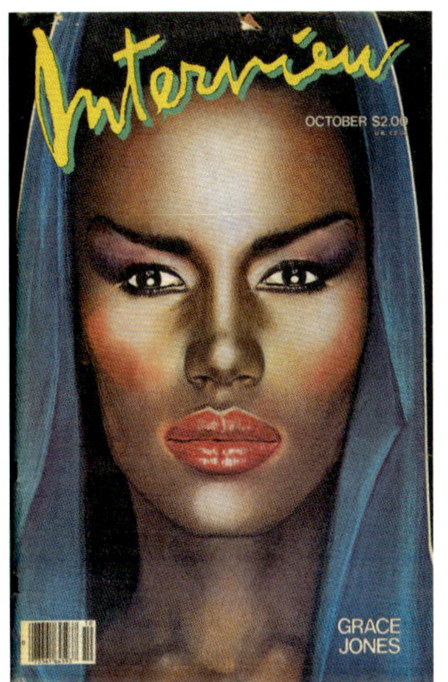

Interview
OCTOBER $2.00
GRACE JONES

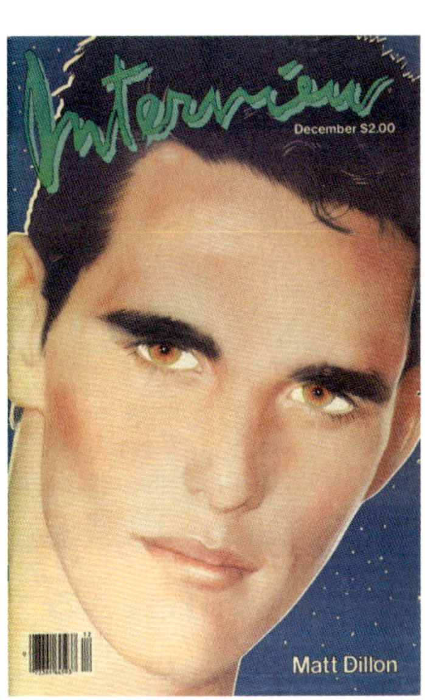

Interview
December $2.00
Matt Dillon

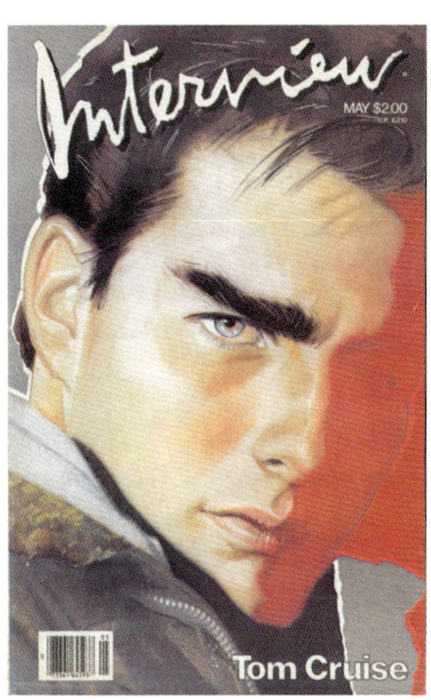

Interview
MAY $2.00
Tom Cruise

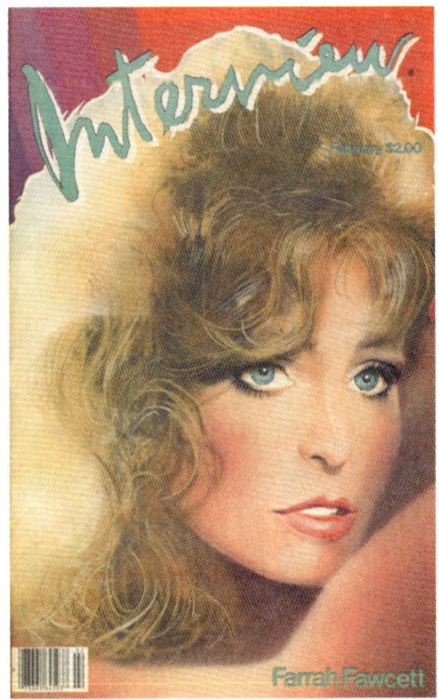

Interview
February $2.00
Farrah Fawcett

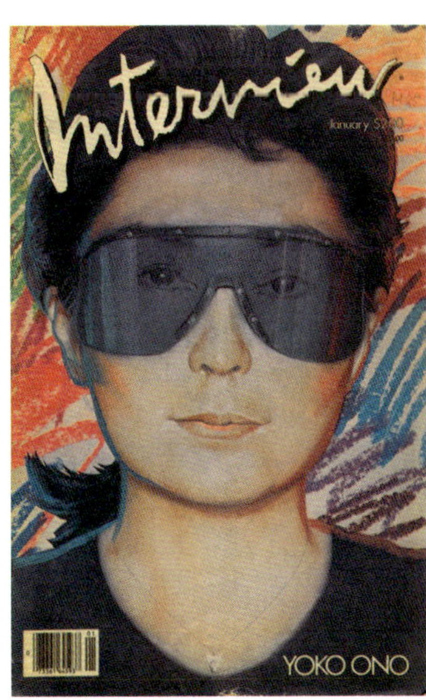

Interview
January $2.00
YOKO ONO

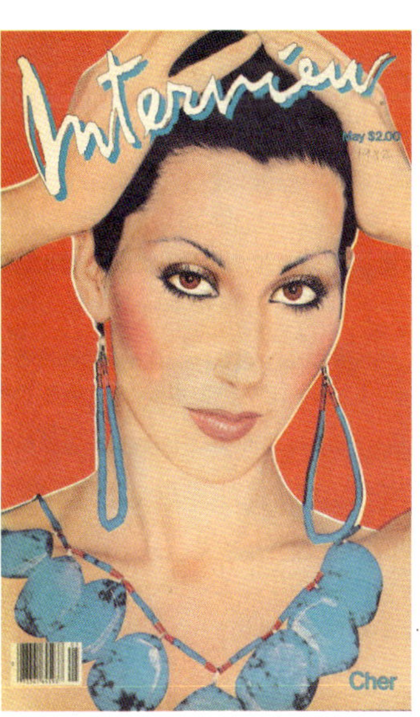

Interview
May $2.00
Cher

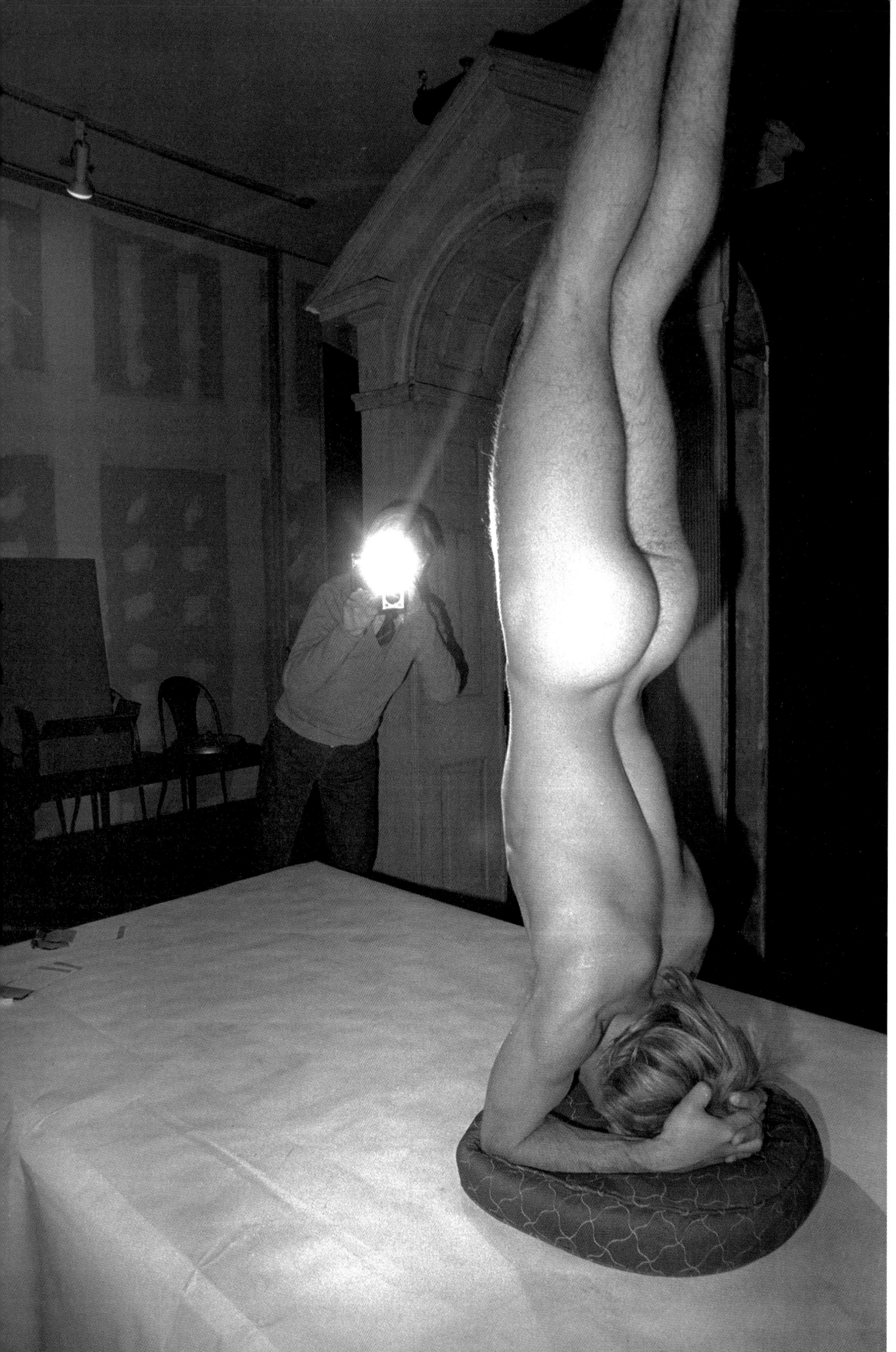

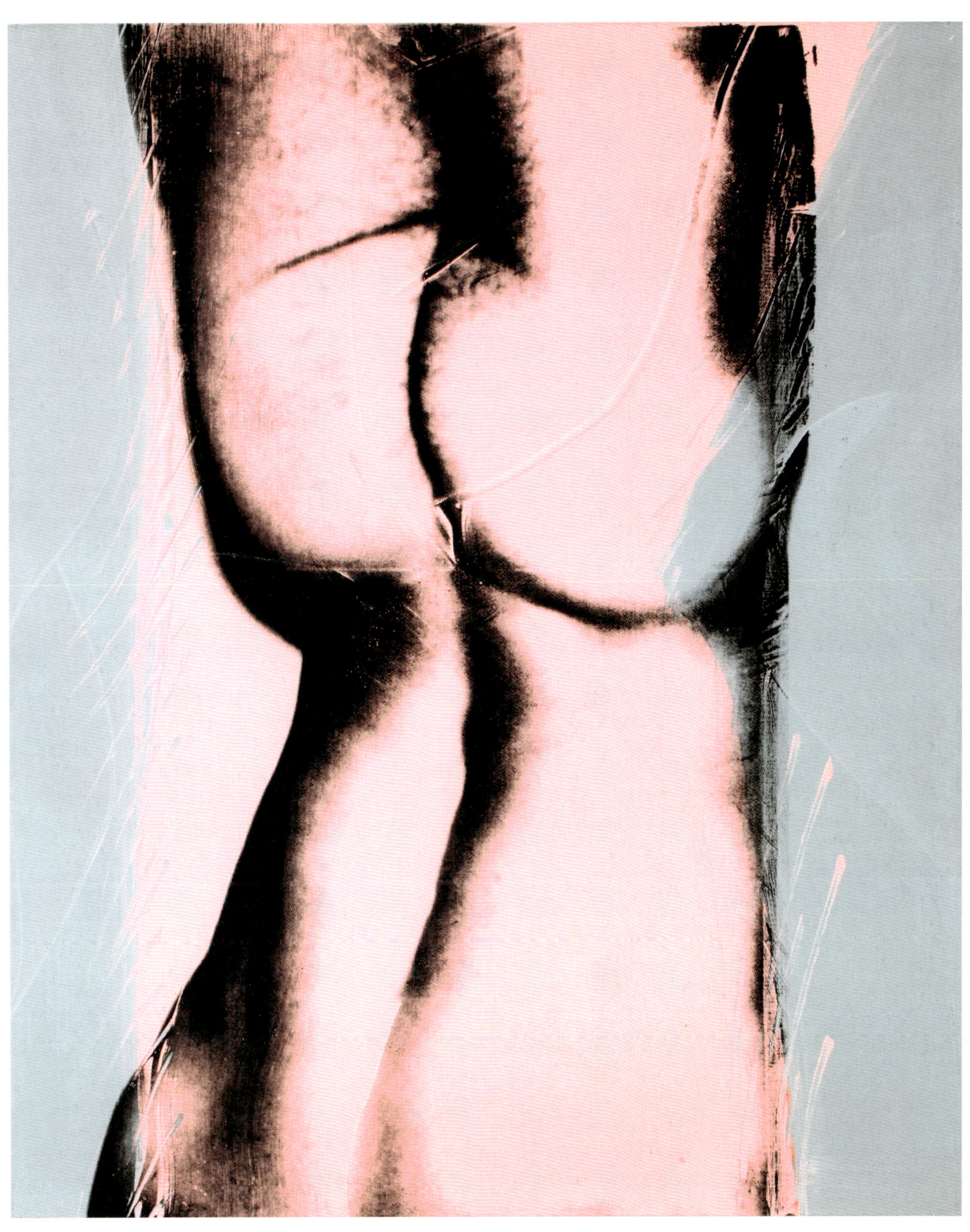

Opposite page
Andy Warhol shooting Bobby
Houston, 860 Broadway
Factory, New York, 1977
Photo by Christopher Makos

Torso 1977
Screenprint and acrylic paint
on canvas
127 x 106.7

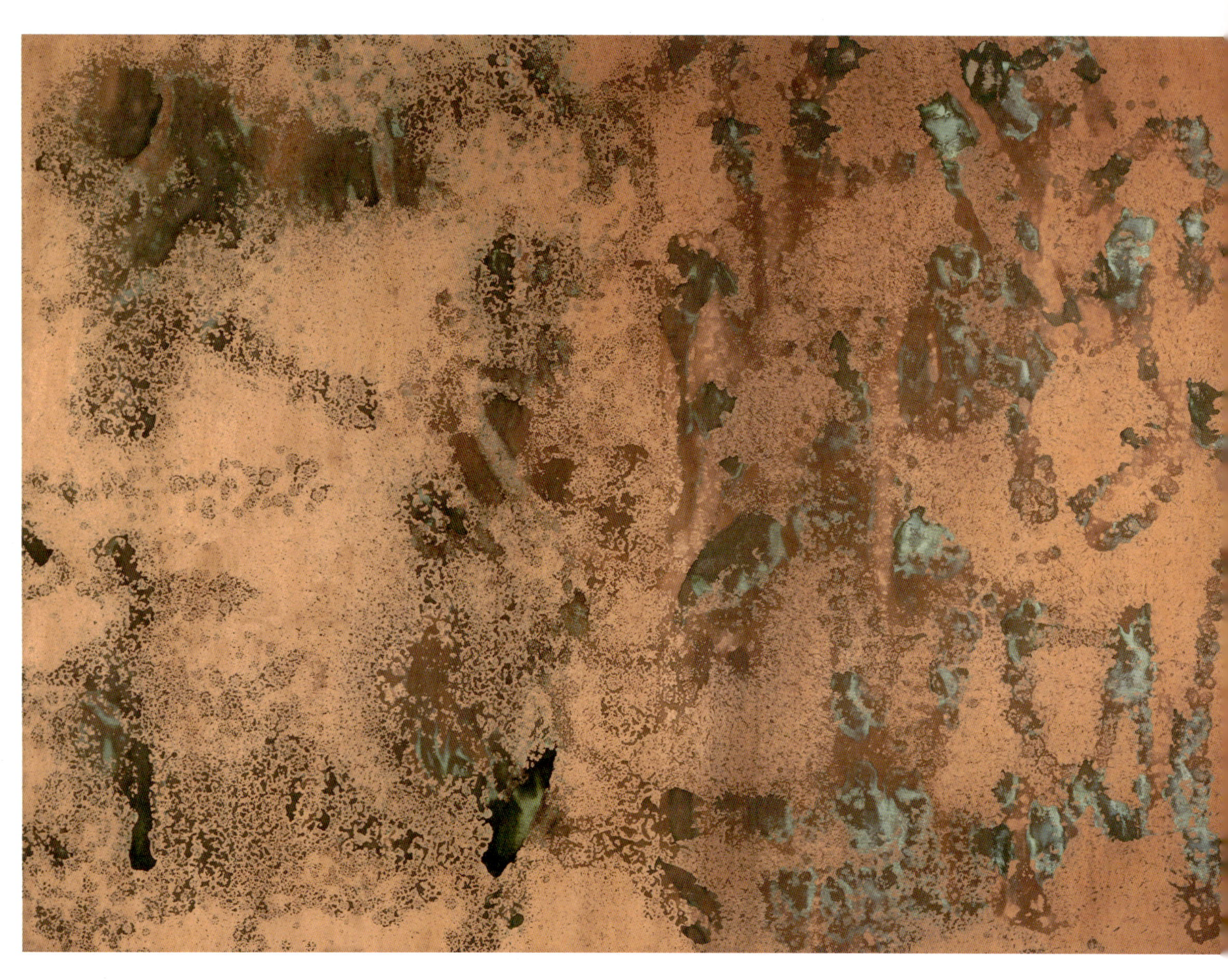

Oxidation Painting 1978
Urine and metallic paint
on canvas
199 x 553.5

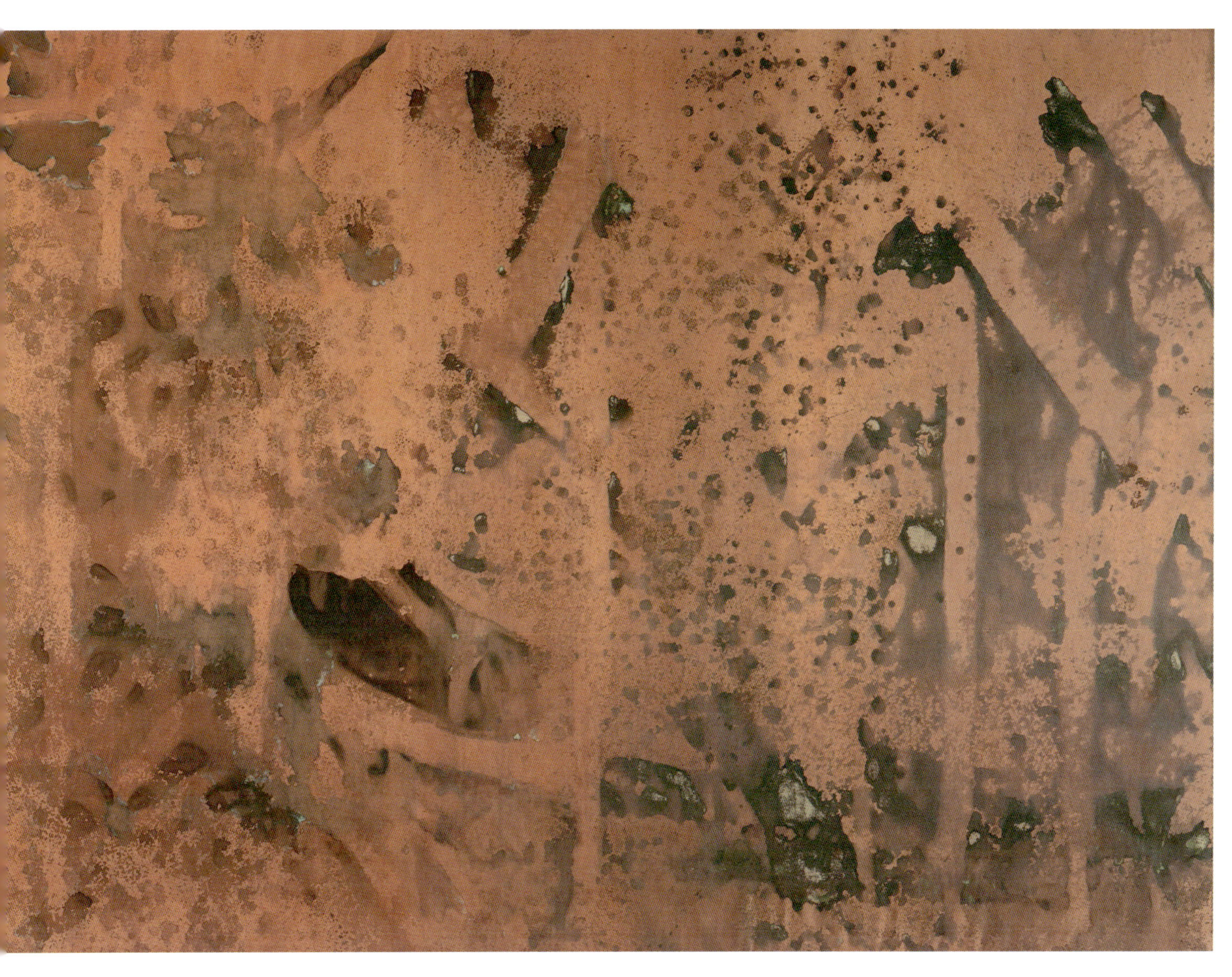

Shadow 1978
Acrylic paint and screenprint
on canvas
198 x 508

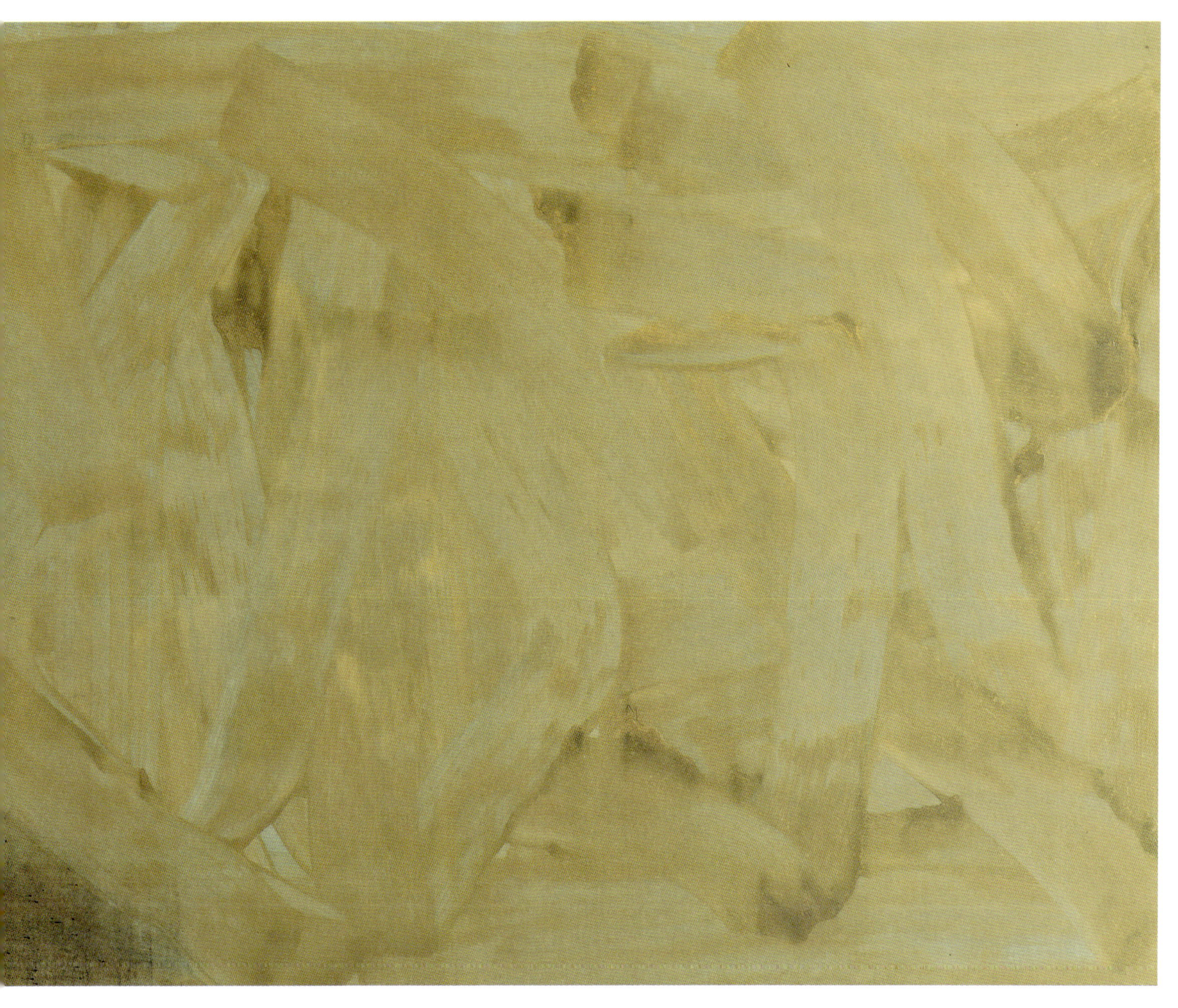

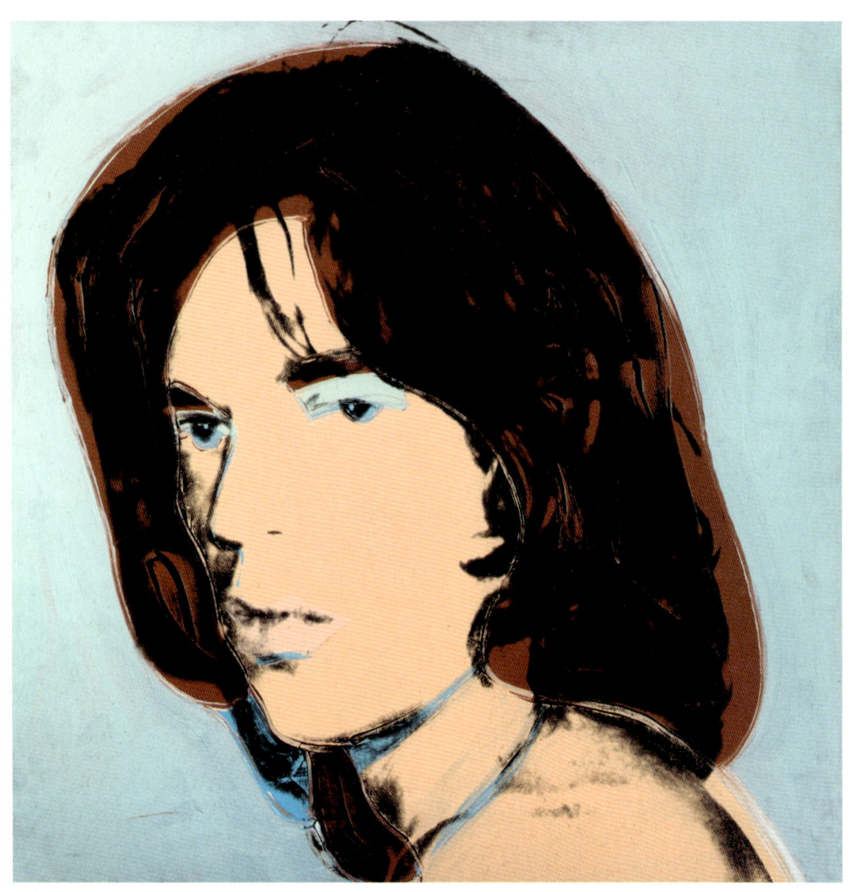

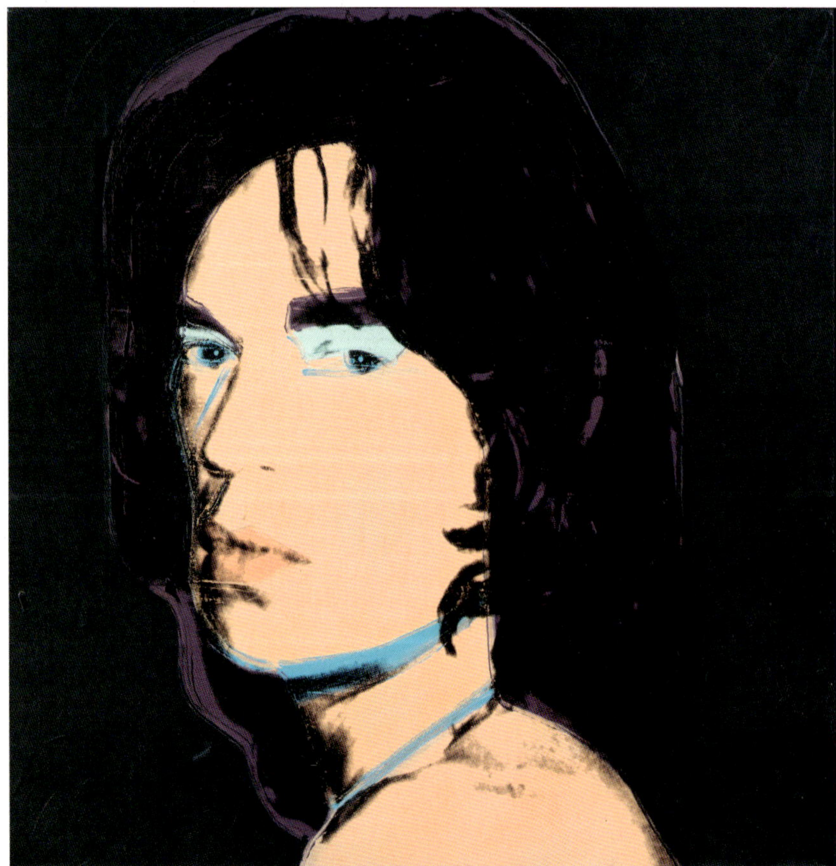

Mick Jagger 1975
Acrylic paint and screenprint
on canvas
101.6 x 101.6 (each)

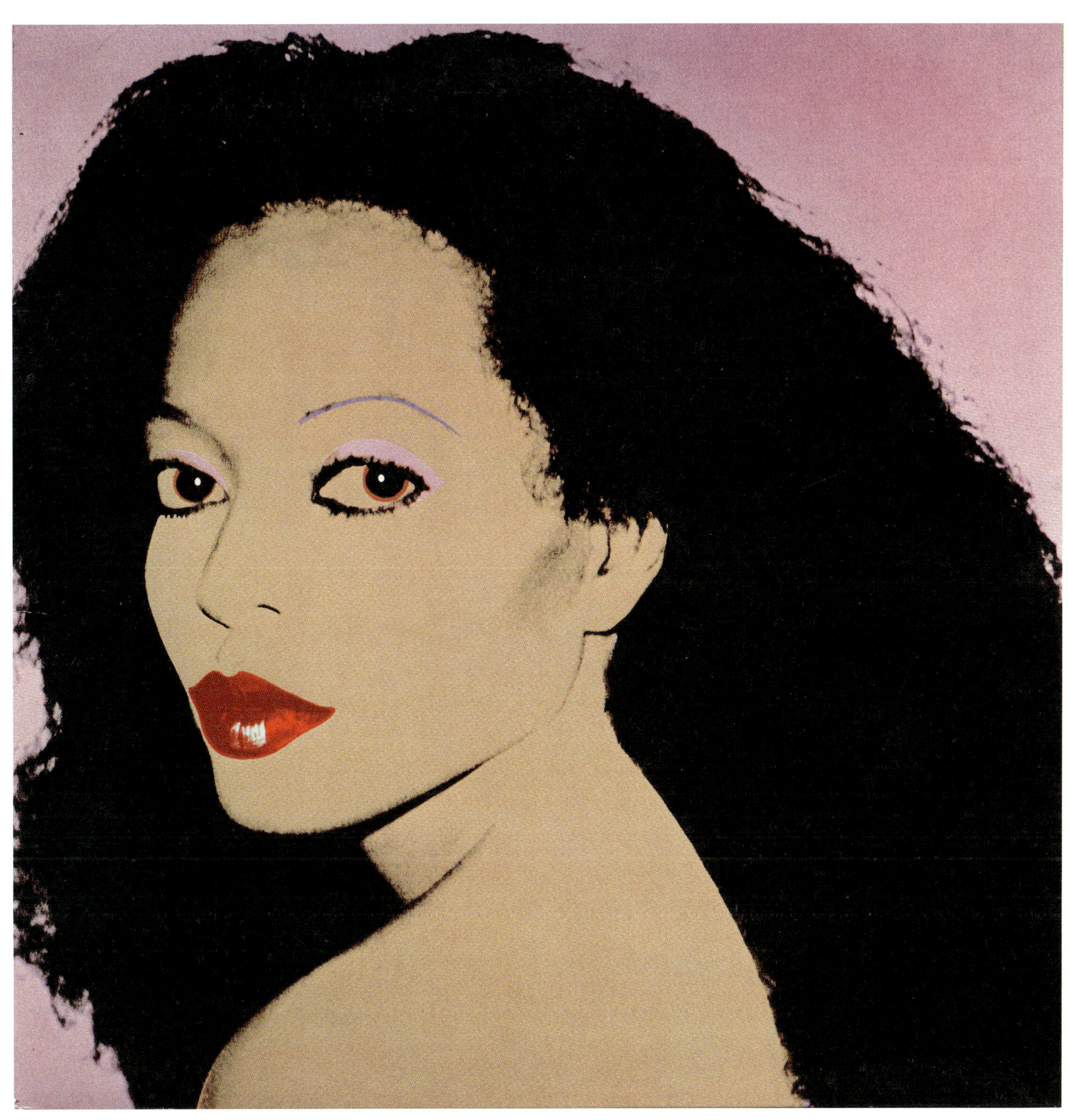

Diana Ross, Silk Electric
1982
Offset lithograph on coated
record cover stock with vinyl
record album
31.4 x 31.4

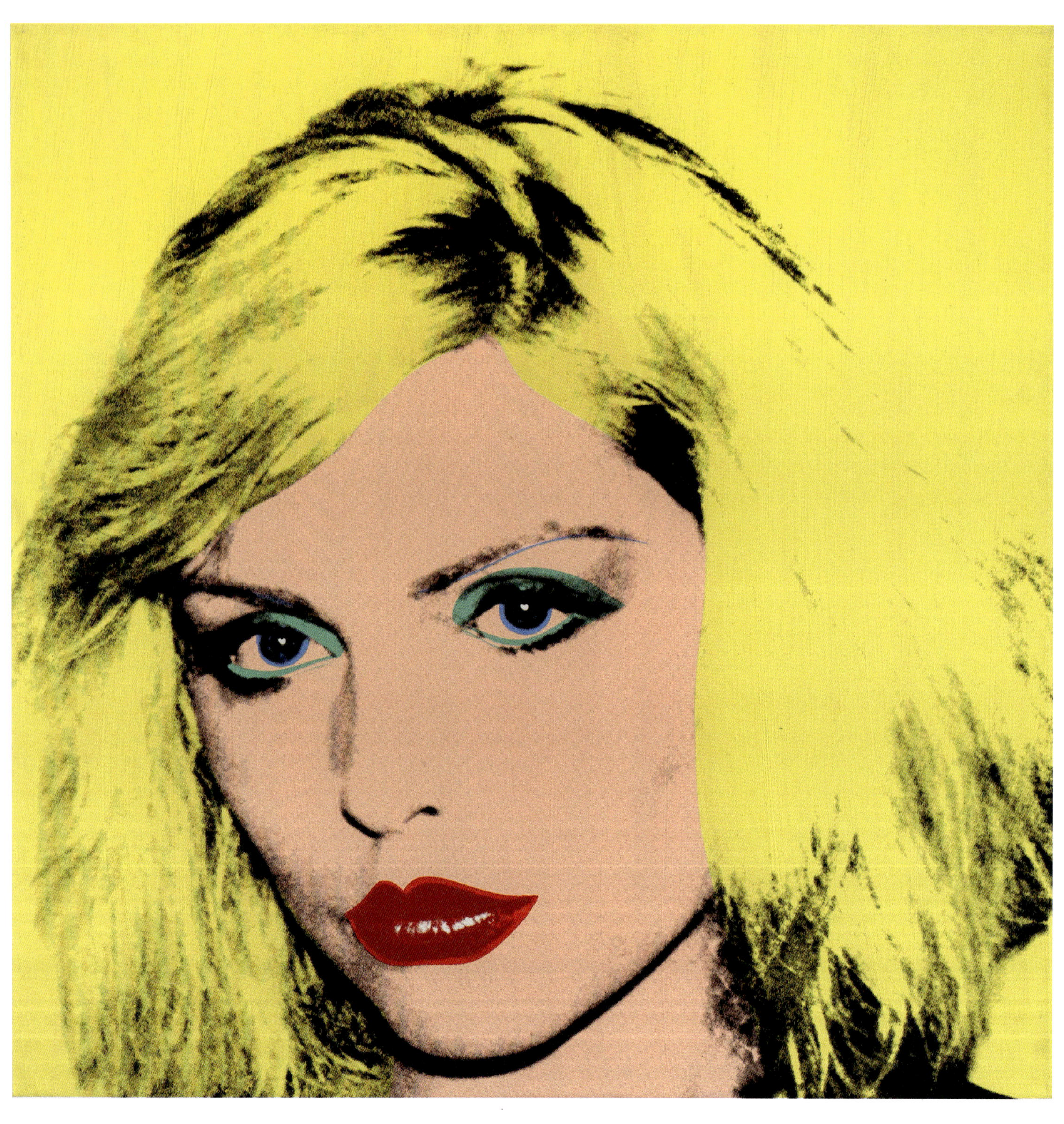

Debbie Harry 1980
Acrylic paint and screenprint
on canvas
101.6 x 101.6 (each)

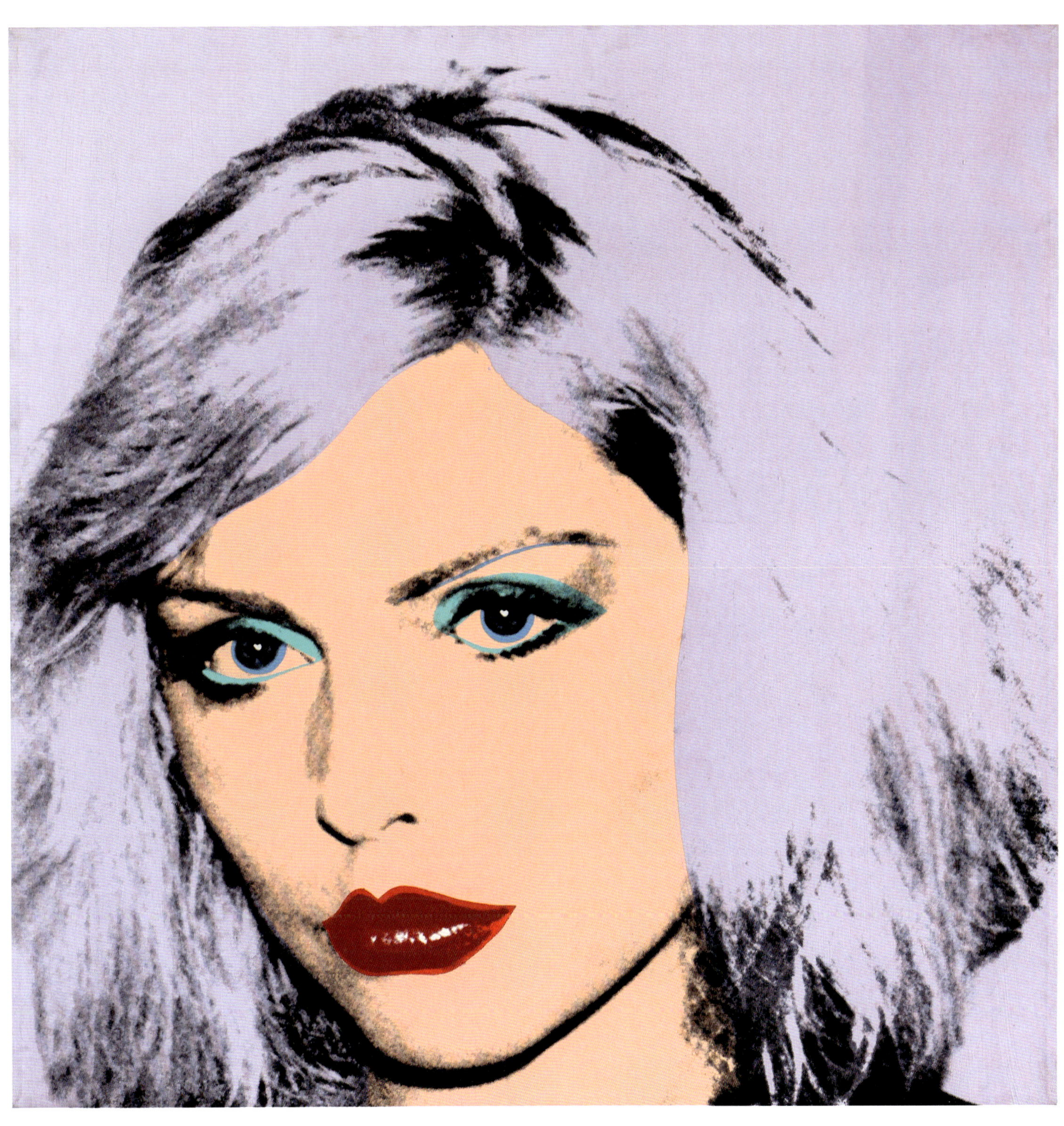

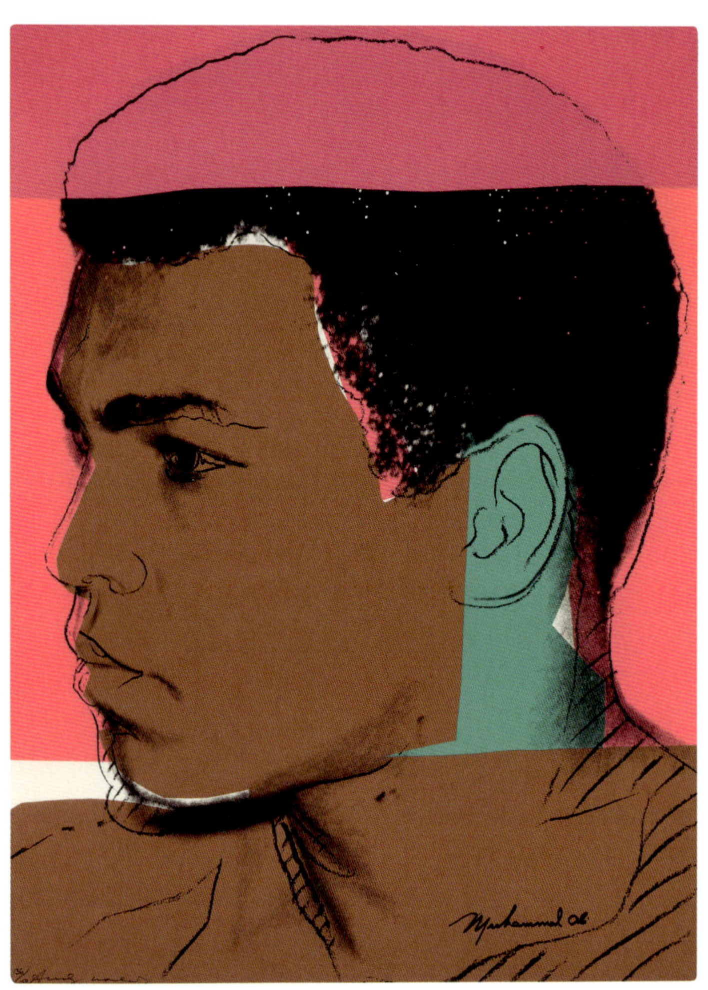

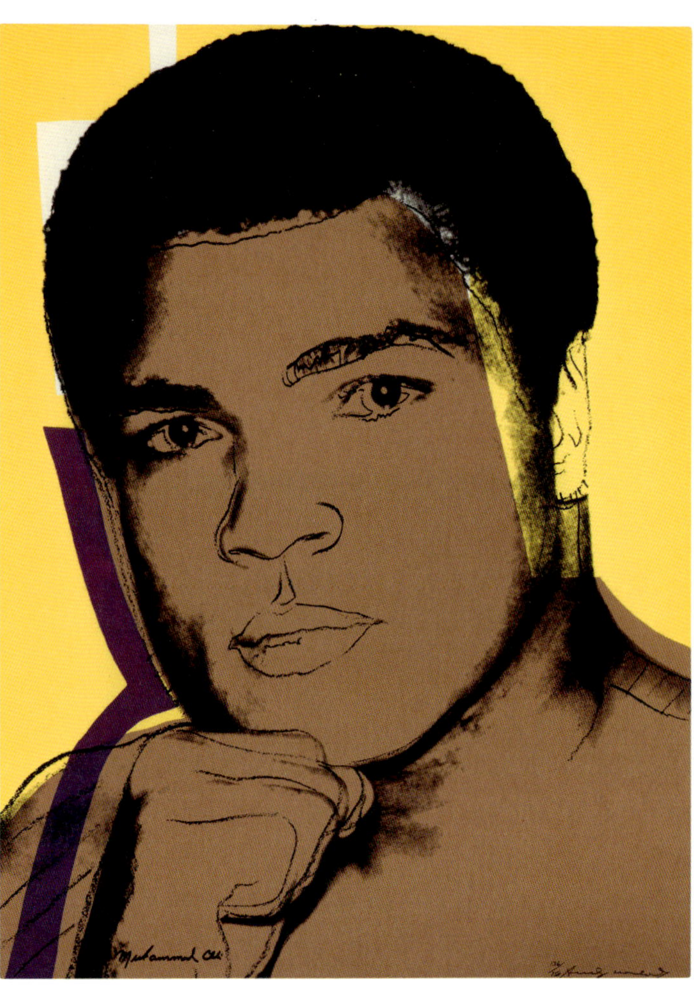

Muhammad Ali 1978
Screenprint on paper
101.6 x 76.2 (each)

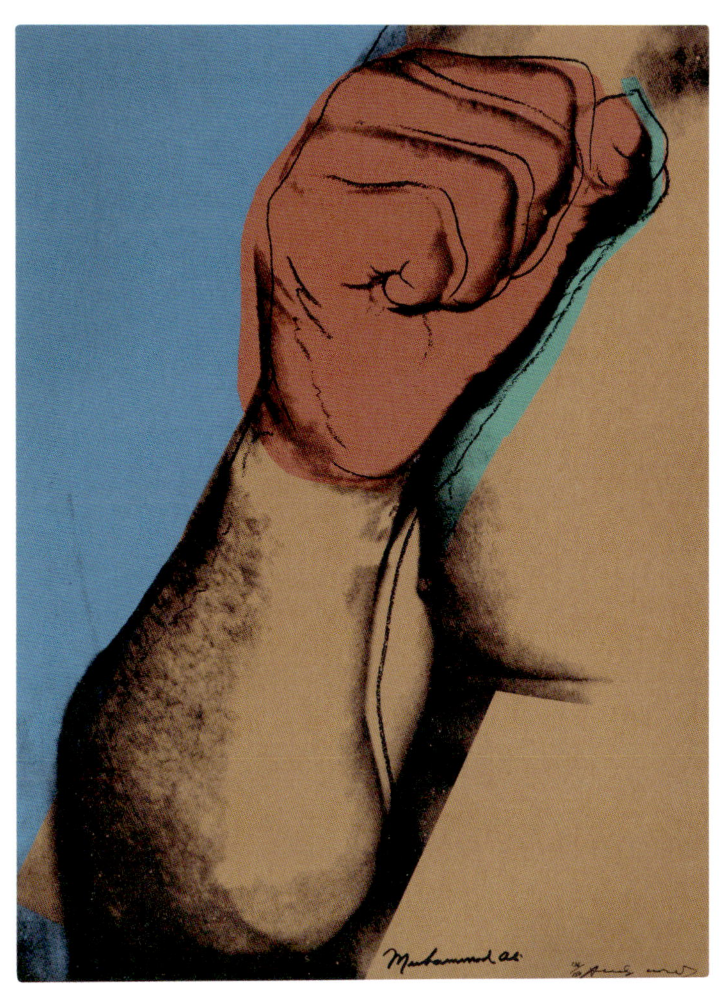
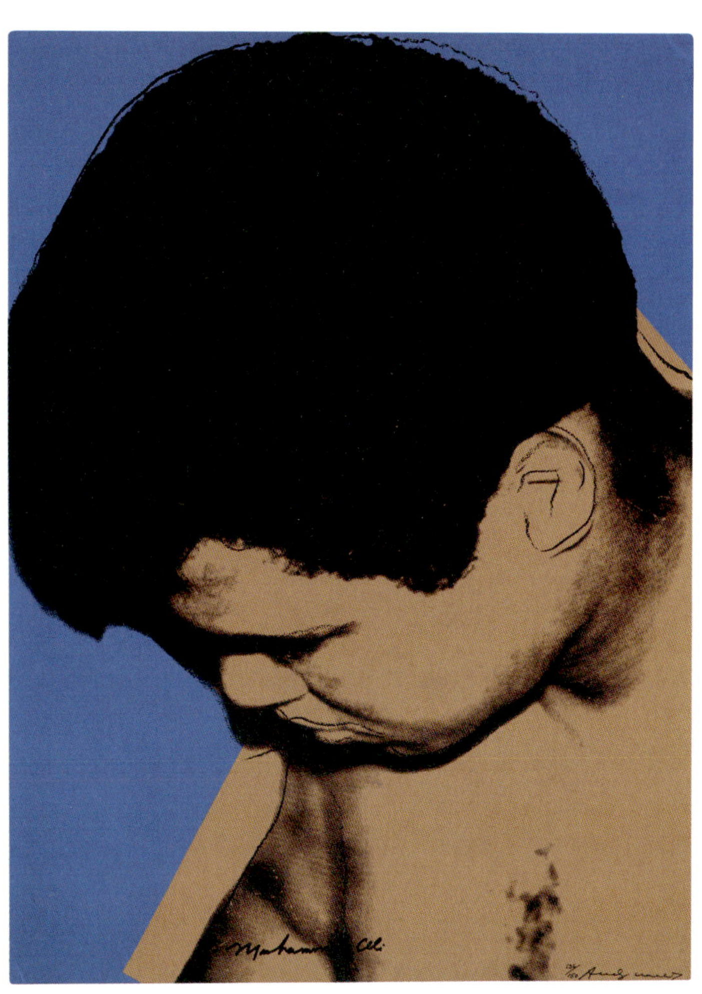

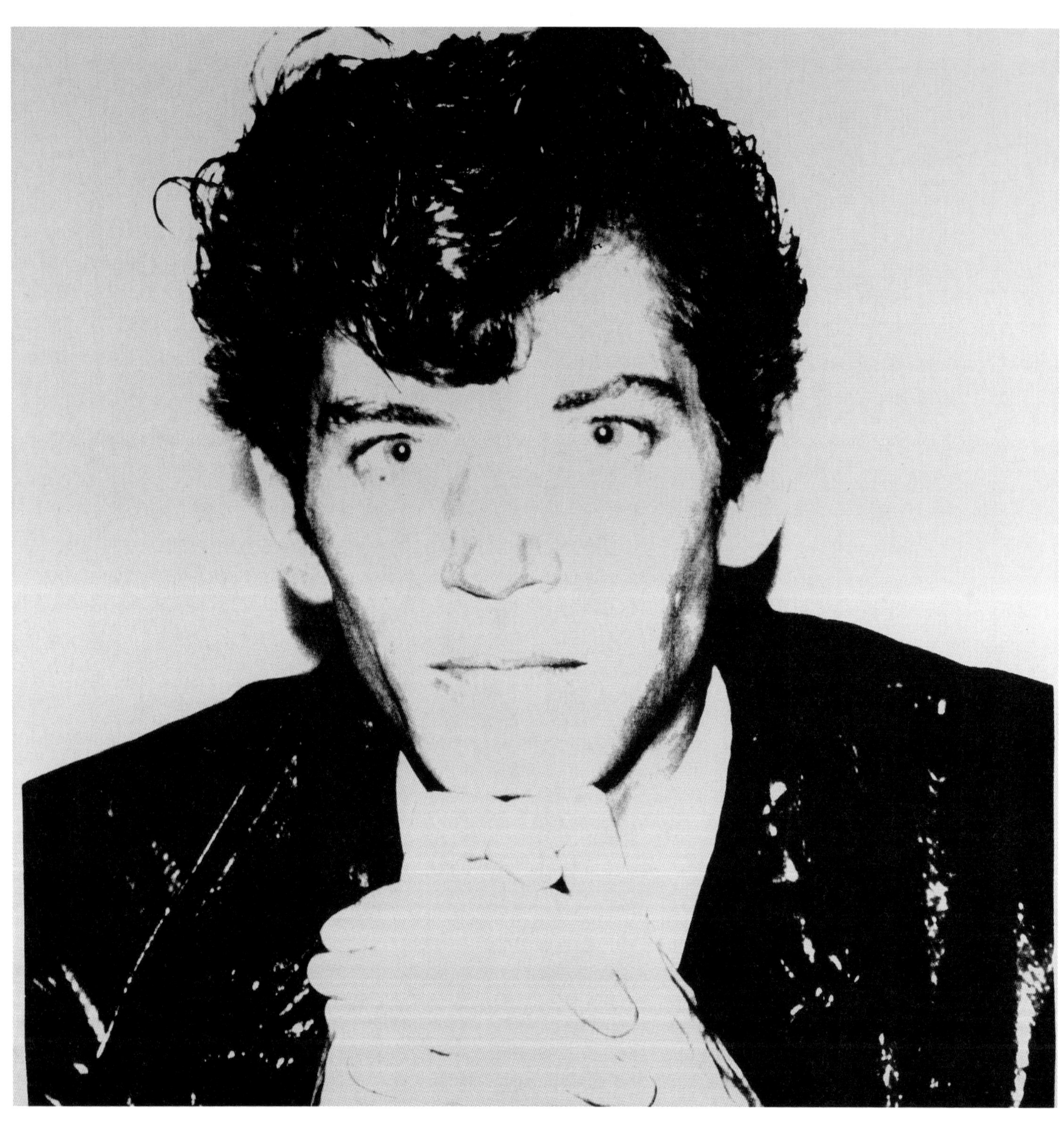

Robert Mapplethorpe 1983
Acrylic paint and screenprint
on canvas
101.7 x 101.7

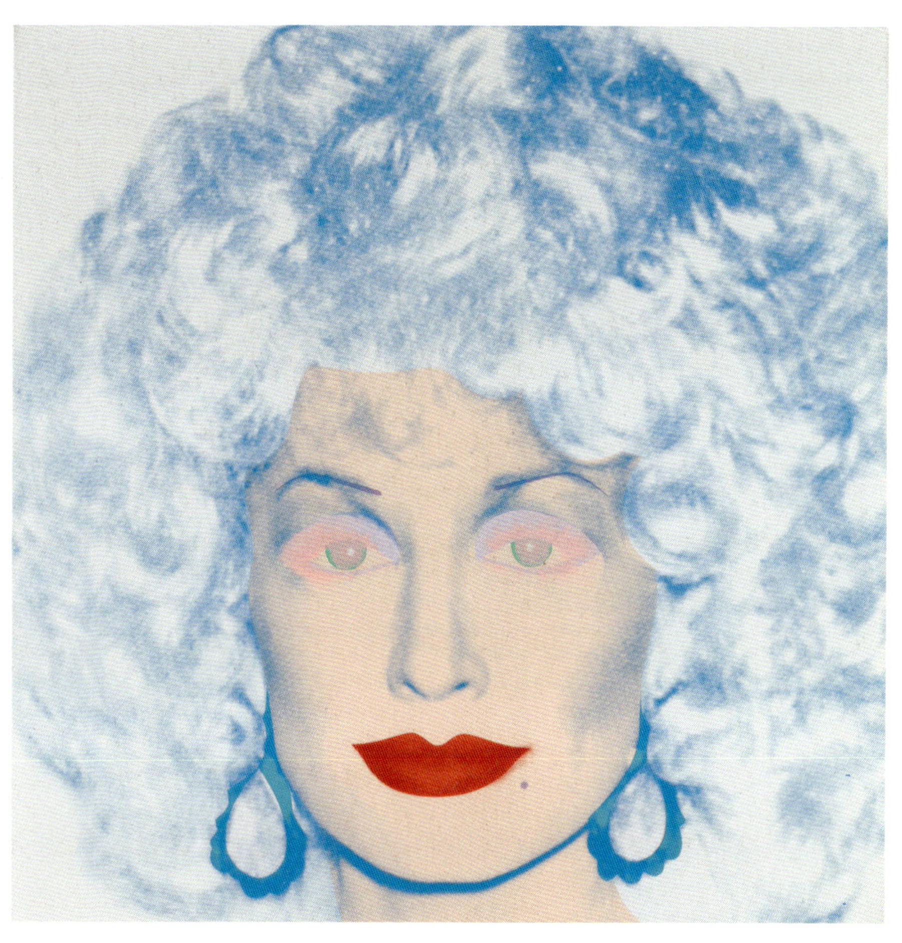

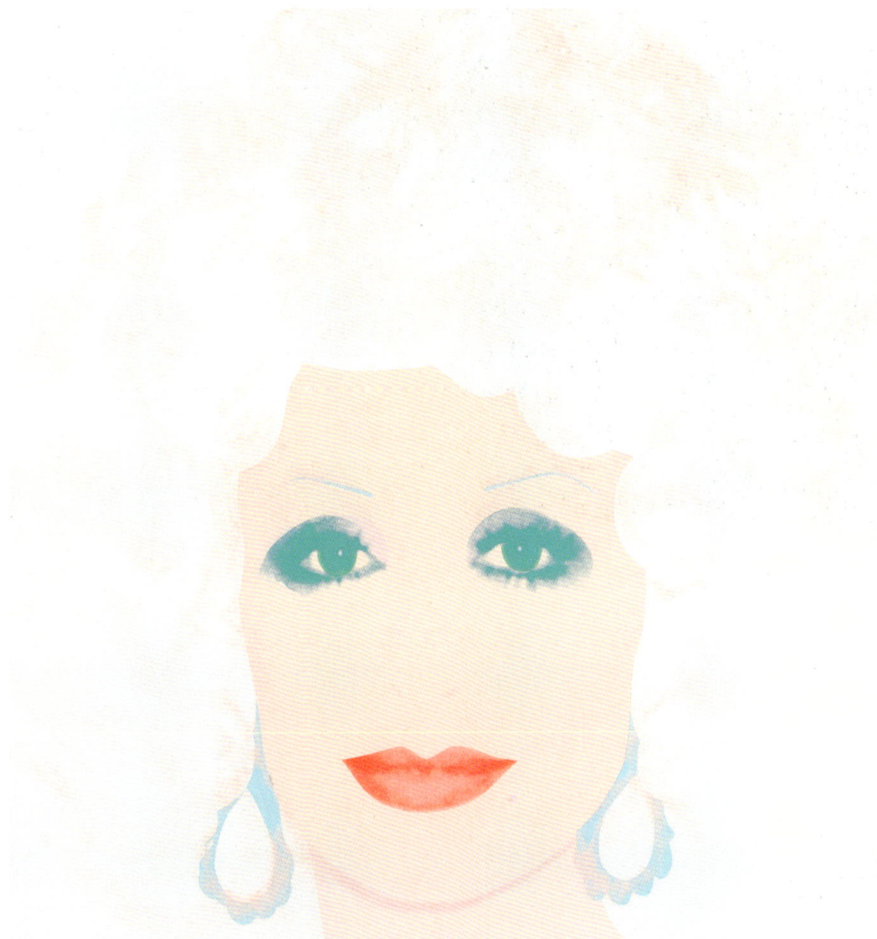

Dolly Parton 1985
Acrylic paint and screenprint
on canvas
106.7 x 106.7 (each)

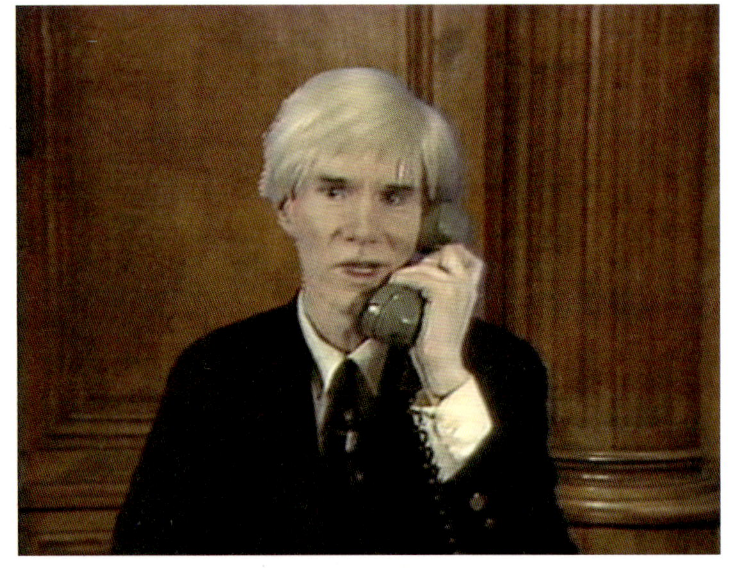

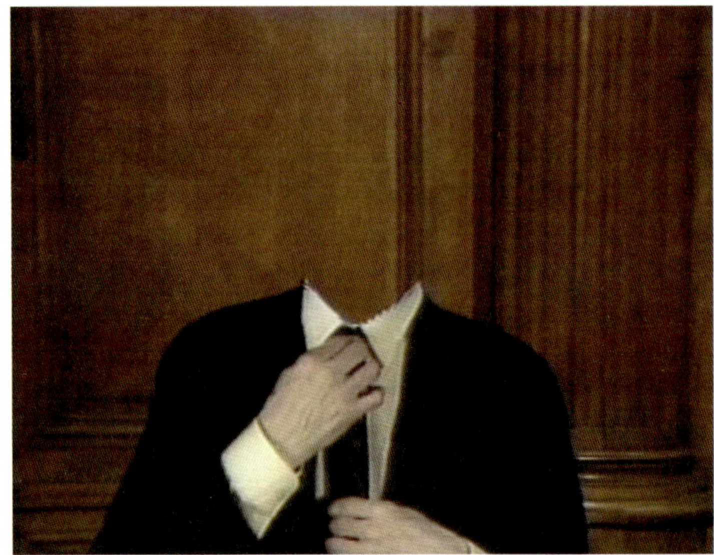

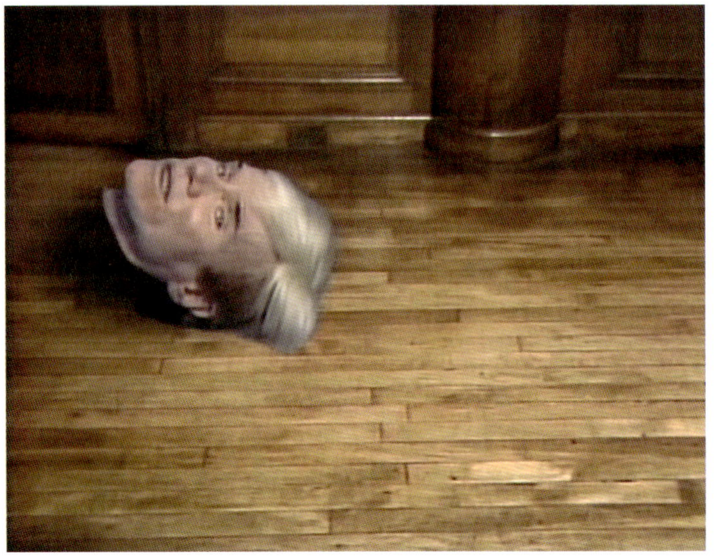

*Andy Warhol's T.V. on
Saturday Night Live
(31 October 1981)* 1981
1-inch videotape,
colour, sound
1 minute

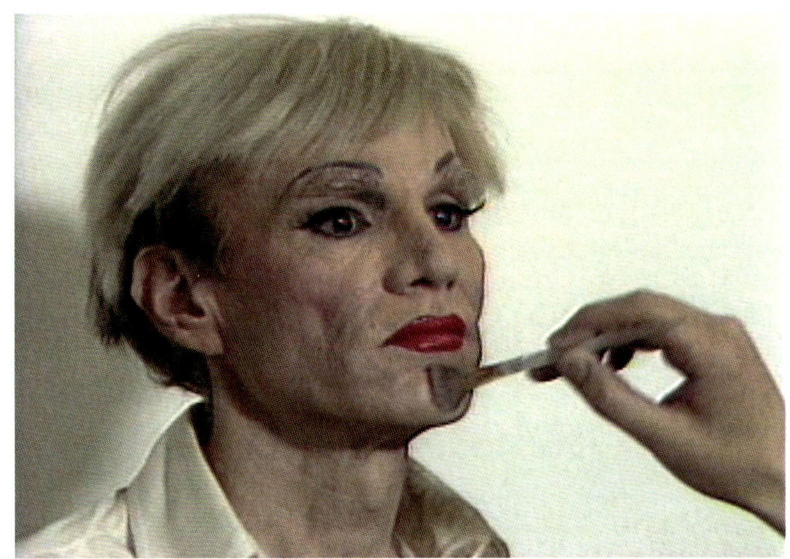

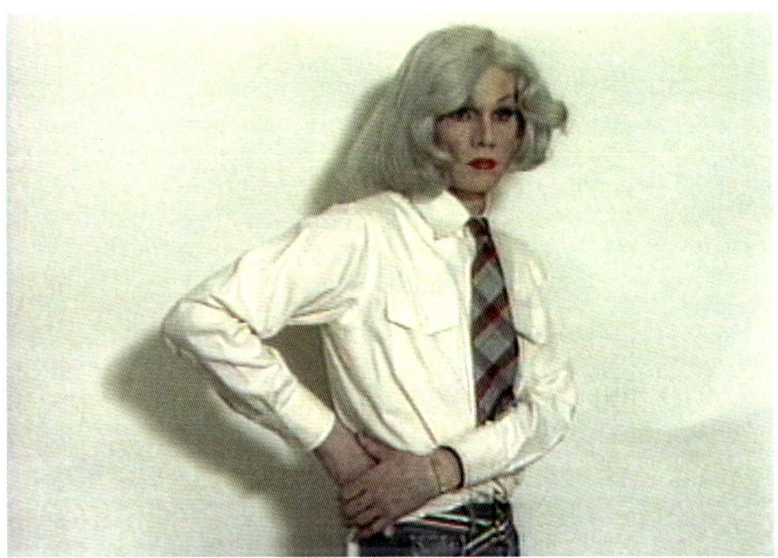

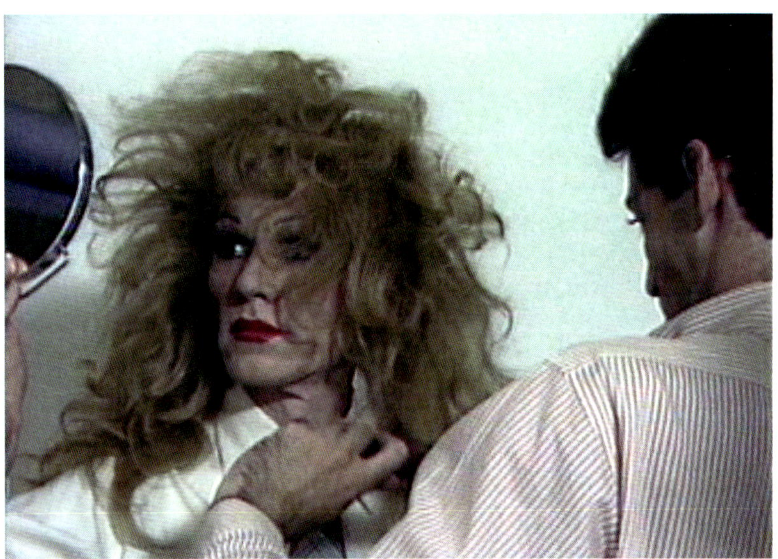

Factory Diary: Andy in Drag,
2 October 1981 1981
¾-inch videotape (3 total),
colour, sound
56 minutes

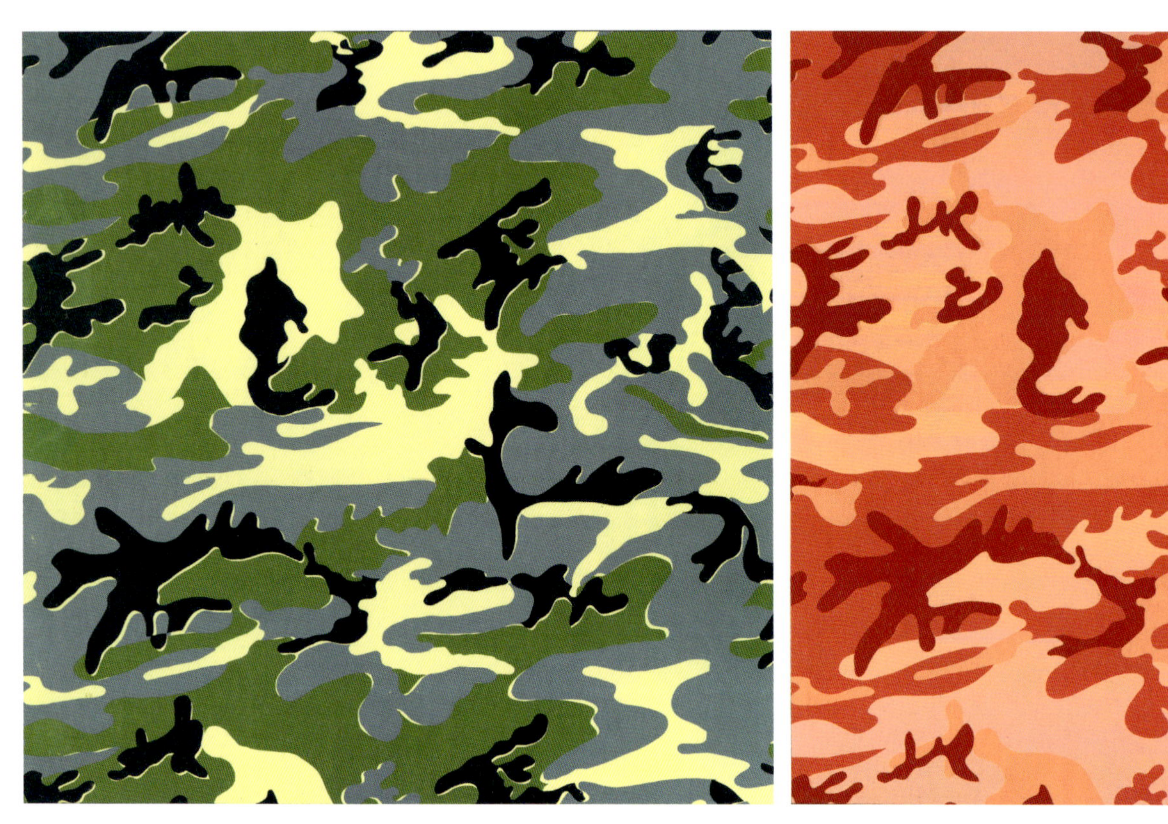
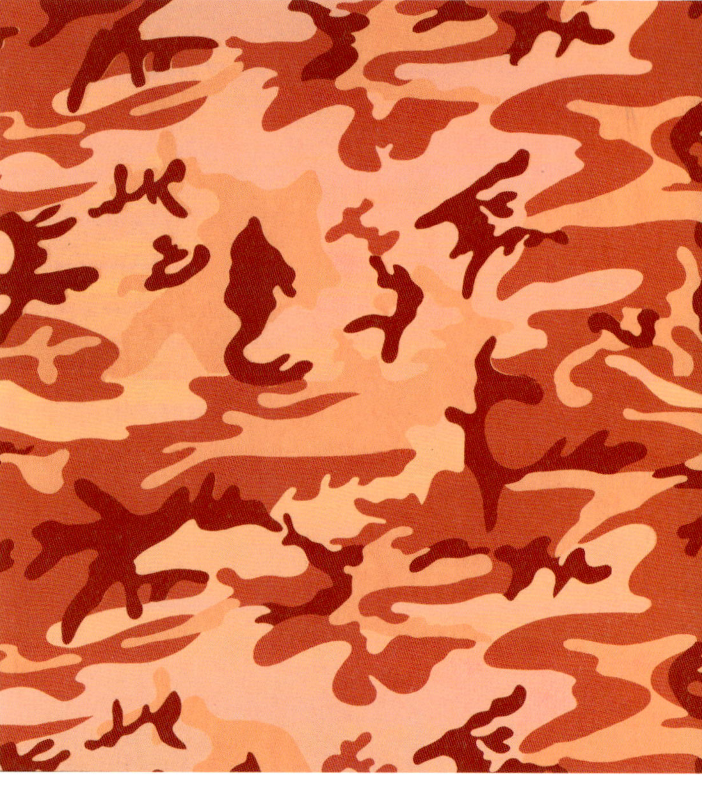

Camouflage 1986
Acrylic paint and screenprint
on four canvases
183 x 183 (each)

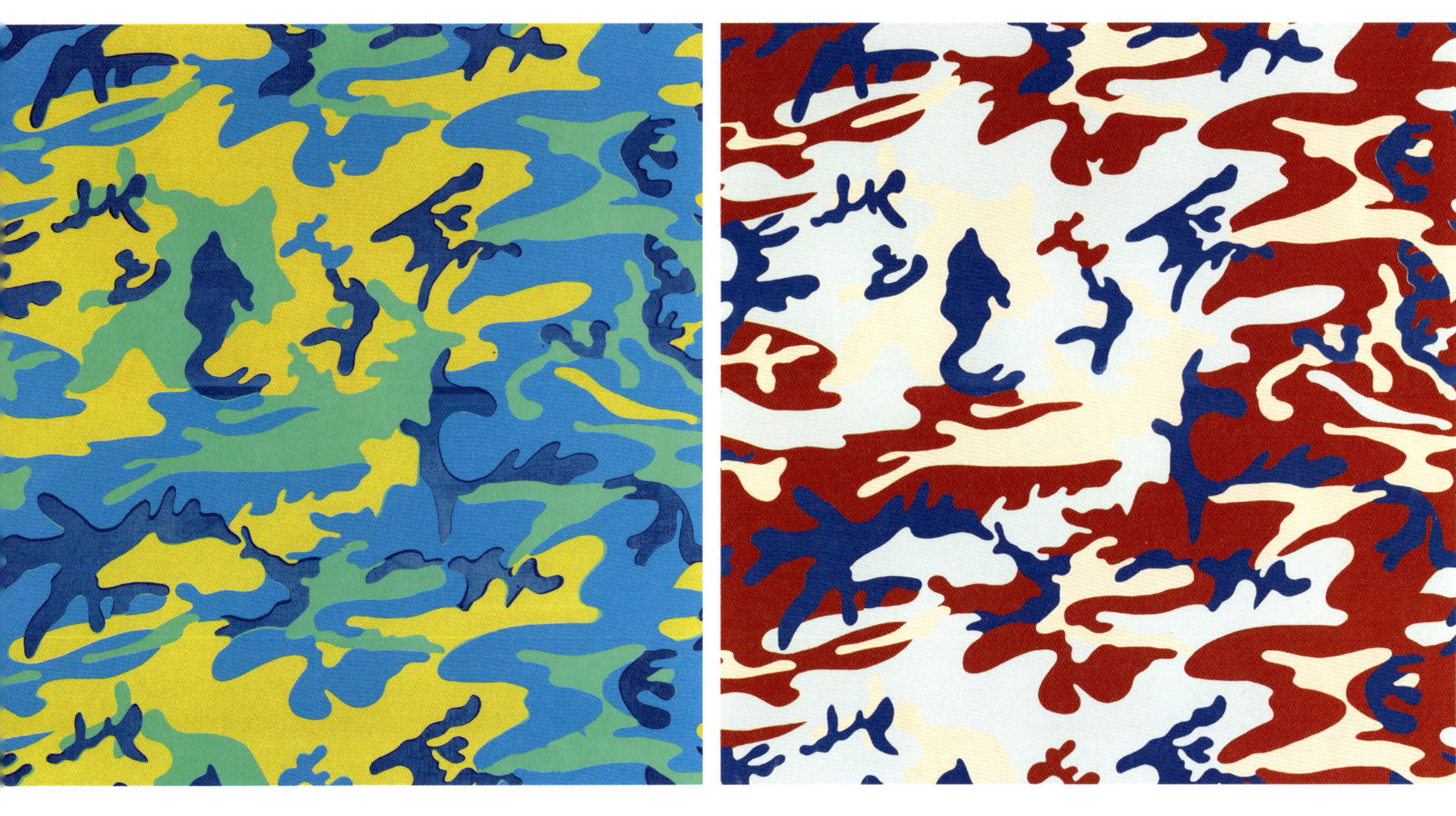

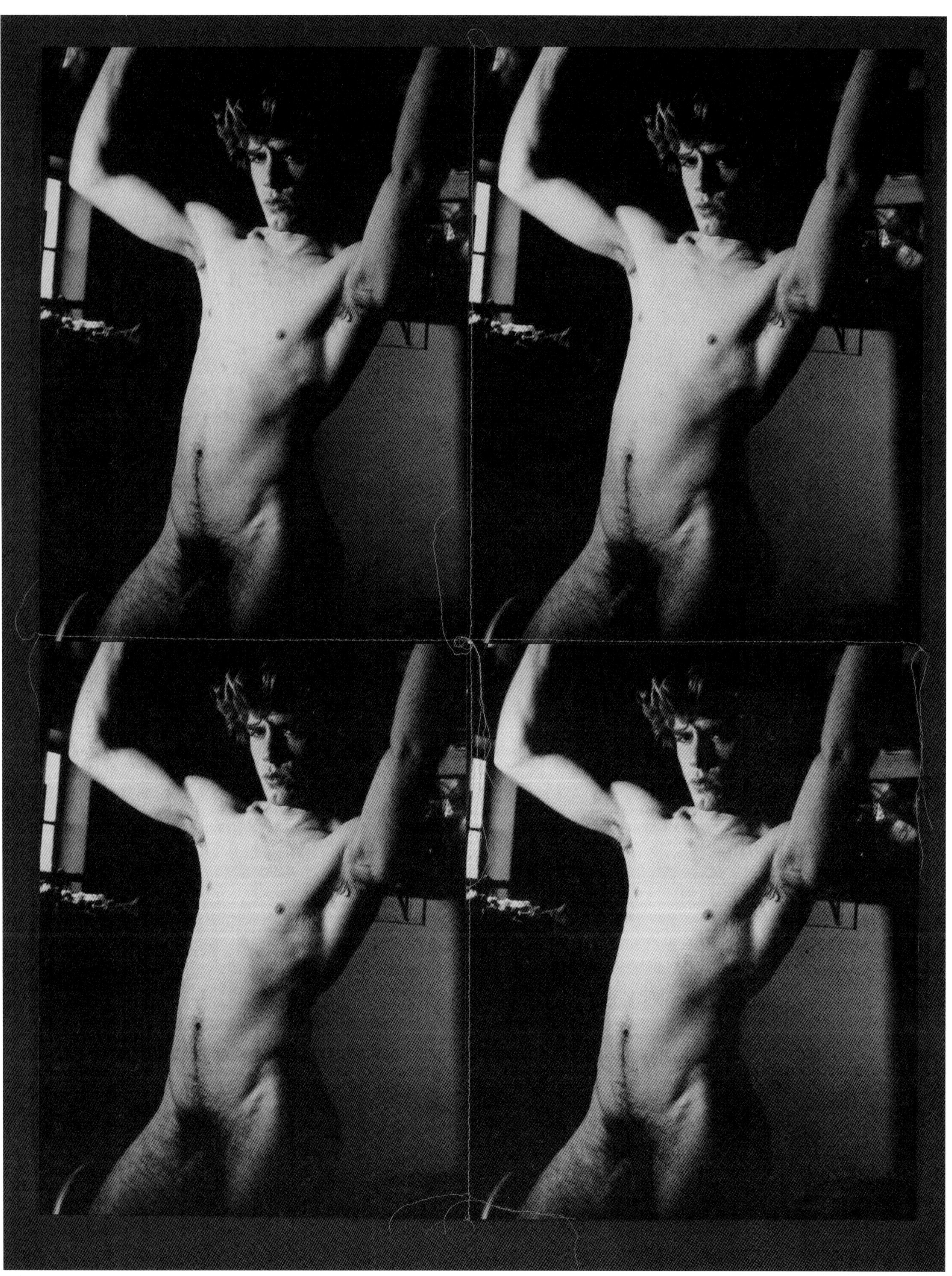

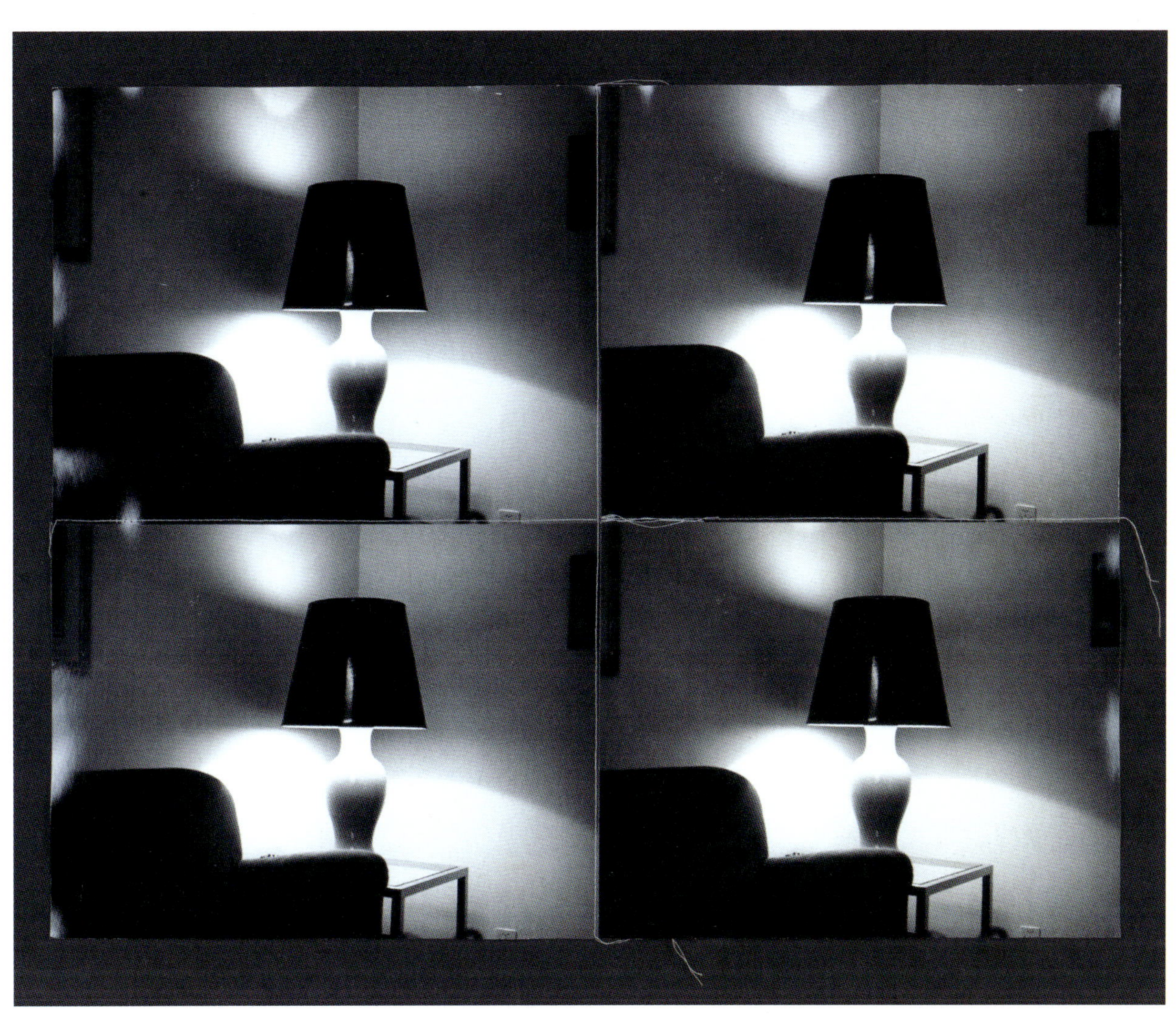

Untitled c.1987
Four photographs; gelatin
silver prints on paper
and thread
53.3 x 68.6

Opposite page
Male Nude 1987
Four photographs; gelatin
silver prints on paper and
thread
71.1 x 55.9

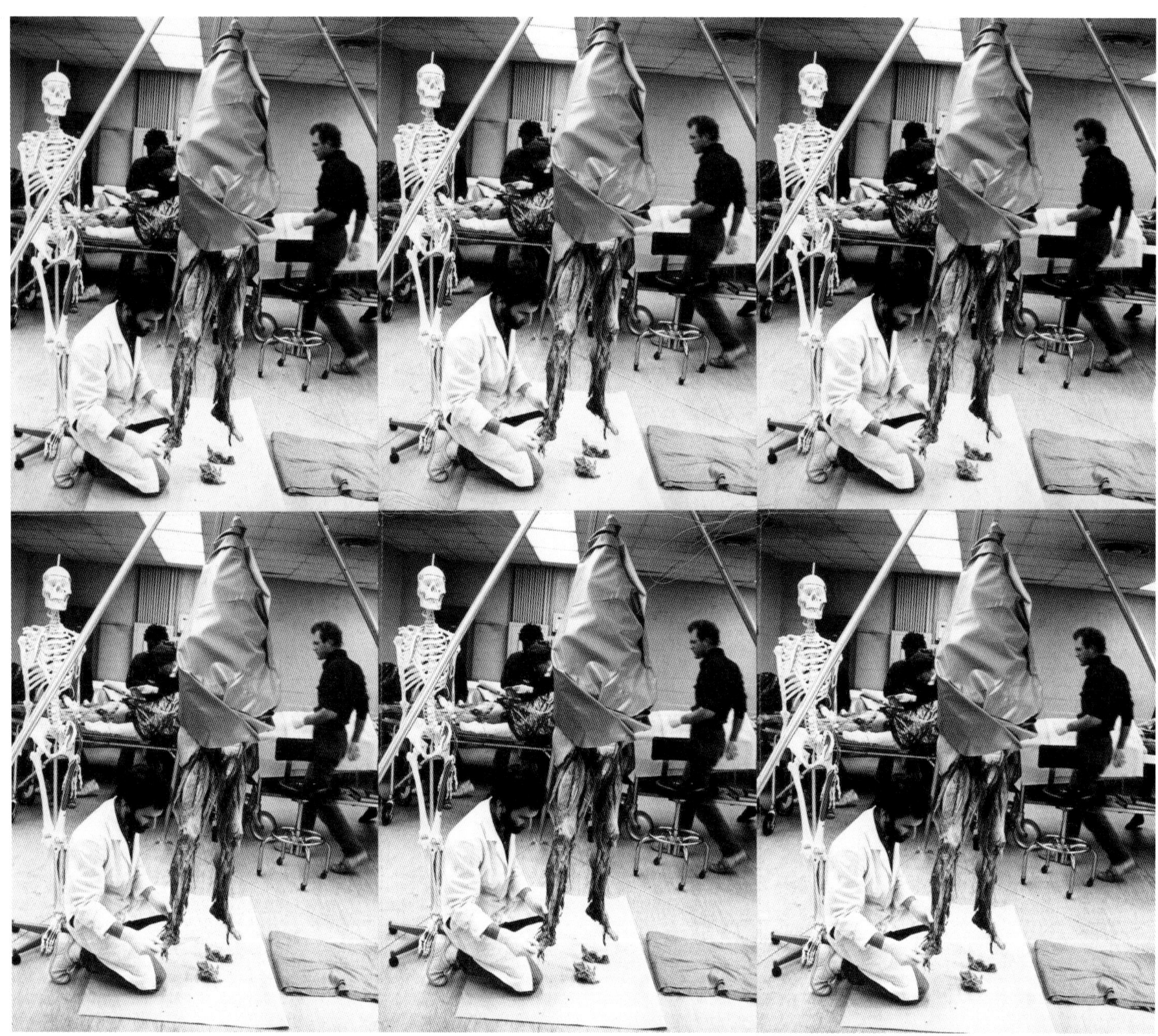

Dissection Class 1986
Six photographs; gelatin silver
prints on paper and thread
69.5 x 80.5

Opposite page
I am Blind 1986
Nine photographs; gelatin
silver prints on paper
and thread
106.7 x 83.8

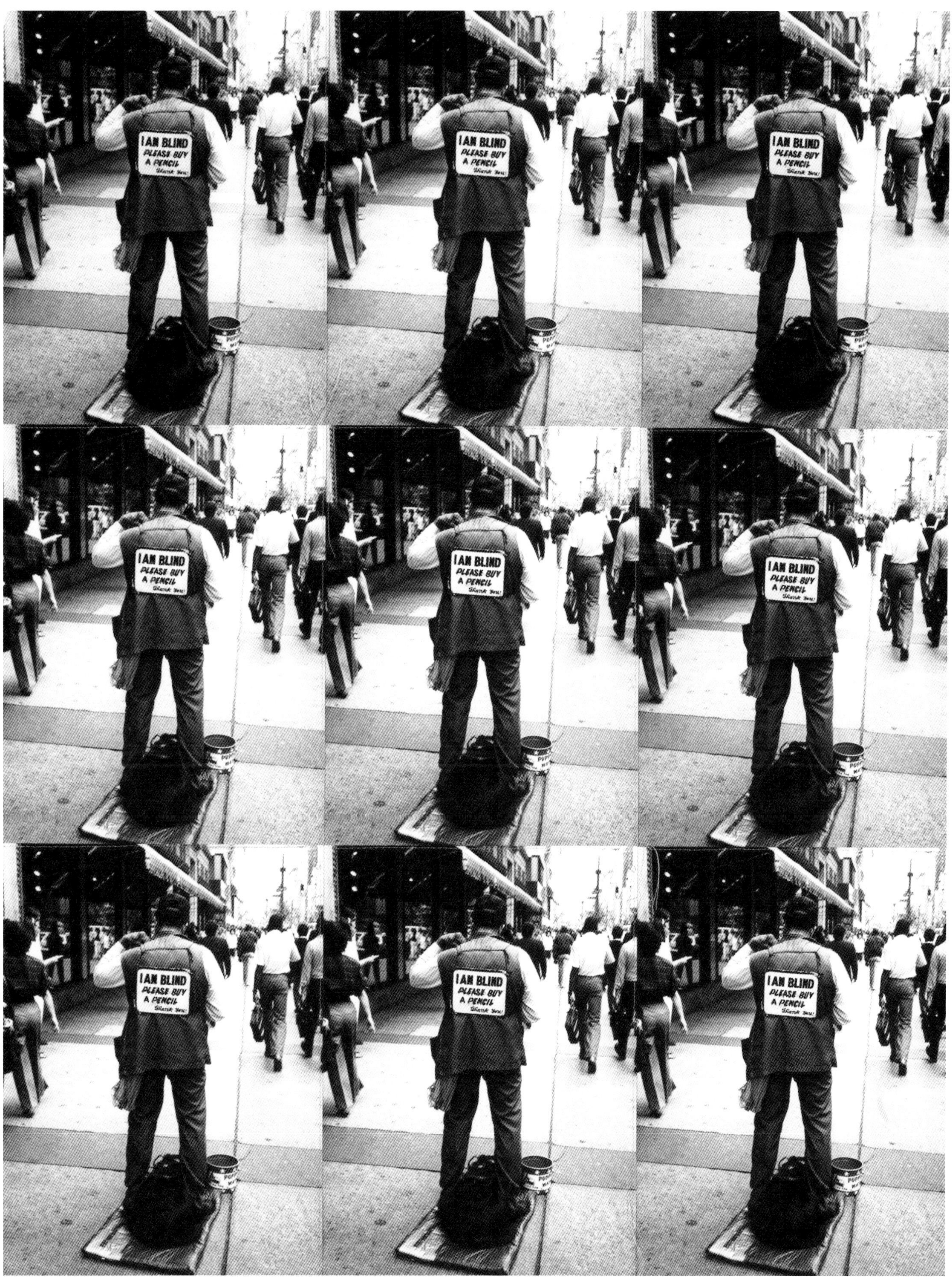

I AM BLIND
PLEASE BUY
A PENCIL
Thank You!

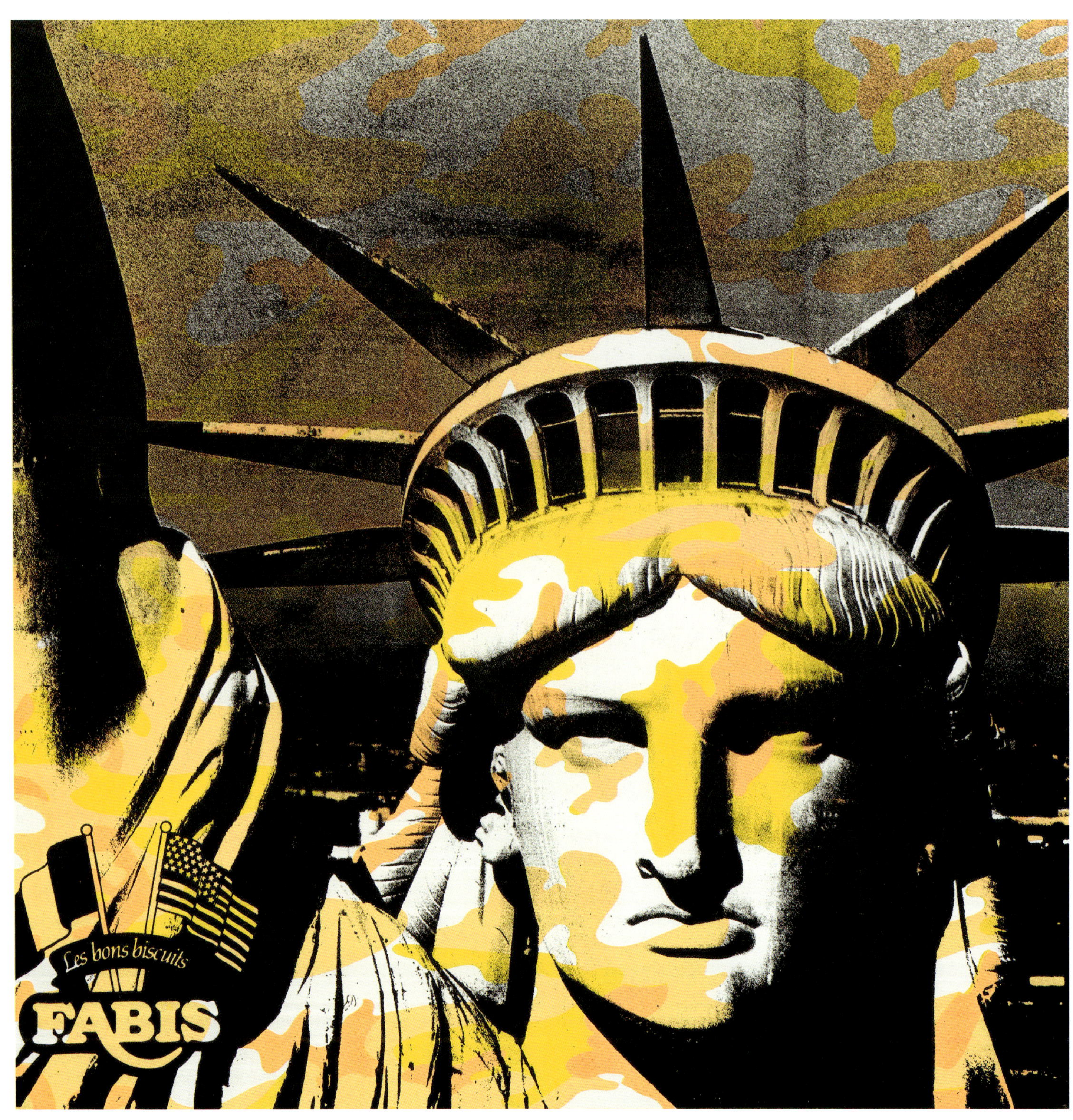

Statue of Liberty 1986
Acrylic paint and
screenprint on canvas
183 x 183

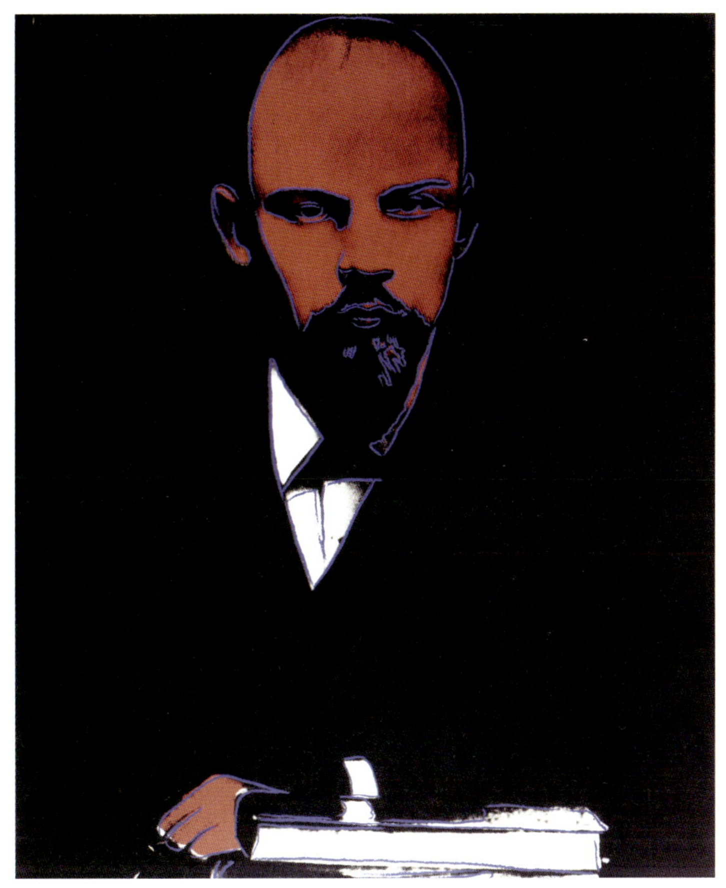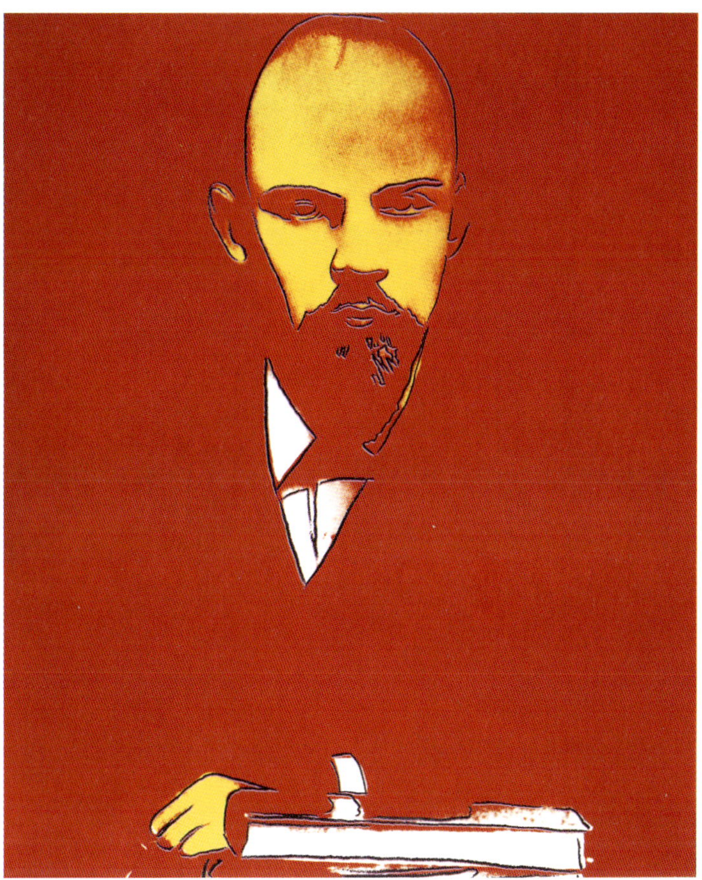

Lenin 1986
Screenprint and acrylic
paint on canvas
213 x 178 (each)

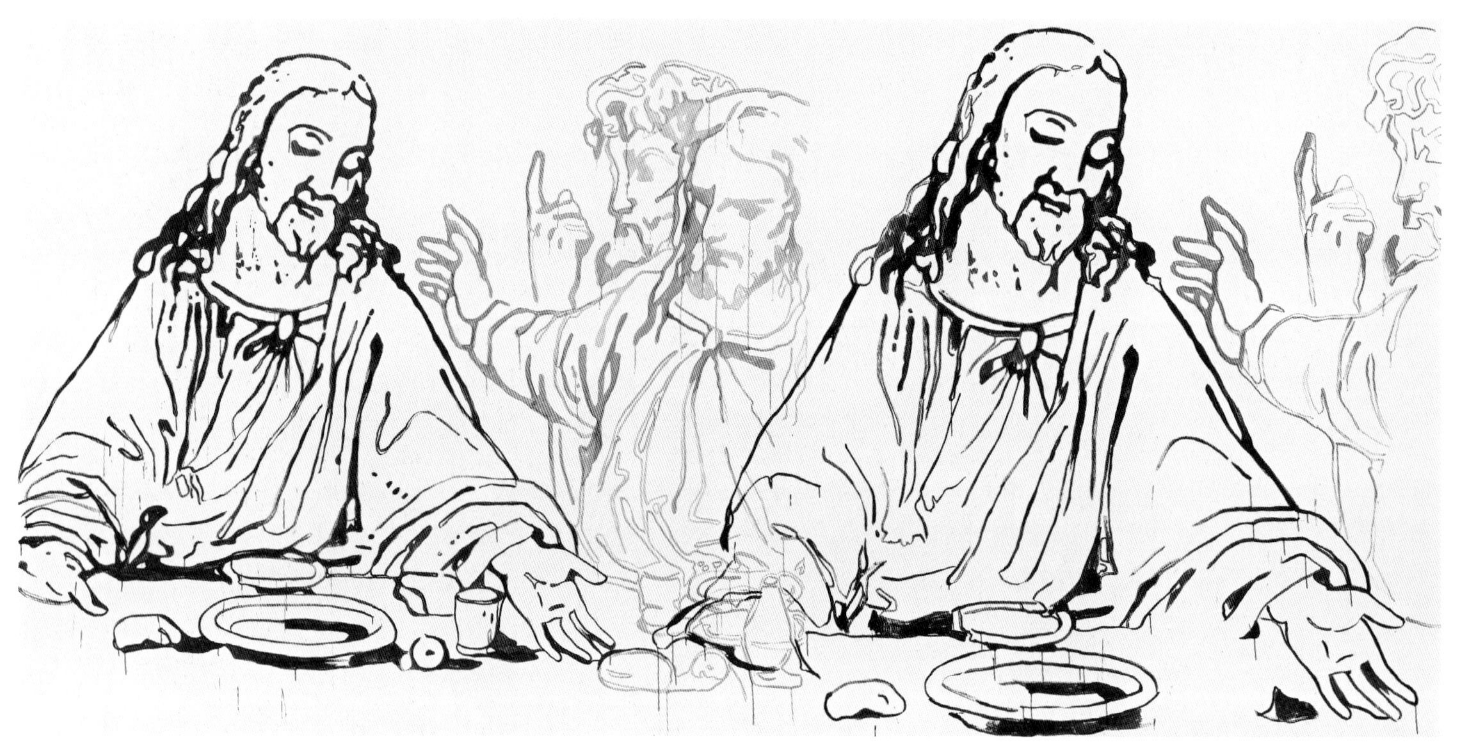

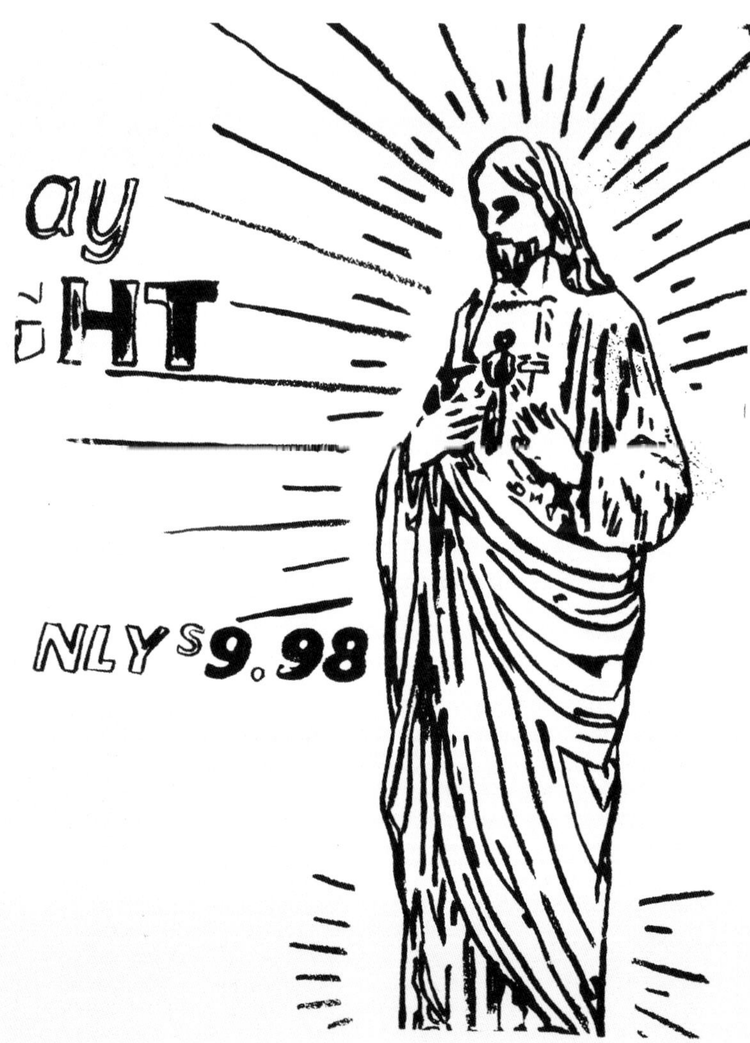

Details of the Last Supper
1986
Acrylic paint on canvas
288 x 580.1

Christ $9.98 (positive)
1985–6
Acrylic paint and
screenprint on canvas
203.7 x 183.2

Opposite page
Rorschach 1984
Acrylic paint on canvas
418.3 x 293.6

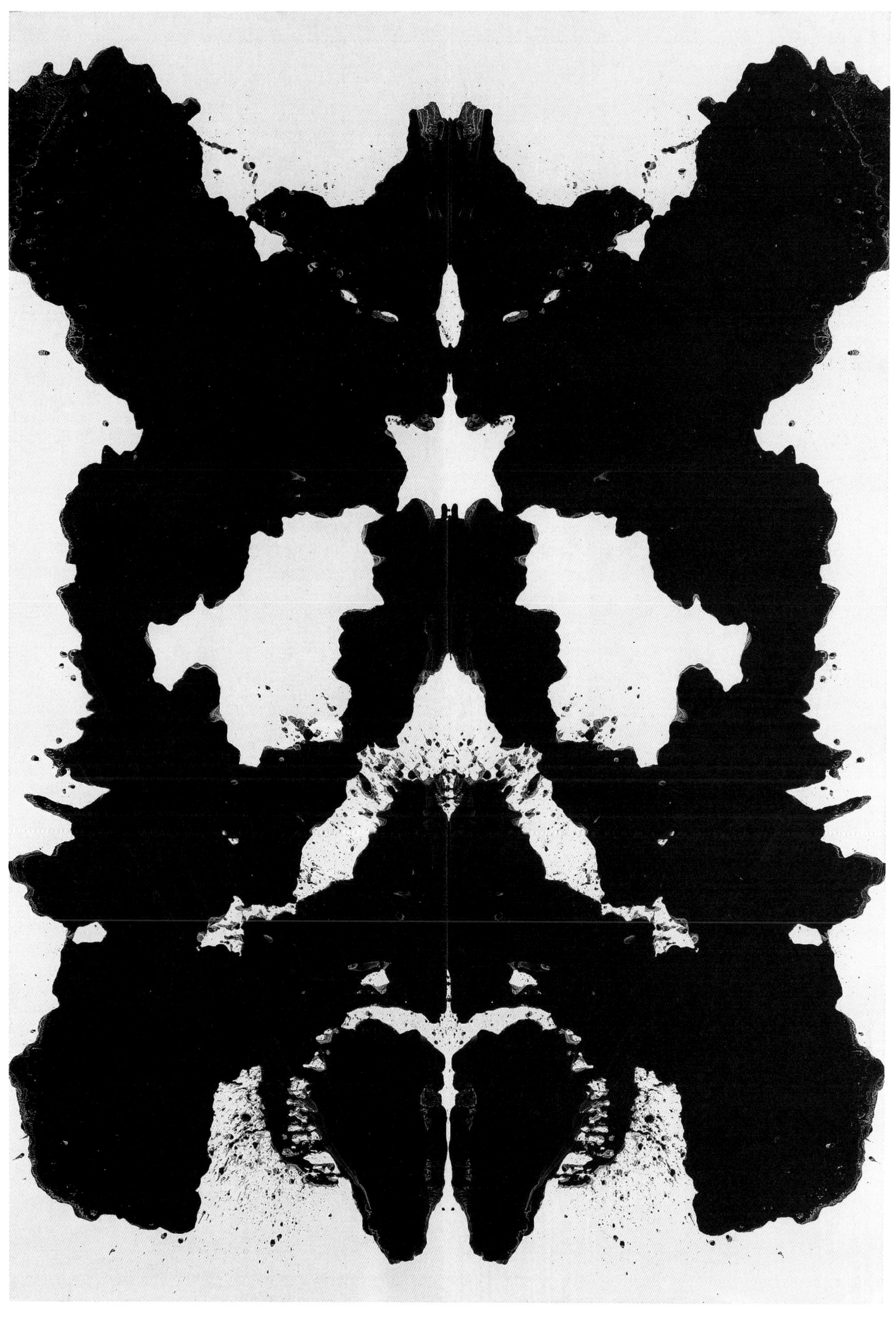

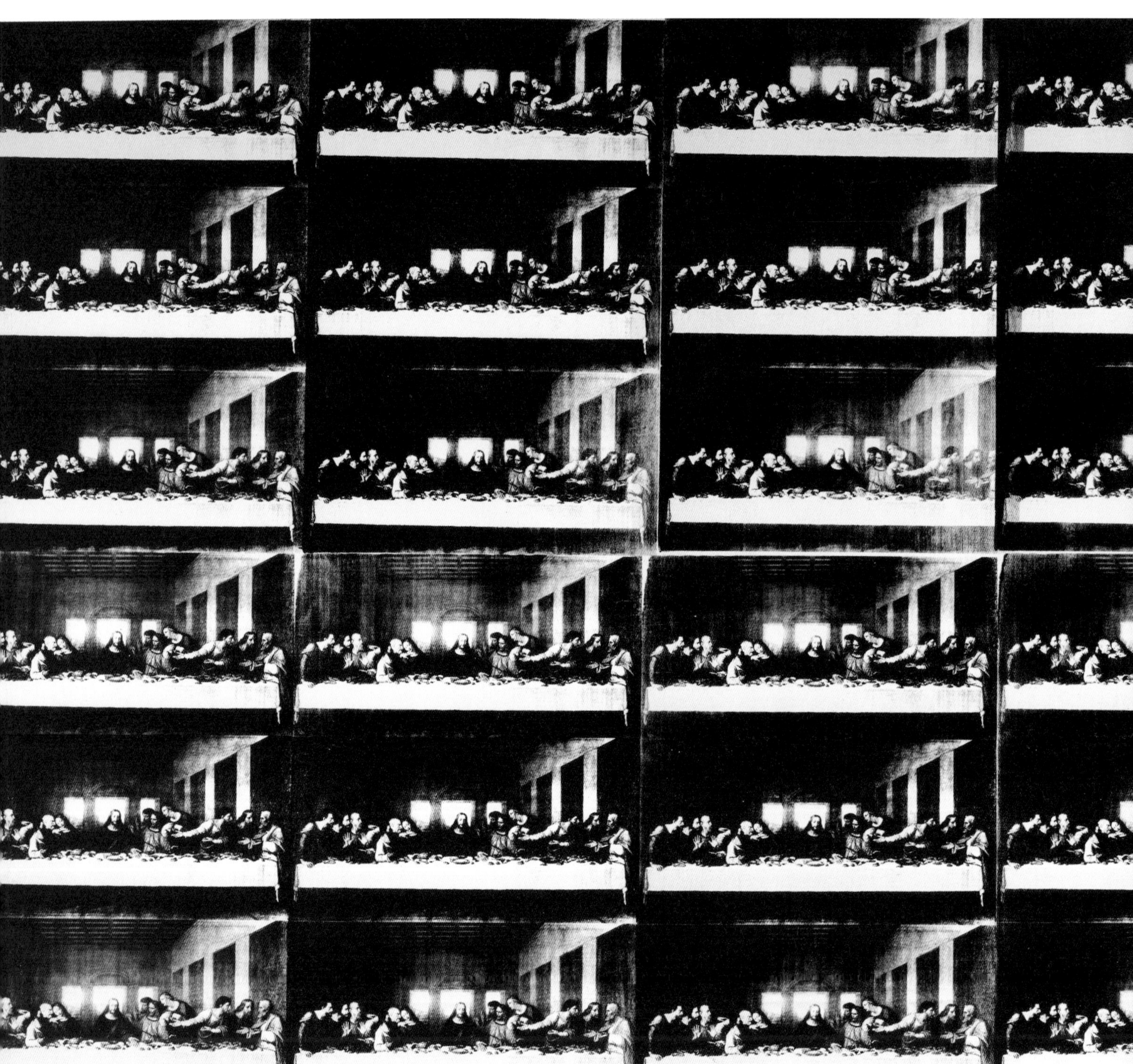

Sixty Last Suppers 1986
Acrylic paint and
screenprint on canvas
294.6 x 998.2

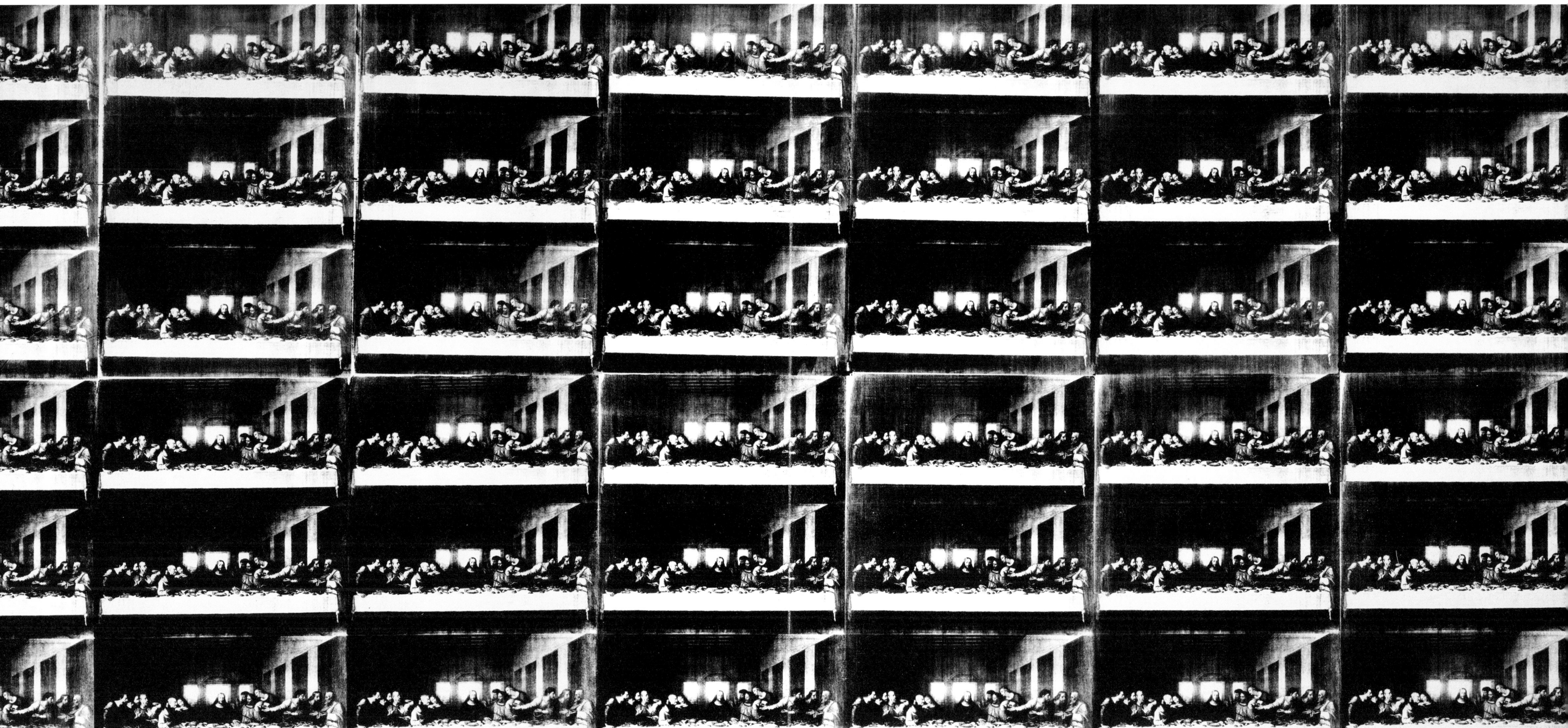

Self-Portrait 1986
Acrylic paint and
screenprint on canvas
203.2 x 203.2

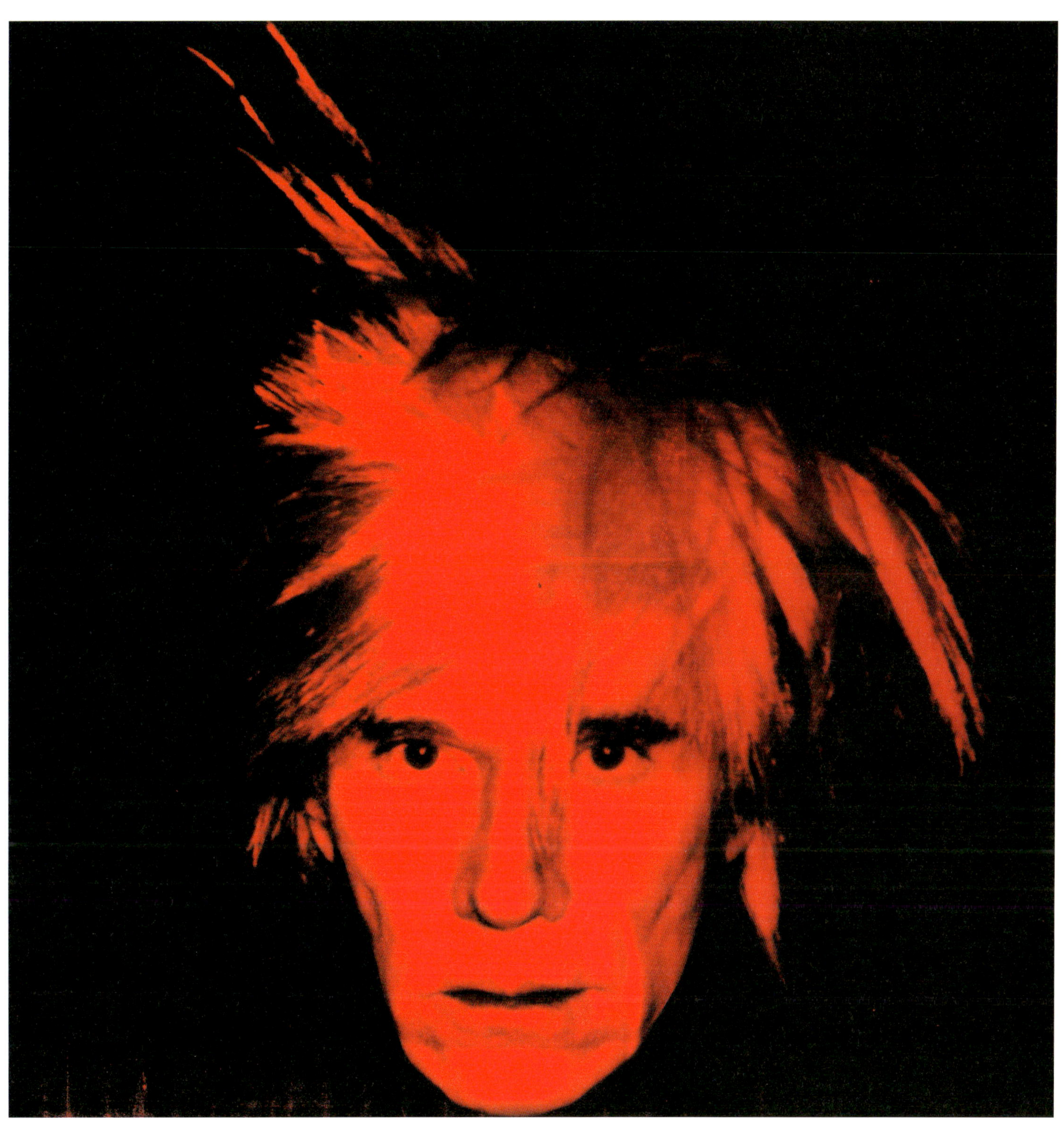

NOTES

Andy Warhol: Outsider on the Inside? pp.10–19

1. Andy Warhol, *The Philosophy of Andy Warhol: From A to B and Back Again*, London and New York 2007 [1975], pp.27–8.
2. Ibid., pp.100–1.
3. Nathan Gluck, *Andy Warhol's Art and Films*, Ann Arbor, MI 1988, p.333. 'Commonism' was previously referenced in 'Deus Ex Machina', *Harper's Bazaar*, November 1962, pp.156–9.
4. Slavoj Žižek, *The Perverts Guide to Ideology*, Sophie Fiennes (dir.), Slavoj Žižek (screenplay), United Kingdom, 2012.
5. Andy Warhol, *America*, New York 1985, p.223.
6. Caroline A. Jones, *Machines In The Studio*, Chicago 1996, p.192. Jones credits Philip Klein, 'The Ethnic Community', in Roy Lubove, ed., *Twentieth Century Pittsburgh*, New York 1976, pp.147–8.
7. Paul Warhola in Michal Cihlár and Rudo Prekop, *Andy Warhol and Czechoslovakia*, Prague 2012, p.66.
8. John Warhola in Cihlár and Prekop 2012, p.47.
9. 'When I thought about it later, when I was already older, I realised why that lady didn't want us in the photograph with her son. They were people who had a fine apartment, they were better dressed than us, just people from a higher class. But those sort of people were shameless. They used to call us "Damn Hunkies". Quote from John Warhola, in Cihlár and Prekop 2012, p.46.
10. Wayne Koestenbaum, *Andy Warhol: A Biography*, London 2009, p.7.
11. All quotes from Gene Swenson's interview with Andy Warhol are from '"What is Pop Art?" A Revised Transcript of Gene Swenson's 1963 Interview with Andy Warhol', transcribed and edited by Jennifer Sichel, *Oxford Art Journal*, Vol.41, Issue 1, March 2018, p.88.
12. Jennifer Sichel, 'Do you think Pop Art's queer? Gene Swenson and Andy Warhol', in *Oxford Art Journal*, Vol.41, Issue 1, March 2018, p.70. In March 2016, Sichel discovered a set of cassette tapes in the archive of critic and curator Gene Swenson. The tapes contain recordings of Swenson's original conversations with various pop artists, including Andy Warhol.
13. Bob Colacello, *Holy Terror: Andy Warhol Close-Up*, New York 1990, p.491.
14. Bankowsky confesses this in his *Artforum* review of the 2018 exhibition at the Whitney Museum of Art, New York.

A La La La: An Andy Warhol Alphabet, pp.20–5

1. Andy Warhol, *The Philosophy of Andy Warhol: From A to B and Back Again*, London and New York 2007 [1975], p.5.
2. Ibid., p.61.
3. Ibid., p.71.
4. Andy Warhol, *The Andy Warhol Diaries*, ed. Pat Hackett, New York 1989, p.807.
5. Andy Warhol and Pat Hackett, *POPism: The Warhol Sixties*, London and New York 2007 [1980], p.362.
6. The author has been unable to source the clip, but the link is here: https://www.youtube.com/watch?v=HNqYH6B1sls
7. Warhol 1989, p.806.
8. Warhol 2007 [1975], p.155.
9. Ibid., p.26.
10. Ibid., p.92.

Silver Clouds: Making Donald Judd Float, pp.26–31

1. Although *Silver Clouds* travelled to four additional cities in 1966–7 (Cincinnati, Hamburg, Cologne and Boston), this essay discusses only the installation at Leo Castelli Gallery,

New York. For a discussion of the process of manufacture of the version of *Silver Clouds* exhibited at Castelli from 2 to 27 April 1966, see Georg Frei and Neil Printz, (eds.), *The Andy Warhol Catalogue Raisonné: Paintings and Sculpture, 1964–1969*, vol.02B, London 2004, pp.207–8 and cat. no.1868 on p.223. See also David Bourdon, *Andy Warhol*, New York 1989, pp.229–30.
2. That anchoring their corners to the floor with string and lead fishing weights was Warhol's preferred method for installing *Silver Clouds* is discussed in Frei and Printz 2004, vol.02B, p.208, and Bourdon 1989, p.230. Warhol mentions the lead fishing weights as part of the process of installing *Silver Clouds* in Andy Warhol, *The Philosophy of Andy Warhol: From A to B and Back Again*, Orlando 1975, p.150, and Andy Warhol and Paul Hackett, *POPism: The Warhol Sixties*, San Diego 1980, p.168.
3. See Robert Pincus-Whitten, 'Turner, Museum of Modern Art; Andy Warhol, Castelli Gallery; Paul Thek, Pace Gallery; Herbert Crowley, Windsor McCay, Metropolitan Museum of Art; 5-Man Show, Royal Marks Gallery', *Artforum* 4, no.10, June 1966, p.54.
4. Strangely, William Berkson is the only reviewer of the Leo Castelli Gallery exhibition to mention that Warhol liberated one of the clouds on opening night. See W[illiam] B[erkson], 'Andy Warhol', *Arts Magazine* 40, no.8, June 1966, p.46.
5. Quoted in Alan Solomon, 'Introduction', in *Andy Warhol*, Boston 1966, unpag.
6. Warhol in a 1966 interview with curator Alan Solomon as quoted in Rainer Crone, *Andy Warhol*, New York 1970, p.30.
7. Donald Judd quoted in Bruce Glaser, 'Questions to Stella and Judd' (1964), ed. Lucy R. Lippard, *Art News* 65, no.5, September 1966, p.57. This interview was aired on WBAI-FM, New York.
8. This is the term American artist Frank Stella uses to describe part-by-part composition; see ibid., p.55.
9. Ibid., pp.55, 57–8.
10. Ibid., p.57 (emphasis in the original).
11. Ibid., p.58.
12. Quoted in Glaser 1966.
13. Donald Judd, 'Specific Objects', *Contemporary Sculpture*, special issue of *Arts Yearbook* 8, 1965, p.77.
14. James Meyer discusses Judd's particular dislike for Warhol's work in his *Minimalism: Art and Polemics in the Sixties*, New Haven 2001, pp.46–7 and p.279n.15.
15. D[onald] J[udd], 'Six Painters and the Object', *Arts Magazine* 37, no.9, May–June 1963, p.108.
16. D[onald] J[udd], 'Kenneth Noland', *Arts Magazine* 37, no.10, September 1963, p.54.
17. Judd 1965, p.78.
18. Warhol's box sculptures were included in his exhibition at Stable Gallery, New York, 21 April – 9 May 1964, and in a group exhibition entitled *Boxes* at Dwan Gallery, Los Angeles, 2–29 February 1964. See Georg Frei and Neil Printz (eds.), *The Andy Warhol Catalogue Raisonné: Paintings and Sculpture, 1964–1969*, vol.02A, London 2004, pp.53, 58 and 86.
19. See Patrick S. Smith's 1 November 1978 interview with Ronald Tavel in his *Andy Warhol's Art and Films*, Ann Arbor, UMI Research Press 1986, pp.495–6. According to Tavel, Warhol read every review of his work.
20. The stack of galvanised iron boxes that was on display at Leo Castelli in 1966 is listed as cat. no.78 in Brydon Smith, *Donald Judd: Catalogue Raisonné of Paintings, Objects and Wood-Blocks, 1960–1974*, Ottawa 1975, p.135. As James Meyer notes in Meyer 2001, p.298n.66, although Judd's stack comprises ten boxes, only

seven were shown as a result of the height of the wall at Castelli. The first time Judd exhibited a stack of galvanised boxes was at the Moderna Museet, Stockholm, from 26 December 1965 to 13 February 1966.
21. According to Warhol, he was working on *Silver Clouds* with David Whitney and David White of Leo Castelli Gallery in February 1966. See Warhol and Hackett 1980, p.149.
22. The term belongs to Charles F. Stuckey, who argues that in 1961 Warhol made paintings of cans of Campbell's soup and Del Monte peaches in response to Jasper Johns's 1960 sculpture of cans of Ballantine ale. See Stuckey, 'Warhol in Context', in Gary Garrels (ed.), *The Work of Andy Warhol* (*Discussions in Contemporary Culture*, 3), New York and Seattle 1989, p.7.
23. In 1965 Stella repudiated many of the arguments he espoused in the February 1964 radio interview with Glaser and Judd, particularly the notion that his paintings lacked illusionism. For a discussion of Stella's shift in viewpoint in 1965, see Meyer 2001, pp.121–2.
24. Judd 1965, p.82.
25. Quoted in Glaser 1966, p.60.
26. Judd 1965.
27. John Coplans makes this important observation in 'Andy Warhol and Elvis Presley', *Studio International* 181, no.930, February 1971, p.53n.6. Stella's aluminium paintings were first exhibited at Leo Castelli Gallery, New York, from 27 September to 15 October 1960.
28. Warhol 1975, p.150.
29. Quoted in Warhol and Hackett 1980, pp.64–5.
30. D[onald] J[udd], 'Robert Morris', *Arts Magazine* 39, no.5, February 1965, p.54.
31. Ibid.
32. Charles F. Stuckey is one of the only writers in the Warhol literature who specifically mentions Morris's *Cloud* as a possible source of inspiration for Warhol's *Silver Clouds*. See Stuckey 1989, p.22.
33. See Warhol and Hackett 1980, p.168, where Warhol writes, 'I preferred to have all the pillows float scattered – exactly halfway to the ceiling.'
34. Quoted in Otto Hahn, 'Rembrandt vidé de Rembrandt', in his *Andy Warhol: The Thirteen Most Wanted Men*, Paris 1967. The translation is mine. The quote in French reads: 'Quand vous parlez de ce que je fais, ne dites pas Marilyn, Lis, Fleurs, dites seulement "Les choses qu'il aime", ou "les nuages". Il n'y a pas de Marilyn, ni de Fleurs, ni de Chaise Electrique, il n'y a que mes nuages ...'.
35. Judd 1965, p.80.
36. Jacques Derrida, 'Structure, Sign and Play in the Discourse of the Human Sciences' 1966, in Richard Macksey and Eugenio Donato (eds.), *The Structuralist Controversy: The Languages of Criticism and the Sciences of Man*, Baltimore 1970, pp.264–5. Derrida's lecture, which was delivered in French, was originally entitled 'La structure, le signe et le jeu dans le discours des sciences humaines'.
37. Ibid., p.261.
38. An audiotape during one of the test runs of inflated Scotchpak that occurred on the roof of the Factory in late 1965 recorded Warhol saying, 'Oh, this is fantastic! Oh! Oh! ... It's going to fly away! ... This is one of the most exciting things that has ever happened to me! It is so beautiful. Oh, Billy, it's infinite, because it goes in with the sky.' Quoted in Wayne Koestenbaum, *Andy Warhol*, New York 2001, p.111.

Reproduction and Reality, pp.32–7

1. It should be noted that the term 'uniqueness' used here has been translated from the German 'Einmaligkeit', literally meaning 'oneness'. It is a kind of temporal uniqueness to which Benjamin

refers, in which something can only happen once, at a particular moment. Whether it happens again for others, or elsewhere, we do not know; the very thing to which we refer will be over by then.
2. In Walter Benjamin, *Selected Writings Volume 2: 1927–1934*, trans. Rodney Livingstone et al., ed. Michael W. Jennings, Howard Eiland and Gary Smith, Cambridge, MA and London 1999, pp.507–31.
3. Ibid., p.527.
4. Walter Benjamin, 'Das Kunstwerk im Zeitalter seiner technischen Reproduzierbarkeit (erste Fassung)', in *Gesammelte Schriften*, vols.I and 2, Frankfurt am Main 1991, pp.431–69, p.455.
5. Crone talked at length with Warhol about this: 'I heard that Brecht wanted all people to think alike, I want all people to think alike', quoted in Rainer Crone and Wilfried Wiegand, *Revolutionäre Ästhetik*, exh. cat., Moderna Museet, Stockholm 1968.
6. Wilfried Wiegand, 'Die Filme Warhols', in Crone and Wiegand 1968, p.101n.52.
7. By his 'middle-period' films I mean those that were produced after his experimental films (*Sleep, Eat, Blow Job, Empire*) and before the films made with/by Paul Morrissey after Warhol was attacked by Valerie Solanas (*Flesh, Trash*, etc.).
8. Douglas Crimp, 'Our Kind Of Movie', in *The Films of Andy Warhol*, Cambridge, MA 2012, p.98.
9. Craig Owens, *Beyond Recognition*, Berkeley, CA 1994, pp.198–202.
10. Crimp 2012, pp.20–38.

The Faces of Warhol, pp.38–47

1. Andy Warhol, cited in Eva Windmöller, 'Ich liebe altes Geld und neue Schecks', interview with Andy Warhol, *Stern*, 42, 8 October 1981, p.196.
2. Bob Colacello, 'Andy Warhol's Portraits, A Personal View', in *Andy Warhol. Headshots, Drawings and Paintings*, exh. cat., Jablonka Galerie, Cologne 2000, unpag.
3. 'Friday, June 6, 1986', in Andy Warhol, *The Andy Warhol Diaries*, ed. Pat Hackett, New York 1989, p.737.
4. See Alain Cueff, 'Cosmetique de l'ombre', in *Le grand monde d'Andy Warhol*, exh. cat., Grand Palais, Paris 2009, p.24ff.
5. Hilton Kramer, 'Art: Whitney Shows Warhol Works', *New York Times*, 23 November 1979.
6. Robert Hughes, 'Mirror, Mirror on the Wall', *Time*, 3 December 1979, p.73.
7. Richard Meyer, 'Warhol's Jews', in *Warhol's Jews. Ten Portraits Reconsidered*, exh. cat., The Jewish Museum New York 2008, p.18.
8. In the run-up, a scandal arose when four portraits of Yves Saint Laurent were withdrawn from the exhibition by his former partner Pierre Bergé. They were to have appeared in the 'Glamour' section, alongside portraits of Sonia Rykiel and Giorgio Armani, which Bergé felt was inappropriate.
9. Tom Wolfe, 'Bob and Spike', in T. Wolfe, *The Pump House Gang*, New York 1968 (4th edn 1973), p.181.
10. Keith Hartley, 'Andy Warhol. Der Fotoautomat als Porträtstudio' in Dietmar Elger (ed.), *Andy Warhol. Selbstporträts*, exh. cat., Kunstverein St Gallen, Ostfildern 2004, p.45.
11. Ethel Scull quoted in *Andy Warhol Photography*, exh. cat., Hamburger Kunsthalle, Hamburg, and The Andy Warhol Museum, Pittsburgh 1999, p.90.
12. It is interesting to compare both with Richard Hamilton's photo collage *My Marilyn (Paste-up)*, produced just a little later, in 1964. Hamilton took black-and-white photographs of a series of colour photos of Marilyn Monroe on the beach from a magazine, originally taken

by photojournalist George Barris. These had been published after her death. Monroe herself checked them as promotional material, making crosses or ticks against them. Hamilton arranged them together in a patchwork design, with different degrees of enlargement, highlighting those that Monroe commented on in colour. While Warhol's use of colour gave his photo-booth images of Ethel Scull a pulsating dynamic, Hamilton's black and white versions of the colour snapshots of Monroe robbed them of their casual *joie de vivre*. In both cases, however, the artists chose from a large number of options according to certain criteria and applied a specific arrangement, so that the casting-like nature of the presentation is evident as the actual creative act within the work, despite the different effect.

13. Thomas Miessgang, 'Der Marilyn-Madonna-Komplex', in Christopher F. Laferl and Anja Tippner (eds.), *Leben als Kunstwerk*, Bielefeld 2011, p.252.

14. Cueff 2009, 'Cosmetique de l'ombre', p.29.

15. See Jane Daggett Dillenberger, *The Religious Art of Andy Warhol*, New York 1998, p.28.

16. See e.g. Cueff 2009, p.29, and Trevor Fairbrother, 'Picture Portraits: Miss Warhol Knows What the Client Wants', in *Andy Warhol: From A to B and Back Again*, exh. cat., Whitney Museum of American Art, New York 2018, p.67. The iconostasis of St John Chrystosom was renovated in the 1970s. Some new icons were installed, so that the current condition no longer corresponds to the picture in Warhol's church visits during the 1930s and 1940s.

17. See Cueff 2009, p.27.

18. See Heiner Bastian, 'Death and Disaster im Werk von Andy Warhol. Ein Tag wie jeder andere' in *Andy Warhol. Death and Disaster*, exh. cat., Kunstsammlungen Chemnitz 2014, pp.15–32.

19. The *Philosophy of Andy Warhol: From A to B and Back Again*, New York and London 1975, p.92.

20. Meyer 2008, p.13.

21. Colacello 2000.

22. Cueff 2009, p.33

23. Bob Colacello (ed.), *Andy Warhol's Exposures*, London 1979, unpag.

24. Warhol: 'There's a new kind of Society. Now it doesn't matter if you came over on the Mayflower, so long as you can get into Studio 54. Anyone rich, powerful, beautiful, or famous can get into society. If you're a few of those things you can really get to the top.'

25. Fairbrother 2018, p.71.

26. Henry Geldzahler, 'Der jungfräuliche Voyeur: Andy Warhol', in *Andy Warhol Porträts*, exh. cat., Anthony d'Offay, London, Munich and New York 1993, pp.13–28, p.28.

27. 'Wednesday, May 25, 1977 – Paris', in Warhol 1989, p.45.

28. Based on Émilia Philippot's piece 'Debbie Harry. Du polaroid à la peinture, migration et transformation des images', in *Le grand monde d'Andy Warhol*, exh. cat., Grand Palais, Paris 2009, pp.57–62.

29. Simon Watney, 'The Warhol Effect', in Gary Garrels (ed.), *The Work of Andy Warhol* (*Discussions in Contemporary Culture*, 3), New York and Seattle 1989, pp.115–22, p.119.

30. See here and below, Elizabeth Hoover, 'Andy Warhol's Trans Subjects Finally Get Named' *Paper*, 24 August 2018. http://www.papermag.com/andy-warhol-drag-queen-portraits-2598476112.html (accessed 17 July 2019).

31. Simon Watney, 'Queer Andy', in Jennifer Doyle, Jonathan Flatley and José Esteban Muñoz (eds.), *Pop Out: Queer Warhol*, Durham, NC and London 1996, p.22.

32. Ibid. pp.24–5.

33. Geldzahler 1993, p.27.

34. First published in 1965 under the title *Quotations from Chairman Mao Tse-tung*, this key text of Maoism comprises quotations and writings. The frontispiece was based on Zhang Zhenshi's official portrait of Mao in 1952.

35. See Cueff 2009, pp.31–2.

36. Vincent Fremont, 'Andy Warhol's Porträts', in *Andy Warhol Porträts*, exh. cat., Anthony d'Offay, London, Munich and New York 1993, p.30.

37. Warhol 2007 [1975], p.62.

38. See Reva Wolf, 'Through the Looking-Glass', in Kenneth Goldsmith (ed.), *I'll Be Your Mirror, The Selected Andy Warhol Interviews*, Cambridge, MA 2004, p.XI.

39. Cueff 2009 p.31.

40. Fremont 1993, 'Andy Warhols Porträts', p.30.

41. See Mark Francis and Margery King (eds.), *The Warhol Look*, exh. cat., Whitney Museum of American Art, New York et al. 1997, pp.188–9.

42. Ibid., p.248.

43. Ibid.

44. See Dillenberger 1998, p.29.

45. Pat Hackett, 'Introduction' in Warhol 1989.

46. Dietmar Elger, 'Die beste amerikanische Erfindung überhaupt – einfach verschwinden zu können', in D.Elger (ed.), *Andy Warhol. Selbstporträts*, exh. cat., Kunstverein St Gallen, Ostfildern 2004, p.94.

47. Referring to an unpublished interview with Paul Warhola, Donna De Salvo refers to the painted gesture of nasal drilling in response to a habit of Andy Warhol's nephew (see Donna De Salvo, 'Andy Warhol: I Work Seven Days a Week', p.17). In the work not explicitly described as self-portrait, Warhol probably used this familiar gesture to to visualise the condition of his own inner self.

48. Barbara Straumann, 'Diva Warhol. Mediale Performance und Versteckspiel', in Rolf Bier and Nils Büttner (eds.), *Who Is That Pale Man? Neues zu Andy Warhol*, Munich 2010, pp.195–216, p.199.

49. Eve Kosofsky Sedgwick, *Epistemology of the Closet*, Berkeley and Los Angeles 1990.

Exhibitionism, pp.56–63

Thanks to Isabella Maidment and Celia White for providing feedback on drafts of the text and to Pauline Moran for taking me to the *Warhol* exhibition at Tate Modern in 2002.

1. Philip Core, *Camp: The Lie That Tells the Truth*, New York 1984, p.189.

2. Radio interview with Mary Woronov, 1995. https://youtu.be/baJ5 ofFChc (accessed February 2019).

3. *Raid the Icebox* opened at the Institute for the Arts, Rice University in Houston (29 October 1969 – 4 January 1970), and travelled to the Isaac Delgado Museum in New Orleans (17 January – 15 February 1970), before finishing at the Museum of Art, Rhode Island School of Design (23 April – 30 June 1970). No further exhibitions under the title *Raid the Icebox* took place.

4. Daniel Robbins, 'Confessions of A Museum Director', in *Raid the Icebox*, exh. cat., Institute for the Arts, Rice University, Houston, Isaac Delgado Museum, New Orleans, and Museum of Art, Rhode Island School of Design 1969, p.14.

5. Ibid., p.15.

6. Mario Amaya's interview for *The Autobiography and Sex Life of Andy Warhol by John Wilcock with a cast of thousands*, New York 1971 (2010 edn), p.26, is illuminating here: 'I do remember one thing Gene [Swenson] was saying; I don't know whether it was from that article, or whether he just said it verbally. He said that everything Andy did was just a souvenir of an exhibition, that they were not really "works of art," that you had to take each thing as a souvenir of that particular exhibition.'

7. Esther Newton, *Mother Camp: Female Impersonators in America*, Chicago 1972, pp.105, 107. Emphasis in original.

8. Susan Sontag, 'Notes on "Camp"', *Partisan Review*, New York 1964, republished in S. Sontag, *Against Interpretation* 1966.

9. 'Introduction', in Jennifer Doyle, Jonathan Flatley and José Esteban Muñoz (eds.), *Pop Out: Queer Warhol*, Durham, NC and London 1996, pp.4–5; see also Trevor Fairbrother, 'Tomorrow's Man', in Donna De Salvo, *'Success is a Job in New York': The Early Art and Business of Andy Warhol*, exh. cat., Grey Art Gallery and Study Center, New York University, and Carnegie Museum of Art, Pittsburgh 1989; and Kenneth E. Silver, 'Modes of Disclosure: The Construction of Gay Identity and the Rise of Pop Art', in *Hand-Painted Pop: American Art in Transition 1955–62*, exh. cat., The Museum of Contemporary Art, Los Angeles 1993. The term 'queer' is used in this essay for the way it draws together a wide range of practices that oppose normative heterosexuality; see Catherine Lord and Richard Meyer, *Art and Queer Culture*, London 2013.

10. Samuel R. Delany, 'Coming/Out', *Shorter Views: Queer Thoughts and the Politics of the Paraliterary*, Hanover and London 1999, pp.82, 89–91. See also George Chauncey, *Gay New York: Gender, Urban Culture, and the Making of the Gay Male World, 1890–1940*, New York 1995, p.7: 'coming out of what is now referred to as the gay closet referred more to coming out into a gay society, just as debutantes came out to the society of their class.'

11. Anonymous, 'A Holey Curiosity', *Baedan 3: Journal of Queer Time Travel*, 2015, p.21.

12. Andy Warhol and Pat Hackett, *POPism: The Warhol Sixties*, London 1980, pp.12–13. For additional context, the star of *Sleep* and briefly Warhol's lover, John Giorno, wrote:

The art world was homophobic, and an everpresent threat. Anyone who was gay was at a disadvantage. An artist overtly with a boyfriend was at a complete disadvantage, and could ruin his career. De Kooning, Pollock, Motherwell, and the male power structure were mean straight pricks. No matter their liberal views, they deep down hated fags. Their disdain dismissed a gay person's art. On top of it, those guys really hated Pop Art ... Andy got around homophobia by making the movie *Sleep* into an abstract painting: the body of a man as a field of light and shadow.

(John Giorno, *You Got to Burn to Shine*, New York 1994, pp.132–3.)

13. Judith Butler, 'Performative Acts and Gender Constitution' in Michael Huxley and Noel Witts (eds.), *The Twentieth Century Performance Reader*, London 2002, p.120.

14. Peter Wollen describes how Warhol's films brought together the realms of camp and minimalism 'in a paradoxical and perverse new combination'. P. Wollen, 'Raid the Icebox', in Michael O'Pray (ed.), *Andy Warhol: Film Factory*, London 1989, pp.14–27. It is also important to consider Warhol's interest in performance in relation to Michael Fried's accusation of 'theatricality' in the work of minimalist sculpture, 'Art and Objecthood', *Artforum*, June 1967, republished in Gregory Battcock (ed.), *Minimal Art: A Critical Anthology* (1968), Berkeley and Los Angeles 1995, pp.116–47.

15. Catherine Wood, *Performance in Contemporary Art*, London 2018, p.67–8.

16. The quote was originally published in Gretchen Berg's article, 'Andy Warhol: My True Story', *The East Village Other*, November 1966, pp.9–10; in *Los Angeles Free Press*, 17 March 1967; and as 'Nothing to Lose', *Cahiers du Cinéma*, no.10, May 1967, pp.38–43. Although frequently quoted and associated with Warhol, it was an amalgamation mostly created by Berg. The original transcript reads:

Berg: It's all there on the surface then; it's what we can see.
Warhol: Well, I like – I guess, yeah.
Berg: What do you like?
Warhol: The surface.
Berg: Then that's all that we can see; if we want to know about Andy Warhol, we just look at your paintings and your films and that's –
Warhol: Yeah.
Berg: There's nothing profound underneath –
Warhol: No.

Published in Matt Wrbican, 'The True Story of "My True Story"', in Eva Meyer-Hermann (ed.), *Andy Warhol: Other Voices Other Rooms*, exh. cat., Stedelijk Museum, Amsterdam 2008, p.57.

17. Amelia Jones, 'The "Pollockian Performative"', in *Body Art / Performing the Subject*, Minneapolis and London 1998, pp.69–70.

18. Warhol and Hackett 1980, p.248.

19. Bob Colacello, *Holy Terror: Andy Warhol Close Up*, New York 1990 (2014 edn), pp.557–60: 'Almost every night that winter, she [Brigid Berlin] came to my place, or I went to hers, and after I smoked two or three joints, I dictated to her, turning myself into Andy, imitating the way he talked and, as best I could, the way he thought.' For more on the process of making Warhol's publications see Lucy Mulroney, *Andy Warhol, Publisher*, Chicago 2018, and Melissa Ragona's paper 'Warhol Sounding' presented at the symposium *Andy Warhol: After Pop* at the Whitney Museum of American Art, 1 March 2019, https://youtu.be/ZiWkCDUfY9U?t=14477 (accessed 20 March 2019).

20. Warhol and Hackett 1980, p.3.

21. Warhol and Hackett 1980, pp.131–3. Emphasis in original.

22. Originally mentioned in Wayne Koestenbaum's *Andy Warhol*, London, 2002, p.57, the notebook is in the archives of The Andy Warhol Museum, Pittsburgh, identification number TC21.3.1.

23. Richard Dyer, 'Introduction', in *Heavenly Bodies*, London 1986 (2nd edn 2004), p.15.

24. Newton 1972, p.112.

25. For an in-depth discussion of the 1950s drag drawings see Nina Schleif, *Drag & Draw: Andy Warhol – The Unknown Fifties*, Munich 2018.

26. Colacello 1990 (2014 edn), pp.296–7.

27. For an in-depth record of the series and information on the models see Neil Printz's entry in *The Andy Warhol Catalogue Raisonné: Paintings and Sculpture, late 1974–1976*, vol.4, London 2014, pp.22–203.

28. Peggy Phelan, 'The Golden Apple: Jennie Livingston's Paris Is Burning', in *Unmarked: The Politics of Performance*, London 1966, pp.93–111.

29. Judith Butler, 'Bodies in Alliance and the Politics of the Street', in *Notes Toward a Performative Theory of Assembly*, London 2015.

30. Warhol and Bob Colacello, *Andy Warhol's Exposures*, London 1979, p.19.

31. Jessica Beck, 'Warhol's Confession: Love, Faith, and AIDS', in *Andy Warhol – From A to B and Back Again*, exh. cat., Whitney Museum of American Art, New York 2018, pp.84–94.

32. Delaney 1999, p.67.

Andy Warhol through the Eyes of Bob Colacello, pp.64–9

1. Excerpt taken from this very interview, p.66.

2. Bob Colacello, *Holy Terror: Andy Warhol Close-Up*, New York 1990.

EXHIBITED WORKS

The works listed appear in all four exhibition venues unless otherwise indicated (venue key below).
All works are by Andy Warhol, unless otherwise
specified. Works are organised chronologically.
Measurements are given in cm, height before
width and depth. Page references to the works
illustrated are given at the end of the entries. All
information was correct at the time of printing.

Venue key:
TM (Tate Modern, London
ML (Museum Ludwig, Cologne)
AGO (Art Gallery of Ontario, Toronto)
DMA (Dallas Museum of Art, Texas)

I Like Dance 1947
Oil paint on board 61.7 x 61.7
Paul Warhola Family Collection
ML, AGO and DMA only
p.73

Girl in Park 1948
Tempera on Masonite 61 x 50.8
Paul Warhola Family Collection
ML, AGO and DMA only
p.14

Male Figure 1948
Tempera on Masonite 61 x 50.8
Paul Warhola Family Collection
ML, AGO and DMA only
p.14

Nosepicker I: Why Pick on Me 1948
Tempera and ink on Masonite 76 x 63.5
Paul Warhola Family Collection
ML, AGO and DMA only
p.72

Three Children 1949
Tempera and ink on Masonite 86.4 x 122
Paul Warhola Family Collection
ML, AGO and DMA only
p.73

Two Dogs Kissing 1949
Tempera on Upson Board 94 x 61
Paul Warhola Family Collection
ML, AGO and DMA only
p.72

Unidentified Male c.1954
Ink on paper 42.5 x 35.6
Cheim & Read, New York

Boy Licking his Lips 1956
Ink on paper 42 x 35.5
ARTIST ROOMS. Acquired jointly by Tate and
the National Galleries of Scotland through
The d'Offay Donation with assistance from the
National Heritage Memorial Fund and the Art
Fund 2008
p.76

Male Torso 1956
Ink on paper 42.5 x 34.5
ARTIST ROOMS. Acquired jointly by Tate and
the National Galleries of Scotland through
The d'Offay Donation with assistance from the
National Heritage Memorial Fund and the Art
Fund 2008
p.74

Reclining Male Nude 1956
Ink on paper 42.5 x 35.4
Galerie des Modernes, Paris
ML, AGO and DMA only

Untitled [Head of a Man] 1956
Ink, graphite and gold leaf on paper
45.4 x 42.2
Collection of John Cheim
p.74

Charles Lisanby c.1956
Ink on paper 42.5 x 35.5
Cheim & Read, New York
p.77

Leon Danielian c.1956
Ink on paper 42.5 x 35.5
Cheim & Read, New York
p.76

Male Nude with Flower c.1956
Ink on paper 42.6 x 35.5
Galerie des Modernes, Paris
ML, AGO and DMA only

Male Partial Figure c.1956
Ink on paper 42.6 x 35.3
Galerie des Modernes, Paris
ML, AGO and DMA only

Reclining Male c.1956
Ink on paper 42.5 x 35.5
Cheim & Read, New York
p.77

Unidentified Female c.1956
Ink on paper 42.5 x 35.5
Cheim & Read, New York
p.76

Unidentified Male c.1956
Ink on paper 43.2 x 35.5
Cheim & Read, New York

Unidentified Male c.1956
Ink on paper 43.2 x 35.5
Cheim & Read, New York
p.76

Unidentified Male c.1956
Ink on paper 42.5 x 35.5
Cheim & Read, New York
p.79

Boy with Flowers 1955-7
Ink on paper 42.5 x 35
ARTIST ROOMS. Acquired jointly by Tate and
the National Galleries of Scotland through
The d'Offay Donation with assistance from the
National Heritage Memorial Fund and the Art
Fund 2008
p.74

Kneeling Male Over Male Lower Torso 1955-7
Ink on paper 42.7 x 35.3
Galerie des Modernes, Paris
p.79

Resting Boy 1955-7
Ink on paper 41.8 x 34.5
ARTIST ROOMS. Acquired jointly by Tate and
the National Galleries of Scotland through
The d'Offay Donation with assistance from the
National Heritage Memorial Fund and the Art
Fund 2008
p.74

Madame Helena Rubinstein 1956-7
Ink on paper 43.2 x 35.5
Cheim & Read, New York
p.77

Male Nude 1956-7
Ink on paper 42.5 x 35.5
Galerie des Modernes, Paris
p.77

Seated Male Nude 1956-7
Ink on paper 42.9 x 35
Galerie des Modernes, Paris

Standing Male Nude 1956-7
Ink on paper 42.8 x 34.9

Galerie des Modernes, Paris
ML, AGO and DMA only

**Andy Warhol 1928-87 and
Julia Warhola 1891-1972**
A Gold Book 1957
Offset lithograph and Dr Martins Aniline dye on
paper and coated metallic paper, with buckram
board cover 38.1 x 29.8 x 1.3
The Andy Warhol Museum, Pittsburgh; Founding
Collection, Contribution The Andy Warhol
Foundation for the Visual Arts, Inc.
1998.3.2427.1

A Gold Book 1957
Offset lithograph and Dr Martins Aniline dye on
paper and coated metallic paper, with buckram
board cover 38.1 x 29.8 x 1.3
The Andy Warhol Museum, Pittsburgh; Founding
Collection, Contribution The Andy Warhol
Foundation for the Visual Arts, Inc.
1998.3.2427.2

A Gold Book 1957
Offset lithograph and Dr Martins Aniline dye on
paper and coated metallic paper, with buckram
board cover 38.1 x 29.8 x 1.3
The Andy Warhol Museum, Pittsburgh; Founding
Collection, Contribution The Andy Warhol
Foundation for the Visual Arts, Inc.
1998.3.2427.3
pp.84-5 (those illustrated here are from
an alternative collection)

Untitled [Head of a Male] 1957
Ink and graphite on paper 45.4 x 30.5
Collection of John Cheim

Male Nude with Shells c.1957
Ink on paper 43.6 x 35.9
Galerie des Modernes, Paris
ML, AGO and DMA only

Standing Male c.1957
Ink on paper 61 x 46
Cheim & Read, New York
p.78

Unidentified Male c.1957
Ink on paper 43.2 x 35.5
Cheim & Read, New York

Unidentified Male c.1957
Ink on paper 42.5 x 35.5
Cheim & Read, New York
p.79

Advertisement 1960
Acrylic paint and wax crayon on canvas
183 x 137
State Museums of Berlin, National Gallery,
Marx Collection
TM and ML only
p.87

Before and After [3] 1961
Casein paint on canvas 137.5 x 178.4
The Doris and Donald Fisher Collection at the
San Francisco Museum of Modern Art
pp.88-9

$199 Television 1961
Acrylic paint and oil stick on canvas
172.7 x 132.7
Whitney Museum of American Art, New York
Gift of The American Contemporary Art
Foundation, Inc., Leonard A. Lauder, President
TM and ML only
p.93

100 Campbell's Soup Cans 1962
Casein, acrylic paint and graphite on canvas
182.9 x 132.7

MMK Museum für Moderne Kunst Frankfurt
am Main, former collection of Karl Ströher,
Darmstadt
p.94

129 Die in Jet! (Plane Crash) 1962
Acrylic paint and graphite on canvas
254.5 x 182.5
Museum Ludwig, Cologne / Donation Ludwig
Collection 1976
p.98

Close Cover Before Striking (Pepsi Cola) 1962
Acrylic paint and sandpaper on canvas
183 x 137
Museum Ludwig, Cologne / Donation Ludwig
Collection 1976
ML only
p.86

*Dance Diagram [1] [Fox Trot: 'The Double
Twinkle Man']* 1962
Casein and graphite on canvas 183.5 x 137.8
MMK Museum für Moderne Kunst Frankfurt
am Main, former collection of Karl Ströher,
Darmstadt. Inv. Nr. 1981/60
ML, AGO and DMA only
p.90

Green Coca Cola Bottles 1962
Acrylic paint, screenprint and graphite on
canvas 210.2 x 145.1
Whitney Museum of American Art, New York;
Purchase, with funds from the Friends of the
Whitney Museum of American Art
TM and ML only
p.95

Round Marilyn 1962
Acrylic paint, screenprint and metallic paint on
canvas. Diam. 45.2
Udo and Anette Brandhorst Collection
TM and ML only
p.101

Marilyn Diptych 1962
Acrylic paint on two canvases
205.4 x 144.8 each
Tate. Purchased 1980
pp.102-3

Marilyn Monroe's Lips 1962
Acrylic paint, screenprint and graphite on
two canvases 210.2 x 205.1; 210.2 x 209.2
Hirshhorn Museum and Sculpture Garden,
Smithsonian Institution, Washington, DC,
Gift of Joseph H. Hirshhorn, 1972
TM only
pp.104-5

Two Dollar Bills (Front and Rear) 1962
Screenprint on canvas 210 x 96
Museum Ludwig, Cologne / Donation Ludwig
Collection 1976
p.99

A Woman's Suicide 1962
Screenprint and graphite on canvas 313 x 211
Kunstsammlung Nordrhein-Westfalen, Düsseldorf
TM and ML only
p.106

*Black and White Disaster #4 (5 Deaths 17 Times
in Black and White)* 1963
Acrylic paint, screenprint and graphite on two
canvases 261.9 x 209 each
Kunstmuseum Basel
TM and ML only
pp.112-13

Red (Pink) Race Riot 1963
Screenprint and acrylic paint on canvas
325.8 x 210.8

Museum Ludwig, Cologne / Donation Ludwig
Collection 1976
TM and ML only
p.114

Silver Liz (aka Liz Taylor) 1963
Aluminium paint and screenprint on canvas
104.1 x 107.9
Private collection
TM and ML only
p.123

Sleep 1963
16mm film, black and white transferred to
digital file, silent
5 hours 21 minutes at 16 frames per second
© 2019 The Andy Warhol Museum, Pittsburgh,
PA, a museum of Carnegie Institute. All rights
reserved.
pp.25, 122

*13 Most Wanted Men No.10, Louis Joseph
M.* 1963
Screenprint on two canvases 123.7 x 100.1;
124 x 100
Städtisches Museum Abteiberg
Mönchengladbach
TM only

Campbell's Boxes 1964
Screenprint ink on wood 25.5 x 48 x 24 each
Museum Ludwig, Cologne / Loan Peter and
Irene Ludwig Foundation 1986
ML only
p.97

Elvis I and II 1963–4
Screenprint and acrylic paint [blue canvas];
screenprint and spray paint [silver canvas]
on canvas 208.3 x 208.3 each
Collection Art Gallery of Ontario, Toronto.
Gift from the Women's Committee Fund, 1966
65/35
pp.110–11

Flowers 1964
Fluorescent paint and screenprint on canvas
208.3 x 208.3
Private collection
p.132

Flowers 1964
Acrylic paint on canvas 208 x 328
Museum Ludwig, Cologne / Loan Peter and
Irene Ludwig Foundation 1982
ML only

Jackie Frieze 1964
Screenprint, acrylic paint and metallic paint on
canvas 50.8 x 325 x 3.8
Source image: photograph-Henri Dauman,
1963
Collection Museum of Contemporary Art
Chicago, gift of Beatrice Cummings Mayer
2007.32
pp.116–17

Jackie Triptych 1964
Screenprint and acrylic paint on three canvases
53 x 124 overall
Museum Ludwig, Cologne / Donation Ludwig
Collection 1976
ML, AGO and DMA only
pp.118–19

Most Wanted Men No.1 John M. 1964
Screenprint on two canvases 124.5 x 95.9 each
Herbert F. Johnson Museum of Art, Cornell
University. Acquired with funds provided by the
National Endowment for the Arts, and through
the generosity of individual donors
76048a,b
p.109

Most Wanted Men No.7, Salvatore V. 1964
Screenprint on two canvases 199 x 99 each
Museum Ludwig, Cologne / Donation Ludwig
Collection 1976
ML only
p.109

Self Portrait 1964
Acrylic paint and screenprint on canvas
50.8 x 41.2
Fondation Louis Vuitton, Paris
TM only
p.121

White Brillo Boxes 1964
Screenprint ink on wood 44 x 43 x 35.5 each
Museum Ludwig, Cologne / Loan Peter and
Irene Ludwig Foundation 1986
TM and ML only
p.96

Screen Test: Jack Smith [ST315] 1964
16mm film, black and white, silent
4 minutes 30 seconds at 16 frames per second
©2019 The Andy Warhol Museum, Pittsburgh,
PA, a museum of Carnegie Institute. All rights
reserved
p.124

Screen Test: Susan Sontag [ST321], 1964
16mm film, black and white, silent
4 minutes 18 seconds at 16 frames per second
©2019 The Andy Warhol Museum, Pittsburgh,
PA, a museum of Carnegie Institute. All rights
reserved.
p.124

Screen Test: Ann Buchanan [ST33] 1964
16mm film, black and white, silent
4 minutes 30 seconds at 16 frames per second
©2019 The Andy Warhol Museum, Pittsburgh,
PA, a museum of Carnegie Institute. All rights
reserved
p.125

Screen Test: Lucinda Childs [ST52] 1964
16mm film, black and white, silent
4 minutes 30 seconds at 16 frames per second
©2019 The Andy Warhol Museum, Pittsburgh,
PA, a museum of Carnegie Institute. All rights
reserved
p.125

Screen Test: Kyoko Kishida [ST183] 1964
16mm film, black and white, silent
4 minutes 30 seconds at 16 frames per second
©2019 The Andy Warhol Museum, Pittsburgh,
PA, a museum of Carnegie Institute. All rights
reserved
p.125

Screen Test: Rufus Collins [ST61] 1964
16mm film, black and white, silent
4 minutes 18 seconds at 16 frames per second
©2019 The Andy Warhol Museum, Pittsburgh,
PA, a museum of Carnegie Institute. All rights
reserved
p.124

Screen Test: Ivy Nicholson [ST230] 1964
16mm film, black and white, silent
4 minutes 30 seconds at 16 frames per second
©2019 The Andy Warhol Museum, Pittsburgh,
PA, a museum of Carnegie Institute.
All rights reserved
p.124

Screen Test: Dennis Hopper [ST155] 1964
16mm film, black and white, silent
4 minutes 18 seconds at 16 frames per second
©2019 The Andy Warhol Museum, Pittsburgh,
PA, a museum of Carnegie Institute. All rights
reserved

Screen Test: Peter Hujar [ST157] 1964
16mm film, black and white, silent
4 minutes 24 seconds at 16 frames per second
©2019 The Andy Warhol Museum, Pittsburgh,
PA, a museum of Carnegie Institute. All rights
reserved
p.125

Screen Test: Mario Montez [ST222] 1965
16mm film, black and white, silent
4 minutes 30 seconds at 16 frames per second
©2019 The Andy Warhol Museum, Pittsburgh,
PA, a museum of Carnegie Institute. All rights
reserved
p.125

Screen Test: Jane Holzer [ST142] 1964
16mm film, black and white, silent
4 minutes 30 seconds at 16 frames per second
©2019 The Andy Warhol Museum, Pittsburgh,
PA, a museum of Carnegie Institute. All rights
reserved
p.124

Screen Test: Edie Sedgwick [ST308] 1965
16mm film, black and white, silent
4 minutes 36 seconds at 16 frames per second
©2019 The Andy Warhol Museum, Pittsburgh,
PA, a museum of Carnegie Institute. All rights
reserved
p.126

Screen Test: Marcel Duchamp [ST80] 1966
16mm film, black and white, silent
4 minutes 24 seconds at 16 frames per second
©2019 The Andy Warhol Museum, Pittsburgh,
PA, a museum of Carnegie Institute. All rights
reserved
p.125

Screen Test: Bob Dylan [ST83] 1966
16mm film, black and white, silent
4 minutes 36 seconds at 16 frames per second
©2019 The Andy Warhol Museum, Pittsburgh,
PA, a museum of Carnegie Institute. All rights
reserved
p.125

Screen Test: Allen Ginsberg [ST115] 1966
16mm film, black and white, silent
4 minutes 30 seconds at 16 frames per second
©2019 The Andy Warhol Museum, Pittsburgh,
PA, a museum of Carnegie Institute. All rights
reserved
p.125

Cow Wallpaper [pink on yellow] 1966,
reprinted 1994
Screenprint on wallpaper
Strip 71.1 wide; overall dimensions variable
The Andy Warhol Museum, Pittsburgh
IA1994.7
Displayed in café and restaurant at TM

Double Marlon 1966
Screenprint on unprimed canvas 213.4 x 243
Yageo Foundation Collection Taiwan
TM only
p.131

Exploding Plastic Inevitable 1966,
reconfigured 2020
16mm film transferred to digital file, black and
white, soundtrack
Equipment: 17 ceiling mounted projectors with
media players, 1 sound system, 4 speakers,
2 disco balls
The Andy Warhol Museum, Pittsburgh
IA2015.5

Silver Clouds 1966
[*Warhol Museum Series* 1994]
Helium-filled metalised plastic film (Scotchpak)

87.6 x 126.4 each
The Andy Warhol Museum, Pittsburgh
IA1994.13
pp.27–8, 138–9

Big Electric Chair 1967
Acrylic paint and screenprint on canvas
137.2 x 185.5
Froehlich Collection, Stuttgart
ML only
p.107

Self Portrait 1967
Acrylic paint and screenprint on canvas
183.2 x 183.2
Tate. Purchased 1971
p.133

[no title] [Electric Chair] 1971
Screenprint on ten sheets of paper
90 x 121.6 each
Tate. Purchased 1982
ML, AGO and DMA only
pp.154–5

Factory Diary: Julia Warhola in Bed c.1970–2
½-inch reel-to-reel videotape transferred to
digital file, black and white, sound 23 minutes
© 2019 The Andy Warhol Museum, Pittsburgh,
PA, a museum of Carnegie Institute. All rights
reserved.
p.54

Mao 1972
Acrylic paint and screenprint on canvas
208.3 x 144.8
Yageo Foundation Collection Taiwan
TM and ML only
p.158

Mao Wallpaper 1974, reprinted 1994
Screenprint on wallpaper
Strip 71.1 wide; overall dimensions variable
The Andy Warhol Museum, Pittsburgh
IA1994.9

Ladies and Gentlemen (Alphanso Panell) 1975
Acrylic paint and screenprint on canvas
81.3 x 66
Italian private collection
p.163

Ladies and Gentlemen (Alphanso Panell) 1975
Acrylic paint and screenprint on canvas
35.6 x 27.9
Italian private collection
p.165

Ladies and Gentlemen (Iris) 1975
Acrylic paint and screenprint on canvas
35.6 x 27.9
Italian private collection
p.171

Ladies and Gentlemen (Alphanso Panell) 1975
Acrylic paint and screenprint on canvas
81.3 x 66
Italian private collection
p.164

Ladies and Gentlemen (Alphanso Panell) 1975
Acrylic paint and screenprint on canvas
35.6 x 27.9
Italian private collection
p.165

Ladies and Gentlemen (Marsha P. Johnson)
1975
Acrylic paint and screenprint on canvas
127 x 101.6
Italian private collection
p.169

Ladies and Gentlemen (Wilhelmina Ross) 1975
Acrylic paint and screenprint on canvas
300 x 200
Italian private collection
p.162

Ladies and Gentlemen (Alphanso Panell) 1975
Acrylic paint and screenprint on canvas
81.3 x 66
Italian private collection
p.163

Ladies and Gentlemen (Lurdes) 1975
Acrylic paint and screenprint on paper
127 x 101.6
Italian private collection
p.168

Ladies and Gentlemen (Iris) 1975
Acrylic paint and screenprint on canvas
35.6 x 27.9
Italian private collection

Ladies and Gentlemen (Iris) 1975
Acrylic paint and screenprint on canvas
35.6 x 27.9
Italian private collection
p.170

Ladies and Gentlemen (Broadway) 1975
Acrylic paint and screenprint on canvas
35.6 x 27.9
Italian private collection
p.166

Ladies and Gentlemen (Iris) 1975
Acrylic paint and screenprint on canvas
35.6 x 27.9
Italian private collection
p.171

Ladies and Gentlemen (Iris) 1975
Acrylic paint and screenprint on canvas
35.6 x 27.9
Italian private collection
p.171

Ladies and Gentlemen (Iris) 1975
Acrylic paint and screenprint on canvas
35.6 x 27.9
Italian private collection
p.171

Ladies and Gentlemen (Iris) 1975
Acrylic paint and screenprint on canvas
35.6 x 27.9
Italian private collection
p.170

Ladies and Gentlemen (Helen/Harry Morales)
1975
Acrylic paint and screenprint on canvas
35.6 x 27.9
Italian private collection

Ladies and Gentlemen (Helen/Harry Morales)
1975
Acrylic paint and screenprint on canvas
35.6 x 27.9
Italian private collection
p.167

Ladies and Gentlemen (Alphanso Panell) 1975
Acrylic paint and screenprint on canvas
81.3 x 66
Italian private collection

Ladies and Gentlemen (Broadway) 1975
Acrylic paint and screenprint on canvas
35.6 x 27.9
Italian private collection
p.166

Ladies and Gentlemen (Broadway) 1975
Acrylic paint and screenprint on canvas
35.6 x 27.9
Italian private collection

Ladies and Gentlemen (Broadway) 1975
Acrylic paint and screenprint on canvas
35.6 x 27.9
Italian private collection
p.166

Ladies and Gentlemen (Wilhelmina Ross) 1975
Acrylic paint and screenprint on canvas
127 x 101.6
Italian private collection
p.2

Ladies and Gentlemen (Alphanso Panell) 1975
Acrylic paint and screenprint on canvas
81.3 x 66
Italian private collection
p.164

Mick Jagger 1975
Acrylic paint and screenprint on canvas
101.6 x 101.6
Private collection
p.184

Mick Jagger 1975
Acrylic paint and screenprint on canvas
101.6 x 101.6
Private collection
p.184

Hammer and Sickle 1976
Acrylic paint and screenprint on canvas
305 x 407.5
Udo and Anette Brandhorst Collection
TM and ML only
p.159

Skull 1976
Acrylic paint and screenprint on canvas
182.9 x 203.2
Collection of Larry Gagosian
TM only
p.161

Skull 1976
Acrylic paint and screenprint on canvas
184.2 x 204.5
Collection of Larry Gagosian
TM only
p.160

Skull 1976
Acrylic paint and screenprint on canvas
182.9 x 203.5
Collection of Larry Gagosian
TM only
p.161

Skull 1976
Acrylic paint and screenprint on canvas
184.2 x 204.5
Collection of Larry Gagosian
TM only
p.160

Torso 1977
Acrylic paint and screenprint on canvas
127 x 101.5
Udo and Anette Brandhorst Collection
ML, AGO and DMA only
p.18

Torso 1977
Screenprint and acrylic paint on canvas
127 x 106.7
ZOYA Gallery, Slovakia
p.179

Oxidation Painting 1978
Urine and metallic paint on canvas 199 x 553.5
Private collection
pp.180–1

Andy Warhol's T.V. [Season 1, Episode 3] 1980
¾-inch videotape transferred to digital file,
colour, sound. 30 min
With Halston, Betsey Johnson, Lisa Robinson,
David Johansen, Andy Warhol, Lenny Kaye, the
Ritz, Jerry Brandt, Sherri Beachfront, Zecca, Jim
Carroll, Johnny Thunders, Danceteria, Hurrah's,
Daniela Morera, Giorgio Armani, the Rock
Lounge, Howard Stein, Walter Steding, Robert
Boykin, Secret Affair, Jim Fouratt, Neil Bogart,
Diana Vreeland, Henry Geldzahler, Debbie
Harry, Chris Stein
© 2019 The Andy Warhol Museum, Pittsburgh,
PA, a museum of Carnegie Institute. All rights
reserved

Debbie Harry 1980
Acrylic paint and screenprint on canvas
101.6 x 101.6
Private Collection of Phyllis and Jerome Lyle
Rappaport
p.187

Debbie Harry 1980
Acrylic paint and screenprint on canvas
101.6 x 101.6
Private Collection of Phyllis and Jerome Lyle
Rappaport
p.186

Andy Warhol T.V. Productions
*Andy Warhol's T.V. on Saturday Night Live
(October 3, 1981)* 1981
1-inch videotape, colour, sound. 1 min
©2019 The Andy Warhol Museum, Pittsburgh,
PA, a museum of Carnegie Institute. All rights
reserved.

*Andy Warhol's T.V. on Saturday Night Live
(October 10, 1981)* 1981
1-inch videotape, colour, sound. 1 minute
©2019 The Andy Warhol Museum, Pittsburgh,
PA, a museum of Carnegie Institute. All rights
reserved.

*Andy Warhol's T.V. on Saturday Night Live
(October 31, 1981)* 1981
1-inch videotape, color, sound, 1 minute
©2019 The Andy Warhol Museum, Pittsburgh,
PA, a museum of Carnegie Institute. All rights
reserved.
p.192

Factory Diary: Andy in Drag, 2 October 1981
1981
¾-inch videotape (three total) transferred to
digital file, colour, sound. 56 minutes
Filmed by Vincent Fremont
© 2019 The Andy Warhol Museum, Pittsburgh,
PA, a museum of Carnegie Institute. All rights
reserved
p.193

Cross 1981–2
Acrylic paint and screenprint on canvas
229 x 178
KOLUMBA, Cologne
Inv.1998/0319
ML only
p.13

Robert Mapplethorpe 1983
Acrylic paint and screenprint on canvas
101.7 x 101.7
ARTIST ROOMS. Acquired jointly by Tate and
the National Galleries of Scotland through
The d'Offay Donation with assistance from the
National Heritage Memorial Fund and the Art
Fund 2008
p.190

Dolly Parton 1985
Acrylic paint and screenprint on canvas
106.7 x 106.7
The Doris and Donald Fisher Collection at the
San Francisco Museum of Modern Art
p.191

Dolly Parton 1985
Acrylic paint and screenprint on canvas
106.7 x 106.7
The Doris and Donald Fisher Collection at the
San Francisco Museum of Modern Art
p.191

Christ $9.98 (positive) 1985–6
Acrylic paint and screenprint on canvas
203.7 x 183.2
Udo and Anette Brandhorst Collection
ML, AGO and DMA only
p.202

Repent and Sin No More! (negative) 1985–6
Screenprint and acrylic paint on canvas
203.5 x 183.4
Udo and Anette Brandhorst Collection
ML, AGO and DMA only

Andy Warhol's Fifteen Minutes [episode 1]
1986
1-inch videotape transferred to digital file,
colour, sound. 30 min
Andy Warhol T.V. Productions for MTV Network.
Conceived by Andy Warhol. Directed by
Don Munroe. Produced by Vincent Fremont.
Executive Director, Andy Warhol. Associate
Producer, Fred Hughes. Writers, Don Munroe,
Andy Warhol, Vincent Fremont.
With Robin Leach, Jerry Hall, Andy Warhol,
Debbie Harry, the Pyramid Club, Jelly Joplin,
Hapi Phace, John Kelly, Dagmar Onassis, Lady
Bunny, Dean Johnson, Terry Toy, Area, 4D,
Katharine Hamnett, Marla Kay, Anna Johnson,
Eric Perram, Tracy Johns, Paulina Porizkova,
Sally Kirkland, The Parachute Club, Bryan
Adams, John Oates, Andy Warhol, Billy Bryans,
Lorraine Segato, Moon and Dweezil Zappa,
Curiosity Killed the Cat, Tama Janowitz,
Lypsinka, Carla Steimer
© 2019 The Andy Warhol Museum, Pittsburgh,
PA, a museum of Carnegie Institute. All rights
reserved
p.37

Camouflage 1986
Acrylic paint and screenprint on four canvases
183 x 183 each
ARTIST ROOMS. Acquired jointly by Tate and
the National Galleries of Scotland through
The d'Offay Donation with assistance from the
National Heritage Memorial Fund and the Art
Fund 2008
ML, AGO and DMA only
pp.194–5

Lenin 1986
Screenprint and acrylic paint on canvas
213 x 178
Städtische Galerie im Lenbachhaus und
Kunstbau Munich
TM and ML only
p.201

Lenin 1986
Screenprint and acrylic paint on canvas
213 x 178
Städtische Galerie im Lenbachhaus und
Kunstbau Munich
TM and ML only
p.201

Self Portrait 1986
Acrylic paint and screenprint on canvas
203.2 x 203.2
Tate. Presented by Janet Wolfson de Botton
1996
p.207

Sixty Last Suppers 1986
Acrylic paint and screenprint on canvas
294.6 x 998.2
Nicola Erni Collection
TM only
pp.204–5

Statue of Liberty (Fabis) 1986
Acrylic paint and screenprint on canvas
183 x 183
Collection Thaddaeus Ropac, London, Paris,
Salzburg
p.200

Knife Display 1976–86
(sewn posthumously in 2014)
Gelatin silver prints stitched together with thread
53.3 x 68.9 overall
Museum Ludwig, Cologne. Gift of The Andy
Warhol Foundation for the Visual Arts, Inc.,
2015. © The Andy Warhol Foundation for the
Visual Arts, Inc.
ML only

Man on the Street, China 1976–86
(sewn posthumously in 2014)
Gelatin silver prints stitched together with thread
53.7 x 69.1 overall
Museum Ludwig, Cologne. Gift of The Andy
Warhol Foundation for the Visual Arts, Inc.,
2015. © The Andy Warhol Foundation for the
Visual Arts, Inc.
ML only

Man Wearing Interview Scarf 1976–86
(sewn posthumously in 2014)
Gelatin silver prints stitched together with thread
68.8 x 53.5 overall
Museum Ludwig, Cologne. Gift of The Andy
Warhol Foundation for the Visual Arts, Inc.,
2015. © The Andy Warhol Foundation for the
Visual Arts, Inc.
ML only

Pieta Relief Sculpture 1976–86
Gelatin silver print on paper 27.7 x 35.6
Museum Ludwig, Cologne. Gift of The Andy
Warhol Foundation for the Visual Arts, Inc.,
2015. © The Andy Warhol Foundation for the
Visual Arts, Inc.
ML only

Skulls (Close-Up) 1976–86
(sewn posthumously in 2014)
Gelatin silver prints stitched together with thread
54 x 69 overall
Museum Ludwig, Cologne. Gift of The Andy
Warhol Foundation for the Visual Arts, Inc.,
2015. © The Andy Warhol Foundation for the
Visual Arts, Inc.
ML only

Standing Nude 1976–86
(sewn posthumously in 2014)
Gelatin silver prints stitched together with thread
58.5 x 53.6 overall
Museum Ludwig, Cologne. Gift of The Andy

Warhol Foundation for the Visual Arts, Inc.,
2015. © The Andy Warhol Foundation for the
Visual Arts, Inc.
ML only

Male Nude 1987
Four photographs; gelatin silver prints on paper
and thread 71.1 x 55.9 overall
ARTIST ROOMS. Acquired jointly by Tate and
the National Galleries of Scotland through
The d'Offay Donation with assistance from the
National Heritage Memorial Fund and the Art
Fund 2008
p.196

Male Nude 1987
Four photographs; gelatin silver prints on paper
and thread 69.6 x 54 overall
ARTIST ROOMS. Acquired jointly by Tate and
the National Galleries of Scotland through
The d'Offay Donation with assistance from the
National Heritage Memorial Fund and the Art
Fund 2008

Male Nude 1987
Four photographs; gelatin silver prints on paper
and thread 69.5 x 54 overall
ARTIST ROOMS. Acquired jointly by Tate and
the National Galleries of Scotland through
The d'Offay Donation with assistance from the
National Heritage Memorial Fund and the Art
Fund 2008

Male Nude 1987
Four photographs; gelatin silver prints on paper
and thread 71.1 x 55.9 overall
ARTIST ROOMS. Acquired jointly by Tate and
the National Galleries of Scotland through
The d'Offay Donation with assistance from the
National Heritage Memorial Fund and the Art
Fund 2008

Untitled [lamp on sidetable] 1987
Four photographs; gelatin silver prints on paper
and thread 53.3 x 68.6 overall
Collection of John Cheim
p.197

Archival documents

Family images (photographers unknown)
*Julia Zavacky Warhola (far right) with family
members in Mikova* c.1910
Facsimile of original gelatin silver print and
vellum on paper 11.7 x 8.3
The Andy Warhol Museum, Pittsburgh; Founding
Collection, Contribution The Andy Warhol
Foundation for the Visual Arts, Inc.
T3257 (facsimile 01)

*Julia Zavacky Warhola in a photograph made
for her passport* 1920
Facsimile of original gelatin silver print on paper
9.7 x 7.3
The Andy Warhol Museum, Pittsburgh; Founding
Collection, Contribution The Andy Warhol
Foundation for the Visual Arts, Inc.
T3256 (facsimile 01)

*Julia Warhola (left) with family members includ-
ing her sister Mary Preksta (Andrej Warhola
may be in between Julia and Mary; Andy may
be the small child wearing a bonnet)* c.1930
Facsimile of original gelatin silver print on paper
12.9 x 8.9
The Andy Warhol Museum, Pittsburgh; Founding
Collection, Contribution The Andy Warhol
Foundation for the Visual Arts, Inc.
T3260 (facsimile 01)

Julia, John and Andy Warhola 1932
Facsimile of original sepia print on paper

5.7 x 4.1
The Andy Warhol Museum, Pittsburgh; Founding
Collection, Contribution The Andy Warhol
Foundation for the Visual Arts, Inc.
1998.3.5247 (facsimile 05)

Andy Warhol as a young boy c.1936
Facsimile of original hand-coloured sepia print
on paper 15.2 x 12.1
The Andy Warhol Museum, Pittsburgh; Founding
Collection, Contribution The Andy Warhol
Foundation for the Visual Arts, Inc.
1998.3.5218 (facsimile 03)

*Andy Warhol (right) with Julia Warhola (centre)
and neighbour Margie Girman (left) in the
Warholas' backyard on Dawson Street* c.1936
Gelatin silver print 5.1 x 7.3
The Andy Warhol Museum, Pittsburgh; Founding
Collection, Contribution The Andy Warhol
Foundation for the Visual Arts, Inc.
T3255 (facsimile 01)

*Andy Warhol, Julia Warhola, George Guke
and Mrs Mary (Zavacky) Preksta* 1937
Facsimile of original sepia print 9.2 x 6
The Andy Warhol Museum, Pittsburgh; Founding
Collection, Contribution The Andy Warhol
Foundation for the Visual Arts, Inc.
1998.3.10540.1 (facsimile 01)

Paul, Andy and John Warhola 1940
Facsimile of original gelatin silver print on paper
12.9 x 8.9
The Andy Warhol Museum, Pittsburgh; Founding
Collection, Contribution The Andy Warhol
Foundation for the Visual Arts, Inc.
T3519 (facsimile 01)

John, Andy and Paul Warhola 1942
Facsimile of original photograph on paper
12.7 x 8.9
The Andy Warhol Museum, Pittsburgh; Founding
Collection, Contribution The Andy Warhol
Foundation for the Visual Arts, Inc.
T597 (facsimile 01)

*Andy Warhol with the family's dog, Lucy, and
Julia Warhola at Dawson Street* c.1946
Facsimile of original gelatin silver print on paper
8.6 x 6.4
The Andy Warhol Museum, Pittsburgh; Founding
Collection, Contribution The Andy Warhol
Foundation for the Visual Arts, Inc.
1998.3.2691 (facsimile 01)

Warhola Family 1946–7
Facsimile of original photograph on paper
7 x 11.7
The Andy Warhol Museum, Pittsburgh; Founding
Collection, Contribution The Andy Warhol
Foundation for the Visual Arts, Inc.
1998.3.10540.2 (facsimile 01)

Artist books and magazines

Aspen, Vol.1, no.3: Fab Issue (December) 1966
Roaring Forks Press, Inc., New York; Phyllis
Johnson, Editor
Printed ink on paper in coated, printed box
31.1 x 23.5 x 1.9
Tate Library

Andy Warhol's Index 1967
Book; offset lithograph on paper, lenticular
photograph on buckram board cover and
printed ink on plastic bag 28.6 x 22.2 x 1.6
The Andy Warhol Museum, Pittsburgh; Founding
Collection, Contribution The Andy Warhol
Foundation for the Visual Arts, Inc.
1998.3.2457.2a-b

Andy Warhol's Index 1967
Book; black and white photographs, text, fold-
out pages, colour pop-up images and various
objects (folded cardboard, balloon, paper-disc
record, band, metal) fixed between pages,
stitch-bound, soft cover 29.8 x 23.5 x 1.6
The Andy Warhol Museum, Pittsburgh; Founding
Collection, Contribution The Andy Warhol
Foundation for the Visual Arts, Inc.
1998.3.2457.4

Andy Warhol's Index 1967
Book; black and white photographs, text, fold-
out pages, colour pop-up images and
various objects (folded cardboard, balloon,
paper-disc record, band, metal) fixed between
pages, stitch-bound, soft cover 28 x 21.7 x 1
Tate Library (two copies)
TM only

Andy Warhol / Moderna Museet, Stockholm
exhibition catalogue 1968
(Exhibition: February–March 1968)
Photos by Stephen Shore b.1947, and
Billy Name 1940–2016
Book; printed ink on paper 26.7 x 21 x 2.5
The Andy Warhol Museum, Pittsburgh; Founding
Collection, Contribution The Andy Warhol
Foundation for the Visual Arts, Inc.
TC74.2.1.2

Andy Warhol / Moderna Museet, Stockholm
exhibition catalogue 1968
(Exhibition February–March 1968)
Book; printed ink on paper 27 x 21
Courtesy of Gregor Muir
TM only

Andy Warhol / Moderna Museet, Stockholm
exhibition catalogue, reprinted 1969
(original edition 1968)
(Exhibition February–March 1968)
Book; printed ink on paper 27 x 21
Tate Library
TM only

a, A Novel 1968
Book; printed ink on paper 23.5 x 16 x 3.5
Tate Library and Tate Curatorial (two copies)

Interview, Vol.1, no.1 1969
Printed ink on newsprint 41.9 x 29.5
© 1969 by Poetry on Film, Inc., New York, NY.
Published by Andy Warhol.
The Andy Warhol Museum, Pittsburgh; Founding
Collection, Contribution The Andy Warhol
Foundation for the Visual Arts, Inc.
1998.3.6318.1
p.174

Blue Movie 1970
Book; print on paper
17.5 x 10 x 1 (two copies)
Tate Curatorial
*The Philosophy of Andy Warhol: From A to B
and Back Again)* 1975
Book; print on paper 19.8 x 12.9
Tate Library and Tate Curatorial (two copies)

Interview magazine 1970–87
Covers designed by Richard Bernstein
1939–2002
Printed ink on paper. Dimensions variable
Tate Library
Issues displayed at TM: December 1972,
December 1978, June 1979, September 1979,
October 1981, December 1981, May 1982,
October 1984, May 1985, June 1985, Decem-
ber 1985, March 1986, June 1986
(Other venue selections not confirmed at time
of printing)

Publications

'Deus Ex Machina', *Harper's Bazaar*, Vol.96, no.3012, pp.158–9, November 1962
Magazine; print on paper 33 x 24
Tate Modern Curatorial

Exhibition announcement (The Personality of the Artist / Stable Gallery, New York, April 21 – May 9 1964) 1964
Offset lithograph on coated paper 34 x 24.1
The Andy Warhol Museum, Pittsburgh; Founding Collection, Contribution The Andy Warhol Foundation for the Visual Arts, Inc.
TC5.61.2

'Mothers', *Esquire*, November 1966
Magazine; print on paper 33.7 x 25.9
Tate Curatorial

Film Culture, No.45, Summer 1967
Designed by George Maciunas; edited by Gerard Malanga b.1943; Editor-in-Chief, Jonas Mekas 1922–2019
Magazine; printed ink on paper
26.7 x 21 x 0.3
The Andy Warhol Museum, Pittsburgh; Founding Collection, Contribution The Andy Warhol Foundation for the Visual Arts, Inc.
TC-17.118

'Actress shoots Andy Warhol/ cries "He controlled my life"', *New York Daily News*, Final****, 4 June 1968
Facsimile from an original newsprint clipping 39.4 x 27.9
The Andy Warhol Museum, Pittsburgh; Founding Collection, Contribution The Andy Warhol Foundation for the Visual Arts, Inc.
TC1.131 (facsimile 01)
p.151

Raid the Icebox 1969
Book; printed ink on paper 21.3 x 17.5 x 1
Tate Curatorial (two copies)

Ephemera

Norelco® audio cassette recorder 1964
Audio cassette recorder, moulded plastic with metal parts 5.4 x 19.7 x 11.4
The Andy Warhol Museum, Pittsburgh; Founding Collection, Contribution The Andy Warhol Foundation for the Visual Arts, Inc.
T499

Steve Paul's THE SCENE Poster 1966
Screenprint on paper 55.6 x 35.5
ARTIST ROOMS. Acquired jointly by Tate and the National Galleries of Scotland through The d'Offay Donation with assistance from the National Heritage Memorial Fund and the Art Fund 2008

S.C.U.M. (Society for Cutting Up Men) Manifesto 1967
Book; print on paper 10.5 x 18
Tate Curatorial (two copies)
Notebook c.1969
Pen and felt-tipped marker on paper
17.8 x 10.8 x 1.6
The Andy Warhol Museum, Pittsburgh; Founding Collection, Contribution The Andy Warhol Foundation for the Visual Arts, Inc.
TC21.3.1

Wig box n.d.
Cardboard wrapped in faux snakeskin paper
26.7 x 20.3 x 10.8
The Andy Warhol Museum, Pittsburgh; Founding Collection, Contribution The Andy Warhol Foundation for the Visual Arts, Inc.

T3146.1a-b
Wig box n.d.
Cardboard wrapped in coated paper 26.7 x 20.3 x 10.8
The Andy Warhol Museum, Pittsburgh; Founding Collection, Contribution The Andy Warhol Foundation for the Visual Arts, Inc.
T3105.1a-b

Paul Bochicchio (designer)
Wig (Blond and Brown) 1980s
Natural and synthetic hair on dyed cloth
31.8 x 29.2 x 2.5
The Andy Warhol Museum, Pittsburgh; Founding Collection, Contribution The Andy Warhol Foundation for the Visual Arts, Inc.
T3105.2

Paul Bochicchio (designer)
Wig (Blond and Brown) 1980s
Natural and synthetic hair on dyed cloth
35.6 x 29.2 x 2.5
The Andy Warhol Museum, Pittsburgh; Founding Collection, Contribution The Andy Warhol Foundation for the Visual Arts, Inc.
T3105.3

Paul Bochicchio (designer)
Wig (Silver and Brown) 1980s
Natural and synthetic hair on dyed cloth
29.2 x 24.8 x 2.5
The Andy Warhol Museum, Pittsburgh; Founding Collection, Contribution The Andy Warhol Foundation for the Visual Arts, Inc.
T3146.2

Record Covers
The selection of exhibited covers varies across venues. The following covers are exhibited at Tate Modern only.

Diana Ross *Silk Electric* 1982
Print on paper 31.43 x 31.43
Courtesy of Gregor Muir
p.185

The Velvet Underground & Nico 1967
Print on paper 31.1 x 31.1
Museum of Applied Arts Cologne / Collection Ulrich Reininghaus
p.144

The Velvet Underground & Nico 1967
Print on paper 31.1 x 31.1
Museum of Applied Arts Cologne / Collection Ulrich Reininghaus
p.144

Other Artists

Richard Avedon 1923–2004
Andy Warhol, artist, New York, 20 August 1969 1969, printed 1975
Gelatin silver print on paper 147.5 x 118
Nicola Erni Collection
TM only
p.153

Michael Kostiuk b.1944
Photographs of Andy Warhol, *Art in Process V Exhibition, Finch College Museum of Art* 1972
Seven photographs; prints on paper
26 x 21 each
Exhibition records of the Contemporary Wing of the Finch College Museum of Art, Archives of American Art
pp.154–5

Stephen Shore b.1947
Edie Sedgwick 1965–7, printed 2017
Photograph; fibre-based gelatin silver print on paper 32.4 x 48.3

Nicola Erni Collection
TM only
p.127

Andy Warhol & Lou Reed 1965–7, printed 2017
Photograph; fibre-based gelatin silver print on paper 32.4 x 48.3
Nicola Erni Collection
TM only
p.128

Edie Sedgwick & Ingrid Superstar 1965–7, printed 2017
Photograph; fibre-based gelatin silver print on paper 32.4 x 48.3
Nicola Erni Collection
TM only
p.129

Andy Warhol 1965–7, printed 2017
Photograph; fibre-based gelatin silver print on paper 32.4 x 48.3
Nicola Erni Collection
TM only

Edie Sedgwick, Andy Warhol, unidentified guests 1965–7, printed 2017
Photograph; fibre-based gelatin silver print on paper 32.4 x 48.3
Nicola Erni Collection
TM only
p.129

Benedetta Barzini, Julie Garfield, Andy Warhol, Lou Reed, Sterling Morrison 1965–7, printed c.2007
Photograph; fibre-based gelatin silver print on paper 32.4 x 48.3
Nicola Erni Collection
TM only

Paul Jasmine & Gino Piserchio 1965–7, printed c.2008
Photograph; fibre-based gelatin silver print on paper 32.4 x 48.3
Nicola Erni Collection
TM only
p.128

Paul Morrissey & Edie Sedgwick 1965–7, printed c.2008
Photograph; fibre-based gelatin silver print on paper 32.4 x 48.3
Nicola Erni Collection
TM only

CREDITS

Copyright

All Artworks by Andy Warhol © 2020 The Andy Warhol Foundation for the Visual Arts, Inc. / Licensed by DACS, London.

Film and video material by Andy Warhol © 2020 The Andy Warhol Museum, Pittsburgh, a museum of the Carnegie Institute.

Copyright © The Richard Avedon Foundation 148–9, 153

Brillo® is a registered trademark of the Armaly Sponge Company. All rights reserved. 96

Burger King is a trademark of Burger King Corporation. Used with permission. All rights reserved. 11

Rudy Burckhardt © ARS, NY and DACS, London 2019 27

The Campbell's images and trademarks are used with permission of Campbell Soup Company. 94, 97

COCA-COLA ®, COKE ® and the Contour Bottle Design are trademarks of The Coca-Cola Company. ©The Coca-Cola Company. All Rights Reserved 95

© Bob Colacello. Courtesy the artist and Vito Schnabel Projects 65–9

© Estate of Leila Davies Singelis 58 bottom

© Nat Finkelstein Estate 28

© Gaumont 145 centre right

Interview published by Crystall Ball Media, interviewmagazine.com 174–7

© Judd Foundation/ARS, NY and DACS, London 2019 29 bottom

© Michael Kostiuk 156–7

Courtesy of The Kraft Heinz Company 11, 97

© Jørgen Leth 11

LIFE and the LIFE logo are registered trademarks of TI Gotham Inc. used under license. 1963 The Picture Collection Inc. All rights reserved. Reprinted/Translated from LIFE and published with permission of The Picture Collection Inc. Reproduction in any manner in any language in whole or in part without written permission is prohibited. 115

Copyright: Peter and Irene Ludwig Foundation 44

Marilyn Monroe™; Rights of Publicity and Persona Rights: The Estate of Marilyn Monroe LLC. marilynmonroe.com cover (paperback)

© The Estate of Robert Morris / Artists Rights Society (ARS), New York / DACS, London 2019 30 bottom, 31

Billy Name © ARS, NY and DACS, London 2019 138

NY Daily News Archive via Getty Images 151

© Pepsico 86–7

POPEYE © King Features Syndicate, Inc. TM

Hearst Holdings, Inc. 92

© RCA 144 top left, top right, centre left

© Promotone BV and the Warhol Foundation 145 top right, centre left

© Courtesy of Sony Music Entertainment 144 top left, top right, centre left, 145 bottom right

© Stephen Shore. Courtesy 303 Gallery, New York 127–9, 139

Sony Japan 145 bottom left

© Frank Stella. ARS, NY and DACS, London 2019 29 top

© Universal Music 144 centre right, 185

Courtesy The Velvet Underground Trust 144 bottom left and right

©2019 The Andy Warhol Museum, Pittsburgh, PA, a museum of Carnegie Institute. All rights reserved. 22, 25, 33–7, 50–5, 58 top, 61, 122, 124–6, 130, 136–7, 140–1, 146–7, 192–3

Photographic

Samuel Adams Green Collection 60

Photo by John Ardoin/Serendipity 3 15

Martin Argyroglo / Fondation Louis Vuitton 121

Art Gallery of Ontario /Gift of Mrs. Else Landauer, in memory of her husband, Walter Landauer, 1979: 79/114 30 top; /Gift from the Women's Committee Fund, 1966 65/35 110–111

Photograph by Richard Avedon. Copyright © The Richard Avedon Foundation 148–9, 153

Photography by Zachary Balber Zacharybalber. com 186–7

Courtesy Bill Bell Collection / Photograph by Douglas M. Parker Studio 39

Photograph by Rudy Burckhardt /Leo Castelli Gallery records, c.1880–2000, bulk 1957–1999. Archives of American Art, Smithsonian Institution, Washington, DC. 27

© Patrick A.Burns / New York Times 108

Photography by Cathy Carver. Hirshhorn Museum and Sculpture Garden 104–5

COLLECTION JOHN CHEIM 74 top left

COURTESY CHEIM & READ, NEW YORK 76 top, 76 bottom right, 77 top, 77 bottom right, 78, 79 left and bottom

Photo © Christie's Images / Bridgeman Images 42, 84, 188-9, 204–205

© Bob Colacello. Courtesy the artist and Vito Schnabel Projects 65–9

Photograph by Jack Delano / Library of Congress, Prints & Photographs Division, FSA/OWI Collection / LC-USF34- 043202-D [P&P] LOT 1347 2

Photo: Charles Duprat, 2019 Collection Thaddaeus Ropac, London • Paris • Salzburg 200

Photograph © Nat Finkelstein Estate 28

Froehlich Collection, Stuttgart 18, 107

Courtesy Gagosian 161 top; photo: Rob McKeever 160, 161 bottom

© Galerie des Modernes, Paris 77 bottom left, 79 top

Iris & B.Gerald Center for Visual Arts at Stanford University; Gift of the Andy Warhol Foundation for the Visual Arts, Inc. 63

Photograph by Patrick Goetelen 180–1

Photography by Patrick Goetelen / © Tate, London 2020 4, 162–71

Photo by Bernard Gotfryd/Getty Images 59

Photograph courtesy of the Herbert F. Johnson Museum of Art, Cornell University 109 top

Photo: Nils-Göran Hökby. Moderna Museet, Stockholm 96

Photograph by Ken Heyman 97

'Andy Warhol Eating a Hamburger' by Jorgen Leth and Andy Warhol. Photo: Ole John 11

Michael Kostiuk, photographer. Exhibition records of the Contemporary Wing of the Finch College 156–7

Kunstmuseum Basel, Sammlung 112–3

Ludwig Forum for International Art Aachen, loan of the Peter and Irene Ludwig Foundation; photo © Ludwig Forum for International Art 92

Copyright: Peter and Irene Ludwig Foundation 44

PHOTO: Christopher Makos 1977 178

© 2019. Image copyright The Metropolitan Museum of Art/Art Resource/Scala, Florence 120, 134–5

Charles Moore/Getty Images 115

Museum of Art, 1943–1975. Archives of American Art, Smithsonian Institution 156–7

Collection Museum of Contemporary Art Chicago, gift of Beatrice Cummings Mayer, 2007.32. Photo: Nathan Keay, © MCA Chicago 116–17

© 2019. Digital image, The Museum of Modern Art, New York/Scala, Florence 85

MUSEUM MMK FÜR MODERNE KUNST, Foto: Axel Schneider 90, 94

The Billy Name Estate / Art Resource, NY 138

© 2019 Pawsburgh Photography. All Rights Reserved. This use license shall be governed by the laws of the Commonwealth of Pennsylvania in the United States of America 43

Photo by Robin Platzer/Twin Images/The LIFE Images Collection via Getty Images/Getty Images 172–3

Private collection / photo: Adam Reich 132

Rheinisches Bildarchiv Köln 86, 91, 98, 99, 109 bottom, 114, 118–19, 144 bottom left, 145 top left and right, centre right

Courtesy of the RISD Museum, Providence, RI 57

Photography by Kevin Ryan / © Tate, London 2019 123

The Doris and Donald Fisher Collection at the San Francisco Museum of Modern Art 29 top, 88–9; /photo: Katherine Du Tie 191

© 2019. Photo Scala, Florence/bpk, Bildagentur fuer Kunst, Kultur und Geschichte, Berlin 19, 75, 87, 101, 106, 159, 182–3, 202–3

Städtische Galerie im Lenbachhaus und Kunstbau München 201

Photo by Steve Schapiro/Corbis via Getty Images 6, 142–3

© Stephen Shore. Courtesy 303 Gallery, New York 127–9, 139

Courtesy of Sonnabend Gallery, NY 30 bottom, 31 top

© Tate, 2020 cover, 21, 74 top right, 74 bottom, 76 bottom left, 102–3, 144 top right and centre right, 145 bottom, 190, 194–9; /Sam Day 29, 60; /Andrew Dunkley 184; /Matt Greenwood 174–7; /Joe Humphrys 133, 154–5; /David Lambert and Rod Tidnam 207, cover (hardback)

© The Andy Warhol Foundation for the Visual Arts, Inc. / DACS/Artimage 2019 13, 40 top

©2019 The Andy Warhol Museum, Pittsburgh, PA, a museum of Carnegie Institute. All rights reserved. Film still courtesy The Andy Warhol Museum 22, 25, 33–7, 50–5, 58 top, 61, 122, 124–6, 130, 136–7, 140–1, 146–7, 192–3

The Andy Warhol Museum, Pittsburgh; Founding Collection, Contribution The Andy Warhol Foundation for the Visual Arts, Inc. 80, 81, 82–3; /1998.3.10540.2 12 top; /1998.1.680 16; /1998.1.2276.48, 1998.1.2276.8, 1998.1.2276.87, 1998.1.2276.5 45; /2001.2.1727 46; /1998.3.3539 144 top left; /1998.3.6342.1-1998.3.6342.3b 145 centre right; /TC7.100 151; /1998.3.6318.1 174 top; /2001.2.1727 185

The Andy Warhol Museum, Pittsburgh; Gift of Jay Reeg 2014.10 144 bottom right

The Andy Warhol Museum, Pittsburgh; Gift of Leila Davies Singelis 1994.22.9.1 58 bottom

Paul Warhola Family Collection 12 bottom, 14, 72–3

© 2019. Digital image Whitney Museum of American Art / Licensed by Scala 40 bottom, 93, 95

Yageo Foundation Taiwan 131, 158

photo by Stan Wolfson/Newsday RM via Getty Images 150

ZOYA Gallery, Bratislava, Slovakia 179

INDEX

SUPPORTING TATE

London Borough of Southwark
John J Studzinski, CBE
Tate Americas Foundation
Tate Members
Julie-Anne Uggla
Lance Uggla
Viktor Vekselberg
Nina and Graham Williams
Manuela and Iwan Wirth
The Wolfson Foundation
and those who wish to remain anonymous

Tate Modern Benefactors and Major Donors
A/Political Foundation
Estate of Pacita Abad
Alireza Abrishamchi
Abrishamchi Foundation
Etel Adnan
AKO Foundation
Alan Cristea Gallery
Raad Zeid Al-Hussein
Alison Jacques Gallery
Estate of Edward Allington
Estate of Lord Jeffrey and Mary Archer
The Late Marion MacCallum Archibald
Art Fund
Art Mentor Foundation Lucerne
The Arts & Humanities Research Council
Arts Council England
The Austrian Federal Chancellery
Mr Petr Aven
Axel Vervoordt Gallery
Miroslaw Balka, in honour of Sir Nicholas Serota
Lionel Barber
Wilhelmina Barns-Graham Trust
Estate of Maria Bartuszová
Beckett-Fonden
Melvin Bedrick
Leanne and Caitlin Bennett, in memory of
    and admiration for Gordon Bennett
Richard Billingham
James Birch
José Luis Blondet
Bloomberg Philanthopries
The Charlotte Bonham-Carter Charitable Trust
Pontus Bonnier
Estate of Louise Bourgeois
Frances Bowes
Ivor Braka
The Estate of Dr Marcella Louis Brenner
Laurel and Paul Britton
The Broad Art Foundation
Rory and Elizabeth Brooks Foundation
Beatrice Bulgari | In Between Art Film
Susan and John Burns
Estate of Lady Sheila Caro
James Chanos
Trustees of the Chantrey Bequest
Henry and Constance Christensen III
Anne Christopherson in memory of
    her husband John Christopherson
The Clore Duffield Foundation
The Clothworkers' Foundation
Denise Coates Foundation
Edwin Cohen and Dillon Cohen
Sadie Coles
Contemporary Art Society
Corinne Bellow Charity
Douglas S Cramer
Sorcha Dallas
Fortes D'Aloia and Gabriel Galeria
Danish Arts Foundation
Danish Ministry for Culture and
    The Embassy of Denmark, London
Dimitris Daskalopoulos
Harry G David
Olga de Amaral
Tacita Dean, in honour of Sir Nicholas Serota
The Jay DeFeo Foundation
Tiqui Atencio Demirdjian and Ago Demirdjian
Department for Business, Innovation and Skills

Department for Digital, Culture, Media and
Sport
The Destina Foundation
Anthony and Anne d'Offay
Peter Doig, in honour of Sir Nicholas Serota
Joe and Marie Donnelly
Peter Dubens
The Easton Foundation
George Economou
Joan Edlis
Maryam and Edward Eisler
Olafur Eliasson
John Ellerman Foundation
Endeavor
European Union
Carl Faker
Elisabeth Fantino, in memory of Dr Alfredo Fantino
Monir Shahroudy Farmanfarmaian
Faurschou Foundation
The Estate of Mary Fedden and Julian Trevelyan
Sebastiano Ferrante
Estate of Rose Finn-Kelcey
Jeanne Donovan Fisher
Wendy Fisher
Peter Fleissig
Fondation Walter & Nicole LeBlanc
Ford Foundation
Eric and Louise Franck
The Estate of Thomas Frangenberg
Freelands Foundation
The Estate of Lucian Freud
Froehlich Foundation, Stuttgart
Gagosian
Frank Gallipoli
Gary and Denise Gardner
Georg Geyer
The Estate of Mr Graham Gibson Miller
Galeria Gisela Capitan
Glenstone Foundation
Nan Goldin, in honour of Sir Nicholas Serota
Sir Nicholas and Lady Goodison
David and Maggie Gordon
Antony Gormley
Lydia and Manfred Gorvy
The Granville-Grossman Bequest
Guaranty Trust Bank Plc
Guy Halamish
Maggi Hambling, in Honour of Maria Balshaw
Halley K Harrishurgh and Michael Rosenfeld
The Drue Heinz Charitable Trust
Thilo Heinzmann
Sanford Heller in honour of Sir Nicholas Serota
Susan Hendricks
Barbara Hepworth Estate
David Herro and Jay Franke in Memory of
    Carol Djanogly
The Hintze Family Charitable Foundation
Roger J Hiorns
Damien Hirst
David Hockney
The Estate of Howard Hodgkin
Andy Holden
Rebecca Horn
Trustees of Lord Howard of Henderskelfe's
    Will Trust
The Estate of Mr John Hoyland
Ministry of Foreign Affairs and Trade of Hungary
Huo Family Foundation (UK) Limited
Iran Heritage Foundation
The Estate of Albert and Beatrice Irvin
The J Isaacs Charitable Trust
John Janssen
Tim Jefferies, in honour of Sir Nicholas Serota
Amrita Jhaveri
Pamela J. Joyner and Alfred J. Giuffrida
Isaac Julien, in honour of Maria Balshaw
Peter and Maria Kellner
J. Patrick Kennedy and Patricia A. Kennedy
Ku-lim Kim
Ph. Konzett, Vienna
Kurimanzutto Gallery

Estate of Tseng Kwong Chi
Lachaise Foundation
Catherine Lagrange
David and Amanda Leathers
Edward and Agnès Lee
Eric Lefkofksy
Legacy Trust UK
The Leverhulme Trust
Lin Lougheed
Henry Luce Foundation
Andrew Lugg
LUMA Foundation
Peder Lund
The Estate of Sir Edwin Manton
The Manton Foundation
Marian Goodman Gallery
Marie-Louise von Motesiczky Charitable Trust
Helen Marten, in honour of Sir Nicholas Serota
Agnes Martin Foundation
Danica and Eduard Maták
Theo Matoff
Lord McAlpine of West Green
Mr Ronald and the Honourable Mrs McAulay
Mark McCain
The Estate of Kenneth McGowan
Steve McQueen
The Andrew W. Mellon Foundation
Paul Mellon Centre For Studies In British Art
Adrian Mibus
The Mikati Foundation
Naomi Milgrom Foundation
Lisa Milroy, in honour of Sir Nicholas Serota
Modern Forms
Montana
The Ronald Moody Trust
Henry Moore Foundation
Jacqueline Morreau Estate
Mottahedan Family
Angela Mullane
The Estate of Jenifer Ann Murray
Museum of Contemporary Art Australia,
    donated through the Australian Government's
    Cultural Gifts Program by Martin Gascoigne
National Heritage Memorial Fund
The National Lottery Community Fund
The National Lottery Heritage Fund
The National Trust
New Carlsberg Foundation
David and Sonya Newell-Smith
Novatek
Outset Germany_Switzerland
Pace Gallery
Maureen Paley
Martin Parr
Paul Hamlyn Foundation
Yana and Stephen Peel
Brigid Peppin
Peter Peri
Catherine Petitgas
The Pivovarov Family
The Porthmeor Fund
David W. Posnett, OBE
Gilberto Pozzi
Serena Prest
Pretzel Gallery
Stephen Prina
Emilio Prini
Qantas Foundation
Qatar Museums Authority
Fiona Rae, in honour of Sir Nicholas Serota
Chandru Ramchandani
Carla Rapoport
Robert Rennie
Simon Reynolds
Dianne Roberts
Roman Family Collection
The Estate of Eugene and Penelope Rosenberg
Edward Ruscha
Sean Ryerson
Keith and Katherine Sachs
The Estate of Simon Sainsbury

Gillian and Simon Salama-Caro
Sammlung Hoffmann Gbr
Gregor Schneider
Karsten Schubert
Jake and Hélène Marie Shafran
Jack Shear
Leo Shih
Sara and John Shlesinger
Taryn Simon
The Estate of Sylvia Sleigh
Jay Smith and Laura Rapp
Wendy Smith
Alan Sprince
The Stanley Picker Trust
Lord Stevenson of Coddenham, CBE
Emile Stipp
The Estate of Michael Stoddart
Norman and Norah Stone
Mercedes and Ian Stoutzker
John Studzinski
Maria Sukkar
Surgo Donor Advised Fund
Marjorie Susman
Swiss Arts Council Pro Helvetia
Swiss Cultural Fund UK
Beth Swofford
Tamares Real Estate Holdings, Inc. in
    collaboration with the Zabludowicz Collection
Tanya Bonakdar Gallery
Tate 1897 Circle
Tate Africa Acquisitions Committee
Tate Americas Foundation
Tate Asia-Pacific Acquisitions Committee
Tate European Collection Circle
Tate International Council
Tate Latin American Acquisitions Committee
Tate Members
Tate Middle East and North Africa
    Acquisitions Committee
Tate North American Acquisitions Committee
Tate Patrons
Tate Photography Acquisitions Committee
Tate Russia and Eastern Europe
    Acquisitions Committee
Terra Foundation for American Art
The Lord Leonard and
    Lady Estelle Wolfson Foundation
The Estate of Mr Nicholas Themans
Thomas Gibson Fine Art Advisory Services
Wolfgang Tillmans, in honour of
    Sir Nicholas Serota
Tim Van Laere Gallery
Tommy Tisch
Bill and Ruth True
The Estate of William Turnbull
Luc Tuymans
V-A-C Foundation
Sir David and Lady Verey
Erika Verzutti
The Estate of Mollie Winifred Vickers
Mercedes Vilardell
Kemang Wa Lehulere
Mark Wallinger
Dr Anne Walmsley
Michael Werner, in honour of Sir Nicholas Serota
Clarence Westbury Foundation
Angela Westwater
White Cube Ltd
Rachel Whiteread
Isabel Wilcox
Hannah Wilke Collection and Archive
Jane and Michael G Wilson
The Worshipful Company of Arts Scholars and
    The Company of Arts Scholars Charitable Trust
Erwin Wurm
Juan Yarur Torres in honour of Felipe Lecaros
YOUNG-HAE CHANGE HEAVY INDUSTRIES
    (Young-Hae Chang, Marc Voge)
The Estate of Mr Anthony Zambra
Qiao Zhibing, in honour of Gregor Muir
Roman Zubal

Federica Baretta
Lucy Barry
Mr Richard Bazzaz
Katrina Beechey
Penny Johanna Beer
Dr Maya Beyhan
Dorothee Boissonnas
Erin Booth
Kit Brennan
Alexandre Carel
David Carpenter
Lauren Carpenter
Sean Carpenter
Marie-Louise Chaldecott
Thibaud Chaligne
Alexandra and Kabir Chhatwani
Aidan Christofferson
Bianca Chu
Thamara Corm
Stephanie Courmont
Tara Wilson Craig
Averil Curci
Helena Czernecka
Sophie Da Gama Campos
Scarlett Dalton
Henry Danowski
Grantland D'Avino
Mr Joshua Davis
Raphaele Deghaye
Countess Charlotte de la Rochefoucauld
Giacomo De Notariis
Agnes de Royere
Emie Diamond
Indira Dyussebayeva
Alexandra Economou
Eleanor A Edelman
Yasmina El Muslemany
Danae Filioti
Kate Finefrock
Thomas Forwood
Jane and Richard Found
Sylvain Fresia
Laurie Frey
Brian Fu
Magdalena Gabriel
Mr Andreas Gegner
Rajasekhar Ghanta
Elissa Goldstone
Mr Taymour Grahne
Beth Greenacre
Miles Greenberg
Alex Haidas
Ayano Hattori
Ari Helgason
Simona Houldsworth
Kyu Hwang
Kamel Jaber
Karim Jalbout
Aled Jones
Miss Meruyert Kaliyeva
Mrs Vasilisa Kameneva
Zoe Karafylakis Sperling
Tamila Kerimova
Zena Aliya Khan
Marika Kielland
Ms Chloe Kinsman
Maria Korolevskaya
Daria Kravchenko
Zoe Kuipers
Dominic Lamotte
Nicholas M Lamotte
Ms Aliki-Marcadia Lampropoulos
Patricia Lara
Nadja Laub
Hena Lee
Alexandra Lekomtseva
John Lellouche
Alexander Lewis
Ines Leynaud
Melissa Lilley
Claire Livingstone
Tessa Lord
Mr J Lueddeckens
Lucy MacLeod
Yusuf Macun
Frederic Maillard
Ms Sonia Mak
Dr Christina Makris

Mr Jean-David Malat
Daria Manganelli
Ignacio Marinho
Zain Masud
Magnus Mathisen
Charles-Henri McDermott
Frederick McDonald
Fiona McGovern
Mary McNicholas
Shahid Miah
Miss Nina Moaddel
Mr Fernando Moncho Lobo
John-Christian Moquette
Olga Nikolskaya
Ikenna Obiekwe
Aurore Ogden (Co-Chair, Young Patrons
    Ambassador Group)
Reine and Boris Okuliar
Berkay Oncel
Chloe O'Sullivan
Periklis Panagopoulos
Alexandrina Pereira
Harsha Perera
Alexander V Petalas (Co-Chair,
    Young Patrons Ambassador Group)
Victor Petitgas
Robert Phillips
Mr Mark Piolet
Christopher Pullen
Chelsea Purvis
Ms Catherine Quin
Mr Eugenio Re Rebaudengo
Georgina Rees
Dave Reynolds
Sydney Rogers
Nour Saleh
Sophie Samuelson
Paola Saracino Fendi
Veronica Scarpati
Count Indoo Sella Di Monteluce
Myriam Semere
Robert Sheffield
Ms Marie-Anya Shriro
Amar Singh
Evgenia Slyusarenko
David Smeralda
Jana Soin
Katarina Stojanovic
Dominic Stolerman
Daniel Story
Melisa Tapan
Nayrouz Tatanaki
Vassan Thavaraja
Mr Leo Thetiot
Soren S K Tholstrup
Omer Tiroche
Charles Towning
Mr Giancarlo Trinca
Mr Philippos Tsangrides
Ms Navann Ty
Giada Vaghi
Mr Lawrence Van Hagen
Sophie van Rappard
Steffan Vaughan Griffiths
Damian Vesey
Alina Voronova
Luning Wang
Yge Wang
Alexandra Werner
Ewa Wilczynski
Anna Wilde
Elizabeth Wilks
Kim Williams
Alexandra Wood
Edward Woodcock
Tyler Woolcott
Vanessa Wurm
Ms Eirian Yem
HRH Princess Eugenie of York
Nadia Zayan
Evgeny Zborovsky
Yuejia Zhou
Marcelo Osvaldo Zimmler
and those who wish to remain anonymous

International Council Members
Segun Agbaje
Staffan Ahrenberg, Editions Cahiers d'Art

Geoff Ainsworth, AM
Michael J. Audain
Maria Baibakova and Mr Adrien Faure
Anne H Bass
Nicolas Berggruen
Pontus Bonnier
Paloma Botín O'Shea
William Bowness, AO
Ivor Braka
The Deborah Loeb Brice Foundation
Elizabeth Brooks
Andrew Cameron, AM
Nicolas and Celia Cattelain
Christina Chandris
Richard Chang (Vice Chair)
Pierre Chen, Yageo Foundation, Taiwan
Euisun Chung and Mrs Geesun Chung
Mr and Mrs Attilio Codognato
Sir Ronald Cohen and Lady Cohen
Dimitris Daskalopoulos
Mr and Mrs Michel David-Weill
Miel de Botton
Suzanne Deal Booth
Tiqui Atencio Demirdjian and Ago Demirdjian
Joseph and Marie Donnelly
Olga Dreesmann
Füsun and Faruk Eczacibasi
Stefan Edlis and Gael Neeson
Fares and Tania Fares
HRH Princess Firyal of Jordan
Doris Fisher
Wendy Fisher
Amanda and Glenn Fuhrman
Belma Gaudio and The Butters Foundation
Candida and Zak Gertler
Yassmin Ghandehari
Alan Gibbs
Lydia and Manfred Gorvy
Laurence Graff
Xavier Guerrand-Hermès
Mimi and Peter Haas Fund
Margrit and Paul Hahnloser
Susan Hayden
Ydessa Hendeles
Marlene Hess and James D. Zirin
Maja Hoffmann
Vicky Hughes
Ishikawa Foundation
Mrs Sangita Jindal
Dakis and Lietta Joannou
Monica Kalpakian
Richard and Pamela Kramlich
Grazyna Kulczyk
Andreas and Ulrike Kurtz
Catherine Lagrange
Pierre Lagrange
The Lauder Foundation – Leonard and
    Judy Lauder Fund
Agnès and Edward Lee
Seo Hyun Lee
Jacqueline and Marc Leland
Joyce Liu
Panos and Sandra Marinopoulos
Mr and Mrs Donald B Marron
Victoria Mikhelson
Naomi Milgrom, AO
Simon and Catriona Mordant
Yoshiko Mori
Dr Mark Nelson
Mr and Mrs Takeo Obayashi
Mr and Mrs Eyal Ofer
Andrea and José Olympio Pereira
Hideyuki Osawa
Simon Palley and Midge Palley
Irene Panagopoulos
Young-Ju Park
Véronique Parke
Yana and Stephen Peel
Daniel and Elizabeth Peltz
Catherine Petitgas (Chair)
Sydney Picasso
Lekha Poddar
Dee Poon
Miuccia Prada and Patrizio Bertelli
Laura Rapp and Jay Smith
Maya and Ramzy Rasamny
Patrizia Sandretto Re Rebaudengo and
    Agostino Re Rebaudengo

Rennie Foundation
Frances Reynolds
Michael Ringier
Hanneli M Rupert
Sevil Sabanci
Dame Theresa Sackler, DBE
Lily Safra
Muriel and Freddy Salem
Rajeeb and Nadia Samdani
Alejandro Santo Domingo
Dasha Shenkman, OBE
Dr Gene Sherman, AM
Jon and Kimberly Shirley
Uli and Rita Sigg
Norah and Norman Stone
Julia Stoschek
John J Studzinski, CBE
Maria and Malek Sukkar
Christen Sveaas
Lorraine Tarabay
Warly Tomei
Richard and Maggie Tsai
Ninetta Vafeia
Paulo A W Vieira
Mercedes Vilardell
Robert and Felicity Waley-Cohen
Angela Westwater and David Meitus
Diana Widmaier Picasso
Christen and Derek Wilson
Sylvie Winckler
The Hon Dame Janet Wolfson de Botton, DBE
Dr Terry Wu
Poju Zabludowicz and Anita Zabludowicz, OBE
Michael Zilkha
and those who wish to remain anonymous

Africa Acquisitions Committee
Kathy Ackerman Robins
The African Arts Trust
Adnan Bashir
Priti Chandaria Shah
Mrs Kavita Chellaram
Harry G David
Lana de Beer David
Mr and Mrs Michel David-Weill
Ladi Delano
Robert and Renee Drake
Mrs Wendy Fisher
Diane B. Frankel
Andrea Kerzner
Othman Lazraq
Matthias and Gervanne Leridon
Caro Macdonald
Dale Mathias
Pascale Revert Wheeler
Emile Stipp
Pulane Tshabalala Kingston
Liese Van Der Watt and Stephan Pretorius
Josef Vascovitz and Lisa Goodman
Mercedes Vilardell (Chair)
Alexa Waley-Cohen
Peter Warwick
and those who wish to remain anonymous

Asia-Pacific Acquisitions Committee
Matthias Arndt
Bonnie and R Derek Bandeen
Lito and Kim Camacho
Mr and Mrs John Carrafiell
David Chau
Adrian Cheng
Jonathan Cheung
Lawrence Chu
Marcel Crespo
Mr Yan d'Auriol
Dani Duclos
Mrs Yassmin Ghandehari
Esther Heer-Zacek
Philippa Hornby
Shareen Khattar Harrison
Mr Chang-Il Kim
Mr Jung Wan Kim
Ms Yung Hee Kim
Ms Ellie Lai
Alan Lau (Co-Chair)
Woong-Yeul Lee
Jasmine Li
Mr William Lim

Lin Qi
Ms Dina Liu
Alan and Yenn Lo
Ms Kai-Yin Lo
Lu Xun
Yoonwhe Leo Moon & Young Ran Yun
Lynn Ou
Mr John Porter
The Red Mansion Foundation
Dr Gene Sherman, AM
Arif Suherman
Mr Patrick Sun
Chikako Tatsuuma
Dr Andreas Teoh
Rudy Tseng
Rachel Verghis
Wang Bing
Yang Bin
Jenny Yeh
Fernando Zobel de Ayala (Co-Chair)
and those who wish to remain anonymous

Latin American Acquisitions Committee
Monica and Robert Aguirre
José Antonio Alcantara
Tiqui Atencio Demirdjian (Chair)
Francesca Bellini
Celia Birbragher
Countess Nicole Brachetti Peretti
Estrellita and Daniel Brodsky
Simone Coscarelli Parma
HSH the Prince Pierre d'Arenberg
Renata Dias de Moraes
Marta Regina Fernandez-Holmann
Barbara Hemmerle Gollust
Julian Iragorri
Aimee Labarrere de Servitje
José Luis Lorenzo
Felipe and Denise Nahas Mattar
Susan McDonald
Gabriela Mendoza
Veronica Nutting
Victoria and Isaac Oberfeld
Silvia Paz Illobre
Catherine Petitgas
Claudio Federico Porcel
Mr Thibault Poutrel
Frances Reynolds
Erica Roberts
Alin Ryan Lobo
Catalina Saieh Guzman
Teresa Sapey
Lilly Scarpetta
Camila Sol de Pool
Teresita Soriano Zucker
Juan Carlos Verme
and those who wish to remain anonymous

Middle East and North Africa Acquisitions Committee
Ahmad and Sirine Abu Ghazaleh
HRH Princess Alia Al-Senussi
Abdelmonem Bin Eisa Alserkal
Mehves Ariburnu
Marwan T Assaf
Perihan Bassatne
Family Boghossian
Ms Isabelle de la Bruyère
Füsun Eczacibasi
Maryam Eisler (Co-Chair)
Shirley Elghanian
Noor Fares
Hossein and Dalia Fateh
Negin Fattahi-Dasmal
Raghida Ghandour Al Rahim
Mareva Grabowski
Aysegül Karadeniz
Mr Elie Khouri
Maha and Kasim Kutay
Falak Naqvi
Dina Nasser-Khadivi
Mr Moshe Peterburg
Ramzy and Maya Rasamny (Co-Chair)
Thomas Rom
Mrs Karen Ruimy
Maria and Malek Sukkar
Faisal Tamer

Berna Tuglular
Sebnem Unlu
Mr Zahid and Ms Binladin
Roxane Zand
and those who wish to remain anonymous

North American Acquisitions Committee
Alireza Abrishamchi
Jacqueline Appel and Alexander Malmaeus
Abigail Baratta
Dorothy Berwin and Dominique Lévy
Lee Broughton
Dillon Cohen
Michael Corman and Kevin Fink
James E Diner
Mala Gaonkar
Jill Garcia
Shari Glazer
Amy Gold
Nina and Dan Gross
Pamela J Joyner
Patricia Kaneb Kelly
Nancy Kaneb Soule
Elisabeth and Panos Karpidas
Christian Keesee
Rachelli Mishori and Leon Koffler
Miyoung Lee
Marjorie and Michael Levine
James Lindon
Kathleen Madden and Paul Frantz
Rebecca Marks
Nancy McCain
Jeff Menashe
Stavros Merjos
Gregory R Miller
Sami Mnaymneh
Shabin and Nadir Mohamed
Jenny Mullen
Alexander Petalas
Amy and John Phelan
Laura Rapp and Jay Smith
Carolin Scharpff-Striebich
Komal Shah
Francis and Eleanor Shen
Kimberly and Jon Shirley
Beth Swofford
Juan Carlos Verme
Charlotte Wagner
Christen and Derek Wilson
and those who wish to remain anonymous

Photography Acquisitions Committee
Ryan Allen and Caleb Kramer
Nicholas Barker
Cynthia Lewis Beck
Carolin Becker
Pierre Brahm
Mrs William Shaw Broeksmit
Elizabeth (Co-Chair) and Rory Brooks
Beth and Michele Colocci
Mr and Mrs Michel David-Weill
Mr Hyung-Teh Do
David Fitzsimons
Lisa Garrison
Emily Goldner and Mike Humphries
Ann Hekmat
Alexandra Hess
Elizabeth and William Kahane
Jack Kirkland
Suling Mead
Sebastien Montabonel
Saadi Soudavar
Nicholas Stanley
Maria and Malek Sukkar
Francois Trausch, in memory of Caroline Trausch
Annie Vartivarian
Michael and Jane Wilson
and those who wish to remain anonymous

Russia and Eastern Europe Acquisitions Committee
Dilyara Allakhverdova (Co-Chair)
David Birnbaum
Francise Hsin-Wen Chang
Marian Gazdik
Patrick Hessel
Vilius Kavaliauskas and Rita Kavaliauskiene
Carl Kostyál

Mrs Grazyna Kulczyk
Peter Kulloi (Co-Chair)
Enikő Leányvári and Gábor Illés
Iveta Manasherova
Eduard Maták
Luba Michailova
Katarzyna Mikolajczak
Maarja Oviir-Neivelt
Florin Pogonaru
Petr Pudil
Neil K Rector
Valeria Rodnyansky
Robert Runták
Ovidiu Șandor
Zsolt Somlói
Elena Sudakova
Miroslav Trnka
Jo Vickery
Veronika Zonabend
Mr Jānis Zuzāns
and those who wish to remain anonymous

South Asia Acquisitions Committee
Shohidul Ahad-Choudhury
Krishna Bhupal
Dr Arani and Mrs Shumita Bose
Krishna Choudhary
Akshay Chudasama
Jai Danani
Shalini Amerasinghe Ganendra
Dr Amin Jaffer
Tarini Jindal
Deepanjana Klein
Simran Kotak and Vir Kotak
Ms Aarti Lohia
Yamini Mehta
Mr Yogesh Mehta
Mohammad N. Miraly
Shalini Misra
Mr Rahul Munjal and Mrs Pooja Munjal
Lekha Poddar (Co-Chair)
Smita Prabhakar
Nadia Samdani
Rajeeb Samdani (Co-Chair)
Mrs Tarana Sawhney
Osman Khalid Waheed
Manuela and Iwan Wirth
and those who wish to remain anonymous

The 1897 Circle
Marilyn Bild
James Birch
David and Deborah Botten
Geoff Bradbury
Charles Brett
Sylvia Carter
Eloise and Francis Charlton
Mr and Mrs Cronk
Alex Davids
Jonathan Davis
Professor Martyn Davis
Sean Dissington
Ronnie Duncan
Joan Edlis
V Fabian
Lt Cdr Paul Fletcher
Mr and Mrs R.N. and M.C. Fry
Tom Glynn
Richard S. Hamilton
L.A. Hynes
John Janssen
Dr Martin Kenig
Isa Levy
Theo Matoff
Jean Medlycott
Miss Sue Novell and Mr Graham Smith
Martin Owen
Simon Reynolds
Dianne Roberts
Dr Claudia Rosanowski
Ann M Smith
Alan Sprince
Deborah Stern
Jennifer Toynbee-Holmes
Estate of Paule Vézelay
D. Von Bethmann Hollweg
Audrey Wallrock
Rosie Watts

Prof. Brian Whitton
Kay and Dyson Wilkes
Simon Casimir Wilson
Andrew Woodd
Mr Zilberberg
and those who wish to remain anonymous

European Collection Circle
Jacques Boissonnas
Karen Cawthorn Argenio
Lonti Ebers
Trustees of the Gaudio Family Foundation (UK) Limited
Annette and Marc Kemmler
Agnès and Edward Lee (Chair)
Narmina Marandi
Danny Rimer
and those who wish to remain anonymous

Tate Modern Corporate Supporters
Bank of America
Bloomberg LP
BMW
C C Land Holdings Ltd
Christie's
Deutsche Bank AG
Hyundai Motor
Laurent Perrier
LetterOne
Qantas
Uniqlo
and those who wish to remain anonymous

Tate Modern Corporate Members
Allford Hall Monaghan Morris
Ashurst LLP
BCS Consulting
Brooks Macdonald
Clifford Chance LLP
Deutsche Bank AG
Dezeen
EY
Finsbury
F-Secure Corporation
Hakluyt & Company Ltd
HSBC
Imperial College Healthcare Charity
JATO Dynamics
LexisNexis
Linklaters LLP
Loyens & Loeff
Morgan Stanley
Rothschild & Co
The Up Group
Wedgewood Britain
and those who wish to remain anonymous

First published 2020 by order of the Tate Trustees by
Tate Publishing, a division of Tate Enterprises Ltd,
Millbank, London SW1P 4RG

www.tate.org.uk/publishing

on the occasion of the exhibition

Andy Warhol

Organised by Tate Modern in collaboration with
Museum Ludwig, Cologne

Presented in The Eyal Ofer Galleries
Tate Modern, London
12 March – 6 September 2020

Museum Ludwig, Cologne (*Andy Warhol. Now*)
10 October 2020 – 21 February 2021

Art Gallery of Ontario, Toronto
27 March – 13 June 2021

Dallas Museum of Art, Texas
11 July – 7 November 2021

The Tate Modern exhibition is in partnership with

With additional support from the Andy Warhol Exhibition
Supporters Circle:
Lydia and Manfred Gorvy

Tate Americas Foundation, Tate International Council,
Tate Patrons and Tate Members

Project Editor: Emma Poulter
Production: Bill Jones
Picture Researcher: Emma O'Neill
Design: The Bon Ton
Originated, printed and bound in Italy by Siz

Measurements of artworks are given in centimetres,
height before width and depth

The Contributors
Kenneth Brummel is Associate Curator of Modern Art, Art Gallery
of Ontario

Stephan Diederich is Curator, Collection of Twentieth-century Art,
Museum Ludwig, Cologne.

Diedrich Diederichsen is a cultural critic in Berlin and teaches theories
of contemporary art at the Academy of Fine Arts in Vienna.

Yilmaz Dziewior is Director of Museum Ludwig, Cologne.

Olivia Laing is a writer, novelist and cultural critic, and author of
The Lonely City (2016).

Fiontán Moran is Assistant Curator, International Art, Tate Modern.

Gregor Muir is Director of Collection, International Art, Tate Modern.

Charlie Porter is a writer.

Martine Syms is an artist who works in video, installation and
performance.

Cover (paperback): *Marilyn Diptych* 1962 (detail). See pp.102–3
Cover (hardback): *Self-Portrait* 1986 (detail). See p.207
Frontispiece: *In working class section of Pittsburgh, Pennsylvania*
Photograph by Jack Delano. Library of Congress Prints and Photographs
Division Washington, D.C
Page 4: *Ladies and Gentlemen (Wilhelmina Ross)* 1975 (detail).
Acrylic paint and screenprint on canvas 127 x 101.6
Page 6: *Andy Warhol Under the Silver Cloud Balloon, Castelli Gallery,
New York, 1965* 1965. Photograph by Steven Schapiro
Gelatin silver print 127 x 101.6

Martine Sym's contribution (pp.48–55) is illustrated with stills from Andy
Warhol's film works. All works, aside from one, are also illustrated and
captioned elsewhere in the book (see below for details). Full caption
information can also be found in the Exhibited Works list.

pp.50–1, 54–5: *Sleep* 1963. See pp.25 and 122
pp.52–3: Selection of *Screen Tests* 1964–6, featuring *Ann Buchanan*
[ST33], *Lucinda Childs* [ST52], *Kyoko Kishida* [ST183], *Ivy Nicholson*
[ST230], *Jane Holzer* [ST142] and *Mario Montez* [ST222]. See also
pp.124–5, and p.211 for full caption details
p.54: *Factory Diary: Julia Warhola in Bed* c.1970–2. See p.211